DOCTOR WHO: THE SCRIPTS

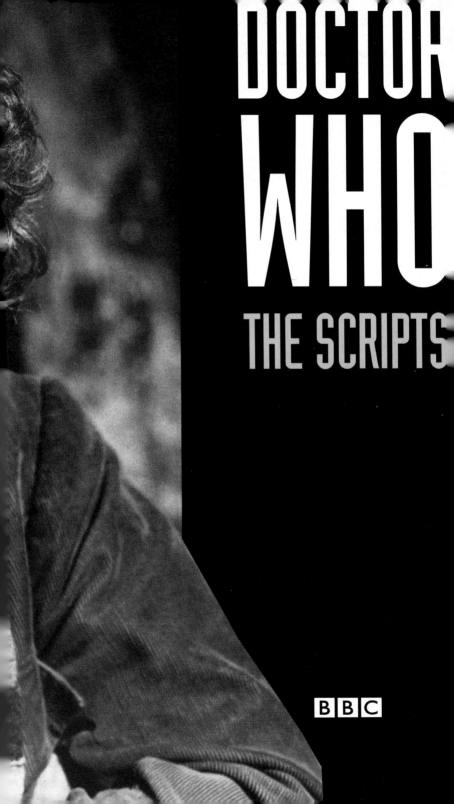

DOCTOR WHO

THE SCRIPTS

BBC

Published by BBC Worldwide Limited
Woodlands, 80 Wood Lane, London W12 0TT

First published 2001
Robot © Terrance Dicks, 2001
The Ark in Space © Robert Holmes, 2001
The Sontaran Experiment © Bob Baker and Dave Martin, 2001
Genesis of the Daleks © Terry Nation, 2001
Revenge of the Cybermen © Gerry Davis, 2001
Additional text © Justin Richards and Andrew Pixley, 2001
Appendix B © Martin J Wiggins, 2001
The moral right of the author has been asserted

ISBN 0 563 53815 5

Commissioning Editor: Ben Dunn
Content Editor: Justin Richards
Associate Editor: Barnaby Harsent
Contributing Editor: Andrew Pixley
Project Editor: April Warman
Art Director: Linda Blakemore
Typesetter: Ben Cracknell Studios

Set in Garamond, Helvetica and Industria
Printed and bound in Great Britain by The Bath Press, Bath
Jacket printed by Lawrence-Allen, Weston-super-Mare

Contents

Preface

A television script goes through various stages and drafts before it is finally realized in front of the cameras.

The scripts as delivered by the author are revised by a script editor to produce the *rehearsal scripts*. The director and production team work from the rehearsal scripts when planning how they make the programme – if these are available. Sometimes schedules are such that this work is done initially from the author's final draft, then refined when the next scripts become available.

The scripts are further refined by the actors in rehearsal, and for technical and aesthetic reasons. When instructions for the camera operators and technical crew are added, the rehearsal scripts are refined into *camera scripts*. It is from these scripts that the programme is made.

Inevitably there are differences between the camera script and the finished programme. Material may be cut from or added to the script in the studio or at the editing stage for reasons of timing, or because these seem like good amendments. Actors may change lines slightly when they say them, or a better exchange between characters may be worked out in the studio. A technical effect may be achieved in a different way from the one that was planned, or may prove to be impossible.

Sometimes a final version of the script is produced that reflects what was actually transmitted – *programme-as-broadcast scripts*.

In this collection we have decided to reproduce the camera scripts. These represent the intention of the production team better than any of the other scripts, while not being merely a simple description of the televised material – all of which is or has been available from BBC Video.

The development of the script to this stage is described in the accompanying production notes and annotations. We have noted major changes at each stage of script development. Scripts that were dropped, or completely rewritten (for example, Christopher Langley's *Space Station* and John Lucarotti's *The Ark in Space*) are covered. For *Revenge of the Cybermen*, which changed considerably, we have provided a synopsis of the original author's scripts (Appendix B). This is because the story as broadcast was still credited to author Gerry Davis, and is a development of his scripts rather than a replacement.

In the interest of making them as accessible and informative as possible, the scripts as reproduced here have been altered from the actual camera scripts in several ways:

- The scripts in this book use the full extent of the column. Studio scenes in the original camera scripts are laid out with camera directions on the left of the page and dialogue and directions on the right (filmed inserts have a slightly different format).
- The camera directions are not reproduced here, but are referenced in the annotations as appropriate.
- The formatting has been altered for readability. In the originals, all directions and character names are in capitals. We have used *italic* for directions, and SMALL CAPITALS for speaking characters.
- Errors of spelling and minor grammatical errors have been corrected unless there is an ambiguity. In that case, the original is preserved with a note to the effect that something else may have been intended. Where a mistake is of interest for some reason (for example the misspelling of the Brigadier's name as Lethbridge Stuart in *Robot*) this is also annotated.
- We have indicated within the body of the script significant differences between the camera script and the programme as transmitted. Omitted dialogue and action is struck through (~~like this~~), and additional material is emboldened (**like this**). Only significant changes are indicated, or ones where meaning or characterization is altered. Transpositions and minor alterations are not shown. For example, in *Genesis of the Daleks* Part One we have not indicated that while Harry's line is scripted as, *'If they can build something like that why are they fighting a war with old-fashioned things like barbed wire and land mines?'* he actually says, *'Why are they fighting a war with old-fashioned things like barbed wire and land mines if they can build something like that?'* Equally, changes between the directions and what actually occurs are only noted if they are significant.

Abbreviations and technical terms

To save space, we have preserved technical and linguistic abbreviations within the text. Technical abbreviations you may find include:

CSO Colour Separation Overlay (also called Chromakey or, nowadays, blue screen). This is a process of overlaying part or all of the image from one camera over part or all of the image from another. For a full explanation see page 77.

CU Close Up. This indicates that the subject should be highly prominent on the screen.

OB Outside Broadcast. The process of creating video (rather than filmed) images on location, or the resulting video material.

OOV Out Of View. Indicates that a character is heard but not seen.

POV Point Of View. Used to explain that a particular event or sequence is shown as if seen from a particular character's viewpoint.

TK Telecine. A filmed sequence.

VO Voice-Over. Indicates that a character is not seen.

Scene numbering

We have preserved the scene numbering of the original scripts. Scenes are generally numbered in order, but there are exceptions:

- If a scene was deleted late in the schedule, it may simply be omitted to save retyping and renumbering the entire script.
- If a scene was added late in the schedule, it may have the same number as the scene it follows, with a suffix 'A'. For example, *Revenge of the Cybermen* Part One has a Scene 21A.
- Scenes planned for filming on location, in the BBC film studios at Ealing, or as model or effects shots, are numbered separately from studio scenes. The scene number for these is marked TELECINE (or its abbreviation, TK) if it is to be realized on film, or OB if it is planned for Outside Broadcast video.

Production credits and information

Dates

Note that dates given for *Doctor Who* (and other television) programmes refer to the date of first-run transmission of the first episode, unless otherwise stated. For example, we refer to *Spearhead from Space* (1970), although that story was actually made in 1969.

Cast

This list includes all credited cast as billed on the programme. Unless otherwise stated, all cast members were credited on all episodes of a serial. For those who were not, the episodes on which they are billed are given in square brackets after their name. Cast were billed in order of on-screen precedence. Discrepancies in billing are footnoted.

Uncredited

All extras and walk-ons not credited on the programme are identified by roles by episode. If different people appear in different episodes, the numbers are given after their names; if all the people in a particular role appear in the same episodes, these are given after the role.

Crew

This list includes all credited crew as billed on the programme. Footnotes indicate if a crew member only worked on one section of a programme. Uncredited crew are not listed unless they made an additional contribution to a credited role.

Production History

This lists all the principal days of production – i.e. filming or recording. Rehearsals are omitted (but usually referred to in the body of the production notes). The date is given along with the nature of the work undertaken, the venue/location/studio and, where known, the times of work. The scenes filmed/recorded on the day – as far as can be determined – are then listed, but note that in some cases these are from planned schedules only and may not reflect the actual production schedule.

Music

Details of the music used on the serial, with a total for specially recorded material, recording dates and venues and information on any library material composed. This information comes from the programme-as-broadcast sheets.

Original Transmission

This lists details of the original broadcast with episode, transmission date, scheduled transmission time, actual transmission time, duration, audience size (in millions), weekly television chart position and audience reaction index (indicating the perceived quality of show). If information is omitted it is because it was not collected or is not available.

Acknowledgements

This book is a collaborative venture. In an attempt to be comprehensive and accurate, we have drawn on the help of many people, all of whom we thank.

The following people provided help and support above and beyond what we hoped for, and we thank them especially:

The staff of the BBC Written Archive Centre, in particular Neil Somerville and Mike Websell.

Jac Rayner for general help, support and research. Peter Anghelides and J Jeremy Bentham for permission to quote from *In-Vision*.

Richard Bignell, David Brunt, Andy Mariott, Stephen James Walker, Julie Rogers and Gary Gillatt for general material, and John Peel for permission to quote from his interview with Terry Nation.

Alistair Lock for telling us everything we ever wanted to know about ring modulators.

Martin J Wiggins for all sorts of material, for keeping us honest, and for providing the *Return of the Cybermen* synopsis for Appendix B.

And Terrance Dicks, of course.

Introduction

by Terrance Dicks

1974 marked the end of an era.

I'd joined *Who* fairly casually in 1968, confidently expecting to be fired in three months. I was to replace Derrick Sherwin who was leaving to take another job, and couldn't get free of *Who* until he'd found a replacement.

The new job didn't work out, Derrick stayed on and there followed a somewhat confused period which ended about a year later when Patrick Troughton left the show, and Jon Pertwee was lined up to replace him.

Derrick and Peter Bryant, the then producer, went off to make *Paul Temple*. Barry Letts took over as producer and I became full script editor, Jon Pertwee arrived as the Doctor and the show went into colour.

Suddenly we had a success on our hands.

There followed five hard but happy years. I always said that working on *Who*, uniquely a series of serials, was like running up a down escalator. You had to run like hell to stand any chance of reaching the top, and if you paused for breath you found yourself at the bottom again.

After about three years Barry and I both tried to move on, but our bosses wouldn't hear of it. We were even asked to create an adult science fiction serial and came up with *Moonbase 3*. In an excess of high-minded BBC rectitude we decided to avoid *Star Trek* type fantasy – no monsters or alien races – and go for grim realism. Reality proved too grim and the public didn't buy it.

But *Who* was still a success and we stayed on for several more years.

Then, after five years, it all came to an end.

Jon approached us on location one day and said hesitantly that he was thinking of leaving. He'd been getting offers of film and stage work, offers he was having to turn down because of his commitment to *Who*. 'If I keep saying no, they'll stop asking,' he said simply.

He'd expected us to reel with shock, and was quite surprised when we both just nodded and said we'd been having similar thoughts for some time.

Suddenly it all fell into place.

Barry started the quest for a new Doctor and the BBC found a keen young producer for *Who*. Bob Holmes was waiting in the wings, ready and eager to take over the script editor's job.

It was, as I said, the end of an era.

To be honest, I think I was the least keen to leave of those concerned. Barry wanted to return to his first love, directing, Jon wanted to move on to stage and film work. On the whole I was still enjoying *Who* – but it seemed absurd to stay on with Jon and Barry leaving. I would have felt like a relic.

So I did what I always do, and went with the flow…

One thing I did want, I decided, was a job to ease my path into freelance life. I invented an instant tradition that the departing script editor always writes the first show of the next season. (At least, I thought I'd invented it, though it turns out that it had happened several times before.)

Barry and Bob were kind enough to go along with the idea, and Bob said he wanted a story about a robot.

I thought, as any science fiction reader would, of Isaac Asimov's robot stories and his Laws of Robotics: 'No robot shall harm a human being. No robot shall allow a human being to come to harm…'

What if a robot's brain should be tampered with, so the Laws of Robotics could be broken? What if the robot developed a conscience and agonized over the harm it had done?

The story began taking shape.

Incidentally, before reading the proofs of this very book, I was genuinely unaware of the similarities between *Robot* and *The Mauritias Penny*. They're undoubtedly there, but the whole process was unconscious at the time.

My old friend Mac Hulke used to say that to write science fiction, or any kind of fiction, you needed a strong original idea.

It didn't have to be *your* strong original idea.

In this case, curiously enough, it was my idea – or rather ours. Still, I don't suppose Mac would have minded.

As I recall, the robot growing to giant size came to me during the actual writing – I wanted to strengthen the *King Kong* element, by having the robot pick Sarah up in a giant hand and stand towering over its enemies. It was an ambitious, perhaps over-ambitious, concept, leading to some slightly wobbly CSO, but Chris Barry made a gallant attempt to make it work. (I won't mention the tank.)

I don't remember very much about the actual shooting of the show, and suspect that I used pressure of work as an excuse to keep away from location filming. As a writer and script editor I always found filming agonizingly boring – like watching the proverbial paint dry. (As a producer, carrying the full responsibility for a show, I found it agonizingly fascinating, but that's another story.)

As for the finished show itself, two things stick in the memory.

Jim Acheson's magnificent robot, the finest ever seen on any screen. Until recently it had a well-deserved place of honour in the Museum of the Moving Image.

Most of all, the young – well youngish – Tom Baker in his first performance as the Doctor. Loping about the set, all teeth and curls, eyes blazing with energy.

The scene where he confronts Harry Sullivan in the laboratory.

'Tell me frankly, what do you think of the ears?'

'Well, I… er… don't really know.'

'Of course you don't. You're a busy man. You don't want to stand here burbling about my ears. I mean – it's neither 'ere nor there, is it?'

His sudden flashing smile near the end when he cancels the missiles.

'The trouble with computers is that they're very sophisticated idiots. They do exactly what you tell them at amazing speed, even if you order them to destroy you. So, if you happen to change your mind it's very difficult to stop them obeying your original order in time… But not impossible!'

With a grin that lights up the set.

Tom's performance in *Robot* secured the Doctor's future for many years.

It's an honour to have been a part of that success.

Terrance Dicks
May 2001

Season Overview

As it reached its 10th anniversary, *Doctor Who* started to go through a series of changes which would see the style and content of the show alter considerably in the next 12 months.

Jon Pertwee was playing the third incarnation of the Doctor and had made the show a notable success once again on BBC1, with a very high profile for its star in contrast to the private nature of his predecessor Patrick Troughton. Both Pertwee and producer Barry Letts had joined *Doctor Who* in late 1969 and by late 1973 they were working on their fifth season together.

Also on the production team was script editor Terrance Dicks, who had joined as an assistant script editor in 1968. When Barry Letts joined as producer in 1969 they hit it off at once. 'Working with Barry meant that my time on *Who*, however stressful, was always enjoyable,' says Dicks. 'We became, and still are, best friends. About six years after we both left *Doctor Who* I returned to the BBC to script edit the *Sunday Classic Serial* which Barry was then producing. Five years after that, when Barry returned to directing, I took over from him as producer.'

During 1973 there had been a series of departures from *Doctor Who*. Letts and Dicks had now been on the show far longer than they had originally intended, and had attempted to leave on previous occasions. During this time, they had been asked to develop an adult science fiction series – *Moonbase 3*. Developed by Dicks in December 1972 and produced by Letts, this had been an attempt to do mainstream science fiction drama on BBC1, and had achieved disappointing ratings. Terrance Dicks: 'We decided to go for grim realism – what life on a moonbase would really be like. We even hired current space pundit James Burke as an adviser. Unfortunately, we overdid the grimness and lost the "sense of wonder" that science fiction is all about.' Barry Letts was also keen to produce a dramatization about the life of Marie Curie, and three scripts based on CS Forester's *Lieutenant Hornblower* had also been commissioned for potential development in 1974. Letts announced his departure from the series during production of *Death to the Daleks* in November 1973.

During the summer of 1973, Dicks had taken the decision not to renew his contract, and to leave *Doctor Who* to become a freelance writer again in spring 1974. At the same time, he had become involved in the new range of *Doctor Who* novelizations being developed by Universal-Tandem for their new Target imprint. So from around October 1973, Dicks was trailed by his old friend Robert Holmes – a regular *Doctor Who* writer since 1968 with a great love of the series – who would take over as script editor in 1974.

In front of the cameras, there had been departures that had upset Pertwee. Katy Manning, who had played the Doctor's assistant Jo Grant, had decided to make the next move in her career, and had left the series in May 1973. Roger Delgado, the suave actor who played the Doctor's arch-enemy the Master, was also planning to leave after a final serial to be made in early 1974, since his semi-regular association with the series was losing him other work. Tragically, while the swansong for the Master was still in development, Delgado was killed in a road accident while filming in Turkey in June 1973. All these events convinced Pertwee that it was time to move on to new projects and end this phase of his career after five happy years. When it came to renegotiating contracts, Pertwee asked for a massive increase in salary if he was to do a sixth season as the Doctor. He was not surprised that his request was turned down by Shaun Sutton, the Head of Television Drama. The series was looking for a new Doctor.

In various respects, the 12th season of *Doctor Who* was late getting off the ground. In terms of scripting, numerous problems had beset Season Eleven, including the extensive rewrites Terrance Dicks undertook in late 1973 on Brian Hayles' *The Monster of Peladon*. As a result, although Season Twelve was due to start production in April 1974, by the end of 1973 very little pre-production work had been completed.

The new producer of *Doctor Who* was to be Philip Hinchcliffe. Hinchcliffe had always been interested in science fiction from his formative years, and recalled a particular fondness for the unearthly adventures of the 1950s BBC radio serial *Journey into Space*. He had also seen the first episode of *Doctor Who* while a student in 1963, and had been less than impressed.

Graduating from university with a degree in English, Hinchcliffe worked for a travel company and as a teacher, joining ATV as a script editor in 1968. There he became an associate producer, working on shows such as the children's comedy-drama *The Kids from 47A* and the daytime drama *General Hospital*. By summer 1973, he had found the options for becoming a drama producer at ATV limited, and had acquired an agent to progress his career. His agent recommended him to Bill Slater (the incoming Head of Drama Serials at the BBC), and Hinchcliffe was called in for an interview. At around this time, Hinchcliffe met Robert Holmes at ATV while Holmes was writing for *General Hospital*, just prior to joining *Doctor Who* himself. In November, Hinchcliffe had been told that he would be taken on by the BBC to produce two series. The first would be an adaptation of *Girls of Slender Means* for BBC2 (after the original producer dropped out) to be made in spring 1974, and this would be followed from the summer by *Doctor Who*. Unfortunately, a production managers' strike hit the BBC early in 1974, and *Girls of Slender Means* was postponed to 1975 (when it was produced by Martin Lisemore). With his first assignment abandoned, the 29-year-old Hinchcliffe moved on to the *Doctor Who* team early and trailed Barry Letts from around March 1974.

Tom Baker is the Doctor

Casting the new Doctor was the job of outgoing producer Barry Letts. He saw the new, less action-orientated Doctor as being a young man trapped in an old man's body, and initially set about looking for older, well-known character actors who could display energy and versatility.

Ron Moody, an actor best known for his appearance as Fagin in the musical *Oliver!*, was again considered (he had been the first choice of producer Peter Bryant to replace Troughton as the Doctor in 1969). However, another favourite this time was Richard Hearne, an elderly comic actor who had gained fame and popularity on television in the 1950s (with shows like *Mr Pastry's Progress* and *Leave it to Pastry*) in his elderly clownish alter ego of Mr Pastry. In 1970, at the age of 61, Hearne had retired from his famed tumbling and slapstick routines, claiming that popular entertainment had become too smutty. Letts attempted to lure him back into television in a pure, wholesome role as a children's hero. However, Hearne seemed to be confused as to what Letts was asking him to do, believing that the producer wanted him to play the Doctor as Mr Pastry, and observing that since Pastry was a comic character, he was totally wrong for an adventure series.

Another favourite of Letts' was Graham Crowden, a Scots character actor with a great deal of film and theatre experience. Letts met with Crowden who was very keen on the idea of replacing Pertwee, but the actor was honest enough to admit that the theatre was his first love, and he did not want to commit to a television role which he might quickly want to leave and return to the stage. (Crowden later appeared in the 1979/80 *Doctor Who* serial *The Horns of Nimon* as Soldeed.)

The next strong candidate was Michael Bentine, a comedy star who had been instrumental in the creation of *The Goon Show* in the 1950s, and had a hit with his surreal comedy series *It's A Square World*. Bentine was extremely keen on the role because he was fascinated by science, and also had a great knowledge of the paranormal. However, it soon became clear that Bentine's desire to write his own material would also extend to working on the scripts for *Doctor Who*, and Letts believed that the series' demanding production schedules would not allow its lead actor this luxury.

Abandoning the notion of an older actor, Letts began discussions with some younger ones. Jim Dale, a former TV host who had become a regular star of the *Carry On* comedy films in the 1960s, was flattered to be considered, but indicated to Letts that he was committed elsewhere for the next twelve months. Another *Carry On* lead to be interviewed was Bernard Cribbins, who had also co-starred in the 1966 Aaru feature film *Daleks – Invasion Earth 2150 AD*. At his meeting with Letts, Cribbins listed off all the talents he could bring to the Doctor – such as diving, dancing, parachuting and golfing – but when he mentioned fighting, Letts told him that the Doctor did *not* fight.

The man who was to become Letts' second choice as the Doctor was Fulton Mackay, a 52-year-old Scots actor who was best known on television as Chief Superintendent Inman in Thames Television's *Special Branch*. A former actor himself, Letts had worked with Mackay for years, and Mackay had played the role of Dr Quinn in *Doctor Who and the Silurians (1970)*, the first *Doctor Who* serial Letts had produced back in 1969. The producer was sure that Mackay could play the Doctor as a character role, in the same way that Patrick Troughton had approached the job. As it happened, within months Mackay would be reprising a role from a one-off comedy he made in 1973, which would bring him fame as Prison Officer MacKay in *Porridge*.

The man who was to become Barry Letts' first choice was not on his initial list. As far as can be ascertained, an out-of-work actor called Tom Baker wrote to Bill Slater, the man who was about to become Letts' new boss as BBC Head of Drama Serials. Baker wrote his letter, asking for work, as he lay on the mattress that served as a bed on the floor of his one-room flat in Bourne Street, Pimlico.

Born in Liverpool in 1934, Baker's desire to act was almost halted when he was prevented from joining the Abbey Theatre in London by his mother, and instead joined a monastic order in the Channel Islands. However, the holy life did not suit him and he returned to the mainland, completing his National Service and serving with the merchant navy. After a troubled marriage had broken down, Baker took up acting as his major career in the 1960s, with work at York Repertory Theatre, the Edinburgh Festival and the National Theatre. His television career was more limited, with small roles in shows like *Dixon of Dock Green* and *Softly, Softly: Task Force*. However, his growing reputation from his stage work secured him the starring role of Rasputin in the 1971 movie *Nicholas and Alexandra*. Now established, other film appearances included *Vault of Horror* and *The Mutations*, while on television he had appeared in *Arthur of the Britons* and in the TV movie *Frankenstein: The True Story* for Universal.

It was the night of Sunday 3 February 1974, and – despite a hopeful movie career – Baker was out of work as an actor. Following a stage production of *Macbeth* which had run until Christmas 1973, Baker had been forced to work on a building site in Ebury Street to sustain a form of income. That evening, he decided to write to Slater, who had been his director in his major television appearance, starring as the Indian doctor in an adaptation of *The Millionairess* for the BBC's Play of the Month strand in 1972. The letter appears to have arrived with Slater on Tuesday 5, the day on which Slater was meeting Letts and discussing the new actor to replace Pertwee.

This meeting made little progress, with Slater having no firm suggestions for the producer, but agreeing to discuss the matter further the next day. That evening, Slater went home with Baker's begging letter and remarked on it to his wife, actress Mary Webster, who also knew Baker. As he did so, he realized that the out-of-work actor could be a suitable choice to star in *Doctor Who*, and was encouraged by his wife to telephone Baker immediately, inviting him to come and discuss 'a role' at Television Centre the following evening. At his Wednesday morning meeting with Letts, Slater suggested Baker. Since Letts was unfamiliar with the actor's work, Slater suggested that he should go and see him starring as the villainous magician Koura in *The Golden Voyage of Sinbad*, a fantasy movie which had been released in December and which was showing at the Victoria Cinema. Returning to collect Terrance Dicks from the production office at Room 505 Union House, Letts went to see the movie that afternoon. Both men were impressed with Baker's rich performance and his screen presence.

After his day on the building site, Baker arrived at the BBC Club that evening for a chat with Slater and was introduced to Letts and to Slater's superior, Shaun Sutton – but left none the wiser as to why Slater had wanted to see him. He then found himself invited back on the Thursday evening for a more formal meeting in Sutton's office, where Letts revealed that after a lot of very positive discussions they wished to offer him the role of the next Doctor Who. Astounded, Baker nodded with delight, and agreed to keep the news to himself for about ten days or so until formal announcements could be arranged. The actor returned to his work on Ebury Street, unable to tell his workmates about his new role.

When Baker became the youngest actor to be offered the role of Doctor Who, it had not been publicly announced that Pertwee was leaving the series. This story was now issued to the press on Friday 8 February while Pertwee was still working on his penultimate serial, *The Monster of Peladon.* (He had also been due to appear as a guest discussing horror films on the BBC2 chat show *Just a Nimmo* on Sunday 3 February, but had been unable to attend on the day.) Many national papers, including the *Daily Mirror, Daily Telegraph* and *Daily Mail* carried the announcement the following day. The *Sun* correctly stated that Pertwee's successor had already been appointed but could not be named until contracts had been worked out, while the *Times* confirmed that the new star would be announced the following week.

They were correct. On Friday 15, Baker put on his most expensive possession – his leather coat – and left his one-room flat to attend his press launch at the Bridge Lounge of Television Centre, accompanied by his friend, the playwright Ted Whitehead. Also present was Elisabeth Sladen who had joined the series in May 1973 as the Doctor's current companion, journalist Sarah Jane Smith. For the press call, Sladen was released from rehearsals for *The Monster of Peladon.* Alongside the two actors was Pat Gorman, a bit-part actor who played monsters on the series, dressed in a Cyberman costume from *The Invasion* to pose for press photographs after Letts' announcement. The new star then went to a small studio for an interview on a regional news show for BBC North West, and also spoke on *Pebble Mill at One.* That evening, the first newspaper to carry the story was the *Evening Standard* which revealed Baker's next job to his amazed colleagues on the Ebury Street site.

The national daily papers covered the story the following morning, with the *Daily Express* doing a feature on Baker at the building site a few days later. In the *Daily Mail,* Baker emphasized that he wanted 'to suggest somebody who is from another world but who has human characteristics', adding that he was fascinated by science fiction. The *Guardian* reported how this former National Theatre Company actor aimed to play the Doctor 'in an individual way... although he has a human body he comes from somewhere else'. In the *Daily Mirror,* Baker explained that he was 'a great fan of *Doctor Who'* (although it actually seems he had seldom seen the show) and that he was looking forward to the security which his one-year contract would offer him. This contract was formalized – for a rather lower fee than Pertwee had received – on Tuesday 19 February. Baker would make an initial 26 episodes of the show between Saturday 20 April and Wednesday 14 May 1975.

In order to flesh out the character for Baker's Doctor, the actor joined Barry Letts, Terrance Dicks and Robert Holmes for a working meal at the

Balzac restaurant in Shepherd's Bush. Here he also met Philip Hinchcliffe who would produce all the serials that followed *Robot*.

The production team knew that although they were casting a younger actor than had been envisaged, they still wanted somebody who would provide a great contrast to Pertwee's version of the Doctor. It was suggested that the Doctor should look eccentric in a similar manner to the images of Albert Einstein. Possibly he could play the violin, rather like Sherlock Holmes.

Feeling that conventional heroes were falling out of fashion, Hinchcliffe suggested a more rebellious, anti-authority figure to contrast with the Pertwee Doctor who had worked for the establishment. Seeing the Doctor as more of a wandering space-gypsy, Hinchcliffe had been struck by the description of Troughton's Doctor as a 'cosmic hobo' (a phrase attributed to Sydney Newman, one of the series' creators) and aimed to combine this with an 'Olympian detachment' to create a character that would appeal to adults and student viewers. However, the producer was not keen to stress the Doctor's alien nature – whereas Holmes believed that this could be conveyed by having the Doctor think laterally or seem preoccupied. Baker himself was delighted by the notion of Hinchcliffe's Bohemian wanderer, seeing him as an innocent figure with an air of continual surprise.

Slowly the discussions led to a vague description which would be given to the writers of the new stories. The Doctor would be a cross between Sherlock Holmes, Professor Bernard Quatermass (the scientist hero of three 1950s BBC TV science fiction serials) and George Bernard Shaw. The new Doctor was conceived of as being witty, sometimes bad-tempered and frequently secretive.

Barry Letts (interviewed in 1987) said of the fourth Doctor: 'We decided to go away from Jon Pertwee. People came up with all sorts of ideas which would have looked like an attempt to duplicate Jon – a poor man's Jon Pertwee. So what we looked for was a strong personality in its own right.'

Terrance Dicks, who wrote *Robot,* Tom Baker's first story as the Doctor, later recalled: 'Tom in the flesh does have this type of loony scatterbrain, so I played on that very much. I also used the device that the new regeneration is always unstable. So he starts off being rather crazy, and gradually quietens down and becomes more reasonable by the end of it. I thought, if they don't like my interpretation of it, or Tom doesn't like that interpretation, they could always say: "Well, he was a bit weird, but he's different now – he's stable." In fact I think they always kept quite a lot of that arbitrary erraticness that I started him off with.'

Dicks was – and is – of the opinion that the changes to the Doctor when he regenerates are superficial. 'It's always the same man, though his surface mannerisms may change. So the dramatic writing of the "serious Doctor stuff" actually changes very little indeed. The flourishes are different.'

Harry Sullivan

As well as a new Doctor, *Robot* had also required the introduction of a new regular character as a contingency until the fourth incarnation of the Doctor had been decided upon.

As action sequences had been a popular ingredient of the show in recent years, it was decided to retain these, and so a young secondary male character was introduced as a new companion. This was Harry Sullivan, a naval surgeon on attachment to UNIT as medical officer. Another change to the UNIT line-up was imminent with the writing out of Captain Mike Yates – a process which began with *Invasion of the Dinosaurs* (made in autumn 1973 and broadcast in 1974) and which would be completed with Jon Pertwee's final story, *Planet of the Spiders*, in which Yates would be back in civvie street. Since this left a gap in the chain of command between the Brigadier and the other UNIT regular – Sergeant Benton – Letts decided to have Benton promoted to Warrant Officer First Class (WO1).

Terrance Dicks recalls: 'The thought was that you might get an "unphysical" Patrick-Troughton-type Doctor. Whenever there was a fight, Troughton tended to hide and send Jamie sailing in. In fact, that didn't work out, which is one of the reasons there were problems with Harry as a companion – there wasn't quite enough for Harry to do.'

Structure of the Season

In April 1974, the structure of the 12th season of *Doctor Who* was planned to comprise five stories running for a total of 26 episodes. This was basically the same structure as all but the first of the Pertwee seasons. The plan seems to have been to start with the two four-parters – *Robot* by Terrance Dicks and *Space Station* by Christopher Langley. These would then be followed by three six-part stories – *Genesis of Terror* (later renamed *Genesis of the Daleks*) by Terry Nation, *Loch Ness* by Robert Banks Stewart (see Appendix A) and another serial that was still to be determined.

Script editor Robert Holmes had always been unhappy about the number of six-part serials in the new season. He recalled that *The Monster of Peladon* had caused particular problems the previous year. He saw the structure of a six-parter as effectively being a four-episode narrative with a two-part storyline tagged on the end to stretch it out. Because of this, in May 1974 Holmes discussed with incoming producer Philip Hinchcliffe the possibility of dropping the uncommissioned final six-parter of the season and replacing it with a two-part serial and a four-part serial. The two-parter could be assigned to the same production team as one of the four-parters so that, although it would be made as if it were a six-parter, the location and studio work would split up into the two separate narrative stories. Hinchcliffe agreed as this would give them more 'first nights' on which to hook a new audience: 'The natural length of a story was probably about four episodes and you were really pushing it after that. On the other hand it's more costly, so I had to argue the next season to have my budget put up, because to do that one extra story you have to build a whole new chunk of sets more. That was a budget battle that I won – so we had more four-parters.'

By the end of May, the shape of the season had changed to comprise six serials: *Robot*; a potential replacement for *Space Station*; the newly commissioned two-part *The Destructors* (later renamed *The Sontaran Experiment*); *Genesis of Terror*; the new four-part *Revenge of the Cybermen* (which would re-use Langley's space-station setting); and a four-part version of *Loch Ness*.

ROBOT

BY TERRANCE DICKS

PART ONE first transmitted 28 December 1974 at 17.35
PART TWO 4 January 1975 at 17.30
PART THREE 11 January 1975 at 17.30
PART FOUR 18 January 1975 at 17.30

Overview

As a showcase for the new Doctor, *Robot* succeeds admirably. The story itself is straightforward, and, with its reliance on the regular UNIT team of the Brigadier and Benton, is reminiscent of the Earth-based Jon Pertwee stories. The notion seems to have been that the new Doctor should be introduced into a setting and structure that was still familiar to the audience. With Jon Pertwee having held the role for longer than either of his predecessors, this was a sensible proposition.

But *Robot* does far more than simply echo the past. The themes it introduces – of rule by elite, of science as the way forward, of 'alien' (in this case, machine) intelligence versus human instinct – would be followed through in each of the other stories of the season. *The Ark in Space* presents an apparently beneficent elitist society of the future in an environment where humanity itself is forced to battle against alien intelligence for control not of the world but of the individual. *The Sontaran Experiment* shows an alien intruder trying to determine the very nature of humanity. *Genesis of the Daleks* presents the flip side of the elitist society of the Ark, and shows us the destructive aspect of scientific 'advancement' in graphic detail. *Revenge of the Cybermen* finally pits humanity directly against what it may become if it succumbs to that advancement.

That *Robot* blends these themes and sets up the debates of the season without apparently becoming heavy or 'preachy' is testament to the quality of the scripts. But with the immensely impressive Robot K1 dominating every scene it is in, and Tom Baker's charismatic portrayal breathing fresh and startling life into the role of the Doctor, it is easy to sit back and let the enjoyment wash over you. Which is, after all, what it's all about.

Origins

The first story of the 12th season of *Doctor Who* was written by outgoing script editor Terrance Dicks. Recalling his commissioning of his predecessor Derrick Sherwin for the serial *The Invasion* when he himself took over as script editor in 1968, Terrance Dicks ensured that he had one freelance project lined up by inventing a 'tradition'. He explained to his successor, Robert Holmes, that an incoming script editor always commissioned their predecessor for their first story.

In fact this had happened several times previously. In 1964, outgoing script editor David Whitaker wrote *The Rescue*, the first script to be edited by his successor, Dennis Spooner. In 1965 Spooner's *The Time Meddler* was the first formal editing job for Spooner's successor Donald Tosh. Both of these had been special cases where freelance writers were not suitable to develop new companions in a limited budget serial.

Having enjoyed working with Dicks, Holmes was more than happy to accept this 'tradition' and Dicks was requested – while still on the BBC staff – to provide the first script for the new Doctor. However, because of the situation with Dicks working for the BBC, the story was not formally commissioned when work began on it in early 1974.

Storyline

One notion which fascinated Holmes concerned the principles by which an artificial intelligence could function; what limitations would be placed on its behaviour – such as the laws of robotics postulated by the Russian-born American science fiction writer Isaac Asimov in 1940. The first of these stated: 'A robot may not injure a human being, or, through inaction, allow a human being to come to harm'. A story about a new, intelligent robot was therefore discussed with Dicks. Since this serial would be a post-regeneration adventure, the production team realized the narrative would be a direct continuation of Pertwee's final story – *Planet of the Spiders* – and that it would therefore be best for the viewers if the Doctor were surrounded by familiar characters such as Brigadier Lethbridge Stewart and the team from UNIT – United Nations Intelligence Taskforce – the paramilitary organization to which the Doctor had been the scientific adviser during his enforced exile on Earth some five years earlier.

Dicks' own desires for a story included a homage to *King Kong*, a classic RKO monster movie from 1933 in which a vast ape is brought back to New York and runs berserk, but is also shown to have affection and feelings towards a beautiful woman. The climax of the film had the massive creature attacked atop the Empire State Building by aircraft and falling to its doom. However, Dicks was interested in the fact that he had once read a critic commenting that the audience for *King Kong* always ended up on the side of the monster; the menacing and intelligent robot suggested by Holmes would therefore have a sympathetic side. Another ingredient for the story was Women's Lib, a topical notion, and Dicks decided to make one of the main villains a strong and independent woman. His story received the simple working title *Robot*, and he set about fleshing the ideas out into scripts.

Scripts

Dicks discussed his four-part storyline fully with Holmes before scripting, and only a few changes were made. With inflation becoming a problem at the time, Holmes suggested a cost-saving revision to the plot of Part Four to remove a sequence where the Doctor's companion, journalist Sarah Jane Smith, was attacked by the Robot while leaving the bunker in her car after the defeat of the principal villains, the Scientific Reform Society (SRS). Dicks reluctantly reworked this. With such minimal changes, *Robot* became Dicks' favourite script of all those he wrote for *Doctor Who*; he was keen to move the format on slightly from the Earth-bound Pertwee serials in developing the new Doctor, and also to leave his own personal stamp as he himself left the series.

In developing the central character of the Robot, Dicks aimed to convey a large and powerful figure which was unaware of its own strength, and whose behaviour softened because of its emotional attachment to Sarah. This aspect was drawn directly from the Oedipus complex (mother-figure attraction) suggested by the behaviour of King Kong towards Ann Darrow, Fay Wray's character in the RKO movie. Dicks also opted to keep the appearance of the Robot hidden until the end of Part One, showing its actions from the machine's electronic point of view. With no idea of how the Robot would look on screen, Dicks' script had it moving in a very versatile way – sinking to its knees, throwing crates at UNIT troops and being quite agile in action sequences. Dicks also wrote the closing sequences with the Robot swollen to giant proportions, knowing that the video-effect technique of Colour Separation Overlay – CSO – would be used to make the Robot massive (for an explanation of CSO, also known as Chromakey or 'blue screen', see page 77).

The sequence of the SRS meeting in Part Three (Scenes 8 and 10) was reminiscent of a similar sequence in *The Mauritius Penny*, an episode of the stylish ABC thriller series *The Avengers* which Terrance Dicks had scripted with his old writing partner Malcolm Hulke in 1962. The episode – recorded on Thursday 18 October 1962 and broadcast Saturday 10 November – concerned a secret organization, 'New Rule', whose purpose was to take control of England and western Europe and reform it under the stronger leadership of a mysterious dictator. The female lead, Mrs Catherine Gale, infiltrated a meeting of the uniformed anti-democracy New Rule fanatics, who were about to be introduced to their leader for the first time. However, her presence at the meeting was detected, and she was exposed as a spy – only to be saved by the arrival of her partner, John Steed. In *Robot*, Sarah infiltrates the SRS meeting where Professor Kettlewell is revealed to be a figurehead for the organization, and the meeting is then disrupted by the arrival of the Doctor after Sarah's discovery.

The scripts were formally commissioned as an in-house project after production had actually begun. On Thursday 23 May, clearance for the departing script editor to write the serial was given; the reasons for this were given in a memo on Friday 10 June as being because of Dicks' 'intimate knowledge of the serial's history required for this particular script (changeover of principal character)'. Even during production, the title of *Robot* was still only provisional. It seems that some documentation issued later in the year referred to it as *The Giant Robot* (the title used for the Target Books novelization of the story). With the script completed, one of Dicks' next assignments was the writing of the new *Doctor Who* stage play *Seven Keys to Doomsday* (see Appendix A).

Baker first attended a studio recording for *Doctor Who* on Tuesday 2 April when he recorded the regeneration scene for *Planet of the Spiders* with Pertwee in Studio 1 at Television Centre. He had not attended rehearsals beforehand and, thrust into the established team, the actor was very quiet and unobtrusive. Hinchcliffe was also present at this session, trailing Letts. Six days later, Baker recorded a guest appearance on *Password*, a BBC TV quiz show.

Picking up on the scatterbrain nature he had seen in his meetings with Baker, Dicks decided to develop the Doctor initially along these lines. He reasoned that if the crazy behaviour of the new incarnation did not work, it could be put down to regenerative trauma and so toned down in later serials. The new Doctor's manner was specified clearly by Dicks in stage directions as having a very different body language to the Pertwee Doctor (for example, in Part One, Scenes 12 and 15, and also when the Doctor is lying down in his lab in Part Two, Scene 4). The remote, preoccupied nature was also specified as he seemed to ignore the Brigadier (Part Two, Scene 18). As a further contrast, in Scene 9 of Part Three, the Doctor's bettering of an SRS thug was achieved more by accident than by any combat skill he would display. Furthermore, Dicks had the new Doctor offer Sarah some sweets at the end of the serial – something the third Doctor would never have done; these were to become jelly babies, one of the icons for the new Doctor. However, elements such as the Doctor's car, Bessie, and his sonic screwdriver were still around as links to the past.

Production Team

The director chosen for Baker's debut was Christopher Barry, an experienced television director who had first worked on *Doctor Who* back in 1963 with the first Dalek serial. Since then, Barry had directed six further *Doctor Who* serials: *The Rescue* (1965), *The Romans* (1965), *The Savages* (1966), *The Power of the Daleks* (1966) – which had introduced Patrick Troughton as the Doctor – *The Daemons* (1971) and *The Mutants* (1972). Since his last *Doctor Who* assignment, Barry had worked for Letts and Dicks as one of the two directors on *Moonbase 3* and was then engaged on episodes of the BBC drama *The*

Carnforth Practice (which had begun production in late 1973). Barry had been keen to move on from *Doctor Who* to direct many other shows, but the prospect of launching another new Doctor lured him back to a show for which he had a very soft spot.

Ian Rawnsley and Judy Clay were both new to *Doctor Who* in their capacities as set designer and make-up designer. James Acheson, assigned to supervise costumes, had first worked on the show back in 1972 alongside Barry on *The Mutants*, since when he had handled *Carnival of Monsters, The Three Doctors* and *The Time Warrior*. (Acheson later won an Oscar for his costume design on *The Last Emperor*.) Unusually for the time, visual effects were contracted outside the BBC to Clifford Culley who ran a small firm, Westbury Design and Optical Ltd., at Pinewood Studios. This team had previously worked on *Planet of the Daleks* and *Invasion of the Dinosaurs* in 1973, and may have been chosen because the technique of making giant monsters using CSO in the latter serial was to be re-employed on *Robot*.

One of Acheson's key tasks was to realize the image for the new Doctor – and Letts wanted a complete contrast to Pertwee's dandified outfit. Keen to develop the Bohemian notion, Baker suggested a hat of some sort to add to the mix, and attended a 'trying on' session at a costume house – the aim being to develop an eccentric rather than flamboyant image. Acheson soon realized that he was influenced by the images of French painter Henri de Toulouse-Lautrec – notably two 1892 lithographs depicting the music hall star Aristide Bruant in advertisements: *Aristide Bruant dans son cabaret* (at Ambassadeurs and Eldorado). In these, Bruant was shown wearing a red scarf and a fedora.

Baker liked the idea of a scarf, and Acheson remembered a distinctive one worn by freelance props-builder Alastair Bowtell (who had been sub-contracted on the serial). It had been knitted by an elderly lady called Begonia Pope, and Acheson sent her a mass of different wools, asking her to produce something for the Doctor. Pope was so delighted to be working for the BBC that she used nearly all the wool – and the scarf ended up incredibly long. Although Baker and Acheson had favoured a long flowing coat for the Doctor, this notion was vetoed and so Baker wore a short red jacket instead, along with woollen trousers, checked shirt, striped tie and paisley cardigan.

Interviewed in 1987, Acheson said of the fourth Doctor's costume: 'It was more eccentric, not flamboyant. Jon Pertwee was very flamboyant, but whereas Pertwee was much more the sartorial, frilly, velvety, greying Doctor Who, Baker was this much more manic, scarecrow-like, slightly more dangerous Doctor Who.'

The Robot

The other key piece of design for the serial was the Robot itself. Unusually, this was also designed by costume designer Jim Acheson and constructed by Bowtell, whom Acheson had worked with on *The Mutants* in 1972. As with the mutant monster costumes, Acheson designed the robot costume by making a model. He later recalled: 'A job like that was not normally something the costume department would be expected to do. So we went out on a bit of a limb and did it anyway.'

The finished product was extremely bulky and cumbersome since, in an attempt to get away from an obvious man in a silvered costume, Acheson opted to have a massive construction built out of very thin aluminium sheeting to make the Robot look truly metallic. 'Aluminium doesn't really come into the realm of the costume department,' he recalled. 'It was a bit daft, really, because the most difficult thing to put on colour separation overlay is a reflective-surfaced costume.'

The Robot's hands and arms were made of balsa wood and covered in aluminium cladding, and ended in a pincer device adapted from an item used in the grocery trade for getting items off high shelves. Inside the costume, the actor would use a radio-mike to have his dialogue modulated in a booming, electronic voice. The head – which was worn as a hat by the actor – contained flashing lights.

The entire costume was very heavy and awkward to wear. Actor Michael Kilgarriff recalls getting scratched and cut by the metal interior as well as suffering from the restricted vision. To alleviate these problems, yet still allow the camera and lighting crews to prepare properly, a lightweight framework with silver foil was built for the actor to use during camera rehearsals (as shown in the picture on page 33).

Cast

Although Tom Baker's casting as the Doctor was the more important of the two regular characters, the first to be cast was in fact Harry Sullivan. Letts recalled Ian Marter, a young actor whom he had been impressed by at a stage play in 1970. He had previously offered Marter a regular role on *Doctor Who* as another member of UNIT, Captain Mike Yates, but Marter had turned the part down. Nevertheless, Letts had then cast Marter as a young 1920s naval officer, Lieutenant John Andrews, in the serial *Carnival of Monsters* which had been recorded in 1972. Marter had never intended to be an actor, but when he left university in 1969 he applied for work at the Bristol Old Vic and was astounded to land the job of assistant stage manager which led him into acting on stage. His theatre work included appearances in the West End, in Dublin and at the Edinburgh Festival with parts in *The Importance of Being Earnest* and *The Rivals*. Meanwhile, his television roles included playing Quentin Ingrams in *Crown Court* as well as appearances in *The Brothers, The Venturers* and Play for Today. Some time after completing *Carnival of Monsters*, Marter had been extremely ill and close to death for two weeks during 1973. It was at the end of six months' recuperation that Letts approached him concerning the role of Harry Sullivan; after a lunchtime meeting where Letts and Holmes outlined Harry as an old-fashioned *Boy's Own* young hero, Marter happily accepted the role. The actor attended two costume fittings for his new part on Tuesday 26 February and Tuesday 5 March.

Elisabeth Sladen and Ian Marter were contracted for the 26 new episodes on Tuesday 16 April, and the following day Nicholas Courtney and John Levene were booked to reprise their semi-regular roles as the Brigadier and Benton. Both had worked on the first studio recordings for *Planet of the Spiders* along with Baker and Sladen a fortnight earlier.

In terms of the guest characters, Barry cast Patricia Maynard – then the partner of actor Dennis Waterman – as Miss Winters, the head of the SRS, because of her ability to be very superior. Winters' assistant, Arnold Jellicoe, was played by Alec Linstead whom Barry had used as UNIT Sergeant Osgood in the 1971 serial *The Daemons*. Also considered for this role was Colin Baker, an actor whom Barry had just worked with on *The Carnforth Practice* (and who would later play the sixth incarnation of the Doctor). To operate the demanding robot costume, Barry selected the tall actor Michael Kilgarriff, whose considerable radio experience and deep voice would be especially valuable for a performance where his face would not be seen. Kilgarriff was used to such work, having appeared on *Doctor Who* in 1967 as the Cyberman Controller in *The Tomb of the Cybermen* and as an Ogron in *Frontier in Space* (1973). In comparison to the massive Robot, the role of its creator, Professor J.P. Kettlewell, went to Edward Burnham because of his small stature; Burnham had played a scientist before in the series – Professor Watkins in *The Invasion*. He was very keen to make all manner of suggestions as to how he should play the eccentric Kettlewell, including the wild hair and thick spectacles (although during production it was necessary to curtail some of the actor's more outrageous suggestions as they grew increasingly camp).

In the smaller roles, Pat Gorman – who had been the Cyberman at Baker's photocall – appeared as the Thinktank guard on location in Part One. Gorman was a walk-on and small part actor who had first worked on *Doctor Who* in *The Dalek Invasion of Earth* in 1964; since then, he had played many guards and monsters, including an uncredited coven member in *The Daemons* for Barry. Similarly, John Scott Martin – playing the vault guard – had first worked on *Doctor Who* in *The Web Planet* in 1965, and regularly operated a Dalek on the series. In this capacity he had worked with Barry on *The Power of the Daleks* as well as being a villager in *The Daemons* and the main Mutt in *The Mutants* for the director (amongst his many other roles). Stunt man Terry Walsh played the SRS bouncer with whom the Doctor has a tussle in Part Three; Walsh had worked on *Doctor Who* since *The Smugglers* in 1966, and had been the fight arranger and a stunt guard for Barry on *The Mutants*. Appearing as Short was Timothy Craven, whom Barry had cast before in *Paul Temple*; Craven had made two previous appearances in *Doctor Who* as a cell guard in *Frontier in Space* and as Robinson in *Invasion of the Dinosaurs* (1974).

Outside Broadcast

Prior to production starting on *Robot*, Letts had been contacted by Barbara Derkow on Monday 1 April. Derkow was the director of a new BBC Further Education series provisionally entitled *Television Drama* which was proposing to film the production of *Robot* to show how a drama series was made; Letts met with Derkow on Thursday 4 and agreed to the study of his final serial as

producer. This was confirmed by the *Television Drama* producer David
Hargreaves on Friday 5 (see Appendix D for further details).

Because of the problems encountered on *Invasion of the Dinosaurs* with
keying a studio element (such as a model dinosaur) into filmed location
material using CSO, Letts decided to use Outside Broadcast (OB) electronic
cameras on *Doctor Who* for the first time, as this would give a more stable
background to the images behind the gigantic Robot in the final episode.
Although lightweight electronic cameras (with cables running back to a
scanner van) had been used for some time to cover sporting events, the use of
them in drama at the BBC had only started in the last few years.

The location recording for *Robot* was scheduled to overlap with the final
studio recordings on *Planet of the Spiders*. Because all the UNIT scenes had
been recorded for Pertwee's final serial at the start of April, Sladen would be the
only cast member to have to divide her time between the two serials. Barry
therefore scheduled his location work around her availability since she would
be needed at Television Centre on Tuesday 30 April and Wednesday 1 May to
record *Planet of the Spiders* which was being directed by Barry Letts.

The main location selected by Barry was BBC property – the Engineering
and Training Centre at Wood Norton in Hereford and Worcester (which had
previously been used in 1969 for Pertwee's debut serial *Spearhead from Space*).
The estate offered a variety of buildings which could appear as the bunker,
Thinktank, Emmett's Electronics, the meeting hall and the home of Professor
Kettlewell. The cast and crew travelled down on Saturday 27 April to start
recording the following day.

Sunday 28 April made the most of Sladen's day off from Letts' serial;
numerous shots of Sarah were recorded although – because Sladen did not
drive – all the shots of Sarah driving her mustard-coloured MG sports car were
left for later on and performed by a double. Baker was rather nervous recording
his first scenes, and was somewhat daunted by the fact that he was an
'unknown' taking on this major role – and a role which he had to make
different from the ways his three predecessors had played it. The presence of
another 'new boy' in the form of Marter helped to relieve some of the pressure.
Sladen found Baker a very different actor to work with when compared to
Pertwee, but just as professional; Baker took to Sladen immediately because she
was kind to him and laughed at his jokes. With Marter, Baker would do the
daily crossword in *The Times* between shots, and the new star also struck up a
friendship with Courtney.

Work on Monday 29 required careful lining up of camera shots for later
integration with CSO material in studio with the massive Robot. The next day,

the cast were issued with their contracts to allow their material to be used in *Television Drama*, and Sladen was busy back in London recording *Planet of the Spiders*. Over the next couple of days, numerous CSO background shots and sequences to be shown on the bunker monitors in studio were also taped. The factory vault used on Wednesday 1 May was an outbuilding hurriedly selected by Barry when he was denied permission to shoot in the real underground studio on the estate (Part Three, Scene 18).

Sladen rejoined the team on Thursday 2 and posed for a photocall which would introduce Baker to the public in costume, as well as revealing the Robot for the first time. The day – which involved several sequences with the Robot – was a very demanding one, and there were disagreements between Culley and production unit manager George Gallaccio about how long Kilgarriff could work inside the costume. The actor became very weak very quickly, and found it difficult to breathe; he almost collapsed during the final take of the scene in which the Robot breaks out of Kettlewell's lab at the start of Part Three. When he got home that night, Kilgarriff was plagued with nightmares of being trapped inside a metal submarine. When he woke the next morning, he was barely able to stand, and had to spend days getting his strength back before his next recording.

Taping resumed at Wood Norton on Sunday 5 May, with the vault, hastily dressed by Rawnsley's team, now acting as the bunker entrance. Recorded on Monday 6 was an effects shot which nobody was very happy with: the abortive attack on the Robot by a tank (Part Three, Scene 29).

Because various BBC productions had been plagued by a scenery shifters' strike, Barry also provisionally booked Tuesday 7 as a stand-by day and used it for miscellaneous pick-up shots. It was also on Tuesday 7 that Derkow confirmed arrangements for *Television Drama* – commenting to Letts that she had very much enjoyed Part One of *Planet of the Spiders* (broadcast the previous Saturday).

Recording

With the film crew of the *Television Drama* documentary in attendance, the first read-through of *Robot* took place at St Nicholas Church Hall on Bennett Street in Chiswick on Friday 10 May. Regular rehearsals for the first studio session started the following Monday. As rehearsals began, Baker was still a rather nervous loner, but soon established himself as the show's new star during the run-up to the first studio session. Baker made use of every opportunity to suggest something novel that his character could do to emphasize his alien values; this included comedy business with breaking a brick by karate (see Part One, Scene 6), as well as using the Doctor's long scarf both to measure the hole left by the Robot (Part One, Scene 25) and to pick up a component at Thinktank (Part Two, Scene 16). A close bond was also forming between Marter and Sladen; when Marter discovered that Sladen and her husband lived close to him in Ealing, the pair started to travel to rehearsals together (particularly when the rehearsal venue was later moved to the BBC's custom-built rehearsal rooms at Acton).

It was intended to record Parts One and Two of *Robot* on Tuesday 21 and Wednesday 22 May, with Barry noting in the camera script that at the end of the scene where Sarah was introduced to the Robot at the start of Part Two he would, 'hope to record at least to here on 1st day'. However, industrial action by the scenery shifters prevented any recording taking place on the first day – forcing Barry Letts to rapidly arrange a remount. Christopher Barry revised his studio schedule to give a list of scenes he believed could be taped the next night. One particular problem was a stepladder left in the middle of the set for Kettlewell's lab. The crew did not dare to move it for union reasons, and so attempted to shoot around it. Barry used the evening of Wednesday 22 to do some technical shots such as effects inserts, the Doctor selecting his new costume and the like.

Because of the dispute, the sets for *Robot* were left standing in Studio 3. This meant that the next day's live transmission of the children's magazine programme *Blue Peter* from that studio saw the show presented from these locations. The edition began with the *Doctor Who* theme replacing the show's usual 'Barnacle Bill' signature tune. Peter Purves (who had played the Doctor's companion Steven Taylor between 1965 and 1966) then emerged from the TARDIS into the UNIT laboratory. John Noakes appeared from the hole in the bunker floor and Lesley Judd closed the massive safe door – all seen by BBC1 viewers some seven months before *Robot* went out. As Noakes commented, 'Well, no doubt you're a bit surprised to see us in the world of *Doctor Who* – well, we're a bit surprised too…'

The episodes of *Robot* were recorded without opening and closing credits; on Thursday 23 May, a request for a new set of filmed titles featuring Tom Baker's face was made, to be added to *Robot* during editing (see page 116).

On Friday 24 May, rehearsals for Parts Three and Four began, and Letts managed to reschedule the abandoned session at short notice for Saturday 1 and Sunday 2 June. Christopher Barry chose to salvage very little material from his earlier problematic recording (aside from the theft from the Government Office, the Doctor's costume routine, the scenes in the vault, the Doctor's visit to Kettlewell's, Sarah's SRS visit and the attack on Chambers). Over the two days, the cast and crew caught up with the schedule, completing the first few scenes for Part Three which continued directly on from Part Two.

By this time, it seems as if the notion for the *Television Drama* team to film work in the studio session for Parts Three and Four had been abandoned; the project was formally cancelled by producer David Hargreaves on Friday 7 June. Taping of Parts Three and Four of *Robot* went ahead as planned on Thursday 6 and Friday 7 June, with regular recording pauses to ready Kilgarriff's heavy costume before all his scenes. Part Four was done on the final evening and was made largely in order, although the final UNIT HQ scene was taped before all the OB sequences, which required the addition of complex CSO elements.

For this, the Robot, UNIT soldiers and other items were placed against a yellow background and keyed into the location scenes recorded by Barry's team weeks earlier. This complex and experimental work was, however, more difficult to execute than expected; overrunning their allocated studio time by 35 minutes, the effects shots were not completed as production wrapped for the summer. For the cast and crew, this was the end nine months of work which had begun in September 1973 with *Invasion of the Dinosaurs*. Production would resume in September with the remaining 22 episodes planned for the new season.

On Monday 17 June, Letts explained that the overrun was due to the ambitious nature of their attempts to mix CSO work with OB video recording:

> Although the show itself was completed, a number of these trick shots remain
> to be picked up at a later date. In my opinion the results are remarkable; this is
> some of the best CSO we have achieved.

Barry began his editing of *Robot* on Monday 24 June, and the initial edit – as far as could be done with neither a complete set of CSO effects sequences nor opening and closing credits – was completed by Thursday 4 July. Only minor trims were made to Parts One and Two.

Because of the BBC strikes and other issues, Letts' move to *Marie Curie* was delayed as the production was deferred and he was now waiting to succeed John McRae as a producer on the Sunday classic serials. Thus, over the summer of 1974, Letts found himself acting as an adviser to his successor as producer, Philip Hinchcliffe.

Since some of the CSO sequences had not been completed – and because Barry Letts and Christopher Barry felt they could improve on others – on Wednesday 14 August Letts arranged a remount for Studio 3 on Friday 11 October which would require only Sladen and Kilgarriff to re-record some of the CSO material. (This was between the location recording for the third story in broadcast order, *The Sontaran Experiment*, and prior to studio recording for the second, *The Ark in Space*.) Christopher Barry fitted this around his commitments to the BBC police series *Z Cars*. As it turned out, this recording was rescheduled to the small Studio 7 on Thursday 24 October. Barry completed his CSO techniques – again with an overrun of 25 minutes. Accounting for the expensive overrun in a memo five days later, Letts justified this by observing again that, 'the results were in fact excellent'.

Christopher Barry saw the new titles for the first time at an edit on Friday 6 December, and they were inserted into the finished Part Four on Thursday 12 December. Incidental music for the series was composed by the show's regular musician Dudley Simpson; the Australian composer had first worked on *Doctor Who* in 1964 with *Planet of Giants* and had done most of the specially commissioned scores since 1967. The score was recorded from October through to December. Dubbing then took place on Monday 16 and Tuesday 17 December (for Parts One and Two), Friday 20 December (for Part Three) and during the transmission period on Tuesday 7 January 1975 (for Part Four).

Promotion and Reaction

Although the production team had been happy with Baker's first adventure as the Doctor, the seal of approval from above came when the BBC Head of Drama Serials, Bill Slater, attended the playback of *Robot* and indicated he was happy with it. *Doctor Who* formed part of the BBC1 New Year re-launch, and attracted a lot of press attention for the broadcast of *Robot* Part One on Saturday 28 December. Broadcast of the series had been advanced one week during the autumn; originally Baker's debut was scheduled for Saturday 4 January 1975.

To lead into the new series and recap the events leading up to the Doctor's metamorphosis, a 105-minute compilation repeat of *Planet of the Spiders* was scheduled for the afternoon of Friday 27 December (a compilation repeat of a *Doctor Who* serial had been a Christmas tradition on BBC1 since *Doctor Who and the Daemons* in 1971). The Christmas *Radio Times* ran a composite photograph showing Pertwee turning into Baker – the first time in five years that the start of the new season had not been given the *Radio Times* cover (since *Robot* was starting in the Christmas fortnight).

The programme attracted a lot of press coverage, although the *Daily Mail*'s Roderick Gilchrist's guess at what the show's new star was earning was several times higher than the truth:

> Although Tom… is believed to have a £1000-a-week contract as Dr Who, he promises his frugal bachelor lifestyle won't change. 'I live in a £6-a-week one-room flat, own one suit and can't be bothered with a car' he said.

In the *Daily Express*, Baker told Mary Duffy that,

Playing the Doctor is not so different from the life I
led for six years when I was in a monastery… There I
was trying to save my soul. Here I save the world –
and sometimes the universe – in four episodes…
What I like is the way the children respond to the
Doctor. They know that though they go through
terror with him, they will always be safe in the end.

The *Sun* printed a recent publicity
photograph of Baker with a Cyberman (taken on
the set of *Revenge of the Cybermen*) and got some
quotes on the new Doctor from Christopher Barry,
who observed:

This Dr Who's whole life-style is different. His
intellect will be as sharp as ever, but he'll be a
somewhat more flamboyant character than the
previous Doctors. We will explain his physical
appearance by saying he is just recovering from a
body change.

On ITV the alternative to *Doctor Who* in its
usual 5.30 p.m. slot was varied. The talent show *New
Faces* was scheduled on three of the major regions –
London Weekend Television (LWT, in London),
Yorkshire and Granada (Northwest England). ATV
in the Midlands screened the extremely popular quiz
show *Sale of the Century* while Southern broadcast
episodes of the imported science fiction film series
Planet of the Apes against *Doctor Who* most weeks.

The audience size for *Robot* was comparable to those over Christmas
1973, although the reaction index scores – which measured the enjoyment of
the programme by a sample audience – were below average. However, on
Saturday 4 January, *Robot* Part Two took *Doctor Who* back into the Top 20
shows of the week. Commenting on the first two episodes in the *Daily Mail*
on Saturday 11 January, Martin Jackson was unsure about Baker's comic
portrayal of the new Doctor:

Mr Baker, in long straggling scarf and large floppy hat makes Dr Who look
like Harpo Marx from *Horse Feathers*. 'We are not playing Dr Who for laughs,'
Tom Baker assured me. 'I was trying to stress his strangeness, that he is not of

Page 74

Letters

Fantasy v reality

Dr Who (Saturdays, BBC1)
was once a fantasy adven-
ture serial for children.
Not any more though; in
today's episode we saw
the Doctor and his friends,
lost in a corpse-strewn
minefield, wrenching gas-
masks from the faces of
dead soldiers in order to
survive an attack by poi-
son gas themselves, cap-
tured by Nazi-pattern
storm-troopers and finally
pursued through a foggy,
nightmarish landscape by
the repulsive results of
'failed experiments in
human genetics.'

It was brutal, violent
and revolting – totally
without point or plot – yet
convincingly enough done
to be really terrifying for
many normal children,
and to put some very
nasty ideas into the heads
of some of the growing
number of disturbed ones.

Does the producer of
this unpleasant effort
really expect a not-too-
bright child to know the
difference between grim
reality on the Falls Road
or in Cambodia, and a
jolly little Saturday romp
with the Doctor?
Alison Duddington
London, N10

Despite positive press reaction to
Tom Baker, *Genesis of the Daleks*
Part One prompted this letter to the
Radio Times (see page 207).

this world, not human, therefore his reactions would be different from ours…
I take Dr Who very seriously. He has to be genuinely lovable, not pleased by
violence and he must be honest. Humorous, but never comical.

On Thursday 16 January, the official BBC audience research report on
Robot Part One was composed from comments sampled from 180 viewers; the
reaction to Baker was very mixed, with many of those interviewed still missing
Jon Pertwee a great deal. However, the Robot itself had been deemed
impressive (see Appendix E). Commenting on Part Three, the *Daily Express*
said that the Doctor was able to survive in the fight against the Robot by using
his 'human unpredictability'. On Saturday 18 January, Patrick Stoddard of the
Evening News commented of 'Doctor Who IV':

> Despite the nervous mumbles of one or two conservatives at the BBC and a
> handful of viewers who think the new Doctor's a bit silly, the tall, shock-haired
> and wide-eyed Tom has given the old fellow a new image… a whole generation
> away from William Hartnell, the original marque.

Stephen Briscoe of the *Yorkshire Post* was also very positive about the new
cult figure. While unimpressed with the *King Kong* homage of *Robot*'s
narrative, on Friday 24 January the *New Statesman*'s Elizabeth Thomas
admitted to liking Baker's eccentric new portrayal. Junior opinion in *Time Out*
on Thursday 30 January was that the new Doctor's introduction was
'disappointingly crude'.

The Making of *Doctor Who*

The production notes for each story detail how that particular story was made.
But generally location work (up until now done on film), and any filmed inserts
were done ahead of the studio sessions. This means that *The Sontaran
Experiment* was made ahead of *The Ark in Space*.

At this stage, *Doctor Who* was studio-recorded with two episodes made every
fortnight (an efficient method of working introduced by Barry Letts in 1970).
But occasionally, to make best use of cast or sets needed primarily for particular
episodes, scenes for one pair of episodes would be recorded with another. For
example, the scenes requiring General Ravon and his headquarters in *Genesis of
the Daleks* are limited to the first episode except for Scenes 17 and 20 in Part
Three. These later scenes were recorded in the same block as Part One, to save
re-erecting the set or hiring the actor for another studio session.

Selected Merchandise

- NOVELIZATION: *Doctor Who and the Giant Robot*: novelization by Terrance Dicks. Published March 1975 by Target Books/Universal-Tandem (paperback) and April 1986 by W.H.Allen (hardback). Simplified edition as *Junior Doctor Who and the Giant Robot* – published May 1979 by W.H. Allen (hardback) and 1980 by Target/W.H. Allen (paperback). American edition: 1978/1980 by Amereon (hardback). Revised Target edition as *Doctor Who – Robot* published May 1992.
- VIDEOTAPE (ETC.): *Doctor Who – Robot* (BBC Video BBCV 4714) issued January 1992. American edition: (Fox #8103) issued 1994.
- GIANT ROBOT TOY (Denys Fisher Toys UK, 1977).

Production Details

4A: Robot

Projects: 2344/7042–7045

Cast

Doctor Who	Tom Baker
Sarah Jane Smith	Elisabeth Sladen
Harry Sullivan	Ian Marter
Brigadier Lethbridge Stewart	Nicholas Courtney
Sergeant Benton*	John Levene
Miss Winters	Patricia Maynard
Robot	Michael Kilgarriff
Professor Kettlewell	Edward Burnham
Jellicoe	Alec Linstead
Short	Timothy Craven[2]

* Despite the credit, Benton's rank is Warrant Officer First Class (WO1) as stated in Part Two

Uncredited:
UNIT Stretcher-Bearers [1]: Leslie Weekes, Nigel Stevens
Double for Robot (hands) [1]: John East
Ministry of Defence Guard [1]: John Scott Martin
Thinktank Guard [1]: Pat Gorman
Double for Sarah Jane Smith [1]: Elizabeth Cassidy
UNIT Drivers [1,4]: Jack Parker, Colin Hamilton
UNIT Soldiers [1,3-4]: Bill Bingham, Steve Rivers, David Parker, Fred Garratt, Norman Littlejohns, Allan Hinton, Douglas Read, Roger Squires, Christopher Carrington, Peter Isley, Gordon Wall, Brian Fellows
UNIT Guard (corpse) [1]: George Howse
Extras [1]: Joe Phillips*, Evan Ross*, David Melbourne, Judy Clay
SRS Scientist [2]: Jay McGrath
Joseph Chambers MP [2]: Walter Goodman
Thinktank Scientist (Philips) [2-3]: Clive Barrie
SRS Bouncer [2]: Terry Sartain* .
UNIT Soldiers [2]: David Pelton, Brian Moorhead
Bouncer [3]: Terry Walsh

UNIT Soldiers [3]: Ian Young, Desmond Verini, David Playdon, Hugh Ward, Dennis Lycett
UNIT Soldiers [3-4]: David Patterson, Raymond Savage, Allan Bicini, Norman Colson, Richard Martin, John Milner
SRS Bouncer/SRS Officers/SRS Audience [3]: Eric French, Alan Crisp, Donald Stratford, Tim Blackstone, Douglas Domingo, Alan Thomas, Leslie Weekes, Geoffrey Witherick, Derek Parks, Alex Hood, Roy Pearce, David Pelton, Barry MacDonald, Jay McGrath, Michael Reynel, Nigel Stevens, Noel Crowder, David Enyon, Leon Maybank
SRS Audience [3]: Penny Lambirth, Elizabeth Broom, Nancy Adams, Maureen Nelson, Pamela Dale, Pat Pelton.
UNIT Soldiers [4]: Ray Knight, Geoff Farnall

* Not in finished programme

Crew

Written by — Terrance Dicks
Title Music by — Ron Grainer & BBC Radiophonic Workshop
Title Sequence — Bernard Lodge
Production Assistant — Peter Grimwade
Production Unit Manager — George Gallaccio
Incidental Music by — Dudley Simpson
Special Sound — Dick Mills
Lighting — Nigel Wright*, John Mason**
Sound — John Holmes** [1-2]
Trevor Webster** [3-4]
Vic Godrich*
Visual Effects Designer — Clifford Culley
Costume Designer — James Acheson
Make-up — Judy Clay
Script Editor — Robert Holmes
Designer — Ian Rawnsley
Producer — Barry Letts
Directed by — Christopher Barry

* Studio ** OB

Production History

OB Recording - BBC Engineering & Training Centre, Wood Norton, Hereford & Worcester
Sunday 28 April 1974:
- Ext. Thinktank - Part One: scenes 14, 28
- Ext. Kettlewell's House - Part One: scene 27
- Ext. Thinktank Workshop - Parts One: scenes 16, 29 and Part Two: scenes 15, 17
- Ext. Country Road - Part Two: scene 21 and Part Four: scene 1

Monday 29 April 1974:
- Ext. Woodland – Part Four: scenes 29, 31, 32, 34
- Ext. Wooded Area – Part Four: scenes 1, 3, 17, 19, 22

Tuesday 30 April 1974:
- Ext. Countryside – Part Two: scene 2 and Part Four: scene 37
- Ext. Bunker Area – Part Four: scene 40
- Ext. Wooded Area – Part Four: scenes 34, 35, 38, 41, 42

Wednesday 1 May 1974:
- Ext. Wooded Area – Part Four: scenes 29A, 34, 41, 42
- Ext. Factory – Part One: scene 18
- Ext. Bunker – Part Three: scenes 18, 29 and Part Four:
- Int. Bunker – Part Three: scene 19 and Part Four: scene 2
- Ext. Road – Part Two: scene 21
- Int. Factory Vault – Part One: scene 23
- Ext. Government Establishment – Part One: scene 2

Thursday 2 May 1974:
- Int. Factory Vault – Part One: scene 23
- Ext. Factory Vault – Part One: scene 19
- Ext. Thinktank Gate – Part One: scenes 14, 28
- Ext. Factory – Part One: scenes 18, 21, 24
- Ext. SRS HQ – Part Three: scene 12
- Ext. Kettlewell's House – Part One: scene 27 and Part Three: scenes 1A, 2

Sunday 5 May 1974: 8.15am–8.00pm
- Ext. Fence – Part One: scenes 9, 12, 15
- Ext. Factory – Part One: scene 18
- Ext. Bunker – Part Three: scenes 18, 20, 22, 26

Monday 6 May 1974: 8.00am–8.00pm
- Ext. Bunker – Part Three: scenes 26, 27, 29 and Part Four: scene 1
- Ext. Wooded Area – Part Four: scenes 7, 9/10, 17, 19, 26, 28
- Ext. Factory – Part One: scene 18

Tuesday 7 May 1974: 8.30am–7.30pm
- Miscellaneous pick-up shots

Studio Recording – Television Centre Studio 3
Tuesday 21 May 1974: 7.30pm–10.00pm
- Planned recording of Part One – abandoned because of industrial action

Wednesday 22 May 1974: 7.30pm-10.00pm
* Planned recording of Part One and Two – rescheduled because of industrial action. The only scenes used were Part One: scene 30 and Part Two: scenes 1, 2, 3, 5, 9, 16, 14, 19

Saturday 1 June 1974: 7.30pm-10.00pm
* Part One – including some scenes recorded on Wednesday 22 May
* Part Two: scenes 1 to 5

Sunday 2 June 1974: 7.30pm-10.00pm
* Part Two – including some scenes recorded on Wednesday 22 May and excluding scenes 1 to 5
* Part Three: scene 1

Thursday 6 June 1974: 7.30pm-10.00pm
* Part Three – except scene 1
* Part Four – possible recording on some control room and corridor scenes

Friday 7 June 1974: 7.30pm-10.35pm [35 min overrun]
* Part Four

Studio Recording – Television Centre Studio 7
Thursday 24 October 1974: [25 min overrun]
* Part Four – remount of CSO sequences with Sarah and Robot

Music
* Specially recorded incidental music by Dudley Simpson and Ad Hoc Orchestra. Recording Dates: Wednesday 16 October, Tuesday 10 December and Monday 23 December 1974 at Lime Grove. Total: 45'16"

Original Transmission – BBC1
Part One	Saturday 28 December 1974	5.35pm	5.35pm	24'11"	10.8M	25th	53
Part Two	Saturday 4 January 1975	5.30pm	5.32pm	25'00"	10.7M	17th	53
Part Three	Saturday 11 January 1975	5.30pm	5.30pm	24'29"	10.1M	22nd	–
Part Four	Saturday 18 January 1975	5.30pm	5.31pm	24'29"	9.0M	30th	51

ROBOT

by Terrance Dicks

Part One

OPENING TITLES

1. INT. UNIT HQ. DOCTOR'S LAB. DAY. ②

Sarah and the Brigadier are looking down at Doctor Who, who lies on the ground.

BRIGADIER Now just a minute!

SARAH Look, Brigadier, look! I think it's starting!

Doctor Who is starting to glow with a golden light.

BRIGADIER Well, here we go, again.

Close-up of Doctor Who's features as they change into those of his new incarnation. ③

But even when the change is complete, Doctor Who twists and writhes, muttering deliriously.

Sarah kneeling by him, looks up at the Brigadier, who rushes to a wall phone, and dials a couple of digits.

BRIGADIER *(Into phone)* Get me the ~~M.D.~~ medical officer. ~~Doctor?~~ Lieutenant Sullivan. ④ Emergency! Come to the lab at once, please!

He slams down the phone and turns back to Sarah who is trying to calm Doctor Who. He is twisting and muttering.

DOCTOR WHO *(Indistinctly)*… typical Sontaran attitude… stop Linx… perverting the course of human history…

BRIGADIER *(OV)* What's he talking about?

SARAH Something that happened when we first met.

DOCTOR WHO I tell you Brigadier, there's nothing to <u>worry</u> about. The Brontosaurus is large, and placid… ⑤

> *The door opens and Harry Sullivan dashes in. He's a large burly young man in naval uniform. His social manner bit 'hearty' but he becomes calm and professional when at work.*
>
> *Two UNIT soldiers with a stretcher follow him into the lab.*

HARRY This the patient, sir?

DOCTOR WHO … and stupid. *(Sits up)* If the square of the hypotenuse equals the sum of the squares on the other two sides, why is a mouse when it spins? Never did know the answer to that one.

> *Without waiting for a reply Harry kneels beside the Doctor and starts to examine him.WO1 Benton enters, carrying a clipboard and some papers.*

BENTON Excuse me sir, the daily reports –

> *He breaks off at the sight of Doctor Who.*

HARRY Get him to sickbay. I'll make a proper examination there.

> *The stretcher-bearers assisted by Harry and Sarah getting Doctor on to stretcher.*

BENTON Who's… ~~that, sir~~?

BRIGADIER That, Mr. Benton, is the Doctor.

BENTON You mean he's done it again, sir? Changed?

> *The Brigadier nods.*

BRIGADIER **Apparently.** Saw it happen, this time. ⑥

> *Benton shakes his head, baffled.*
>
> *Doctor Who is carried out on the stretcher, Sarah and Harry going with him. Harry is last out and the Brigadier stops him at the door.*

BRIGADIER Lieutenant Sullivan.

HARRY **Yes sir?**

BRIGADIER I'm placing the Doctor in your personal charge. He's to have your full attention.

> *Harry looks puzzled, but doesn't argue.*

HARRY ~~Yes, of course,~~ **Right-ho**, sir.

> *He goes off down the corridor.*
>
> *Automatically Benton hands his papers to the Brigadier, who starts looking through them.*

BRIGADIER Anything urgent, Mr. Benton?

BENTON No, sir. Just routine.

BRIGADIER *(Looking at papers)* Yes, ~~good~~, everything seems pretty quiet.

2. EXT. GOVERNMENT ESTABLISHMENT. (OB) NIGHT. ⑦

[Note: This sequence could be day, but night, day-for-night, ⑧ or at least a suggestion of atmospheric murk and gloom would obviously be preferable.

We shan't see very much of this location or of any of the other locations which are the scene of the Robot raids. It is suggested that they might well be odd bits of Thinktank locations redressed. All that is necessary in each case is to convey the impression that somewhere heavily guarded and secure is being broken into.

We don't get a full look at the Robot until the end of the episode.]

> *Subjective camera-sequence is seen through the eyes of the Robot.* ⑨ *It's a massive seven-foot-high metal figure. A special optical effect indicates when we are looking through the Robot's eyes.* ⑩ *We can also hear an electronic heartbeat.* ⑪
>
> *Camera moves through concealing bushes towards a heavy gate. On it a sign reads:*
>
> *Ministry of Defence. Weaponry Research Centre. No admittance without pass. Guard dogs patrolling.*
>
> *A UNIT sentry is on guard.* ⑫
>
> *Camera moves out of the bushes and advances towards him. We see his horrified and amazed reaction. As camera moves nearer he raises his gun to fire but the gun is wrenched from his grasp and he is struck down.*
>
> *Camera moves in on the gate. Two metal hands come into shot and snap the chains holding the gate closed. The gate is pushed open, and the camera moves on through.* ⑬
>
> *Hold for a moment on the shattered chains and the felled sentry.*
>
> *Resume subjective camera – we are moving along a path. A guard dog dashes up barking*

furiously. ⑭ *Then reacting to what it sees, it backs away from camera growling, and then makes off, howling dismally.*
   We close in on the door. A blow from a metal fist smashes it open.
   Camera moves through. ⑮

3. INT. GOVERNMENT OFFICE. NIGHT.

The room is in darkness.
   Light from the window illuminates a massive safe. Camera moves up to it, and metal hands grip the handle and rip the door off.
   A metal hand reaches for a folder inside.

4. INT. UNIT HQ. DOCTOR'S LAB. DAY.

The Brigadier is reading letter. While talking to Sarah.
BRIGADIER *(Reading)* The complete set of plans for the disintegrator gun. ⑯
SARAH Stolen? Who by?
BRIGADIER No one saw them. Probably enemy agents. A small commando-squad. ~~We~~ **They** found heavy vehicle tracks. *(Severely, realizing what he is doing)* ~~Naturally~~ **You realize of course, Miss Smith**, all this is top secret, ~~Miss Smith~~!
   Sarah can't resist teasing him.
SARAH Then why are you telling me?
BRIGADIER Because... because
He stops, splutters, gestures round the empty laboratory. It is eloquent of Doctor Who. Bits of some half-completed experiment litter a lab bench. The TARDIS stands sadly in the corner. Because there's no-one else I can tell.
SARAH *(Understanding)* The Doctor's still unconscious?
   The Brigadier nods.
BRIGADIER He'll be all right. I know he will.
   But she obviously isn't convinced.
BRIGADIER He used to drive me mad, but I miss having him about! He'd have been interested in this robbery, you know. Some very strange features...
   The Brigadier is embarrassed by his own display of feeling. Sarah changes the subject.
SARAH Actually I came here to ask a favour.
BRIGADIER *(Absently)* Yes, of course.

SARAH You know Thinktank? The frontiers-of-science research place. All the latest in everything under one roof.
BRIGADIER Oh yes. Er, what about it?
   Sarah gives a winning smile.
SARAH Well, now and again, exceptionally favoured journalists are allowed to visit it. And for ~~absolutely~~ ages now I've been dying to – ~~get in there~~.
   She looks at him appealingly.
BRIGADIER You want me to get you a visitor's pass?
SARAH Oh~~? Oh, yes,~~ please.
BRIGADIER Nothing simpler. Come along to my office, and I'll fix it up right away.
   They move towards the door. Sarah pauses.
SARAH And could I see the Doctor before I go?
BRIGADIER Yes, of course.
SARAH Are you sure you've got the right man to look after him?
BRIGADIER ~~Lieutenant~~ **Young** Sullivan? ~~First class~~ **Very fine** chap. ~~Very fine~~ **First-class** doctor.
SARAH He seems ~~sort of~~ **a bit** old-fashioned.

5. INT. UNIT CORRIDORS. DAY.

Corner, where the Doctor, jacket over pyjamas, comes creeping along the corridor clutching his boots in his hand. He hears the approaching voices and ducks out of sight behind a cupboard (or another turn of wall) just as the Brigadier and Sarah appear.
BRIGADIER Nothing wrong with that, Miss Smith. You may not have noticed but I'm a ~~little~~ **bit** old-fashioned myself.
SARAH Nonsense, Brigadier. You're a swinger.
   By now they have reached the corner. They turn it, and go on their way. As soon as they are out of sight, the Doctor emerges from his hiding place and makes off down the corridor towards the laboratory.

6. INT. UNIT HQ. DOCTOR'S LAB. DAY.

The room is empty. After a moment the door opens. The Doctor pops his head in. He sees the room is empty, looks pleased and comes in, closing the door behind him.

For a moment he looks lost, as if he can't quite remember what he's there for. Then he spots the TARDIS and beams.

He crosses to it, tries to open the door. It's locked. This seems to baffle him for a moment. He frowns. Then cheers up.

DOCTOR WHO Key! Key, key, key!

He starts looking in all the pockets of the jacket he wears over his pyjamas. He can't find it and looks baffled. Then he remembers the boots he is carrying. He tips out first one and then the other. The key falls from the second boot on to the palm of his hand. **17**

DOCTOR WHO Yes of course. Obvious place!

He is just about to put the key in the lock when the door opens.

Harry Sullivan bustles in, wearing white coat and stethoscope. He is full of professional good cheer. He is obviously relieved to have found the Doctor, and gives him a reproving look.

HARRY **There you are!** Come on Doctor. You're supposed to be in the sickbay.

DOCTOR WHO Am I? Do**n't** you mean the infirmary?

HARRY No, I do not mean the infirmary, I mean the sickbay! You're not fit yet.

DOCTOR WHO Not fit? I'm the Doctor. **18**

HARRY No Doctor, I'm the doctor. And I say that you're not fit.

DOCTOR WHO You may be <u>a</u> doctor, but I am <u>the</u> Doctor. The definite article, you might say.

HARRY Look here, Doctor, you're not fit –

DOCTOR WHO *(Indignantly)* **Not** fit? **Not** fit? Of course I'm fit. All systems go.

Watched by the baffled Harry, the Doctor has a little burst of physical activity, touching his toes, **19** *running on the spot, and finishing with a few rapid push-ups. Then he leaps to his feet, strides across to Harry. The Doctor takes the stethoscope, pops the earpieces in Harry's ears and applies the business end to his own chest.*

HARRY I say! Look…

The Doctor's manner is brisk, hearty, hyperactive. He is running on overdrive, after his long rest.

DOCTOR WHO Heartbeats.

By professional reflex Harry takes the Doctor's heartbeat. The Doctor moves the stethoscope to the other side. Harry reacts.

HARRY **I say,** I don't think that can be right.

DOCTOR WHO Both a bit fast, **are they**? Still, must be patient. A new body's like a new house. Takes a bit of time to settle in!

He wanders to a mirror and examines his face critically, talking rapidly all the time.

As for the physiognomy – well **nothing's perfect…** ~~we~~ have to take the rough with the smooth… Mind you, I think the nose is definitely an improvement. **20** But the ears well, I'm not too sure.

He tugs at his ears experimentally, seems to accept that they're fixed and turns to Harry.

Tell me, frankly what do you say to the ears?

HARRY Well, I don't know.

DOCTOR WHO Of course you don't, why should you? You're a busy man, you don't want to stand here burbling about my ears. Neither ear, nor there, is it? Eh? But I can't waste any more time. Things to do, places to go. I'm a busy man too, you know.

The Doctor shakes Harry warmly by the hand.

DOCTOR WHO Well, thank you for a most ~~enjoyable chat~~ **interesting conversation**. Must be on my way.

Harry is still not amused. He blocks the way to the TARDIS.

HARRY ~~I'm sorry Doctor, but there's~~ **There is absolutely** no question of your leaving, **Doctor**. You'll go back to the infirmary, I mean sickbay, get into bed, and stay there till <u>I</u> say you can get up.

He advances purposefully on the Doctor, who backs away, apparently intimidated.

DOCTOR WHO How can I prove my point? *(He grabs wire and skips)* ~~Come on then.~~

HARRY I feel I ought to warn you, Doctor that there's grave danger of minor cardial infarction, not to mention pulmonary…

Harry joins in with the Doctor: **21**

DOCTOR WHO *(Song)*

Mother, mother I feel sick
Send for the doctor, quick, quick, quick
~~Doctor, doctor,~~ **Mother, dear,** shall he die?
Yes my darling, bye and bye.
One, two, three, four…

7. INT. UNIT CORRIDORS. DAY.

The Brigadier and Sarah rushing along towards the laboratory.

BRIGADIER ~~If he's not in the sickbay,~~ there's only one place he can be.

SARAH I thought you said Doctor Sullivan was looking after him.

BRIGADIER He's supposed to be…

By now they are at the laboratory doors. The Brigadier opens it for Sarah and they rush in.

8. INT. UNIT HQ. DOCTOR'S LAB. DAY.

The laboratory appears quiet and empty. They look round. Then they hear a muffled thumping from a corner cupboard.

SARAH Cupboard!

Sarah rushes across to it and opens it. Harry Sullivan, tied up, falls out.

BRIGADIER ~~What are you doing there?~~

SARAH **What are you doing down there? Where's the Doctor?**

SARAH ~~What happened?~~

HARRY *(Indignant)* ~~Picked me up and flung me in the cupboard~~ **Tied me up and hung me in here** like a pair of **old** boots.

BRIGADIER Where is he?

The familiar groaning sound of the TARDIS answers the question.

BRIGADIER Hah! Too late.

Sarah rushes to the TARDIS door and hammers on it with her fists.

SARAH Doctor, Doctor, wait, ~~please. Don't go rushing off.~~ Doctor, listen, **please it's Sarah! Doctor!**

The TARDIS noise subsides. After a moment the door opens and the Doctor pops his head out. ㉒

DOCTOR WHO *(Taking in the scene)* Yes? Ah, come to see me off, have you? Well, I hate goodbyes. I'll just slip quietly away.

Starts to re-enter the TARDIS, but is stopped by Sarah's anguished cry.

SARAH Doctor, you can't go!

DOCTOR WHO Can't? Can't! No such word as can't. ㉓ Why not?

He asks the question straightforwardly, in a tone of a child-like curiosity. Sarah racks her brains.

SARAH *(To Doctor)* Well, because **you're not** w– er, because the Brigadier needs you. Don't you, Brigadier?

BRIGADIER What? Oh yes, yes of course. Depending on you.

DOCTOR WHO What for?

The Brigadier gives Sarah an anguished look. He has no idea.

Sarah answers for him.

SARAH There's been this robbery, **hasn't there** Brigadier – some kind of secret weapon.

BRIGADIER Ah yes. Very serious business.

SARAH *(To Doctor)* I mean, you are still UNIT's Scientific Adviser. **Remember?** You can't go **rushing** off and leave them in the lurch.

DOCTOR WHO Can't I? Goodbye.

Closes door.

HARRY Excuse me, sir. Could you oblige?

BRIGADIER Oh, yes.

DOCTOR WHO Excuse me.

BRIGADIER What?

DOCTOR WHO Haven't we met somewhere before?

BRIGADIER ~~Well…~~

DOCTOR WHO No, don't tell me. Alexander the Great! No? Hannibal? No. **Ah!** Brigadier? Brigadier Alastair Gordon Lethbridge Stuart. ㉔ How are you?

Shakes hands.

BRIGADIER Very well, thank you but…

DOCTOR WHO And Sarah Jane ~~Smith~~. **Well now isn't this nice.** Now what was that you said about a secret weapon?

The Doctor looks thoughtful then, to everyone's relief, he comes out of the TARDIS. He looks round enquiringly.

9. EXT. FENCE. DAY.

Robot's POV subjective camera. We are approaching a heavy electrical fence bordering a small compound of buildings.

Two metal hands come into shot and grasp the strands of wire. There is a crackle of electricity and sparks flash round the hands.

Obviously unaffected the hands snap first one, then another strand of the heavy wire in two, with effortless ease.

10. INT. STOREROOM. DAY.

A small electronic storeroom, lined with crates and boxes. A bored security guard sits reading a paper. **25** *Suddenly he hears the massive clump, clump, clump of footsteps coming towards the door from the corridor outside. He looks at the door. The footsteps come nearer and the doors are shaken by a thump from the outside.*

The guard rushes to the door as it is shaken by a second thump. He puts a massive steel bar across the door, but as the door is forced inward from the outside the bar begins to bulge and bend. **26** *The guard backs away in horror. He looks round wildly and then moves towards a wall phone. As he approaches it there is a shattering crash from behind him.*

We cut to a close-up of the guard as the doors burst open.

He reacts in amazement and horror at what he sees. He backs away, again making for the wall phone.

Cut to a close-up of the wall phone as he grabs for it. A metal hand is there before him, ripping the phone out of the wall.

Cut to a close-up of the terrified guard as he is struck down.

Cut to Robot's POV subjective camera, as it scans the rows of boxes and cartons. It pauses at one, and then reaches for it, placing it to one side. The scan is repeated and then it reaches for another box, obviously making a careful selection, working quickly and accurately.

11. INT. UNIT HQ. DOCTOR'S LAB. DAY.

Harry Sullivan is sitting listening to his own heartbeat when the Brigadier comes rushing in.

BRIGADIER Doctor, there's been another ~~one!~~ –
He pauses, seeing only Harry.

BRIGADIER Where is he?
Harry nods towards the TARDIS.

HARRY In there.
Brigadier suspiciously moving towards the TARDIS.

BRIGADIER But he promised…

DOCTOR WHO *(VO)* Ah, Brigadier!
Cut to the doorway of the TARDIS.

There stands the Doctor, resplendent in a huge bearskin jacket. **27**

BRIGADIER Doctor, we must get moving. ~~There's been a second…~~
He breaks off, seeing the Doctor.
The Doctor notices.

DOCTOR WHO Something wrong?

BRIGADIER You've changed.

DOCTOR WHO Oh no, not again.
He rushes to the mirror and peers critically at his face, prodding and poking it.

BRIGADIER I didn't mean your face, ~~Doctor.~~ I meant your clothes.

DOCTOR WHO *(Sadly)* You don't like them?

BRIGADIER UNIT is supposed to be a security organization.

DOCTOR WHO You think I might attract attention?

BRIGADIER It's just possible.

DOCTOR WHO One moment.
He darts back inside TARDIS and instantly reappears in an even more eccentric costume. **28**

DOCTOR WHO No? No!
He looks at their horrified faces.
He goes back inside and reappears in what is basically his new costume.

DOCTOR WHO How about this?

BRIGADIER Much better, Doctor. Now if we're finished with your wardrobe, ~~there's an urgent…~~

DOCTOR WHO I'll try again if you like.

BRIGADIER Let's settle for that! ~~Now, Doctor, there's been~~

DOCTOR WHO Time we were off!

BRIGADIER Off?

DOCTOR WHO To visit the scene of the crime.

BRIGADIER Thing is, there's been another ~~robbery.~~

DOCTOR WHO *(Over his shoulder)* Tell me on the way, Brigadier. Tell me on the way. You must cultivate a sense of urgency! ~~Procrastination is the thief of time.~~
The Brigadier gives Harry an exasperated look. Harry represses a grin, and they set off after the Doctor.

12. EXT. FENCE. (OB) DAY.

The Brigadier is indicating the broken fence. Harry looks on.

BRIGADIER Millions of volts running through the wretched thing and for all the ~~use~~ **good it was, it might j–** … Doctor?

The Doctor is sitting cross-legged on the grass, staring in absorption at something on the ground in front of him.

BRIGADIER Doctor, will you please pay attention.

DOCTOR WHO Oh but I am. I assure you. Look.

He picks the something carefully from the ground and extends it on the palm of his hand towards the Brigadier.

Cut to a close-up of the Doctor's hand. On it is a daisy, squashed absolutely flat, like a pressed flower in a book.

BRIGADIER Doctor, I have every respect for your concern for the ecology, but one squashed ~~daisy~~ dandelion…

DOCTOR WHO Not just squashed. Flattened. Almost pulverized.

He blows on the daisy and it flies into powder.

DOCTOR WHO Now, how did it get like that?

HARRY *(Impatiently)* I suppose it was stepped on.

DOCTOR WHO Exactly. And according to my estimation of the resistance to pressure of vegetable fibre it was stepped on by something that weighed a quarter of a ton.

The Brigadier and Harry react, and the Doctor leaps up and goes through the gap in the wire.

Harry and the Brigadier scrabble hurriedly after him.

13. INT. STOREROOM. DAY.

The Doctor looks at the rifled but not empty shelves – Harry there.

BRIGADIER Funny thing is, they left a lot of valuable and top secret stuff behind. Here's a list of all they actually took.

He hands over a list. The Doctor scans it briefly.

DOCTOR WHO Just what you'd need for the control circuitry of one, compact, powerful technological device. A disintegrator gun, for instance…

BRIGADIER What do you know about that?

Again they react.

The Doctor winks and puts a finger against his nose.

14. EXT. THINKTANK. (OB) DAY.

The Thinktank is a big, secluded country house taken over by a wealthy foundation and converted to scientific research. ㉙

GUARD Yes, miss?

Jellicoe, a fussy, elegant man in his thirties is standing by the front entrance. He wears elaborate, ultra-trendy clothes.

Beside him is Miss Winters. About the same age as Jellicoe, she is dressed fashionably but simply, and might be a very superior executive secretary. Her manner, in contrast to that of Jellicoe, is utterly calm and relaxed, pleasant but a little cool.

JELLICOE That journalist girl is arriving. The one with the UNIT pass.

A car ㉚ has drawn up at the gate. The driver, Sarah, is showing an armed security guard her pass. At a nod from the guard, Sarah gets out of the car, and enters the building.

The guard points towards Miss Winters and Jellicoe on the steps.

Cut back to Jellicoe and Miss Winters.

JELLICOE It's something of a nuisance at the present moment in time…

There is tension beneath his words.

WINTERS We shall treat Miss Smith exactly ~~like the others~~ **as any other visitor**.

JELLICOE I suppose so, I suppose so…

Sarah comes up to them, a little hesitantly. She addresses herself to Jellicoe.

SARAH Hello. You know it's awfully ~~It's very~~ good of you to allow this visit, Director.

Jellicoe looks embarrassed. Miss Winters rises and moves towards Sarah.

WINTERS I hadn't expected male chauvinist attitudes from you, Miss Smith.

SARAH I'm sorry?

WINTERS I'm the director. Hilda Winters. This is Arnold Jellicoe, my assistant.

15. EXT. FENCE. (OB) DAY.

The Brigadier and Harry are standing by the UNIT Land Rover. The Doctor is stretched out in the back of the Land Rover, his feet poking over the side.

He has a general tendency to adopt gawky, sprawling attitudes.

BRIGADIER So what are we looking for?

DOCTOR WHO Something that brushes aside chains and electric fences like cobwebs. Something intelligent, that ~~selects~~ **takes** only what it needs, and leaves the rest. Something that kills a man as casually as it crushes a ~~daisy~~ **dandelion**.

BRIGADIER What sort of a something? Is it ~~a~~ human?

The Doctor considers and then shakes his head.

DOCTOR WHO I doubt it, Brigadier. More than human, perhaps.

BRIGADIER Well, whatever it is, how do we find it?

DOCTOR WHO By locking the next stable door in good time.

BRIGADIER What?

DOCTOR WHO It – whatever <u>it</u> may be – has stolen the plans for the new disintegrator gun. It has also in its possession the necessary control circuitry.

HARRY You think it wants to build the gun?

DOCTOR WHO Why else steal the plans and the circuitry? Assuming I'm right – and I invariably am – what is the third vital ingredient?

For a moment the Brigadier looks baffled, then he gets it.

BRIGADIER The focusing generator!

The Doctor nods approvingly, like a master who has at last got a dimmish pupil to understand a simple theorem.

DOCTOR WHO Exactly Brigadier. **Exactly.**

The Brigadier snatches his RT.

BRIGADIER Greyhound leader to trap one. **Over.** ~~Red priority.~~

Benton's voice comes through on the RT.

BENTON (VO) Trap one, we read you Greyhound leader. **Over.**

BRIGADIER **Mr Benton – Red priority.** Emmett's Electronics, ~~Benton~~. Smallish factory in Essex. **I want blanket security.** ~~Full security seal,~~ every available man. Air cover as well. I'll meet you there in *(looking at watch)* ~~fifteen minutes~~ **one hour**, and by then I want that

place better guarded than Fort Knox. ~~Greyhound~~ out.

The Land Rover is already moving, and the Doctor has to jump to scramble in as it whizzes out of sight.

16. EXT. THINKTANK. (OB) DAY.

Sarah, Miss Winters and Jellicoe strolling through the grounds. They are somewhere at the rear of the building.

~~**SARAH** I really can't thank you enough. It's been a fascinating tour.~~

JELLICOE As you've seen, we do mostly what's called 'frontiers of science' research here.

WINTERS As soon as our work reaches the practical stage, it's handed over to someone. Someone with more resources and a bigger budget.

JELLICOE Usually the Government!

This is a well-rehearsed double act.

SARAH Like the new disintegrator gun. You pioneered the research on that, didn't you?

Reaction from Jellicoe and Winters.

WINTERS Well, yes. But I'm not sure you should know about that.

SARAH **Oops!** Sorry, talking out of turn.

Embarrassed she looks round for a diversion. They're just passing a long, low-lying building.

SARAH What's in here?

She pops through the door, ㉛ *before they can stop her.*

17. INT. THINKTANK. KETTLEWELL'S WORKSHOP. DAY. ㉜

A spotlessly clean but empty concrete room. Doors at the far end.

Sarah looks round curiously. She looks at a faded notice. Winters and Jellicoe have followed her in.

JELLICOE *(Sharply)* There's nothing here. Nothing at all. ㉝

WINTERS *(Pleasantly)* As you can see, it's empty.

Sarah looks up from the notice.

SARAH *(Reading)* J. P. Kettlewell. Robotics Section. He left ~~you~~ some time ago, didn't he? **That's right,** There was ~~quite a~~ **all that** fuss about it in the press.

WINTERS Indeed there was. As you probably heard, he turned against conventional science altogether.

JELLICOE Spends his time on alternative technology – whatever that may mean.

SARAH What's through there?

She indicates the massive metal doors on the other side of the room.

JELLICOE Storeroom. The professor left some valuable equipment. We're keeping it till he deigns to come and collect it.

Sarah's journalistic instincts tell her there's something up, but she can't very well press the matter. She nods, then stops and sniffs.

SARAH Funny musty sort of… oops!

She takes a few steps forward, and then skids, before she can finish her sentence. Jellicoe grabs her arm and saves her from a nasty fall.

WINTERS Are you all right?

SARAH *(Gasping)* Just about. **Thank you.**

WINTERS Let's be on our way Miss Smith. Still quite a lot to see, you know.

SARAH Oh yes, of course. **Thank you.**

She takes Sarah firmly by the other arm and leads her out.

18. EXT. FACTORY. (OB) DAY.

A simple factory compound (if possible some previous location doubled).

A montage of shots showing UNIT troops setting up observation posts, hidden machine-gun emplacements, men with rifles and Sten guns in cover – enough to give the impression that a hidden ring of armed men is surrounding the factory.

Stock shot. Cut to a helicopter patrolling overhead.

Cut to WO1 Benton, wriggling through cover, checking patrols and placing new ones.

Over all this the Brigadier's voice.

BRIGADIER *(VO)* I tell you Doctor. I've got the whole place covered. Armed patrols have every inch of the perimeter under observation. Helicopter patrols overhead. Inside that factory is a vault. Not a safe, Doctor, a vault. There's a sentry outside it.

As the Brigadier speaks the picture changes

19. DOOR OUTSIDE FACTORY VAULT. (OB) DAY.

Close up of sentry guarding a massive door.

BRIGADIER *(VO)* Inside the vault…

20. INT. FACTORY VAULT.

A tiny room. On a table inside it stands a metal casket.

BRIGADIER *(VO)* There's a **casket – a** metal casket containing every focusing generator in the place.

21. EXT. FACTORY. (OB) DAY.

BRIGADIER *(VO)* Believe me Doctor, the place is impregnable.

End the sequence of shots to show the Land Rover parked in the cover of some trees near the factory gate.

The Brigadier and Harry are in front, the Doctor is sprawled at the back.

DOCTOR WHO Never cared for the word impregnable. Sounds too much like 'unsinkable'.

HARRY What's wrong with unsinkable?

DOCTOR WHO ~~Always reminds me of your 'Titanic'.~~ **Nothing. As the iceberg said to the *Titanic*.**

HARRY What?

DOCTOR WHO Glug, glug, glug!

He makes a sinking gesture.

The Brigadier snorts, Benton comes up to the Land Rover and salutes.

BENTON All patrols posted sir.

BRIGADIER Everything secure?

BENTON Yes, sir. The lads are so close to each other they're standing on each other's **feet.** ~~toes, sir.~~

BRIGADIER Good! You see, Doctor! Not even a rat could get through that cordon. Protected from every side, and from above.

DOCTOR WHO *(Thoughtfully)* That still leaves one direction.

The Brigadier looks puzzled.

The Doctor points downwards.

22. INT. FACTORY VAULT. MODEL SHOT. DAY.

All is quiet.

Cut to close-up of the floor.

The floor of the vault begins to crack.

Suddenly, huge metal fist punches its way through the concrete.

23. EXT. FACTORY VAULT. (OB) DAY.

The sentry outside the door reacts to the sounds of crashing masonry – the Robot is enlarging the hole.

The sentry unbars the door and flings it open. He reacts in horror.

Cut to subjective camera, Robot's POV. The horrified sentry stares at the Robot, levels his Sten gun and blazes away.

24. EXT. FACTORY. (OB) DAY.

Doctor Who and co. react to the sound of shots. There is a choking scream and the shooting stops abruptly.

The Brigadier, Benton, Harry and Doctor Who sprint for the factory.

25. INT. FACTORY VAULT. DAY.

The vault is empty, except for the UNIT sentry crumpled in a corner. There is a large circular hole in the middle of the floor.

The Brigadier and Benton rush in, guns waving. They stop, amazed.

Harry and the Doctor appear behind them.

Harry goes to the soldier and starts to examine him.

The Doctor looks at the hole. 🕄

DOCTOR WHO There seems to be a very large rat about, Brigadier.

BRIGADIER ~~Well, what do we do now?~~ **Rat?!**

DOCTOR WHO Possibly we should obtain the services of a very large cat.

26. INT. KETTLEWELL'S LAB. DAY.

Kettlewell, a whiskery, Einstein-type scientist is talking to Sarah. He is smoking a pipe.

KETTLEWELL I'm sorry Miss Smith. I cannot help you, and I don't know why you came here.

SARAH I'm not too sure myself to be honest. I just felt something in the atmosphere at the Thinktank.

KETTLEWELL I severed all connection with that establishment some time ago, when I became totally disillusioned with the path all our research was taking – the path to ruination.

I have now devoted my life to alternative **energy** technologies.

SARAH Solar cells, heat from windmills, that sort of thing?

KETTLEWELL As you say, that sort of thing. It is a rich and complex field, and I have a great deal of work to do.

He rises pointedly. Sarah is forced to rise too. She makes a last effort.

SARAH I just wondered if they might be carrying on your work in Robotics.

KETTLEWELL No one is carrying on my work in Robotics Miss Smith, because no one **has the ability to do so** ~~else would be capable of it.~~ Good day.

He turns to his work.

SARAH ~~Good afternoon. Thank you.~~ Goodbye.

KETTLEWELL Good day, Miss Smith.

She pauses a moment, sniffs the air, her suspicions aroused. Then she leaves.

SARAH ~~Goodbye.~~ Just going.

Once she has gone, he rises and looks through the window. 🕄

27. EXT. KETTLEWELL'S HOUSE. (OB) DAY.

Sarah goes back to the car, sits for a moment behind the wheel. Cut to Sarah's bag, on the seat beside her. We see her hand fish out a pass. Close in on pass. It reads 'Institute for Advanced Scientific Research. One day visitor's pass. Valid until 4pm.' 🕄 *Sarah looks at her watch. She still has enough time. Cut to a long shot of the car as Sarah drives away.* 🕄

28. EXT. THINKTANK. (OB) DAY.

Sarah's car parked at the checkpoint.

CU Sarah in the car. She is looking up appealingly.

SARAH ~~You see~~ I left my notebook in one of the empty labs. I know exactly where it is, I can see myself putting it down. So if ~~I could~~ **you could let me just** pop in and get it, I needn't let your Director know what an idiot I've been. <u>Please</u> – my pass is still valid for *(looking at her watch)* ~~nearly~~ **another** ten minutes **yet**.

GUARD I'll check for you.

He turns and goes to a phone. Sarah slips out of the car and runs towards the bunker.

29. EXT. THINKTANK. (OB) DAY.

Sarah creeps along. All is silent. Spooky and deserted.

She comes to the door to Kettlewell's workshop and enters cautiously.

30. INT. THINKTANK. WORKSHOP. DAY.

Sarah comes in and looks round. All is quiet. She goes to the point where she fell, runs her finger on the ground and sniffs.

SARAH It was oil. I knew it.

While she is peering thoughtfully at the oil patch, there comes a shattering metallic crash. Sarah jumps, and looks up as the far doors open – cut to Sarah's POV.

Low-angle shot of the Robot, looking enormous as it stalks towards her seen full frontal for the first time. It speaks in a tremendous, booming voice.

ROBOT Who are you? Why are you here? **39**

CLOSING TITLES **40**

---

1 'Robot' is listed on the camera script as a 'working title'.

2 With the exception of the regeneration itself, the opening of this scene was re-recorded for *Robot*, despite being a reprise of *Planet of the Spiders*. Partly this was simply to allow Christopher Barry to 'pick up' Courtney and Sladen for the next shot, allowing their position and movement to be fluid between the two. Although the recording of *Robot* overlapped with the recording of Jon Pertwee's final story, *Planet of the Spiders*, the regeneration scene was actually shot in the first recording block of the Pertwee story. Otherwise Tom Baker would have recorded scenes as the Doctor ahead of recording his regeneration into the role.

3 The regeneration itself was achieved by 'roll-back-and-mix'. This is the technique that is usually used for the TARDIS materialization/dematerialization. A camera is locked off (i.e. fixed), and records a scene. The camera is then stopped, the tape wound back, and the scene continues but with a change – in this case one actor is replaced with another. The final output image is then achieved by mixing from the scene as recorded before the change to the scene after the change, so that the alteration appears to take place in real time – one person's features fade into those of another, or the TARDIS seems to appear or fade away.

4 Dr Sullivan is mentioned in *Planet of the Spiders* – a later change to that story to tie in with the new regular character of Harry. The original *Spiders* script apparently referred to Dr Sweetman (a reference preserved in Terrance Dicks' novelization). It is possible that Harry's surname was originally to be Sweetman.

5 These are references to *The Time Warrior* (1973–4) and *Invasion of the Dinosaurs* (1974). The Doctor quotes this line from Malcolm Hulke's *Dinosaurs* script which Terrance Dicks always liked.

6 The decision to have the Brigadier and Sarah witness the Doctor's regeneration was deliberate. Terrance Dicks: 'We didn't want people saying, "But you can't be the Doctor – he doesn't look like that!" which is always a bugbear. So we decided to have the change take place under everybody's nose. The Brigadier knows it's the Doctor because he's seen the change. The identity of the Doctor was never in doubt – we'd already done all that.'

7 A note on the script indicates that director Christopher Barry considered making this the first scene of the story – ahead of the reprise of the Doctor's regeneration.

8 This was indeed a night shoot.

9 In fact there is a 'normal' establishing shot of the sentry in his sentry box at the gate. This serves to demonstrate the difference when we see from the Robot's POV.

10 This is a mosaic-type view. Christopher Barry: 'I wanted to get the feeling that we were into the Robot's head. You can buy mosaic mirror in sheets to stick in glitzy discos, and the view was just reflected off a monitor in a sheet of that. We reversed the phase on the picture going into the monitor, so it came out the right way round, and then put a camera on it.'

11 The sound effects do include a 'pulsing' sound which speeds up whenever the Robot nears its target or is attacked.

12 He is not seen to be a UNIT soldier.

13 The subjective view of the Robot's hands and arms was achieved by having them held in front of the camera by tall actor John East.

14 The dog was supplied by Mrs Wickett.

15 This scene required eight takes. The best was take 6. Take 8 was abandoned, according to the editing notes, because 'Dog did not look cowardly when coming back through shot'.

16 The Brigadier's line is voiced over the end of the previous scene as we see that the folder the Robot has removed from the safe is labelled 'TOP SECRET'.

17 This is a continuity reference back to *Spearhead from Space* where the Doctor has his key stored in his shoe. Terrance Dicks: 'Wherever possible one remembered and put in these little cross-references, almost automatically. People who notice them, notice them. And for people who don't, it doesn't do any harm.'

18 This amusing exchange is not in the camera script, so it is likely it was worked out between Tom Baker, Ian Marter and Christopher Barry during rehearsals.

19 He actually karate chops a (pre-cut) brick in half before running furiously on the spot.

20 This was one of Dicks' in-jokes – a reference to how sensitive Jon Pertwee had been about the size of his nose.

21 Not through choice!

22 A production note points out that the Doctor is still in his pyjamas. In fact he wears the third Doctor's velvet jacket over his nightshirt.

23 The Doctor shuts the TARDIS door. After a moment, he re-emerges for his next words.

24 This is the first time that we learn the Brigadier's full name. Note the misspelling of Stewart.

25 During camera rehearsals, John Scott Martin was seen reading a copy of the 1972 Piccolo Book *The Making of Doctor Who* rather than the prop newspaper he had been given. (*The Making of Doctor Who*, by Malcolm Hulke and Terrance Dicks, was subsequently updated, using *Robot* as an example of how *Doctor Who* was made.)

26 This required several takes – first the bar did not bend when the doors were pushed, later it bent but did not break.

27 The Doctor is wearing full Viking regalia, including a horned hat.

28 This sequence was a locked-off camera effect. The camera was set in position so that it did not move between the sequences, and they could be run together as continuous despite the breaks to allow the Doctor to change his costume. He emerges from the TARDIS first as the King of Hearts and then as a Pierrot clown (to which the Brigadier shakes his head) before adopting his new costume. This 'entrance' is enhanced by a musical cue based on the *Who* theme music.

29 We open from Sarah's POV as she drives up to the main gate where a guard is on duty. The guard signals for her to stop and approaches the car. The gate has signs on it saying: 'KEEP CLEAR for emergency access', 'HALT', and 'NO ADMITTANCE WITHOUT A PASS'.

30 Sarah drives an MG, registration number RMF654L.

31 The door is marked 'Positively no admittance'.

32 This is preceded by a sequence of the characters walking along a short corridor to the main workshop.

33 An echo effect was added to the dialogue within Kettlewell's workshop.

34 Although the scene is listed as a model shot, in fact only the floor was a model. This foreground miniature was matted into the vault set using CSO (with yellow as the keying colour). The model floor was then cracked and broken from below to allow the Robot's metal digging tool (also a model) to emerge into the vault.

35 He measures the hole's diameter with his scarf.

36 After recording this scene there was a recording break to ensure the robot costume was ready for the next scene where the Robot makes its first full appearance in the studio.

37 The pass gives the Thinktank's title as '*National* Institute for Advanced Scientific Research'. It also gives the date as 4 April (no year is given).

38 Scene 2 from Part Two was inserted here.

39 The final shot of the episode is Sarah as she backs away, seen from the Robot's POV – making the point that the robot Sarah has found is indeed the one responsible for the break-ins and deaths.

40 The closing credits erroneously billed John Levene as 'Sergeant Benton' for all episodes despite his promotion to Warrant Officer (as mentioned in Part Two, Scene 22).

ROBOT

by Terrance Dicks

Part Two

OPENING TITLES

1. INT. THINKTANK WORKSHOP. DAY.

Reprise last scene of Part One, ❶ *to the point where Sarah looks up and sees the Robot.*

ROBOT Who are you? Why are you here?

Seeing the terrifying figure of the Robot bearing down on her, she backs away in fear then turns and runs...

2. EXT. COUNTRYSIDE. (OB) DAY. ❷

Doctor Who, Brigadier, Harry and WO1 Benton are looking at a hole about six feet in diameter, dug into the side of the hill.

BENTON We think this is the other end of it, sir. Only...

BRIGADIER ~~Well?~~ Only? Only what?

BENTON Only, it's not a proper tunnel, sir. No props or anything, just the earth shoved aside. Whoever went through it wouldn't be able to breathe.

DOCTOR WHO Whoever went through it didn't need to breathe.

BENTON ~~And we found these.~~ Then there were these, sir.

We close in on a row of Robot footprints, leading away from the hole. ❸

2. INT. CORRIDOR. DAY.

Sarah comes charging out, slap into Miss Winters.

WINTERS **Hello,** Miss Smith..!

SARAH Look out! There's a great Robot **in there…**

WINTERS **Yes, I know.** Don't worry. My assistant's dealing with it. ~~Shall we go back inside? It's quite all right.~~

~~**SARAH** *(At door)* Ah… after you.~~

3. INT. THINKTANK WORKSHOP. DAY.

Winters enters, cautiously followed by Sarah. No sign now of the Robot.

WINTERS I'm sorry if our little joke upset you.

SARAH Joke?

WINTERS You were determined to see the Robot. So we arranged it for you. That is what you wanted, isn't it?

SARAH Very kind of you… *(Sits)*

Jellicoe enters from the Robot room.

JELLICOE **When** we heard you were in the building, **we guessed what you were up to.** ~~and guessed the reason.~~ So I nipped in here ahead of you and activated it.

Sarah gives a fearful look towards the door.

SARAH Is it still in there?

WINTERS Oh yes. Would you like to see it again?

There is a hint of challenge in her voice. Sarah braces herself.

SARAH Thank you. I'd like to very much…

Miss Winters nods to Jellicoe, who walks through the door.

4. INT. UNIT HQ. DOCTOR'S LAB. DAY.

Open close on the Brigadier.

BRIGADIER Well, Doctor, what are we dealing with? Invasion from outer space again?

Cut to Doctor Who, stretched out at full length on a laboratory bench like a crusader on a tombstone. His eyes shut.

It is a characteristic of his new incarnation that he always tends to lie, lean, hang or perch in some unlikely position, rather than sitting conventionally.

DOCTOR WHO Why should some alien life form raid Earth just to steal a new weapon? If they

were that advanced they'd have weapons of their own.

Doctor Who jumps off the bench and strides about.

DOCTOR WHO Rather a splendid paradox, **eh** Brigadier, ~~don't you think~~? The only ones that could do it – wouldn't need to!

Doctor Who is delighted with his conclusion. The Brigadier sighs and perseveres.

BRIGADIER Enemy agents?

DOCTOR WHO They might steal the plans – but why steal the circuits and the generators? An enemy government would have those resources itself.

BRIGADIER So where does that leave us?

DOCTOR WHO I think your enemies are home-grown, Brigadier. People with access to technological information and a very unusual weapon. A weapon that walks, and thinks. In a word – anthropomorphic.

BRIGADIER Well, I suppose that narrows the field a bit. Do we know anything else about these people? *(Looks outside doors)*

DOCTOR WHO Only that they're prepared to kill to protect themselves. *(Pause)* Where's Sarah?

5. INT. THINKTANK WORKSHOP. DAY.

Miss Winters standing over Sarah, who is waiting nervously.

SARAH What's the hold-up?

WINTERS Mr Jellicoe is checking over its circuits.

SARAH Why's he taking so long?

WINTERS We must be sure that everything's safe.

SARAH Safe?

She looks at Miss Winters in alarm. There is a shattering clang as the metal doors are opened. The Robot stalks forward, Jellicoe behind.

WINTERS Stop.

The Robot stops. Sarah looks at it.

SARAH It's very impressive. ④ What's it for?

WINTERS Ask it! It's voice-controlled.

SARAH *(To Robot)* What do you do?

ROBOT Insufficient data. Please be more specific.

JELLICOE It has a terribly literal mind.

SARAH *(To Robot)* What is your purpose? Your function?

ROBOT I am an experimental prototype Robot K1. My eventual purpose is to replace the human being in a variety of difficult and dangerous tasks. Tasks for which I am programmed are: ~~The operation of exploration vehicles on alien planets!~~ Mining operations of all kinds! Operations involving radioactive materials…

WINTERS *(To Robot)* Terminate.

The Robot obeys.

JELLICOE It would go on for hours!

SARAH Why all the mystery? Why didn't you show him to me when I first came?

WINTERS My dear Miss Smith, why should we? You were a privileged visitor here. You abused that privilege to pry into matters on the secret list.

Sarah has to accept defeat.

SARAH You're right of course. I apologize.

JELLICOE Not a bit of it, you were just following the instincts of a good journalist. Now if you've seen enough…

He makes to lead her out. She fires a sudden question.

SARAH It isn't <u>dangerous</u>, is it?

Reaction from Jellicoe and Winters.

WINTERS Of course not. Why should it be?

SARAH It strikes me that it could be a very powerful weapon – if it got into the wrong hands. It could be – misused.

WINTERS Like this, you mean? *(To Robot)* This girl is an intruder and a spy. She must not leave here alive. Destroy her.

The Robot swings round and lumbers towards Sarah.

Sarah is in such a position that she cannot reach the door. She is backed into a corner.

WINTERS Destroy her!

The Robot's hands reach for her… Then it stops moving.

ROBOT I cannot obey. This order conflicts with my prime directive.

WINTERS *(VO)* You must obey. You are programmed to obey.

ROBOT I must obey. I cannot obey. I must obey. I cannot…

The Robot falls to its knees, head bowed as if in agony.

WINTERS ~~The order is withdrawn.~~ **Terminate.**

The Robot stands motionless and silent.

Sarah is shaken and furious. She turns on Miss Winters.

SARAH Another of your little jokes?

WINTERS A practical demonstration. You must admit it was a convincing one.

JELLICOE Prime directive, you see. It's built into the Robot's very being that it must serve humanity and <u>never</u> harm it.

Sarah looks at the Robot.

Then she turns back to Miss Winters.

SARAH That was a cruel thing to do.

WINTERS Cruel? It isn't human, you know. It has no feelings.

SARAH It's got a brain, hasn't it. It walks and talks like us, how can you be sure it doesn't have feelings too?

Sarah goes up to the Robot.

SARAH Are you all right?

ROBOT My functioning is unimpaired.

SARAH But you were distressed… I saw…

ROBOT Conflict with ~~the~~ **my** prime directive causes imbalance in my neural circuits.

SARAH I'm sorry. It wasn't my idea.

ROBOT The imbalance has been corrected. It is not logical that you should feel sorrow.

WINTERS Really, Miss Smith, this is absurd. I think you must be the sort of girl who gives motor cars pet names.

Sarah falls silent, abashed and angry.

WINTERS *(To Robot)* Deactivate!

The Robot stands silent. And motionless.

WINTERS You see. It's just a lump of metal.

Sarah controls herself with a mighty effort.

SARAH *(Formally)* Thank you for a most interesting demonstration. I think I'd better leave now.

She moves towards the door.

Miss Winters moves to bar her way.

WINTERS One moment, Miss Smith.

Sarah stops.

There is a moment of tension.

WINTERS If I were to make a formal complaint about your behaviour **here**, you ~~would be~~ **might find yourself** in a very difficult position.

JELLICOE Dangerous thing, curiosity, you know. Can get you in a lot of trouble.

WINTERS So I'll make a bargain with you. Keep quiet about what you've discovered, and I'll keep quiet about how you discovered it.

SARAH Goodbye Miss Winters, Mr Jellicoe. Please don't bother to see me out.

Stiff with anger, Sarah marches off down the corridor.

Jellicoe looks after her and when she has gone, turns back to Miss Winters.

JELLICOE That was an appallingly dangerous thing to do – telling it to destroy her. The inhibitor's only just been reset. You know there have been problems. Suppose it had obeyed you?

Miss Winters shrugs.

WINTERS It made an interesting test. ⑤

6. INT. UNIT HQ. DOCTOR'S LAB. DAY.

The Doctor and the Brigadier.

BRIGADIER And where do I start looking for this precious conspiracy?

DOCTOR WHO Oh, it's surely not that difficult, Brigadier. **Ah, thank you.** ⑥ There can't be many groups of people in the country with the money and resources to design and build something **like**…

The door is flung open and Sarah bursts in talking to Harry, but also coincidentally finishing the Doctor's sentence for him.

SARAH …~~like~~ an enormous robot, well over seven feet tall!

The Doctor looks up pleased.

DOCTOR WHO Yes, something like that. However did you guess?

SARAH Guess? I've just <u>seen</u> it. I've been <u>talking</u> to it. Brigadier, there's something very odd going on at the Thinktank…

7. INT. THINKTANK. WORKSHOP. NIGHT.

Winters and Jellicoe are working on the Robot standing beside a ladder.

The laboratory is in darkness except for one small lamp illuminating its body.

JELLICOE Screwdriver!

Winters passes him small electronic screwdriver. He adjusts something and an arm twitches.

~~JELLICOE Swab.~~

He and Winters exchange looks.

WINTERS Careful!

JELLICOE **Swab.**

Jellicoe tries again. Winters takes back screwdriver and hands him swab. Head is replaced. ⑦

Winters looks on. ⑧

JELLICOE There. I think that's it.

WINTERS Think? You'd better be sure.

JELLICOE It's a delicate job. I'm not really trained in this sort of work.

WINTERS We'd better test it.

She reaches for the control unit.

Jellicoe puts out a hand to stop her.

JELLICOE This time, emphasize the recall instructions. You know it refused to return after that last business. I found it wandering near Kettlewell's place.

WINTERS How touching. Perhaps Miss Smith was right –

JELLICOE What about?

WINTERS Perhaps it does have feelings ~~after all~~. It misses Daddy. *(To Robot)* Activate!

She activates the Robot. ⑨

The Robot seems to come alive.

WINTERS Prepare for visual scanning.

ROBOT I am ready.

Miss Winters activates a slide projector.

Pictures of a middle-aged politician, Chambers, taken from newspaper files begin to flash up on a screen.

WINTERS This man is an enemy of the human race. He must be destroyed.

8. INT. UNIT HQ. DOCTOR'S LAB. NIGHT.

The Doctor, Sarah, Harry and the Brigadier.

The Doctor, seemingly ignoring them, is building a tower from odds and ends on the lab bench, carefully balancing one thing on another with childlike pleasure.

SARAH But it's obvious that Thinktank lot are involved. Why don't you raid the place and arrest the lot of them?

BRIGADIER I very much doubt if I'd get the authority. And if I did, it'd cause so much fuss they'd have plenty of time to hide the evidence. I must have more to go on.

SARAH More than just my word, you mean?

The Brigadier looks embarrassed.

Harry chimes in.

HARRY You need an inside man.

BRIGADIER What?

HARRY **Well, you know** – someone planted on them to keep his eyes and ears open.

SARAH You know, that's not a bad idea…

BRIGADIER Have to be someone they'd accept. Someone with the proper scientific qualifications.

The Doctor speaks, without looking up from the tower.

DOCTOR WHO Scientific – or medical.

They all look at Harry.

HARRY I say – me?

SARAH **Well, why not?** Your chance to be a real James Bond.

BRIGADIER It might work. We could fix you up with a cover story…

HARRY I could wear a disguise!

The Doctor is placing a last unlikely object on top of his tower. He stands up.

DOCTOR WHO ~~I think~~ I'd like to talk to…

Putting the last object on.

DOCTOR WHO Professor Kettlewell! ⑩

9. INT. KETTLEWELL'S LAB. NIGHT.

Doctor Who, Sarah, and the Brigadier with Kettlewell.

Kettlewell is very angry.

KETTLEWELL I tell you, as I told this young woman, I know nothing of the Thinktank, or its activities. I have severed <u>all</u> connection…

SARAH But, I <u>saw</u> the Robot!

KETTLEWELL **What's that? Oh, that's** impossible. ~~The Robot was destroyed~~. **I gave orders for him to be dismantled.**

BRIGADIER Professor Kettlewell, this <u>is</u> an official enquiry, and I must ask you –

The Doctor has been wandering around looking at various bits of Kettlewell's work. Kettlewell notices.

KETTLEWELL Will you kindly put those papers down, sir?

The Doctor is looking at a bundle of notes and drawings.

DOCTOR WHO ~~Design~~ **Plans** for a new solar battery.

KETTLEWELL That~~'s~~ **folder is private and** confidential.

DOCTOR WHO This'll never do, ~~will it?~~ **you know.** If Theta over X coalesces with your disputed factor. ~~There you are Professor, the error is in the third part of the calculation.~~ You're losing half your output.

KETTLEWELL Rubbish. I checked these calculations myself.

DOCTOR WHO Look, the error is in the third ~~stage~~ **part** of the calculation.

KETTLEWELL Bless my ~~buttons~~ **soul**!

He looks at the Doctor with new respect.

DOCTOR WHO You're doing vital work, Professor. Earth's human race should have started tapping solar power long ago.

KETTLEWELL This new ~~form of~~ solar battery will give **an** endless ~~non-pollutant~~ **supply of pollution-free** energy at a fraction of the present cost and they haven't the wit to see it…

DOCTOR WHO **Well, there you are.**

KETTLEWELL I've told them time and again till I'm blue in the face.

DOCTOR WHO People can never see what's under their noses above their heads!

The Brigadier finds himself ignored.

BRIGADIER Concerning this Robot…

KETTLEWELL ~~Don't interrupt~~ **Do be quiet,** young man. Ever since **the days of** Gallileo…

DOCTOR WHO ~~Or~~ **And** Copernicus.

KETTLEWELL **And Copernicus.** Scientists ~~throughout the ages…~~ **have had to put up with** –

DOCTOR WHO *(Gently)* Professor! I think you'd better tell us about the Robot.

Kettlewell sighs, accepting defeat.

KETTLEWELL It was the last project I worked on before I decided to leave. I gave orders for him to be ~~disassembled~~ **dismantled**. It was like putting my own son to death, but I thought it **was for the** best. Its power, its capacity to learn had begun to frighten me.

SARAH But it <u>wasn't</u> destroyed, was it?

KETTLEWELL I don't know. That woman Winters might have countermanded my orders…

BRIGADIER Could the Robot have been ~~used~~ **made** to carry out these break-ins?

KETTLEWELL **No, no, no…** You said people were hurt – **even** killed?

The Brigadier nods.

KETTLEWELL Then it's out of the question. *(To Sarah)* ~~It~~ **You said he** refused to harm you, didn't ~~it~~ **you**? I gave him my own brain pattern. It has <u>my</u> ideals, <u>my</u> principles…
DOCTOR WHO The circuitry you built could be altered – tampered with.
KETTLEWELL Doctor, **not even** I ~~myself~~ could ~~not~~ effect such changes. And as for Jellicoe or Miss Winters, they're incompetent nincompoops.
SARAH Maybe. But I wouldn't put it past them to try…
KETTLEWELL If they **force him** ~~try to make it~~ **to** go against ~~its~~ **his** prime directive, they'll destroy ~~its~~ **his** mind. ~~It~~ **He** will go mad.

10. INT. FOR EXT. POLITICIAN'S DOORWAY. NIGHT.

The doorway to a house. The shadow of the Robot appears across the door. Its metal hand holds a gun.

11. INT. POLITICIAN'S STUDY. NIGHT.
Sounds of chaos and confusion. Alarm bells ringing, shots, yelled orders. ⓫ *The door is opened and Chambers, the politician we saw in the photographs shown to the Robot, hurries in, locking the door behind him. He wears pyjamas and dressing gown, and is panic-stricken and dishevelled. He goes at once to a cupboard in the corner of the room and opens it. Behind the cupboard door is the massive steel door of an enormous vault.*
Chambers reacts with relief seeing that the vault is still untouched. Then he turns towards the desk and reaches for a red telephone.
Before he can speak there is a hiss. He turns to see that the Robot has smashed through the door and wall. ⓬
Chambers gasps and backs away in horror.
ROBOT You are an enemy of humanity. I must destroy you.
The Robot corners Chambers and strikes him down. It goes to cupboard, guns it open.
Robot starts to wrench off steel door of vault. ⓭

12. INT. UNIT HQ. DOCTOR'S LAB. NIGHT.
The Brigadier is showing the Doctor and Sarah a sheaf of scene-of-crime type photographs. One is of the smashed lock on the door of Chambers' house.
BRIGADIER There was a triple security therma lock on that door made from case-hardened dynastreem. It was completely disintegrated~~; vanished away~~.
DOCTOR WHO *(With a look)* Disintegrated!
SARAH But there's nothing that could do that! **Dynastreem's indestructible.**
DOCTOR WHO I think the Brigadier has an idea – eh, Alistair?
BRIGADIER Hmm – anyway, the neighbours heard a commotion but by the time the police arrived, it was all over. The safe was empty.
The Doctor indicates a photograph of Chambers. ⓮
DOCTOR WHO Who was this man?
BRIGADIER Joseph Chambers – cabinet minister. He had certain special responsibilities in the area of security.
The Brigadier's tone is embarrassed and it is obvious he won't say any more. The Doctor notices but doesn't press him. The Brigadier changes the subject.
BRIGADIER Yes, I've been running a full security check myself on those Thinktank people.
DOCTOR WHO Anything interesting?
BRIGADIER Not really. Seem to be an exemplary lot. Just one oddity… quite a few of them were members of something called the Scientific Reform Society.
DOCTOR WHO Really, and who might they be?
BRIGADIER Little tinpot organization founded years ago. Wants to reform the world on scientific and rational lines. You know the sort of thing. Harmless bunch of cranks **if you ask me**. But recently~~, as far as I can see…~~
DOCTOR WHO ~~What happened?~~ Yes, go on then.
BRIGADIER Well, they got a sudden rush of new members. ~~Some of them quite~~ **Quite a few** well-known scientists. Younger people too, computer technicians and so on.
SARAH Miss Winters is a member?
BRIGADIER Apparently. Jellicoe too. And quite a few of the Thinktank lot.

SARAH *(Thoughtfully)* Doesn't sound their style, does it?

Sarah gets decisively to her feet.

SARAH Ah well…

BRIGADIER And where are you off to?

SARAH Home to bed. Busy day tomorrow. I am still a working girl, you know.

BRIGADIER Quite right. You leave all this business to us.

Sarah pauses at the door.

SARAH One thing about reform ~~movements~~ societies… they're never adverse to a bit of free publicity.

Sarah exits. The Brigadier turns to the Doctor, only to find him gazing into space, rapt with thought.

BRIGADIER **Well, Doctor – what do you think..?** Doctor! What are we going to do? Or shall we leave it all to Miss Smith?

The Doctor snaps awake and beams at the Brigadier.

DOCTOR WHO Let's pay a visit to the Thinktank tomorrow Brigadier. We can ask them to demonstrate Professor Kettlewell's Robot! Goodnight!

13. INT. KETTLEWELL'S LAB. NIGHT.

Kettlewell is working late. He hears sounds outside, locks up.

KETTLEWELL ~~What is it?~~ Who's there?

There comes a knock on the door. Not a hammering, but a measured knock, knock.

KETTLEWELL ~~Who is it?~~ Rats?

Again measured knocks. Kettlewell goes to door.

KETTLEWELL Then it's true.

Opens it. Standing there is the Robot.

ROBOT *(Confused)* I – I – I…

Kettlewell backs away. The Robot comes in.

KETTLEWELL What's the matter?

ROBOT ~~I have done wrong.~~ I have been given orders that conflict with my prime directive.

KETTLEWELL Oh no!

ROBOT They say there is no conflict. Yet I know there <u>is</u> conflict. I do not understand. Help me. ~~I do not understand.~~

14. INT. SRS HQ. LOBBY. DAY.

The lobby/office area of a larger hall, which we shall see in Part Three. All very shabby and run down.

Sarah is interviewing a short, Himmler-like little man in rimless glasses. There is a gleam of fanaticism in his eye, a muscular thuggish young man in slacks and rollneck sweater hovers menacingly.

Sarah is wearing a trouser suit or a mini skirt. Something to arouse disapproval in the ultra-conventional. She is reading through some SRS brochures.

SARAH As I understand it then, Mr. Short, you advocate rule by a sort of self-appointed elite?

SHORT It's only logical. Superior types should rule. They're best equipped for it!

SARAH And the 'inferior types'?

SHORT They'd be guided, helped. Kept away from harmful ideas and influences. For instance…

SARAH Do go on…

SHORT Your own attire, ~~for instance~~. Is it really suitable..?

SARAH *(Politely, but with edge)* **Trousers?** ~~Isn't~~ **Well, surely** that's a matter for me to decide?

SHORT As things are at the moment, it is. But in a more rationally ordered society…

SARAH I'd wear what you thought was good for me. **I see.** And think what you thought was good for me, too?

SHORT *(Fiercely)* It would be for your own good.

Sarah represses her answer. She looks at papers on Short's desk, unashamedly reading them upside down.

SARAH I see you're having a meeting here tonight. ~~Would it be possible…~~ **Do you think it would be possible for me to come?**

A short reaction from Short. He snatches the papers away. The young man closes in menacingly.

SHORT Sorry, out of the question. Private meeting, ~~no press.~~ Members only. **No press.**

SARAH But <u>if</u> I joined?

SHORT I really don't think you'd qualify. We have very high standards.

He stands, bringing the interview to an end, and Sarah stands too.

SARAH *(Sweetly)* Well, thank you so much for your time, Mr Short, and for telling me your most interesting ideas.

SHORT I do hope you'll include us in your article. We've been sadly misrepresented…

Sarah, now about to leave, pauses for a parting shot.

SARAH Really! ~~Oh yes.~~ **Well,** we're covering a number of fringe organizations, and I'm sure ~~we've~~ **we'll find** a place for you. Somewhere between the flying saucer people and the Flat Earthers. ~~Goodbye.~~

Sarah marches out, clutching her brochures.

Short stands looking after her, now looking far more sinister than benevolent. He goes to a table and picks up a phone.

15. EXT. THINKTANK WORKSHOP. (OB) DAY. ⑮

The Doctor and Brigadier are coming along the path that leads to Kettlewell's workshop. Miss Winter is escorting them.

DOCTOR WHO I can't thank you enough for the ~~tour~~ **visit**. It ~~really~~ has been most amusing.

WINTERS I suppose it all seems very elementary to a scientist of your standing Doctor…

DOCTOR WHO Yes it does rather. Still, never mind. Got to start somewhere, eh?

She isn't pleased. By now they are near Kettlewell's workshop.

DOCTOR WHO ~~Now here's something I'm really~~ **But there is one thing I'm** looking forward to – ~~though~~ Professor Kettlewell's Robot. **It's** in here, isn't it?

The Doctor dives into the workshop and the rest have to follow.

16. INT. THINKTANK WORKSHOP. DAY. ⑯

The Doctor stands looking round expectantly.

DOCTOR WHO Come on then! Where's your Tin Man?

WINTERS I'm afraid I must disappoint you, Doctor.

DOCTOR WHO Oh dear. I do so hate being disappointed. I was determined to see that Robot!

There is a steely undertone in his words.

WINTERS We had to dismantle it.

DOCTOR WHO What? Such a harmless creature too.

WINTERS ~~Since~~ **After** the visit of your friend, Miss Smith, it became unstable. She introduced it to concepts it was not equipped to deal with.

DOCTOR WHO Compassion and concern – useless things like that?

WINTERS We decided it would be safer to follow Professor Kettlewell's original ~~directive~~ **instructions**.

DOCTOR WHO Now that is a pity. **You see, one of our problems, Miss Winters, is that –** ⑰ I say! You haven't still got the bits have you? Maybe I could put ~~them~~ **it** together **again**. I'm ~~quite~~ **really rather** good at that sort of thing.

WINTERS We have our own furnaces in the basement. The Robot has been utterly destroyed.

BRIGADIER I could get authority to search.

WINTERS You might find it difficult Brigadier. But I won't stand on formalities. Search by all means if you wish.

DOCTOR WHO In that case, I'm sure we needn't bother. Come along, Brigadier. Miss Winters has a great deal to do.

Doctor Who, Miss Winters and the Brigadier are walking back along the corridor. Jellicoe hurries up to them – with a guard. ⑱

JELLICOE Miss Winters, there's a visitor – oh I'm sorry.

WINTERS Would you forgive me?

DOCTOR WHO Please, don't let **us** detain you.

WINTERS ~~The guard~~ **Philips** will show you a short cut **back to your car**.

DOCTOR WHO You know, I have a feeling we shall meet again.

With murmured farewells they part, Doctor Who, the Brigadier and guard going one way. We stay with Jellicoe and Miss Winters, going the other.

DOCTOR WHO **Come along, Brigadier.**

17. EXT. THINKTANK WORKSHOP. (OB) DAY.

JELLICOE Did they believe you?

WINTERS Of course not. But it doesn't matter. By the time they can act it'll be too late.

JELLICOE Someone from the Ministry of Health has turned up. Apparently under some obscure regulation they've just remembered, we have to have a complete check-up on the medical records of our staff.

WINTERS What an odd coincidence – at a time like this.

A bowler-hatted, umbrella'd type is waiting peering into a window.

JELLICOE Director, this is Doctor Sullivan – from the ministry.

The man in the window turns round and we see that it is Harry.

18. INT. UNIT HQ. DOCTOR'S LAB. DAY.

Doctor Who and the Brigadier are talking. ⑲

BRIGADIER Did you believe them?

DOCTOR WHO Of course not. And they know I didn't. And I know that they know I didn't. And they know that I know that they know I didn't. And –

BRIGADIER All right Doctor. So where is ~~it~~ the Robot?

DOCTOR WHO Either they've hidden it or it's wandered off somewhere by itself.

The Brigadier looks at his watch.

BRIGADIER I must be off. Got to try and persuade the minister to let ~~us~~ me raid the Thinktank. What are you going to do? Don't tell me – more thinking?

DOCTOR WHO I beg your pardon, Brigadier I was just thinking.

The Doctor nods.

The Brigadier sighs, and bustles off. Doctor Who is about to enter the TARDIS.

The phone rings and he picks it up.

DOCTOR WHO Yes? Yes of course I'll talk to him. I'll talk to anybody. (Pause) Professor Kettlewell? Yes, this is the Doctor.

19. INT. KETTLEWELL'S LAB. DAY.

Close on Kettlewell on the telephone. He is very agitated.

KETTLEWELL Doctor, you've got to help me. The Robot ~~– it came~~ has come to my house. I've got ~~it~~ him hidden. **But he's** ~~It's~~ very unstable… ~~I'm not sure if I can~~ **may not be able to** control ~~it~~ him… We <u>must</u> keep ~~it away from the~~ **him** out of the hands of those Thinktank people. They've driven ~~it~~ **him** almost insane…

(Pause) Yes at ~~the cottage~~ **my house**… I'll be waiting ~~for you~~ **at the gate**.

Kettlewell puts down the phone. ⑳ *He looks nervous and frightened. There is a knock on the door. He opens it. Facing him menacingly are Jellicoe and Miss Winters. He falls back, afraid.*

20. INT. UNIT HQ. DOCTOR'S LAB. DAY.

The Doctor stands thinking for a moment.

He finds a sheet of paper and begins to write – breaks pencil ㉑ *and grabs typewriter and feeds in paper.* ㉒

He finishes the note, fastens it where it can be seen and exits.

21. EXT. ROAD. (OB)

Doctor Who, driving along in Bessie.

22. INT. UNIT CORRIDORS. DAY.

Sarah, carrying SRS brochures, is walking with Benton. Sarah points to his new rank badges.

SARAH ~~What's happened to your stripes? Aren't you still a sergeant?~~ **Oh, I like that.** ㉓ **What is it?**

BENTON That's promotion, Miss. **To WO1.**

Sarah looks blank.

SARAH WO what?

BENTON Warrant Officer. You see, technically speaking the Brig should have a major and a captain under him. But the **UNIT** budget won't run to it, so they settled for promoting me!

SARAH Congratulations! About time, too!

BENTON Thank you.

She enters the laboratory, Benton follows.

23. INT. UNIT HQ. DOCTOR'S LAB. DAY.

SARAH (Calling) Doctor, I went to see those SRS people…

She spots the note, takes it and reads it, ㉔ *dropping her SRS brochures on the bench.*

SARAH (Reading) **Sarah** – Professor Kettlewell tells me that he has the Robot hidden at his ~~college~~ ㉕ **house**. Gone to meet him. PS. It is of course possible that this message is a trap. If it is I can deal with it. PPS. I am leaving this note in case I can't!

Sarah gives the note to Benton.

SARAH The idiot! He thinks he can cope with anything.

BENTON We'd better get after him. I'll get some men…

SARAH Right. I'll see you there.

She starts to rush out.

BENTON Wait for us ~~Miss~~. We'll go together.

But Sarah has already gone.

24. INT. KETTLEWELL'S LAB. DAY.

The shutters are up, the room in semi-darkness. The Doctor enters.

DOCTOR WHO Professor Kettlewell..? **Professor Kettlewell?… Professor?**

No reply. The Doctor advances cautiously. **26**

The giant form of the Robot appears. The Doctor looks at it with interest rather than fear.

ROBOT You are the Doctor?

DOCTOR WHO ~~Yes, yes, of course.~~ How do you do? I've been looking forward to meeting you.

ROBOT Please confirm your identity. There must be no mistake. You are the Doctor?

DOCTOR WHO Yes, **yes** of course.

ROBOT You are an enemy of the human race. I must destroy you.

The Robot advances menacingly on the Doctor. He backs away. It moves so that he cannot get away through the door and backs him into a corner.

ROBOT Please do not resist. I do not wish to cause you unnecessary pain. **27**

DOCTOR WHO How very kind of you.

Doctor leaps over bench. **28**

DOCTOR WHO ~~Wait!~~ **Prime directive!** What is your prime directive?

This key phrase gives the Robot pause.

ROBOT I must serve humanity, and never harm it.

DOCTOR WHO Then you must not harm me. I am a friend of humanity.

Backs to other column.

ROBOT No! You are ~~the~~ **an** enemy. You must be destroyed.

Robot walks into scarf and knocks down pillar. **29**

Robot smashes door and Doctor puts hat on Robot's head. **30**

The Robot is surprisingly agile for its size (we hope) but the Doctor is in the early stage of the chase, quickly moving. However, his new body is still not fully recovered and the Doctor begins to show signs of dizziness. He tries to defend himself with various bits of lumber dotted about the laboratory – a chair, lab bench, etc. But the Robot smashes through and casts aside all obstacles. One of its blows catches the Doctor a glancing blow on the head.

The Doctor staggers and recovers, but from then on is perceptibly slower. The Robot is gaining on him, and the end is only a matter of time. **31**

CLOSING TITLES

---

1 The episode starts with Sarah examining the oil on the floor.

2 This scene was edited into the closing stages of Part One, between Scenes 27 and 28, as Part Two was too long.

3 The Doctor walks in the footprints, making the point that they are indeed footprints, and that they are very large.

4 Terrance Dicks was especially pleased with the meticulous design and realization of the Robot: 'I do think that it was one of the most beautiful robots that has appeared in the history of science fiction! It was everything I wanted.'

5 At this point, Kilgarriff was removed from the robot costume, and the suit was then used on the set as an empty prop for Scene 7.

6 The Doctor is building a tower out of various components. At this point he takes a small metal bar from the Brigadier and adds it to his tower.

7 A line of Jellicoe's was deleted from here late on.

8 There was a recording break here to allow Michael Kilgarriff to get back into the robot costume.

⑨ One of the prop arms used in the Robot POV shots is visible on a bench – presumably a spare.

⑩ The scene closes with the Doctor's carefully built tower collapsing. The camera direction is 'Pan down as tower falls'.

⑪ There is just the alarm bell. The implication is that Chambers is alone in his house, unguarded.

⑫ The Robot uses the disintegrator gun to make a hole in the wall. CSO was used to merge the necessary images: a mask superimposed on the study wall to show the disintegrated hole and then, as another image, the Robot beyond. A red glow was added as the wall dissolves.

⑬ The Robot uses the disintegrator gun to open the safe/vault. The sequence is shown from inside the safe, the door glowing and then fading away to reveal the Robot as it reaches in for the envelope.

⑭ Several monochrome photographs of extra Walter Goodman as Joseph Chambers were taken as props for the serial.

⑮ This short scene required three takes, with one shot being cut in from take 2.

⑯ As with Part One, Scene 17, this is preceded by a brief sequence of the characters walking along a short corridor to the main workshop.

⑰ The Doctor's scarf has been 'sweeping' along the floor. He breaks off mid-sentence as he finds it has picked up a component.

⑱ In fact, the Doctor opens the doors to reveal Jellicoe standing – listening – outside. There is a white-coated man – Philips – with him.

⑲ The Doctor is examining the component he found.

⑳ A production note indicates that a sound effect of a car drawing up was to be added at this point. But there is none.

㉑ In the event, the Doctor uses the typewriter first. In his novelization of the story, Terrance Dicks has the Doctor handwriting the note. This may have been changed late on to set up the fact that the Doctor can type incredibly fast – an ability that is vital to his aborting the nuclear launch in Part Four, Scene 13.

㉒ This sequence was recorded on a videodisc borrowed from the Sports Department so that it could be speeded up. The Doctor then sticks the note to a convenient piece of Blu-tak on the TARDIS. Christopher Barry: 'We had to go cap in hand to the Sports Department, because they were the only people who had a videodisc at the BBC. You really had to beg, borrow, or steal it.'

㉓ In the original drafts, Benton was still a sergeant, and the promotion was clarified by this short scene.

㉔ The note which Sarah and Benton find is not the one the Doctor left – the Doctor types only two lines on his piece of paper (Scene 20). This note has 13 lines of double-spaced capitals in three paragraphs.

㉕ Presumably a misspelling of 'cottage'.

㉖ As he looks round, the Doctor opens and closes the back door, then switches on the light. A retake was necessary when the set wall wobbled as he pressed the light-switch.

㉗ The Robot smashes a (sugar glass) window as the Doctor ducks away.

㉘ The Doctor throws a handful of ball bearings at the Robot, but it crushes them under foot. Then he tries the back door, but it is now locked.

㉙ The stage direction for the Doctor tying his scarf between two pillars is missing, though preserved in the camera instructions. He also swings a heavy chain at the Robot, to little effect.

㉚ The Robot halts as its head is covered, as if deactivated. But when the Doctor approaches to check, it lashes out and strikes him. This sequence required a retake as the hat refused to stay in position.

㉛ The episode ends with the Doctor falling unconscious from the blow as the Robot looms over him.

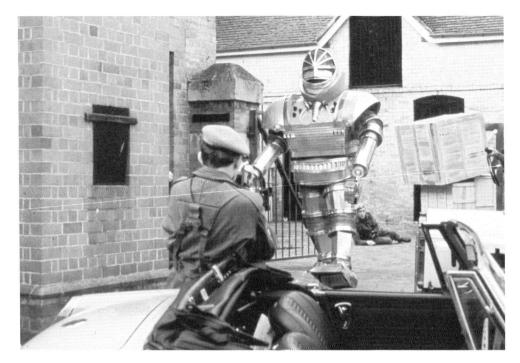

ROBOT

by Terrance Dicks

Part Three

OPENING TITLES

1. INT. KETTLEWELL'S LAB. DAY.

The shutters are up. The room in semi-darkness.

The Doctor enters.

DOCTOR WHO Professor Kettlewell?

No reply.

The Doctor advances cautiously.

The giant form of the Robot appears. The Doctor looks at it with interest rather than fear.

ROBOT Are you the Doctor?

DOCTOR WHO How do you do? I've been waiting to meet you.

ROBOT Please confirm your identity. There must be no mistake. You are the Doctor?

DOCTOR WHO Yes, of course.

ROBOT You are an enemy of the human race. I must destroy you.

The Robot advances menacingly on the Doctor. He backs away. It moves so that he cannot get away through the door, then backs him into a corner.

ROBOT Please do not resist. I do not wish to cause you unnecessary pain.

DOCTOR WHO How very kind of you.

The Robot, now very close, aims a smashing blow.

DOCTOR WHO Wait! What is your prime directive?

This key phrase gives the Robot pause.

ROBOT I must serve humanity, and never harm it.

DOCTOR WHO Then you must not harm me. I am a friend of humanity.

Backs to other column.

ROBOT No! You <u>are</u> the enemy. You must be destroyed.

Robot walks into scarf and knocks down pillar.

Robot smashes door and Doctor puts hat on Robot's head.

The Robot is agile for its size but the Doctor is quicker moving.

Doctor approaches Robot which hits him.

The Doctor staggers and recovers, but from then on is perceptibly slower. The Robot is gaining on him, and the end is only a matter of time.

1A. EXT. KETTLEWELL'S LAB. (OB). ❷

Sarah runs round the corner.

Sarah sees the Doctor's car, the hole in the door made by the Robot (from the inside) and hears crashing from the inside of the warehouse. She runs to the door and struggles to open it.

1B. INT. KETTLEWELL'S LAB. DAY.

Finally the Doctor is driven into a corner. He is trapped, he stumbles, and the Robot raises its arm for the final blow. ❸

SARAH *(VO)* No! **No!**

The Robot stops. It turns. Sarah runs into the laboratory.

SARAH You mustn't harm him.

ROBOT He is an enemy of humanity.

SARAH No, he isn't. He's a good man. ~~He's~~ A <u>friend</u>.

The Robot looks over to her.

ROBOT You were at the laboratory. You were concerned for me… You felt… <u>sorrow</u>.

SARAH That's right. And you refused to harm me even when you were ordered to. Those people are evil. They are lying to you. They've altered your programming to make you act **all** wrongly.

The Robot begins to reel in distress.

ROBOT I am confused. I do not understand. ~~I am distressed. I am in~~ I feel pain.

It swings in the direction of the door as there comes the sound of running feet.

BENTON *(VO)* Miss Smith, keep down!

Cut to Sarah's POV. In warehouse doorway stands Benton with a couple of UNIT soldiers

SARAH No… don't shoot!

Shots ring out.

The Robot turns and starts advancing towards Benton and the soldiers.

Soldier's POV as the Robot starts advancing towards them.

Ignoring the shots, the Robot scatters the soldiers and exits through door with hole.

2. EXT. KETTLEWELL'S LAB. DAY.

❹ *More soldiers are waiting outside. They open fire. The Robot picks up an enormous crate and hurls it at them.*

The soldiers are scattered or crushed. The Robot makes off.

3. INT. KETTLEWELL'S LAB. DAY.

Sarah is bending over the unconscious Doctor. Benton runs up.

BENTON *(Drops on knee)* Is he all right?

SARAH I think so.

BENTON We **just** couldn't stop it. ❺

SARAH What did you have to start shooting for? It wouldn't have ~~hurt~~ **harmed** you.

BENTON Well, you could have fooled me! It <u>was</u> trying to kill the Doctor, wasn't it?

SARAH Yes, but that was **because** – oh ~~never mind~~ **it doesn't matter**, it wasn't your fault. I suppose. You did your best.

BENTON *(Bitterly)* Thanks very much. The US Cavalry never get treated like this.

~~**SARAH** I'm sorry.~~

Suddenly they hear a muffled thump, and a groan.

SARAH Listen.

The sound comes again.

BENTON There…

In the corner there is a cupboard. Benton approaches it, gun in hand. Cautiously he pulls the door open. Out tumbles the semi-conscious figure of Professor Kettlewell.

4. INT. UNIT HQ. DOCTOR'S LAB.

Kettlewell, shaken but apparently recovered, is talking to Sarah. She is bathing a bruise on his forehead.

Kettlewell is in the middle of recounting something to Sarah. He is drawn and haggard, and seems to have a compulsion to talk.

KETTLEWELL The Robot came to find me last night… it was in terrible distress. They'd just forced it to commit another crime…

Sarah nods.

SARAH Yes. Yes, I know.

KETTLEWELL They've altered ~~its~~ **his** circuitry to overcome ~~the~~ **his** prime directive. They succeeded, but at a terrible cost.

SARAH He became unbalanced?

He nods.

KETTLEWELL Then Jellicoe and Miss Winters came, while I was waiting for the Doctor. They programmed the Robot to kill him. I protested, but they… they… they…

He shudders.

SARAH Never mind. You're safe now.

KETTLEWELL When I think of that Robot's potential! I invented the metal ~~its~~ **he's** made from, you know. I call it living metal! It actually has the capacity ~~for~~ **to**…

Benton enters with mugs of tea.

KETTLEWELL … grow~~th~~ like an animal organism.

SARAH It's quite big enough for me now, thank you.

KETTLEWELL That's how I made my other discovery, **you know,** the metallic equivalent to a virus. ~~It consumes metal: destroys it utterly.~~ **It breaks down metal into easily recyclable form.** *(Eagerly)* You see what that could mean? ~~A way~~ **It means we shall be able** to get rid of all the metallic waste polluting this planet.

BENTON *(Handing Kettlewell a mug of tea)* **Professor.**

Suddenly Kettlewell notices an SRS brochure. He picks it up.

KETTLEWELL ~~Where do these come from?~~ **What's that doing there?**

SARAH I went to see them – rather unpleasant.

KETTLEWELL *(Reading)* Scientific Reform Society. **Oh yes, yes…** Just before I left Thinktank they persuaded me to join.

I **remember I** went along to a meeting~~, I remember~~. Very odd bunch. Never went again.

Sarah is thinking hard.

SARAH **Well now,** there's a meeting tonight. Suppose you were to turn up, Professor. Would they let you in?

KETTLEWELL Very probably. I think I've still got my membership card **about me** somewhere.

SARAH If I came along too, with a camera and a tape recorder, you could smuggle me in. We could get the goods on them for the Brigadier.

BENTON Now hold on you two…

SARAH What do you say, Professor. Shall we try it? **Of course,** it could be dangerous.

KETTLEWELL If there's anything I can do to help defeat those people…

BENTON **But,** the Brig**adier** would go spare. So would the Doctor.

SARAH Well one's away and the other's asleep. Help him up.

BENTON ~~I'd better~~ **Well, I'll go and** wake the Doctor and ~~ask him~~ **see what he says**.

SARAH Don't you dare. He had a nasty knock on the head, and he needs to rest.

BENTON In that case it's just… not on then… I'm sorry.

SARAH *(Fiercely)* Mr Benton! Are we members of UNIT?

BENTON Well, no, of course not.

SARAH Are we under arrest?

BENTON *(Patiently)* No, Miss.

SARAH Well, in that case, where we go and what we do is no**ne of your** business ~~of yours~~ is it? **Come along, Professor.**

BENTON But ~~Miss…~~ **wouldn't it be best if –**

SARAH So **just** you go and blanco your rifle, or something. Come along, Professor.

With that she marches the professor out. Benton sighs.

5. INT. LOBBY. SRS HQ. EVENING.

Jellicoe ⑥ sits at a table checking membership cards as people file into hall. Thuggish henchman is at his side.

One or two members go through. Jellicoe glances at next card. He stiffens, looks up. Kettlewell is standing there nervously.

Jellicoe exchanges a look with thug.

JELLICOE **Professor Kettlewell.** How nice to see you again so soon, ~~Professor…~~

He hands Kettlewell's card back and motions him into the hall.

6. INT. UNIT HQ. DOCTOR'S LAB.

Benton on the carpet before a grim-faced Brigadier.

BRIGADIER *(Angry)* What the blazes were you thinking of Mr Benton? You should never have let them go.

BENTON *(Wearily)* Maybe you could have stopped 'em sir, but I couldn't. As the young lady pointed out, they're not really under our jurisdiction. Excuse me sir, but did you get permission to raid the Thinktank?

BRIGADIER *(Grimly)* No, Mr Benton. I did not.

DOCTOR WHO *(VO)* Then you must act without it!

The Brigadier turns. The Doctor is standing in the doorway, a bit shaky but otherwise normal.

~~BRIGADIER Ah, Doctor. Are you alright?~~

DOCTOR WHO I know what they're up to now. Worked it all out while I was having my little nap. It's all tied up with the information stolen from that poor fellow Chambers. He must have been ~~custodian~~ **the guardian** of some kind of ultimate threat.

The Brigadier reacts in amazement.

BRIGADIER How on earth ~~do you know that? I never mentioned –~~

DOCTOR WHO I don't know exactly <u>what</u> it is – just the <u>kind</u> of thing it has to be. Well, am I right?

Doctor moves and sits on bench. The Brigadier's manner is grim.

~~DOCTOR WHO You know I am.~~

The Brigadier comes forward.

BRIGADIER A few months ago, the superpowers, Russia, America, China, decided upon a plan to ensure peace. All three powers have hidden atomic missile sites. All three agreed to hand over details of the sites, plus full operation instructions to another neutral country. In the event of trouble, that country could publish <u>everyone's</u> secrets and cool things down. Naturally enough the only country that could be trusted with such a role was Great Britain.

DOCTOR WHO Naturally, I mean the rest were all foreigners.

BRIGADIER Well exactly. The destructor codes for firing the missiles were in Chambers' house, stored in a special dynastreem safe. The Robot killed Chambers ~~and used~~ **blasted the safe open with** the disintegrator gun ~~to open the safe~~ and ~~take~~ **took** the codes.

BENTON So what can they do with them now they've got 'em?

BRIGADIER They could set off every atomic missile in the world, **Mr Benton.**

DOCTOR WHO Yes. And start a nuclear holocaust that would turn this little planet of yours into a radioactive cinder, suspended in space.

(Jumps down, goes through)

There is a stunned silence.

BENTON You mean they'll use the information to blackmail the world – do things our way, or we light the blue touch-paper?

DOCTOR WHO *(Back to them)* I'm afraid so.

BRIGADIER We think they've been using this Scientific Reform Society as a front, Doctor.

He picks up one of the brochures for the Scientific Reform Society left by Sarah, hands it to Doctor Who. The Doctor looks at it. The Brigadier glares at Benton

BRIGADIER I've just heard from Benton that Miss Smith's gone off with Kettlewell to try and get into one of their meetings.

Doctor Who reacts to the name.

DOCTOR WHO *(Horrified)* Kettlewell? You let ~~her~~ **Sarah** go off somewhere with <u>Kettlewell</u>?

7. INT. REAR ENTRANCE. SRS HQ. DAY.

A section of corridor with a door in it. Kettlewell comes along and opens the door a crack.

KETTLEWELL Miss Smith – are you there?

Sarah slips inside.

SARAH How's it going, **Professor?**

KETTLEWELL All right, I think. They were a bit suspicious ~~at first~~ **to start with** but I've found ~~a place where you can~~ **somewhere for you to** hide.

They move along the corridor.

71

8. INT. HALL. SRS HQ. DAY (EVE).

A small group of people gathered for the meeting. They are plainly dressed, but all have a quality of fanaticism. Burly, tallish guards in rollneck sweaters are standing around the walls. Short is at a table on the dais. Miss Winters is with him.

Miss Winters is finishing a speech.

WINTERS And as you know, my friends, tonight is the culmination of many ~~many~~ years of work and planning. A brilliant and audacious scheme is about to come to its climax…

There is fierce applause of a mini-Nuremberg kind. ❼

During the speech we cut to Sarah, hiding behind some filing cabinets at the other end of the hall.

She has switched on a small tape-recorder and is busily photographing the audience with a miniature camera.

WINTERS You have all waited long and patiently during the years of scorn and ridicule, the days when we were laughed at as cranks. Now a new and better future is almost within our grasp. A future in which we, the elite, will rule as is our right!

More applause.

WINTERS We owe it all to one man, the man whose unrivalled scientific genius has put us in the commanding position we now hold. Professor Kettlewell!

Kettlewell enters. Cut to Sarah to see her amazed reaction, and then back to Kettlewell.

WINTERS He brings with him the symbol of our movement. The creature whose intelligence and power make him a fitting emblem for our scientific new order.

Behind Kettlewell appears the Robot. It stands looming over him, to the awe-stricken gasps of the audience.

9. INT. LOBBY. SRS HQ. DAY.

Just inside the door, Doctor Who is arguing with the large and muscular bouncer whose job it is to keep out undesirables.

Doctor Who is pretending to search for his membership card.

He is producing various documents and scraps of paper from his pockets. He pulls out an ornate scroll.

DOCTOR WHO Now where is that pass? It must be somewhere. Freedom of the City of Scaro… ❽ no… *(Producing a plastic card)* Pilot's licence for the Mars Venus rocket run… no… Galactic passport. Do you travel much..? *(Producing another note)* ~~How about this…~~ Honorary Member of the Alpha Centaurian ❾ Table Tennis Club. Very tricky opponents those chaps, six arms; of course, six bats. Really keeps you on your toes. Tell you what. I'll just pop out and ~~try another entrance~~ find…

Doctor Who tries to slip past the bouncer. The bouncer grabs for him but the Doctor isn't there. The bouncer trips and crashes to the ground.

~~**DOCTOR WHO** I'm terribly sorry!~~

The Doctor seems to go to help the bouncer up.

Immediately the bouncer takes a swipe at him, misses, trips over Doctor Who's foot and knocks himself out against the wall. ❿

DOCTOR WHO Oh dear! **I'm terribly sorry.** You lie there and rest, I'll go and get some help. And don't worry now. Everything's going to be all right.

He goes past the bouncer and towards the hall.

This incident is typical of the new Doctor's form of self-defence, which might be described as unintentional aikido. Doctor Who never seems to take any aggressive action, but his opponents invariably come to grief in some apparently accidental way.

10. INT. HALL. SRS HQ. DAY.

WINTERS With the aid of this Robot we shall seek out and destroy all those who try to harm us.

ROBOT Seek out and destroy.

At nod from Kettlewell the Robot stalks through the audience, ⓫ *making straight for Sarah's hiding place. It reaches the filing cabinet behind which she is hiding and sweeps it aside.*

Sarah is revealed, complete with camera and tape recorder. There is a growl of anger from the crowd.

They move menacingly towards her. She tries to run, but the Robot bars her way.

WINTERS *(To the audience)* She's a spy. Deal with her.

Everyone has moved from the dais end of the hall to surround Sarah.

DOCTOR WHO *(VO)* Good evening, everyone!

They all swing round. Doctor Who is standing in the centre of the little stage at the other end of the room.

The crowd moves back towards him, so that he has rather the appearance of a performer on a stage.

DOCTOR WHO Now please, please ~~be seated~~ **stay calm, everyone keep your seat.** Now then, what can I do to entertain you all, till my friend the Brigadier arrives? A little song? Just a little dance?

He performs a couple of steps.

DOCTOR WHO Anyone for cards?

WINTERS Don't just stand there, you idiots. Get him.

A couple of guards make for the dais.

~~**DOCTOR WHO** Anyone for cards?~~

Doctor Who produces a pack of cards and does a fancy shuffle.

DOCTOR WHO Now for my next trick, I shall require the assistance of a member of the audience.

By now the first of his attackers is about to jump on to the stage.

DOCTOR WHO I say – haven't we met somewhere before? Let me help you up. What a pity! Any other sporting ~~gentleman~~ **member of the audience**?

But by now others have crowded on to the platform.

Doctor Who is overwhelmed and dragged from the platform and into the body of the hall, where he and Sarah are held captive before Kettlewell and Miss Winters.

DOCTOR WHO Tell me one thing, Professor Kettlewell. Why?

KETTLEWELL **For years** I've been trying to <u>persuade</u> people to stop spoiling this planet ~~for years~~ Doctor. Now, with help from my friends, here, I can <u>make</u> them ~~stop~~.

DOCTOR WHO Aren't you forgetting – in science, as in morality, the end never justifies the means.

JELLICOE *(To Miss Winters)* What are we going to do with them?

WINTERS Kill them, of course.

KETTLEWELL No! No!

WINTERS They're far too dangerous to us.

KETTLEWELL We could lock them up…

WINTERS And have them escape? It's too late to be squeamish, Professor.

Doctor Who looks at Kettlewell, almost sympathetically.

DOCTOR WHO You see what I mean, Professor.

WINTERS Take them away.

There is a move to drag them away. A shot rings out.

BRIGADIER *(VO)* Stay where you are. My men have this building surrounded.

They all turn to see the Brigadier and Benton at the rear entrance.

Benton has just fired a shot in the air. There is a panic in the audience. Doctor Who seizes his chance, breaks free from his captors.

Cut to a close-up of Winters and Kettlewell.

WINTERS Is the transport still there?

JELLICOE Outside.

WINTERS Quick, the front way.

BRIGADIER Stop! Stay where you are!

KETTLEWELL *(To Robot)* Protect us! **Protect us!**

The Robot backs away, and Kettlewell and Miss Winters make their escape, using it as shelter.

Miss Winters grabs Sarah, and uses her as a shield.

The Brigadier raises his gun, but is reluctant to fire for fear of hitting Sarah.

Kettlewell, Jellicoe, Miss Winters, Sarah and the Robot all exit through the front entrance.

EXT. FRONT AREA. SRS HQ. (OB) DAY.

Kettlewell and Miss Winters, shielded by the Robot, come out with Sarah as their prisoner and retreat towards a waiting horsebox. ⓬

The UNIT soldiers are firing at the Robot, which ignores the bullets and smashes down any soldier who comes within reach.

Miss Winters gets into the front of the horsebox and revs it up. Kettlewell, followed by

Sarah and the Robot, gets in the back. The rear doors are slammed and the horsebox roars away, crashing through a UNIT barricade and disappearing into the distance.

12A. INT. REAR LOBBY. SRS HALL. DAY.
Thugs escaping.

13. INT. HALL. SRS HQ. DAY.
A general air of mopping up. The last few SRS members being hustled away.
   The Doctor is sitting on the dais talking to the Brigadier.

BRIGADIER Well, Doctor…

DOCTOR WHO ~~Of course Kettlewell had to be involved.~~ It had to be Kettlewell.

~~**BRIGADIER** Why?~~

DOCTOR WHO Only ~~with his knowledge~~ he could ~~they~~ have **attempted to** reprogram~~med~~ the Robot to overcome its prime directive – ~~and luckily, they weren't completely successful.~~

BRIGADIER Then all that business about ~~Kettlewell~~ being knocked ~~out~~ **on the head** and ~~locked~~ **pushed** in the cupboard…

DOCTOR WHO Faked. ~~They faked it all~~ **Faked** to gain your confidence.

~~**BRIGADIER** Well, they got the destructor codes.~~

DOCTOR WHO And they still have the destructor codes. And Sarah~~, didn't they~~!

~~**BRIGADIER** What do you imagine they will do now?~~

DOCTOR WHO And now they'll hide ~~away~~ **up** somewhere and try their blackmail plan, I suppose.

BRIGADIER How can they? If they start a nuclear war, they'll go up with the rest of us.

DOCTOR WHO I rather imagine that has occurred to them. You'd better find them Brigadier – and soon.

BRIGADIER I agree, but how? ~~They could be anywhere.~~

~~**DOCTOR WHO** I agree.~~

   Benton comes in with an RT set.

BENTON Excuse me sir. Call for you from Dr Sullivan, sir. Linked in from HQ.

   The Brigadier takes RT.

BRIGADIER Thank you. Sullivan, are you still at Thinktank? Over.

14. INT. THINKTANK CALLBOX. DAY.
A section of corridor, with a public telephone.
   Harry is on the telephone.

HARRY Yes, **sir. But** I may not have much time. Listen, **sir,** I managed to **give them the slip** ~~hide myself~~, I think they've forgotten about me. They~~'re~~ **seem to be** pulling out, sir. Whole place is being evacuated.

15. INT. HALL. SRS HQ. DAY.
BRIGADIER **Listen,** Sullivan, this is urgent. Do you know where they're going. Have you got any idea at all?

HARRY *(Distort)* Well, sir I heard somebody mention the bunker. Seemed to be a kind of jo–

   There is a clunk and then silence, the Brigadier jiggles the RT.

BRIGADIER Sullivan! Are you **still** there?

16. INT. THINKTANK CORRIDOR. DAY.
Cut to Harry unconscious on the floor.
   Jellicoe stands over him with a blunt instrument.
   There is a thuggish guard, dressed as a white-coated technician *beside him.*

JELLICOE *(To technician)* We'll take him with us. He'll make a useful hostage.

   They start to drag him away.

17. INT. HALL. SRS HQ. DAY.
The Brigadier abandons the RT.

BRIGADIER No good. Broken connection.

DOCTOR WHO Or broken head, if someone overheard him calling us.

BRIGADIER He said something about going to a bunker…

18. EXT. BUNKER. (OB) DAY.
A concrete area surrounding the main entrance. Its dominating feature is a heavily fortified main door.
   This needn't be particularly big. The bunker itself of course is hidden well underground. What we are looking at is virtually the fortified head of a lift shaft.
   Brigadier's army arrives in a small convoy of Land Rovers.

The Brigadier, the Doctor, 🔞 *and Sergeant Benton are in the first one.*

The convoy draws up a discreet distance away from the entrance.

BRIGADIER This is the place – an atomic shelter designed and built by the Thinktank people back in the Cold War days.

DOCTOR WHO So if their bluff <u>is</u> called – they'll stay down there safe and sound, and emerge to rule the survivors – if any.

BENTON You really think they're in there! Sir?

BRIGADIER We'll soon find out… **Right Benton.**

BENTON *(To troops)* **Fall out!**

Everyone starts getting down from the vehicles.

19. INT. BUNKER CONTROL ROOM. DAY.

A small underground control room with a monitor screen.

Jellicoe, Miss Winters, Kettlewell are watching the monitor screen.

Sarah stands captive, guarded by a thug.

WINTERS Activate the automatic defence system.

KETTLEWELL Shouldn't we talk to them first?

WINTERS We'll talk afterwards. First we must show them the strength of our position.

Jellicoe presses various buttons. On the screen the Brigadier and Benton and some UNIT troops can be seen approaching the main door.

Miss Winters notices Sarah.

WINTERS Put her with the other one.

The thug bundles Sarah.

20. EXT. BUNKER. (OB) DAY.

The Brigadier and his men start moving towards the doors.

The Doctor is looking about keenly. 🔞 *Suddenly he catches a flash of metallic movement from a high point commanding the corner. He stands up on the Land Rover, cups his hands and yells.*

DOCTOR WHO **Down** Brigadier – ~~down all of you~~. **Everybody,** get down.

As he yells, a chatter of machine-gun fire breaks out, and a murderous crossfire sweeps the area in front of the doors.

Thanks to the Doctor's warning the Brigadier and his men are able to drop and wriggle back out of danger.

The Brigadier and Benton come back to the Land Rover.

BRIGADIER Well of all the cheek! They've got troops here!

DOCTOR WHO I don't think so, Brigadier. Automated machine-gun nests, I fancy. ~~Probably~~ Activated by body heat as you get within range.

There is a crackle from Benton's RT. He fiddles with it.

DOCTOR WHO *(To Benton)* Shhh!

BENTON It's not me, Doctor. Someone's trying to get through on our frequency ~~sir~~.

DOCTOR WHO Good man.

21. INT. BUNKER CONTROL ROOM. DAY.

BENTON Greyhound leader, receiving you. Over.

WINTERS Let me speak to the Brigadier

Miss Winters is talking on a radio set-up.

BRIGADIER Lethbridge Stuart. 🔞

WINTERS Brigadier – can you hear me?

BRIGADIER *(VO filter)* I hear you, Miss Winters. Come out and give yourselves up **or we shall attack.**

WINTERS We hold two of your friends as hostages.

22. EXT. BUNKER. (OB) DAY.

The Brigadier reacts to this threat. He glances at the Doctor, then steels himself.

BRIGADIER That will not deter me ~~from my duty~~. I repeat, give yourselves up or we shall attack.

23. INT. BUNKER CONTROL ROOM. DAY.

WINTERS You'll never reach those doors alive, Brigadier – and if you did you'd never get through them. By now the governments of the world will have received our demands. Unless they are agreed to in full, the destructor codes will be used. We have associates standing by all over the world. <u>You</u> have 30 minutes in which to surrender.

24. EXT. BUNKER. WOODED AREA. (OB) DAY.

The Brigadier is furious.

BRIGADIER Mr. Benton… Take a party with grenades. Find those machine-gun nests and knock them out.

BENTON Sir!

He moves away.

BRIGADIER I'll show that wretched woman.

25. INT. BUNKER STORAGE BAY. DAY.

Simply sectioned-off bits of concrete wall.
Harry is firmly bound to a chair.
The Robot stands guard over him.
Harry struggles to free himself.

ROBOT Do not move. If you attempt to escape I must destroy you.

Harry keeps very still.
Sarah is shoved in by the thug. He pushes her into a chair and starts tying her up.

HARRY Oh, I say Miss Smith. I'm awfully sorry.

GUARD Shut up!

Guard exits.

SARAH *(Turning to Harry)* James Bond!

26. EXT. BUNKER. (OB) DAY.

A series of explosions comes from the points where we have established the machine guns. 20 *Benton comes running up.*

BENTON That's the lot, sir.

BRIGADIER Right. Prepare to advance!

DOCTOR WHO Just a moment, Brigadier.

He fishes around in his pockets and produces his trusty sonic screwdriver.

He makes a few adjustments until it produces high-pitched buzz and a flashing light.

Doctor Who sweeps the ground before the entrance with the sonic screwdriver.

There are a number of spectacular explosions as concealed mines are detonated.

Doctor Who turns to the UNIT troops who are looking rather stunned.

DOCTOR WHO Come along then!

They march up to the door and start examining it.

BENTON Shall I get some explosives sir?

BRIGADIER Yes.

DOCTOR WHO Oh no must you? I really do think we've had enough bangs and flashes for a bit. Hang on.

Doctor Who makes more adjustments to the sonic screwdriver.

DOCTOR WHO *(Proudly)* Turns it into a miniature sonic lance you see.

BRIGADIER And what do you propose to do with that, ~~Doctor~~?

DOCTOR WHO Cut out the lock for you. Shouldn't take ~~very~~ long.

He draws a circle round a selected part of the doors with the sonic screwdriver. To everyone's astonishment it is cutting through the metal. 21

27. INT. BUNKER CONTROL ROOM. DAY.

Doctor Who can be seen at work on the monitor.

Dials are flickering madly on the console.

JELLICOE They're getting through… it isn't possible.

WINTERS *(To Kettlewell)* Very well. **We shall have to** use the destructor codes. Show them we're not bluffing.

KETTLEWELL *(Panicky)* ~~It takes time~~ **It would take too long** to set up the sequence. They'll be in here long before that. You said we'd have plenty of time.

WINTERS Then we must gain time, ~~Prof~~. We shall have to use your metal friend, Professor. This time, he'd better not let us down. *(To Jellicoe)* Is the disintegrator gun ready yet?

JELLICOE Yes.

Jellicoe nods.

WINTERS Then fit it and send him out. *(To Kettlewell)* Come on, Professor. Start getting the destructor codes operational. Maybe they'll listen when the first few missiles are fired.

Jellicoe hurries out.

~~**TELECINE**~~

~~*Missile shots*~~ 22

28. INT. BUNKER STORAGE BAY. DAY.

Sarah and Harry still tied to chairs, guarded by the Robot.

Jellicoe hurries in and, ignoring Harry, unpacks a wooden crate, fetching out a kind of massive sci-fi rifle. ㉓

He hands it to the Robot.

JELLICOE Enemies of humanity are attacking us. You ~~will~~ **must** take this weapon and destroy them.

Reaction of Sarah and Harry.

SARAH No – no you mustn't!

29. EXT. BUNKER. (OB) DAY.

Doctor Who stops his cutting. He frees the doors.

DOCTOR WHO They're opening! Back, everybody, back.

BRIGADIER Maybe they're going to surrender.

DOCTOR WHO I very much doubt it. Get your men back, Brigadier, if you don't want them killed!

The Brigadier signals his men to move back. As they move back to a safe distance:

BENTON Back – fall back to the woods.

The doors start to open.

The Robot stands there. Gun in its hands. Steps out. The door closes behind it.

The last man to pull back is still quite close to the doors.

When the Robot emerges the last man spins round and opens fire at it. The Robot levels the gun, there is a flash and an electronic shriek.

The soldier glows ㉔ *and vanishes.* ㉕

BRIGADIER *(Grimly)* I brought along something to deal with it!

DOCTOR WHO I very much doubt it, Brigadier.

He waves a signal. A tank lumbers slowly towards the Robot. ㉖

The Robot levels the gun, and fires. The tank, too, glows brightly and then vanishes. The Robot stands menacing the soldiers. It speaks in a great, booming voice.

ROBOT Go! Go now, or I shall destroy you all!

CLOSING TITLES

CSO – That's Why They Call It the Blues

Colour Separation Overlay, also known as Chromakey or blue screen, is a way of combining two images. The technique works by having areas of a specified colour in one image replaced by elements from a second image. Blue is typically used as the so-called 'keying' colour, though yellow was also used quite often on *Doctor Who* – not least as the TARDIS is blue, and would disappear if blue was the keying colour. Yellow was used for *Robot*.

CSO is a remarkably versatile tool. A single key-coloured rectangular area can become a large screen display showing the whole of another video image. Or a character standing alone in front of a key-colour backdrop can be added to another set – even a model. In the opposite case, a model can be added to a live-action scene and appear full size.

The disadvantages of CSO were that it could take a long time to set up, and often there was a coloured 'haze' around the CSO area. Reflective surfaces also gave problems as they could reflect the key colour and therefore 'disappear' into the other image.

The most obvious use of CSO in *Robot* was to add the giant-sized Robot into live-action scenes with UNIT soldiers, Sarah and other characters. For these scenes, the Robot was recorded acting against a yellow backdrop. The yellow colour was then replaced by video previously recorded on location.

Producer Barry Letts recalled that:

'*Robot* was done on outside broadcast video quite deliberately because we knew we were going to use CSO to put the Robot into the location background with him in the studio. When we tried that as an experiment before – in *Carnival of Monsters* (1973) where the Drashig came up out of the hold, and more extensively in *Invasion of the Dinosaurs* (1974) – we used film for the location work. With the Drashig it was fine, just a quick shot. With the dinosaurs we had quite lengthy sequences. And the trouble with film is that no matter how carefully it's shot, the picture floats slightly. What happens if you put something absolutely rigid from video into a film background is that the eye thinks the background is still and the foreground floating slightly.

'I hated the stuff in *Invasion of the Dinosaurs*. That's no reflection on the people who did it, just that we were trying it too early. So the only solution was to put both the background and the foreground on video, because it's absolutely rock steady. It was only because we could do that that we accepted the idea of doing *Robot* as we did. There was an OB unit at that time set aside for drama. You had to make a special bid for it.'

The images here show how two soldiers were CSO'd into a scene of the giant Robot (already added with CSO) attacking other soldiers on location.

1. A composite image of the Robot and soldiers on location.

2. The soldiers to be added into the picture, performing against a yellow backdrop. The yellow will then be replaced with another video image (1, opposite).

3. The resulting composite image – actually three layers deep: the video recorded on location; the Robot added from the studio; the soldiers added to that composite image.

① For production notes and amendments on the reprise, see the end of Part Two.

② This scene is cut in before the point where the previous scene ended in Part Two.

③ Although it is a different shot, the Robot is now at the point over the Doctor where it was at the end of Part Two.

④ We see the Robot smashing through the door from outside. Even the thinnest balsa wood prop door presented problems for Kilgarriff, whose movement inside the robot costume was badly restricted.

⑤ In the camera script this line is mistakenly also given to Sarah.

⑥ Jellicoe is wearing his SRS 'uniform'. It has stylized a 'SRS' on the collar, and the SRS emblem on the left sleeve. This emblem is based on the shape of the Robot's head. It is also reminiscent of a swastika.

⑦ Christopher Barry called this her 'Hitler from the pulpit' speech.

⑧ Note the misspelling of Skaro, a planet the Doctor will visit again in *Genesis of the Daleks*.

⑨ A one-eyed, six-armed native of Alpha Centauri appeared in *The Curse of Peladon* (1972) and in the previous year's *The Monster of Peladon* (1974).

⑩ Regular stunt man Terry Walsh played the SRS bouncer and performed a couple of simple action sequences with Baker in this scene and the next. Christopher Barry suggested that Baker use his scarf to trip up Walsh in this scene.

⑪ A cut-away shot to Sarah's worried reaction was used to mask the fact that the Robot could only manage the final step down from the dais on its own.

⑫ Although not mentioned, Jellicoe is the last out. He guides the Robot down the steps from the entrance to the 'meeting hall', as it is labelled, and helps it up the ramp into the horsebox.

⑬ A production note at this point – 'RELAX ROBOT' – indicates that Michael Kilgarriff was able to rest for the next few studio scenes (until Scene 25).

⑭ Harry is calling from the pay phone in the short corridor outside Kettlewell's workshop at Thinktank.

⑮ It is Philips (from Part Two, Scene 16).

⑯ The intention had been to shoot the entrance to the Thinktank bunker at the real entrance to an underground studio at Wood Norton. But as Christopher Barry explained, this ran into problems with the Official Secrets Act: 'The underground studio was supposed to be a regional broadcasting centre in the event of war. This was one reason we went, of course – the vault would have been marvellous. Then suddenly they said, "Oh it's secret – you can't show that!" So we had to build on the hillside. Ian Rawnsley [the designer] probably had to knock it up fairly fast, and it also had to be incredibly tall for the Robot to get in the door, which didn't make it easy to have a thing sliding into the hillside.'

⑰ The Doctor and the Brigadier are in Bessie, leading the convoy. Benton joins them after they arrive.

⑱ The Doctor is looking through a small telescope. There is an inserted shot of the gun emplacement above the main door to the bunker, using a circular mask to give the telescope POV.

⑲ Again, Stewart is misspelled.

⑳ Three machine-gun nests are destroyed, courtesy of Visual Effects' pyrotechnics.

㉑ This was done using a hot blade inside the door to cut through a thin plastic area.

㉒ Christopher Barry planned to have some stock film of missiles being readied for launch, but this was abandoned before studio (see also Part Four, following Scene 7).

㉓ The facts that the disintegrator gun is first described here, and Miss Winters asks if it is ready (in the previous scene), suggest it was a late decision to have the Robot use it in Part Two.

㉔ A pulsing, electronic effect added in post-production. Also used for the destruction of the tank.

㉕ Achieved using 'roll-back-and-mix' (see Part One, Scene 1.)

㉖ The attack by an armoured tank was achieved on location by means of a locked-off camera and a foreground miniature. With no money or time left to build a tank from scratch, Clifford Culley's visual effects team simply used a toy Scorpion tank made by Palitoy for their Action Man range. This appeared as a foreground miniature which Christopher Barry found disappointing although the effect had been suggested to him by Letts. Barry Letts: 'I was intrigued by the idea, as I always have been, of using models... Chris Barry didn't want to at all. Chris wanted to get the army in and sort out a location shoot. But we couldn't afford the time and the money as far as I was concerned. I thought we'd get away with it, but obviously we didn't.'

ROBOT

by Terrance Dicks

Part Four

OPENING TITLES

1. EXT. BUNKER. DAY. ❶

The doors to the bunker open. The Robot stands there, disintegrator gun in its hands. It steps out. The doors close behind it.

The last man to retreat is still quite close to the doors. When the Robot emerges he spins round and opens fire at it.

The Robot reveals the gun, there is a flash and an electronic shriek.

The soldier glows and vanishes.

BRIGADIER *(Grimly)* I've brought along something to deal with it.

He waves a signal. A tank lumbers slowly towards the Robot.

The Robot raises the laser gun and fires again. The tank, too, glows brightly, and then vanishes.

The Robot stands menacing the soldiers. It speaks in a great booming voice.

ROBOT Go! Go now, or I shall destroy you all!

2. INT. BUNKER CONTROL ROOM. DAY.

Miss Winters, Jellicoe and Kettlewell are watching the scene on monitor.

Kettlewell is busy at a computer control nearby. A file of computer codes open in front of him. A countdown clock is clicking backwards from 600, 2 *599, 598…*

WINTERS ~~That~~ Everything seems to be very satisfactory. *(To Kettlewell)* How are you getting on, **Professor**?

KETTLEWELL ~~I'm starting~~ I've just finished **making** the preliminary link-ups. You don't really intend to <u>use</u> the destructor codes, do you?

WINTERS I want everything in readiness.

KETTLEWELL If they don't agree – if they call our bluff then we'll surrender, won't we?

WINTERS No. We shall fire the missiles. *(Smiles)*

KETTLEWELL We can't. It'll ~~start~~ **mean** a nuclear war.

WINTERS You want a better world, don't you? We shan't gain it without <u>some</u> sacrifices. **Now, start the countdown, Professor.**

Kettlewell looks at her, appalled.

3. INT. BUNKER STORAGE BAY. DAY.

Freed from the supervision of the Robot, Sarah and Harry are making tremendous efforts to free themselves.

They have moved their chairs round, back to back.

Sarah is trying to undo Harry's bonds with her still-freed fingers.

HARRY How are ~~you~~ we doing, Miss Smith? ~~It's coming – I think!~~

SARAH OK.

HARRY Yeah, I think it's coming.

4. INT. BUNKER CONTROL ROOM. DAY.

Miss Winters turns to Jellicoe.

WINTERS What about food and water? How long can we hold out if the worst happens?

JELLICOE I'm not really sure.

WINTERS Then you should be. Take me to the food storage. We must make a proper check. *(To Kettlewell)* Keep an eye on our friends outside, Professor.

5. INT. BUNKER CORRIDOR. DAY.

Miss Winters and Jellicoe come along the corridor ~~with a thug~~. They pass the storage bay in which Sarah and Harry are imprisoned. They look in at them. They are slumped on their chairs, tied up, the chairs moved hurriedly apart.

JELLICOE Wait – what do you do about <u>them</u>? 3

6. INT. BUNKER STORAGE BAY. DAY.

WINTERS ~~They're~~ Obviously no use as hostages, and we can't afford useless mouths to feed. They'll have to be disposed of.

The thug moves towards Harry and Sarah.

WINTERS Later!

They close doors as soon as they are out of sight, Harry and Sarah come to life.

HARRY That was a near one!

SARAH We're nearly there, I think.

They shuffle the chairs back to back again, and Sarah resumes trying to undo Harry's bonds. 4

7. EXT. WOODED AREA. (OB) DAY.

The Brigadier and the Doctor have withdrawn to a safe distance. They are watching the Robot as it patrols the entrance to the bunker.

BRIGADIER What's the range and power of that weapon, Doctor?

DOCTOR WHO Power – ~~more or less~~ **almost** unlimited… Range, well, it could drill a hole in the surface of the moon.

BRIGADIER And knock out anything we send against it?

The Doctor nods.

DOCTOR WHO Yes… well, no use standing here is it? Brigadier, you prepare your men for an attack ~~on the Robot. See if you can~~ **Try and** draw ~~it~~ **the Robot** away from the door. I'll slip **round** behind it and finish cutting ~~through~~ the lock.

BRIGADIER We don't stand much chance you know, ~~Doctor.~~

DOCTOR WHO I know. But we have to try.

The Brigadier looks at him and nods, accepting the risk.

BRIGADIER Right. We'll cover you as long as we can. **Right, Benton…**

~~Telecine~~

~~Missile shots.~~ 5

8. INT. BUNKER CONTROL ROOM. DAY.

6 *Kettlewell, in a very agitated state, is punching out instructions on a computer terminal. Suddenly he stops, throws the file with the codes aside.*

KETTLEWELL I can't do it. I won't!

Jellicoe appears at steps. **7**

KETTLEWELL ~~No, and it isn't going to be. I won't go on with it.~~

Jellicoe produces a revolver.

JELLICOE Don't try and stop it, Professor!

He indicates the file. **8**

JELLICOE Let it run!

Kettlewell, terrified, starts punching buttons again.

Sarah and Harry appear behind Jellicoe. Harry jumps him. There is a short sharp struggle in the control room.

Harry manages to knock the gun from Jellicoe's hands, and after a further struggle knocks out Jellicoe with a classic upper cut.

KETTLEWELL Thank heavens you've come.

SARAH ~~Thank heavens you've come~~. **9** *(To Kettlewell)* **Can you** cancel what you've been doing?

Kettlewell is already punching buttons.

KETTLEWELL ~~It would take too long~~. **There's not time.** I'll punch in a hold signal.

Kettlewell punches the hold signal. **10**

HARRY Right, now open the main gates, ~~Prof.~~ We're going outside.

Kettlewell operates more controls.

9. EXT. WOODED AREA. (OB) DAY.

The Brigadier and the Doctor are ready for their kamikaze mission.

Suddenly the Doctor points.

Cut to their POV.

Behind the Robot the massive main gates are opening.

BRIGADIER ~~We've still got to get past that thing.~~ **Wait – the doors!**

10. EXT. BUNKER. (OB) DAY.

The Robot rounds on Sarah, aiming its gun.

Harry and Kettlewell can be glimpsed in the doorway behind her.

SARAH Doctor! Please, don't shoot. ~~I'm~~ **We're** no danger to you.

ROBOT You must go. The soldiers must go.

SARAH You've got to let ~~them~~ **him** in there.

ROBOT They are enemies of the human race.

SARAH No. **They're** the enemies ~~are~~ in there. They want to start an atomic war, kill millions of people.

The Robot shows signs of confusion.

The Doctor, the Brigadier and his men begin to advance.

ROBOT ~~Go, or I will shoot. I must shoot.~~ **You must go, or I will kill… I must destroy you.** **11**

Sarah doesn't move.

ROBOT I must destroy you.

It raises the gun just as Kettlewell emerges from the doors.

Harry is behind him.

KETTLEWELL No, don't! She was telling…

HARRY ~~Professor! Look out!~~

The Robot has already fired.

Kettlewell is blown to the ground.

He glows and vanishes. **12**

The Robot gives a cry of almost human agony.

ROBOT I have killed the one who created me.

The Robot hurls the gun down, and crashes to the ground.

DOCTOR WHO Now's our chance!

The Brigadier and the Doctor rush into the bunker. So do Harry and Sarah.

Benton, in passing, scoops up the disintegrator gun.

11. INT. BUNKER CONTROL ROOM. DAY.

Miss Winters comes in and sees the prostrate Jellicoe. She looks at the monitor, sees UNIT troops are on their way in. She sees the file on the floor and picks it up.

She sits at the computer keyboard and starts punching buttons.

12. INT. BUNKER CORRIDORS. DAY.

Doctor Who, Sarah, Brigadier and Harry, running for the control room.

Benton and UNIT troops behind.

13. INT. BUNKER CONTROL ROOM. DAY.

The open file beside Miss Winters.

Doctor, Brigadier, Benton, Sarah and co. appear in the doorway plus two soldiers.

BRIGADIER Get away from that keyboard!

Miss Winter carries on punching buttons.

WINTERS You won't shoot, Brigadier?

Cut to the Brigadier; he is nonplussed.

SARAH *(VO)* Maybe he won't, but I will!

Cut to Sarah. She has snatched up Jellicoe's gun from the floor and is covering Miss Winters.

SARAH Move away.

Miss Winters looks up at Sarah, sees she means it and stands up.

WINTERS Why not? It's finished. The firing instructions have gone out.

BRIGADIER ~~Cancel them~~. **I can still get the major powers to use their fail-safe procedures.**

WINTERS Too late, **Brigadier.**

BRIGADIER Cancel the destructor codes!

Indicating the countdown clock.

WINTERS When that reaches zero, the missiles will be fired. No one could send the cancel codes in time.

DOCTOR WHO She~~'s~~ **may be** right, Brigadier.

The clock is now reading 41 – it is clicking down 40, 39, 38, 37 etc. as we watch. ⓭

BRIGADIER Get her out of here!

Benton and soldiers march her out. Brigadier turns to the Doctor.

Doctor Who is already at the keyboard, leafing through the file at amazing speed.

BENTON Move!

As Miss Winters is hustled, and Jellicoe dragged, out, the Doctor starts punching buttons, his fingers moving in a positive blur of speed. The countdown clock continues its ticking: 20, 19, 18, 17.

Everyone watches tensely as Doctor Who works. Doctor Who himself, however, seems quite unruffled, and he chats amiably, as he punches the keyboard.

DOCTOR WHO The trouble with computers, of course… is that they're very sophisticated idiots… they do exactly what you tell them at amazing speed… even if you order them to kill you… so if you do happen to change your mind… it's very difficult to stop them obeying the original order!

As he finishes this speech the countdown clock clicks down to 4, 3, 2 and it registers 600. ⓮

The Doctor sits back beaming.

DOCTOR WHO But not impossible!

General signs of relief. They crowd round the Doctor, congratulating him.

HARRY ~~Sir, well done!~~ **Congratulations, Doctor!**

Cut to Sarah. A sudden thought seems to strike her. She slips away unseen.

The Brigadier turns to Harry and Benton and the Doctor.

BRIGADIER Well, it's over. Now for a little mopping up!

BENTON Right, sir.

14. INT. BUNKER CORRIDOR. DAY.

Sarah comes along and passes the storage bay entrance. Suddenly the Robot appears from the gloom, and grabs her.

15. EXT. WOODED AREA. (OB) DAY.

The Brigadier is with Harry, the Doctor, and Benton.

BRIGADIER Vanished? How can they have vanished?

BENTON We were all pretty busy inside sir – mopping up the rest of that Thinktank lot. We noticed the Robot was gone when we came out and everyone assumed someone else had got it.

DOCTOR WHO And Sarah?

BENTON Well, we thought… Thought she'd just gone home…

DOCTOR WHO ~~So nobody~~ **Gone home? You mean that not one of you** connected the ~~vanishing~~ **disappearance** of Sarah with the vanishing of the Robot?

BRIGADIER You're sure there is a connection?

DOCTOR WHO Oh I think so, don't you?

HARRY Why Sarah?

DOCTOR WHO The Robot killed Kettlewell, remember, the man who created it. It must be in a state of tremendous emotional shock. What more natural than that it should turn to the one person who ever showed it kindness?

BRIGADIER Hmm. Keep looking Benton.

BENTON Right, sir.

16. INT. BUNKER STORAGE BAY. DAY.

Sarah and the Robot huddled in darkness.

SARAH Honestly – they're bound to find us.

ROBOT Anyone who finds us will be destroyed.

SARAH Why? What's the point of more killing? I keep telling you, it's all over. What can you do alone?

ROBOT I can bring about the destruction of humanity.

Sarah gasps. The Robot touches her almost tenderly on the shoulder.

ROBOT But do not fear, Sarah. You alone will be ~~spared~~ saved. **The bunker is cleared.** Come.

They exit.

17. EXT. WOODED AREA. (OB) DAY.

The Doctor, Harry and the Brigadier still waiting, by the vehicles.

Benton approaches and they all look up eagerly.

BRIGADIER Well?

BENTON Still nothing. We're spreading the search radius wider and wider, sir, but – *(Shrugging)* the bigger the area to cover, the harder it gets.

DOCTOR WHO **There is just one teeny-weeny little thing.**

BRIGADIER What's that?

DOCTOR WHO Something else ~~we~~ you haven't thought of – what are we going to do when we find it?

BRIGADIER Yes… you know, just once I'd like to meet an alien menace that <u>wasn't</u> immune to bullets.

Benton, about to leave, pauses in the doorway. ⑮

BENTON Excuse me, sir?

BRIGADIER ~~Well, Benton?~~ Hmm?

BENTON When Professor Kettlewell was here – talking to Miss Smith, he said the Robot was made of some kind of 'living metal'. He even said it could grow…

DOCTOR WHO Did he now?

BENTON Yes. And he was going on about some kind of 'metal virus'… something that attacked the living metal.

DOCTOR WHO In the same way ~~that a~~ disease attacks animal tissue.

BENTON Well something like that. Anyway, I just wondered, **if we could**…

He realizes that everyone is looking at him.

DOCTOR WHO Yes?

BENTON Sorry. It's probably a daft idea.

The Doctor leaps to his feet, claps Benton on the shoulder.

DOCTOR WHO **Wonderful, Mr Benton! Wonderful.** Brigadier, I must get to Kettlewell's place at once. You find that Robot.

The Doctor jumps into Bessie.

BRIGADIER *(To Harry)* Better go with him. ~~Take this.~~

~~The Brigadier gives Harry an RT.~~

HARRY Right, sir.

BRIGADIER Keep in RT contact.

Harry jumps in next to the Doctor, and they roar away.

18. INT. BUNKER CORRIDOR. DAY.

Sarah and the Robot move along the corridor. Suddenly they run full tilt into a UNIT sentry.

The sentry raises his gun, and the Robot lifts its arm to strike him down.

SARAH No! Don't hurt him. **Let him go.** He's not important. ~~Let him go.~~

Sentry and Robot freeze. Sarah turns to sentry and speaks in a low urgent voice.

SARAH Don't shoot. Just leave, now.

The sentry looks as if he will argue.

SARAH Don't worry about me. Just go.

The sentry edges past them and runs down the corridor. Sarah and the Robot move towards the control room. The sentry runs for the door.

19. EXT. WOODED AREA. DAY.

The Brigadier and Benton.

BENTON Look sir.

Cut to their POV:

Bunker doors closing as a UNIT sentry runs out.

20. INT. BUNKER CONTROL ROOM. DAY.

Sarah and the Robot. The Robot operates the control and the door. It sits at the computer terminal ⑯ *and begins to tap the keys.*

The countdown clock has gone back to 600 ⓱ *(i.e. 10 minutes in seconds – the time the missile firing sequence takes) then it starts to count down again. 599, 598, 597…*

SARAH No! No!

She tries to drag the Robot away, but of course makes absolutely no impression. It gives a casual flick of its arm which sends her flying across the room. She hits the wall and slides down towards the floor.

SARAH But why? Why?

ROBOT I destroyed Kettlewell. I must see that his plan does not fail.

SARAH But he changed his mind. He wouldn't want you to continue.

ROBOT Mankind is not worthy to survive. Once it is destroyed I shall build more machines like myself. Machines do not lie.

Ignoring Sarah the Robot goes on with its work. The countdown clock continues to count down.

21. INT. KETTLEWELL'S LAB. DAY.

The Doctor has pieced together apparatus from the wreckage. Watched by Harry and surrounded by bubbling flasks and vials, the Doctor is engaged on a complicated experiment with materials he has rigged up from Kettlewell's equipment. He is peering at a dilapidated sheaf of Kettlewell's notes which he has found. He sighs.

DOCTOR WHO Why didn't the silly man write up his experiments properly?

The UNIT RT beside Harry crackles into life.

BRIGADIER *(VO filter)* Doctor, this is the Brigadier can you hear me?

HARRY This is Lieutenant Sullivan, sir. The Doctor's rather busy at the moment.

The Doctor is pouring fluid from one flask to another. It fizzes, smokes and bubbles.

DOCTOR WHO Tell him to stop pestering me. I've found the metal virus and I'm trying to prepare an active solution. He must give me time.

22. EXT WOODED AREA. (OB) DAY.

The Brigadier is on the RT.

BRIGADIER Sullivan, tell the Doctor we've found it, the Robot!

HARRY *(VO filter)* Well done sir. Where is it?

BRIGADIER ~~In the bunker.~~ It's shut itself inside the bunker – with ~~Sarah~~ Miss Smith!

23. INT. KETTLEWELL'S LAB. DAY.

The Doctor is thinking hard.

DOCTOR WHO *(To himself)* Yes… yes of course. Suppressed Oedipus complex leading to excessive guilt and over-compensation.

BRIGADIER ~~This is no time to talk Oedipus.~~ Doctor, Oedipus is not, surely –

He grabs RT from Harry.

DOCTOR WHO The Robot will try to carry out Kettlewell's plan. Is the computer terminal in the bunker still active?

BRIGADIER *(VO filter)* As far as I know… don't suppose anyone thought to…

DOCTOR WHO Can you ~~cut off the power~~ switch off the electricity supply?

BRIGADIER *(VO filter)* Yes – no. It's on a special sealed circuit.

DOCTOR WHO Then warn all the major powers. The emergency is not over. They must operate full fail-safe procedures, at once. ~~We may have only seconds!~~

24. INT. BUNKER CONTROL ROOM. DAY.

The Robot is still at the keyboard.

Sarah looks on helplessly. The countdown clock is down into double figures, 20, 19, 18… ⓲

Suddenly the computer flashes a sign: fail-safe mechanism operative. ⓳ *The Robot continues its work but the countdown clock ticks slower and slower, 8, 9, 7, and then stops. The computer is silent.* ⓴

SARAH You see – They've operated the fail-safe mechanism – ~~please, won't you~~ give up now! Please!

The Robot turns to Sarah, brooding and menacing.

ROBOT Humanity must be destroyed. It is evil, corrupt.

SARAH You can't take on the whole world. Don't you understand, they'll destroy you.

ROBOT Do not fear. I cannot be destroyed. Come.

The Robot grabs her and leaves.

25. INT. KETTLEWELL'S LAB. DAY.

DOCTOR WHO Come ~~on~~ along, man, come ~~on~~ along.

He has distilled couple of pints of seething solution. He is taking out a couple of drops with some kind of dropper.

On the bench in front of him is a small bar of silvery metal. ㉑

HARRY This any good?

The Doctor drops a few drops of the solution onto the metal. We don't see the result, but we see Harry's reaction of amazement.

DOCTOR WHO ~~I've~~ We've done it, Harry… ~~I've~~ We've done it!

26. EXT. WOODED AREA. (OB) DAY.

Benton and the Brigadier observing the bunker doors. They see them open.

BENTON Sir!

For a moment nothing happens. Then the Robot emerges, Sarah (double ㉒ *) following. (This is in long shot)*

BRIGADIER No one's to open fire: she may get a chance to get clear.

We cut to a man with a bazooka, or some other form of light artillery, standing ready. Other men have grenades.

We cut to the Robot, seen over Sarah's shoulder, as she stands in the doorway.

ROBOT Stay here.

The Robot marches steadily towards the soldiers.

BENTON It's going to attack us sir. Shall we pull back?

The Brigadier looks round, harassed. Then his eye falls on the disintegrater gun, in the back of the Land Rover.

BRIGADIER Yes of course! ~~The answer were here all along! We don't need the Doctor's mumbo-jumbo!~~ The very thing! I think just for once we're not going to need the Doctor.

The Brigadier grabs the gun and advances towards the Robot. He aims the gun and fires. The Robot is bathed in a golden glow. Then, to the Brigadier's amazement, it begins to swell in size. Soon it has grown to an enormous height, towering over them like a giant. (Intercut the process with reaction shots) ㉓

Cut to over-the-shoulder shot of Sarah (double) looking at the Robot. It is now so large that only its legs are in frame.

Sarah decides to make a dash for it. She starts running towards the UNIT troops.

Cut to long shot of Sarah (double) running across towards the woodland. She trips and falls. ㉔

27. CSO SHOT.

The giant Robot pursuing Sarah to the wooded area.

28. INT. FOR EXT. SECTION OF WOODS. (CSO SHOT) DAY.

High-angle shot of Sarah in terror, against an expanse of looming woodland.

Giant metal CSO? hand reaches down for her ㉕

29. EXT. WOODED AREA. (OB) DAY.

We see the giant Robot pick up Sarah and perch her on the gable of a high building. ㉖

30. INT. FOR EXT. GABLE. DAY.

Sarah perched precariously on the gable. (CSO Shot) ㉗

Cut to her POV. The giant face of the Robot. When it speaks, its voice is even more booming.

ROBOT You will be safe. See how I deal with our enemies. ㉘

31. EXT. WOODLAND. (OB) DAY.

Cut to the Brigadier and his men.

BRIGADIER Follow me and hold your fire until ordered. ㉙ She's out of the line of fire. ~~Try the bazooka, and the grenades~~ Launcher and grenades.

BENTON Smith, Ashton – get down here quickly with the launcher.

Benton signals the soldiers to open fire, they blaze away with the bazooka and hurl grenades.

32. CSO SHOT.

The Robot turns towards them. ㉚

33. EXT. COUNTRY ROADS. (OB) DAY.

The Doctor and Harry driving along in Bessie.

34. MODEL SHOTS.

A montage sequence showing as much of a rampage as we can imagine.

Using real people in conjunction with the Robot, enlarged by CSO, and the Robot in its actual size shown with model cars, buildings, or even people.

We see the giant Robot advancing, ignoring the shots. A close shot of a soldier fleeing from a giant hand (or foot). ③①

BRIGADIER Right – pull back!

We see the Robot stamp on a Land Rover, and destroy part of a building. ③②

The Brigadier and his men pull back defeated.

35. EXT. WOODED AREA. (OB) DAY.

The Doctor and Harry drive up to the area. They look out of the car in amazement.

36. MODEL SHOT.

The triumphant Robot, seen against model buildings. ③③

HARRY Curiouser and curiouser.

DOCTOR WHO Said Alice.

HARRY Exactly. ③④

37. EXT. COUNTRYSIDE. (OB) DAY.

The Doctor drives up to the point to which the Brigadier and his men have fallen back. He gets out of his car.

DOCTOR WHO ~~What happened?~~ I see our little problem seems to have grown. ~~And~~ Where's Sarah?

BENTON She's safe enough, **Doc.**

BRIGADIER I gave it a blast with the disintegrator gun.

BENTON It left her on a roof.

DOCTOR WHO ~~I see.~~ Really, Brigadier, you should be more careful with your **little** toys. You gave it just the infusion of energy it needed.

BRIGADIER *(Grim)* I've called for artillery and the RAF are on the way.

DOCTOR WHO I hope none of that'll be necessary.

Doctor Who goes back to his car, taking from it a plastic bucket with a lid.

BRIGADIER What's that?

DOCTOR WHO Another piece of brilliance from the late Professor **Kettlewell**. One that will solve our problem, I hope. **Drive on, Harry.** Wish me luck, **Brigadier.**

~~**HARRY** I'll drive you Doctor.~~

Harry gets behind the wheel, the Doctor beside him with the bucket.

BRIGADIER Doctor! Now just a moment!

Harry drives off. ③⑤

SARAH *(VO) (Distant)* ~~Help..!~~ Hey – hey, get me down!

BRIGADIER Oh… well, don't just stand there, Mr Benton. ~~You heard Miss Smith: go and assist her...~~ Go and help Miss Smith.

BENTON Right sir.

38. CSO SHOT. (OB).

The Brigadier's POV of Harry driving Doctor Who towards the giant Robot.

39. CSO SHOT.

The Doctor's car coming closer to the Robot. ③⑥ *A metal hand reaches down to grab it as Harry drives between the Robot's legs.* ③⑦ *The Doctor dashes the contents of his bucket at one giant foot, and Harry whizzes the car away.*

40. EXT. BUNKER AREA. (OB) DAY.

Harry drives back to the Brigadier.

BRIGADIER What is that stuff?

DOCTOR WHO Some of Kettlewell's metal virus in an active solution.

BRIGADIER Will it work, now the thing's that size?

DOCTOR WHO Even faster, I hope! Look!

41. MODEL SHOT.

The Robot seen against model buildings. A brown stain ③⑧ *is seen spreading over the Robot's body from the foot upwards.*

At the same time the Robot begins to shrink to its normal size.

42. EXT. WOODED AREA. (OB) DAY.

Reaction shots of the Doctor, Brigadier and co.

DOCTOR WHO It's thrown the growth mechanism into reverse.

HARRY Oh well done, Doctor!

DOCTOR WHO **Thank you, Harry.**

Cut to the Robot now normal size. It staggers and collapses.

The Doctor and the Brigadier walk slowly up to the Robot. They look down at it. It is curled in a foetal attitude. The brown stain mottles its silvery form.

BRIGADIER I'll have it taken away and broken up. Just in case.

DOCTOR WHO ~~No need.~~ **No, Brigadier, no – that won't be necessary.** Look!

43. CSO SHOT.

The Robot crumbles into dust. **㊴**

44. INT. UNIT HQ. DOCTOR'S LAB. DAY.

Sarah sits at a bench gazing sadly into space. The Doctor enters, doesn't say anything then:

DOCTOR WHO Sarah? Sarah? **Would you like a** jelly baby? **㊵** I had to do it, you know.

SARAH Yes… yes ~~of course~~ **I know**. It was insane and it did terrible things. ~~It was just that,~~ **But,** at first… it was so human…

DOCTOR WHO It was a wonderful ~~being~~ **creature**. Capable of great good, and great evil.

He sighs.

DOCTOR WHO Yes, I think you could say it was human. *(Cheerily)* You know, what you need is a change. How about a little trip in the TARDIS, I'm just off!

SARAH But you can't just go!

DOCTOR WHO Why not? Its a free cosmos!

SARAH The Brigadier…

DOCTOR WHO The Brigadier wants me to address the Cabinet, have lunch at Downing Street, dinner at the palace, and write 17 reports in triplicate. Well, **I won't do it.** I won't, I won't, I won't!

He bangs his fist on a brick, hurts it, winces, and sucks his knuckles.

DOCTOR WHO Why should I?

SARAH Doctor, you're being childish.

DOCTOR WHO Well of course I am! No point in being grown up if you can't be childish sometimes. Are you coming?

Sarah considers. It is at this point that she really accepts the new Doctor as the Doctor. He looks at her appealingly, offering sweet. Sarah nods.

Doctor Who beams and opens the door of the TARDIS with a flourish.

As she is about to enter the door to the lab opens and Harry Sullivan bustles in.

HARRY Hullo, ~~hullo, and what are we~~ **and what are you two** up to now, **eh?**

Doctor Who glares at him.

DOCTOR WHO We're just going for a little trip. Would you like a jelly baby?

Harry laughs heartily.

HARRY ~~Going for~~ A little trip – **what,** in that old police box?

DOCTOR WHO *(Acidly)* Yes, as a matter of fact, in that old police box.

HARRY *(Heartily)* **Come along,** now ~~then~~ Doctor, ~~you're a~~ **we're both** reasonable ~~man~~ **men,** ~~and I'm a reasonable man.~~ **Now** we both know police boxes don't go careering ~~round in Time and Space~~ **around all over the place**.

DOCTOR WHO Do we?

HARRY Of course we do! The whole idea's absurd.

DOCTOR WHO Is it? You wouldn't care to step inside for a moment? Just to demonstrate it's all an illusion?

HARRY Well, if it will do any good.

DOCTOR WHO Oh yes. It will make me feel much better!

SARAH *(Warningly)* Doctor…

He gives her a wicked grin.

DOCTOR WHO *(To Harry)* In you go!

HARRY Right-oh!

Harry enters, followed by Sarah and Doctor Who. Just as the door closes, we hear Harry's awed voice.

HARRY Oh, I say!

We hear the TARDIS making its groaning sound.

A few seconds later and the Brigadier comes rushing in.

BRIGADIER Doctor, about that dinner at the palace, **Her Majesty…**

The TARDIS dematerializes. **㊶**

BRIGADIER **Yes…** Well, I'll tell them you'll be a little late. **㊷**

CLOSING TITLES

1   For production notes and amendments on the reprise, see the end of Part Three.

2   The countdown is shown on a screen – a colour-tinted image of a digital countdown clock was fed through using the graphics device Anchor. The countdown starts at 300, at the end of this scene.

3   This line is actually spoken at the start of the next scene.

4   The end of the direction is missing from the camera script – the bold text inserted here is assumed.

5   Christopher Barry planned to have some stock film of missiles being readied for launch, but this was abandoned before studio (see also Part Three, following Scene 27).

6   A production note puts the countdown clock at 65, but it is actually at 93.

7   Jellicoe's line, which motivates Kettlewell's deleted response, is missing from the camera script.

8   Kettlewell goes for Jellicoe with a chair, but Jellicoe has a gun, and forces Kettlewell back to the console.

9   Presumably a misprint, as it makes more sense for Kettlewell to have this line.

10   A production note says 'Countdown stops at 40'; in fact it stops at 58.

11   While the second take of this scene was better than the first, Michael Kilgarriff got this line wrong. Take 2 was used, with the Robot's line from take 1 dubbed in.

12   Again, 'roll-back-and-mix' was used for Kettlewell's disintegration, with Tom Baker, Ian Marter and Elisabeth Sladen keeping still as Edward Burnham left the camera's view, then reacting to his 'death'.

13   The countdown is actually at 21.

14   It freezes at 2.

15   This suggests this scene may have been relocated to the wooded area from an interior set, possibly UNIT's mobile HQ which featured in several earlier stories such as *The Claws of Axos* (1971). Benton's mention of 'here' in his next line could also imply the scene was located in the Doctor's lab.

16   The rigid robot costume precluded this.

17   The clock is still frozen at 2. A production notes says: 'See it go back. 600'. It actually resets to 300.

18   Production note: 'Number 20', which is indeed where the countdown has reached.

19   Production note: 'Flashing red light Q – Buzzer?' The red light was not used, though there is a pulsing sound effect.

20   After 8, the screen changes to read 'FAIL SAFE', with 'Countdown Aborted' between the words. This shot was done at the end of the scene and edited back in.

21   Harry brings the Doctor a strip of metal.

22   Since location work for *Robot* overlapped with the studio production of *Planet of the Spiders*, Elisabeth Sladen was working on both stories at the same time. A double was not actually used, but was considered for some of the location scenes, including this one.

23   CSO was used to show the Robot growing. The camera showing the Robot against a yellow backdrop zoomed in, so that when the shot was matted on to the background of the bunker exterior, the Robot appeared to grow. A red glow was added in post-production.

24   Christopher Barry: 'Obviously it was in the back of one's mind that it was a homage to *King Kong*. But I certainly was not trying to do a pastiche of any shots in *King Kong*… I think if I'd done that it would have become coy and arch. One just had to be aware that there was a precedent and try and make it as believable as possible – unfortunately with toy tanks rather than model aeroplanes!'

25   CSO was indeed used to show the Robot's hand close on Sarah and lift her. There were three merged images – the Robot's hand, Sarah lying on the ground and the grassy-bank background.

26   This scene was achieved using CSO to show the giant Robot carrying a mannequin of Sarah.

27   CSO was used to show the giant Robot holding Sarah against a background of roofs and chimneys.

28   The Robot's line, after another insert of the Brigadier and his men, was a CSO shot of Sarah holding on to a (CSO'd) chimney, with the Robot's huge head CSO'd behind. The shot alters to show Sarah CSO'd against a chimney, her hand positioned as if holding a drainpipe for support.

29   This was cut into Scene 29 as the Robot carries Sarah.

30   The CSO'd Robot stands in front of buildings. Visual Effects rigged an explosion on the face of the building behind.

31   At one point, the Robot picks up two UNIT men – actually Action Man toys – and drops them.

㉜ Two of the CSO scenes in this sequence were specifically constructed to give depth to the shots. One was where the Robot's giant foot crushes a soldier as another fires from behind. The other is where the Robot follows soldiers up the road as another two fire from behind him (see page 79). Christopher Barry: 'It meant another pass on CSO, but it made it seem three-dimensional – that the Robot was in the middle of things.'

㉝ CSO was used to show the giant Robot among the buildings as the Doctor and Harry arrive in Bessie.

㉞ After an insert shot of Sarah on the rooftop (CSO again), the Robot walks into power cables (a prop against a CSO background). Electric blue flashes were provided by a spark machine as the Robot pulls the cables down. A retake was needed when the spark generator used to make these flashes was positioned too high, so the flashes appeared in the wrong place.

㉟ Scene 38 is inserted here.

㊱ As with several sequences in the giant Robot section, we see again from the Robot's POV.

㊲ Bessie drives past the Robot as the Doctor throws the virus solution.

㊳ The stain was an electronic effect added in post-production.

㊴ The supine, damaged Robot – a 'mini-robot' prop – with its electronically overlaid stain was added with CSO, then faded away.

㊵ Jelly babies were to become a standard feature of the fourth Doctor. This is the first time he offers one to anyone.

㊶ This used a split-screen/roll-back-and-mix effect so that the Brigadier could apparently watch the TARDIS dematerialize. A second take was needed, as on the first take the TARDIS disappeared too fast.

㊷ This final line was added by Nicholas Courtney during rehearsals.

THE ARK IN SPACE

BY ROBERT HOLMES

PART ONE first transmitted 25 January 1975 at 17.35
PART TWO 1 February 1975 at 17.30
PART THREE 8 February 1975 at 17.30
PART FOUR 15 February 1975 at 17.30

Overview

The Ark in Space is at once a horror story and a testament to the endurance and resilience of humanity. Confined to the television studio, the huge, impressive sets and bright lighting counterpoint the inherent claustrophobia of a story that deals with turning the human body itself into a battlefield.

Possession was a theme that Robert Holmes and Philip Hinchcliffe would continue to explore. But it is rarely more poignant and unsettling than here where we see Noah's body slowly consumed by the Wirrn.

The transformation, and the group consciousness that Noah inherits, is reminiscent of the first *Quatermass* serial of over 20 years earlier. But from our perspective today, it is the parallels with Ridley Scott's *Alien* (released four years after *Ark* was transmitted) that are more evident.

But most of all, this is the story in which Tom Baker's Doctor firmly stamped his impression on the role and made it his own. His 'humanity' speech in the first episode (Scene 24) still resonates today, and it is through the very qualities that the speech espouses that the Wirrn are defeated.

Origin

With the introductory serial for the new Doctor being written in-house by a tried and trusted old hand on the show, the original plan was that the second adventure for the season should come from a writer new to the series – and apparently new to television. Little is known about Christopher Langley, who it was planned would write the space-bound serial to follow the Doctor's regenerative story. His name does not feature elsewhere in the BBC Radio and Television Drama Writers Index. He lived in Hemel Hempstead and on Thursday 24 January 1974 was commissioned by script editor Robert Holmes for a storyline referred to as *Space Station* – although since the 'target delivery date' for this was Sunday 30 December 1973, it is likely that an outline had already been submitted 'on spec' before this date, and that Robert Holmes was now formalizing his intention to have Langley's submission used in the series. The writer's name also appears on an active story list for *Doctor Who* issued by the Drama Department on Monday 11 February 1974. Subsequent to this, all four scripts for *Space Station* were commissioned, and Langley delivered these on Tuesdays at weekly intervals from 19 March to 9 April 1974.

When he arrived on *Doctor Who*, incoming producer Philip Hinchcliffe found that several stories were already in development. *Space Station* was already in place, there had been discussions and a gentleman's agreement with Terry Nation for a Dalek serial, and Barry Letts had decided to bring back the Cybermen in a serial by Gerry Davis. The new producer had a strong desire to take *Doctor Who* into the real arena of science fiction, aiming to explore it in a more convincing and adult manner than his predecessors. Aware of the show's popularity, he particularly wanted to expand the audience to take in more adults who already made up a large proportion of the viewers. Looking to the more experienced Holmes – 15 years his senior – for support and guidance, Hinchcliffe was delighted to find that his script editor also believed in increasing the standard of scripting on *Doctor Who*, which would include extensive in-house rewrites if necessary. The two men formed a solid working partnership, finding that they sparked each other off with ideas. Tom Baker was also keen to move in a more adult direction with the series. While waiting to take over fully from Barry Letts, Hinchcliffe did a lot of reading of science fiction novels to reacquaint himself with the genre, and decided that he wanted to make the new series full of exciting and dramatic adventures, along the lines of radio serials such as *Dick Barton – Special Agent* and *Journey into Space* which he had enjoyed as a youngster.

There is no record of what befell Langley's *Space Station* scripts, but the problem seems to have occured between early April and mid-May. Certainly it seems that the original intention was that *Space Station* was to be made and broadcast second in the new season.

Storyline

Writer John Lucarotti was asked to provide a space-bound replacement, using the same setting as Langley's story. Robert Holmes had already asked Gerry Davis to work this space station setting into his Cybermen story to save money on sets.

Lucarotti had worked on *Doctor Who* regularly between 1963 and 1965. His first script was *Marco Polo* (1964) followed by *The Aztecs* (1964). But his association with the series had ended after problems with a four-part serial he had been commissioned to write under the title *War of God* about the 1572 massacre of the Huguenots in Paris. The script was refined by story editor Donald Tosh to become *The Massacre of St Bartholomew's Eve* (1966). Since then, Lucarotti had worked on other fantasy series including *Joe 90* and drama series such as *The Borderers, The Expert, Paul Temple* and *Brett* as well as being a regular writer on the BBC oil-firm drama *The Troubleshooters.*

Lucarotti had also been in discussion about novelizations of some of his ITV children's television serials with Universal Tandem, and while at their offices in early 1973 had bumped into Terrance Dicks who was discussing the new range of *Doctor Who* novelizations with the company, to be published under their 'Target' imprint. Noting Lucarotti's experience on SF shows, Dicks

subsequently commissioned the writer for two scripts on *Moonbase 3* which
was to be made that summer – between Seasons Ten and Eleven of *Doctor
Who*. These scripts – 'The Dark Side of the Moon' and 'The Gentle
Rain' (renamed 'Castor and Pollux' and 'Achilles Heel') – were commissioned
from Lucarotti on Monday 25 January 1973. He was then commissioned on
the *Lieutenant Hornblower* project that Barry Letts and Terrance Dicks were
planning on Wednesday 11 April 1973. *Moonbase 3* entered production in
April 1973, but was not renewed beyond its first six episodes. *Lieutenant
Hornblower* never entered production, although all three scripts had been
delivered by January 1974.

It seems that in late 1973 there were discussions between Lucarotti and
Dicks about a storyline concerning the human race being held in a form of
suspended animation. Nothing seems to have been formally commissioned at
this time. Shortly before this, Lucarotti had been working on an unused pilot
script for another science fiction series – Gerry and Sylvia Anderson's *Space:
1999* which had started shooting at Pinewood Studios for ITC.

Lucarotti was briefed on the story's requirements by Robert Holmes and
Barry Letts while visiting London from his home in Corsica (where he lived and
worked on board his yacht) around May 1974. Lucarotti accepted the assignment
and was commissioned for the four replacement scripts under the title *The Ark in
Space* on Wednesday 5 June. With pre-production planned for August, the writer
was requested to submit his work by a deadline of Wednesday 17 July.

Lucarotti's storyline concerned an immense spaceship, containing the
entire human race in suspended animation – a sort of space ark. The vessel also
included a landscaped countryside about the size of Kent where flora from
Earth were kept alive so that the world could be reseeded after the impending
disaster from which humanity was escaping. The Doctor directed the TARDIS
to this space ark to keep a rendezvous of some sort, and discovered on arrival
that the station's systems had broken down. Alien beings called the Delc were
now at work in the ark.

The Delc came in two variant species. The first was a race of beings which
were effectively floating heads without bodies – these did the thinking and
mental reasoning for the aliens. The rest of the Delc took orders and were
bodies without heads – undertaking all the physical tasks and able to reproduce
themselves in an instant. Since the Delc were a form of fungus, they spread
through space in the form of spores and had become caught on the
infrastructure of the space station. From this stage, the spores had germinated
and the Delc now threatened the sleeping humans. The Doctor discovered that
to blast the aliens was ineffective, since the Delc simply exploded and released

more spores like a dandelion; however electrocution was an effective means of defence ('just like frying mushrooms really,' as the Doctor comments). At the end of the story, the Doctor used a golf club to drive the Delc heads off into space, and so save the ark.

Following the format of early *Doctor Who* serials in which each episode had an individual title (a concept dropped in 1966 after Lucarotti had left the series), Lucarotti subtitled the first episode of *The Ark in Space* as 'Puffball' (referring to the way the Delc spore reproduced) while the fourth and final episode in which the Doctor repelled the Delc was 'Golfball'; the other episodes also had titles ending in '…ball'.

Scripts

The first script for *The Ark in Space* was delivered on Sunday 23 June and Lucarotti's storyline was formally accepted for development two days later. However, there was some immediate concern about this first submission from Holmes, Letts and incoming producer Philip Hinchcliffe. The content and style was not what the production team had in mind, and they attempted to contact Lucarotti in Corsica to guide him with reference to the remaining three instalments. On his yacht in the Mediterranean, Lucarotti had completed his next three episodes already and despatched them, but the scripts were held up in a postal strike and not delivered to the BBC until Friday 12 July. Without direct communication with the BBC, the writer's development of the narrative had moved even further from the original concept discussed with Holmes and Letts.

Reading the submissions, Barry Letts immediately realized that *The Ark in Space* as it stood was far too complex to fit *Doctor Who*'s family slot. According to Letts, 'What came in was too clever by half. What John had done was so involved… Too hard, too difficult, too complicated and sophisticated for the slot.' Robert Holmes later recalled: 'It was really overwritten, and had these elaborate special effects sequences, like this damn great hydroponic garden floating in space, and there was no way we could afford to do it.'

By now, Lucarotti was very busy on other writing projects, and the postal disputes continued to dog communication between London and Corsica. During August it became clear that the scripts were proving unworkable, even with adjustments made by the production team. One of Hinchcliffe's first actions as producer was therefore to arrange for Holmes to write a new version of *The Ark in Space* from scratch as an in-house project – under similar circumstances to *Robot* only to a more urgent deadline. Hinchcliffe:

> Basically, I leaned on Bob and said 'Look, you've got to write this'. So Bob
> disappeared and sweated blood and wrote the story. I encouraged him to follow

his own bent really, and wangled his payment out of the BBC. He did a marvellous job. I thought, 'We've got something really good here!' Bob got us out of a terrible hole, and did something rather brilliant.

Production of *The Ark in Space* was handled by the same team as the story that was to follow it, *The Destructors*. The crew would make *The Destructors* first on location, followed by a studio-bound version of *The Ark in Space* at BBC Television Centre. Because of inflation at the time, and as had been planned all along, Holmes wrote his scripts on a very cost-conscious basis, fitting the settings in with some elements of Davis' problematic scripts for what was now entitled *Return of the Cybermen*. Since Hinchcliffe had experience as a script editor from his time at ATV, he was to act as editor on Holmes' writing.

Holmes rewrote the scripts from top to bottom in 18 days, matching them in with the plot of *The Sontaran Experiment* (as *The Destructors* had now been retitled). As Holmes' scripts took shape, copies were sent to Hinchcliffe – who was on leave at the time in Lancashire. Amongst other comments, Hinchcliffe questioned the term 'cryogenic'. Explaining his terminology on Monday 5 August, Holmes commented:

> 'Cryonic' is a term used in America for the, as yet theoretical, art of storing people in deep freeze. I cannot trace 'cryogenic' but with its implication of genetics I think it's a reasonable neologism.

On Tuesday 20 August, Hinchcliffe despatched the first two of Holmes' revised scripts for *The Ark in Space* to Lucarotti, via his agent Stephen Durbridge. In a covering note, the producer commented:

> As you will see they have turned into completely fresh scripts. You will recognize some elements of the original story but we have lost the 'floating head' and much more is made of the arrival.
>
> Episodes 3 and 4 will follow in a week or two. Meanwhile, I would be grateful if you would let me know quite soon how you would like to be credited in view of the extensive rewrites.

The formal agreement allowing Holmes to write a new version of *The Ark in Space* was made on Monday 30 September. By now, Lucarotti had agreed not to take a credit on the serial, and would receive no residual fees from sales or merchandising associated with it. To clarify matters with his superiors, Hinchcliffe wrote to Peter Wineman – the assistant to Bill Slater – on Tuesday 8 October, explaining the necessity for Holmes' staff contribution:

The scripts originally commissioned for this serial turned out to be unusable and four new scripts had to be written in a hurry. I felt that Robert Holmes was the only person who could do the job satisfactorily in the time available.

As a result, a payment deal for Holmes was resolved by Thursday 10 October – shortly before production was due to begin.

The conclusion of Part Four (Scene 57) was rewritten by Holmes on Tuesday 8 October. Originally, Holmes had the Wirrn going off into space at the end and surviving – but it was suggested that it was probably better for the younger audience to show the alien threat destroyed. Hinchcliffe agreed that the Wirrn should be destroyed in the transport ship.

On Monday 14 October, Part One material between the Doctor and Harry in the control room (about the cricket ball – Scene 17) and the transom (in which they saw the Wirrn larvae – Scene 21) was rewritten. Although the finished scripts were almost entirely Holmes' dialogue, character and narrative flow, Lucarotti was still credited with the storyline in BBC documentation because of the work he had done on the initial concept and setting. The BBC's internal 'early warning synopsis' for the story actually lists John Lucarotti as the author, 'adapted by Robert Holmes'.

Production Team

The same production team handled both *The Ark in Space* and the subsequent story *The Sontaran Experiment* – although the two would be made in reverse order. The director was Rodney Bennett, who had joined BBC Radio producing talk shows. With the launch of BBC2 in 1964, Bennett decided he wanted to move into television and soon found himself directing an episode of *Z Cars*. Attached to the Drama Department, Bennett directed editions of *Thirty Minute Theatre* and then went freelance in 1970, continuing to work at the BBC on serials such as *Lord Peter Wimsey* and plays like *The Case of Eliza Armstrong*. Barry Letts asked that Bennett work on the two stories at the time when Hinchcliffe was just joining *Doctor Who*, and Hinchcliffe had enjoyed Bennett's work on TV drama serials he had seen. Contracted on Tuesday 11 June, Bennett joined the *Doctor Who* team on Monday 19 August for a four-and-a-half-month stint.

The designer, Roger Murray-Leach, was new to *Doctor Who* and had been working on some ambitious light-entertainment series where his imaginative work was noted by Hinchcliffe, who requested that Murray-Leach be given an opportunity to work on drama series such as *Doctor Who*. He was to be delighted with his work. A notable aspect of Murray-Leach's interior sets were that they often incorporated ceilings, which was a rarity in studio design.

Make-up was handled by Sylvia James who had worked on all the Patrick Troughton serials from *The Abominable Snowmen* in 1967 to *The War Games* in 1969 as well as *The Sea Devils* and *The Curse of Peladon* in 1971/2. Barbara Kidd, who had supervised *Robot*, returned in charge of costumes for both stories. Visual effects were handled by John Friedlander and Tony Oxley; Friedlander was known primarily as a specialist sculptor, and had worked on *Doctor Who* in various capacities as an assistant since *The Ark* in 1966, mainly creating masks for aliens such as the Ogrons (*Day of the Daleks*: 1972) and the Exxilons (*Death to the Daleks*: 1974). These two serials were to be Friedlander's first credits as visual effects designer; the same went for Oxley. On Tuesday 30 July, Dudley Simpson was commissioned to provide the music score on both serials.

Cast

Playing Noah was Kenton Moore, an actor who had appeared in series such as *Jason King* and *Elizabeth R* and who played regular PC Logie in *Z Cars*.

Wendy Williams, who played Vira, was married to Hugh David, an actor-turned-director who had directed two *Doctor Who* serials: *The Highlanders* (1966/7) and *Fury from the Deep* (1968). She had appeared in series such as *Danger Man* and was a regular alongside her husband in Granada's *Knight Errant Ltd*. At the time she was making *The Ark in Space*, she had just completed work on the BBC2 costume drama *The Pallisers*.

Christopher Masters was cast as Libri with Australian actor John Gregg – a lead actor in the antipodean series *Delta* – as Lycett. Richardson Morgan, cast as Rogin, had appeared as Corporal Blake in *The Web of Fear* (1968), and in the ITV computer play *ADAM* the previous year.

Performing the roll of the main Wirrn were two stunt men, Stuart Fell and Nick Hobbs. Both had joined *Doctor Who* in 1970 as part of the HAVOC stunt team (and were booked via HAVOC in mid-October 1974). Hobbs had been in *The Ambassadors of Death* and Fell in *Terror of the Autons*. Both had gone on to play various small roles (often monsters) in serials such as *The Curse of Peladon*. Fell would double as the Wirrn version of Noah in Part Four.

Providing the voices heard in Part One were Gladys Spencer and Peter Tuddenham; Tuddenham was later to become well known for the voices of computers such as Zen, Orac and Slave on the BBC SF adventure series *Blake's 7*. Spencer and Tuddenham recorded their voices on Wednesday 16 October before main rehearsals began.

Filming

The only pre-filming on the serial was a small amount of model work shot by Oxley and Friedlander on silent 16mm film for Part Four; this showed the Wirrn making their way around the hull of Nerva, along with the launch and destruction of the transport ship. This filming took place in early October 1974, and used small puppet Wirrn suspended on wires.

Recording

Rehearsals in Room 402 of the BBC's rehearsal facility in Acton began on Thursday 17 October, with Baker having recovered from the broken collarbone which he had sustained while making *The Sontaran Experiment* on location in Dartmoor several weeks earlier. When Fell was not available for rehearsals, Friedlander stood in for him, wearing the Wirrn larvae costume which he himself had created from polythene bubble-wrap material – then a new invention – which had been sprayed green. Letts was still around for the recording of this serial since *Marie Curie* was still in production limbo.

Part One was recorded on Monday 28 October (Ian Marter's 30th birthday). This first evening included the early scenes of Part Two for which guest cast members were not required. Recording was generally in sequence apart from the three scenes of Sarah on the tranquiller couch which were taped together. Many of the control panels seen on board Nerva were stock items from previous serials, and several had been made in 1969 for the ITC/Century 21 television series *UFO*, while others came from earlier Supermarionation shows.

Murray-Leach and Bennett had both considered Holmes' original suggestion for the Cryogenic Chamber (see Part One, Scene 24) but felt unhappy with the tunnel concept, which they had thought could be achieved using mirrors. Instead, Murray-Leach came up with the notion of the vertical stacking of the pallets containing the sleepers. Each plastic and fibreglass pallet was numbered starting at ground level D with level E above it; D1 was Vira, D2 was Noah, D3 was Dune, D6 was Libri, D8 was Rogin, D9 was Lycett and Sarah occupied D12. High camera angles used by Bennett helped to make the already impressive set seem larger than it really was; a mirror was also employed to create the illusion of another chamber beyond the first by reflecting the main set. Hinchcliffe and his crew were astounded by Murray-Leach's cryogenic chamber which became the centrepiece for the serial.

The white costumes for the Nerva sleepers had colour-coded trimmings: Prime Unit Lazar (Noah) and Rogin had red flashes, First Medtech Vira had yellow, Lycett and Libri had green and Sarah's was edged with blue. The first evening of recording began later than planned by 17 minutes because of 'the CSO not functioning properly', as Hinchcliffe explained in his memo two days later to account for a 15 minute overrun beyond the 10 p.m. deadline.

The taping for Part Two on Tuesday 29 included an hour of pre-recording effects inserts. Recording in the evening was generally in sequence apart from scenes of the Wirrn in the infrastructure which were made together. This instalment saw the introduction of the raised infrastructure set built around the solar stacks. It had also been intended to record the first six scenes of Part Three at the end of the evening but when the crew fell behind schedule, only the first scene of the next episode was actually performed, and the rest left to remount a fortnight later.

After rehearsals from Thursday 31 October, Parts Three and Four were recorded on Monday 11 and Tuesday 12 November; these saw the introduction of the two full-size Wirrn costumes which Friedlander had made using fibreglass for the head and a moulded latex abdomen over a bamboo frame (a third static prop had been made for the dead queen Wirrn used in the first studio session). The original hope had been to show the Wirrn eating their way through the bulkheads, crawling along on their feelers or hanging from their abdominal pincers; all these notions were abandoned as impractical. With the abdomens in fact barely hiding the feet of Hobbs and Fell, Bennett arranged all his shots to keep the base of the Wirrn off the screen.

Because of the make-up changes required for the mutating Noah – and the fact that the early scenes for Part Three had not been pre-recorded as planned – parts of the script were rewritten and simplified (adding Harry's remarks that the

High Minister is a woman) and recorded on the second studio day. The first day was thus devoted largely to Part Three, with some scenes taped for Part Four. Most of the scenes in the cryogenic chamber were left to the end of the evening.

The second day had a photocall on the impressive cryogenic chamber set, mainly concentrating on Tom Baker. In the afternoon, effects inserts were pre-recorded along with the opening scenes for Part Three. The main recording in the evening was effectively Part Four, taped mainly in sequence apart from some scenes on the crew deck of the shuttle.

The episodes were edited during December, and the music score was recorded during January 1975 by Dudley Simpson, with the episodes being dubbed only weeks before transmission. For the first time in his tenure as producer, Hinchcliffe felt that one scene (Part Three, Scene 11) had overstepped the mark regarding suitability for a family audience and asked Bill Slater if he agreed it should be cut. Slater concurred, and the scene was toned down in editing.

Promotion and Reaction

The Ark in Space was broadcast on Saturdays from 25 January 1975. Part One was scheduled to start five minutes later than the others because of BBC1 coverage of the FA Cup Draw. As with the opposition to *Robot*, LWT and Granada ran *New Faces* while ATV screened *Sale of the Century*. Meanwhile, Yorkshire and Southern overlapped *Doctor Who* with items such as re-runs of the 1960s *Tarzan* series starring Ron Ely and another family film series, *The Adventures of Black Beauty*.

In terms of audience size, *The Ark in Space* was a major improvement over *Robot*. Part Two saw the largest audience for a *Doctor Who* episode since the first episode of *The Web Planet* in 1965. With over 13 million viewers, the instalment reached number five in the TV charts for the week.

Selected Merchandise

- NOVELIZATION: *Doctor Who and the Ark in Space*: novelization by Ian Marter. Published April 1977 by Allan Wingate (hardback) and May 1977 by Target Books/Wyndham (paperback). Revised Target edition as *Doctor Who – The Ark in Space* published May 1991.
- SOUND EFFECTS: *Doctor Who – Sound Effects No. 19* (BBC Records REC 316/ZCM 316) issued May 1978; includes a fission gun.
- SOUND EFFECTS: *Doctor Who – 30 Years at the Radiophonic Workshop* (BBC CD 871) issued July 1993; includes 'Wirrn in the Infrastructure'.
- SOUND EFFECTS: *Doctor Who at the BBC Radiophonic Workshop: Volume 2 – New Beginnings* (BBC WMSF 6024-2) issued May 2000; includes 'Nerva Beacon Infrastructure & T-Mat Couch'.
- INCIDENTAL MUSIC: *Doctor Who – Pyramids of Mars* (Silva Screen FILMCD 134) issued September 1993; includes five bands of incidental music (new recordings by Heathcliff Blair made late 1992/early 1993).

- VIDEOTAPES (ETC.): *Doctor Who – The Ark in Space* (BBC Video BBCV 4244) issued in edited form June 1989. Unedited reissue (BBC Video BBCV 5218) issued February 1994. American edition: (Playhouse #5420) issued 1991. Laserdisc issue (Encore Entertainment EE 1158) in 1996.

Production Details

4C: The Ark In Space

Projects: 2344/7048-7051

Cast

Doctor Who	Tom Baker
Sarah Jane Smith	Elisabeth Sladen
Harry Sullivan	Ian Marter
Vira	Wendy Williams[2-4]
Noah	Kenton Moore [2-4]
Libri	Christopher Masters [2]
Rogin	Richardson Morgan [3-4]
Lycett	John Gregg [3]
High Minister's Voice*	Gladys Spencer[1,3]
Voices*	Peter Tuddenham [1]
Wirrn Operators	Stuart Fell [3 4], Nick Hobbs [4]

* Credited jointly as *Voices* on Part One

Uncredited:

Double for Vira in pallet [1]: Jan Goram
Double for Rogin in pallet [1-2]: Barry Summerford
Double for Lycett in pallet [1-2]: Sean Cooney
Doubles for Noah in pallet [1]: Roy Brent
Doubles for Libri in pallet [1]: Rick Carroll
Bodies in pallets [1-2]: Tina Roach, Peter Duke, Richard Archer
Dune [1,3]: Brian Jacobs
Wirrn Grub Operator [2-3]: Stuart Fell
Bodies in pallets [3-4]: Richard Archer, Lyn Summer, Geoffrey Brighty

Crew

Written by	Robert Holmes*
Production Assistant	Marion McDougall
Production Unit Manager	George Gallaccio
Title Music by	Ron Grainer & BBC Radiophonic Workshop
Title Sequence	Bernard Lodge
Incidental Music by	Dudley Simpson
Special Sound	Dick Mills
Visual Effects Designers	John Friedlander, Tony Oxley
Costume Designer	Barbara Kidd

Make-up	Sylvia James
Lighting	Nigel Wright
Sound	John Lloyd
Designer	Roger Murray-Leach
Producer	Philip Hinchcliffe
Directed by	Rodney Bennett

* Story idea by John Lucarotti

Production History

Voice Recordings – Spur Sound Studio
Wednesday 16 October 1974: 3.00pm–5.00pm
* Parts One and Three: Gladys Spencer and Peter Tuddenham

Studio Recording – Television Centre Studio 3
Monday 28 October 1974: 7.30pm–10.15pm [15 min overrun]
* Part One
* Part Two: start of scene 1
* Part Three: Control room 1, control room 2 and cryogenic chamber POV inserts

Tuesday 28 October 1974: 2.30pm–3.30pm & 7.30pm–10.00pm
* Part Two
* Part Three: scenes 1 to 6

Studio Recording – Television Centre Studio 1
Monday 11 November 1974: 7.30pm–10.00pm
* Part Three: scene 7 onwards, except scene 16
* Part Four: scenes 2, 3 and 53

Tuesday 12 November 1974: 2.30pm–3.30pm & 7.30pm–10.00pm
* Part Four: except scenes 2 [control room 2], 3 and 53 [transom]
* Part Three: scenes 1 to 6D (remount), 16 [grille], 17, 19 [effects inserts].

Music
* Specially recorded incidental music by Dudley Simpson and orchestra. Recording Dates: Wednesday 15 January 1975 (Parts One and Two) and Thursday 30 January 1975 (Parts Three and Four) at Lime Grove. Total: 29'45"
* *Concerto Grosso Opus 3 Number 2 – Largo*, composed by Handel, played by the Academy of St Martin in the Field. 1'41" used in Part One for sequence of Sarah being tranquillized.

Original Transmission – BBC1

Part One	Saturday 25 January 1975	5.35pm	5.36pm	24'58"	9.4M	27th	–
Part Two	Saturday 1 February 1975	5.30pm	5.30pm	24'49"	13.6M	5th	–
Part Three	Saturday 8 February 1975	5.30pm	5.32pm	24'05"	11.2M	17th	–
Part Four	Saturday 15 February 1975	5.30pm	5.31pm	24'37"	10.2M	24th	–

THE ARK IN SPACE

by Robert Holmes

Part One

OPENING TITLES

1. SPACE STATION IN ORBIT.

A space station in Earth orbit. ②
    We are moving towards it.
    Our approach speed appears to increase as we get nearer.
    Soothing, eerie 'space music' rises to a climactic shriek of exultation as we plunge into impact with the satellite's scarred and ancient surface.
    The screen goes black.
    The silence is absolute. ③

1A. INT. CRYOGENIC CHAMBER. ④

Still subjective camera. ⑤ *We are inching painfully across the floor of the chamber.*
    The only light is the dim green luminescence given out by the abyssal eye. The only sound is the laboured rasp of our dying lungs.
    Distinctly ahead of us now, only feet away, we see a low pallet. A plastic survival shroud, like a pup tent, covers the bed. ⑥ *Reaching forward with one gelatinous tentacle, we pull the shroud aside. The body of a man, waxen and immobile, lies on the bed. With a last great effort, we drag ourselves up and over the body.*

1B. SPACE STATION IN EARTH ORBIT.
Model of space station.

2. INT. CONTROL ROOM 1.
In darkness and silent as the grave. Then the TARDIS materializes. ❼ *After a moment the door opens and the Doctor steps out.*
DOCTOR WHO Clumsy, ham-fisted idiot – !
He flashes a torch around.
HARRY *(VO)* ~~But I was only trying~~ Well I said I was sorry, didn't I?
DOCTOR WHO What? *(Turns)* Come out ~~of there~~. And don't <u>touch</u> anything!
Harry and Sarah emerge. She carries a lantern. ❽
HARRY I was only trying to open the door – oh, I say! We've gone!
SARAH Who's gone?
HARRY I mean this isn't… We aren't where we were when… ~~Good heavens,~~ I'm going mad!
SARAH That's how I felt the first time. Where are we, Doctor?
DOCTOR WHO I've no idea.
SARAH A little trip to the moon, you said, just to prove to Harry that –
DOCTOR WHO I didn't expect him to start messing about with the helmic regulators.
He looks around.
Harry is dazedly staring into the TARDIS. The Doctor drags him away.
DOCTOR WHO Come away from there, Harry!
He closes the door.
HARRY You could sell that thing, Doctor.
DOCTOR WHO I could <u>what</u>?
HARRY Well. Jolly useful in Trafalgar Square. Hundreds of bobbies hiding inside it.
SARAH Harry.
HARRY Eh?
SARAH Stop burbling.
HARRY Yes, well… shock, I expect. I **must say**, I feel ~~quite~~ **very** strange.
The Doctor lets his yo-yo unwind from a still hand. It hangs at the extent of its string.
DOCTOR WHO Not much oxygen. **Still**, nothing to worry about.
SARAH Suffocation is nothing to worry about?
DOCTOR WHO We can survive for quite a time yet.
SARAH While you play with that yo-yo?

He lets it slip down again.
DOCTOR WHO Just a simple gravity reading, Sarah. Yes, almost certainly we're inside some kind of artificial satellite… Now isn't that interesting?
SARAH Not very.
DOCTOR WHO I think it is.
He shines his torch around with keen interest.
SARAH It's dark and cold and it's getting very airless –
DOCTOR WHO All we have to do is get the power back on. Let's see what's over here.
He moves off.
SARAH *(To Harry)* Well we might as well have a look around. **You** coming ~~for a walk, Harry~~?
HARRY Better stick with the Doctor don't you think?
They follow.
The Doctor has found a control console. He plays around with it. Lights come on.
DOCTOR WHO Yes. That's better.
One entire wall of the chamber is a complicated and elaborate control bank.
The Doctor studies the mass of gauges and hydraulic pipes.
DOCTOR WHO Incredible…
HARRY ~~What's it all for?~~ I say! What's all that for?
DOCTOR WHO I've never seen anything quite like it. ❾
~~**HARRY** Sarah~~.
SARAH Hey, Doctor!
The Doctor looks.
DOCTOR WHO Definitely built on Earth but I can't **quite** place the period.
Sarah is studying the far wall. A panel opens in it. She looks through.
SARAH ~~Doctor!~~ Doctor, look!
DOCTOR WHO In a moment, Sarah.
Doctor Who is making a close study of some part of the machine.
HARRY None of it seems to work now, anyway.
Sarah pulls a face at the Doctor's back and steps through the panel.

3. INT. CONTROL ROOM 2.
Sarah finds herself in an even more complex machine room. This section contains the main

computers. *They are dead and silent. Behind her the panel slides shut.*

4. INT. CONTROL ROOM 1.

DOCTOR WHO Judging by the macro-slave drive and that modified version of the Bennett oscillator, ⑩ I'd say this was built in the early thirtieth century.

HARRY Oh, no…

DOCTOR WHO You don't agree?

HARRY ~~The~~ **Early** thirtieth century?!

DOCTOR WHO Late twenty-ninth, early thirtieth, I feel sure.

Harry looks as though he's been hit with a wet sandbag.

5. INT. CONTROL ROOM 2.

Sarah, meanwhile, is doing her tour of the second section. She's finding it increasingly hard to breathe. She turns back, sees the blank wall, hurries over.

SARAH Doctor..! Doctor..! There's ~~no~~ **hardly any** air in here. Doctor, please!

She hammers the wall. Fear and exertion increase her distress.

6. INT. CONTROL ROOM 1.

~~**DOCTOR WHO** Of course, with something as old as this it's difficult to be exact.~~

HARRY Doctor, I'm a simple sort of chap… Are you trying to tell me that we're now in the middle of the thirtieth century?

DOCTOR WHO Good ~~gracious~~ **heavens** no! Well beyond that.

HARRY Beyond the thirtieth!

DOCTOR WHO You gave that helmic regulator quite a twist, I'm afraid.

HARRY Well – where are we?

DOCTOR WHO It's difficult to say. ~~This~~ **All this stuff** has obviously been here for some time. Several thousand years at least – what was that?

~~**HARRY** I didn't say a word. I'm beyond words.~~

7. INT. CONTROL ROOM 2.

Sarah, with the last of her strength, again strikes the wall with a metal stanchion. Then collapses.

SARAH Doctor… I can't… breathe…

8. INT. CONTROL ROOM 1.

The Doctor is staring around.

DOCTOR WHO Sarah! Where can she have got to?

HARRY ~~Back~~ In the TARDIS?

DOCTOR WHO Impossible. I've got the key… I've told her time and again about ~~this sort of thing!~~ going off by herself – **Sarah?!**

HARRY But there's only one door and I swear she didn't go out ~~there~~ **that way**.

DOCTOR WHO Then there must be another exit.

HARRY **A sort of** hidden deck hatch or something?

DOCTOR WHO Vacuum-tight panel, ~~probably~~ **more likely**; **they** used them a lot in these early space ~~ships~~ **vessels**. *(He finds the panel)* Yes, just as I thought!

HARRY No door knob.

DOCTOR WHO **There must be** a remote control. You haven't touched anything, have you Harry?

HARRY Me?

DOCTOR WHO There are only two of us in here and your name is Harry.

HARRY Yes… I did just try one switch.

DOCTOR WHO Which switch, **Harry**?

HARRY But **absolutely** nothing happened.

DOCTOR WHO Which switch?

HARRY Which switch? ~~Oh – this one.~~ **Well, I think it was…** ~~No, wait a mo'~~… I think perhaps it was… Well, I might have been standing further along.

DOCTOR WHO Try and remember, Harry.

HARRY I am trying. But it's ~~frightfully~~ **awfully** difficult, ~~you know~~. **I can hardly breathe.**

DOCTOR WHO ~~Just~~ Think where you were standing.

HARRY It was this one.

DOCTOR WHO Sure?

HARRY ~~Positive~~. **Yes.** But ~~absolutely~~ nothing happened –

DOCTOR WHO ~~Press it.~~ Go on. Press it.

Harry does. They turn as the panel opens. The Doctor goes to it.

~~**DOCTOR WHO** Sarah!~~

9. INT. CONTROL ROOM 2.

He runs into the computer section and bends over Sarah.

Harry joins him.

HARRY Crikey. She's cyanosed.

DOCTOR WHO No air in here. Help me to get her back…

They start to carry her out. The panel closes. Harry drops his end and makes a dive to stop it closing. He's too late.

HARRY ~~Confound it~~. Now what **do we do**?

DOCTOR WHO There ~~should~~ **must** be a reverse ~~control~~ **mechanism**.

He searches for it.

HARRY I've always hated sliding doors. Ever since I ~~got~~ **caught** my nose ~~stuck~~ in one in Portsmouth **barracks**.

He is easing Sarah into a relaxed breathing position.

DOCTOR WHO How is she, Harry?

HARRY ~~Oh, not bad. She'll recover quite quickly once she's out of here.~~ **She'll be OK if we can get her out of here.**

The Doctor has settled on two switches. He tries one with no effect. He depresses the other. Again nothing.

DOCTOR WHO Must be a broken circuit…

HARRY What?

DOCTOR WHO Nothing… Nothing seems to be working **properly** in here.

HARRY Oh.

He is sweating and struggling for breath. The Doctor is not yet affected.

DOCTOR WHO Ah, I've found the oxygen control!

HARRY ~~Oh Good…~~ **Well done.**

The Doctor turns a wheel marked 'oxygen bleed'. He puts an ear down and listens. We can tell the bad news from his expression.

DOCTOR WHO Not good, Harry.

HARRY No luck, eh?

DOCTOR WHO *(To himself)* Why is nothing functioning?

HARRY Couldn't we smash… a way out **or something**, ~~Doctor~~?

DOCTOR WHO With our bare hands?

Harry, suffering heavily, looks at Sarah.

HARRY It's all my… fault.

DOCTOR WHO ~~No,~~ I got us into this Harry.

HARRY Not enough… enough puff to argue.

DOCTOR WHO Then lie down. Conserve the oxygen while I…

The Doctor is checking the cable-run between junction boxes by the wall.

DOCTOR WHO Do what I can… That's odd…

HARRY What?

DOCTOR WHO These cables have been sheared clean through… ~~Right!~~ Oxygen valve servo-mechanism.

The Doctor traces the run back to the oxygen system.

DOCTOR WHO Yellow, black, green…

HARRY Uh?

He starts re-connecting leads to terminals.

DOCTOR WHO Yellow, black, green… yellow, black, green…

Harry is nearly unconscious.

The Doctor is clearly groggy himself. He works slowly and clumsily and with great effort. Once he drops his sonic screwdriver and its recovery is a physical ordeal. Gulping for air, beaded with sweat, eyes blurred, he makes the final connection. We hear the sweet hiss of oxygen through the valve. The Doctor drags himself to the nearest ball-vent and sucks air into his lungs. Then he directs the vent towards Harry and Sarah. He crosses to them.

DOCTOR WHO Harry… **Harry**…

Harry stirs.

The Doctor turns to Sarah, listens to her breathing.

Harry struggles to sit up.

HARRY Is she… she OK?

DOCTOR WHO Just in time… Are you feeling better?

HARRY Convalescent… All I need now is a couple of weeks at the seaside.

DOCTOR WHO Good. Give me a hand to lay her on that couch. It's near the vents.

HARRY Good thinking.

They carry Sarah to a segmented leather couch.

DOCTOR WHO I'll just ~~fix~~ **repair** the rest of those cables.

HARRY Sheared, you said?

The Doctor studies them again.

DOCTOR WHO Or… bitten.

HARRY Eh?

DOCTOR WHO *(Working)* There's a mystery here, Harry. Something happened a long time ago…

HARRY Bitten?

DOCTOR WHO It looks like it. The interesting question is why? Clearly deliberate therefore done for a purpose. Therefore whatever it was ~~possessed~~ **had** a reasoning intelligence.

HARRY And very large teeth.

DOCTOR WHO Splendid. Now let's see if that panel's working.

He crosses and tries switch no. 1 again. The panel opens. The Doctor smirks.

DOCTOR WHO All systems go, wouldn't you say?

HARRY She's coming round.

Sarah's eyes flicker and open.

DOCTOR WHO Good.

HARRY ~~Take it easy~~ **Steady on**, old girl. **Steady on.**

SARAH Harry…

HARRY Yes. I'm here.

SARAH Call me 'old girl' again and I'll spit in your eye.

DOCTOR WHO Welcome back, Sarah Jane.

HARRY ~~Spot of brandy would be the thing, you know.~~

SARAH I couldn't breathe…

HARRY **A drop of brandy would be the thing now**.

DOCTOR WHO There's some in the TARDIS.

HARRY You'll be as right as ninepence in a ~~little while~~ **minute**. We're going to get you ~~a drop of~~ **some** brandy, **all right?**

SARAH I hate brandy.

Harry ad libs as he follows the Doctor.

10. INT. CONTROL ROOM 1.

The Doctor is in the other section staring at a metal rod with a kind of radar-dish top which is lowering from the ceiling. ⓬

HARRY Do you think you could persuade… **I say** – what ~~the deuce~~ is that?

DOCTOR WHO Get down, Harry!

He jumps and carries Harry with him behind the shelter of a bench. A lightning bolt flashes from the rod, ⓭ *striking Harry's shoe as he vanishes. He gives a yelp of pain. His shoe lies smouldering two yards away.* ⓮

HARRY Oh, crikey! What~~'s happening~~ **is it**?

DOCTOR WHO Keep your head down!

11. INT. CONTROL ROOM 2.

SARAH Doctor?!

Sarah moves a limp arm, thinks about sitting up, and decides to rest a little longer. She closes her eyes. There is a distant sleigh-bell sound, a shimmer of light plays over the couch, Sarah dematerializes. ⓯

12. INT. CONTROL ROOM 1.

Using an extensible probe the Doctor cautiously raises his hat above the bench. There is a second thunderbolt. He brings the hat down with its crown burning and ruefully beats out the flames. ⓰

DOCTOR WHO We seem to be trapped, Harry.

HARRY What is it?

DOCTOR WHO Some sort of automatic guard. I wasn't bargaining for this when I repaired the circuits. I wonder?

HARRY ~~What?~~

DOCTOR WHO Of course! That's why they were cut in the first place! ~~I begin to understand it now –~~

HARRY What about Sarah? **If she comes –**

DOCTOR WHO Tell her to stay where she is.

HARRY Sarah! Sarah!?

13. INT. CONTROL ROOM 2.

On the empty couch.

HARRY *(VO)* Can you hear me, old girl? ~~Stay where you are. Don't come near the door – understand?~~ **Keep away from the door, do you understand? Keep away from the door.**

14. INT. ACCESS CHAMBER. ⓱

Sarah lying on an identical couch. Classical music ⓲ *echoes through the room. Coloured spotlights drift mesmerizingly over her body. Suddenly her eyes snap open. She stares around.*

SARAH Where am I?

A calm and gentle voice issues soothingly from a speaker.

VOICE Welcome, sister. Welcome to Nerva.

Sarah, startled, begins to sit up.

VOICE No, do not move. It is dangerous to move from the tranquiller couch. Please remain in contact with the biocryonid vibrations.

Sarah, already under the influence, sinks back.

VOICE In five minutes the final phase of your processing must commence. If you have any personal possessions that you wish to have preserved, please place them in the casket adjacent to your right hand. Shortly you will hear the recorded voice of the High Minister speaking personally to you. At the conclusion of the minister's message there will be a two-minute interregnum preceding the commencement of irradiation. ~~You may use this time to record any final message that you wish to have conveyed to the members of your commune. Please state the name and district number of your commune at the beginning and end of your message.~~

~~Sarah dreamily unclips her brooch, ear-rings, bracelet, or whatever, and opens the casket.~~

15. INT. CONTROL ROOM 1.

The Doctor lowers his all-purpose extensible probe. He taps his teeth with it.

~~HARRY Does that help? We're organic.~~

DOCTOR WHO Apparently it's not activated by movement. Unless what's moving is organic.

HARRY Hardly helps us, does it. We're organic. ⑲

DOCTOR WHO Not ~~under~~ **down** here, we're not, Harry.

HARRY Ah, yes! Good bit of logical deduction, Doctor.

DOCTOR WHO *(Acidly)* Thank you.

Out with sonic screwdriver. He sets to work on the studs holding the bench down. ⑳

16. INT. ACCESS CHAMBER.

As before, Sarah is bemusedly watching the play of light. Suddenly a woman's voice issues from the speaker.

VOICE Greetings, Citizen Volunteer. This is the High Minister speaking:

Sarah raises a sleepy hand in greeting.

VOICE On behalf of the World Executive I salute you who are about to make the supreme sacrifice. In a few minutes you will pass beyond life. In case there is any fear in your heart, any doubt in your mind at this awesome moment, let me remind you that you take with you all our pasts. You carry the torch that has been handed down from generation to generation…

SARAH What's happening?

For a second she shows a frightened awareness. Then she relaxes back into the soothing vibrations of the couch.

17. INT. CONTROL ROOM 1.

The bench is free. The Doctor and Harry ease it across the floor.

HARRY Where are we going with it?

DOCTOR WHO To this wall. Inch it round your way.

HARRY OK.

DOCTOR WHO One slip, Harry, and we'll be charcoal.

Grunting with effort, they manoeuvre against the control wall. The Doctor peers up.

~~**DOCTOR WHO** Back to you, Harry.~~

~~**HARRY** OK.~~

DOCTOR WHO Ah! There it is.

HARRY What?

DOCTOR WHO Trouble is ~~I~~ **we** can't reach it from here.

HARRY What can't ~~you~~ **we** reach?

DOCTOR WHO The autoguard, cut-out, up there, see..? Never mind. ~~The~~ Faithful old scarf.

He unwinds it and prepares to throw it over a lever marked 'auto-guard'. ㉑ He flings it. The lightning crackles, his scarf falls back in two sections, the ends burning.

HARRY Hard luck. Jolly good try, though.

The Doctor extinguishes his scarf.

DOCTOR WHO This isn't **a game of** cricket, ~~you know~~, Harry.

HARRY Sorry. ~~No.~~ Mind you, if ~~only~~ I had a cricket ball I'd jolly soon knock that switch –

He stares as the Doctor produces a battered ball from his trouser pocket. He polishes it on his leg and hands it to Harry.

DOCTOR WHO Will this do?

Harry spits on his hand.

HARRY Watch this.

He throws the ball. The lightning crackles. ㉒ The ball descends in blazing fragments.

HARRY Organic… of course.

DOCTOR WHO Afraid so.

HARRY ~~Well~~ – now what?

DOCTOR WHO There's only one thing left. Risky. ~~I must try it.~~ **But it might work.** You don't ~~need~~ **want** your other shoe do you, ~~Harry.~~

HARRY Suppose not.

111

DOCTOR WHO Slip it off, ~~old chap~~… Now I want you to throw it across the room. When I give you the word. Understand? ~~Ready — now!~~
~~HARRY What are you going to do?~~
DOCTOR WHO I'm **going to** tr~~ying~~ to distract it.
He sets himself for a spring.
DOCTOR WHO Let's just hope it's not double-barrelled. **Ready?**
HARRY Ready.
DOCTOR WHO Now!
Harry hurls the shoe. The lightning blasts. The Doctor springs, pulls the lever and drops in one movement. Harry's shoe burns brightly. ㉓
DOCTOR WHO I think we've done it, Harry.
Very cautiously he edges from under the bench. He straightens
DOCTOR WHO Pity about the scarf. Madame Nostradamus made it for me. A witty little knitter. (Calls) All right, Sarah, you can come through now. Never get another like it.
HARRY ~~What about~~ **Look at** my shoes!~~?~~
DOCTOR WHO Sarah!
He goes through to the other section. Harry stares at his stockinged feet.
~~HARRY The Lords of the Admiralty are never going to believe this.~~

18. INT. CONTROL ROOM 2.
~~Harry enters.~~
    ~~The Doctor silently indicates the empty couch.~~
~~HARRY Oh, not again..!~~

19. INT. ACCESS CHAMBER.
A Perspex cylinder slides from the wall, enclosing the couch on which Sarah lies. A smoky red vapour hisses into the cylinder, coiling about her, rapidly thickening. ㉔

20. INT. CONTROL ROOM 2.
The Doctor removes the leather sections from the couch. The base is a metal grid. It looks like the inside of a wireless set.
DOCTOR WHO Oh, what a fool! ~~Why didn't I realize..?~~ **Of course.**
HARRY What is **it** ~~that thing~~?
DOCTOR WHO **Why didn't I realize?** Short-range matter transmitter. But the strange thing is…
He turns and studies the computer.

DOCTOR WHO It's just an internal relay, Harry.
HARRY I haven't the foggiest notion what you're talking about, Doctor.
DOCTOR WHO Never mind. It means Sarah~~'s not can't be~~ far away. All we have to do is find her. Come along.
He leads the way out.

21. INT. THE TRANSOM.
The transom is a curving passage that circles the Ark, at 90 degrees if possible: it should appear endless. ㉕ *There is dim indirect lighting. The Doctor and Harry emerge into it.*
DOCTOR WHO I think we'll try this way first.
They come to a door marked 'armoury'. ㉖
HARRY I say, what about in the armoury?
DOCTOR WHO Not very likely.
They move on and find their way barred by doors. ㉗
MECHANICAL VOICE (OOV) (Barks out) This is a sterile area! Keep out!
HARRY **Just** like ~~a~~ hospital.
The Doctor presses the control button. The doors slide open. The Doctor motions Harry through.
HARRY Ought we, d'you think?
DOCTOR WHO ~~Why not?~~ **Don't be nervous, Harry.**
Harry shrugs. He goes through.
    Cut to a subject shot from inside, the same as in Scene 1 accompanied by an eerie, loud breathing. ㉘ *Harry steps through first, stares directly at camera. He stops with a shocked gasp.*
    Cut to Harry's POV. Just for a fraction of a second, we see a glistening glob. It is shapeless, about the size of a sack of flour and it slithers out of sight round the corner. ㉙
DOCTOR WHO What is it?
HARRY I saw something… moving.
DOCTOR WHO Nonsense, ~~old chap~~ **Harry.**
HARRY I'm positive I **saw something move** –
DOCTOR WHO Trick of the light.
HARRY It wasn't a trick of the light. I saw something moving… ~~Just about here.~~
The Doctor stops and stares down. He bends. We see it now. A slimy silvery trail about two feet wide, it stops in an iron grille.

~~**DOCTOR WHO** Nothing could have lived in here... Nothing.~~

He scratches a fingernail over the trail. He rubs a stickiness off his fingers distastefully.

~~**HARRY** What d'you make of it, Doctor?~~

DOCTOR *(Musing)* It's like the trail left by a gastropod mollusc.

HARRY A slug?

The Doctor rises. He looks about abstractedly.

DOCTOR WHO Or a snail?

HARRY That size..? ~~Never~~ **Impossible!** Anyway it couldn't have got through ~~there~~ **this grille**.

DOCTOR WHO **Very** interesting. A multi-nucleate organism?

HARRY Eh?

DOCTOR WHO Come on, let's find Sarah first. This looks promising...

He opens a door marked 'green badge personnel only.' [30]

22. INT. CUBICLE.

In a small lift, doors either side. The Doctor closes the door, and the lift moves. [31]

HARRY She's obviously not in here.

DOCTOR WHO Decontamination chamber. ~~Better hold your breath~~. **Might make you feel a bit dizzy.**

23. INT. CROSS CHAMBER. [32]

Door opens. Doctor Who helps a wheezing Harry out.

He props him against the wall and looks about with high interest.

He crosses and studies the segmented couch, a replica of that in the control room.

DOCTOR WHO I've a feeling we're getting warm, Harry.

There is a door with a wheel lock.

It is marked 'Animal-Botanic'.

Doctor Who peers in through the observation port.

DOCTOR WHO Animal and botanic. Yes of course! That explains everything. Do you realize what this is, Harry?

HARRY Uuh..?

DOCTOR WHO Aren't you feeling better ~~yet~~?

HARRY No. I'm not ~~feeling better~~.

DOCTOR WHO Pull yourself together. This is fascinating. A cryogenic repository.

HARRY A repository for what?

DOCTOR WHO Everything. Well, everything they considered worth preserving. And just look at this!

One entire wall of the chamber is a filing cabinet.

He opens drawers.

DOCTOR WHO Microfilm... It's a complete record, ~~Harry.~~ History. Music. Architecture. Literature. Engineering... Incredible! The entire body of human thought and achievement.

HARRY Yes, but what**'s it all** for?

DOCTOR WHO Posterity? *(Shrugs)* I don't know... Why build all this and send it into space?

HARRY I say. Couldn't be some sort of survival kit, could it?

DOCTOR WHO Survival? ~~of course~~.

HARRY You know the kind of thing they shove in lifeboats **and things**.

DOCTOR WHO You're improving, Harry.

HARRY Am I **really**?

DOCTOR WHO Your mind is starting to work. It's entirely due to my influence**, of course**. You mustn't take any credit for it. **Now** – what's missing?

HARRY ~~Eh?~~ **Missing?**

DOCTOR WHO **Yes.** If we are to assume that some great cataclysm struck the Earth and just before the end they launched this lifeboat... then the most obvious missing element ~~appears to be~~ **is** man himself. What has happened to the human species, Harry?

He brings a hand down in declamatory fashion.

The hand smacks a button. There is a hissing noise and a panel slides open.

They look at each other.

24. INT. CRYOGENIC CHAMBER.

Harry and Doctor Who enter.

Rows of low pallets retreat into mirrored infinity.

Each is shrouded in plastic.

Waxen human figures lie immobile on the pallets. [33]

HARRY **I say!** What a place for a mortuary!

DOCTOR WHO This isn't a mortuary, **Harry**. Quite the reverse.

HARRY The reverse? Well, I'd hardly call it a nursery… **34**

DOCTOR WHO Cryogenic chamber. Old principle but I've never seen it applied on this scale. There must be hundreds here. Look at them!

HARRY When you've seen one corpse you've seen 'em all.

DOCTOR WHO Corpse? These people aren't dead, Harry – they're asleep. ~~This is the whole~~ **The entire** human race awaiting the trumpet blast!

Doctor Who moves off along the beds.
Harry spins his head.
He pulls aside the plastic shroud from the highest pallet and feels for a pulse beat.

HARRY Dead as a door knocker.

He digs out his stethoscope.

DOCTOR WHO **35** Homo sapiens. What an inventive, invincible species… It's only a few million years since they crawled up out of the mud and learned to walk. Puny, defenceless bipeds, they survived flood and famine and plague. They survived cosmic wars and holocausts. And now ~~they're out here~~ **here they are, out** among the stars, waiting ~~for~~ **to begin** a new life… ready to outsit eternity. They're indomitable! **Indomitable!**

He delivers this speech to himself, on the move, and returns to see Harry using his stethoscope.

DOCTOR WHO What do you think you're doing, Harry?

HARRY Sorry to contradict you, Doctor. There's not a flicker of life.

DOCTOR WHO Suspended animation.

HARRY But there are no metabolic functions at all. ~~Look at this one.~~ **I mean, look at him.** Even in the deepest coma the hair and fingernails don't stop growing. The epidermis –

DOCTOR WHO <u>Total</u> suspension, Harry. ~~That's the whole point of a cryogenic chamber.~~ You can't survive ten thousand years in a coma.

HARRY Ten thousand years?

DOCTOR WHO Fifty thousand years. A hundred thousand. ~~The length of~~ Time is immaterial.

He pauses for a last look about.

DOCTOR WHO Amazing sight, isn't it? The entire human race in one room. All colours. All creeds, all differences finally forgotten.

HARRY **Doctor** – are you serious? The entire human race.

DOCTOR WHO Well, its chosen descendants. The operation must have been meticulously planned. Come on.

HARRY Now where are we going?

DOCTOR WHO First to find Sarah – then we'll shut down the systems and leave. We're intruders here, you know.

HARRY Just a minute Doctor. ~~D'you mean~~ **Are you trying** to tell me this is ~~how~~ **where** it's all going to end? In here?

DOCTOR WHO Not ~~the~~ end, Harry. Just a pause.

HARRY But there are only a few hundred corpse… bodies here – I mean what happened to the rest of ~~mankind~~ **humanity**? ~~There must have been~~ **Some global** catastrophe?

DOCTOR WHO Yes. And they saw it coming so they made provision **for it** as best they could. Don't forget ~~that~~. It's something for you to feel proud of.

Harry looks around with appropriate awe.
Suddenly his expression changes.

HARRY Doctor, look!

He points. We pan to the silvery trail on the floor.
Again they study it.

DOCTOR WHO *(To himself)* Oxygen. Radiant heat… This deep in space. I wonder..?

HARRY Perhaps it's some sort of mould.

DOCTOR WHO Mould?

HARRY ~~The other~~ **And that** trail we saw in the corridor.

DOCTOR WHO ~~But the~~ **And that** thing you saw moving **in the corridor..?**

HARRY Dust? That grille **thing** is ~~probably~~ a dust extractor. We opened the doors after umpteen years and ~~there was~~ **caused** a bit of a draught…

DOCTOR WHO ~~Yes~~ Very convincing. All the same we'll just check some of the beds while we're here.

They move off.

HARRY What are we checking for exactly?

DOCTOR WHO Just making sure everything's in order.

Harry shrugs. He ambles along his row of beds.

HARRY **Right-ho.**

Suddenly he stops. He pulls aside a shroud.

His expression changes to one of horror.

HARRY Doctor! ~~Doctor, over here quick!~~

Doctor Who hurries over.

DOCTOR WHO What have you found?

He stops, appalled, staring at the bed.

We pan down. Sarah lies there, waxen and motionless.

Doctor Who takes her shoulders.

DOCTOR WHO Sarah..! Oh, Sarah Jane…

HARRY ~~There's nothing we can do for her now.~~ We can't help her now.

DOCTOR WHO No. She'll be like this for three thousand years at least.

HARRY ~~There must be something we can do!~~

DOCTOR WHO Even if we had a resuscitation ~~tank~~ unit it's probably too late to revive her now.

HARRY There must be something we can do! ~~Resuscitation tank? What does it look~~ ~~like?~~ What would a resuscitation unit look like?

Harry hurries to them. ③⑥

DOCTOR WHO Very similar to an oxygen cylinder. You'll recognize it if there is one.

He bends over Sarah again, checking for any sign of life.

Harry opens one cupboard – hurries to the next.

He pulls open the door.

A seven-foot-high 'thing': gelatinous, jointed tentacles bristling with coarse hair, huge single faceted 'eye', and ferocious, open-gaping mandibles swings down upon him.

Harry gives a cry and falls back. ③⑦

CLOSING TITLES

---

❶ Some documentation refers to the story simply as *Ark in Space*.

❷ The opening model shot was a CSO combination of a photo caption of stars, a telejector slide of planet Earth and Tony Oxley's model of Nerva.

❸ The subjective Wirrn POV is not used until Scene 1A. Scene 1 is mixed into Scene 1A.

❹ This sequence, up to Scene 2, was recorded 'in full' for editing into Part Three, Scene 19 where the Doctor relives the Wirrn queen's experiences. Also pre-recorded here was the autoguard attacking the queen, and the Wirrn queen's sabotage of the control systems. These were POV shots, edited into Part Three, Scene 19.

❺ A green 'Aida' lens smeared with gel was used on the camera to give the POV Wirrn shots.

❻ The cryogenic chambers were actually constructed upright, not as horizontal beds (see page 117 for the original design model and drawings).

❼ Rather than the usual 'roll-back-and-mix' effect, the TARDIS materialization was achieved simply by having the police-box lamp begin to flash on the darkened set accompanied by the materialization sound effect.

❽ An oil lamp similar to one Sarah takes from the TARDIS in *Death to the Daleks* (1974).

❾ As the Doctor speaks, Harry presses a button and a section of wall in front of Sarah slides open (hence her next additional line).

❿ An in-joke – the Bennett oscillator was named after director Rodney Bennett.

⓫ Harry starts his line from the beginning of the next scene.

⓬ The autoguard prop was lowered from the studio's camera/lighting gantry. The original intention was for it to rise up from the floor.

⓭ A spark generator produced the lightning effect, which was then overlaid on to the picture.

⓮ Harry's smouldering shoe was recorded after Scene 18 and inserted here.

⓯ The effect of Sarah's disappearance was achieved using 'roll-back-and-mix' (see *Robot* Part One, Scene 1) with a 20-second overlap.

⓰ There was a brief recording break to fill the hat with smoke.

⓱ The scenes of Sarah on the couch in the access chamber (Scenes 14, 16, 19) were all recorded together after Scene 20.

Title Sequence

Keen not to spend too much money on a new title sequence, producer Philip Hinchcliffe suggested to graphics designer Bernard Lodge reusing the same basic idea as the 'slit-scan' titles which had been introduced with *The Time Warrior* in 1973. Hinchcliffe also suggested incorporating the image of the TARDIS police box into the shapes generated.

The slit-scan technique used a camera mounted on a motorized arm erected vertically above the motorized animation table which could move from side to side. On the table was a piece of back-lit vacuum-formed plastic chrome material, above which was placed a static caption mask with gaps such as two slits (for the TARDIS-shaped tunnel) or a circle (for the vortex tunnel). The camera tracked up and down the armature with the shutter locked to a single frame of film, and as a result exposed different parts of the frame to different sections of the pattern which was moved sideways beneath the mask. The time-consuming process meant that the cycle of moving the camera had to be repeated with each and every frame to build up the finished sequence. Various versions of the titles were made. One retained the Jon Pertwee vortex opening instead of the TARDIS, while another used a striking TARDIS-shaped corridor.

The new 35mm title sequence was first used on *The Ark in Space* and *The Sontaran Experiment* in October 1974. The titles for *Robot* were taped on Tuesday 12 November along with the final studio session on *The Ark in Space*.

For *The Ark in Space*, a greener colourization of the new 35mm opening titles, different from all other episodes, was used. The opening and closing credits for *The Sontaran Experiment* were also transferred the same evening, using the blue/lilac tint which would be used as standard on all other episodes through to *Shada* in 1979.

18 *Concerto Grosso Opus 3 Number 2 – Largo*, composed by Handel, played by the Academy of St Martin in the Field was used.
19 The camera script mistakenly places this line ahead of the Doctor's previous line.
20 An inserted shot shows a close-up of the bolt unscrewing – achieved by twisting the bolt from beneath on a model.
21 The control – a slider – is not labelled.
22 A blue lighting effect accompanying the sound of the autoguard firing.
23 Harry's second smouldering shoe was recorded after the first shoe, before Scene 18 and inserted here.
24 A visual effects document gives the original requirement for the couch: 'A smokey red vapour hisses into the cylinder, coiling about her, rapidly thickening.' To achieve this, a Perspex screen was lowered across the side of the couch, then dry-ice vapour was pumped in. A red light was shone through the vapour.
25 Windows along the length of the transom give out into space. The star field was added using CSO.
26 The door is not shown. Harry's inserted line removed the need for a sign.
27 The doors are labelled 'AREA Q'.

28 Again, as with Scene 1, an Aida lens was used for the Wirrn grub's POV shot of Harry.

29 The grub disappears through a vent – the prop was pulled through from behind. This shot and the Wirrn POV shot of Harry were recorded separately after Scene 22 and inserted.

30 The sign actually reads 'YELLOW BADGE PERSONNEL ONLY'.

31 A green lighting effect was used in this scene.

32 This is the same set as the access chamber. The couch the Doctor finds is the one where Sarah was cryogenically frozen in Scene 19.

33 The sets for *The Ark in Space* are impressive – especially the cryogenic chamber. Producer Philip Hinchcliffe later recalled: '[Designer] Roger [Murray-Leach] came up with a clever way of creating scale in the cryogenic storage chamber, by giving the whole set a sense of great height. And he used a mirror to create a false-perspective effect for the camera, so that it looked as though there was an endless series of these honeycomb chambers… I remember going in through the studio doors and being just blown away. It was absolutely amazing… This thing was 18 to 20 feet high, and people were coming in from other studios and programmes and staring at it in disbelief… I don't think anything that big had ever been put up in the studios before.'

34 This is misprinted in the camera script as 'I'd hardly call it a nunnery…'.

35 There was a recording break either side of this speech. This was to adjust the set so that it seemed that the Doctor was in a second, vast cryogenic chamber joining the first. The set was actually the same one, but with the main doorway replaced by more cryogenic pallets.

36 Harry passes a sign that says (all in capitals) 'Do not enter cryogenic area when light is on or floor is in motion'. The first cupboard that Harry opens is labelled 'Medic 2'.

37 The episode ends with the screen going black as the Wirrn queen falls towards it.

A model and designs for the Cryogenic Chamber for *The Ark in Space*.

THE ARK IN SPACE

by Robert Holmes

Part Two

OPENING TITLES

1. INT. CRYOGENIC CHAMBER. ❶

Harry falls back with a cry.
   The Wirrn swoops down on him.
   *It drops beside him with a soft thud,
scattering bits of its desiccated tentacles.*
   *Harry, pop-eyed with shock, pulls himself up.
The Doctor is standing behind him, staring at
the creature.*

HARRY Well, it's dead **anyway**…

DOCTOR WHO Very dead.

He picks up a piece of tentacle.

DOCTOR WHO ~~Practically~~ **Almost** mummified.

HARRY What is it?

*For a second the Doctor gazes blankly at
Harry, deeply introspective. Then he shakes his
head.*

DOCTOR WHO That's something we can leave till
later. No sign of a ~~resuscitator~~ **resuscitation
tank**, eh?

HARRY ~~I didn't get chance to see.~~ **I hardly had
a chance to look for one.**

*The Doctor lifts a case from the cupboard.
Opening it –*

DOCTOR WHO ~~Some kind of~~ **Emergency** medical
kit wouldn't you say? ~~These look like drugs.~~

*Harry shakes his head over the futuristic
implements.*

HARRY Bit beyond me, I'm afraid. ~~I'm a leeches man myself.~~

DOCTOR WHO *(Frustrated)* There <u>must</u> be something in this that would help Sarah. But what? What?

HARRY Doctor… look! ②

For a second the Doctor gazes blankly at Harry, deeply introspective. Then he shakes his head.

A low flicker of multi-coloured lights shows under one of the shrouds. ③

They cross to it.

Vira, an exotic, dark-skinned woman ④ *in a short white tunic, is motionless on the pallet.*

The lights seem to be flowing over her. We hear the whining hum of a dynamo rising in pitch and volume.

The Doctor looks at the coils of hosepipe plugged in at the head of the pallet.

DOCTOR WHO Of course they don't need a tank! The resuscitation phase is programmed in~~,~~ ~~Harry~~! Look she's starting to breathe!

HARRY *(A beat)* ~~Great Scott~~! **Yes,** I think she is.

DOCTOR WHO No doubt about it.

HARRY ~~Then there's some~~ **That means there's** hope for Sarah. Look she's moving.

Vira is briefly visited by an ague.

~~DOCTOR WHO~~ ~~Just the nervous system reporting for duty.~~

Vira slowly raises her arms. Her eyes open in a blank stare.

The humming noise and the flicker of lights die away.

There is no response from Vira but after a few deep breaths she sits slowly upright. A staring gaze, whispered speech and hyperslow movements are recognized by Haitians as characteristic of the living dead. Now her head turns slowly towards them.

~~VIRA~~ ~~Who are you?~~

~~DOCTOR WHO~~ ~~Don't be alarmed. We're friends.~~

He smiles reassuringly. There is no response from Vira but her gaze falls on the medical kit. She reaches slowly towards it.

HARRY Something you want?

He holds the case open for her.

She takes out a thing like a small paint sprayer. Reaches again and takes out one of the phials. She fits this into the butt of the sprayer.

HARRY ~~I'll do that if you like~~ **Can't I do that for you..?** *(To Doctor)* Independent sort of bird, isn't she?

Vira opens her tunic and places the end of the sprayer over her heart. She pulls the trigger. There is the hiss of compressed gas.

Vira gives a choked cry and falls back, writhing in pain.

Harry bends over her.

DOCTOR WHO Leave her, Harry.

HARRY But she's –

DOCTOR WHO Nothing you can do. She ~~understands~~ **knows** what she's doing.

The spasm passes.

Vira sits up again and swings her legs off the pallet. Her reactions are nearly normal now.

VIRA Explain yourselves.

DOCTOR WHO Well, **there isn't very much to explain**. We're just travellers in space – like yourself.

VIRA That is not adequate.

She has the natural arrogant authority that goes with an IQ of around 400. She walks around them critically.

HARRY My name's Sullivan, ~~ma'am~~… uh… Surgeon-Lieutenant Harry Sullivan, **actually**. And ~~this is~~ – this is the Doctor.

VIRA You claim to be medtechs?

HARRY Sorry?

DOCTOR WHO My doctorate is purely honorary. And Harry here is only qualified to work on sailors.

VIRA My name is Vira. I am a first medtech.

DOCTOR I'm delighted to hear it. You see we're in rather desperate need of medical help. ~~If you'll just come over here Vira –~~

He leads her to Sarah's pallet.

VIRA This female is a stranger.

HARRY She's a friend of ours. She got caught in the machinery ~~or something~~.

VIRA She was not among the chosen.

HARRY Well, she's among the chosen now, isn't she?

DOCTOR WHO Is there ~~some~~ **any** way of reversing the cryogenic process?

VIRA That can be dangerous. How long since she underwent tissue irradiation?

HARRY Can't be more than an hour, can it, Doctor? We haven't been here an hour altogether.

Vira takes a meter from her kit. She attaches leads to Sarah's temples. The gauge needle flickers slightly.

VIRA Receding neural activity.

HARRY Is there anything you can do for her?

VIRA Is she of value?

HARRY Value? She's a human being ~~just like you and me~~ like ourselves! What kind of a question **is that?**

The Doctor grips Harry's arm.

DOCTOR WHO The answer is yes.

VIRA Your comrade is a romantic.

DOCTOR WHO Perhaps we both are.

Vira screws another phial into the butt of her injector.

VIRA I will inject a·monod block.

She opens Sarah's blouse. **5**

HARRY That'll do the trick, eh?

VIRA Your colony speech has no meaning.

DOCTOR WHO ~~Will it bring her round – reverse the process?~~

HARRY I mean it will bring her round – reverse the process?

Vira presses the trigger. Again the hiss of air.

VIRA She will either survive or die. The action of **the** antiprotonic is not predictable.

DOCTOR WHO I see… You've turned her body into a battlefield!

VIRA Battlefield..? I hyped in classicals but you dawn-timers have a language **all** of your own!

DOCTOR WHO We do seem to have a slight communication problem.

Vira again uses her meter to check Sarah's neural loading.

HARRY I wish there was something I could do. ~~to help her?~~

VIRA It is done. There is nothing further.

She collects her kit and moves down towards the end of the chamber.

VIRA As she revives her electrical field will draw power from the bionosphere.

She indicates a pallet where the lights are now flickering.

VIRA Here is our Prime Unit.

HARRY Prime Unit?

VIRA Our… leader, **I think** you would say. Noah.

HARRY Noah? Oh, I see. As in Noah's Ark, eh!

VIRA It is a name from mythology. His real name is Lazar. We called him Noah as… as an amusement.

HARRY Joke.

VIRA Joke? Oh, yes. There was not much joke in the last days.

She reaches into the shroud and measures the sleeper's neural activity. There is an unconscious tenderness in the way she touches Noah that even Harry might notice.

He is a dark-bearded man in his thirties. He wears a tunic similar to Vira's distinguished by rank badge, and white shorts. **6**

DOCTOR WHO What happened in those last days ~~on earth~~ Vira?

She looks at him surprised.

VIRA Has your colony no records – no history? Where are you from?

HARRY London… ~~You know~~ —England..? Earth actually.

VIRA That is not possible. Earth is dead.

DOCTOR WHO I'm afraid you're probably wrong about that.

VIRA The solar flares destroyed all life on Earth.

DOCTOR WHO Solar flares? I see…

VIRA Our scientists calculated it would be five thousand years before the biosphere became viable again.

DOCTOR WHO Oh, yes, the absolute minimum I would say. But I'm afraid I've a bit of a shock for you, Vira.

VIRA Shock?

DOCTOR WHO Yes. You've overslept by several thousand years… You see when we ~~arrived~~ came here we found a massive systems failure.

VIRA The systems have no capacity for failure~~, Doctor~~.

DOCTOR WHO Possibly not. But a long time ago, while you were dormant, you had a visitor. Come, let me show you.

He leads her across to the Wirrn. She stares.

VIRA Is it… ~~something~~ from space? How did it get ~~in~~ here?

DOCTOR WHO I don't know yet but observe the size of that brain-pan. It had a purpose in coming here and once inside it severed most of your satellite's control systems… including your alarm clock, **so to speak**.

VIRA *(To herself)* What purpose..?

2. INT. INFRASTRUCTURE. ⑦

Very dark. A place of gantries, iron steps and girder supports. The only light, a bright phosphorescent glow, shines from the circular, armoured-glass window in the service hatch of a concrete dome.

We track towards the light source. The mass of Wirrn larvae ⑧ *is hanging on the side of the dome like some giant fungus. It is dark green, blotched with brown, and its surface throbs sluggishly. As we move closer a lump protrudes above the mass of larvae. It extends further and further out and finally resolves into a gelatinous forearm and hand. The hand moves to the locking wheel of the service hatch.* ⑨

3. INT. CRYOGENIC CHAMBER.

Harry is looking at Sarah. The Doctor joins him.

HARRY No change.

DOCTOR WHO No… For once in my life I feel surplus to requirements. ~~I'm not used to it, Harry.~~

~~Harry looks at Vira who is attending Noah.~~
~~HARRY She certainly seems very competent.~~

3B. CRYOGENIC CHAMBER.

The lights under Noah's shroud suddenly start to flicker on and off. The noise of the dynamo stops and starts in sync. Vira checks the pipe connections.

VIRA Doctor…

DOCTOR WHO *(Crossing)* What is it?

VIRA There is a technical fault in the bionosphere.

DOCTOR WHO *(Checking swiftly)* I don't think ~~it's~~ **the fault's** at this end. It's your main power supply.

VIRA It must be corrected~~, Doctor~~! If his heart stops now there is nothing I can do.

DOCTOR WHO Don't worry. I noticed your Ark has a secondary power ~~system~~ **supply**. You **stay here and** keep an eye on things here, Harry.

HARRY Right-oh.

The Doctor exits. Vira stares at the flickering lights.

VIRA Yes – but… The Ark was designed to have a negative fault capacity.

HARRY Gremlins get into everything, old girl. First law of the sea.

~~5. INT. THE TRANSOM.~~

~~*The Doctor steps out into the Transom and hurries along. He stops suddenly and stares at the grille.*~~

~~*There is now a double slug-track to and from it.*~~

~~*He recollects his mission and hurries on.*~~

~~6. INT. CRYOGENIC CHAMBER.~~

~~**VIRA** I should have gone myself. Your comrade has no knowledge of the Ark.~~

~~**HARRY** Do you understand solar power systems?~~

~~**VIRA** Only the principles… But your Doctor is a dawn-timer! What can he do?~~

~~**HARRY** He's a wizard with bits of wire and things. Just you wait and see. He'll have it ticking over in no time.~~

7. INT. CONTROL ROOM 2.

The Doctor has lifted the plastic cover off a power box and is manually adjusting a pair of large induction coils. He replaces the cover and operates a series of trips.

8. INT. CRYOGENIC CHAMBER.

In Noah's pallet the swirl of light resumes its former steady pattern.

The dynamic hum ceases its hiccuping.

HARRY ~~Told you, didn't I? Chap's a top-class boffin.~~ There you are – what did I tell you? Doctor's a first-class boffin.

Vira checks Noah's neural reactions again.

VIRA Good. He will soon revive.

DOCTOR WHO *(VO)* Harry!

HARRY I say – that was fast!

He hurries out to meet the Doctor.

9. INT. ACCESS CHAMBER.

Harry enters and checks, mystified.

HARRY Doctor..? Where are you?

DOCTOR WHO *(VO)* In the control ~~centre~~ **room**.

Harry sees the speaker from which the voice emanates.

DOCTOR WHO Have you got the power back on in there?

10. INT. CONTROL ROOM 2.

The Doctor is at the intercom switchboard.

HARRY *(VO)* Yes, we have. Everything's shipshape now.

DOCTOR WHO Splendid. The fault seems to be in the main solar stack. I'm going to take a look at it.

HARRY *(VO)* Ah… OK.

11. INT. ACCESS CHAMBER.

HARRY Ah, I say. Don't be long, will you?

There is an uncommunicative crackle from the speaker.

Harry turns back towards the cryogenic chamber.

12. INT. CRYOGENIC CHAMBER.

Vira is giving Noah a shot over the heart from the injector as Harry enters.

Noah groans and thrashes in a spasm of agony.

He looks up at Vira and his eyes clear.

NOAH Vira…

VIRA Welcome, Commander.

He sits up and takes her hand.

NOAH Then it's over… It's over, Vira. You and I are alive again.

VIRA And together~~, Noah~~.

These tender pleasantries are broken as Noah catches sight of Harry.

NOAH Who is this?

HARRY ~~The name's Sullivan. Harry Sullivan – uh – sir.~~ Lieutenant Sullivan, sir.

NOAH A regressive? Here…

HARRY I'm not a regressive. I'm a naval officer. *(He spins away)*

HARRY *(Seeing Sarah's pallet light up)* Sarah!

NOAH Clearly a regressive. His speech patterns prove it. How did he get here?

VIRA They claim they are travellers in space~~, Noah~~.

NOAH They?

VIRA There are three **of them**. Another male called the Doctor and that female. They say she was irradiated by error.

HARRY *(Calls)* Vira! She's coming round!

NOAH There was a regressive faction among the volunteers for colony nine.

VIRA With a zero zero survival predic. One generation.

NOAH Even so… Our genetic pool has been balanced, cross-matched, compat-evaluated. Three random units could threaten our survival.

HARRY Vira!

Vira picks up her kit.

VIRA The Council can decide, Noah. The plan had a seven per cent stretch factor.

She goes over and studies Sarah. She checks her neural waves.

HARRY I think she's going to be all right.

VIRA She will revive soon.

Harry slaps her on the shoulder in his relief – an action not well received.

HARRY Oh, thank heaven for that! The Doctor'll be delighted.

NOAH Where is… the Doctor?

HARRY ~~Gone to have a look at the thingummy. Says you've got a fault in it.~~ He said you've got a spot of bother in your, erm… Anyway, he's – he's gone to fix it.

NOAH What?

HARRY Um – Solar stack, I think he said. ~~Hey, look~~ Yes, she's breathing!

Noah exits.

13. INT. INFRASTRUCTURE.

The Doctor is moving stealthily, like a Sioux tracker, across the decking. Occasionally he flashes his torch into some dark recess. He stops and bends suddenly. In the light of his torch we see the slug trail on the decking.

14. INT. THE TRANSOM.

On the archway door. It opens and Noah comes out. He is buckling on a blaster gun.

15. INT. CRYOGENIC CHAMBER.

Vira is preparing an injection.

Sarah's eyes are open but she is not receiving much.

HARRY Soon have you up and about, old thing. ~~Not to worry~~ —this won't hurt a bit.

Vira shoots the injection into Sarah's chest. She twists in pain.

HARRY Well, perhaps just a **little** bit.

VIRA If you are space travellers, as you claim, you should leave now.

HARRY That's a bit brusque, isn't it? If it hadn't been for the Doctor –

VIRA Noah will not permit contamination of the genetic pool. All regressive transmitters have been eliminated.

HARRY Oh, come on – We're not contaminating anybody.

VIRA He has the authority to initiate condign action. Personally I consider your destruction is not necessary.

And she goes off about her medtech duties.

HARRY Well, thanks very much…

SARAH Harry…

HARRY ~~How are you feeling?~~ Yes – do you think you can ~~you~~ stand? Gently, mind – there's a step down.

SARAH *(As he helps her)* I'm so muzzy… **What's this?** What's happening?

HARRY All right, it's all right.

15A. INT. INFRASTRUCTURE.

The Doctor is cautiously approaching the solar stack. After a thoughtful appraisal he touches the locking wheel. He wipes its stickiness from his fingers and, with a nod of understanding, sidles along to the observation window. Shielding his eyes against the glare, he peers in.

15B. INT. INFRASTRUCTURE (MODEL SHOT). ⑩

From the Doctor's POV we see the incandescent, furnace-like interior of the stack. The glob is just distinguishable in the blazing light.

It is a throbbing, bloated mass. It looks much larger and friskier than in previous shots.

15C. INT. INFRASTRUCTURE.

Doctor Who has seen enough. He springs to the wheel and starts to lock the hatch.

A froggy, globular eye in a ball of jelly rears up to the window.

It moves, stares at Doctor Who.

He spins the locking wheel desperately.

The eye disappears and from inside the stack there is a great howl, not unlike a bronchial factory hooter.

Something of enormous power crashes against the hatch.

The whole stack shudders.

Doctor Who backs away, awed.

The thing trapped inside the stack is going mad. It surges against the hatch with screams of rage.

Doctor Who turns and hurries out.

16. INT. CRYOGENIC CHAMBER.

Harry is still explaining the details of their situation to Sarah.

Vira is checking her patients on two pallets where the lights are flashing.

The lighting effect starts under yet another shroud.

HARRY ~~Going to be quite a population here soon.~~

SARAH Ten thousand years?

HARRY According to the Doctor.

SARAH It's unbelievable, Harry!

She sees the Wirrn and starts back.

SARAH What's that?

HARRY Dunno. We found it in the cupboard.

SARAH In the cupboard?

HARRY Sort of galactic woodworm, I suppose.

SARAH It is dead isn't it?

HARRY Oh, yes. Been dead for years. Nothing to worry about.

Vira draws back the shroud from the third pallet.

She stares in disbelief. The bed is empty. ⑪

VIRA Come here!

HARRY What's the trouble?

VIRA What have you done with Dune?

HARRY ~~Eh?~~ Dune?

VIRA *(Points to bed)* Where is he? Answer me!

17. INT. CONTROL ROOM 2.

Doctor Who is figuring out the control systems. He finds the solar-stack control panel and gives a smile of satisfaction.

As his hand reaches for the lever Noah enters from behind.

He levels the blaster.

NOAH ~~Stand back!~~

DOCTOR WHO *(Smiling)* Ah there you are! Awake at last.

NOAH Move away.

DOCTOR WHO ~~Certainly~~. I'm just ~~about to shut down the solar stack.~~ **shutting** down the power in the main stack.

NOAH Touch that ~~lever~~ **switch** and I'll atomize you!

DOCTOR WHO Noah!

NOAH Earth is ours.

DOCTOR WHO My dear man if you think **for one moment** we're laying claim to Earth? You couldn't be more mistaken. **We're here to help you.**

NOAH By deactivating the main solar stack?

DOCTOR WHO Precisely. There's something trapped inside that stack, Noah, but from the rate at which it's absorbing ~~power~~ **energy** it won't be trapped much longer. The stack must be shut down!

Noah chuckles, the chuckle turns into a laugh.

NOAH If you'd been down there with me **Noah, you** –

Casually, still laughing, Noah shoots him. ⑫

Doctor Who turns into a waxwork image, one admonitory hand still raised. ⑬

NOAH ~~Time you were shut down, Doctor… and your two comrades.~~

~~He makes cursory inspection of the Doctor's pockets.~~

NOAH ~~Degenerate ninth colonists!~~

~~He throws the stuff down and goes to the speaker console.~~

18. INT. INFRASTRUCTURE (MODEL SHOT). ⑭

The armoured-glass window in the dome bursts outwards. The hoarse factory hooter emits a triumphant screech. Glob starts to foam nauseatingly through the window.

19. CRYOGENIC CHAMBER.

As before.

VIRA The revivification pattern ~~is~~ **was** inbuilt. Dune was allotted pallet three.

SARAH Perhaps he recovered early?

HARRY ~~That's right. After all, some chaps don't need a lot of sleep~~ —Yes, that's possible isn't it? I mean, after all, some people need more sleep than others.

VIRA ~~The revivification pattern is inbuilt. Dune was allotted pallet~~.

NOAH *(VO)* Vira? Hear me. Hear me…

Vira exits.

20. INT. ACCESS CHAMBER.

Vira crosses to the speaker.

VIRA Yes, Noah? Where are you?

21. INT. CONTROL ROOM 2.

NOAH Main control. I found the Doctor here about to sabotage the power system. He's been dealt with.

22. INT. ACCESS CHAMBER.

On Vira. Angle to show Harry and Sarah listening.

VIRA Noah, we have a problem ~~here~~. Pallet three is empty.

23. INT. CONTROL ROOM 2.

NOAH Explain…

VIRA *(VO)* Technician Dune is missing. There is no explanation.

NOAH The explanation is that the regressives have taken him. Any other problems?

VIRA *(VO)* No, Commander.

NOAH Then proceed with the schedule. I'm about to check the ~~solar~~ **power** stacks.

He cuts the speaker, glances at the motionless Doctor, then exits purposefully.

24. INT. ACCESS CHAMBER.

VIRA Commander Noah will question you on his return. Complete truth is advisable.

She brushes past them and goes into the cryogenic chamber. Sarah and Harry look at each other.

HARRY Cocky bunch, aren't they?

SARAH What do you think's happened to the Doctor?

HARRY I think we'd ~~ought to~~ **better** find out, ~~old girl~~ **don't you?** Come on **then**.

25. INT. INFRASTRUCTURE.

Noah is moving towards the dome. He sees the shattered window and checks, staring incredulously.

Something moves on his right and he spins quickly. The blaster gun roars. From his left there is a flicker of movement, like a lunging snake. Noah gives a great bellow of pain, clutching at his left hand… then he stiffens and falls to the floor. **15**

26. INT. CONTROL ROOM 2.

On the motionless Doctor. Harry and Sarah enter.

SARAH Doctor! *(They run over)* What's wrong with him?

HARRY ~~How do I know?~~ I haven't a clue, Sarah.

SARAH Well, you're supposed to be ~~the~~ a Doct–

HARRY He's alive, anyway. ~~I can hear his heart beating.~~ His hearts are beating.

SARAH Oh, Doctor… ~~Do something, Harry!~~

HARRY ~~Such as what?~~ It's incredible. He's absolutely rigid. ~~No responses — look.~~

SARAH Harry, please – do something!

HARRY There's no response at all.

He snaps his fingers in front of the Doctor's eyes. The Doctor blinks.

DOCTOR WHO – you wouldn't find it quite so amusing… Eh?

Sarah hugs him.

DOCTOR WHO Ah, Sarah, you're back. Splendid. Where's Noah?

~~HARRY Oughtn't you to sit down or something?~~

The Doctor rubs his head.

DOCTOR WHO Oh, he shot me, did he? Cut off in mid-sentence. I might have been saying something important. I <u>was</u> saying something important!

SARAH Are you all right?

DOCTOR WHO Blinding headache, **that's all**. I hate stun guns. Where is he?

SARAH Who?

DOCTOR Noah~~. Noah~~ of course! Who else?

HARRY We **over**heard him on the intercom **thing** saying something about checking the solar stacks –

DOCTOR WHO **What?!** The idiot! Quick – there might still be time –

HARRY *(Holding him)* Doctor, you're sure you're all right?

DOCTOR WHO Never mind **about** me, Harry… There's a man in danger!

He staggers out.

Sarah and Harry run after him.

27. INT. INFRASTRUCTURE.

Noah picks up his blaster gun. He gets slowly to his feet. His left hand is concealed. Before he turns towards the camera he thrusts it deep into his tunic pocket. In the reflected flare of light from the solar stack his expression seems strangely inhuman. He is like a dead man walking. He moves out of frame.

28. INT. THE TRANSOM.

The Doctor, Sarah and Harry moving along.

HARRY Strange how they give us the run of the ship. Why didn't Vira try to stop us?

DOCTOR WHO Not her function, Harry.

HARRY How do you mean?

DOCTOR WHO By the thirtieth century human society was highly compartmentalized. Vira is a medtech. And I suspect we're an executive problem.

NOAH Right, Doctor.

He looms in front of them, gun in hand.

NOAH But not a difficult one. You can be… easily eliminated.

DOCTOR WHO Unlike that thing **you saw** in the solar stack, Noah. ~~You saw it?~~

NOAH I saw a pathetic attempt at sabotage. The observation port is damaged.

DOCTOR WHO Then we're too late! It's escaped…

He stands considering this latest development.

SARAH What's escaped?

NOAH Turn about. We will return to the cryogenic section.

DOCTOR WHO You're absolutely right. *(He leads off briskly)* Come along. We've no time to lose.

29. INT. CRYOGENIC CHAMBER.

Vira is attending to the latest survivor, a lean young man named Libri. He is semi-comatose until she gives him a burst from the injection.

As she tightens and Libri convulses in established fashion the others enter.

Noah brings up the rear, covering them with his blaster.

~~NOAH Stop.~~

LIBRI Vira…

VIRA Welcome.

He takes her hand.

Noah goes over. ⑯

NOAH Welcome Libri.

Libri, still dazed, stares at Noah with an expression of fear. He shrinks back.

LIBRI Keep back – keep away!

As Noah leans forward over him he cries out in terror and tries to strike Noah.

The Doctor watches keenly.

NOAH What's ~~wrong~~ **the matter** with him?

VIRA **I don't know.**

NOAH Is it his mind?

VIRA His ~~responses~~ **reactions** were normal. ~~I don't understand~~. Libri, this is Noah. You remember ~~our~~ Commander Noah?

Libri looks round as though recovering from a bad dream.

LIBRI I'm sorry… I saw something standing **there**…

DOCTOR WHO What was it you saw, Libri?

NOAH Silence! You're here to answer questions, not to ask them.

LIBRI It was horrible! A shape… I'm sorry. I'm all right now.

VILA Temporary neuro-ocular confusion.

She helps Libri from the pallet.

DOCTOR WHO *(To himself)* The process is much too slow. They aren't going to make it.

SARAH What?

NOAH *(Threatening)* No further warnings.

HARRY *(Contemptuously)* You'd shoot, too, wouldn't you? Nice fellow!

NOAH Libri.

Noah hands his blaster to Libri.

NOAH Keep these three under guard. Kill them if they give any trouble.

LIBRI Yes, sir.

VIRA Where are you going, Noah?

NOAH ~~I must shut down the system.~~ **The system must be shut down.**

VIRA What?

NOAH The revivification has to be stopped.

VIRA Why? I don't understand…

For a second or so, Noah himself seems to share her confusion. Then he turns firmly.

NOAH It is an order. I am the commander.

VIRA But the first phase isn't completed. We need the technical crew, Noah, to operate the station.

NOAH Yes… No! No. The plan is changed. Hear me. Hear me. The plan is changed.

VIRA ~~What's wrong, Noah?~~ **Noah, what is it?** Is it something to do with Dune?

NOAH Dune?

VIRA Technician Dune. I reported him missing…

NOAH **But** I'm here. I'm Dune. ⑰

VIRA What?

NOAH The system ~~must… (He chokes for a moment)~~ must be shut down now! No more aliens!

He rushes out.

VIRA Noah come back!

DOCTOR He must be stopped.

VIRA Something has happened to his mind! There was a power fault during his revival.

DOCTOR WHO Get after him, man!

LIBRI *(Wavering)* No… No, he gave me an order.

DOCTOR WHO Don't be an imbecile! Tell him Vira!

VIRA There is no procedure for stopping the revivification programme. It could be damaging, Libri.

LIBRI But he is our commander.

DOCTOR WHO Can you be sure?

LIBRI What?

DOCTOR WHO When you first saw him you had a subconscious impression of something… horrible, you said. That wasn't Noah, was it?

LIBRI No…

The Doctor uses his full personal magnetism.

DOCTOR WHO Believe me – he must be stopped.

Libri hesitates no longer. He hurries out.

DOCTOR WHO **Good.**

VIRA It is not advisable for you to try to escape.

DOCTOR WHO You take some convincing that we're on your side, don't you? Now what was all that about a missing technician?

VIRA ~~Look —~~ Pallet three. I found it empty.

The Doctor crosses to the bed.

~~DOCTOR WHO Not entirely empty…~~

SARAH Noah thinks we're to blame.

HARRY Chap's jumped the ship **that's all** ~~somehow. Always happening.~~ **Happens all the time.**

The Doctor extends his probe into the pallet.

SARAH **Oh come on** – a space satellite is a bit different from a ship, Harry.

HARRY ~~Not much. But~~ **Oh I don't know, Sarah – I bet you** there's the equivalent of a dinghy missing.

DOCTOR WHO Not quite empty.

VIRA What's **that** ~~is it Doctor~~?

The Doctor has screwed in his eyeglass and is examining a strip of tripe-like tissue held in the end of the probe.

DOCTOR WHO Membrane…

VIRA Membrane?

DOCTOR WHO Part of the egg shell.

VIRA Where **is** ~~has~~ it ~~come~~ from?

DOCTOR WHO *(A beat)* It's almost too horrible to ~~believe~~ **think about**…

He gestures towards the dead Wirrn.

DOCTOR WHO The egg-tube is empty.

VIRA That thing..?

DOCTOR WHO The progenitor. The queen colonizer.

SARAH I don't understand, ~~Doctor~~.

DOCTOR WHO Ever heard of **the** Eumenes?

HARRY Eumenes? ~~Isn't she~~ One of our frigates?

DOCTOR WHO It's a genus of wasp that paralyses caterpillars and lays its eggs in their bodies. When the larvae emerge they have ~~an~~ ~~immediate~~ **ready-made** food supply.

SARAH Oh, no!

DOCTOR WHO Strange how the same life patterns recur throughout the universe.

HARRY You mean that slug thing –

DOCTOR WHO Ciliated larvae, Harry. *(To Vira)* Dune was power systems technician, I imagine?

VIRA Yes, but how did you **know** –

DOCTOR WHO It – or they – went directly to the solar stack.

They look at him.

VIRA You mean Dune's knowledge –

DOCTOR WHO Has been thoroughly digested, I'm afraid.

SARAH ~~Do you have to~~ **Don't** make jokes like that, Doctor~~.~~**?**

DOCTOR WHO When I say I'm afraid, Sarah… I'm not **making jokes.** ~~joking at all.~~

30. INT. CONTROL ROOM 1.

Libri is moving cautiously towards the second control room, gun in hand. Suddenly Noah appears in the doorway.

LIBRI Commander…

Noah advances, holds out his right hand.

NOAH Give me the gun!

LIBRI *(Backing)* I'm sorry, Commander.

NOAH Give me the gun!

LIBRI No… You're not well.

NOAH I order you!

LIBRI I-I can't…

Noah continues advancing. He reaches for the gun.

LIBRI Stay back, Commander… Please. Don't force me to…

Noah calmly takes the gun from him and steps back.

NOAH You fool, Libri.

He shoots Libri. [18] *The blast is longer than he directed at the Doctor.*

> *Libri lights up and collapses.*
> *Noah turns on his heel and exits.*

31. INT. CONTROL ROOM 2.

Noah enters. He stands looking at the systems switches, his face registering some deep conflict.

He takes his left hand from his tunic pocket and gazes at it. There is no shape left. The hand is a formless suppurating glob. [19]

Noah raises it slowly to the main systems lever. [20]

CLOSING TITLES

1 The reprise starts with a close-up of Sarah in cryogenic suspension and the Doctor's line from Part One: 'Oh Sarah Jane.'

2 The scene up to this point was recorded with Part One. This was a convenient break-point as the first non-regular character is introduced.

3 Camera directions refer to Vira's pallet as 'Pallet 1' for the lighting cue.

4 Holmes seemingly had a more multi-racial view of the survivors on board Nerva than was seen in the finished programme.

5 Vira injects herself over the heart, through her own tunic. She injects Sarah in the wrist.

6 Noah had no beard, and wears the same design of tunic and (long) trousers uniform as the others. Colour shoulder flashes are used to denote rank/responsibility.

7 This scene is preceded by a short model shot of Nerva in space, which then mixes to the Wirrn larva crawling round the solar stack.

8 The Wirrn grub was designed by John Friedlander and made from bubble-wrap, which was then a new material. Because Stuart Fell was not available for all rehearsals, Friedlander wore the costume himself for those sessions.

9 The shot of the Wirrn larva's 'hand' operating the locking wheel was omitted from this scene and inserted as Scene 3A ahead of Scene 3B. (This was planned ahead of recording, the edits and inserts being marked on the camera script.)

10 Together with Scene 18, this model shot was pre-recorded ahead of the rest of the episode. While listed as a short scene in its own right, it was edited in as three short inserts in 15A and 15C.

11 It was planned to record a close-up of the empty pallet at the end of the scene. In the event no close-up was inserted.

12 Noah's gun was a working prop made by Tony Oxley and enhanced by a video effect. A pale blue circle was placed on the end of the gun while a different blue halo effect was superimposed over the target. These shots showing the blaster's effect were done at the end of the main recordings for this scene, as inserts to be edited back in.

13 The Doctor freezes for a moment, then collapses to the floor.

14 Together with Scene 15B, this model shot was pre-recorded ahead of the rest of the episode.

15 The close-ups of Noah's gun, the firing effect and the Wirrn larva wiping across his hand were recorded as inserts at the ends of the scene and edited back in.

16 Two of the cryogenic pallets immediately to Libri's right were removed to allow the camera to shoot Noah and Libri's confrontation from behind Libri's shoulder. The pallets were repositioned during a recording break before Noah's line: 'You're here to answer questions…'

17 This is one of several references to *The Quatermass Experiment*, a 1953 BBC Television serial that had been the first specially written adult SF venture on television. Written by Nigel Kneale, the six episodes told the tale of how an astronaut on mankind's first space mission was returned to Earth as an amalgam being – containing the memory and knowledge of his two colleagues who had vanished in the space rocket. The knowledge obtained by the astronaut, Victor Carroon, was mirrored in Holmes' *Ark* scripts by the manner in which the insectoid Wirrn gained the intelligence and experience of those they absorbed. (See also Scene 31.)

18 The CSO inserts of the gun, the blue light that fires from it, and the star-shaped effect that hits Libri (c.f. the halo round the Doctor for the stun setting) were recorded at the end of the episode, after Scene 31.

19 Noah's infected hand was made by Sylvia James from bubble-wrap covered in green make-up.

20 Part Two ended with Noah seeing his own hand, mutated and swollen by infected Wirrn flesh. This drew upon the cliffhanger of *The Quatermass Experiment* Episode Four in which Carroon's hand was seen to be a lumpy, misshapen mass after his changed form had come into contact with a cactus. (See also Scene 29.)

THE ARK IN SPACE

by Robert Holmes

Part Three

OPENING TITLES

1. INT. CONTROL ROOM 2.

The final moments of Part Two… ❶
Noah looks at his formless hand, then raises it towards the main systems lever.

Before his hand quite touches it, a noise not unlike a bosun's whistle echoes through the ship.

Then the voice of the High Minister issues from every speaker.

VOICE ❷ Hullo, Space Station Nerva. This is the Earth High Minister. ❸ The fact that you are hearing my voice in a message recorded thousands of years before the day in which you

are now living, is a sure sign that our great undertaking, the salvation of the human race, has been rewarded with success.

Noah, at first frozen with shock, turns towards the speaker. The voice of his great leader has clearly, if only temporarily, returned him to the human fold.

2. INT. CRYOGENIC CHAMBER.

The lights on two more pallets are flickering and the occupants, Lycett and Rogin, are awakening. But they are temporarily unheeded as Vira, the Doctor, Sarah and Harry listen to the voice.

VOICE You have slept ~~for~~ longer than the recorded history of mankind. And you stand now at the dawn of a new age. You will return to an Earth purified by flame – a world that we cannot guess at. If it be arid you must make it flourish. If it be stony you must make it fertile. The challenge is vast, the task enormous, but let nothing daunt you. ④ Remember, Citizen Volunteers, that you are the proud standard bearers of our entire race…

HARRY Sounds like a sort of a pre-match peptalk, ~~isn't it?~~

The Doctor doesn't answer. He is absorbed.

VOICE Of the millions that walk the world today, you are the chosen survivors. ⑤

3. INT. CONTROL ROOM 2.

On Noah.

VOICE You have been entrusted with a sacred duty – to see that human culture, human knowledge, human love and faith shall never perish from the universe. Guard what we have given you with all your strength.

Noah is suffering great schizophrenic agony. He takes his alien left arm in his right hand and hammers it repeatedly across the sharp edge of a control desk.

Nothing drops off. He reels towards the speaker switchboard.

3A. INT. TRANSOM.

VOICE And now, across the chasm of the years, I send you the prayers and hopes of the entire world. ⑥

4. INT. CRYOGENIC CHAMBER.

VOICE God speed you to a safe landing.

HARRY Well, I bet that did your female chauvinist heart a power of good.

SARAH Why?

HARRY Well, I mean, fancy a member of the fair sex being top of the totem pole?

NOAH *(VO)* Vira! Vira…

VIRA That's Noah!

She exits.

5. INT. ACCESS CHAMBER.

Vira goes to the speaker. As the others enter:

VIRA Yes, Commander?

NOAH *(VO)* Vira hear me. This is an order. Expedite revivification. Commence main phase now.

VIRA But, Noah, the safety checks –

6. INT. CONTROL ROOM 2.

Noah is ashen-faced, battling to retain control of his mind.

NOAH Ignore safety checks. We… You are in danger. Get our… your people to Earth before…

VIRA *(VO)* Noah?

NOAH Before the Wirrn… Vira, take command! Hear me. You take command.

VIRA *(VO)* What has happened..? Commander, are you there? ⑦… ~~Hullo!~~

NOAH ~~The~~ Wirrn are here… ~~in the Ark~~… They will… We shall absorb the humans! The Earth shall be ours!

He staggers towards the control panel, glob hand raised. His good right hand fights it back.

VIRA *(VO)* Noah… Noah! ⑧

NOAH *(Weak)* Vira… no time. They're in my mind. Getting stronger… Libri's dead. You will all die… must save our people. You must!

With an effort of will, keeping his left arm pinioned, Noah fights his way from the control room.

VIRA *(VO)* Noah! ⑨

7. INT. ACCESS CHAMBER.

HARRY Chap sounds in a bad way…

VIRA What did he mean – they're in his mind?

DOCTOR WHO Absorb… We shall <u>absorb</u> the humans. Endo-parasitism?

SARAH *(To Vira)* He talks to himself sometimes because he's the only one who understands what he's talking about.

DOCTOR WHO If the Wirrn can do that we've no chance at all! A complete physical absorption.

VIRA Of us?

DOCTOR WHO They'll literally eat us alive. Vira, we've got to talk with Noah. You'd better come with me. He trusts you.

VIRA My duty is to supervise the revivification –

DOCTOR WHO No, Noah has passed **the** command to you. Your duties have been widened.

VIRA *(A beat)* What is your intention?

DOCTOR WHO To find out exactly what it is we're facing. And only Noah knows that.

VIRA I can't leave until the last of our technical section have awakened.

DOCTOR WHO Harry can handle that for you. Can't you Harry?

HARRY ~~Eh?~~ Well, I –

DOCTOR WHO You've watched Vira. You know the procedure.

HARRY ~~Well—~~ Yes, I…

Vira hands over her equipment.

VIRA One gramme of scropoline when the neural register enters the red zone.

HARRY ~~I see.~~ Right.

DOCTOR WHO He'll be all right ~~Vira~~.

VIRA *(Leaving)* And the injection must be right over the pectoralis major.

HARRY Ah, yes – now that, I do understand…

SARAH *(Following the Doctor and Vira)* Good luck.

DOCTOR Sarah, you stay with Harry.

The Doctor and Vira exit. Harry looks at Sarah.

HARRY ~~All right,~~ Yes, come along nurse Smith?

They go through to the cryogenic chamber.

8. INT. CRYOGENIC CHAMBER.

Lycett's eyes are open.

Harry takes a neural reading.

HARRY ~~Well, he's~~ Yes, you see – this chap's in the red zone.

He undoes Lycett's tunic.

SARAH There's another one seems to be awake here.

HARRY After ten thousand years, **Sarah**, he can't be in **that much of** a hurry.

SARAH I hope you know what you're doing.

HARRY Oh, yes. It's dead simple, really. Medicine by numbers.

He turns the injector over in his hands.

SARAH **Oh yes.** Dead simple?

HARRY ~~Just a matter of fitting a fresh thingummy jig into this whatsit. Here, you have a look.~~ Just a question of fitting a fresh ampoule thing into here.

9. INT. THE TRANSOM. ⑩

~~Vira is with the Doctor.~~

~~**VIRA** Doctor, you spoke of parasitism.~~

~~**DOCTOR WHO** Just a guess. No this way. I think he'll have left the control room.~~

~~**VIRA** And you believe Noah has become a host for this creature?~~

~~**DOCTOR WHO** I might be wrong, Vira –~~

~~**VIRA** No, that is why you said he knows about the Wirrn. Your postulate is a multi-nucleated organism with shared consciousness?~~

~~**DOCTOR WHO** I believe it must be something of that kind.~~

~~**VIRA** Then the logical progression is that Noah will ultimately become part of the Wirrn?~~

~~**DOCTOR WHO** There's no need to assume the worst. There may be something we can do. But we must talk to him while he's still emotionally a…~~

~~**VIRA** A human being? Yes, I understand.~~

~~*The Doctor looks at her. He leads on.*~~

~~10. INT. CRYOGENIC CHAMBER.~~

~~*Sarah hands back the injector.*~~

~~**SARAH** There. That should work.~~

~~**HARRY** Thanks. What a useful little thing you are.~~

~~*Sarah looks murder but Harry is bent over Lycett. He operates the trigger.*~~

~~*The injection hisses. Lycett chokes and writhes.*~~

~~*Harry eyes him solemnly during this.*~~

~~**SARAH** *(Shivers)* Oh do hurry. It reminds me of Dr. Frankenstein.~~

~~**HARRY** I can't rush these jobs. In any case, I've another patient over there.~~

~~*He indicates Rogin who is rising slowly from the dead.*~~

~~*Harry crosses and pushes him gently back.*~~

~~**HARRY** I say. Steady, old chap. No sleepwalking.~~

11. INT. THE TRANSOM.

Vira and the Doctor come to a sterility shutter. ⓫ *The Doctor raises a hand to break the locking cell. The shutter slides back. Noah stands on the further side in right profile. The blaster is held in his right hand.*

VIRA Noah..!

He turns towards them. The whole left side of his body is horribly distorted by scabrous green swellings.
 Vira reacts.

NOAH Keep back! Don't touch me…

VIRA Noah, please –

NOAH Keep away, I said.
 He raises the blaster.

DOCTOR WHO Noah, tell us one thing. How much time do we have?

NOAH Time?

DOCTOR WHO Before the Wirrn reach their adult form?

NOAH It feels near. Very near. The tearing free and then the great blackness… rushing through ⑫… ~~wirren-wirrennn… burning fire-life-ecstasy!~~
 ~~*He rolls against the shutter, panting for breath. His voice cracked.*~~
~~**NOAH** Oh Vira… Oh, Vira!~~
 ~~*She stares at him.*~~
~~**VIRA** Are you in pain?~~
~~**NOAH** Pain? I'm in torment! These creatures…~~
 ~~*He throws the blaster at the Doctor's feet.*~~
~~**NOAH** Vira. Shoot me!~~
~~**NOAH** Kill me! Please…~~
~~**NOAH** For pity's sake, kill me!~~
 ~~*Noah is a convulsed, shuddering bundle. The Doctor's jaw tightens.*~~
 ~~*Vira passes a hand over the locking cell. The shutter slides back into place.*~~
 ~~*A muted moan of despair from Noah. Then silence.*~~
~~**VIRA** I'm sorry.~~
~~**DOCTOR WHO** I couldn't have done it, anyway.~~
 ~~*Doctor picks up gun.*~~
~~**VIRA** I showed weakness. But there is something you should know… Noah and I –~~
 Her eyes close for a moment, her only concession to emotion. ⑬

VIRA Noah and I were pair-bonded for the new life.
 The Doctor looks at her sadly, then touches her shoulder.

DOCTOR WHO Let's go back.

12. INT. CRYOGENIC CHAMBER.
Rogin and Lycett are looking grim.

ROGIN Dune, Libri and Noah?

SARAH I'm sorry. It must be a horrible shock for you.

LYCETT So there's just two of us **left** to check the ship?

SARAH And Vira. **She** has taken command.

LYCETT Where is she?

SARAH She's gone with the Doctor. They're trying to contact Noah.

ROGIN ~~A snitch-up already!~~ **There's been a snitch-up!** Didn't I tell you, Lycett? Five thousand years ago I said there'd be a snitch-up!

LYCETT Ten thousand.

ROGIN Beautiful! We should've taken our chance **with the solar flares and gone into** ~~in~~ the thermic shelters. We'd have been happily dead by now.

LYCETT What was it that killed them? Their lungs, was it?

HARRY Hm?

LYCETT Dune and Libri? We were told our lung tissue might atrophy.
 Harry looks at Sarah.

HARRY Well, no, actually ~~it was – ah –~~

SARAH Something got in here.

HARRY That's right. Some sort of space creature.

ROGIN Eh?

SARAH It cut through your alarm clock system.

ROGIN What?
 Sarah indicates the dead Wirrn. They react.

SARAH Look. ~~Don't worry.~~ **It's OK.** It's dead.

DOCTOR WHO *(Behind them)* But unfortunately its larvae are **still** very much alive.
 They turn.

LYCETT Vira…

ROGIN Vira, what's gone wrong?

VIRA Welcome, Lycett… Rogin. You feel well?

LYCETT Yes, Commander.

12A. INT. THE TRANSOM. ⑭
Grub makes its way up transom to cryogenic chamber.

~~## 12B. INT. CRYOGENIC CHAMBER.~~
~~**SARAH** Did you find Noah?~~
 ~~*Doctor Who is squatting, studying the Wirrn corpse.*~~

~~DOCTOR WHO Yes, but it wasn't such a good idea. He couldn't tell me what I need to know… however, this might. Vira? Vira. Do you have a scalpel?~~
~~VIRA A scalpel?~~
~~DOCTOR WHO An instrument for cutting tissue.~~
~~VIRA Oh, yes.~~
~~*She finds one in trolley.*~~

~~12C. INT. TRANSOM.~~ ⑮
~~*Grub makes its way up Transom to Cryogenic Chamber.*~~

12D. INT. CRYOGENIC CHAMBER.
HARRY What are you going to do **with it**?
DOCTOR WHO How much of your anatomy do you remember, Harry?
HARRY Quite a lot **I think** but you need a blooming entomologist for that thing.
DOCTOR WHO **We need to find its weaknesses and we need to find them quickly.**
VIRA Can we help?
DOCTOR WHO Ah – not at the moment, ~~I'm afraid~~ **thank you.**
VIRA Then we will start the main phase. Lycett. Rogin.
They exit. Doctor Who is already probing absorbedly.
After a moment he gazes up.
DOCTOR WHO What was that she **just** said?
SARAH They're going to start the main phase.
DOCTOR WHO ~~Oh no, they're not!~~ **What?!**
He scrambles to his feet and hands the scalpel to Harry.
DOCTOR WHO Carry on with that thoracic incision. Not too deep, ~~though~~.

13. INT. ACCESS CHAMBER.
LYCETT But the safety checks?
VIRA We shall override them.
ROGIN Why?
LYCETT **We can't!**
VIRA That is my decision.
She moves to a wall panel.
VIRA Take your operating stations.
DOCTOR WHO *(Enters)* Vira, the main phase must wait.

VIRA Noah said we should expedite the revivification programme. Get our people to Earth –
DOCTOR WHO Noah was wrong. How long would it take?
VIRA Seventy-two hours for complete revivification. ~~We could evacuate the Ark in another twenty-four~~. **Another 24 to evacuate the Ark.**
DOCTOR WHO Four whole days. The rate at which the Wirrn are developing they'll have pupated to imago long before that. You know what that means.
VIRA We must try.
DOCTOR WHO You can't ~~make~~ **do** it Vira. The Ark will be crawling with those ~~things~~ **creatures**.
Pointing to the next room.
DOCTOR WHO Within hours.
VIRA Doctor, the fate of all humanity might be decided in the next few hours!
DOCTOR WHO Vira, if you fail your people are going to die in pain and fear. If I fail, they'll die anyway, but, at least, only the six of us will know anything about it.
VIRA You have an alternative plan?
DOCTOR WHO Between the larval and imago forms there must be a pupal stage. The Wirrn will be dormant and defenceless. If ~~I~~ **we** can find their weaknesses…
VIRA We might destroy them…
DOCTOR WHO Yes.
VIRA Very well. *(To the others)* Stand down.
LYCETT There's a power flutter in section four, Commander.
VIRA What does that indicate?
LYCETT Some external fault. Shall I check the stacks?
DOCTOR WHO No. ~~You can't.~~ The larvae have taken over the infrastructure. They seem to need solar radiation.
He exits. Vira follows.
ROGIN We should have stayed on Earth, Lycett. I liked the Earth. I <u>like</u> heat.

14. INT. CRYOGENIC CHAMBER.
Harry is staring into the Wirrn.
HARRY Curious lung structure… *(As the Doctor crosses)* Look at this, Doctor?

The Doctor gazes into the chest cavity.

DOCTOR WHO Oh, yes! A superb adaptation… Fascinating!

SARAH What is it?

DOCTOR WHO Obviously the **creature's** lungs recycle the ~~creature's own~~ wastes. Almost certainly by enzymes. Quite wonderful! Carbon dioxide back to oxygen.

SARAH You mean the way plants make oxygen –

DOCTOR WHO ~~Absolutely~~ **Exactly** right, Sarah. It must live in space, probably just occasionally visiting a planetary atmosphere for food and oxygen the way a whale rises from the ocean.

HARRY But judging by ~~those~~ **his** mandibles ~~it~~ **this chap** doesn't live on plankton.

The Doctor picks up the scalpel and goes back to work.

VIRA Noah spoke of the great blackness… rushing ~~through~~ **in**… he meant space. But how did he know?

DOCTOR WHO He now has the race memory of the Wirrn.

He removes with delicate care an eye section with ganglia attached.

DOCTOR WHO Symbioticatavism to be precise. I'm going to need your help now, **Vira**.

He carries the bundle of tissue away.

15. INT. ACCESS CHAMBER.

The Doctor hurries in, sets his specimen down, and opens the wall control-panel. Vira and the rest enter.

DOCTOR WHO Have you got any spare extension leads, Rogin..?

Rogin indicates yes.

ROGIN Yes, but…

DOCTOR WHO Hurry man. Fetch them!

VIRA What are you **going to** do~~ing~~ Doctor?

DOCTOR WHO A little experiment. Circuit display, Lycett~~, quickly.~~

VIRA It is forbidden to alter those circuits!

DOCTOR WHO ~~Come along Lycett, give a man some room.~~ I need the use of your neural cortex amplifier. Not for long, don't worry.

He attaches two electrodes to his tissue specimen and runs a plugged lead from the wall panel to the nearest video monitor.

16. INT. CRYOGENIC CHAMBER. ⑯

A soft bubbling and slurping noise like the tide quietly rising under a pier. We pan over to a grille. Glob is pushing up against it, forming into a mass.

17. INT. ACCESS CHAMBER.

DOCTOR WHO Right, Lycett. Switch on the video circuit, will you?

Lycett does so. The screen flickers but remains grey.

DOCTOR WHO It'll take a while to warm up…

He adjusts his connections.

HARRY What are you trying to do exactly, Doctor?

DOCTOR WHO Sometimes latent neural impressions can be revived.

HARRY Really?

DOCTOR WHO Yes.

HARRY I've never heard of that.

DOCTOR WHO Advanced technology. Gipsies used to believe the eye retained its last image after death. ~~Not quite right but~~ not so far out… **No…** It's not going to work. Switch off, Lycett.

SARAH Now what?

DOCTOR WHO It should work… *(Thoughtful)* The coil isn't ~~producing~~ **giving** a strong enough stimulus. I'll have to link in my own cerebral cortex. That's the only ~~answer~~ **thing**.

VIRA That is highly dangerous~~, Doctor~~.

DOCTOR WHO I know. Two more leads, Rogin.

He takes another lead from the control panel.

VIRA The power could burn out a living brain.

DOCTOR WHO An ordinary brain, I agree. But mine is exceptional.

VIRA I cannot permit it. The shock might kill you.

DOCTOR WHO I think not. Unless, of course, the experiment is interrupted. That could be dangerous.

He attaches a pair of electrodes to his head.

SARAH Do you have to do it, Doctor?

HARRY Doctor, why take the risk –

DOCTOR WHO If I can find out what it was that killed that creature, we might have a chance of fighting the Wirrn. That**'s** ~~might be~~ our only hope.

SARAH Yes but **do you** have to be the one –

DOCTOR WHO It's not just our ~~survival that's in the balance~~ existence that's at stake, Sarah – it's ~~that of~~ the human race ~~itself~~. It may be irrational of me but human **beings** are quite my favourite species. *(He touches his pocket)* Oh, Vira…

VIRA Yes, Doctor?
He hands her the blaster.
DOCTOR WHO ~~You'd better keep~~ **Take** this. Don't hesitate to use it if anything goes wrong. You won't have much time.
HARRY What d'you mean?
DOCTOR WHO ~~Secure me Rogin… The switch, please, Lycett~~… **Switch on, Lycett**… Lycett!
The Doctor convulses, arches rigidly then slumps unconscious.
SARAH Doctor!
VIRA He's joining his mind to the Wirrn. He could remain a part of it… for ever.
A spatter of flashes shows on the screen.
ROGIN Look… it's working…
There is a loud metallic clatter from the next room.
LYCETT What was that?
ROGIN We'd better ~~see~~ **look**.
They head for the cryogenic chamber.
On the screen a swirling pattern slowly establishes and becomes – our opening model shot. It is spotted and foggy – not a perfect picture.
Establishes Sarah and Vira watching. The Doctor is unconscious but his face reflects the Wirrn emotions as the space station swims nearer – anguish, effort and finally triumph. ⑰

18. INT. CRYOGENIC CHAMBER.
Rogin and Lycett look around. The grille has been smashed inwards.
Lycett crosses to it.
LYCETT ~~See~~, over here! *(He bends to examine the grille)* Case-hardened diranium bent like tin!
The glob, a palpitating evil mass high up the wall, ⑱ *slithers down towards him.*
ROGIN Look out, Lycett! Behind you!
Lycett spins round. He tries to get away but, in his fright, trips over a pallet. The glob flows up to him and remorselessly over him. He vanishes into it, screaming.

Rogin stares in horror.
ROGIN Shut the door! ⑲
Lycett's screams die as he disappears.
ROGIN Shut the door!
Harry comes hurrying in.
HARRY What's going –?
He stares. The glob starts moving towards the two men.
ROGIN Get out, man! Get out!
They run.

19. INT. ACCESS CHAMBER.
On the video monitor another foggy, subjective sequence shows us the interior of control room 1.
Harry and Rogin burst in. They lock the door.
ROGIN **They've killed Lycett.** ~~Lycett's been killed~~. There's ~~a~~ **some sort of** huge grub in there.
HARRY Stop the experiment.
SARAH No. You can't. ~~Harry~~ You'll kill him!
VIRA The armoury, Rogin! Get the fission ~~hoses~~ **guns**!
ROGIN Right.
HARRY I'll come with you.
The men hurry out.
On the screen the autoguard is rising from the floor. Lightning sizzles from its radar-dish head, flashing directly at us. The Doctor writhes in pain.
We smash into the control room and close on the cable circuit. Blackness.
The door between the cryogenic and access chambers shudders as the Wirrn larva pounds against it. Its 'breathing' is a hoarse, bronchial roar.
Sarah and Vira exchange frightened glances.
VIRA Hurry, Rogin…
SARAH That door won't hold much longer.
On the screen we see again Part One, Scene 1.
The Doctor appears to be in his death throes.
In the dim light of the Wirrn's bio-luminescent eye we inch up over the pallet and across the figure lying there. ⑳
Vira emits a shocked gasp.
VIRA ~~That's~~ Dune!

135

20. INT. THE TRANSOM. ㉑

The door to the armoury is open. Harry and Rogin come out carrying fission hoses – like highly compact flame-throwers. ㉒
They run off to the transom. Noah ㉓ moves in front of them from the cover of the sterility shutter, they skid to a halt, staring. He is hunched and leprous, toad-like in form though still recognizably him. He stares and looks away.

NOAH Fools! Human fools!
Rogin beats him to the trigger and a blast of force jets along the transom. ㉔
Noah falls back but recovers.
They stare in astonishment as he again raises the blaster.

~~**HARRY** Down!~~
~~**NOAH** You cannot stop the Wirrn with your puny weapons.~~
~~*He pulls Rogin down.*~~
~~*Noah advances for the kill.*~~
~~*Rogin shoots.*~~
~~**HARRY** Quick!~~
~~*They leap past Noah and race on down the Transom as he staggers to his feet.* ㉕~~

21. INT. ACCESS CHAMBER.

The door is bulging under the Wirrn's assault. ㉖ Its rasping breath is thunderous.
On the screen there is only grey frazzle. Sarah cuts it off and hurries to the Doctor. She removes the head electrodes.

SARAH Help me with him, **Vira**!
VIRA Wait… Come away.
DOCTOR WHO The Wirrn… the Wirrn…
VIRA Doctor…
His head turns slowly. He looks without recognition and starts to sit up.
VIRA Doctor –?
She raises the gun.
SARAH No! No, you can't, **I won't let you** –
DOCTOR WHO Can't what. Is it time to get up?
SARAH Oh Doctor, you're **going to be** all right…
DOCTOR WHO Is that noise in my head or…
He looks across the access chamber. The door is giving.
~~**DOCTOR WHO** Great heavens!~~

Harry and Rogin hurry in. There is a triumphant scream from the Wirrn larva and the door bursts open. The glob is solid, hanging in the entrance like a wall. Vira blasts at it. ㉗ Harry and Rogin fire the fission hoses. ㉘ The Wirrn howls with pain – and advances. The Doctor totters to his feet.
~~**DOCTOR WHO** What's happening?~~
~~**HARRY** Keep away Doctor!~~
The others slowly retreat in front of the glob, firing all the time. The Doctor staggers towards the glob as though mesmerized by it.
HARRY Doctor – come back!
The Doctor is still moving forward – now almost touching the glob. Sarah runs forward and swings him away.
SARAH Doctor – don't! **Doctor… Doctor!**
He stares at her. Then shakes his head in a brisk recovery.
DOCTOR WHO Aim lower. ~~Aim at its undersection, Harry! Quick…~~
Rogin and Harry switch their fire to the glob's nether regions. It shrieks and retreats. ㉙ They pursue it, forcing it back into the cryogenic chamber. Its cries recede.
ROGIN It's gone back through the grille.
Harry shuts the door panel. The Doctor sits. Sarah holds her face trying to stop shivering. Harry takes her arm gently.
HARRY That was a close one! All right Sarah? Doctor? ~~Doctor, are you all right now? That was close…~~
DOCTOR WHO But why..? Why have they gone over to the attack?
VIRA They want to destroy us.
DOCTOR WHO They've only got to wait. In their adult form they'll be a thousand times deadlier. Fission-~~hoses~~ **guns** will have no effect ~~on them~~ then.
SARAH How many of them will there be?
DOCTOR WHO At a hatching… a hundred ~~or so~~.
HARRY A hundred? We won't stand a chance. ~~Is there any way we can~~ **How can we** fight a hundred of ~~the things~~ **those**?
DOCTOR WHO Electricity. Only with electricity, ~~Harry~~. That's the one thing I ~~remember~~ **found out**.
SARAH Electricity…

DOCTOR WHO Yes. It was the autoguard that killed the queen. Half a million volts.
HARRY ~~But how did the larvae get~~ We found the queen in the cupboard~~.~~?
DOCTOR WHO Amazing will-power. I could feel it ~~fighting of~~ struggling against death until its task was done… Rogin, is there any way we could electrify the infrastructure? ~~That's where the Wirrn are massing.~~
ROGIN Not from here, Doctor. We'd need to run cables from the control centre.
DOCTOR WHO The control centre! *(He starts forward)* Right, then let's go!
HARRY No use that way, Doctor.
ROGIN Noah's waiting out there. Put one foot in the transom and you'll be dead.
The Doctor stops.
DOCTOR WHO ~~Of course~~. Yes, I was forgetting Noah's ~~still a has that~~ extra mobility…
VIRA Then we're trapped?
DOCTOR WHO The Wirrn are using Dune's knowledge of the Ark. But perhaps there's something he didn't know…
He crosses to the segmented couch.
ROGIN Dune was first tech. He knew it all.
VIRA He helped design the systems.
The Doctor is making some adjustments to the apparatus beneath the segments.
DOCTOR WHO Nobody knows it all. Perhaps he's forgotten that these transmat**s** ~~beams~~ are reversible.
ROGIN That's clever.
DOCTOR WHO Isn't it? As you appreciate it, Rogin, you can go first. I'll give you a ~~lift up.~~ hand, come on.
ROGIN *(Shrugs and gets on the couch)* Oh well… I never liked it here, anyway.
The Doctor touches a switch.
Rogin is gone. ㉚
DOCTOR WHO You next, Harry.
The Doctor touches a switch.

22. INT. CONTROL ROOM 2. ㉛
Rogin is standing rubbing his jaw as Harry appears on the couch.
HARRY I say!
ROGIN You all right?
HARRY What a marvellous way to travel!
ROGIN Always sets my teeth on edge.

23. INT. ACCESS CHAMBER.
Sarah gets on to the couch. The Doctor reaches for the switch.
~~**DOCTOR** Ready. Ready. Press!~~
As he does so the lights start to fade. Sarah does not transmat.
DOCTOR WHO There's a power drain.
He goes to the intercom.
DOCTOR WHO Hullo, control centre.
ROGIN *(VO)* Hullo, Doctor. We've got a power failure.
DOCTOR WHO It's general then. Do you have a fault reading?
ROGIN *(VO)* Section four. That's the secondary stack. There's no…
His voice fades out. The lights drop to a firefly glimmer.
VIRA All power systems are self-repairing.
DOCTOR WHO Malicious damage excluded.
Sarah gets off the couch, trying to make light of things.
SARAH Oh well… Obviously I'm not going anywhere.
VIRA The oxygen pumps have stopped~~,~~ ~~Doctor.~~
DOCTOR WHO Of course – ~~why didn't I think of that?~~ The Wirrn won't need oxygen in their pupal stage. An easy way of killing us.
VIRA Well… Suffocation is not the most unpleasant death.
DOCTOR WHO ~~Suffocation.~~ What? We're not finished yet. You two stay here.
SARAH Where are you going~~, Doctor~~?
DOCTOR WHO The infrastructure. If they've entered the pupal stage, they'll be dormant ~~for a few hours. There's a chance I can~~ Give me a chance to get down there and ~~re-connect~~ switch the power back on.
VIRA But you're forgetting Noah.
DOCTOR WHO No I'm not. I think ~~by this time his job is finished~~ his job's done now. He'll be metamorphosing too.
He works the manual door winch.

24. INT. THE TRANSOM.
The Doctor emerges. The transom appears empty. He starts to edge along.

25. INT. INFRASTRUCTURE.

An iron hatch squinches aside. The Doctor enters. He stands on the metal balustrade. In the half-light, immobile pupal forms glisten, one upon the other, into the darkest depths of the chamber... motionless as guardsmen, they are an alien, inimical harbinger of terror yet to come.

If there is sufficient reflected light from the solar stack, we shall see that the pupae are ovoid and translucent and that the form of the adult Wirrn is vaguely discernible under the chrysalis.

The Doctor nerves himself and moves down into the infrastructure. He reaches the solar stack and takes out his torch. Its light shines on a red control handle. There are plus and minus signs on either end of its quadrant.

The lever is hard against minus. The Doctor reaches for the lever. There is a high, insect-type clatter from the darkness behind him. The Doctor spins round.

Noah is advancing towards him. A hardly recognizable Noah. The face is there still. But the shoulders merge into the menacing form of an adult Wirrn, seven foot long. ㉜ *Noah's face is about level with the Doctor's knees. But now, as it comes within striking range, the Wirrn rears up on its hindquarters like a praying mantis.*

The formidable tentacles poise over the Doctor who is backed against the dome. Again it emits the high, shrill rattle...

CLOSING TITLES

---

① The episode starts with Noah pulling his hand from his pocket. This section – up to the end of Scene 6 – should have been recorded at the end of Part Two. In the event time ran out, so it was recorded at the start of Part Four and edited into Part Three.

② As with the voices in Part One, the voice was pre-recorded (on 16 October) and played into the studio.

③ The High Minister's speech starts over the image of Noah and his mutated arm. Then we see Nerva in space, fading to the deserted transom area then back to Noah before cutting to Scene 2 as the speech continues.

④ Harry's line is actually inserted here.

⑤ This line is actually played into Scene 3.

⑥ The transom having been shown in Scene 1, this line is played over a close-up of Vira at the beginning of Scene 4.

⑦ For this line, we cut back to a close-up of Vira in the access chamber (recorded as Scene 6A).

⑧ Again, we cut back to the access chamber for this line (recorded as Scene 6C).

⑨ It was planned to record up to this point with Part Two. In the event, time ran out and these scenes were recorded with Part Four.

⑩ This scene was recorded after Scene 10. Scenes 9 and 10 were cut for reasons of timing.

⑪ The shutter was set into the transom set after the recording of Scene 9.

⑫ The cut-away shot of Noah's gun landing at Vira's feet, recorded at the end of the scene to be inserted, was edited in here to cover the cut sequence. A sound effect over a close shot of the Doctor is used to indicate that the shutter has closed again.

⑬ The complete scene was recorded and included in the initial edit of the episode. But Philip Hinchcliffe was worried that this sequence, with Noah begging Vira to kill him, perhaps went too far. After discussing it with his superior, Bill Slater, Hinchcliffe cut the sequence: 'You got a bit too much anguish. I decided that was perhaps going too far, and referred it up to Bill Slater... There was a bit of devilment in Bob Holmes.' Interviewed for the 1977 *Lively Arts* documentary *Whose Doctor Who?* Hinchcliffe revealed that he had twice had to cut sequences that he felt were too extreme. This was one of them, the other was cut from *The Seeds of Doom* (1976).

⑭ This short scene was recorded after Scene 10 and edited in.

⑮ This short scene was recorded with Scene 12A.

16   This scene was recorded with Part Four.

17   The picture fades between a close shot of the monitor, with the opening of Part One displayed, and a close-up of the Doctor's anguished, contorted face.

18   The grub slithers in from the adjoining chamber.

19   Rogin shouts at Lycett to close the door of the cryogenic chamber to keep the grub away from him.

20   The opening shots of Part One, and the additional material not seen then, was recorded with Part One. The close-ups of the monitor on which this is replayed were recorded with Part Four and edited in.

21   This scene was recorded after Scene 23.

22   The fission hoses became smaller handguns. The fission guns were working props, made by Tony Oxley. The fronts of the guns opened when the trigger was pulled – an effect achieved by fitting elastic bands inside the props. The effect on the victim was a star-shaped pattern of blue lightning strikes produced with a spark generator and overlaid on the picture.

23   Noah is further mutated now. The left side of his face is becoming a huge Wirrn eye.

24   An insert recorded after the main scene shows Rogin's foot pulling back as a blue star-shaped splodge is overlaid on the floor to show the effect of Noah's shot. This is followed by an insert of a fission gunshot hitting the shutter controls. The shutter then closes over Noah as he is still reeling from repeated hits. Presumably Noah has helped himself to another blaster from the armoury, as he threw his first gun to Vira in Scene 11.

25   A more involved sequence was originally planned. A visual effects requirements document describes the sequence: 'Blast from Noah's gun slices metal from the transom. Burst from fission hose sheers the beam above the sterility shutter. Beam falls knocking Noah flat and pinning his right arm.'

26   The Wirrn grub is actually forcing its way around the edge of the door.

27   The first shot we see is a close-up of Vira's gun firing. It is the same design as Noah's gun (see Part Two), which he threw to Vira in Scene 11.

28   CSO was used to show the tissue of the Wirrn grub tearing apart under the fire from the fission guns.

29   An earlier version of the script had the Doctor driving the Wirrn grub away with acid. The initial visual effects requirements document states: 'Carboy of acid to be taken from panel in the Access Chamber. Doctor breaks free from its ceramic connectors. Doctor throws carboy into glob. Carboy bubbles. Glob evaporates in a boiling tumescence of white foam and steam.'

30   This is achieved using the same roll-back-and-mix technique used in Part One, Scene 11.

31   The scene was recorded after Scene 23.

32   One of the adult Wirrn costumes was used for Noah from here on. For a few seconds, Noah's half-larval, half-human face is superimposed over the Wirrn head. Then it fades away.

THE ARK IN SPACE

by Robert Holmes

Part Four

1. INT. INFRASTRUCTURE. ❶

❷ *The noise blends into the cackle of a blaster.* ❸ *Blue tracers slam into the creature. Noah snarls and swings round to meet this new challenge.*

Vira and Sarah are up on the metal balustrade.

SARAH Run, Doctor! **Run!**

The Doctor needs no urging. He is already on his way.

NOAH ❹ Stay Vira… Stay!

~~**VIRA** Noah!~~

The blaster drops from her hand, bouncing off the steps into the chamber. ❺ *She stares with shock at the thing Noah has become. The Doctor swings on to the stairs. The three humans back towards the entrance hatch, expecting at any moment the Wirrn to launch itself across the chamber.*

NOAH Abandon the Ark, Vira. Take the transport ship… Leave now. If you stay you are doomed…

VIRA That would be desertion.

~~**NOAH** Save yourself. You can do nothing now… The Wirrn species must survive.~~

~~**DOCTOR WHO** At the cost of the human species?~~

~~**NOAH** Survival is all.~~

VIRA ~~We cannot abandon the Ark, Noah. You know that.~~

NOAH Then you must die. All of you. When the Wirrn emerge you will be hunted down and destroyed… as you destroyed us.

SARAH We've never destroyed…

She looks at the Doctor.

SARAH What's he mean?

There is a dry rattle from the Wirrn. It drifts a couple of yards nearer. The Doctor and companions edge back tensely.

NOAH Long ago… long ago… humans came to the old lands. For a thousand years the Wirrn fought them. But you humans destroyed the breeding colonies. The Wirrn were driven from Andromeda…

VIRA Andromeda..! So our star pioneers succeeded!

NOAH Since then we have drifted through space searching for a new habitat. The Ark is ours. It must be ours!

DOCTOR WHO But the Wirrn live in space. You don't need the Ark.

NOAH You know… nothing! We live in space but our breeding colonies are terrestrial.

DOCTOR WHO You could leave the Ark and go on… There's ~~enough~~ **plenty of** room in the galaxy for us all.

NOAH In the old lands senseless herbivores – cattle – were the hosts for our hatchings. Now we shall use the humans in the cryogenic chamber. We shall be ~~possessed~~ **informed** with all human knowledge. In one generation the Wirrn will become an advanced technological species. We shall have power.

VIRA That proposition is genetically impossible!

NOAH I already have all Dune's knowledge. High energy physics. Quantum mechanics. Every ramet in the next hatching of Wirrn will possess the sum of your race's learning. That is why you must die.

Suddenly there is a sound like a large paper bag tearing. They look round. Sarah clutches the Doctor's arm. One of the chrysalids is cracking. 6

Even as they look, a gelatinous, bristle-covered tentacle pushes out of the crack.

DOCTOR WHO Time to leave~~, I think~~.

They go out through the hatch.

NOAH *(Motionless)* Leave the Ark, Vira, or die with the rest of your race…

2. INT. CONTROL ROOM 2.

The lights are on here. Rogin is tidying up a harness of wires from one of the control panels. Harry, watching, rubs his jaw with the barrel of his fission hose.

HARRY Something must have happened to them.

ROGIN If we go out there it might happen to us.

HARRY I think we ought to investigate.

ROGIN There are no lights in the rest of the Ark, Harry. After what happened to Lycett I want to see where I am putting my feet.

Harry looks at his own stockinged feet.

HARRY You should worry…

There is a noise from the next room and he jumps for his fission hose.

The Doctor, Sarah and Vira enter.

HARRY Well, Doctor, it took you long enough to get here. I've been worried ~~out of my wits~~ **stiff**!

DOCTOR WHO We ~~ran~~ **bumped** into Noah.

ROGIN Again?

DOCTOR WHO Yes. ~~He was~~ Quite chatty this time. Garrulous even.

VIRA You've got the power on?

ROGIN No, Commander. I'm using photon energy. There's just enough to run the lights.

HARRY **Well** – what did Noah say?

SARAH Vamoose or stick around and get killed.

HARRY Ah, well. I'm ready **to go. Doctor?**

DOCTOR WHO ~~Would~~ anyone ~~care~~ for a jelly baby..? ~~Nobody?~~

He sits down, legs sprawled, jaws munching.

HARRY ~~Doctor we've got the TARDIS.~~ **Well, look, why don't we all just pile into the TARDIS?**

DOCTOR WHO No?

VIRA TARDIS..?

HARRY Sort of **space** ship thing **in there.** There's plenty of room for us all.

DOCTOR WHO Vira has no intention of leaving the Ark – have you?

VIRA I can't.

DOCTOR WHO Of course you can't. So neither can we.

SARAH Oh, well… that settles us.

DOCTOR WHO ~~In any case~~ **Besides,** we can't let the Wirrn eat all those cryogenic sleepers as though they were a lot of…

He looks at the jelly baby he was about to pop into his mouth.

HARRY Jelly babies?

The Doctor drops the sweet back into its bag.

DOCTOR WHO **Exactly.** Let them be turned into **a lot of** surrogate humans! It's the most immoral suggestion I've heard for centuries.

ROGIN How ~~are we going to~~ **can** we stop 'em!

DOCTOR WHO High voltage ~~current~~ **power**… If we could somehow run enough **electrical** power through the bulkheads of the cryogenic chamber –

SARAH ~~You mean~~ Like an electric fence?

DOCTOR WHO Yes. The Wirrn would never **dare to** cross it. The **only** problem is we don't have any electrical power. And they control its sources – the solar stacks.

HARRY We can forget that idea then, **can't we.**

SARAH Doctor –

DOCTOR WHO Unless we can lure them out of the infrastructure.

SARAH Hang on a minute –

VIRA How can we do that?

DOCTOR WHO Bait. Human bait. If ~~we~~ **one of us** could distract them for a few minutes, ~~while one of us slipped~~ **I might be able to get** down and turn~~ed~~ the power on –

SARAH Doctor, **will you** listen ~~to me~~!

DOCTOR WHO Sarah, we're trying to work out a plan.

VIRA That wouldn't work, Doctor. If they have Dune's knowledge they would simply turn it off again.

DOCTOR WHO Not if we electrified the switch itself.

ROGIN That'd take a long time. Those switch-boxes are nonconducting.

There is a heavy silence. The Doctor sighs.

DOCTOR WHO Well, we can't do without oxygen **indefinitely.** What were you trying to say, Sarah?

SARAH Oh, I was just wondering about the transport ship that Noah mentioned.

DOCTOR WHO What about it?

SARAH Surely it has its own power system, hasn't it?

A general look. Out of the mouths of babes…

ROGIN Four granovox turbines! That ship can generate twice the power of the Ark!

DOCTOR WHO How can we reach it?

Vira punches up a plan of the Ark on monitor. ⑦

VIRA Here's the connecting ramp. It's less than a hundred metres from this control room.

Rogin studies the plan.

ROGIN The only trouble is how do we run cable from the ship to the cryogenic chamber? If it's in the open they'll cut it.

DOCTOR WHO Aren't these conduits?

ROGIN Yes, but they're only **about** this wide. We'd need a mechanical cable-runner…

SARAH ~~Doctor~~. Why can't I take the cable through? **Well,** I'm ~~only~~ about that wide.

They stare at her in surprise.

HARRY It's hardly a job for ~~a girl, you know~~ **you, Sarah**.

ROGIN I reckon she might just squeeze through Doctor.

DOCTOR WHO Good girl Sarah… ~~Then~~ **Come on,** we'd better hurry, the Wirrn are going to start moving at any moment. You four go to the **transport** ship and I'll start wiring up the cryogenic chamber.

3. INT. THE TRANSOM. ⑧

~~Doctor, Harry, Sarah, Vira, Rogin emerge into the Transom and separate. Harry looks back.~~

~~HARRY Good luck, Doctor.~~

4. INT. DOCK SECTION.

A hatch opens and Rogin leads his party down a short steel ladder. Headroom is restricted. Harry looks down from the hatch. ⑨

He drops a coil of heavy cable through the hatch.

ROGIN **This is the transport ship. And here's the conduit.** ~~Well,~~ We'll connect one end up ~~there~~ **here** and you'll **have to drag the other end through** ~~carry it through there~~. *(Indicates conduit)*

He opens a conduit cover.

ROGIN Do you think we can manage it?

Harry clambers down to join them. Sarah looks into the conduit.

SARAH I'll have to.

VIRA Good luck! ⑩

HARRY It's very narrow, Sarah… Does that run straight to the cryogenic ~~place~~ chamber?

VIRA No. There are many junctions.

HARRY Then how is she going to ~~know~~ find her way… I mean in the dark and everything?

Rogin is sweating with the effort of opening the hatch to the transport ship. It is directly above him and looks like an upside-down conning tower. It opens with a sigh of released air. He pulls down a short alloy ladder.

VIRA ~~You'll take~~ We'll give her a two-way radio from the ship. We have a plan of the conduits. We can guide ~~her~~ you.

He climbs up into the ship. After a moment light floods down.

ROGIN All right, Commander.

Vira climbs the ladder.

5. INT. CREW DECK.

Vira comes up through the hatch. Sarah and then Harry follow. Rogin is switching on the power. We hear the hum of powerful generators. Rogin looks over the control module and switches on the video scanners.

ROGIN ~~Everything perfect~~ Beautiful… We could head straight home to Earth now. Nothing ~~to~~ could stop us.

Vira gazes at him. He meets her eye at first defiantly and then looks away guiltily.

VIRA ~~Your tests show the ship is in order?~~ You've completed all checks?

ROGIN Yes, Commander.

VIRA ~~Then we must~~ Right – waste no more time. Give ~~Sarah~~ the girl a radio.

Rogin moves to obey.

6. INT. CRYOGENIC CHAMBER.

The Doctor is soldering cable links – with his sonic screwdriver – over the wall sections. After a moment he stops and listens.

7. INT. ACCESS CHAMBER.

A Wirrn enters. ⑪ It starts round, its antennae probing the air.

8. INT. CRYOGENIC CHAMBER.

The Doctor shrugs. He returns to his work.

⑫ ~~10. INT. ACCESS CHAMBER.~~

~~The Wirrn moves towards the cryogenic chamber.~~

11. INT. DOCK SECTION.

Harry is looking at the coil of cable, one end of which now runs into the conduit. He bends over the conduit entrance.

HARRY ~~Are you coping~~ How are you doing, old girl?

SARAH *(Hollow VO)* ~~Elloncy uffa ungay twit…~~ How do you think I'm doing, twit?!

HARRY Sorry. Thought you were stuck. ⑬

No answer. Only a savage jerk on the cable.

12. INT. CRYOGENIC CHAMBER.

The Wirrn enters, it drifts forward, antennae searching, moving among the pallets.

We pick up the Doctor. He is lying frozen under one of the shrouds. The Wirrn pauses beside his pallet. We see its huge body just beyond the Doctor's head.

The Wirrn waves its antennae delicately and drifts on. The Doctor remains rigid but his eyelids sink in relief.

13. INT. CREW DECK.

Vira and Rogin are at the control module, the plan of the Ark in front of them. Sarah's voice issues suddenly from a speaker.

SARAH Hullo, Rogin..? Hullo? I've reached another junction. A sort of Y-fork.

Rogin stabs a finger on the plan.

ROGIN That's good! You're more than halfway… Take the right conduit. Understand?

SARAH *(Filter)* Got you.

Vira also taps the map and gives a look.

ROGIN *(Nodding)* Sarah?

SARAH *(Filter)* Yes?

ROGIN The section you're in now runs right through the infrastructure. Move as quietly as you can.

14. INT. CONDUIT 'A'.
Sarah is lying full length in a dark tube. She wears a headset and throat mike. She is breathing heavily from her exertions.

SARAH Understood…
She inches forward.

15. INT. CRYOGENIC CHAMBER.
The Doctor eases himself up. The chamber is empty. He crosses the room quietly and looks through into the access chamber. He goes back to work on the final section of the wall.

16. INT. INFRASTRUCTURE.
Still only the reflected light from the solar stacks. A Wirrn in a litter of many abandoned shells. The Wirrn moves forward. It lowers its antennae to the conduit that runs along one section of the wall.

Now it moves along the conduit at about the pace Sarah might be supposed to be moving…

17. INT. CONDUIT 'A'.
Sarah is still dragging herself along. Now one side of the conduit is replaced by an inspection cover of extrapolated alloy. The big luminous green eye of a Wirrn presses against the cover. She can see it four inches from her face.

The eye withdraws and there is a high, angry Wirrn rattle. A tentacle smashes into the grille, trying to force through. Sarah gives a cry of terror and wriggles past the grille.

18. INT. INFRASTRUCTURE.
The Wirrn closes its huge mandibles over the conduit and starts ripping away strips of metal. It is rattling furiously and working itself into a right old paddy. 🄯

19. INT. CONDUIT 'B'.
Sarah wriggles along for her life, the sounds of metallic destruction receding behind her.

20. INT. CRYOGENIC CHAMBER.
The Doctor has finished his task. He takes the cover off the conduit and listens… nothing.

21. INT. CREW DECK.
Harry has joined Vira and Rogin.

ROGIN Now it's the second opening you come to on your left. Understand?
SARAH *(Filter)* Yes… *(Heaving breath)*…
Rogin, is it much further?
ROGIN No… another 15 metres. You're almost there.
He takes the end of the cable from Harry and opens junction box.
SARAH *(Filter)* I hope so… ~~I can't~~ **I don't think I can**… go on much longer.
VIRA Yes you can.
HARRY Come along, Sarah. Stick at it~~, Sarah~~!
SARAH *(Filter)* ~~Keep getting stuck –~~ That's the trouble.

22. INT. CONDUIT 'A'.
Sarah, as before, very weary.
SARAH I keep getting stuck
HARRY *(Filter)* Marvellous thing about old Sarah. Terrific sense of humour…
Sarah grits her teeth and inches onward.

23. INT. CRYOGENIC CHAMBER.
The Doctor hears a sound in the conduit. Then a muffled moan of despair.
DOCTOR WHO Come on, Sarah… Hurry!
SARAH *(VO)* Doctor? Where are you?
DOCTOR WHO Straight ahead… look – I'll shine a light…
He flashes his torch in the conduit.
DOCTOR WHO Can you see?
SARAH *(VO)* Yes… *(Voice strained)* Doctor, I can't move!
DOCTOR WHO Of course you can~~, my dear~~. You've got this far.
SARAH *(VO)* No! I'm stuck!
DOCTOR WHO Don't panic, Sarah, **don't panic**… Ease ~~yourself~~ round and try again.

24. INT. CONDUIT 'A'.
Sarah tries desperately to free herself.
SARAH ~~It's no use, Doctor …~~ I'm jammed – I can't move either forward or back!
She starts to sob with frustration and fear.

25. INT. CRYOGENIC CHAMBER.
Sarah's muted sobs. The Doctor rubs his nose.
DOCTOR WHO *(Cruelly)* That's right! Blub away. I might expect that from you!

26. INT. CONDUIT 'A'.

SARAH ~~(Crying) My hips are jammed… I can't move either forward or back… back…~~
DOCTOR WHO *(VO)* Stop whining, girl! You're ~~utterly~~ useless…
SARAH *(Shocked)* Oh, Doctor..?

27. INT. CRYOGENIC CHAMBER.

DOCTOR WHO Oh, Doctor..! Is that all you have to say for yourself? **Stupid foolish girl.** ~~You miserable, hopeless little fool! I tell you, Sarah,~~ We should never have relied on you. I knew you'd let us down…

28. INT. CONDUIT 'A'.

DOCTOR WHO *(VO)* That's the trouble with girls like you. You think you're tough but when you're really up against it… you've no guts at all.

Anger provides the spur. Sarah makes a tremendous wrenching effort. She grips in front, then moves forward.

29. INT. CRYOGENIC CHAMBER.

DOCTOR WHO Hundreds of lives at stake… and you lie there blubbing.
SARAH *(VO)* You wait till I get out!

The Doctor hears her moving. He grins in delight. A moment later Sarah is scrabbling at the entrance to the conduit. He leans in to pull her out.

SARAH I can manage! I don't need your help, thank you!

But she is exhausted. He helps her out and she almost collapses. The Doctor holds her.

DOCTOR WHO Yes you do, yes you do, yes you do… Splendid! You've done marvellously, Sarah! I'm very proud of you! **I really am very proud of you.**

She stares at him, realizing.

SARAH **What?!** Conned again..! You're a brute. ~~You —~~
DOCTOR WHO Me a brute? Don't be ungrateful. I was only encouraging you. Come on.

He unclips her belt with the cable-grip attached. Sarah takes off her head radio.

SARAH *(Into mike)* Hullo, Rogin…

30. INT. CREW DECK.

SARAH ~~(VO filter) I'm in the cryogenic section —~~
HARRY ~~She's made it!~~
SARAH *(VO filter)* The Doctor's connecting the cable now.
ROGIN Beautiful! Let me know when to switch the power through.

31. INT. CRYOGENIC CHAMBER.

The Doctor is making a final connection with his sonic screwdriver.
DOCTOR WHO Close the door to the access chamber, Sarah.

32. INT. ACCESS CHAMBER.

A Wirrn stands in the centre of the chamber, antennae waving. We see it from Sarah's POV then take her reaction as she stands in the doorway.

She gives a cry of fear. The Wirrn rattles angrily and swoops towards her. Sarah slams the access panel into place.

DOCTOR WHO *(OOV)* ~~Come away from that door.~~

33. INT. CRYOGENIC CHAMBER.

A scream of rage from the Wirrn. It crashes into the panel with an impact that seems to shake the Ark. The Doctor picks up Sarah's discarded radio.

DOCTOR WHO Are you ready ~~Rogin~~ man?
ROGIN Yes. **15**
DOCTOR WHO **Switch on** now!
ROGIN Right.

33A. INT. ACCESS CHAMBER.

The Wirrn gathers itself then lurches forward into another battering assault on the door panel. It hits the panel and there is a blasting crackle of high voltage electricity. **16** *The Wirrn screams and falls back, smoking and writhing.*

34. INT. CRYOGENIC CHAMBER.

The cry of the wounded Wirrn lessens. The Doctor's tension recedes.
DOCTOR WHO Not bad for a lash up!
SARAH Has it gone, do you think?

DOCTOR WHO *(Nods)* Reporting to the others. They'll know where we are now.

VIRA *(VO filter)* Hullo, Doctor… **Are you all right down there?**

DOCTOR WHO ~~So far so good~~. **For the moment.**

35. INT. CREW DECK.

VIRA You lack confidence?

DOCTOR WHO *(VO filter)* The Wirrn ~~aren't beaten yet~~ **don't give up that easily**. They need the Ark ~~and they won't give up easily~~. How is it your end?

VIRA There's been no sign of them in this part of the Ark.

~~**DOCTOR WHO** *(VO filter)* Get Rogin to run a cable round the entrance hatch. Once they work out where the power is coming from you'll be in trouble.~~

~~*Rogin takes over the speaker.*~~

~~**ROGIN** Hullo, Doctor. That won't work. The ship's held to the Ark by synestic locks.~~

36. INT. CRYOGENIC CHAMBER.

~~**DOCTOR WHO** You mean if you electrify –~~

~~**ROGIN** *(VO filter)* We'd reverse the magnetism and the ship would be just pushed out into space.~~

~~**DOCTOR WHO** Well, you'd better think of something, Rogin, before the Wirrn think of you.~~

~~**ROGIN** *(VO filter)* Don't worry. I've got a scanner on the decking-funnel. If they try coming through there I'll just turn on the motors and fry them.~~

SARAH Doctor – !

DOCTOR WHO I think we've got some more visitors. Don't let the power drop.

Faintly, from the access chamber, we hear the Wirrn rattle.

37. INT. ACCESS CHAMBER.

Two Wirrn are facing the cryogenic chamber. They turn towards each other. Their antennae lock for a few seconds. Then one of the Wirrn backs off and makes his way out of the chamber.

38. INT. CRYOGENIC CHAMBER.

The Doctor and Sarah close to the wall, listening…

DOCTOR WHO Gone away…

SARAH I think so. I can't hear anything now.

DOCTOR WHO *(Frowning)* **Either** discretion **is** the better part of valour. Or…

SARAH Or what?

DOCTOR WHO **Or** they're planning something.

He looks at his home-built electrocution outfit.

SARAH Yes, but we're safe here, aren't we?

DOCTOR WHO Unless they chew through the floor. I've left a free-running cable just in case… *(He kneels and prods at the floor)* The insulation should stand up to it.

Suddenly, from the grille broken by the larva Wirrn, a tentacle whips out and lassoes Sarah's legs. She screams in terror as she is dragged towards the grille. The Wirrn screams in triumph. ⑰

The Doctor drops his spare cable – unable to use it without electrocuting Sarah. He grabs one of the fire axes from a chest. The Wirrn is forcing up through the grille with incredible power. Metal is rending around the grille.

The Doctor chops savagely at the Wirrn tentacle. The Wirrn roars. At the third slashing blow it releases Sarah. The tentacle whips towards the Doctor. He jumps back, carrying Sarah with him. They fall. The Wirrn powers further up through the grille.

The Doctor is up on his feet. He snatches up the spare cable, and rips off the insulating cap. He runs at the Wirrn, holding the cable like a wire hose. The tentacle lashes towards him.

The Doctor catches it on the cable end. There is a flash and a ball of smoke. The tentacle blazes and falls. The Wirrn shrieks, tries to reverse out of the grille. But it is wedged. The Doctor stabs the naked power cable into its head. The Wirrn burns and dies. As the smoke clears the Doctor turns shakily away. Sarah is wan-faced. She sits weakly on a pallet.

~~**SARAH** Oh, Doctor…~~

DOCTOR WHO Cheer up. We're still on our feet.

He replaces the insulation cap on the cable.

SARAH Those things are so… so venomous! They'll never give up.

DOCTOR WHO And neither shall we, Sarah. What we're ~~defending~~ **protecting** here is too precious.

39. INT. INFRASTRUCTURE.

Close on the control panel of the solar stack. Wirrn 🔞 *tentacle moves on to the lever and pushes it over the quadrant.*

40. INT. CONTROL ROOM 2.

A Wirrn 🔞 *hovers over the switchboard. As the full lights come on it moves a tentacle across the row of switches.*

41. INT. CRYOGENIC CHAMBER.

Full lighting. Sarah and the Doctor look around.

SARAH Why have they turned the power **back** on?

DOCTOR WHO *(Shrugs)* ~~I've no doubt~~ We'll find out soon enough.

NOAH *(VO)* Vira! Can you hear me?

DOCTOR WHO *(Facing speaker)* She can hear you. What do you want, Noah?

NOAH *(VO)* Your resistance is useless. We control the Ark.

DOCTOR WHO And we control the cryogenic chamber. I repeat – what do you want?

42. INT. CONTROL ROOM 2.

NOAH *(In his Wirrn guise)* We offer you safe passage from the Ark. Surrender now and your lives will be spared.

DOCTOR WHO *(VO)* Not a chance.

NOAH What does Vira say?

DOCTOR WHO *(VO)* She agrees with me.

42A. INT. CREW DECK.

DOCTOR WHO *(VO)* **Don't you, Vira.**

NOAH *(VO)* Let Vira speak. She is the commander.

DOCTOR WHO She's busy – resuscitating more humans.

43. INT. CRYOGENIC CHAMBER.

NOAH *(VO)* You lie!

DOCTOR WHO Listen Noah – now hear me. You're beaten. The Ark is of no value to you without its humans… so why don't you just leave us in peace?

44. INT. CONTROL ROOM 2.

NOAH Humans require two mass-pounds of oxygen a day to stay alive, Doctor. We Wirrn can live for years without fresh oxygen. If you refuse to surrender we shall shut down the oxygen pumps.

45. INT. CRYOGENIC CHAMBER.

DOCTOR WHO And if we ~~do~~ surrender?

NOAH *(VO)* I have said. You will be allowed to leave the Ark.

DOCTOR WHO The Wirrn hate all humans. Once we step outside this chamber we'd be attacked.

NOAH *(VO)* I am the swarm leader. I guarantee your safety. The Wirrn will spare your lives… but leave the sleepers for us! 🔞

~~**DOCTOR WHO** Those are impossible conditions. We can never accept them.~~

~~**NOAH** *(VO)* Then die slowly. In the end it will be the same. The Wirrn must triumph!~~

DOCTOR WHO Noah, listen to me. If there's any part of you that's still human… if you've any memory of the man you once were… Leave the Ark. Lead the swarm ~~out~~ into space.

46. INT. CONTROL ROOM 2.

DOCTOR WHO *(VO)* That's where the Wirrn belong. Not on Earth – not where you were born~~, Noah~~. Remember the **wind and the sun,** **the** fields and ~~the woods, the wind and the sun,~~ the blue sky… That's the Earth, Noah. It's for ~~people — it's for~~ the human race. **Don't abandon it.** ~~Don't destroy them.~~

The Wirrn has backed from the switchboard. Its antennae move restlessly.

NOAH *(VO)* I have no memory of the Earth.

47. INT. CREW DECK. 🔞

Harry starts suddenly. He peers closer at the scanner.

HARRY I say, Rogin!

~~**ROGIN** Yes?~~

HARRY I don't want to be an alarmist but I think ~~there's~~ **I saw** something moving ~~out there~~.

Rogin leans over and looks at the scanner. It shows the dock section. Rogin trims the scanner. Edging into the shot are the legs and antennae of a Wirrn. Then a second Wirrn.

ROGIN You're right! They're coming up the funnel, Commander.

VIRA Start starboard four.

ROGIN *(On control module)* Starboard four running.

VIRA Negative thrust out.

ROGIN Neg thrust… *(Moving control)* out!

VIRA Full boost.

ROGIN Full boost… *(Presses button)* Check. *Dials flicker. Lights flash. A digital display flicks from five down to zero* 🟢 *and – boom! We hear the blast of a rocket motor. On the scanner the picture of the dock section disappears in a blast of fire and smoke.*

VIRA Close boost.

ROGIN Close boost.

VIRA Close starboard four.

ROGIN And close starboard four. *The look at the scanner. The smoke is sucked away through exhaust ducts. The dock section is empty.*

HARRY ~~By Jove, that must have~~ I bet that singed their whiskers, ~~eh?~~ for them.

ROGIN They won't try that again ~~Commander~~.

VIRA I wonder if Noah…

ROGIN Noah?

VIRA It's not important.

DOCTOR WHO *(VO filter)* Are you all right over there?

HARRY ~~Hello,~~ Ahoy there, Doctor! Yes, we're fine, thanks.

DOCTOR WHO *(VO filter)* We heard a rocket engine.

HARRY Just a warning blast. How are things with you?

48. INT. CRYOGENIC CHAMBER.

DOCTOR WHO *(Into radio)* ~~We're holding our own.~~ All right at the moment.

HARRY *(VO filter)* Oh. Good.

DOCTOR WHO Keep in touch.

HARRY ~~*(Filter)* Jolly good.~~

The Doctor puts the radio down.

SARAH I don't know if it's my imagination but it seems to be getting stuffy in here.

DOCTOR WHO It is **your** imagination.

SARAH You'd say that, anyway…

50. INT. CREW DECK. (MODEL SHOT)

Wirrn over hull. 🟢

VIRA They're coming in through the reversion vents!

ROGIN Look at them! There's ~~an~~ whole army **of them** out there… 🟢

VIRA *(On radio)* Doctor – the Wirrn have space-walked round the Ark and have broken into the cargo hold.

51. INT. CRYOGENIC CHAMBER.

DOCTOR WHO *(On radio)* How many of them are there, Vira?

VIRA *(VO filter)* We cannot say. But it looks as though the entire swarm is attacking.

DOCTOR WHO *(On radio)* And how long will it take them to reach your control deck?

VIRA *(VO filter)* A few minutes only. The interior bulkheads have a low stress factor.

The Doctor wastes two seconds in thought. He snaps his fingers.

DOCTOR WHO Tell Rogin to cut the power. We're coming out!

52. INT. CREW DECK.

Rogin cuts the power.

ROGIN Power off, Doctor.

DOCTOR WHO *(VO filter)* **Good.** Set ~~all~~ the controls on automatic **take-off** and evacuate the ship. Hurry!

Rogin looks at Vira.

VIRA We'll do as you say, Doctor.

53. INT. TRANSOM. 🟢

The Doctor bursts into the transom, he drags Sarah after him.

DOCTOR WHO **Come on, Sarah. Come on.** Run, ~~Sarah~~ **girl**! Run!

They sprint off down the transom.

54. INT. CREW DECK.

Harry opens a plate on the forward bulkhead. An armoured window behind the plate gives a view of the forward compartment. But the view is immediately obscured by a Wirrn pushing up against the window. Its menacing rattle sounds faintly. Harry slams the plate.

HARRY The hull's absolutely ~~solid~~ **crawling** with the brutes!

As if to emphasize his point there is a heavy crash against the bulkhead.

ROGIN Are you coming or staying?

Harry turns. Vira is already descending through the floor hatch.

55. INT. DOCK SECTION.

The Doctor helps Vira off the ladder.

DOCTOR WHO Into the Ark, fast you can! You, too, Sarah… *(As Harry drops off the ladder)* Go with the girls, Harry… ㉖ Rogin, help me with the synestic locks.

ROGIN I thought that was your idea.

There are three locking bars attached to the base of the ship. The Doctor and Rogin struggle to remove the corroded plates that control the magnetic flow. Harry looks back.

HARRY What are you ~~trying~~ **going** to do, Doctor?

DOCTOR WHO Just… look after Sarah for me, Harry.

Harry exits.

The Doctor breaks his plate free and drops it into his jacket pocket. ㉗ Rogin removes his plate.

DOCTOR WHO ~~All right.~~ Leave this one to me.

He is already at work on the third plate.

ROGIN You know what happens when you cut that lock?

DOCTOR WHO Get into the Ark, man! No point in both of us being killed by the blast.

ROGIN We don't want trouble with the space technician's union, Doctor. That's my job.

He chops the Doctor over the carotid sinus, catches him as he collapses and drags him across the dock section.

56. INT. CREW DECK. ㉘

A Wirrn is bursting through the bulkhead. ㉙ It gives a triumphant shriek.

On the scanner we see Rogin, craning upwards, working just under camera vision. He moves back and we see the synestic plate in his hand.

Then there is a roar from the rocket motors. Rogin and the picture of the dock section disappear in a blast of white vapour.

TELECINE 3 (MODEL SHOT) ㉚

The Ark from space POV.

Suddenly its forward rocket section separates from the rest of the Ark. It lifts, gathers speed, and moves out into space.

The rocket ship moves through space.

57. INT. CONTROL ROOM 2.

T/c 4 on a monitor. Vira, Harry and Sarah staring silently. ㉛

VIRA They must both have died instantly.

Sarah sniffles. Harry gives her a clumsy squeeze.

HARRY Come on, ~~old girl~~ **Sarah**. He'd **have** want**ed** you to be brave.

The Doctor enters. They stare in shock.

VIRA Doctor! Where's Rogin?

DOCTOR WHO Rogin's dead. I woke up in a protection hatch…

Sarah runs over to him.

SARAH Oh, Doctor, ~~you did get away~~ **you're safe.**

DOCTOR WHO Yes… We're all safe now, Sarah. Thanks to ~~one man's~~ **Rogin's** bravery and perhaps something else…

VIRA Something – else?

DOCTOR WHO Some vestige of ~~the~~ human spirit. Was Noah ~~one move ahead of us – and~~ on our side **and one step ahead of us** at the end?

VIRA You mean by leading the swarm into the shuttle?

HARRY Look – !

A call light is flashing on the console. ㉜ Vira flicks a switch down.

VIRA Space station Nerva.

NOAH *(VO filter)* Goodbye Vira… ㉝

~~VIRA~~ ~~Noah?~~

Even as she speaks the rocket in the monitor picture, now only a bright speck in the distance, explodes in a little ball of light, and as it fades we hear the explosion through the radio loudspeaker. ㉞

SARAH The shuttle's blown up!

VIRA ~~Noah~~ **He** must have known that would happen. ~~He~~ **Noah** deliberately neglected to set the rocket stabilizers.

DOCTOR WHO ~~Perhaps~~ **More than a vestige of** ~~the~~ human spirit.

~~VIRA Noah neglected to set the rocket stabilizers. He must have known that would happen.~~

He walks over to the clover-leaf kiosk of the matterbeam.

DOCTOR WHO It can all begin now, **Vira. Mankind is safe.**

VIRA I must get my people back to Earth. Now that I've lost the transport ship I'll have to rely on this matter transmitter.

DOCTOR WHO Yes.

VIRA It will be a long operation. It can only convey three people at a time.

The Doctor plays with the controls.

DOCTOR WHO It could if it was functioning properly. The signal's faulty. Probably your diode receptors. I'll **just** beam down and check them.

SARAH To Earth?

The Doctor hands the TARDIS key to her.

DOCTOR WHO Yes, that's where the trouble is. Fetch me a coat from the TARDIS. ~~You remember the weather down there.~~ **You never know what the solar flares have done to the weather.**

Harry and Sarah exchange glances and exit.

VIRA ~~Do you think it's~~ **It isn't** anything serious?

DOCTOR WHO ~~It may be nothing~~ **Probably no** more than a spot of corrosion – whatever it is it shouldn't take too long to fix. ~~I'll also be able~~ **And it'll give me a chance** to see if the planet is fully viable again. ~~Where have they got to?~~ **What's keeping them..?** Sarah?

He looks round. Harry is hurrying back struggling into a duffel coat and clutching a pair of shoes. Sarah is swathed in a yellow anorak suit and putting on a woolly hat.

SARAH Coming… Here's your coat.

DOCTOR WHO ~~Did I say anything about you two coming?~~ **I don't remember inviting you two.**

SARAH No, you didn't but **here** we are.

HARRY ~~Don't forget~~ **Well**, the Brigadier told me to ~~stay~~ **stick** with you, Doctor, and orders is orders.

The Doctor shrugs helplessly and looks at Vira with a smile.

DOCTOR WHO I hope you don't mind ~~us leaving you~~ **being left**.

VIRA ~~There is much to be done.~~ **Well, I won't be alone for long.** Life is returning to the Ark and soon to the world.

DOCTOR WHO ~~Oh Vira. Have one of these…~~ **Have a jelly baby, Vira.** 🟤35

VIRA **Thank you.**

The three travellers step into the transmat kiosk. The Doctor presses a control and waves. They vanish. 🟤36

VIRA Thank you. 🟤37

CLOSING TITLES

🔘1 This scene together with Scene 2 was recorded at the end of Part Three.

🔘2 The episode starts with the adult Noah Wirrn approaching the Doctor.

🔘3 It is Vira's blaster (with same blue star-burst effect) rather than a fission gun.

🔘4 Noah is the only speaking Wirrn. The lines were spoken by Kenton Moore into an off-stage microphone, treated, and played into the studio in real time.

🔘5 We hear the blaster fall, and when we next see Vira she no longer has it.

🔘6 This was originally planned as an inserted model shot. In fact a full-size prop was used.

🔘7 Three telejector slides showed a diagrammatic layout of the Ark on a monitor. The first shows the Ark from the outside as a cross-section; the second the Ark from above; the third a close-up of the central section of the Ark where the transport ship is located.

🔘8 This scene was recorded with Part Three to save re-erecting the transom set.

🔘9 The hatch is actually at 'ground' level, and Vira leads the party through to the transport ship.

🔘10 Rogin operates a control and a ladder drops down from the bottom of the transport ship.

⑪   Three adult Wirrn were made – two costumes, and the 'prop' Wirrn queen with her pincer claw at the base. All three were constructed from latex and fibreglass over a bamboo frame. Philip Hinchcliffe was slightly disappointed with the Wirrn: 'The bodies were a bit too shiny and new, they just didn't look organic enough. You had Noah being ravaged by this green virus, and the make-up department had a field day with that, but the finished creature didn't quite have the right impact.'

⑫   There is no Scene 9 in the camera script – it was deleted before studio recording, and this is noted on the script ('No Scene 9').

⑬   While recording the scenes in which Sarah had to crawl along the sections of ducting, Elisabeth Sladen really did become stuck – only to be 'unglued' when one of her fellow actors went around the rear of the set and slapped her behind.

⑭   The Wirrn rattles at the grille, but does not rip away the metal.

⑮   Rogin's line is blank in the camera script.

⑯   A spark generator provided the electrical discharge, enhanced by a pyrotechnic flash and smoke.

⑰   This sequence is simplified and the axe is not used. The Doctor drags Sarah away from the Wirrn, is grabbed himself but breaks free, then dispatches it with the power cable, amidst smoke and a flash. There is a brief cut-away to a close-up of Sarah reacting – which is actually re-used from Part Three, Scene 21 where she is watching the fission guns' effect on the Wirrn grub.

⑱   The Wirrn in this scene was played by Nick Hobbs.

⑲   The Wirrn in this scene (and in the following scenes in control room 2) – Noah – was played by stunt man Stuart Fell.

⑳   For this line we cut back to Noah/Wirrn in the control room.

㉑   The sequences shown on the monitor in this scene, together with monitor sequences for Scene 56, were recorded ahead of the rest of Part Four, and played back on the screen.

㉒   The countdown clock was a prop provided by Century 21 (Gerry Anderson's company), as were some of the other control systems used in this story.

㉓   29 seconds of model film showing the 'puppet' Wirrn crawling over the Ark's hull is played on to the transport ship's monitor. Only a few seconds of the material is seen, cut in here.

㉔   Part of a second model sequence (lasting 18 seconds in total) is cut in here – a closer shot favouring the Wirrn leader (presumably Noah).

㉕   This scene was recorded with Part Three to save re-erecting the Transom set.

㉖   Cut in here is a brief insert of a Wirrn on the crew deck of the ship.

㉗   This is the piece of synestic lock that saves the Doctor's life when Styre shoots him in *The Sontaran Experiment*, Part Two, Scene 15.

㉘   The sequences shown on the monitor in this scene, together with monitor sequences for Scene 47, were recorded ahead of the rest of Part Four, and played back on the screen.

㉙   The Wirrn are on the crew deck – we do not see them breaking in.

㉚   Telecine 1 and 2 were the filmed model sequences shown on the monitor in Scene 50. Like those inserts, this was a model sequence shot on 16mm film. The total duration of the film work for this sequence was 23 seconds.

㉛   T/c 4 was 17 seconds of 16mm film showing the (model) transport ship travelling through space.

㉜   It is accompanied by a sound effect – actually the same sound effect used for Davros' life-support systems' failure in *Genesis of the Daleks* Part Five, Scene 6.

㉝   After this line a brief shot of two Wirrn on the transport ship is inserted. The image is 'peaked' to white-out.

㉞   Telecine 5, 16mm film of the shuttle exploding, was played on to the monitor. The model sequence of the shuttle travelling in space then exploding lasted 24 seconds, of which only about three seconds was used. The sequence is silent, with no explosion heard through the speaker.

㉟   He throws the bag to her.

㊱   This was achieved by 'roll-back-and-mix' (see *Robot* Part One, Scene 1).

㊲   Having smiled as she says that life is returning to the Ark, Vira laughs on her final line – the first overt emotion she has displayed.

THE SONTARAN EXPERIMENT

BY BOB BAKER AND DAVE MARTIN

PART ONE first transmitted 22 February 1975 at 17.30
PART TWO 1 March 1975 at 17.30

Overview

The contrast to *The Ark in Space* is marked. While the previously transmitted story was set in a claustrophobic, sterile environment, *The Sontaran Experiment* takes place on the open, undisciplined landscape of a deserted future Earth.

And while the action of *The Ark in Space* builds slowly over its four episodes as the Wirrn develop and take control, *The Sontaran Experiment* hits the ground running. Even in the first episode, before the true nature of the threat is revealed, the Doctor and his companions are in a rush. They don't stop running from one place to another until the end of the story.

Which is just as well. The script is accomplished and the tension and action build over the course of the story. But the notion that an entire invasion fleet is waiting for Styre's rather circumspect report on the human race – which is no longer on Earth anyway – does not really stand up to scrutiny. But this is a minor quibble when set against the elements of this story that do succeed – the continuing development of the new Doctor's character; the detailed background and characterization of the Sontarans; the interplay and suspicion between the colonists… It may be a minor league story in terms of its length and its content, but *The Sontaran Experiment* is expertly told.

Origin

Having agreed with Philip Hinchcliffe to abandon one of the three six-part stories planned for Season Twelve, and replace it with a four-parter and a two-parter, Robert Holmes set about looking for a suitable writer for the scripts, which were needed at short notice to begin the main production block in September. Terrance Dicks and Barry Letts suggested to him the Bristol-based writing partnership of Bob Baker and Dave Martin.

Baker and Martin had been submitting material to *Doctor Who* since 1969 and had so far developed three broadcast serials: *The Claws of Axos* (1971), *The Mutants* and *The Three Doctors* (1972/3). Although Holmes knew of Baker and Martin, he had not worked with them before and rang them up to see if they were interested in the assignment of producing a quick filler. Baker and Martin had recently been writing for series such as ITC's *SkiBoy* and had also developed a science fiction serial for HTV entitled *Sky*.

Storyline

The briefing which Holmes gave Baker and Martin concerned the outline discussed with John Lucarotti for *The Ark in Space* – the notion of an Earth of the far future evacuated because of an impending disaster. The desolate Earth would be the setting for the serial, which could be made entirely on location.

Although he generally disliked reusing old monsters, Holmes also suggested that the villain of the piece should be a Sontaran. The Sontarans, a war-loving clone species, had been created by Holmes the previous year for the serial *The Time Warrior* (1973/4), while he was still a freelance writer, which meant that he would receive a small copyright fee for their use.

It was believed that the costume for Linx, the only Sontaran seen in *The Time Warrior*, was still in storage along with the spherical Sontaran spaceship from that serial. This would help reduce costs for the story, and Holmes told the writers to include only one Sontaran in their script. Fascinated by the concept of his own creation, Holmes outlined the character of the Sontaran field major he envisaged for the serial, and the brutal military assessment survey which the Sontaran would be conducting.

Having considered the brief, Baker and Martin called Holmes back to discuss a storyline with him. Interviewed in 1988, Bob Baker said: 'We phoned the storyline to him. I don't think we even did an outline. We talked through the story and he said, "Get on with it!" It's wonderful when that happens – writing outlines can sometimes take longer than writing the script.'

Since the serial would be made totally on location, Baker and Martin suggested some of the remote and bleak West Country venues which they had written into *Sky* and proposed Dartmoor as the setting for a ruined London. Baker: 'The idea was of this lovely landscape, like the *Planet of the Apes* film where the Statue of Liberty is sticking up out of the beach. We'd have loved to have had the top of Nelson's Column sticking out through the grass, but you can't afford that. I mean, it's *Doctor Who!*'

The storyline, entitled *The Destructors*, was formally commissioned on Thursday 23 May, and Baker and Martin were asked to deliver their basic idea within four days (although the formal date given was Thursday 20 June).

Scripts

To aid the writing process with regard to the new incarnation of the Doctor, Baker and Martin travelled to London and were shown a rough edit of *Robot*. The pair immediately warmed to Tom Baker's interpretation of the character. They were also given more information about the basic ideas behind Lucarotti's *The Ark in Space* which would precede their story in broadcast order. As a result, the writers did their usual scientific research for a factual basis upon which to develop their story. They envisaged an Earth of the future purified by the solar-flare activity, and effectively re-evolving all over again from nothing in an act of rebirth. This notion also linked in with *Entropy*, a short film which Bob Baker had made in 1956.

The first script for *The Destructors* was commissioned on Wednesday 5 June (despite the fact that Baker and Martin's storyline was not formally delivered until Wednesday 12 June). The target for delivery of the first script was set for Monday 1 July to allow plenty of time for any re-writes before pre-production began in August. The first script was delivered on Saturday 6 July – the same day that the second was commissioned for delivery by Monday 15 July. The final version of this arrived at the BBC on Friday 12 August. Both scripts were rapidly accepted by Holmes.

The GalSec crew encountered by the Doctor's party originally numbered nine. In the scripts, no accent for the GalSec team was mentioned, although Roth's lines used the term 'yunnerstand?', Vural said their landing on Earth was for a 'looksee' and Erak used the phrase 'musta gone bush' (Part One, Scenes 17 and 24). In various pre-production documents, the GalSec characters were usually referred to as 'South Africans' and Roth was originally referred to as 'Savage'. A later list of characters dated Tuesday 3 September gave some more background on the ranks and posts of the GalSec astronauts: Roth was the 'navigator', Vural was the 'leader officer', Erak was a 'younger officer', Krans was the 'chief engineer' and the prisoner was an 'engineer'. The other GalSec character seen, Zake, was not named until very shortly before location work began.

When developing the robot used by Sontaran Field Major Styre in their scripts, Baker and Martin gave minimal description – although the notion of something like a golf buggy was discussed. The writers had originally visualized a machine that could jump across short distances at the speed of sound, suddenly appearing at a particular stop after moving invisibly across the landscape. Bob Baker: 'It was supposed to move almost at the speed of sound for very short distances – just whip across the landscape and *be* somewhere. Almost invisible, just *arrive.*'

Reading the scripts, Philip Hinchcliffe was struck by several aspects, as he commented to Robert Holmes and Barry Letts on Tuesday 23 July:

1. Story background

Not enough references to Earth as the forbidden planet, linking with the Ark story. The Sontaran 'master plan' is unclear – perhaps Styre reports to his superiors near end.

2. Loose ends

The savage – how did he get there? Who is he? Needs to be clearer. Is he mentally unbalanced or is his regression due to contact with Styre or the 'golf buggy'?

THE SONTARAN EXPERIMENT: OVERVIEW

3. Vural et al

How does their space patrol link with the frozen humans in the Ark? Is the manacled prisoner in the dungeon one of Vural's crew members?

4. The Dr as hero

The new scenario is more or less as follows:

At the end of Episode 1 the Dr eludes Vural & Co who are themselves captured by the 'golf buggy'. The Dr reaches the priory (perhaps escaping via the pit or following the 'golf buggy') and stumbles across the Sontaran spacecraft. There he 'fixes' the energizing probe. Meanwhile Sarah and Harry are at the point of death. Enter the Dr to save them, with the added twist that he has to play for time before luring Styre back to the spacecraft where he is blown up by the faulty energizing probe.

It strikes me that in this new version we shall have to lose the sub-plot of Vural's mind being 'taken over' by Styre and the battle of moral wills. This does not break my heart because we want the Dr in physical action at the climax of the story but perhaps we could keep the idea of the Dr's <u>moral</u> supremacy somehow.

5. Ending

Very difficult in the space of two episodes, I know, but we need to round off the story more emphatically, linking back to the *Ark* and forward to the Dalek adventure.

6. Special effects

How crucial to the story are the boa constrictor and the bird/crab monster which are used to torture Sarah and Harry? My guess is these will prove expensive, not an argument against them in itself!, but are they a bit melodramatic and fanciful for our Sontaran? Could we think of alternatives?

The version of the scripts as delivered included various design elements which would increase the cost of the production, and on Tuesday 23 July Hinchcliffe asked Letts for advice on costing items such as a lean-to hut required for Vural's encampment, and the elements to make the remains of the priory where Styre sets up his base. This was described by Hinchcliffe as 'comprising a corridor, two dungeons… and a courtyard with an underground entrance covered by a flagstone in the centre'.

At this point, the production team debated whether or not to blow up the Sontaran spacecraft, and extra scenes of Harry and Sarah in danger were being considered. When the cost estimates were returned from Raymond Cusick – a

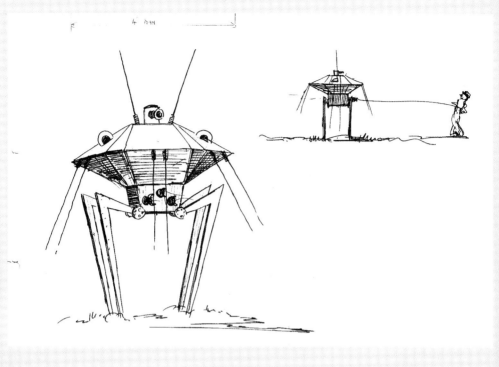

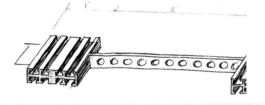

Visual Effects and Graphic Design

This page, top: Visual effects design sketches for Styre's robot, giving an idea of scale and how the robot would capture its victims.

This page, middle: Visual effects design for Styre's gravity bar and its control box (Part Two, Scene 19).

This page, bottom: Visual effects design for the matterbeam globe. Note the removable panel.

Opposite page, top: A graphic of the Sontaran fleet in space, intended to be used at the close of Part Two, Scene 12 (see the accompanying footnote).

Opposite page, bottom: Visual effects designs for the various guns used by the colonists and Styre's new gun (bottom right).

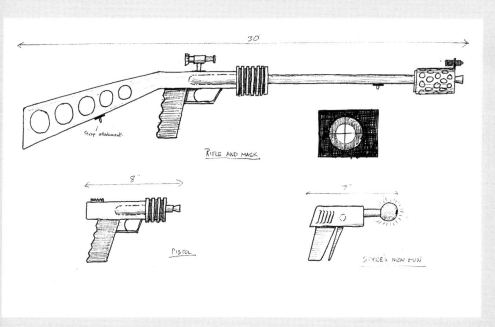

former *Doctor Who* designer who had created the Daleks and was now acting chief assistant to Head of Television Design (Drama) – the notion of the lean-to was abandoned, along with the priory elements in Baker and Martin's scripts and any notion of showing the interior of Styre's spacecraft (which would now be replaced by a single monitor unit seen on location). Sending a copy of the first script to Tommy Thomas (in charge of OB lighting) on Tuesday 30 July, Hinchcliffe observed that:

> The choice of location is obviously crucial – we may end up with something other than a Priory – and it is possible the action will have to be adapted to what we can find. Anyway, this will give you an idea of the scope of the action.

Considering the script of Part Two, Hinchcliffe felt that the change in setting would mean a number of alterations, as he outlined to director Rodney Bennett on Thursday 22 August:

> Now we are going for a prehistoric rather than a medieval setting the wine press device used to torture the Savage is anachronistic. Bob [Holmes] agrees it would be more plausible if Styre had brought a piece of futuristic equipment with him to carry out this test. Could we think more along these lines therefore, designing something which can still be operated by Vural & Co.
>
> Likewise we should lose the metal breastplate the Dr finds on p.33 and Bob will adjust the script accordingly.

Holmes' editing on the scripts was minor, involving a few changes to Styre's dialogue to bring him more in line with the character of Linx from *The Time Warrior*. As can be seen from the camera script, references to the priory and Vural's encampment remained, despite the decision to abandon the use of recognizable ruined buildings. During August, a few other changes were made to insert continuity references which would tie up with *The Ark in Space*, which Holmes was then rewriting. The Doctor's character was also still settling down into its new persona, and in the scripts the Doctor referred to Harry as 'old chap' and was to be humming the tune 'If You Were The Only Girl in the World' to himself as he worked on the transmat.

An agreement between the BBC and Holmes over the use of the Sontarans in *The Destructors* (in which Hinchcliffe erroneously indicated the serial would re-use 'Lynx' [sic]) was made on Tuesday 10 September. On Wednesday 18 September, Holmes wrote to the 'Bristol boys' (Baker and Martin) concerning the alterations he had made to their scripts, just before production began (and also referring to the problems on the scripts for *Revenge of the Cybermen*):

I believe you already have copies of your scripts. The story will probably be screened as 'The Sontaran Experiment'.

You will realize that it became necessary to do some further work to them to fit the action to the location.

The story is being done on location amid some curious rock formations on Dartmoor. This may be within your range in a fast motor car so I also enclose a copy of the shooting schedule in case you wish to visit the scene of the crime.

I'm having some Cybermen trouble so I won't be able to get down there, unfortunately, but I know you would be welcome visitors.

Keep in touch. Next season is sooner than you think.

Baker and Martin were unhappy about this late change in title, since it spoiled the cliffhanger in which the villain of the piece was revealed. The title *The Destructors* continued to appear on a lot of the BBC paperwork; the camera script had the new title typed below the original in brackets. The show was still referred to as *The Destructors* on the programme-as-broadcast log for its BBC1 transmission the following year, as well as in the track listings for the BBC's *Doctor Who Sound Effects* record issued in 1978.

Production Team

The production team for *The Destructors* was the same as that which would go on to make *The Ark in Space*. Rodney Bennett joined as director in mid-August, with Roger Murray-Leach as the set designer, Sylvia James on make-up, Barbara Kidd on costumes, and John Friedlander and Tony Oxley sharing the visual effects designs.

Friedlander concentrated on the sculpting and design of the monsters and remodelled his original design for the Sontaran mask (made for *The Time Warrior*), partly because the original mould had been destroyed but also to allow more ventilation. Kevin Lindsay, the actor who had played Linx the previous year, had complained of the weight of the mask.

Although Friedlander later claimed that a lapse of memory caused him to model the new Sontaran hands with five fingers rather than the three seen previously, a set of special effects requirements drawn up on Tuesday 27 August proves that this was a conscious design decision: 'Possible remaking of feet (enlarged and looking more like the foot section of medieval warrior) and hands (five fingers with very long nails stretching from first joint to fingertips. Also replacing thumb with claw-like shape).' A handwritten note adds: 'JOHN: Model hands gnarled, stunted (like roots of a tree).'

At the same time, a requirement for Styre's head to deflate was also added.

An original idea of having an operator inside the Sontaran robot was rejected early on and Oxley's design for the machine ended up as a lightweight sheet-aluminium construction with rotating head, illuminating eye and twitching antennae which was mounted upon a camera dolly. This would be pulled along camera tracks specially laid on location, but kept out of camera shot to suggest that the robot actually floated along (or at the very least had a more glamorous base). Notes made at a special effects meeting on Tuesday 27 August referred to:

> A metal robot to move along 'Elemack tracks'. The 'chap' must have a revolving eye, at least 3 spring arms, length as discussed, for reverse film/video disk edit… The body to be non-spheric.

On location, Oxley's operation of the robot would be assisted by Peter Pegrum. The prop itself turned out to be very delicate and prone to breaking down. Oxley's original design sketches are reproduced on page 158.

Cast

Kevin Lindsay was cast as both Field Major Styre and the marshal. Lindsay had played Linx in *The Time Warrior*, and some months earlier had been cast as Cho-je in *Planet of the Spiders* (1974). Of the GalSec crewmen, only Donald Douglas (Vural) and regular stunt man Terry Walsh (Zake) were not native South Africans. Playing Krans was actor/writer Glyn Jones who had written a four-part *Doctor Who* story for William Hartnell's Doctor entitled *The Space Museum* (1965). Since then he had worked on *The Gold Robbers* and his own children's film series *Here Come The Double Deckers!* Jones had submitted a further story idea for *Doctor Who* to Terrance Dicks in 1970, but this had been rejected.

A late addition to the team was Stuart Fell who would double Lindsay for action sequences involving Styre. Around this time, Hinchcliffe took the decision that one of his areas of saving on *Doctor Who* would be in terms of stunts; with a new style of show, he felt the action should take second place to the scripts and during September explained to Walsh that the stunt requirement on future *Doctor Who* serials would probably be reduced. Rather than hire teams of stunt men, certain artists – such as Walsh and Fell – would be called upon for a variety of roles.

Location Recording

When it was not possible to find priory ruins or suitably demolished buildings in London, the production team instead decided to use a natural landscape of a cleansed Earth with plenty of rocky outcrops and gullies. Production assistant

Marion McDougall knew the West Country settings which Baker and Martin had envisaged quite well, and suggested that the serial was made on Dartmoor.

Following on from the use of OB videotape for the location sequences on *Robot*, production unit manager George Gallaccio had been even more impressed with a documentary he had seen about the potential benefits of the new lightweight equipment and felt that this would be beneficial on *The Destructors*. Most notably, capturing the images directly on two-inch tape would allow a videotape editor to assemble parts of the programme in the scanner van while on location, saving on editing costs later on. Unfortunately, the scanner van available could not offer CSO or film transfer facilities, meaning the idea of using CSO for Styre's robot had to be dropped; similarly, the opening and closing titles would have to be added later during the recordings for *The Ark in Space*. Bennett was happy to use OB cameras rather than a film crew, having done a play on OB for Thirty Minute Theatre some years earlier.

Room 501 at BBC Acton saw the *Doctor Who* regular cast reassemble on Tuesday 17 September after their summer break since recording *Robot*; in the intervening months, Baker had been starring in a television film *The Author of Beltraffio* (broadcast in November 1976) and had also appeared on stage at the Playhouse in *The Trials of Oscar Wilde*. By this time, Baker had left his Bourne Street flat and was a man of 'no fixed abode'. He could be contacted through his agent, Jean Diamond, if needed by the production office. Baker's home address was a closely guarded secret. He took his public image very seriously, being careful never to use bad language, misbehave or smoke in public where the children who would watch him on television might be present.

There were to be five days of rehearsal on the serial before the team departed for location. Early on the morning of Monday 23, the cast and crew set out from London to their Dartmoor location in Devon. Because of the autumn weather and the exposed nature of the venue, the OB schedule carried a warning:

---

* AN IMPORTANT REMINDER !

TO ALL CONCERNED WITH OUTSIDE REHEARSALS ON LOCATION:

PLEASE, FOR YOUR OWN SAKES, BRING WARM CLOTHES, STRONG FOOTWEAR – PREFERABLY WATER-PROOF OR AT LEAST WATER REPELLENT, A CHANGE OF SOCKS AND OVERCOAT. IT'S GOING TO BE B----- (SLIGHTLY) COLD.

Bennett had opted to use some of his rehearsal time on location to familiarize the cast and crew with their surroundings. However, as the crew arrived at Warren House Inn near Postbridge and disembarked from the minibus, the heavens opened and the team were drenched in rain. Rapidly, Bennett set about locating additional wet-weather gear for the team from a shop in a local town, and the regular cast members acquired extra coats and waterskins to wear for their performances. That evening the crew dried out at the base hotels in Chagford. Rehearsals then continued on Tuesday 24 at Hound Tor near Manaton – some way to the east of Warren House Inn. The cast were then given the day off on Wednesday, with the rest of the OB team – including Philip Hinchcliffe and Barry Letts – arriving from London that day.

In contrast to the initial rehearsal period, the crew enjoyed good weather as recording began on Thursday 26 on the estate of Headland Warren Farm at Postbridge. Taping of the scenes was done using two of the three cameras which were available (because of the condensation caused by the cold, a third camera was apparently drying out back at one of the base hotels, ready to replace either of others should the moisture take effect). The two active cameras were linked back to the OB scanner van – one was generally mounted on a static tripod while the other was hand-held, allowing scenes to be recorded from two angles at once as in a studio.

With the scanner van 200 yards away from the cameras, Bennett opted to direct from the van, relaying instructions to the cast and camera crew via Hinchcliffe, McDougall or one of his assistants. Now far more settled in their roles, the regular cast started to experiment with ad-libbing small elements of their shared dialogue. Bennett also encouraged the notion of the Doctor keeping a lot of junk in his pockets, notably a yo-yo which the Doctor would use later on in *The Ark in Space*; Baker very much valued discussing the developing persona of the new Doctor with the director.

Walsh completed all his acting scenes as Zake on the first day, and so spent the next day – Friday 27 – doubling Marter and Baker for falls into the pit. Saturday 28 saw some bright but cold weather for the crew, and Marter was not needed on this day. Lindsay – who had returned to London after the initial rehearsals – travelled back to Dartmoor to rejoin the crew for the following day's work.

It was on Sunday 29 September that the sleet and rain really hit the crew on their first day at Hound Tor, a different section of the Dartmoor wilderness near Manaton owned by Wing Commander Longsden of Leighton; this was where the rest of the story would be recorded. This was the first day with Lindsay in his new Styre outfit. During recording of *The Time Warrior* it had been discovered that the actor suffered from a heart condition that often meant he was weak and exhausted. To reduce the strain on Lindsay, the actor only wore the Sontaran helmet over his latex mask once in the serial. Tragically,

Lindsay was to suffer a fatal heart attack in spring 1975. Sladen was uncomfortable for much of this day while her torture scenes were recorded – she was left to sit for hours in a nappy-style arrangement amidst the drizzle.

At around 5 p.m. on Sunday, Bennett and Hinchcliffe became aware in the scanner van that the crew had stopped work during a scene in which the Doctor confronted Styre at 'Sarah's dungeon'. Marion McDougall arrived back at the OB vehicle with the news that there had been an accident. While enacting the sequence for Part Two, Scene 15 in which Styre flung the Doctor away from him, Tom Baker had been running forward, taken the 'blow' from Lindsay, slipped on the wet grassy surface and fallen heavily on his left shoulder. Baker was in considerable pain and looked terribly pale; his arm was cradled in his scarf as a makeshift sling. The Dartmoor rescue team were summoned to get the immobile Baker to hospital, and the crew watched with great concern as he was wrapped in tin foil to retain his body heat and carried down the hillside to a car park from where he could be driven to Torquay Hospital. The final four scenes for the day were effectively abandoned.

With the injuries to Baker still unknown, Hinchcliffe and Bennett considered ways in which *The Sontaran Experiment* could be completed without the series' new star – and indeed the impact if Baker were in a worse state than hoped. The crew returned to the base hotel that night and were amazed when Baker strolled into the bar at 9 p.m. with his arm in a sling and sporting a neck brace. It transpired that Baker had cracked his collarbone and should be fully recovered in a fortnight. For the remaining location days, Bennett and Hinchcliffe revised their plans to keep any physical movement for the actor down to a minimum and shoot him mainly in close-up or with Terry Walsh doubling.

After the traumas of Sunday, Monday 30 saw more work at Hound Tor on the opposite side of the crags to the previous day. Walsh now doubled Baker in any long shots, or scenes where the Doctor had to climb or walk, allowing Baker to remain as motionless as possible for his close-ups (sometimes sitting in a chair). Baker's neck brace was hidden by the Doctor's coat and scarf.

Recording was attended by the local newspaper – the *Mid-Devon Advertiser* – as well as by a BBC publicity photographer. Baker also did an interview for the local BBC radio show *Morning South-West* about the local filming.

As the sun came out, work began on some new unscripted sequences for Part Two which had been added to pad out the loss of some other material for the later instalment. For the fight between the Doctor and Styre, Walsh and Fell doubled for Baker and Lindsay; Fell had to be careful not to damage the Styre outfit since only one version of the mask had been made.

Shots involving the 14-foot Sontaran spacecraft were taped on Tuesday 1 October, with the crew attempting to protect the polystyrene prop – salvaged from *The Time Warrior* – from the adverse weather on the tor.

A new unscripted scene of the Doctor defeating the Sontaran robot had been developed for insertion into Part Two. Because of the poor weather and accident, Bennett ended up recording on his stand-by day of Wednesday 2, requiring only the three regular cast members and his two stunt men.

The episodes were edited over two days between Wednesday 9 and Wednesday 16 October. Even with numerous trims and cuts, the edited Part Two still ran to its 25-minute maximum. The titles for the serial were recorded on Monday 28 October during the first of the two studio sessions for *The Ark in Space* (using Studio 3's telecine transfer facility).

The Radiophonic Workshop's Dick Mills was sent a two-page list of required sound effects for the story on 11 September. Final dubbing of the episodes – along with music and film – was undertaken on Saturday 15 February 1975 for Part Two, and on Friday 21 February for Part One. Dudley Simpson again composed and recorded the incidental score.

Promotion and Reaction

The serial was broadcast on BBC1 on Saturday 22 February and Saturday 1 March 1975. The broadcast of Part Two coincided with an article in the *Sun* in which Eve Kenworthy, the 13-year-old daughter of television reviewer Chris Kenworthy, commented that she did not find Baker's Doctor to be as good as Jon Pertwee's and denounced him as being a bit 'wet'. In addition to Hinchcliffe's comments, that in that day's episode the Doctor had 'a face-to-face fight with an evil Alien', Baker was allowed to respond to the criticisms:

> I get around two hundred letters a week, most of them in favour. But I suppose kids who saw Jon Pertwee as a father figure will be a bit against me. As for the scarf, it appears to be very popular. One lady told me she was gathering wool to make one and I sent her some. The hat comes from a smart shop in Bond Street. It was only after I sat on it a couple of times and went through one or two explosions that it became battered and floppy looking.

With both episodes in the Top 20 programmes for the week, the story sustained the large audiences achieved by *The Ark in Space*. The popular *Sale of the Century* continued on ATV and *New Faces* remained on Granada, while LWT dropped the talent show and replaced it with *The Adventurer*, a lacklustre ITC thriller series starring Gene Barry which had been made some years before. *The Adventures of Black Beauty* remained the main opposition show on Southern and Yorkshire.

Selected Merchandise

- NOVELIZATION: *Doctor Who and the Sontaran Experiment*: novelization by Ian Marter. Published November 1978 by W.H. Allen (hardback) and December 1978 by Target Books/W.H. Allen (paperback).
- SOUND EFFECTS: *Doctor Who – Sound Effects No. 19* (BBC Records REC 316/ZCM 316) issued May 1978; includes 'Styre's Scouting Machine'.
- SOUND EFFECTS: *Doctor Who – 30 Years at the Radiophonic Workshop* (BBC CD 871) issued July 1993; includes 'Threat to Sarah'.
- VIDEOTAPES (ETC.): *Doctor Who – The Sontaran Experiment/The Genesis of the Daleks* (BBC Video BBCV 4643) issued October 1991. American edition: (CBS/Fox #5946) issued 1994.

Production Details

4B: The Sontaran Experiment

Projects: 2344/7046-7047

Cast

Doctor Who	Tom Baker
Sarah Jane Smith	Elisabeth Sladen
Harry Sullivan	Ian Marter
Vural	Donald Douglas
Krans	Glyn Jones
Erak	Peter Walshe
Styre and the Marshal	Kevin Lindsay*
Roth	Peter Rutherford
Zake	Terry Walsh [1]
Prisoner	Brian Ellis [2]

* Credited on Part One as Styre.

Uncredited:

Stunt Double for Harry Sullivan [1]: Terry Walsh
Stunt Double for Doctor Who [1-2]: Terry Walsh
Stunt Double for Styre [2]: Stuart Fell

Crew

Written by	Bob Baker and Dave Martin
Fight Arranger	Terry Walsh [2]
Production Assistant	Marion McDougall
Production Unit Manager	George Gallaccio
Title Music by	Ron Grainer & BBC Radiophonic Workshop
Title Sequence	Bernard Lodge
Incidental Music by	Dudley Simpson
Special Sound	Dick Mills
Visual Effects Designers	John Friedlander, Tony Oxley
Costume Designer	Barbara Kidd
Make-up	Sylvia James
Lighting	Tommy Thomas
Sound	Vic Godrich

Script Editor   Robert Holmes
Designer   Roger Murray-Leach
Producer   Philip Hinchcliffe
Directed by   Rodney Bennett

Production History

OB Recording - near Warren House, Postbridge, Devon
Thursday 26 September 1974: 10.00am–5.00pm
- Ext. Matterbeam – Globe area – Part One: scenes 1, 4, 6, 9, 11 and Part Two: scene 23
- Ext. Matterbeam – Walk area – Part One: scenes 2, 8, 21, 23, 25
- Ext. Matterbeam – Swamp area – Part One: scene 13

Friday 27 September 1974: 10.00am–5.00pm
- Ext. Pit – Top area – Part One: scenes 5, 7, 12, 15, 17, 27 and Part Two: scene 4
- Ext. Pit – Bottom area – Part One: scenes 1, 10 and Part Two: scenes 2, 6

Saturday 28 September 1974: 10.00am–5.00pm
- Ext. Encampment – Part One: scenes 14, 18, 22, 24, 26

OB Recording - Hound Tor, near Manaton, Devon
Sunday 29 September 1974: 10.00am–5.00pm
- Prisoner's dungeon – Part Two: scenes 3A, 5A, 17A
- Sarah's dungeon – Part Two: scenes 7, 9, 11, 13, 15, 17, 21
- Ext. Tunnel exit – Part One: scene 16 and Part Two: scene 12A
- Ext. Street area – Part Two: scenes 3, 8, 12B, 14
- Staircase – Part One: scene 28

Monday 30 September 1974: 10.00am–5.00pm
- Ext. Courtyard – Talk area – Part Two: scene 18
- Ext. Courtyard – Torture area – Part Two: scenes 19, 22
- Ext. Courtyard – Control area – Part One: scene 19 and Part Two: scenes 10, 12, 20, 22B

Tuesday 1 October 1974: 10.00am–5.00pm
- Spacecraft area – Part One: scenes 28A, 30 and Part Two: scenes 1, 16, 22A

Wednesday 2 October 1974:
- Stand-by day

Music
- Specially recorded incidental music composed by Dudley Simpson (commissioned 30 July) and performed by Ad Hoc Orchestra. Recording Date: Monday 17 February 1975 at Lime Grove (another recording for Part Two on Monday 24 February was cancelled). 5'06" of music was composed for Part One, of which 4'10" was used. 7'28" of music used for Part Two, giving a total of 11'38" for the story.

Original Transmission – BBC1

Part One Saturday 22 February 19755.30pm 5.30pm 24'27" 11.0M 18th –
Part Two Saturday 1 March 1975   5.30pm 5.30pm 25'00" 10.5M 17th 55

THE SONTARAN EXPERIMENT

by Bob Baker & Dave Martin

Part One

OPENING TITLES

1. EXT. HEATHLAND. (OB) DAY. MATTERBEAM GLOBE AREA ②

Undulating sandy scrub like an old tank-training ground. Plenty of bumps and hollows, fern and gorse-type vegetation. Establishing shot of a fairly level patch in the midst of the scrub.

Here and there, glinting in the sunlight, flashes of reflected light as the camera pans around a circle of stainless-steel globes ③ comprising the reception area of the matterbeam.

A humming noise emanates from the globes, rising to a crescendo and then cutting abruptly. The Doctor appears in the circle. He looks round for the others. The humming crescendo again and Harry appears. Then promptly disappears and the Doctor reacts.

Harry is on the blink. Here-gone-here-gone. Finally here. ④

HARRY Ah, Doctor.

DOCTOR WHO Are you ~~staying~~ coming or going? Or going or ~~staying~~ coming?

HARRY I feel **a bit** like a Morse message. Slightly scrambled.

DOCTOR WHO ~~Now~~ Yes, **well**, let's get on with it.

Takes out sonic screwdriver and stoops to examine one of the globes.

DOCTOR WHO These must be the refractors. ~~Now then –~~

HARRY Oh – Doctor?

DOCTOR WHO *(Already preoccupied)* ~~Mmmm?~~ Yes?

HARRY I can see you're busy but – er – what about Sarah?

DOCTOR WHO ~~Oh, yes.~~ Sarah.

From the distance muffled:

SARAH *(OOV)* He-elp..!

DOCTOR WHO ~~Oh, dear –~~ That sounds like Sarah.

They look round the surrounding gorse.
Pan to Sarah's legs sticking up out of a gorse bush.

SARAH *(OOV)* Help me – ouch!

DOCTOR WHO *(Frowns)* Mmm… it's not only oscillating, it's ellipsing as well… You'd better give her a hand, ~~old chap~~ Harry…

HARRY Righty-oh.

DOCTOR WHO Yes, I see the problem. Focus gone a bit fuzzy.

He stoops to clear away the earth from around the globe closest to him.
Harry pulls Sarah out of the gorse.

HARRY Okay, old thing?

SARAH Harry – I am not a thing…

HARRY Doctor says it's the refractors.

SARAH Is it? Ouch –

HARRY I say, not hurt are you?

SARAH Only ~~in the~~ my…

She pulls a very spiky piece of gorse off her behind.

SARAH dignity…

They approach the Doctor. Still on his knees – he has cleared the globe and is operating on the pedestal beneath which contains the control circuits.

DOCTOR WHO Ah, Sarah! You're looking well. ⑤

Sarah sniffs.

DOCTOR WHO Look – ah – this is going to take some time to do the whole lot.

He indicates the circle of globes.

DOCTOR WHO So why don't you make the most of it?

SARAH Make the most of what?

DOCTOR WHO ~~I mean it's a~~ Glorious day, beautiful unspoilt countryside – no one's set foot here for thousands of years –

SARAH What you're trying to say is that you're busy and you'd like us to push off.

DOCTOR WHO ~~Pithily put.~~ I would phrase it more elegantly **myself**, of course. **But, yes.**

HARRY Might as well have a recce while we're here. Coming old – coming, Sarah?

Sarah sighs with exasperation and moves off with Harry.

DOCTOR WHO **Enjoy yourselves.** *(Points)* Trafalgar Square should be that way.

SARAH Trafalgar Square?

DOCTOR WHO If this is Piccadilly…

SARAH You're joking… aren't you?

DOCTOR WHO Mind the traffic!

The Doctor grins and bends to his work.

~~2. EXT. ANOTHER AREA OF HEATH. (OB) DAY. WALK AREA (2)~~

~~*Harry bends to study the vegetation. Sarah glares around.*~~

2A. EXT. ANOTHER AREA OF HEATH. (OB) DAY.
MATTERBEAM WALK AREA (2)

SARAH Trafalgar Square, my foot! Not a pigeon in sight!

HARRY Don't suppose many of our feathered friends survived, you know. There's not much in the way of life, is there?

~~**SARAH** I imagine lizards and things came off best.~~

~~**HARRY** And bacteria.~~

~~**SARAH** Everything's so still. It's rather creepy.~~

~~**HARRY** Well, you wouldn't expect much noise. I mean bacteria are pretty quiet little bugs.~~

SARAH ~~I don't like it here, Harry.~~ It's rather creepy. It doesn't seem like Earth at all.

HARRY Oh, I dunno. It's nice and ~~clean~~ tidy, anyway – no lolly sticks.

SARAH *(Flatly)* It's not what I expected.

HARRY Well, it'll ~~soon~~ **all** change when they get down from Nerva. Their animal-botanic section is packed with stuff.

SARAH *(Grabbing him)* What was that?

HARRY What?

SARAH Shh. Listen!

HARRY I can't hear anything.

He marches to the top of the next rise. There is a distinct sound of movement in the bracken behind Sarah. **6**

SARAH Over there!

Harry turns, looks, sees nothing.

HARRY Come on, **Sarah – you're imagining things.** It's pure imagination.

Sarah does not move.

HARRY Sarah – there's been no life on Earth – not of any size – for ten thousand years!

SARAH We don't know that, **do we.** Not for sure. There could **be anything here**… well, there could be things here.

HARRY Such as what?

SARAH I don't know. Mutations… creatures.

HARRY Oh, Come on!

She lets him pull her to the top of the rise.
Something unseen rustles through the bracken after them.

7 **4. EXT. GLOBE CIRCLE. (OB) DAY.**
MATTERBEAM AREA

The Doctor working on the third silver globe. He tumtitums: 'If You Were the Only Girl in the World'.

Another angle:

A rifle barrel parting the bracken and sighting on the Doctor's back. It is a modern weapon, very unlike a present-day rifle. **8**

Two men, scruffily bearded, uniformed, gazing down at the Doctor. Erak hands his rifle to Zake.

ERAK Keep him covered Zake. I'll get the others…

Doubled, keeping out of the Doctor's vision, he hurries back up the slope.

5. EXT. ANOTHER AREA. (OB) DAY.
PIT AREA (TOP)

Harry, leading the way, turns to call Sarah.

HARRY Come on, Sarah – Hey, **Sarah – come and have a look at this…**

And down he goes into a pit cunningly covered over with bracken. **9**

Sarah runs to the hole.

Harry is sprawled at the bottom of the pit. It is about 12 feet deep.

Harry groans and stirs.

SARAH Harry! Are you all right? Harry!

6. EXT. ENCAMPMENT. (OB) DAY.

Erak comes hurrying into the camp area where Krans is preparing a root stew. **10**

ERAK Krans! Krans! I've seen a guy… *(Panting)* Some stranger –

KRANS What?

ERAK Zake's watching him. He's down by that circle. I thought maybe Vural **ought to know** –

KRANS No, no, no. He's gone out looking for grub. **Down** by the circle, eh?

ERAK Yeah… Could be he's something to do with this mess, huh?

Krans picks up his rifle.

KRANS *(Grim)* **Well** we'll soon find out!

7. EXT. THE PIT. (OB) DAY.
PIT AREA BOTTOM

Harry sits up.

HARRY No bones broken, I don't think.

He gets to his feet.

HARRY All the same, I'm stuck. Aren't I?

SARAH **Harry**… Harry. There's something wrong here… I mean **The edge of** this hole was **has been** covered…

HARRY Of course it was **has.** That's why I fell into it… Oh, I see what you mean! Deliberate trap, eh?

SARAH I'll go and get the Doctor.

Harry's worried reaction… Then a rueful smile.

HARRY **All right.** I'll – er – wait here **then.**

We take his POV of Sarah vanishing from the edge of the pit.

7A. EXT. HEATH. (OB) DAY.
MATTERBEAM AREA

Zake lies in the scrub watching the Doctor.

Suddenly the machine **11** *appears over a crest.*

Zake looks round and gives a gasp of shock.

He jumps to his feet and runs. The machine zooms after him.

7B. EXT. GLOBE CIRCLE. (OB) DAY.
MATTERBEAM AREA

The Doctor has removed a piece of globe mechanism. His sonic screwdriver is on the ground beside him as he polishes the corroded metal.

7C. EXT. HEATH. (OB) DAY.
HEATHLAND – NEAR MATTERBEAM AREA

The machine is gaining on Zake. He looks back fearfully, misses his footing.

7X. EXT. HEATH. (OB) DAY.

2ND HALF OF SCENE 7C
WALK AREA (3)

Zake falls into gully.

7D. EXT. GLOBE CIRCLE. (OB) DAY.
MATTERBEAM AREA

The Doctor hears a distant cry. He springs up.
DOCTOR Harry!
He runs. **12**

7E. EXT. HEATH. (OB) DAY.
WALK AREA (3)

The spaceman is lying in a crumpled heap at the foot of the rocks. No sign of the machine.
   The Doctor arrives, looks about, sees the spaceman. He scrambles down into the gully and examines the man.
DOCTOR WHO Broken neck…
He stares at the body, weighing up this new development. He starts to scramble out of the gully.
   As he gets to the top, Krans and Erak arrive on the further side. Krans swings the rifle up.
KRANS Hold it –!
DOCTOR WHO Is he a friend of yours?
Erak stares down at Zake.
ERAK He's killed Zake!
DOCTOR WHO No – I –
The Doctor ducks and runs for it. Krans aims and fires. **13** *The Doctor pitches forward.*

8. EXT. ANOTHER AREA. (OB) DAY.
WALK AREA (2)

Sarah running back over their tracks towards the reception area.
   She sneaks backward glances the whole time, scared that something is after her.

9. EXT. GLOBE CIRCLE. (OB) DAY.
MATTERBEAM GLOBE AREA

A silver globe in foreground. Tilt up to show Sarah running into the circle.
SARAH Doctor? *(Looking around)* Doctor?
With increasing fear, she paces round the circle. Comes to the globe the Doctor was working on. There, on the ground, is his sonic screwdriver. **14**

10. EXT. THE PIT. (OB) DAY.
PIT AREA (BOTTOM)

Close on Harry examining the sandy walls of the pit.
   A noise makes him desist. He looks up.
HARRY Sarah?
But all he sees is the edge of the pit crumbling under some unseen foot… and sand and stones falling into his face.
HARRY Hello? Hey. Who's there?
No reply: only something moving away through the bracken.
HARRY Hey! Now look here –
A large rock is hurled with force into the pit:
   Harry crouches down in the corner of the pit, flattening himself against the wall.
   Another stone crashes down. And another.
   Harry starts scrabbling away at the scrub and bushes at the bottom of the pit, desperately trying to make an overhang for himself. His efforts reveal the keystone of an arch. There is a narrow gap under it, another rock crashes down from above, dangerously close. Harry wriggles into the hole.

11. EXT. GLOBE CIRCLE. (OB) DAY.
MATTERBEAM GLOBE AREA

SARAH Doctor!
The faint echo of her shout mocks her. She feels very alone. She looks at the sonic screwdriver in her hand. Then up around the empty heathland. She realizes it is no use calling any more, pockets the screwdriver and heads off back towards the pit. Fear soon makes her break into a run.

12. EXT. THE PIT. (OB) DAY. ⑮
PIT AREA (TOP)

Sarah arriving, heaving for breath, at the edge of the pit and looking down.

SARAH Harry, Harry – I can't find… him.

She sees the floor of the pit covered in rocks and dislodged earth.

SARAH ~~Oh no…~~ Harry?

She collapses on to the ground. For a second or two it is all too much for her. Then she pulls herself together and looks around. A piece of the bracken used to cover the pit catches her eyes. It confirms her earlier fears. The end of the bracken has been freshly cut.

Still holding on to the bracken as the only clue she has, Sarah stands up and takes a good look around for signs of any lurking enemy.

13. EXT. HEATHLAND. (OB) DAY. ⑯
WALK AREA (3)

Low shot of boots and torn trousers tucked into them marching along the track.

The leading pair of boots passes camera then we see the Doctor, slung on a pole like a dead stag, unconscious. ⑰ *Then a second pair of boots passes camera.*

There is a rustling in the bracken beside the track. The fronds part and the gaunt, manic face of Roth peers out furtively.

14. EXT. ENCAMPMENT. (OB) DAY.

A lean-to of branches and ferns. ⑱ *The two men come staggering into the encampment. They are scruffily bearded and wear what is recognizably some sort of military uniform.*

They drop the Doctor unceremoniously on the floor and stretch their backs. The older, Krans, blows life into the smouldering fire in front of the hut.

ERAK How long before the dope wears off?

KRANS He's coming round now.

CU the Doctor: a flicker of consciousness.

KRANS Cut him loose, Erak. Leave his hands tied.

Erak takes a machete and cuts the Doctor free from the pole. They haul him to his feet. Krans takes a burning brand ⑲ *from the now glowing fire and pushes it towards the Doctor's face. The Doctor's eyes open.*

~~**DOCTOR WHO** What the –~~

Krans throws the brand back in the fire and grabs the Doctor by the collar.

KRANS All right. Now talk!

DOCTOR WHO Certainly. What would you like me to ~~say~~ **talk about**?

KRANS *(Shaking him)* What have you done with our crewmates?

15. EXT. PIT AREA. (OB) DAY.
PIT AREA (TOP)

Sarah is dragging a rotten tree trunk about ten foot long towards the pit. As she reaches the edge she pauses for breath… again the rustling in the bracken.

She looks round nervously. The bracken moving. Nothing else.

16. EXT. RUINS. (OB) DAY. ⑳
SARAH'S DUNGEON

Rocks.

Harry in and starts to climb.

16A. EXT. RUINS. (OB) DAY.

The tunnel exit.

Harry appears and exits L.

16B. EXT. RUINS. (OB) DAY.
APPROACH (1)

Harry runs for cover among rocks.

17. EXT. PIT AREA. (OB) DAY.
PIT AREA (TOP)

Sarah is lowering the log into the hole, intending to use it as a sort of ladder.

Suddenly a dirty hand clamps round Sarah's neck and across her mouth and she is dragged backwards.

Roth, dressed in ragged space gear, pinions Sarah to the ground. She struggles and tries to scream, but he is preventing her from making any sound.

There is a low, humming noise some way off and approaching the pit is a silvery circular machine with two telescopic antennae waving about. Roth throws himself flat beside Sarah.

The machine, bleeping away, sensors waving, stops at the pit. Its sensors study the hole. Then it trundles carefully round the shaft and on out of sight.

SARAH What on Earth –

ROTH Sssh!

He waves her to silence and gets up nervously to check that the machine has really gone.

ROTH Who are you? Where are you from?

SARAH ~~Funny.~~ That's just what I was going to ask you. **OK,** my name's Sarah. What's yours?

ROTH Sarah…

SARAH What's your name?

ROTH Roth.

SARAH And do you live here, Roth? No – those are space clothes, aren't they?

Roth edges over to the pit, looks in.

ROTH I covered this, yunnerstan? ~~That machine shoulda gone down.~~ **To catch the machine.**

SARAH Tell me about the machine. Why are you **so** frightened of it~~, Roth~~?

ROTH The machine serves him. Catches my crewmates –

SARAH Serves who?

ROTH The thing in the rocks, ~~yunnerstan?~~ I'll **not** ~~don't~~ get caught, not again. ~~No, no.~~

SARAH ~~Roth listen – listen –~~ No, wait – what thing in the rocks?

ROTH ~~Over there.~~ The alien, **in the rocks.** The machine catches us, takes us for torture. *(He shows ugly marks on his body)* **㉑** I got away, see.

SARAH **Those are burns, aren't they? Did the alien do that –** ~~The alien did that –~~ **is that what you're saying?** ~~They're burns, aren't they?~~

ROTH He killed Heeth and Splier, I got away, yunnerstan?

SARAH I think I'm beginning to… Look, take me to where these rocks are.

ROTH Na… na…

SARAH Roth, you've got to help me! I came here with two friends and they've both vanished, yunnerstan? I mean, you understand?

ROTH I saw ~~'em~~.

SARAH Then it was you following us?

ROTH One of your friends is with Vural.

SARAH Vural?

ROTH He was in the circle. I saw 'em take him.

SARAH ~~You mean~~ Then you know where the Doctor is?

18. EXT. ENCAMPMENT. (OB) DAY.

Krans is questioning the Doctor.

DOCTOR WHO I told you, I've just got here –

ERAK How? We've seen no ship.

DOCTOR WHO I didn't use one~~, old chap~~. I came by transmat beam.

VURAL That's a lie!

He enters frame.

DOCTOR WHO ~~I assure you I am not in the habit of lying.~~ **That's the truth.** ~~And~~ Who are you?

VURAL Vural. I am the leader of this party.

To others.

VURAL Where did you find him?

ERAK First saw him creeping about that circle.

DOCTOR WHO Not creeping – I was repairing –

KRANS Shut up!

KRANS Time we caught up with him he was bent over Zake.

KRANS Killed him.

DOCTOR WHO I did not kill him. I heard a cry and found him lying in a gully with his neck broken. An accident, I imagine.

VURAL *(A beat)* You say you came here by transmat beam?

DOCTOR WHO That's right.

VURAL There's no transmat system ~~for~~ **on** this planet. The Earth's been junked.

DOCTOR WHO Temporarily abandoned, perhaps, but not junked. Oh no.

VURAL It's worn out, useless, and too far from the freight routes. Nobody comes here so there's no transmat system. Check?

ERAK Check.

VURAL So **you'd better** start telling the truth or you'll find things getting a little rough.

DOCTOR WHO I'm sorry to keep contradicting you but there is a transmat beam from Space Station Nerva.

KRANS From where?

DOCTOR WHO Space Station Nerva.

The three gaze at each other. Erak shakes his head.

ERAK Is he crazy?

KRANS A joker.

VURAL You don't expect us to believe that!

DOCTOR WHO Nerva. Transmat beam. Earth. It's as simple as that. Why don't you believe me?

VURAL Because Nerva doesn't exist, that's why. There's no such place.

DOCTOR WHO Fascinating… You don't believe it exists and yet you've obviously heard of it.

KRANS Everybody's heard of the Lost Colony.

DOCTOR WHO Lost Colony? You mean it's become a ~~myth~~ legend like Lost Atlantis?

ERAK Like what?

DOCTOR WHO ~~Don't you know about Atlantis? It's a legendary place~~. Lost Atlantis. It's a legendary city… Oh never mind. ~~Well, that's immensely~~ This is extremely interesting. Are you going to ~~untie me~~ cut me loose?

VURAL We're going to get the truth out of you first!

KRANS Too right.

DOCTOR WHO Very colonial. You are from a colony, I take it?

VURAL GalSec.

DOCTOR WHO Of course, on Nerva they know that various colony ships left Earth. They'll be delighted to hear they're not the sole survivors of the human ~~species~~ race. You are human?

KRANS What do you mean?

ERAK Course we are.

DOCTOR WHO Oh, no offence. No offence.

The Doctor looks at Vural. Camera closes on a device on Vural's shirt front. ㉒

DOCTOR WHO Do you mind if I take a close look at that?

Reactions.

19. EXT. RUINS. (OB) DAY. COURTYARD CONTROL AREA

The Doctor on a monitor screen. ㉓

DOCTOR WHO *(Filter)* D'you mind if I take a closer look?

His face bends forward into a close shot.

DOCTOR WHO I'd say it's not a product of human technology, eh, Vural?

Vural shoves the Doctor back.

VURAL *(Filter)* You're a freak!

A talon-hand comes into frame and cuts the picture. It moves to another switch on the console. There is a sharp series of bleeps and pings. ㉔

20. EXT. RUINS. (OB) DAY. STAIRCASE TOP

Harry is wandering cautiously through the dark dank decaying cloisters. A very eerie, haunted sort of place.

Suddenly from the other side of a wall he hears a series of bleeps and pings. Harry freezes.

21. EXT. HEATH. (OB) DAY. ㉕ HEATHLAND – NEAR MATTERBEAM AREA

The machine stops trundling along when it 'hears' the series of bleeps and pings. These noises are its orders: it stops. Turns round, extends its sensors and moves as fast as it can in the direction it has just come from.

22. EXT. ENCAMPMENT. (OB) DAY.

The Doctor still bound, the others talking some way off. ㉖

ERAK ~~He's lying through his teeth –~~ I say get rid of him now and save ourselves the trouble later.

VURAL Krans?

KRANS If he'd landed by ship we'd have heard. Maybe he did come by transmat beam.

ERAK From Nerva?

KRANS Maybe.

VURAL I remember the old story. Back in the days of the Expansion a bunch of survival sleepers went to Space Station Nerva to wait for the Earth to cool down again.

ERAK So Earth's ~~been cool a long time~~ cooled down and they've never come back. And Nerva's never been found. It's just a story.

VURAL Yeah. I reckon if it ever existed it got burnt up in the sunbursts.

KRANS You know what makes me half believe him? It's such a crazy story, that's what.

ERAK You mean if he was ~~lying he'd dream up~~ making it up, he'd think of something better?

KRANS Check.

ERAK Never.

KRANS I'll question him again.

VURAL No. I'll handle this.

23. EXT. HEATH. (OB) DAY. WALK AREA (1)

Sarah and Roth moving warily.

ROTH Sssh! It's just a ways down here…

SARAH Well, what are we waiting for ~~Roth~~?

ROTH Na, na…

SARAH **Roth**, if you were in Vural's crew why are you so frightened of him?

ROTH He's been to the rocks. I saw. I saw.

SARAH What do you mean, **you saw**?

ROTH The alien let him go, yunnerstan? Vural's hooked.

He moves on.

24. EXT. ENCAMPMENT. (OB) DAY.

The Doctor again under interrogation.

VURAL Right. How long have they been in deep freeze on Nerva?

DOCTOR WHO Oh… ten thousand years?

VURAL And you woke up before the others?

DOCTOR WHO ~~Oh~~ Well, no. ~~No,~~ I'm a sort of travelling time… expert. As you can see, Earth has been habitable for ~~a few~~ **several** thousand years. But they didn't wake up. Why? Clock stopped. Overslept. So here I am.

VURAL Clock expert…

DOCTOR WHO Horologist actually. **And chronometrist.** ~~And time expert.~~ Just love clocks – atomic, quartz, grandfather –

ERAK He's still lying.

VURAL **Shut up, Erak.**

DOCTOR WHO Cuckoo clocks…

VURAL ~~Shut up, Erak.~~ You got any proof?

DOCTOR WHO Well, no. I didn't expect to meet anyone. I understood Earth was not inhabited.

KRANS That's what we thought. Until we ~~picked up~~ **got** a distress call from around here.

DOCTOR WHO A mayday? **Then** you're a military expedition, I take it?

VURAL One of our GalSec freighters went missing. We picked up a ~~mayday~~ **distress call** and came down for a looksee. Soon as we left the ship it was vapourized. Nine of us were stuck here.

DOCTOR WHO Nine? Where are the rest?

VURAL Vanished.

ERAK *(Menacing)* And we reckon that circle of yours has got something to do with it!

DOCTOR WHO Oh, ~~no, no~~ **rubbish**. That's simply the reception point for the transmat beam from Nerva.

He looks beyond them and sees Sarah and Roth sneaking up to the encampment.

ERAK Let's kill him **now** and get it over with.

VURAL No.

DOCTOR WHO **That's** wild talk ~~my friend~~ **Erak**. Far from killing me, you should treat me as an honoured guest.

KRANS Why?

DOCTOR WHO You don't want to be stuck here for ever, do you?

VURAL Go on.

DOCTOR WHO ~~Well~~, I might consider helping you.

VURAL How d'you reckon to help us?

DOCTOR WHO Simple. I finish refocusing the matterbeam and we all pop up to Nerva. ~~Then~~ You ~~can~~ get in touch with your headquarters and they~~'ll~~ send a ship for you. ~~I'll have two eggs for breakfast, gently boiled, and not too much butter on the toast.~~

VURAL Listen. If you are one of the Old People, we're not taking orders from your lot. While you were dozing away, our people kept going. And they made it. We've got bases all across the galaxy now. You've done nothing for ~~the last~~ ten thousand years ~~and~~ **while** we've made an empire. Understand?

DOCTOR WHO Oh, absolutely.

VURAL We're not taking any of that Mother Earth ~~claptrap~~ **rubbish** –

KRANS Hey, look! It's Roth!

They spin round. Roth stands on a hillock some 50 yards away.

ERAK ~~It's old Rothy!~~ Hey, Rothy!

They dash towards him. Roth turns and disappears.

KRANS Roth! It's Rothy!

ERAK Rothy..!

Sarah runs into the encampment and cuts the Doctor's bonds with a discarded machete.

DOCTOR WHO ~~Hullo~~ **Good girl**, Sarah. Who's your ~~speedy~~ **fast** friend?

SARAH Explain later. Come on.

They race away.

VURAL *(Calls)* Roth..! Roth!

ERAK *(Panting)* It's no good Krans. He's bunked.

KRANS I saw him… plain as daylight.

VURAL Why'd he run like that? Why'd he run from us?

ERAK He musta gone bush.

They are trudging back to the camp. Vural halts suddenly, staring.

VURAL Hey!

He points. The Doctor's bonds lie severed.

ERAK That freak! He's got away!

VURAL *(Grim)* Get your guns. ㉗

25. EXT. HEATH. (OB) DAY.
WALK AREA (1)

Sarah, the Doctor and Roth.

SARAH ~~This way, Doctor.~~ Doctor, the pit's this way.

DOCTOR WHO ~~No, first things first. I think I dropped my sonic screwdriver by the circle –~~ I've lost my sonic screwdriver – I feel absolutely lost without it.

Sarah hands it to him.

SARAH I've found your sonic screwdriver. Doctor – the pit!

DOCTOR WHO ~~I knew it left it somewhere.~~

SARAH ~~The pit?~~

DOCTOR WHO ~~Lead on, MacSmith.~~ What would I do without you?

26. EXT. HEATH. (OB) DAY.
ENCAMPMENT

Vural, Krans and Erak, all armed, moving like hunters.

VURAL Erak?

ERAK Nothing.

VURAL Keep your eyes peeled. They can't have got far.

27. EXT. PIT AREA. (OB) DAY.
PIT AREA TOP

Halting at the pit edge, the Doctor, Sarah and Roth. They gaze down.

DOCTOR WHO He couldn't have climbed out?

SARAH Not without help.

DOCTOR WHO This machine you told me about – could that have lifted him –

SARAH No, he'd already gone by the time the machine came.

DOCTOR WHO Excuse me…

The Doctor bends and studies the scorched grass. He plucks some of the grass and chews it thoughtfully.

DOCTOR WHO Terullian drive.

SARAH What?

DOCTOR WHO **The machine.** That's **very** interesting because there's no terullian to be found in this galaxy.

ROTH Yeah, alien. Alien, yunnerstan?

He moves his hands over his head, miming a dome shape.

DOCTOR WHO Yes~~, all right~~. **Don't you worry about it**, old chap. ~~Don't you worry about him.~~ *(To Sarah)* He's half demented by shock.

SARAH He's been tortured. Badly by the look of it. He's terrified of everyone now ~~including~~ especially his old crewmates.

DOCTOR WHO Yes, can't say I blame him for being wary of friend Vural, at any rate… You know it's absolutely typical of Harry. How anyone in their proper mind could fall down a whacking great subsidence like… that's it!

SARAH What's it?

DOCTOR WHO Subsidence. A sewer or something. Maybe the Central Line, eh?

SARAH I'm not with you.

DOCTOR WHO I mean there must be a way out from the bottom. Hang on, **Sarah** – I'll just go down and take a look.

SARAH Be careful, Doctor. If you break a leg or something we'll never get you out…

The Doctor is disappearing down the shaft, clinging to the log.

DOCTOR WHO ~~Don't worry Sarah. Perfectly safe –~~ ㉘

Pan Doctor to bottom of pit. ㉙

SARAH Doctor, Doctor!

She turns round. The machine is there. Roth gibbers with fright and falls on his knees in front of the machine.

ROTH Na! Na na na!

The sensor arm swings slowly from the crazed man to Sarah.

28. EXT. RUINS. (OB) DAY.
CLIMBING AREA

Harry is making a laborious climb to a point where he can look down the further side of the stone crag. He gazes down and we establish his reaction.

28A. EXT. RUINS. (OB) DAY. SPACECRAFT AREA

Inside a ruined courtyard ㉚ *is the Sontaran spacecraft.* ㉛

Equipment from the craft has been set up against one wall.

29. EXT. PIT AREA. (OB) DAY. PIT AREA (TOP)

We establish the emptiness. No sign now of the machine – or Sarah or Roth.

The Doctor lies at the bottom. He stirs. ㉜

He sits up groggily and rubs his head.

DOCTOR WHO Sarah… Roth, Sarah..! Sarah, are you there?

No answer.

He rubs his head again, this time in thought.

30. EXT. RUINS. (OB) DAY. SPACECRAFT AREA

Harry crouches lower as he hears the humming noise of the robot machine. It comes into the courtyard area with Sarah and Roth in tow.

The machine pauses, scans the area with its sensors.

But Harry is too well shielded for the machine to sense his presence.

The machine drags its captives over to the spacecraft.

The door section starts to open. Close shot of Sarah held captive by the machine. In the doorway appears the squat figure of Styre, the Sontaran warrior.

STYRE Ah!

SARAH Linx! ㉝

He steps out and moves up to the two new captives. He reaches out and takes Sarah's arm and his claw digs into her flesh.

~~**STYRE** Ah – the female of the species…~~

CLOSING TITLES ㉞

---

① In mid-September 1974, very shortly before recording, the title of the serial was finally changed from *The Destructors* to *The Sontaran Experiment* (on the camera script, this new title is typed in below the original in brackets).

② Most scene titles in the camera script were suffixed by the location in which they were to be recorded.

③ The 'matterbeam globes' were provided by Visual Effects. The requirement, as stated to Visual Effects, was for: '12 "Mushroom Spheres" – one with removable panel. To be "aged". Ring of spheres to be 12' – 15'.' The need for one globe to have a 'blink' effect was dropped, though the Doctor removes a circular access panel from one. Only ten globes were actually used. The original design sketch is reproduced on page 158.

④ Run-ons with a locked-off camera were used for the opening sequence of the Doctor and Harry materializing. Removing these during editing made the characters fade into and out of vision, in a similar technique to 'roll-back-and-mix' (see *Robot* Part One, Scene 1).

⑤ The Doctor says this deadpan, despite the fact that Sarah has pulled her woollen hat down over her eyes.

⑥ The moving bracken was replaced with a fleeting glimpse of Roth running along the horizon. This was recorded at the end of the main scene, and edited in.

⑦ Scene 3 was deleted before recording (a note on the script says 'No Scene 3').

⑧ A view through the gunsight was achieved using a circular lens mask with a cross-hair provided by Visual Effects and fitted to the camera (see design on page 159). This was recorded after the main scene and edited in.

⑨ A close-up of Harry's foot going through the covered edge of the pit was recorded at the end of the main scene, but not used. The fall was performed by stunt man Terry Walsh (who also plays Zake).

⑩ The props list for the fire and colonists' food includes: 'Stuff for Camp Fire – firelighters, matches, 2 sacks of peat, 2 dozen branches, 6-8 newspapers… Food for colonists: sweet potatoes, blackberries or strawberries, figs (if readily available) various nuts (and nutcracker!)'

It's a Mistake to Clutter One's Pockets

By the time of *The Sontaran Experiment* the Doctor had 24 'personal' props in his possession (some of which had featured in *Robot* and would feature in *The Ark in Space*). Most of these were things he kept in his pockets, and were all carefully itemized for the sake of continuity and stored in a cardboard box in Room 509 of Threshold House:

DOCTOR WHO – PERSONAL PROPS USED BY TOM BAKER – COMPLETE TO
THE END OF CURRENT SCHEDULE

1. A GLADSTONE BAG.
2. SONIC SCREWDRIVER.
3. TARDIS KEY ON CHAIN.
4. (THERE ARE TWO OTHER TARDIS KEYS, BEING DUPLICATES FROM VIS. EFFECTS.)
5. 1 × EYE GLASS.
6. 1 × PACK OF PLAYING CARDS.
7. 1 × PACK OF 'TRICK' PLAYING CARDS.
8. 1 × MAGNIFYING GLASS.
9. 1 × TOY GUN. ("COLORADO" – SILVER METAL – CRESCENT TOY CO; GT. BRIT.)
10. 1 × TOY CAR. ("BATMOBILE" – CORGI TOYS.).
11. 1 × PROP. MOUSE.
12. 1 × BLUE YOYO.
13. 6 × TRANSPARENT DICE.
14. 1 × CUCKOO CALL.
15. 1 × GOOSE CALL.
16. 1 × CURLEW CALL.
17. 1 × TELESCOPE. ADJUSTABLE TYPE.
18. 1 × PAIR OF YELLOW PLASTIC GOGGLES.
19. 1 × GALACTIC PASSPORT. THIS IS ONLY A SIMPLE GRAPHIC.
20. FREEDOM OF THE CITY OF SKARO (NAME OF) SCROLL. ON CLOTH.
21. 1 × LEATHER PURSE.
22. 1 × MAGNET.
23. 1 × OLD LEATHER NOTEBOOK AND BALL-POINT PEN.
24. 1 × BATTERED "SELENIUM LOCKING MECHANISM" EX. LIFESAVER OF THE DR.

Many of these props would appear in later stories – the Batmobile toy, for example, in *The Talons of Weng-Chiang* (1977). A handwritten note on the sheet suggests items that might be added to the Doctor's collection, including – intriguingly – 'a bicycle'.

⑪ Visual Effects notes for Styre's robot describe it as: 'Silvery, circular machine with two telescopic antennae – possibly disguised golf truck or small agricultural vehicle…' It is also noted that it will be driven over rough ground. See page 158 for the original visual effects design.

⑫ The sonic screwdriver is left balanced on the top of one of the globes.

⑬ The end of Krans' rifle lights up as it fires (a close-up recorded at the end of the main scene and edited in). See page 159 for the original design drawing.

⑭ It is still balanced on the globe. Sarah picks it up.

⑮ Scene 13 was edited in ahead of this scene.

⑯ This scene was moved ahead of Scene 12.

⑰ The pole was not used.

⑱ The encampment was a small cave in the rock face. The fire is outside the cave mouth.

⑲ The visual effects requirement was for 'Burning brand – with in-built gel or firelighter'.

⑳ These three short scenes (16, 16A, 16B) show Harry's escape from the pit, and the start of his journey into the rocks where Styre has his headquarters.

㉑ Make-up applied the burn marks on Roth's right forearm.

㉒ The transmitter – called a 'kinemitter' in Part Two, Scene 16 – was a simple metal pin-brooch provided by Visual Effects to meet the requirement that it look like 'non-human technology'.

㉓ The sequence for the monitor was recorded at the end of Scene 18 and played on to the screen when this scene was recorded (two days later). The image was slightly distorted by the use of a special lens.

㉔ Scene 21 was inserted here, showing the robot responding – it rises up, turns, then moves off.

㉕ This scene was moved ahead of Scene 20.

㉖ The Doctor is not visible, the colonists are inside their small cave.

㉗ Visual Effects was asked to provide '3 guns – 2 rifles (one to fire), one pistol. Rifles to have shoulder straps, sights of colourless ringed Perspex (to match lens mask)'. Rodney Bennett asked to see and approve the preliminary designs, which are reproduced on page 159.

㉘ The Doctor's cry is unintelligible.

㉙ Terry Walsh doubled for the Doctor and performed the fall.

㉚ The spaceship stands on a shelf of rock. The equipment is not in the same area.

㉛ The same prop was used as appeared in *The Time Warrior* (1973/4).

㉜ The Doctor is woken by water dripping off the twigs at the edge of the pit.

㉝ This line is included at the start of Part Two, though omitted here. Linx is the name of the Sontaran Sarah encountered in *The Time Warrior*.

㉞ The episode closes with Styre removing his helmet and starting towards Sarah and Roth.

THE SONTARAN EXPERIMENT

by Bob Baker & Dave Martin

Part Two

OPENING TITLES

1. EXT. RUINS. (OB) DAY.
SPACECRAFT AREA

In the doorway of the Sontaran spacecraft the squat figure of Styre, the Sontaran warrior.

STYRE Ah!

SARAH Links! ❶

He steps out and moves up to the two new captives. He reaches out and takes Sarah's arm. His claw digs into her flesh.

STYRE Ah, the female of the species… ❷

Styre turns to the machine and bleeps out a message on his pocket bleeper. ❸

The machine withdraws the tentacles from the captives. ❹

SARAH ~~I know you~~. You're Linx ❺ – the Sontaran. But – you were… You were destroyed in the thirteenth century. **You were** blown to smithereens –

On Roth glancing from one to the other, estimating his chances of escape.

STYRE You may have seen one of us.

SARAH But – you're identical – the same ugly…

STYRE Identical yes, the same no. I am Styre, Field Major Styre as you will address me, of the Sontaran G3 Military Assessment Survey. And your ~~observations are~~ **opinion of my**

looks is of no interest to my programme… Female number one. First assessment – would appear to have no military justification. Offensive value therefore nil –

Roth makes a run for it. Styre takes out his handgun ❻ *and tracks Roth's progress.*

ROTH You won't ~~have~~ get me! You won't torture me again!

The handgun makes a high-pitched buzz. ❼
Roth falls.
Sarah screams.

STYRE Why do you make that disagreeable noise?

SARAH You killed him ~~for nothing~~!

STYRE That is my function. I am a warrior.

SARAH You're a murderer. Murderer~~, you mean~~ –

STYRE Silence. The moron was of no further ~~value~~ use to me. I had already tested him. You, as a female, are far more interesting – and soon ~~we~~ I will have the rest of your companions.

Styre gives a bleeped message to the machine which trundles off. ❽

Harry is stealthily climbing down on the further side of the crag.

2. EXT. PIT AREA. (OB) DAY.
PIT AREA (TOP)

The Doctor, struggling a bit, is climbing from the pit by means of the log. He hears some noise above.

DOCTOR WHO Hullo Sarah?

Vural and the others loom at the edge of the pit, guns pointing.

DOCTOR WHO Oh, it's you again. Can't say I'm delighted. No good pretending.

VURAL Just keep climbing. Nice and quiet.

DOCTOR WHO If you insist.

~~3. EXT. RUINS. (OB) DAY.~~
~~STREET AREA~~

~~*Harry is moving through the ruined cloisters with extreme caution. Suddenly he makes a dive for cover – a bush, a pile of rock, whatever.*~~

~~*Styre comes heavily round the corner. He is passing the place where Harry is hiding when he stops. He stares around suspiciously. Harry flattens himself.*~~

~~*After a tense second Styre goes on towards the courtyard.*~~

~~*Styre disappears.*~~

~~*Harry sighs with relief. He heads further into the ruins.*~~

3A. EXT. RUINS. (OB) DAY.
STAIRCASE BOTTOM

HARRY *(Low)* Sarah..? Sarah, old girl… you here anywhere?

He hears a low moan ❾ *and stops.*

HARRY Sarah? Where are you?

3B. EXT. RUINS. (OB) DAY.
PRISONER'S DUNGEON

The moan again.

Harry traces the sound to – depending on location – the ruins of a room, an alcove, or simply the other side of a wall. ❿

A man is manacled against the wall. He is dressed in the same kind of uniform that Vural's party wears. He is obviously dying. He cringes away as Harry bends over him.

HARRY All right, old chap.

PRISONER No… no…

HARRY It's all right, old chap. I'm not going to hurt you. Let's take a look…

PRISONER … Water…

Harry makes a swift professional examination of the man.

4. EXT. PIT AREA. (OB) DAY.
PIT AREA TOP

The Doctor has reached ground level. Vural motions Krans to pull him up.

VURAL Krans.

KRANS No tricks now…

He bends forward.

DOCTOR WHO Behind you!

KRANS I said no tricks –

The Doctor drops back into the pit.
The machine is rolling up to the group.
They open fire with their guns but the tentacles are already lashing towards them. ⓫

~~5. EXT. RUINS. (OB) DAY.~~
~~TUNNEL EXIT~~

~~*Harry has found water.*~~

~~*He soaks a handkerchief in it then heads back into the ruins.*~~

5A. EXT. RUINS. (OB) DAY. PRISONER'S DUNGEON

On the prisoner. Harry arrives and puts the wet cloth between the man's lips. He sucks greedily. Harry tugs at the solid iron rings of the manacles. They are firmly fixed into the wall.

HARRY Look, old chap. I'm going to have to go and get help. You understand?

The prisoner nods weakly.

HARRY The Sontaran put you here? *(Another nod)* What for? Do you know why?

The prisoner gathers his strength.

PRISONER To… die –

HARRY To die? Are there many more of you?

The prisoner nods 🕛 *and then goes limp. Harry feels his pulse, he shakes his head grimly.*

6. EXT. THE PIT. (OB) DAY. PIT AREA BOTTOM

The Doctor is searching the floor of the pit. He pulls aside the bush and uncovers the keystone with the hole below it. He peers in.

DOCTOR WHO Not the Central Line…

He starts to wriggle into the hole, feet first.

7. EXT. RUINS. (OB) DAY. SARAH'S DUNGEON

Any roofless or partly roofed alcove or chamber. Styre is bending over Sarah. She is strapped to a stone plinth. 🕛

STYRE When I ambushed the Galsec ship there were nine survivors. I have **already** used **up** five of them and have been studying the **free** behaviour patterns of the remaining four.

SARAH So?

STYRE So it is useless lying to me. I know you were not on that Galsec ship. Where ~~have~~ **do** you come from? What is your planet of origin?

SARAH ~~I've told you…~~ Earth.

STYRE That is a lie. There has been no intelligent life on this planet since the time of the solar flares.

SARAH How do you know?

STYRE I have ~~seen~~ the reports.

SARAH And they can't be wrong can they?

STYRE Silence!

Styre stomps about. Irritated by Sarah and the possibility of error, he turns on her.

STYRE You are nothing, you understand? You are a mistake, and must therefore be eliminated. According to my data you should not exist. ~~When I have finished with you, the necessary correction will be made, and the plan will go forward as before. It will be as if you never existed.~~

SARAH ~~I see… What plan is this?~~

STYRE ~~The Sontaran invasion programme. But it is of no concern of yours: you will not be alive to see it. Meanwhile, you may have some experimental value, like the others.~~

Styre leaves.

8. EXT. RUINS. (OB) DAY. APPROACH (2)

Harry has armed himself with a length of heavy chain. 🕛 *He comes to a hole where a section of wall has fallen down. He peers through. Styre is climbing towards him.*

Harry drops flat. Styre goes by on the far side of the wall. Harry gets to his feet and climbs through the hole. He heads in the direction Styre came from. 🕛

9. EXT. RUINS. (OB) DAY. SARAH'S DUNGEON

HARRY Sarah?

On Sarah, strapped to the plinth. She struggles against the bonds without effect.

SARAH *(OV)* Harry! **Over here.**

HARRY Sarah!

He is staring in at her, frozen with shock.

SARAH ~~Harry!~~ **Well come on.** Help me!

HARRY Hang on, old thing. ~~I'll have you out of there in a tick!~~

He runs smack into the force wall and falls back. He gets up and tries again. There is a solid invisible barrier he cannot penetrate. 🕛

HARRY ~~What the deuce –?~~ I can't get in.

SARAH It's a force field.

HARRY Eh?

SARAH **That's it,** he's locked me inside a force field. It's no good, Harry.

HARRY *(Baffled)* Well – ~~Look –~~ don't worry, old ~~girl~~ **thing**. I'll find a way! I'll get you out of there if I have to knock his bally head off and grab his keys.

He starts to hurry away and then turns back.

HARRY Just don't **you** worry, Sarah.

He leaves. ⑰

10. EXT. RUINS. (OB) DAY. ⑱
COURTYARD CONTROL AREA

Styre lumbers into a seat in front of it. Into his pocket recorder as he adjusts other switches:

STYRE Experiment seven. Subject female. Project – resistance to fear.

He tunes in on the screen. We see Sarah in her dungeon. ⑲

11. EXT. RUINS. (OB) DAY. ⑳
SARAH'S DUNGEON

Sarah on her plinth, 'seeing' these monstrous things, ㉑ *trying to resist the terror she feels.* ㉒

12. EXT. RUINS. (OB) DAY. ㉓
COURTYARD CONTROL AREA

Styre flicks off the screen and tunes in something else.

STYRE G three intelligence… G three intelligence, Field Major Styre reporting from Earthbase…

The screen deblurs: we see another Sontaran, in a more resplendent costume: that of the Fleet Marshal. ㉔

MARSHAL Well, Styre?

STYRE My report, Marshal –

MARSHAL Get on with it then.

STYRE As we know the Earth has not been repopulated. I have therefore carried out my instructions and have lured a group of humans to the planet for testing. The results of my experiments indicate that they are puny beings with little resistance to physical stress and are totally dependent on organic chemical intake for their energy supply.

MARSHAL Thank you Styre. Then your report is ~~ready~~ **complete**.

STYRE Not quite Marshal.

MARSHAL But why ~~should~~ **must** there be any delay?

STYRE Some inconsistencies have arisen. Small mistakes that will soon be eliminated. My final intelligence report for the assault will be with you within the hour, Marshal.

MARSHAL It must be, Styre, it must be… ~~You will now see how the battle fleet is assembled.~~

And off goes the marshal's image. To be replaced by shot showing battle phalanxes. ㉕

STYRE Very good, sah!

12A. EXT. RUINS. (OB) DAY. ㉖
TUNNEL EXIT

Tunnel exit.

Doctor appears and exits out L.

12B. EXT. RUINS. (OB) DAY. ㉗
APPROACH (1)

Doctor makes a crouching run to the nearest wall, edges along it, and rounds a corner.

~~12C. EXT. RUINS. (OB) DAY.~~
~~STREET AREA~~

~~**HARRY** Whoops!~~

~~*Harry is poised to swat him with the chain. He lowers the chain with a sheepish grin.*~~

~~**DOCTOR WHO** Doctor Sullivan, I presume?~~

~~**HARRY** Sorry about that. I thought you were the pig-faced chap.~~

~~**DOCTOR WHO** Pig-faced chap?~~

~~**HARRY** This potato-headed feller.~~

~~**DOCTOR WHO** Potato-headed… Harry, you'd better start again.~~

~~**HARRY** Ah. Yes. Well. I fell in a pit.~~

~~**DOCTOR WHO** I know. Part of the Whitehall warren. Carry on.~~

~~13. EXT. RUINS. (OB) DAY.~~
~~SARAH'S DUNGEON~~

~~*Sarah, still 'seeing' projected horrors, finally cracks.*~~

~~*She screams with terror.*~~

~~14. EXT. RUINS. (OB) DAY.~~
~~STREET AREA~~

~~**DOCTOR WHO** I see… The Sontarans again –~~

~~**HARRY** Fellow called himself Styre.~~

~~**DOCTOR WHO** Yes, well they're all identical – all clones – ssh!~~

~~*Distinctly: Sarah screams again.*~~

~~**DOCTOR WHO** That's Sarah!~~

~~*He is off immediately.*~~

~~HARRY Doctor, you can't reach her! There's~~
~~some kind of force field…~~
~~But the Doctor has gone.~~
~~Harry shrugs. He decides to follow.~~

15. EXT. RUINS. (OB) DAY.
SARAH'S DUNGEON

*Sarah's terrorization reaches a climax. She is
rigid and screaming, straining against her
bonds.*
*The Doctor arrives at the force wall. He feels
over the area and then locates the Magnox
drive set in the wall. He flicks his sonic
screwdriver to full power and directs its jet at
the Magnox drive.*
*Under the jet of the screwdriver Magnox
drive flares up and falls off the wall. Over
action:* 28

DOCTOR WHO Sarah… Sarah..! Listen to me,
Sarah! It's not real! D'you understand~~, Sarah..?~~
Nothing is happening to you. It's only in your
mind… 29 Fight it, Sarah. Fight it!
*Sarah passes out – or dies? – of sheer terror just
as the Doctor breaks the force wall and gets to
her.*
He bends over, listening for a heartbeat. 30
DOCTOR WHO Sarah…
His face clouds with a terrible resolve.
And as he straightens up –
STYRE Very touching.
DOCTOR WHO You unspeakable abomination.
*The Doctor swings round and grapples with
Styre. Face to face in BCU: flings the Doctor
away.* 31
STYRE Words, earthling, will never prevail
against Sontaran… might!
DOCTOR WHO *(Doctor on ground)* Why did you
do this to her? *(Picks himself up)*
STYRE I did nothing. I merely resurrected those
things which lay buried in the depths of her
~~own~~ pathetic little mind. She was a victim of
her own fear…
Brings up his handgun.
STYRE And now – your turn…
The Doctor glances to the R.
DOCTOR WHO Get him Harry!
*Styre swings round. The Doctor catches hold of
Styre's gun hand and continues the swing,
spinning Styre in the 'extralight' gravity of*

Earth. Leaving him spinning, the Doctor 32
races out.
Styre recovers and rounds the corner.
He fires a blast at the Doctor.
The Doctor spins and dodges towards cover.
Styre takes a steady aim and blasts again.
The Doctor falls.
*Styre walks up to him and kicks the body
contemptuously.*
STYRE Worm!

16. EXT. RUINS. (OB) DAY.
SPACECRAFT AREA

*Enter the machine towing the three spacemen.
It halts and sends out a stream of bleeps.*
KRANS Well, now we know what happened to
our mates.
ERAK We've still got a chance. If this thing
intended to kill us…
He stops as Styre appears.
KRANS Might have been the best thing.
STYRE Good, the final batch of material.
VURAL Not me. No, not me –
STYRE All of you.
VURAL But I helped you! I did everything you
said –
KRANS What?
VURAL You said you'd save me if I –
STYRE ~~A simple test of human gullibility.~~ Why
should I spare you – a traitor to your own
miserable kind?
ERAK You stinking lousy swine, Vural! You
tried to do a deal with this thing?
VURAL It was all I could do – it gave us more
time.
KRANS That first night ~~we were here~~. He was
~~missing~~ gone for hours. Lost, he said…
VURAL ~~It was~~ I did it for us…
*Styre tears the kinemitter device from Vural's
shirt.*
STYRE Enough of this bickering. ~~Take them!~~
The machine tows them off.

17. EXT. RUINS. (OB) DAY.
SARAH'S DUNGEON

*Harry is bending over the unconscious Sarah.
He shakes his head.*
*He leaves her now he sees the sprawled figure
of the Doctor.*

HARRY Doctor!

He hurries to him and turns him over. The Doctor is lifeless.

HARRY Not both of them!

He straightens, looks round in indecision then moves on.

17A. EXT. RUINS. (OB) DAY. PRISONER'S DUNGEON

Harry rounds the next corner. Finds the Prisoner. The man is dead.

HARRY Murdering swine…

Footsteps, Harry backs away out of sight.
Harry takes a firm grip on his length of chain. ㉝

Styre enters, he checks the condition of the prisoner and then starts to dictate into his hand recorder.

STYRE Field Major Styre, Sontaran G Three Military Assessment Survey. Experiment five: human resistance to fluid deprivation; data: subject died after nine days, seven hours. Impairment of mental faculties, motor reflexes and physical co-ordination noted after only three days.

Harry, round the corner, creeps forward with the clear intention of attacking Styre.

STYRE *(VO)* Conclusion: dependence on fluid is a significant weakness which should be exploited in our attack…

A hand taps Harry's shoulder. He spins. It is the Doctor. Groggy but unbowed he motions Harry to silence and pulls him away.

STYRE *(VO)* As a rider to the above, we should also **like to** take account ~~of~~ the successful conclusion of experiment four where immersion in the fluid, H_2O, produced asphyxiation in less than three minutes. Conclusion: the species has little resistance to… immersion in liquids.

18. EXT. RUINS. (OB) DAY. COURTYARD TALK AREA

The Doctor and Harry stop.

~~**DOCTOR WHO** I'm ashamed of you Harry. Hitting a chap from behind!~~
~~**HARRY** I thought you were —~~

~~**DOCTOR WHO** Anyway, it wouldn't have worked unless you'd caught him on the back of his neck. That's his Achilles heel you know.~~

HARRY Doctor, I thought you were **both** dead!

The Doctor opens his jacket. He takes a dented metal plate from the inside pocket.

DOCTOR WHO Not me. ~~Part~~ **A piece** of the sonastic ㉞ locking mechanism from Nerva's rocket. ㉟ ~~Forgot I'd popped it in my jacket.~~

HARRY Fortuitous.

DOCTOR WHO Foresight~~, old chap~~. You never know when these bits and pieces will come in handy. ~~Nails, string, chewing gum, sonastic locking mechanisms…~~ Never throw anything away, Harry.

~~**HARRY** What are you looking for now?~~

DOCTOR WHO Now where's my five-hundred-year diary. ㊱ I remember jotting a few notes about the Sontarans… ~~No I can't find it. Carrying too much rubbish.~~ It's a mistake to clutter one's pockets, Harry.

HARRY Yes, Doctor.

DOCTOR WHO ~~Before he shot me I'd rather hoped to find out what he's doing here.~~ What's Styre doing here?

HARRY Well, he's killing people ~~mostly~~. **This is** some sort of ghastly experiment. **Look what he's done to Sarah.**

DOCTOR WHO Harry, Sontarans never do anything without a military reason. ~~Look you'd better hang on here and see if there's anything you can do for Sarah —~~ **You look to Sarah.**

HARRY ~~Where are you going?~~ **What are you going to do?**

DOCTOR WHO ~~To~~ Find out what's behind all this. ~~Now do try and keep out of trouble, Harry.~~

He leaves. ㊲

19. EXT. RUINS. (OB) DAY. COURTYARD TORTURE AREA

Vural is staked out.
Krans and Erak are holding a metal bar above him.

STYRE Experiment eight: resistance to pressure on the human breast cage and muscular strength. Are you prepared?

ERAK ㊳ **What are you up to – you lump of filth?**

STYRE You are holding a gravity bar. At the moment it is a mere 40 pounds earth weight. I will increase that weight to 200 pounds…

He moves a hand control. Erak and Krans grunt under the sudden weight.

STYRE 300 pounds…

He watches Erak and Krans slowly sinking to their knees.

STYRE We will now increase the weight of the bar to 500 pounds, earth gravity.

He moves a hand control. Erak and Krans grunt under the sudden weight.

STYRE 600 pounds… When you drop it the experiment will end.

He watches Erak and Krans slowly sinking to their knees.

19A. EXT. RUINS. (OB) DAY. 39 SPACECRAFT AREA

The Doctor approaches Styre's ship. 40 *He turns to find the machine behind him.*

DOCTOR WHO Hello… Hello… Don't be alarmed, old thing. I'm not going to hurt you. Everything's going to be all right.

He aims the sonic screwdriver at the robot. The robot collapses. 41

VURAL *(VO)* Please!

19B. EXT. RUINS. (OB) DAY. COURTYARD TORTURE AREA

VURAL Please!

KRANS You murdering fiend!

STYRE ~~Strange.~~ He is not your friend. He is a traitor. And yet you struggle to save his life. ~~700~~ 500 pounds.

The bar drops to Vural's chest. He gives a scream of terror.

Suddenly a stream of beeps call Styre to the control area.

STYRE Enough! I ~~will~~ must delay the experiment.

He turns dial back then leaves.

KRANS Erak – the knife. The knife!

Erak struggles to reach a knife close by.

20. EXT. RUINS. (OB) DAY. COURTYARD CONTROL AREA

Styre comes into the courtyard. He doesn't notice the Doctor watching from the top of a nearby wall. His attention is immediately captured by the video image of the marshal on the screen.

MARSHAL ~~Major!~~ Styre! Field Major Styre! I order you to report.

STYRE This is Field Major Styre, sir.

MARSHAL Styre, your constant delays are causing alarm. We must have your report.

STYRE I am just ~~conducting the~~ completing my final experiment~~, Marshal~~. The compressibility test of human tissue.

MARSHAL The entire invasion fleet is being held up~~, Styre~~. How much longer must we wait?

STYRE ~~Sir,~~ My programme was ordered by the Grand Strategic Council. The invasion cannot begin until all experiments are analysed.

MARSHAL Then get a move on, Styre! The fleet is waiting for my signal.

He fades out.

STYRE Very good, ~~sir~~ Marshal.

He makes some control adjustments. The Doctor has seen enough. He slides backwards off the wall.

21. EXT. THE RUINS. (OB) DAY. SARAH'S DUNGEON

Sarah on her plinth. A hand touches her face, lifts an eyelid. It is Harry. He peers into her eye. Its lid flickers.

HARRY *(Relieved)* About time..! I thought you were a goner…

SARAH Those… awful things! Where are they?

HARRY Steady on, old girl. There's nothing here.

SARAH They seemed so real. I knew it was my mind but…

HARRY Just something friend Styre arranged for you. I've really taken a dislike to that fellow. Now let's get you untied…

Harry starts untying Sarah.

The Doctor enters. 42

SARAH Doctor!

DOCTOR WHO Ah Sarah! Feeling better? No, don't ~~answer~~ tell me – ~~there isn't~~ no time. We've got an invasion on our hands.

HARRY An invasion? You mean Styre –

DOCTOR WHO Him and thousands exactly like him.

SARAH They're going to invade Earth?

DOCTOR WHO ~~Not only Earth this~~ The entire galaxy. ~~I imagine~~ It's suddenly acquired some strategic ~~significance~~ **importance** in their ~~interminable~~ **endless** war against the Rutans.

HARRY But why is Styre torturing – them all.

DOCTOR WHO He's making an assessment of human physical limitations. Sontarans are very methodical people. ~~They leave nothing to chance.~~ And that might give us a slight advantage.

HARRY I haven't noticed, frankly.

SARAH **What are you going to do?**

DOCTOR WHO I'm going to take him on in single combat. It's the only way ~~to stop him~~.

HARRY You're what?

DOCTOR WHO Sontarans never turn down the chance to kill somebody.

SARAH You're not going to let him kill you?

DOCTOR WHO Hope not. Going to try to tire him – he's pretty unwieldy for all his strength and he's not used to Earth gravity. The thing is, if I can get him exhausted he'll have to go back to his ship to re-energize. Are you with me?

HARRY Just about.

DOCTOR WHO While I keep him busy, I want you to get into his ship. Now, once you're **inside, this is what I want you to do, Harry**…

The Doctor hands Harry his screwdriver and Harry gives the Doctor the staff.

22. EXT. RUINS. (OB) DAY.
COURTYARD TORTURE AREA

On Vural choking under the weight on his chest.

STYRE Increase to ~~one thousand~~ **600** pounds.
Suddenly the Doctor appears, Error Flynn style, on the rocks behind him. 43

DOCTOR WHO ~~Turn Hellhound turn!~~ **Styre!** Still about your butcher's ways, Styre?

STYRE ~~Not~~ You..! But I killed you!

DOCTOR WHO Another mistake, Styre. You've fallen right into our trap.

STYRE Trap –?

DOCTOR WHO **Yes.** Those people you've been so cleverly evaluating are not Earth warriors. They are our slave class – the lowest form of human intelligence.

STYRE You lie!

DOCTOR WHO Do you think these puny creatures could conquer half the galaxy? No, Styre…

DOCTOR WHO I represent the true warrior class: evaluate me if you dare!
Styre brings his handgun up.

DOCTOR WHO Is that the Sontaran way? The mighty warrior sheltering behind ~~a~~ **his** gun? I challenge you, Styre! Single combat! Or are you afraid?

STYRE Afraid..? A Sontaran, afraid?
He snatches one of the prisoner's machetes and turns to face the Doctor.

STYRE All right. Come to your death!
The Doctor has a wooden staff 44 *which he uses kendo style: i.e. he stands still as Styre rushes at him and then moves swiftly aside and thwacks Styre, aiming for the probic vent all the time.* 45

While this is going on, Krans and Erak struggle to lay the bar beyond Vural's head.

The fight moves quickly from place to place, using all the natural features of the area.

We see that the Doctor is trying to get Styre to charge about as much as possible – without getting caught by the machete Styre wields with devastating ferocity.

Harry is meanwhile working his way towards the spaceship. 46

Sarah has gone to help Krans and Erak release Vural. 47

DOCTOR WHO Styre – it's not over yet!

STYRE I'll finish with you later.
He moves up the ramp but the Doctor trips him with the staff.

Styre rolls off the ramp but pulls the Doctor down.

They wrestle on the ground.

Styre gets the upper hand and raises his machete for a lethal chop.

Vural runs forward and springs on Styre's sword arm. The combatants roll apart.

Styre kills Vural with a savage blow and again heads for the ramp.

Again the Doctor delays him.

There is a final flurry of action on the ramp. Staff and machete are lost and they grapple face to face.

Harry, holding a piece of machinery, slips out of the craft.

The Doctor sees him, Styre doesn't.

DOCTOR WHO You're weakening, Styre, **you're** weakening…

STYRE Am I?

He makes one last mighty effort and hurls the Doctor off the ramp. He is spread-eagled, apparently unconscious on the ground.

STYRE I shall kill you all now… But first I have more important tasks to ~~complete~~ **perform**.

He staggers into the spacecraft. The Doctor makes an amazing recovery and scrambles to his feet, helped by Harry.

DOCTOR WHO ~~Did you get it?~~

Harry shows him a small piece of electronic gadgetry.

HARRY Is this what you meant?

DOCTOR WHO It had better be – let's get out of here!

SARAH Doctor – Styre's killed Vural. He saved your life. ~~What's happening?~~

DOCTOR WHO I know. ~~Out of here,~~ Everybody out as fast as you can. **Come on.**

They all run for it and reach the safety of a crumbling wall as a loud roaring and rumbling starts to come out of the spaceship.

The rumbling becomes volcanic. And then Styre appears at the door of the ship.

Smoke pouring from him, in his death agonies.

As he screams, we zoom in.

Styre collapses in smoke like a deflated rubber ball. 48

The spaceship blows up with a huge flash of brilliant white light. 49

They are all crouched while dust and plaster rain on them. When all is quiet Sarah looks up.

SARAH What happened ~~Doctor~~?

DOCTOR WHO Ask Harry. He did it.

HARRY What did I do? And what is this ~~bit~~ **thing** anyway?

The Doctor takes the piece of electronic gadgetry from Harry and contemplates it.

DOCTOR WHO It's a sort of terrulian diode bypass transformer – 50

HARRY *(Completely blank)* Oh.

DOCTOR WHO Yes. Sontarans as I told you ~~occasionally~~ **sometimes** need to feed on pure energy. By removing this, you – er – altered things slightly… *(little sad smile)* and the energy fed on him.

KRANS 51 Well. That's **taken care of** one of 'em. ~~What about this~~ **But what about the rest of** the invasion fleet waiting to blast us out of the galaxy?

The Doctor crosses to the communication set-up and switches on.

DOCTOR WHO ~~Well come on you two. I'll just deal with that.~~ Yes, well I'll just attend to that.

22A. EXT. RUINS. (OB) DAY. SPACECRAFT AREA

The fight moves now towards the ship and then round to the rear of it.

This gives Harry a chance to use the sonic screwdriver to gain access.

While Harry does this we lose sight of the two combatants.

But no sooner is Harry inside than Styre appears, staggering and exhausted… and alone.

Styre staggers up the ramp. Then the Doctor, also the worse for wear, appears).

DOCTOR WHO Styre! *(Styre turns)* It's not over yet –

22B. EXT. RUINS. (OB) DAY. COURTYARD CONTROL AREA

The Marshal's rage-contorted face appears.

MARSHAL Styre! Your report, the ~~coordin~~ intelligence – . *(Sees the Doctor)* What is this?

DOCTOR WHO Your Waterloo, Marshal… Your intelligence unit has been destroyed, I'm afraid… And the invasion plans are in our ~~possession~~ **hands**. One move across the buffer zone, Marshal, and your entire fleet will be ~~annihilated~~ **destroyed**…

MARSHAL We shall destroy your planets –

DOCTOR WHO ~~Without the coordinates?~~ 52 ~~Not this time… You're bluffing Marshal. May as well face up to it, you've lost again.~~ **What, without Styre's report?**

MARSHAL Next time, earthling, we shall utt**erly destroy you** –
The Doctor switches him off.
DOCTOR WHO ~~No speeches, thank you. Bye!~~ Not today, thank you. *(The others look at him amazed, he smiles)* Brinkmanship I think they call it.

23. EXT. GLOBE CIRCLE. (OB) DAY. MATTERBEAM GLOBE AREA

The Doctor is making a last adjustment to a globe.
The others are all present.
DOCTOR WHO Sure you won't ~~come with~~ join us?
KRANS We'll wait here till that lot from Nerva get here. Thanks all the same.

ERAK Don't trust those transmat beams. They never work too good.
DOCTOR WHO As you wish.
Krans and Erak move out of the circle and stand at the edge.
DOCTOR WHO I should stand back **if I were you** ~~a bit. Just in case~~. I mean it should be –
Suddenly the Doctor, Harry and Sarah vanish. We hear the Doctor's voice.
DOCTOR WHO *(VO)* All right. But you never know –
The Doctor reappears.
DOCTOR WHO Quite, do you?
And off he goes again, this time for good. 🔵53

CLOSING TITLES

---

❶ This line is included in the script for Part Two, though omitted from the end of Part One. Note the misspelling of Linx.

❷ This was the original ending of Part One. But to help balance the episode lengths, the end of Part One was moved back to Styre's removal of his helmet.

❸ A prop re-used from *The Time Warrior* (1973/4).

❹ This was recorded as two separate shots – the 'tentacle' cables leaving Roth and Sarah, and then the tentacles being pulled back into the robot.

❺ This is a reference to Sarah's first meeting with a Sontaran – Linx – in *The Time Warrior*.

❻ The decision was taken to provide Styre with a different weapon from the stubby 'wand' Linx has in *The Time Warrior*. The requirement stated to Visual Effects was for 'a new gun, v. simple'. The original design drawing is reproduced on page 159.

❼ Styre's gun effect was achieved using a 12"× 9" black card with a red dot to show the gun firing (from the Graphics Department). The red-dot image was positioned and overlaid on a close-up of the gun.

❽ This sequence was recorded, but not used.

❾ The prisoner's moan was recorded with Scene 3B (recorded the previous day) and edited in.

❿ These directions show the original intent for Styre's base to be in a ruined priory. The prisoner is chained to a rock wall, manacles hanging down from above (described to Visual Effects as 'futuristic mangles').

⓫ The OB scanner van had a videodisc unit facility (often used on sports coverage) which allowed shots to be run backwards and re-recorded in reverse. This effect was used for shots where the robot's tentacles captured its prey. The colonists were tied with the ropes, which were pulled back into the robot. When reversed, the effect was to show the ropes shooting out from the robot and wrapping round the colonists.

⓬ The scene ends here – we do not see that the prisoner is dead. (If Harry knew the prisoner was dead here, Scene 17A would make little sense.)

⓭ A device is attached to Sarah's forehead. The visual effects requirements document notes: 'Terminals – head device for Sarah: a circular disc, to be taped to Sarah's forehead using toupee tape.'

⓮ Harry has not found the chain, but brandishes a heavy stick as a potential weapon. Probably this was also the case in Scene 12C, as Harry subsequently has the stick in Scene 17.

⓯ Scene 12A was edited in here.

⓰ No visual effect was provided for the force field – just Ian Marter pushing against the air, and an accompanying sound effect.

⓱ Scene 12B was edited in here.

(18) This scene (together with Scene 11) was moved to come at the end of Scene 12.

(19) The images of Sarah were fed 'live' from another camera in the dungeon area.

(20) This scene (together with Scene 10) was moved to come at the end of Scene 12.

(21) The script did not specify the projected horrors that Sarah endured in Styre's experiment, but it did explain that the cause of the force field which stopped Harry and later the Doctor from reaching Sarah was a Magnox drive, the control panel of which was to be set into the rock face. Sarah sees her rope turn into a snake (a puppet with an opening mouth), then back again. Rapidly moving hand-held camera shots made the rocks above seem to be falling towards her, and finally 'gunge' covered her legs. The videodisc was used to alter the speed of the gunge moving up Sarah's legs.

(22) Dick Mills created one of his favourite sounds, squelching swarfega in his hands, to represent the gunge which terrified Sarah.

(23) This scene was moved to come ahead of Scene 10 (after the repositioned Scene 12B).

(24) Lindsay pre-recorded his dialogue as the marshal against a specially erected set and this was then played back to a monitor from the scanner van so that Lindsay could complete the scene as Styre. The marshal's uniform was identical to Styre's except for two circular 'bosses' on the collar to denote his rank.

(25) A graphic of the Sontaran war fleet in space was actually produced but not used. The scene cuts straight into Scene 10. The requirement for the graphic was stated as: 'Caption for model or whatever to represent radar type blips of Sontaran starships in battle phalanxes.' A handwritten note added: '12"× 9" Graphics – caption drawing of spaceships blurred edge of spacecraft until sides of ships disappearing.' The unused drawing is reproduced on page 159.

(26) This scene was edited in ahead of Scene 9.

(27) This scene was edited in ahead of Scene 10.

(28) For this sequence the script suggests: '(Note: This effect demands that the Magnox drive be constructed of celluloid or some similar inflammable substance. It also requires the sonic screwdriver to be practical. A Ronson blowtorch with a flexible extension running down the Doctor's sleeve to the "Screwdriver"?)'. In the event, a small package with a flash charge was detonated on cue.

(29) This is the point where the Doctor actually destroys the Magnox drive. This was supposed to be recorded – along with Styre's gunshot at the Doctor – at the end of the scene and edited back in. Since Tom Baker was injured, it was actually recorded another day.

(30) The Doctor pushes the device from Sarah's forehead.

(31) It was at this point that Tom Baker slipped and cracked his collarbone. The accident meant that the final four scenes of the day were not recorded until later in the week.

(32) Tom Baker was doubled by Terry Walsh as Baker was injured.

(33) Harry still has the heavy stick.

(34) In *The Ark in Space* it is 'synestic' not 'sonastic'. Other documents call it 'selenium' (see page 172).

(35) Visual Effects was asked to provide two metal plates, one perhaps for use undamaged in *The Ark in Space*: 'the old "before" and "after" bit'.

(36) The second Doctor (played by Patrick Troughton) had a five-hundred-year-diary in some of his earlier stories, such as *The Power of the Daleks* (1966).

(37) Again Terry Walsh doubles for the Doctor as he scrambles up the rocks and along a ledge.

(38) Dialogue was added to explain the gravity-bar experiment, and to provide a more 'natural' breaking point for the inserted scene that follows. The original design for the gravity-bar is reproduced on page 158.

(39) This short scene was worked out on location and added to explain what happens to Styre's robot.

(40) Terry Walsh doubles for the Doctor in long shots.

(41) Since no visual effect was planned for the robot's destruction, it was allowed to collapse down to one side on its 'legs'. Sound effects indicated that the robot was in trouble, and 'dying'.

(42) Harry and Sarah run up to the Doctor (who does not move much in this scene due to Baker's injury).

(43) After a brief shot of Terry Walsh as the Doctor running up over the rocks, Baker is seen in close-up to disguise his injury.

(44) Given him by Harry.

(45) For the fight scene, Terry Walsh doubled for Tom Baker and Stuart Fell for Kevin Lindsay as Styre.

46 Scene 22A was cut into the main action. Harry opens the spaceship door with the sonic screwdriver.

47 Various cut-in shots were recorded separately from the main action to be edited into the scene. These were referred to by code letter and were: (a) *Sarah/Harry crossing to Vural/Krans/Erak;* (b) *Sarah/Erak/Krans releasing Vural;* (c) *Harry starting to climb;* (d) *Harry further up climb;* (e) *Doctor fighting – avoiding Styre's machete, tripping, falling;* (f) *Styre waving machete, burying machete in ground;* (g) *Close-up Doctor's feet;* (h) *Close-up Styre's feet.* After a recording break, four further cut-ins were recorded: (a) *Close-ups Doctor – climbing rocks;* (b) *Close-ups Styre – wielding machete;* (c) *Close-ups Doctor's legs – machete missing ankles;* (d) *2-shot Styre/Doctor, Styre cutting Doctor's stick.*

48 To achieve this, the air was let out of a balloon inflated inside the Sontaran mask positioned above the empty Sontaran costume.

49 The destruction of Styre's craft was done by removing the spaceship prop during a white-out, and editing this with a large explosion set off by Tony Oxley. The detonation was so large that it was heard by the public in nearby villages and the police were contacted.

50 The visual effects requirements sheet lists this as: 'Terruliam Diode Bypass Transformer – Electronic gadgetry prop.'

51 This line was given to Harry.

52 The reference to coordinates may be left over from a previous draft of the script. Possibly Styre was charged with obtaining secret coordinates for the invasion as well as, or instead of, the assessment, and was torturing the colonists to get these coordinates (though this invalidates the subplot about Vural's treachery).

53 As with Part One, Scene 1, this was achieved with a locked-off shot and run-ons were used to show the TARDIS crew vanishing.

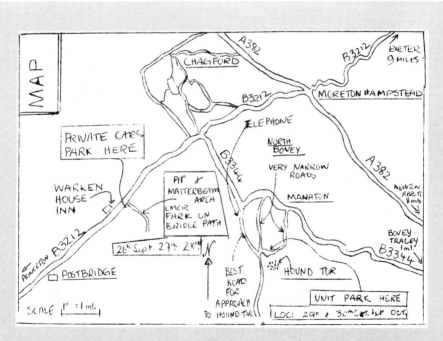

This map, taken from the film schedule, shows the various locations used for *The Sontaran Experiment,* as well as local amenities. A separate sketch map of the Hound Tor area showed the various 'acting areas' in detail.

GENESIS OF
THE DALEKS

BY TERRY NATION

PART ONE first transmitted 8 March 1975 at 17.30

PART TWO 15 March 1975 at 17.30

PART THREE 22 March 1975 at 17.30

PART FOUR 29 March 1975 at 17.30

PART FIVE 5 April 1975 at 17.30

PART SIX 12 April 1975 at 17.30

Overview

Genesis of the Daleks was voted the best-ever *Doctor Who* story by readers of *Doctor Who Magazine*. It isn't hard to see why.

This is a story that has it all – the perfect Doctor pitted against his deadliest enemies for the supreme prize: their very existence. This battle is played out against the backdrop of a thousand-year war on an alien planet, but one where allusions to genetic engineering and Nazi totalitarianism are poignantly presented. In Davros we are presented with the first – and the most convincing – of a series of supervillains that the Hinchcliffe/Holmes team would create. The terrifying thing about him is that he is utterly convincing – his megalomania, his drive, his political acumen, and – most frightening of all – the fact that, in a way, Davros is right. His ideals and goals – the survival of his people – are understandable; it is the way he goes about it, the means to the end that is so abhorrent.

The underlying power of *Genesis of the Daleks*, a story about survival more than anything else, lies in the way the themes and arguments are dramatized. We are with the Doctor as he agonizes about whether he could kill a child who would grow into a dictator; we have seen the suffering the Daleks have inflicted; we know that Davros would indeed release the hypothetical virus…

And it has the Daleks. For all the amusement they seem to cause in the press, the Daleks remain a potent image. Despite the fact that they remain in the background for most of this story, they dominate every scene they are in – upstaging even their creator.

Nothing is perfect. But even with its giant clams, and despite the fact that it is all too obvious that for most of the time there are only three working Daleks, *Genesis of the Daleks* comes about as close as *Doctor Who* gets.

Origin

Since their first appearance in 1963 the Daleks – the ruthless, radiation-mutated race from Skaro confined to mobile metal casings – had been the most popular alien menace on *Doctor Who*. Their creator, Terry Nation, had written or co-written a further three serials (plus a one-off trailer episode) featuring the Daleks through to late 1965. By this time he was involved with commercial film series such as *The Baron*, and later *The Champions, Department S, The Saint, The Avengers* and *The Persuaders!* In 1966 and 1967, two further Dalek serials were written by David Whitaker – with Nation's approval – after which the creatures were dropped for some time. In 1971, producer Barry Letts decided to bring back the Daleks, with Nation agreeing to his 'bad guys' being inserted into an existing Louis Marks script. This became *Day of the Daleks*. Following on from this, there was a 'gentleman's agreement' that Nation would be approached for a Dalek serial in each season; Nation wrote *Destination: Daleks* (retitled *Planet of the Daleks,* 1973) between May and August 1972 for Season Ten, and *Death to the Daleks* during July 1973 for Season Eleven.

In late 1973, Nation considered his Dalek submission for Season Twelve, and engaged in discussions with Letts and Terrance Dicks. The storyline Nation proposed was one that Letts felt re-used too much material from the earlier Dalek serials. *Planet of the Daleks* had already been a partial reworking of the original 1963 Dalek serial. As a fresh starting point, Letts proposed that Nation should investigate how the Daleks were created. This notion fired Nation's imagination. Robert Holmes was not terribly keen to feature a Dalek serial in the season that he would be editing, mainly because he found returning enemies tended to become boring. Also, he had not enjoyed script editing *Death to the Daleks.*

Holmes' feelings were shared by incoming producer Philip Hinchcliffe, who joined the team after the serial had been commissioned. Hinchcliffe felt the Daleks lacked menace, and determined that any serial spanning six episodes would have to be strong drama to appeal to both an adult and child audience. However, Letts' enthusiasm, and the fact that the abuse of genetic engineering – plus its related moral issues – could be brought into a new Dalek storyline made the project more attractive.

This storyline was to become Nation's favourite *Doctor Who* submission, as he set about studying the influences on his creation of the Daleks in 1963 and fleshing out the horrific war that had spawned them. The concept of identical, emotionless, ruthless killers was his embodiment of Adolf Hitler's Nazi regime of World War II, through whose bombings a young Nation had lived in south Wales. This in turn postulated a totalitarian state for the Daleks to emerge from, and also some form of scientific elite. The concept of special people selected to survive a global holocaust was one that terrified Nation. The original neutronic-war scenario led Nation towards a morality tale, which opposed war and totalitarian politics.

The battleground on Skaro was inspired by Nation's memories of a 1936 movie, *Things to Come* directed by William Cameron Menzies – itself an adaptation of H.G. Wells' 1933 novel *The Shape of Things to Come.* This movie depicted various points in the future of mankind, and ultimately a time after a holocaust. Technology had failed and been largely abandoned. The vast majority of the population had returned to a simple way of life, while the rulers made a last-ditch attempt to pour all their remaining science into a vast rocket ship which could whisk a human colony away to populate the stars. Menzies' visions prompted Nation to depict the conflict using old and new technology – space-age weaponry wielded during World War I trench warfare. Survival after catastrophe was also a strong instinct for Nation at this time; since 1973 he had been developing a new BBC drama series called *Survivors* which showed how a small group of survivors would cope after a disease had decimated the world's population.

Storyline

Nation entitled his six-page storyline *Daleks – Genesis of Terror*; this was very close indeed to the six-part adventure which was finally televized. However, without the linking narrative to the previous story, the start of Part One's outline was markedly different:

> The Tardis is in Limbo – it materializes in a <u>garden</u> where a Time Lord is waiting for Dr Who. He directs him to go to Skaro at a time before the Daleks have evolved to try and stop their creation. The Time Lord gives Dr Who a bracelet to transport him with Harry and Sarah to Skaro.

This travel bracelet was a plot device that Nation used to keep the Doctor and his companions involved in the action, akin to the vital TARDIS fluid link stolen by the Daleks in the original 1963 serial. It was also very similar to the 'travel dials' in Nation's 1964 script *The Keys of Marinus*, and the teleport bracelets he would later feature in his BBC space opera *Blake's 7*. The outline for Part One also featured General Greiner who never made it to the finished programmes:

> In a <u>trench</u> [the Doctor's party] endure a gas attack and Dr Who and Harry are captured by the Kaleds and taken to a <u>Command Post</u>. From there they are taken to <u>Command HQ</u> to be questioned by Ravon and later Gen. Greiner who tells them that the Kaleds are winning the war against the Thals and will soon wipe them out completely.

At an early stage, the production team noted that the character of Greiner – who was also present when the Doctor and Harry met the Kaled statesmen in Part Three – 'may be written out and replaced by Ravon'. Tane was originally referred to as 'Gitane'.

Nation specified three races living on Skaro. One of these – the Thals – was a blond humanoid race seen in the original Dalek story and *Planet of the Daleks*:

> Skaro is inhabited by Kaleds, Thals and Mutos (people suffering from radiation effects of old atomic wars).

The Kaleds – a name deriving from an anagram of Daleks as the Doctor points out in Part One – was the race from which the Daleks were to evolve.

The main guest character in the storyline was to be the creator of the Daleks, introduced at the end of Part One:

[Sarah] arrives at a <u>ruin</u> and peers through a hole to see Davros in a wheelchair attended by Gharman. They are obviously carrying out an experiment with a target, then out of the gloom glides a machine – a primitive Dalek which destroys the target to order, much to the satisfaction of Davros.

The storyline for Part Two then observed:

Davros arrives and it is clear that he is the supreme commander and is almost a machine himself.

Some of the episode endings were also different from the finished programmes, with Part Two's climax being:

Some prisoners are shot and Sarah and Sevrin are marooned on the <u>scaffolding of the rocket</u>. Dr Who and Harry are escaping through an <u>air duct</u> when they meet a huge monster.

This narrative began Part Three as:

In the <u>air duct</u> Dr Who and Harry overcome the monster and continue their journey.

And ended (as the camera scripts still do) with:

In the <u>rocket silo</u> Dr Who is trying to sabotage the rocket but is laid out from behind. He comes to in the <u>rocket launch room</u> to hear the count-down for the rocket aimed on the Kaled City. In the <u>Main Lab</u> Kaled scientists are worried. In the <u>rocket launch room</u> the General pushes the fire button and Dr Who realizes that Sarah and Harry must be back in the city by now. He is in despair. In the <u>Main Lab</u> Davros watches the destruction of the Kaled City dome and then orders a Dalek to exterminate Ronson whom he says has betrayed them. Ronson dies.

Part Five was originally to conclude on a more philosophical note (the camera script still retains this ending – see Part Five, Scene 20):

In the <u>corridor</u> Sarah and Harry wait for Dr, who is in the <u>incubator room</u> setting the charge. They call him but receive no answer. Harry rushes in to find the Dr covered in a liquid, he pulls him out into the <u>corridor</u> but he appears unharmed. Worried about the morality of destroying the Dalek race the Dr is full of indecision.

Notable elements missing from this rough outline included the abortive escape from Ravon by the Doctor and Harry in Part One. Part Two's storyline referred to Sarah and Sevrin being held at the Thal dome with a character called Marrass – this is possibly the second Muto who found Sarah at the ruins, or the captured Kaled officer. In Part Three, it was noted that Sarah started to become ill from radiation. In Part Four, Bettan, the Thal woman, was originally a male character, and passing back through the caves, the Doctor, Harry and Sarah come into contact with a huge creature that stings the Doctor. Gharman was also able to get some Elite guards on his side in Part Five, while in the concluding instalment, when Davros learns that the Doctor's party have escaped from his office, he sends the Daleks to kill him.

Concerned about the potential cost of the storyline, Robert Holmes wrote to Terry Nation at his home, Lynsted Park at Sittingbourne in Kent, on Sunday 24 March. Enclosing an annotated version of the storyline, the script editor commented:

> As you will see, we love the story but want it brought down to something the budget will stand. If none of this cuts you too deeply, perhaps you'll ring me and we can discuss possible delivery dates – I need to put a date on the commissioning docket.

Scripts

On Monday 1 April, Nation was commissioned for six scripts for *Daleks – Genesis of Terror*, to be delivered by Sunday 14 July. Part One was rapidly delivered on Monday 22 April, followed by Part Two on Monday 3 July. Scripts for Parts Three and Four were delivered on Saturday 6 July, with the final pair on Friday 19 July.

The character that Nation most enjoyed writing for in his serial was Davros; as an intermediate stage between Kaled and Dalek, Davros could reason in a human fashion, and employ the ruthlessness of the Daleks, meaning that better dialogue could be written for him than was possible with his creations. Careful not to repeat the mistake he made with the Daleks in his original 1963 scripts, Nation specified that Davros' death at the hands of his own creations should not be shown on screen, so that there could be a hint of life left in the character should he be required to return.

Robert Holmes added various references to the scripts to maintain recent continuity and link back to *The Sontaran Experiment*. This included dialogue concerning Nerva Beacon from *The Ark in Space*, and comparing Davros' Elite to the Thinktank organization from *Robot*.

Terry Nation

In March 1988, writer John Peel interviewed Terry Nation for the *Doctor Who* research magazine *In-Vision*. He asked Nation how *Genesis of the Daleks* fitted into his personal vision of the future, as well as established Dalek mythology.

I tried very hard throughout to make *Genesis of the Daleks* fit with what had gone before, to adjust and change where I could but not to step on too many traditions. But obviously everything I knew about the Daleks was already there, and it is much easier to look back. If you look at a formed adult human being now and talk to him you can find out something about his past and his childhood. So I was working from the complete version, and working backwards to how they might have begun.

Later, after the first Dalek story (which was the 'take the money and fly like a thief' one), I began to see some influences in it. By that time I had convinced myself perhaps that they were closer to Nazis than any other political group I could think of. But it worked terribly well for them. I grew up during the war and was aware of the Nazis and their totalitarian state. The Germans seemed to have got totalitarianism into a perfect style by that time.

If you look at *Genesis of the Daleks*, the uniforms, the Elite – all those things – seem to have echoes of what the Nazi regime was like. I was tremendously influenced by that. I would have said that was in the script, but I won't swear to it. So many things change from the moment I put them on the typewriter to the moment they're on the screen. But the Elite was mine, and the general idea was – I believe – mine.

Am I glorifying evil in a way? No, certainly I would have avoided that absolutely. I did try to show them always in the worst possible light – I did destroy virtually all of the Nazi elements there. Remember, there were good guys in that picture too! I think it was a very moral tale.

I do believe that under certain circumstances people, indeed entire races, can be perverted from their original intentions. The burning of Dresden, for instance, was just a war whoop of victory for the British and Americans; it was in some way showing, 'We are the winners, and we will show you just how violently conquerable you are'. I think that was a perversion, it was something that should never have happened.

Genesis of the Daleks was a highly moral tale. It was always intended to be a kind of anti-war piece, an anti-political piece and certainly anti-totalitarianism. Trust no one, especially governments!

The Time Lord mission was the production team's. I was never in on the Time Lords, that was the link situation. We had the time ring because I figured 'How the hell do we get them out?' So we had to give them something. And it's always good to have lost something. If you go back to that very first block of episodes, they had lost the fluid link and had to go back into the Dalek city to get it. That same kind of device worked.

Every time I did a story they would tell me what their overall look was, and what episodes they were coming from – what had been going on. By then they were heavily into the Time Lord stuff, which was something I didn't like. It seemed to me to take authority away from the Doctor.

In *Genesis of the Daleks* we had so many good elements going – we almost overloaded ourselves with elements. We had two different cities, we had two different races of people, we had highly complex political manoeuvring going on. And within all of this we had the Daleks developing. It was a complex story, with a lot of story to tell. It could have gone on for another four episodes in fact.

It's always been one of my favourites because it stayed very true to the script. I had demanded tremendous things of the production—like the rocket ship the Thals were building, and standing on the top of the rocket ship with that dizzying view downwards. I think the producer gave me almost everything I asked for in that show. When I actually sit at the typewriter I see the pictures in front of me, and those pictures were fairly well realized by the time I saw it on the screen— when they'd come out of my head. Never do they come out looking identical to the ones I saw. But that time they came out fairly fully realized. I think the production was brilliant on that show: they did wonderful things.

Production Team

The director chosen for the serial was David Maloney. A former journalist and actor, Maloney had been a production assistant on *Doctor Who* since 1964, working on *The Rescue, The Romans, The Time Meddler, The Myth Makers* (1965) and *The Ark* (1966). In early 1968, he passed the BBC director's course, and was soon directing his first *Doctor Who* serial, *The Mind Robber* (1968); this was followed by *The Krotons* (1968/9), *The War Games* (1969) and his most recent work on the series had been Nation's *Planet of the Daleks* in 1973. By now Maloney had branched out into other BBC drama such as *Softly, Softly: Task Force* and *Z Cars* and was reluctant to become too associated with *Doctor Who*. However, the scripts for *Genesis of the Daleks* impressed him greatly and he soon found that he had a good rapport with Tom Baker. Maloney was contracted to the production on Monday 11 November.

Set design for the serial was handled by David Spode – this was his only *Doctor Who* serial. Visual effects were designed by Peter Day, whose previous *Doctor Who* credits had been *The Evil of the Daleks* (1967), *The Tomb of the Cybermen* (1967), *Fury from the Deep, The Ambassadors of Death, The Daemons, The Sea Devils* (1972) and the previous season's *The Monster of Peladon* (1974). Sylvia James, who had already worked on the current season, supervised make-up, and the same was true for Barbara Kidd in charge of costume (Maloney had requested James Acheson for costume design, but he was not available).

Cast

Cast in the pivotal role of Davros was Michael Wisher, an actor known for his vocal talents who could therefore perform well through a mask. Wisher had just completed a masked role in *Doctor Who* – Magrik in *Revenge of the Cybermen*, which although it was the subsequent serial was recorded before *Genesis of the Daleks*. Wisher's first appearance in *Doctor Who* had been in *The Ambassadors of Death*, followed by *Terror of the Autons* (1971) and *Carnival of Monsters* (1973); he had also provided Dalek voices in *Frontier in Space*, *Planet of the Daleks* (directed by David Maloney) and *Death to the Daleks*.

The actor playing Nyder, Peter Miles, also had experience of *Doctor Who*, having worked on *Doctor Who and the Silurians* in 1969/70 (transmitted in 1970) and *Invasion of the Dinosaurs* in 1973 (transmitted 1974). The role of Sevrin was originally allocated to John Duttine – whom Maloney later cast as the lead in his 1981 version of *The Day of the Triffids* – but was ultimately played by Stephen Yardley, a regular in the BBC series *United!* and *Z Cars*.

Dennis Chinnery had briefly appeared in a 1965 Dalek serial, *The Chase* (1965), and was now cast as Gharman, a role for which David Baillie was considered. Tom Georgeson, who played Kavell, later starred in *The Boys from the Blackstuff* and *Between the Lines*, while John Franklyn-Robbins, playing the Time Lord, had been used by Maloney in his adaptation of *Woodstock*. Hilary Minster, whom Maloney had directed as Marat in *Planet of the Daleks*, was originally considered as Mogran, but was then recast as the Thal who menaces Sarah at the top of the rocket. Both Minster and Guy Siner – who played Ravon – were later stars of *'Allo 'Allo*. Two other Thals were played by Pat Gorman (see *Robot*) and stunt man Max Faulkner. Faulkner had featured in *The Ambassadors of Death*, *The Monster of Peladon* and *Planet of the Spiders*. James Garbutt, playing Ronson, had appeared in *The Onedin Line*. Denys Becler was considered for the part of Tane, but the role went to Drew Wood.

The Daleks were operated by John Scott Martin, Cy Town and Keith Ashley. Martin's long *Doctor Who* career began as a Zarbi in the 1965 serial *The Web Planet*, and he had played a Dalek in every Dalek serial since *The Chase* later that year. Town's Dalek career on *Doctor Who* had begun with *Frontier in Space* (1973), and for Ashley it was his first credited role after being a walk-on since 1966. The Dalek voices were provided by Roy Skelton, who had performed many small roles since his *Doctor Who* debut in 1966 on *The Ark*; Skelton had performed the Dalek voices in *The Evil of the Daleks* and *Planet of the Daleks*. Various small roles requiring stunt work were played by Terry Walsh (see *Robot*) and Alan Chuntz; both had just worked on *Revenge of the Cybermen* with Chuntz's work on the series stretching back to *The Invasion*.

When booking the artists for the serial on Tuesday 3 December, Maloney's assistant Hazel Marriott asked Pauline Mansfield:

> Can you please put on all contracts for the men, 'it may be necessary to have your hair cut short' or words to that effect!
>
> Also, those parts asterisked [i.e. Sevrin and Gerrill] may have to have make-up to make their faces horrible and mutated!

Filming

Recalling the unsatisfactory use of the Daleks on location during *Planet of the Daleks*, Maloney did not schedule any location work involving them. After some rehearsals from around Thursday 2 January, shooting on 16mm film took place the following week at the rat-infested Betchworth Quarry in Surrey (courtesy of Oxted Greystone Lime Ltd, which was paid £300 in fees) which was used for the surface of Skaro; Maloney and his film crew had done a location recce at New Year.

Filming of the action scenes in the Thal rocket silo – which Nation had assumed would be recorded electronically on videotape – took place at the BBC Television Film Studios in Ealing on Monday 13 and Tuesday 14.

On Thursday 16, a small amount of model filming was performed for the serial: the establishing shots of the Kaled dome and its destruction at the end of Part Three. This was a wire frame supported through the bottom of the miniature landscape with rods, and when the small explosive charges were detonated, the rods were pulled down to make the dome collapse.

Recording

Studio rehearsals started at Acton Room 302 on Thursday 16 January; during rehearsals on Monday 20, Tom Baker celebrated his 41st birthday.

Evening recordings started on Monday 27 and Tuesday 28 January, with one episode generally taped each evening. However, to save erecting some sets twice or re-hiring cast, the Kaled command HQ scenes for Part Three were taped with Part One. Similarly, the scenes set in the detention room and its adjoining corridor for Part Four were taped after Part Two.

Also present for camera rehearsals on Part One – and fascinated by Davros – was a group of youngsters aged seven to 16 years old who had won a visit to the studios as a prize in a 'Design-a-Monster' competition organized by Lorne Martin of BBC Enterprises via the *Doctor Who* exhibitions on Blackpool's Golden Mile and at Longleat House in Wiltshire. A special luncheon for the children with Baker, Marter, Sladen, Maloney, Holmes and

Gallaccio was arranged since 'meeting the stars of the show is obviously going to be the high point of their visit'.

A second rehearsal period ran from Thursday 30 January, and this time it was Sladen who celebrated her 27th birthday during her weekend off on Saturday 1 February. These rehearsals culminated with taping Parts Three and Four on Monday 10 and Tuesday 11 February; the rocket silo and ducting scenes for Part Two, and the trench and Thal city scenes for Part Five were also recorded. By now it had been decided that the iron cross worn by Nyder was a little too obvious in terms of Nazi symbolism, and Miles did not wear the prop again; however, the adornment was visible in the detention room scenes (13 and 14) in Part Four which had already been taped.

During this block of recording, Maloney had to abandon one CSO shot of the Daleks and the Thal revellers in front of film footage of the burning dome model, as it was too time-consuming (Part Four, Scene 6). During the taping of Part Three, the CSO shot of the Doctor, Sarah and Harry needed to open *Revenge of the Cybermen* was restaged by Maloney on behalf of director Michael E. Briant.

After rehearsals from Thursday 13 February, the final recording session was on Monday 24 and Tuesday 25 February. On the Monday, Baker and the production team posed with the Daleks for publicity shots outside BBC Television Centre (one of the photos is reproduced on page 11). Recording for Part Five was slightly out of sequence, allowing time for Ian Marter and Elisabeth Sladen to make costume changes to overcome a continuity problem as Sladen had already made *Revenge of the Cybermen* wearing combat gear rather than her clothes from *The Sontaran Experiment*.

The serial's final episode required the use of the five empty 'non practical' (or 'goon' as the crew referred to them) Daleks built for *Planet of the Daleks* for static appearances in the background. The Doctor managed to regain his coat from Part One before the scene outside the incubator room.

Part One was edited on Wednesday 29 January, Part Two on Wednesday 12 February, Part Three on Friday 28 February, Part Four on Monday 3 March and then the final two episodes on several days including Tuesday 4, Sunday 9 and Friday 14 March. The music was recorded over a period of a month from the start of March 1975 by Simpson, with the shows dubbed only days before transmission (Part One was dubbed the day before broadcast).

Promotion and Reaction

The *Radio Times* of Thursday 6 March introduced *Genesis of the Daleks* via an item called 'Master of the Mean Machines' where Nation and Baker discussed the Daleks with Anthony Haden-Guest. The final episode was broadcast during the same week as the first episode of Nation's *Survivors*, so there was a further feature on the writer, including a photo of him with two rare Mark 7 Daleks from the *Radio Times*' 1972 Dalek competition to promote *Day of the Daleks* (see page 249).

Opposition from LWT remained in the form of *The Adventurer, Sale of the Century* continued on ATV and *New Faces* stayed on Granada as well as being scheduled on Yorkshire. Southern continued with re-runs of *Tarzan* and another 1960s adventure-film series about three secret agents with super powers: *The Champions.* The audience response in terms of size and appreciation was generally good, if slightly down on the two preceding stories. On Monday 10 March, two days after the broadcast of Part One, Shaun Usher in the *Daily Mail* observed:

Dr Who [is] facing up to another annual farewell appearance by the Daleks. Terry Nation, who devised these malevolent third-cousins to fairground bumper-cars, and is writing this section of the saga, may be hurt by the reaction, but the Daleks are positively reassuring to those of us who knew *Dr Who* when he was William Hartnell and we were a lot younger.

The *Daily Mail* was also the forum for another attack on the series as unsuitable for young children, by Mary Whitehouse of the National Viewers and Listeners Association, on Thursday 27 March:

Doctor Who has turned into tea-time brutality for tots. The series has moved from fantasy to real-life violence with cruelty, corpses, poison-gas and Nazi-type stormtroopers, not to mention revolting experiments in human genetics… It is now questionable whether it should be shown any time before nine in the evening.

3.0 Dr Who
Genesis of the Daleks
A complete adventure in one programme, starring
Tom Baker as Dr Who
written by TERRY NATION
The Time Lords have a mission for the Doctor. He finds himself stranded on Skaro – the planet of the Daleks where a war of attrition is reaching its bitter final stages.

Sarah Jane Smith.ELISABETH SLADEN
Harry Sullivan............IAN MARTER
Davros................MICHAEL WISHER
Nyder.....................PETER MILES
Sevrin...............STEPHEN YARDLEY

Incidental music by DUDLEY SIMPSON
Producer PHILIP HINCHCLIFFE
Director DAVID MALONEY (Repeat)

The most important mission the Doctor has ever faced – can he prevent Davros creating his Daleks? A complete Dr Who adventure today: 3.0 pm

Radio Times listing (opposite) and artwork from the compilation repeat of the story, broadcast 27 December 1975.

Interestingly, Nation himself later agreed in an interview with Robert Hardcastle on BBC Radio 4 that Maloney's interpretation of his script had included 'elements of visual brutality' which meant that he felt it was now unsuitable viewing for his two children. The criticisms continued into the letters page of the *Radio Times*, also on Thursday 27 March, with a letter from Alison Duddington of London (reproduced in full on page 39):

> *Dr Who* was once a fantasy adventure serial for children. Not any more though… It was brutal, violent and revolting – totally without point or plot – yet convincingly enough done to be really terrifying for many normal children, and to put some very nasty ideas into the heads of some of the growing number of disturbed ones.

Hinchcliffe responded to the criticism, saying:

> Though I am sure that most of our audience realizes they are watching fiction not fact, of course ultimately, we have to rely upon parents in the home to decide whether a programme is suitable for their child. We do take great pains to ensure that we never depict any act of violence which could be dangerously copied by children.

The BBC had an audience research reports compiled on *Genesis of the Daleks* Part Six on Monday 5 May, based on comments by a sample of 228 viewers (see Appendix E).

Selected Merchandise

- NOVELIZATION: *Doctor Who and the Genesis of the Daleks*: novelization by Terrance Dicks. Published July 1976 by Target Books (paperback) and Allan Wingate (hardback). Abridged version included in *Doctor Who and the Daleks Omnibus* from Artus Publishing Ltd in September 1976. American edition: May 1979 by Pinnacle Books (paperback) and included in *The Adventures of Doctor Who* from Nelson Doubleday Inc in 1979. Revised Target edition as *Doctor Who – Genesis of the Daleks* published September 1991.
- SOUND EFFECTS: *Doctor Who – Sound Effects No. 19* (BBC Records REC 316/ZCM 316) issued May 1978; includes 'Dalek gun' and 'hatching tank' effects.
- INCIDENTAL MUSIC: *Doctor Who – Pyramids of Mars* (Silva Screen FILMCD 134) issued September 1993; includes eight bands of incidental music (new recordings by Heathcliff Blair made late 1992/early 1993).
- SOUNDTRACK: *Doctor Who – Genesis of the Daleks* (BBC Records REH 364/ZCR 364) issued October 1979; 58 mins abridged soundtrack with new narration from Tom Baker. Included as part of *Doctor Who – Genesis of the Daleks & Slipback* (BBC Radio Collection ZBBC 1020) in November 1988. Revised and reissued as ISBN: 0563 47857 8, July 2001 (RRP £9.99).
- VIDEOTAPES (ETC.): *Doctor Who – The Sontaran Experiment/The Genesis of the Daleks* (BBC Video BBCV 4643) issued October 1991. American edition: (CBS/Fox #5946) issued 1994. *Doctor Who - Davros Box Set* exclusive to W. H. Smith (BBC Video BBCV7241) to be issued 2001.

Production Details

4E: Genesis Of The Daleks

Projects: 2344/7056-7061

Cast

Doctor Who	Tom Baker	
Sarah Jane Smith	Elisabeth Sladen	
Harry Sullivan	Ian Marter	
Davros	Michael Wisher	
Nyder	Peter Miles	
Gharman	Dennis Chinnery	[1-2,4-6]
Sevrin	Stephen Yardley	[2-6]
Ronson	James Garbutt	[2-4]
Ravon	Guy Siner	[1,3]
Time Lord	John Franklyn-Robbins	[1]
Tane	Drew Wood	[2]
Gerrill	Jeremy Chandler	[2]
Kaled Leader	Richard Reeves	[1-3]
Kavell	Tom Georgeson	[3-5]
Mogran	Ivor Roberts	[3]
Bettan	Harriet Philpin	[4-6]
Kravos	Andrew Johns	[6]
Thal Soldier	Pat Gorman	[2]
Thal Politician	Michael Lynch	[3-4]
Thal Soldier	Hilary Minster	[3]
Thal Guard	Max Faulkner	[3]
Kaled Guard	Peter Mantle	[5]

Thal Soldier	John Gleeson [6]
Dalek Operators	John Scott Martin, Cy Town [3-6],
	Keith Ashley [3-6]
Dalek Voice	Roy Skelton [3-6]

Uncredited:

Stunt man/1st Soldier [1], Stuntman/Muto [2,4]: Terry Walsh
Stunt man/2nd Soldier [1]: Alan Chuntz
3rd Soldier [1]: David Billa
Soldiers [1]: David Cleeve, Tim Blackstone, Julian Hudson
Dead Soldier [1]: Peter Duke
Mutos: Michael Crane [1], John Sowerbutt [1-2], John Delieu
[2-4], James Muir [2-3], Stephen Calcutt [2-4], Christopher
Holmes [2], Roger Salter [3]
Kaleds [1]: Tony O'Keefe, Steven Butler, Michael Bunker
Kaled Boy [1]: Paul Burton
Thals [1]: Dougal Rossiter, Julian Peters. Keith Klugston
Stunt men/Thal Soldiers [1-2]: Terry Walsh [1-2], Max Faulkner
[2-3]
Stunt man/Kaled Soldier [1-2]: Alan Chuntz
Kaled Soldiers [1]: Peter Kodak, Giles Melville
Elite Guards: Barry Somerford [1-4,6], Bob Watson [1], Peter
Kodak [2], Giles Melville [2], Roy Ceaser [3-4,6]
Scientists (inc Fenatin): Richard Orme [2], Harry Van Engel
[2,5-6], Charles Rayford [2-3,6], Pat Travis [2-4,6], William
Ashley [2-4,6], John Timberlake [2-3,6], Charles Erskine [4],
Alan Charles Thomas [6], Mike Reynell [6], Tony Hayes [6]
Dalek Voice [2]: Michael Wisher
Kaled Prisoner [2]: Ken Tracey
Thal Guards: David Cleeve [2,4-5], Patrick Scoular [2,4-5], Reg
Turner [6]
Teddy Driver Guard [2]: John Dunn
Thal Soldiers: David Billa [2-3,6], Tim Blackstone [2-3,6], David
Cleeve [2-3], Philip Mather [4-5], Rick Carroll [4-5], Julian
Hudson [4-5], Ryan Craven [4-5]
Thing! [2]: Dod Watson
Stunt Double for Sarah Jane Smith [2]: Tracey Eddon
Kaled Councillors [3]: Anthony Lang, George Romanoff, Ronald
Nunnery
Stunt men/Thal Guards [3]: Jim Dowdall, Dinny Powell
Thal Officers [3]: David Roy Paul, Keith Norrish
Thal Politician [3]: Peter Whittaker
Thal Generals [4]: John Beardmore, Eric Rayner
Stunt men/Kaled Guards [5]: Alan Chuntz, Jim Dowdall
Stunt men/Scientists [5]: Terry Walsh, Paddy Ryan

Crew

Written by	Terry Nation
Production Unit Manager	George Gallaccio

Production Assistant	Rosemary Crowson
Title Music by	Ron Grainer & BBC Radiophonic
Workshop	
Title Sequence	Bernard Lodge
Incidental Music by	Dudley Simpson
Special Sound	Dick Mills
Visual Effects Designer	Peter Day
Davros' Mask	John Friedlander [6]
Costume Designer	Barbara Kidd
Make up	Sylvia James
Studio Lighting	Duncan Brown
Studio Sound	Tony Millier
Film Cameraman	Elmer Cossey [1-3]
Film Sound	Bill Meekums [1-3]
Film Editor	Larry Toft [1-3]
Script Editor	Robert Holmes
Designer	David Spode
Producer	Philip Hinchcliffe
Directed by	David Maloney

Production History

Filming – Betchworth Quarry, Betchworth, Surrey
Monday 6 January 1975: 8.30am onwards
* Ext. Wastelands – Part One TK 1B, 1C

Tuesday 7 January 1975: 8.30am onwards
* Ext. Wastelands – Part One TK 1C, 1D

Wednesday 8 January 1975: 8.30am onwards
* Ext. Wastelands – Part One TK 1D, 1E, 1F

Thursday 9 January 1975: 8.30am onwards
* Ext. Wastelands – Part One TK 1A, 2, 3, 4

Friday 10 January 1975: 8.30am onwards
* Stand-by Day

Filming – BBC Ealing Television Film Studios Stage 2
Monday 13 January 1975: 8.30am onwards
* Int. Rocket silo – Part Two: TK 1A, 2, 3

Tuesday 14 January 1975: 8.30am onwards
* Int. Rocket silo – Part Three: TK 1, 2, 3, 4

Filming
Thursday 16 January 1975
* Model shots – Part One: TK1, Part Two: TK1, Part Three: scenes
  34-37 and Part Four: scene 2

Studio Recording - Television Centre Studio 1
Monday 27 January 1975: 7.30pm-10.00pm
- Part One
- Part Three: scenes 17, 20 [Command HQ]

Tuesday 28 January 1975: 7.30pm-10.00pm
- Part Two, except scenes 6, 8, 17
- Part Four: scenes 12-14 [Kaled Corridor/Detention Room]

Monday 10 February 1975: 7.30pm-10.00pm
- Part Three: except scenes 17, 20, 34-37
- Part Two: scenes 6, 8 [Rocket Silo], 17 [Section of Duct]
- *Revenge of the Cybermen*: Opening CSO shot

Tuesday 11 February 1975: 7.30pm-10.00pm
- Part Three: scenes 34-37 [Launch Room/Main Lab]
- Part Four: except scenes 12-14
- Part Five: scenes 8, 17 [Trench], 7 [Thal Corridor]

Studio Recording - Television Centre Studio 6
Monday 24 February 1975: 7.30pm-10.00pm
- Part Five: except scenes 7, 8, 17

Tuesday 25 February 1975: 7.30pm-10.00pm
- Part Six

Music
- Specially recorded incidental music by Dudley Simpson and Ad Hoc Orchestra. Recording Dates: Monday 3 March (Part One), Tuesday 11 March (Part Two), Wednesday 12 March (Part Three: planned for Parts Three and Four), Wednesday 26 March (Part Four; planned for Part Five), Tuesday 1 April (Part Five) and Wednesday 2 April 1975 (Part Six) at Lime Grove. Total: 46'26"

Original Transmission - BBC1

Part One	Saturday 8 March 1975	5.30pm	5.30pm	24'30"	10.7M	23rd	-
Part Two	Saturday 15 March 1975	5.30pm	5.30pm	24'51"	10.5M	15th	57
Part Three	Saturday 22 March 1975	5.30pm	5.30pm	22'38"	8.5M	42nd	-
Part Four	Saturday 29 March 1975	5.30pm	5.31pm	23'38"	8.8M	36th	-
Part Five	Saturday 5 April 1975	5.30pm	5.30pm	23'27"	9.8M	30th	57
Part Six	Saturday 12 April 1975	5.30pm	5.31pm	23'30"	9.1M	26th	56

GENESIS OF THE DALEKS

by Terry Nation

Part One

OPENING TITLES

TELECINE 1
EXT. WASTELAND. DAY.

A fog-shrouded desolation. We track through banks of fog that hang close to the ravaged ground. There is no vegetation. It is a lifeless and chilling place.

Suddenly a grey-snouted face and goggle eyes rise behind a ridge of mud. The head pans in a careful survey. Then the soldier waves advance. He rises to his feet and comes down the ridge. More soldiers follow. All wear identical gas masks. Their uniforms are ragged, their weapons motley. ❶

A star shell bursts high overhead. Then there is the K-rump of a distant mortar bomb and the sudden frantic barking of a heavy machine gun. But the action is away on some other part of the line and the soldiers keep steadily on. They disappear into the fog. ❷

We pan to front again and the Doctor is standing there staring after the soldiers. He does a 360 degree survey of his surroundings, totally mystified. As he completes his circle a voice comes from the fog. ❸

TIME LORD Ah, welcome, Doctor.

The Doctor stares. The Time Lord suddenly condenses in the fog and steps forward. ❹

DOCTOR WHO ~~So I've been hijacked!~~ **What's going on?** *(Angry)* Don't you realize how dangerous it is to intercept a transmat beam?

TIME LORD Oh, come, Doctor! Not with our techniques… We Time Lords transcended such simple mechanical devices when the Universe was less than half its present size.

DOCTOR WHO ~~Whatever I did to you — whatever crimes I committed in the past —~~ **Look, whatever I've done for you in the past** – I have more than made up for. I will not tolerate this continual interference in my life!

The Time Lord cocks an eye at him and moves off. The Doctor has, perforce, to go along with him.

TIME LORD Continual? We pride ourselves that we seldom interfere in the affairs of others.

DOCTOR WHO Except mine.

TIME LORD You, Doctor, are a special case. You enjoy the freedom that we allow you. In return, occasionally – not continually – we ask you to do something for us.

DOCTOR WHO I won't do it. Whatever it is, I refuse.

TIME LORD Daleks.

The Doctor stops in his tracks.

DOCTOR WHO Daleks? ~~Well, what about them?~~ **Tell me more.**

TIME LORD We foresee a time when they will have destroyed all other life forms and become the dominant creatures in the Universe.

DOCTOR WHO It's possible. Go on.

TIME LORD We'd like you to return to Skaro at a point in time before the Daleks evolved.

DOCTOR WHO ~~I see. Yes… Yes, yes,~~ **Do you mean** avert their creation~~, eh?~~

TIME LORD Or affect their genetic development so that they evolve into less aggressive creatures.

DOCTOR WHO Mmm… ~~I suppose~~ that's feasible.

TIME LORD Alternatively, if you learn enough about their very beginnings, you might discover some inherent weakness.

The Doctor nods, thinking. He looks up.

DOCTOR WHO All right… All right, just once more.

TIME LORD You'll do it?

DOCTOR WHO If you'll let me have the space-time coordinates I'll set the TARDIS **for Skaro** –

TIME LORD No need for that, Doctor. **You're here.** This is Skaro.

DOCTOR WHO What?

TIME LORD ~~You're here.~~ We thought it would save time if we assumed your agreement.

DOCTOR WHO ~~But I haven't set the TARDIS's time-drift compensators! If she drifts I won't be able to —~~ ⑤ what's this?

He looks at the copper bangle the Time Lord has thrust into his hands. ⑥

TIME LORD A time ring. It will return you to the TARDIS when you've finished here. There's just one thing.

DOCTOR WHO What's that?

TIME LORD Be careful not to lose it. That time ring is your lifeline. Good luck, Doctor. ⑦

DOCTOR WHO Now just a moment – **Don't just disappear!**

The Time Lord dematerializes.

DOCTOR WHO What about ~~my companions —~~ Harry and Sarah?

A staccato burst of small-arms fire in the distance. The Doctor fits the time ring on his wrist and moves off through the fog.

SARAH *(VO)* Doctor..? Doctor?

DOCTOR WHO ~~Sarah! Where are you?~~ **Ah, there you are.**

He hurries forward and almost loses his footing on a greasy bank of mud. Sarah is at the bottom helping Harry out of a patch of bog. ⑧

HARRY *(Shaken)* **I say, Doctor.** That was a **pretty** rough landing. What happened?

SARAH Yes, where are we, Doctor? This isn't the beacon.

DOCTOR WHO There's been a slight change of plan. This is Skaro –

He is interrupted by the rumble of gunfire and the high shriek of shells passing overhead.

HARRY I say, that's gunfire!

DOCTOR WHO Heavy artillery.

SARAH Doctor, it's getting closer!

DOCTOR WHO Creeping barrage. Quick, get down!

And all three jump back into the muddy crater. They huddle together under the rim of the

crater, hands over their ears. The roar of the
bombardment continues for a while longer. A
shell falling very near sprays them with earth.
Then the barrage ends. Cautiously they raise
their heads.

DOCTOR WHO ~~Not what you'd call a friendly welcome.~~ Something's annoyed them!

SARAH Doctor, look!

Sarah gives a shocked cry. She points. There is
the body of a soldier on the other side of the
crater. He lies motionless, rifle pointing at
them. It takes a second or two before they
realize he is dead.

DOCTOR WHO It's all right, Sarah.

He goes across to the body, taking in the
curious gas mask, the tattered uniform
assembled from odd pieces of equipment, the
ancient rifle… Harry bends over the body.

HARRY Nothing to be done for this chap.

The Doctor takes a space-age gun from the
soldier's holster and examines it. He indicates
the rifle. **9**

DOCTOR WHO Strange. There are centuries ~~of technological development separating~~ between
these two weapons.

SARAH What's that on his jacket, Doctor?

~~**DOCTOR WHO** A radiation detector…~~

HARRY A radiation detector… And a gas mask.
The two things don't go together, do they?

SARAH Part of his uniform is made of animal
skins and yet that combat jacket is a modern
synthetic fibre. ~~I don't understand.~~

DOCTOR WHO It's like finding the remains of a
Stone Age man with a transistor radio.

HARRY Playing rock music~~, eh..? Rock?~~

~~**SARAH** We did get the point, Harry.~~

DOCTOR WHO A thousand-year war? Civilization
on the point of collapse?

SARAH What?

DOCTOR WHO Nothing. Just theorizing, that's
all. Come along.

HARRY Where are we going?

DOCTOR WHO Forward.

The trio start to advance again across the
wastelands. They pick their way through the
barbed wire. The Doctor's eye is taken by
something half-buried in the soil. He holds up
a hand to halt his companions.

DOCTOR WHO Halt – don't move.

He indicates what he has seen.

SARAH What is it?

DOCTOR WHO I can see a land mine. ~~I think~~
We're in the middle of a minefield… ~~Look…~~
~~I'll lead the way… Keep close behind and~~
Follow me, and tread in my footsteps…

SARAH ~~You sound like~~ Good King Wenceslas…

The Doctor starts to pick his way forward,
cautiously testing each step. Sarah and Harry
follow keeping precisely to the route Doctor
Who is making.

They continue in this way for some yards
when the Doctor halts suddenly and snaps a
glance off to one side towards a pile of earth.
He stands silent and staring for a few
moments. The others following his gaze.

HARRY ~~You see something?~~ What?

DOCTOR WHO I could have sworn something
moved… And I get the distinct feeling that
we're being watched…

SARAH I've had that feeling too…

HARRY ~~Oh, rubbish.~~ I can't see anything
~~moving out there except fog~~.

DOCTOR WHO Let's hope it's imagination.

He turns to move forward. We angle to the
ground slightly ahead of him. An edge of a
landmine pokes up through the soil.

Doctor Who moves forward with yet
another backward glance at the point where
he thought he saw movement. Unwarily his
foot grates against the edge of the mine.
He freezes.

HARRY What is it?

With care, he edges his foot away from the
mine. Breath-holding from Harry and Sarah.
A trickle of earth falls off the mine and it shifts
slightly as Doctor Who eases the pressure of his
foot. The Doctor speaks very quietly.

DOCTOR WHO Harry… I'm standing on a land
mine. If I let it shift, if I move my foot, it
might detonate it. ~~This thing is likely to shift~~
~~when I move my foot and that could detonate~~
~~it…~~

HARRY Don't move your foot…

DOCTOR WHO I won't!

Harry edges forward and drops to his knees
beside the mine. He grips the edges of it and
then begins to brush the soil away from its top.
Doctor Who's foot remains rigidly in position.

HARRY ~~There's a stone or something underneath…~~ It's rocking ~~slightly…~~

SARAH Can't you wedge something under it to make it firm?

HARRY That's what I'm trying to do.

Again with painstaking care and nerve-racking slowness, Harry edges a small piece of stone beneath the mine. He makes a nervous test of the mine's stability.

HARRY Back up Sarah…

Sarah dumbly moves back a few yards.

DOCTOR WHO You get back as well, Harry. No point in risking both our lives…

HARRY No. You'll have a better chance if I hold it firm…

DOCTOR WHO ~~Now don't be stupid…~~ Please Harry, don't be difficult.

HARRY And don't argue, Doctor. Just lift your foot… **very very** gently.

The Doctor and Harry both brace themselves. Harry gripping either side of the mine and holding it firm. The Doctor lifts his foot and removes it from danger. The sigh of relief is only brief as we watch Harry release his hold on the mine. One hand free, then the second. The mine tilts fractionally. Harry stands. He closes his eyes in relief. Wipes his brow.

DOCTOR WHO Thank you, Harry.

HARRY My pleasure.

DOCTOR WHO Let's go.

The Doctor starts forward again. Sarah and Harry follow. As they move out of shot we angle toward the point where the Doctor thought he saw something move.

As we watch, the vague outline of a head and shoulders appears. A head swathed in a fur hood. ⑩

Another area of the wastelands. Still pocked with shell holes and general devastation. The trio are moving forward through a gap in some rusty barbed wire approaching a slight rise. As they top the rise ~~Sarah~~ Doctor Who halts. Reacts and points.

SARAH ~~Look!~~

DOCTOR WHO Look – what do you think?

TELECINE 1A
EXT. CITY DOME. DAY.

A distant view of a great transparent dome that covers a city. Fog swirls gently around it. ⑪

TELECINE 1B
EXT. WASTELANDS. DAY.

SARAH It's like a huge bubble… ⑫

DOCTOR WHO A protective dome~~, and large enough to cover an entire city~~.

SARAH Large enough to cover an entire city?

DOCTOR WHO Yes.

HARRY If they can build something like that, why are they fighting a war with old-fashioned things like barbed wire and land mines?

The group move forward again.

1. EXT. TRENCH. DAY.

Part of a classic World War I trench complex. Sandbagged and duckboard floors. A number of dead, uniformed soldiers are propped on the firing step. ⑬ *The uniforms have a makeshift quality about them. Rifles are levelled across the top of the trench as though prepared for attack. These vary in type from muzzle loaders to automatic carbines.*

The Doctor and his two companions appear at one end of the trench and stare.

DOCTOR WHO Even the dead have a part to play. Propped up to make the trench appear fully manned.

HARRY Different sort of uniform ~~– such as it is~~ – from the other chap's.

DOCTOR WHO ~~We've probably~~ Yes, we may have crossed the lines…

SARAH Same mixture of ancient and modern, though.

DOCTOR WHO That's why I think this war has been going on for a very long time. They probably started with the most modern equipment but now no longer have the resources… they have to make do.

HARRY A war of attrition, **eh, only backwards.** ~~they'll end~~ **At this rate they're going to finish** up with bows and arrows..?

DOCTOR WHO It would explain the mixture of equipment.

Sarah calls from further along the trench.

SARAH Psst… ~~it's locked.~~

HARRY *(Whispering)* Careful, Sarah.

SARAH *(Whispering)* It's all right, it's locked.

They hurry down to join her. She is standing beside a heavy iron door that is concreted into the side wall of the trench. A very formidable door.

Harry strains to force the door open and fails.

HARRY Some kind of service tunnel, I expect. ~~Pretty solid. A service tunnel perhaps.~~ Might even lead ~~right~~ into the dome… ~~let's see where the trench goes…~~

DOCTOR WHO Let's see where the trench leads.

They start to move away. As they do, a small peephole flap in the door slides aside and an eye peers out. Angle on the trio as they begin to move back the way they have come. They are alarmed suddenly by the descending whine of a shell. They all crouch for cover. ⑭ *There is an explosion beyond the lip of the trench. The Doctor peers over the top.*

DOCTOR WHO It's gas..! ~~a poison~~ gas shell..! ~~the soldiers' respirators… quickly!~~

SARAH Gas?

DOCTOR WHO Poison gas.

HARRY Respirators, quick!

As a cloud of green smoke rolls into the trench they desperately pull the bodies of the troops from the wall of the trench and snatch the gas masks from their packs.

The trio pull the masks over their faces and tighten the straps. There is a sudden burst of rifle fire. Bullets splatter around them.

~~The Doctor again peers over the lip of the trench. His VP: advancing toward the trench is the patrol: they are the Thal troops we saw in the opening. We hear a muffled order yelled by their leader. 'Charge'.~~

In seconds the Thal troops are leaping over the sandbags and dropping into the trench.

The Doctor and Harry are instantly engaged in hand-to-hand fighting as they struggle to defend themselves and Sarah. Much of the battle is blurred and lost in the green smoke but it is obvious from the first that the Doctor's group is outnumbered and has no chance.

Harry is knocked aside by a blow from a rifle butt and he falls semi-conscious. Sarah,

unprotected now, tries to back away. A Thal soldier advances on her. The Doctor jumps on him but is then clubbed from behind. He begins to fall.

The iron door is thrown open sharply and from it pour a squad of Kaled soldiers. They wear respirators and are well armed. One of them has a machine gun. This he blazes along the trench and the Thal troops fall under the hail of fire.

The Kaled troops pull off their gas masks. We now see that they are all very young. 15 or 16 years old. ⑮

One of the boys, obviously their leader, moves forward through the carnage looking about him.

The Doctor, only dazed, starts to sit up. The Kaled leader instantly levels his gun at him. He calls to the young men behind him.

LEADER This one's alive… ~~take him into the tunnel…~~ Get him inside.

Two of the Kaled soldiers drag the Doctor to his feet and pull him towards the iron door and the tunnel behind it. The Doctor is too dazed to protest. The Kaled leader hears a groan and notices Harry.

LEADER There's another one here…

Harry is picked up and dragged off to the tunnel. The Kaled leader takes another quick look around. There is sudden burst of fire from somewhere beyond the trench. Urgently the leader orders his men back into the tunnel.

LEADER Get him inside… hurry… hurry…

They all dash for the tunnel. The door closes with a resounding clang.

Silence returns to the trench. The camera slowly tracks past the victims of the skirmish coming finally to Sarah where she lies unconscious. A trickle of blood oozing from her scalp.

2. INT. TRENCH COMMAND POST. DAY.

This is the small area immediately inside the iron door. The walls shored up with planks. A few rough benches. The minimum items of comfort.

At one side of the room is a small trolley-like vehicle that runs on lines that vanish into a

dark opening in the wall of the command
post. **16**

The young Kaled troops are slumping down
to rest.

Harry, still unconscious, lies on the floor
where he has been dumped.

The Doctor is in a sitting position, his back
against the trolley.

The Kaled leader stoops and pulls the
Doctor's gas mask off.

The Kaled boy (the second in command)
does the same to Harry. They stare down at
the men.

LEADER They don't look like Thals… I wonder?
There've been rumours lately that the Thals
were developing robots… Anyway… Stick
them on the transporter…

Two Kaleds lift the Doctor on to the trolley and
then do the same to Harry.

LEADER I'll be at command headquarters with
General Ravon.

He climbs on to the trolley.

LEADER Count the ammunition and clean your
weapons.

He operates the controls.

The trolley vanishes into the dark opening.

3. INT. COMMAND HEADQUARTERS. DAY.

A room that shows signs of blast damage. There
are maps on the wall, tattered and much
overpencilled, and all the other items one
would expect in a command room. Wherever
possible we show the odd contrast of makeshift
things and ultra-modern items.

The centre of the room is dominated by a
large table on which there is a relief map. **17**
The model shows quite clearly two glass domes
that represent the two warring cities. Between
them are marked the trenches and the general
shape of the 'waste-lands'.

A young officer of about 18, slightly better
dressed than the troops we have thus far seen, is
moving symbols about on the relief map.

Another Kaled soldier is seated at the
communications centre.

The trolley arrives and the Doctor and
Harry are shoved inside the room by the Kaled
leader. The officer, Ravon, glances up.

RAVON Well?

LEADER Two prisoners sir. Captured on section
one oh one…

The Doctor is supporting Harry who is still
groggy.

RAVON For interrogation. Good.

He crosses, staring hard.

RAVON I enjoy interrogations.

DOCTOR WHO Yes, you look the type.

A blow from Ravon sends him spinning.
Harry collapses.

RAVON You insolent Muto!

LEADER Sir?

RAVON What?

LEADER My section totally destroyed the Thal
attackers, except for these two. But our supply
of ammunition is running low –

RAVON Then conserve it! Ammunition is
valuable and cannot be wasted.

LEADER Yes, sir.

RAVON For instance, when I've finished with
these two animals they'll be hanged, not taken
out and shot as in the past.

LEADER I understand, sir.

RAVON Then that will be all. Return to your
unit.

They exchange salutes and the Kaled leader
exits.

RAVON So the Thals have come down to
recruiting Mutos, have they? Turn out your
pockets!

DOCTOR WHO ~~Why not? I do turn them out
every year or so …~~ Certainly.

He starts producing his usual collection of junk
together with one or two complex scientific
instruments. **18**

Ravon notices that the Doctor is shooting
interested glances at the relief map. He sneers.

RAVON Take a good look… In a few weeks we
are going to change the shape of that map for
ever… We will wipe the Thals from the face of
Skaro.

DOCTOR WHO I've heard that before.

RAVON What?

DOCTOR WHO ~~You're going~~ I was just wondering
how you propose to wipe the Thals from the
face of Skaro with boy soldiers, no
ammunition – and very young generals!

RAVON You've had one warning about your
insolence!

The Doctor shoots a glance at the soldier on the communications set. His back is turned.

DOCTOR WHO ~~Sorry. It just seemed you might have a less logistic problems in this final campaign.~~ Yes, I do beg your pardon.

He smiles.

Ravon glowers, unsure of the Doctor's meaning. **19**

RAVON When victory is ours we shall wipe every trace of the Thals and their city from the face of this land. We will avenge the deaths of all Kaleds who have fallen in the cause of right and justice and build a peace that will be a monument to their sacrifice. Our battle cry will be… Total extermination of the Thals!

DOCTOR WHO That's very impressive. You mean you're going to sweep right across these wastelands –

He flings out an arm, strikes Ravon on the arm – the gun falls.

Harry scoops up Ravon's gun and levels it at the Kaled soldier as he turns.

DOCTOR WHO Did I hurt your fingers?

RAVON You won't get out of here alive!

DOCTOR WHO Yes, so you said.

He takes the soldier's gun **20** *and destroys the communications set with a few well-judged blows. It sparks and burns. Over action:*

DOCTOR WHO So you're Kaleds, eh?

RAVON Even you Mutos know the difference between Thals and Kaleds!

DOCTOR WHO K-a-l-e-d-s… Why, that's an anagram of… Interesting. Are you fit to move, Harry?

HARRY Never felt fitter.

DOCTOR WHO ~~I wouldn't have guessed.~~ Now then Alexander the Great lead us out of here.

RAVON Never.

DOCTOR WHO You won't get a medal for being stupid, ~~Colonel~~ General. **21** In fact you won't get any more medals for anything.

There is a disturbing hardness about the Doctor. He and Harry look a desperate couple. Ravon shrugs.

RAVON Where d'you want me to take you?

DOCTOR WHO Back to the wastelands.

RAVON Yes… that's home to you, isn't it? But you won't get far, I promise you.

HARRY Come on, we're wasting time.

Ravon starts to lead the way out. Harry and the Doctor follow.

4. EXT. TRENCH. DAY.

Sarah regains consciousness. She gets up dazedly. She is surrounded by dead men. Fear and revulsion grip her. She picks her way through the bodies strewn along the trench calling gently in the silence.

SARAH Doctor… Doctor? Harry?

When she finds neither of them she seems lost for a moment. She starts to scramble out of the trench. Then she returns and takes a pistol from the belt of one of the fallen. Holding it nervously she clambers out of the trench.

5. INT. CORRIDOR. DAY.

Ravon comes into the passage still followed by Harry and the Doctor.

HARRY Where are we? This isn't leading to the surface.

RAVON There's a platform lift at the end. You must have seen it.

HARRY You're still making the same mistake, General. We're not, whatever they are.

RAVON Only Mutos live in the wastelands.

DOCTOR WHO Come on.

HARRY I hope ~~we find~~ Sarah's all right!

DOCTOR WHO Yes.

Ravon stops by a lift door. He gives a harsh laugh.

RAVON If you've ~~a~~ friends up there, ~~he~~ they won't last much longer.

DOCTOR WHO What d'you mean?

RAVON Night's coming on. The Mutos start moving at night.

He presses the lift button.

He hurries forward and looks round the corner. Nyder is coming down the passage. He is clearly one of the Elite, exuding arrogance and confidence; his uniform and equipment are immaculate.

Doctor Who turns back to Ravon.

HARRY **22** Just remember we're your friends.

He reinforces the remark with a pistol jammed in Ravon's back. Harry stands close on Ravon's other flank, gun concealed in his jacket pocket. Nyder turns the corner and checks.

NYDER General Ravon…

RAVON Nyder.

Nyder looks curiously at the Doctor and Harry.

NYDER I wish to see you.

Ravon licks his lips nervously. Angle to show the gun pressing against his kidneys.

RAVON If you'll wait in my office, Nyder. I'll ~~only~~ be a few minutes.

DOCTOR WHO Perhaps you should introduce us, General?

RAVON Security Commander Nyder – uh –

NYDER You're civilians, I see?

DOCTOR WHO ~~Only here on a brief visit. However,~~ Yes, but we're not staying long – don't let us detain you.

NYDER You won't.

He goes on down the corridor.

Doctor Who and Harry urge Ravon in the other direction.

Nyder suddenly swings round, gun in hand.

NYDER Down, Ravon!

Ravon flings himself flat. Nyder fires. The bullet whines past Harry's ear, clipping a lump from the wall. ㉓

DOCTOR WHO Run, Harry!

They race off round the corner as Nyder fires again.

Nyder springs to a wall alarm and presses the button.

NYDER *(Into speaker)* Alert all guards! Two Thal intruders in the Command complex!

Instantly a high klaxon alarm blares through the corridors.

Armed Kaleds appear on all sides.

6A. INT. CORRIDOR (ANOTHER SECTION). DAY. ㉔

Doctor Who and Harry running for their lives.

Suddenly Kaled guards spill out into the corridor ahead of them.

They skid to a halt.

DOCTOR WHO This way!

They dive down a side passage as the first shots ring out.

6B. INT. CORRIDOR. DAY.

Ravon is dusting himself down.

Nyder is with him.

RAVON They took me by surprise.

NYDER Fool! What kind of soldier lets two unarmed prisoners overpower him in his own headquarters?

RAVON There's something… different about those two. They're not Thals and they're not Mutos.

NYDER We'll find out what's different about them – by autopsy.

6D. INT. CORRIDOR. DAY. ㉕

The Doctor and Harry creep out of a doorway. The corridor is empty.

The Doctor shakes his head.

DOCTOR WHO Listen!

Footsteps. Squads of men coming from both directions. The klaxon, which sounds distant from this section, dies away with gurgle. ㉖

HARRY We're trapped…

Suddenly in front of them the lift doors open. There is no time to think. They dive in.

The Doctor stabs frantically at the operating button.

The first Kaled soldiers round the corner. They see the Doctor and Harry and raise their guns.

The lift doors close. A burst of gunfire rattles off the metal doors. The soldiers rush forward to stop the lift but are too late.

Nyder comes into shot and sizes up the situation in a flash. He seizes the nearest wall set.

NYDER Alert surface patrols to watch for intruders in the area of platform lift seven!

TELECINE 2
EXT. WASTELANDS. DAY.

The Doctor and Harry jerk to a halt on the surface. They are standing on a silver platform flush with the muddy surface.

HARRY Now what?

DOCTOR WHO ~~Just~~ keep running~~, Harry~~!

HARRY What?

DOCTOR WHO Keep running!

They race off into the mist. A Kaled patrol looms up in front of them and is momentarily taken by surprise. Harry and the Doctor bound like gazelles over obstacles and have gone before the first ragged fusillade drills holes in the mist.

As they keep running we heard the crack of rifles, the whine of ricochets, and the muffled shouts of their pursuers converging on them.

Harry slips and goes down with a thud that winds him. The Doctor helps him up and with many an anxious backward glance forces him on through the wastelands. We cut to Kaled soldiers spread out, moving steadily in military order, rifles at the ready.

Another angle:

The Doctor and Harry still running but turning now.

Another angle:

A tripwire running to the prong of an anti-personnel mine. We pan up to show the Doctor and Harry stumbling up the rise. They come nearer and nearer. The Doctor's foot catches the tripwire. He feels it and instantly recognizes it for what it is.

DOCTOR WHO Down, Harry!

He flings Harry forward into the mud. There is a big explosion within yards of them.

They are showered with filth and rocks.

DOCTOR WHO Are you all right?

HARRY That was a lucky escape.

As they recover from the shock and start to sit up we see the Doctor reacting.

His POV: Four Kaled soldiers advancing, rifles pointing. He raises his hands.

DOCTOR WHO ~~All right… Kamerade…~~ I wouldn't say that, Harry.

The Kaled soldiers surround them and drag them to their feet.

7. INT. COMMAND HQ. DAY. ㉗

~~Nyder is studying the pile of objects removed from the Doctor's pockets. Ravon puts down his handset.~~

~~**RAVON** The prisoners have been recaptured. They are being brought here.~~

~~**NYDER** Excellent. They should never have escaped… You're not even efficient at your staff duties, I see.~~

~~**RAVON** What?~~

~~**NYDER** That map is out of date.~~

~~**RAVON** In what way?~~

~~**NYDER** A heavy Thal offensive has taken a thousand yards of our trenches in section 17.~~

~~**RAVON** I've not been informed. I'll mark it up at once.~~

~~Nyder smiles at having put Ravon down. He turns his back and picks up one of the articles from the table.~~

~~**NYDER** Interesting…~~

TELECINE 3
EXT. WASTELANDS. DAY.

Sarah is picking her way through the barbed wire with no very clear idea of where she is going.

SARAH Doctor, Harry..? Doctor, Harry?

She has the feeling that she is not alone but can see nothing in the fog.

Suddenly she comes upon the lift platform. She bends and touches it but doesn't step in it, uncertain as to what it might be. She walks carefully around it and goes on into the mist.

As she is swallowed from view we get a vague glimpse of a huge, lurching animal form that is obviously trailing her. ㉘

8. INT. COMMAND HEADQUARTERS. DAY.

㉙ The Doctor and Harry have been brought in. They are mud-stained and bruised but face Nyder defiantly. He holds up some instruments.

NYDER This is yours?

DOCTOR WHO Yes.

NYDER What is its function?

DOCTOR WHO It's an etheric beam locator. It's also handy for detecting ion-charged emissions.

NYDER Oh really? It is not of Thal manufacture.

DOCTOR WHO Naturally not. My friend and I are not from your planet.

NYDER Aliens?

HARRY Humans… Well, I am, anyway.

NYDER I have heard Davros say there is no intelligent life on other planets. So either he is wrong or you are lying.

DOCTOR WHO We're not lying.

NYDER And Davros is never wrong. About anything.

DOCTOR WHO Then he must be exceptional. Even I am occasionally wrong about some things… Who is **this** Davros?

NYDER Our greatest scientist. He is in charge of all research at the Bunker.

RAVON They could be Mutos, Nyder. Intelligent Mutos who've developed a technology –

DOCTOR WHO Tell me, what exactly are Mutos?

NYDER Mutos are the scarred relics of ourselves, monsters created by the chemical weapons used in the first century of this war. They were banished into the wastelands where they live and scavenge like animals.

DOCTOR WHO Genetically wounded, in other words?

NYDER We must keep the Kaled race pure. Imperfects ~~children~~ are… rejected. Some of them survive out there.

DOCTOR WHO That's a very harsh policy.

HARRY That's horrible.

NYDER Your views are not important. General Ravon, I'll take these two back to the Bunker for interrogation by the special unit.

RAVON They are the army's prisoners.

NYDER Then you will release them to me. The special unit will get more out of them than your crude methods ever would.

RAVON Very well – if you insist…

NYDER I do insist, General. Oh, and I have a list of requirements here. All these items are to be sent to the bunker immediately.

He hands Ravon a list.

Ravon looks at it and reacts strongly.

RAVON I can't spare this equipment. These spare parts alone will take more than half my supply.

NYDER You'll notice the requisition is countersigned by Davros himself. If you would like to take the matter up with him…

RAVON ~~… Though how~~ I'm expected to fight a war without equipment… **Very well,** I'll have these things out to the Bunker by dawn.

NYDER By midnight, General. The order specifies midnight.

RAVON By midnight…

NYDER Good.

He salutes and turns on his heel.

NYDER Bring the prisoners.

His soldiers move in on the Doctor and Harry.

TELECINE 4
EXT. WASTELANDS. DAY. 30

Sarah spins round in sudden terror. We see a blurred outline of some shaggy creature seem to loom up menacingly behind Sarah. She turns, sees it, and starts to run in terror.

Another angle, Sarah running desperately in fear. She trips and falls, sprawling. As she lies still there is the sound of movement all around. Soft rustling sounds and low moaning noises.

Sarah stares about her in fear then reacts to something she sees. She scrambles to her feet and begins to run towards a section of stone-built wall. The remains of what might once have been a house, but so badly damaged it is hardly recognizable.

Sarah runs up to the wall, then with natural caution slows down and moves silently to peer through a shell hole. 31

9. INT. SHATTERED WALL. NIGHT.

The other side of the wall is what is left of a room. There is a slightly cleared floor space amongst the rubble.

In a wheelchair of very complex design is the huddled figure of Davros. (Of him and his special chair, more in a later episode.) We have no clear picture of him as he is hidden in flickering shadows.

Another man, Gharman, in the same Elite uniform as Nyder, stands some little distance away propping up a target designed as the outline of a soldier.

We see Sarah watching through the hole.

The target fixed in position, Gharman moves back towards Davros and reports.

GHARMAN Ready, Davros…

DAVROS Observe the test closely my friend… this will be a moment that will live in history…

Davros' gloved and claw-like hand presses a control on the panel of his wheelchair. There is a whirring sound from the darkness.

We see Sarah's reaction, and then show a Dalek glide out of the shadows. The Dalek is not as we now know it. More primitive. Less well equipped. 32

There is no mistaking that it is a Dalek even though it has no sucker arm. Its movements are slow and clumsy. Faltering. As it advances

Davros gives softly spoken orders to which it reacts.

DAVROS ~~Left… left… forward… now right. Stop.~~ Halt… Turn right… Halt.

The Dalek is now facing the target.

DAVROS Now… exterminate.

The Dalek's gun roars and the target bursts into explosive flame. ㉝

DAVROS Perfect. The weaponry is perfect. Now we can begin. ㉞

CLOSING TITLES

---

❶ Shooting on 16mm film took place the week of 9 January 1975 at the rat-infested Betchworth Quarry in Surrey which was used for the surface of Skaro.

❷ The patrol is gunned down as they rise and advance. The action is shown in slow motion, the survivors stepping over their comrades' bodies as they head off into the mist.

The only aspect of the finished production which Nation disliked was this brutal massacre sequence in the wastelands, added by David Maloney.

In retrospect, Maloney seemed to agree with him: 'The move during that era was towards being quite frightening and violent. I pushed that and actively participated in it. My chief designer and I conceived all these strange images, particularly for the beginning sequence, although I think all that slow-motion death was a bit much in retrospect.'

❸ Achieved by having the camera pan through an area of mist, then as the Time Lord says 'Ah' back again to reveal the Time Lord standing there.

❹ This opening was rewritten from Nation's original setting by director David Maloney who felt that the serial needed a grim and shocking opening. The sequence was inspired by the image of a knight playing chess with the dark figure of Death in Ingmar Bergman's 1957 film *The Seventh Seal*.

Maloney: 'Terry had started it with the Doctor meeting a Time Lord in a beautiful garden. I switched that and conceived the figure of the Time Lord after the Bergman *Seventh Seal* monk figure: a man cowled and with no face playing chess on a hill with a knight. That was a direct pinch, hence John Franklyn-Robbins' costume.'

❺ This deleted line explains the TARDIS drifting back through time on Nerva beacon between *The Ark in Space* and *Revenge of the Cybermen*. It is also picked up on in a line in *Revenge* (recorded before *Genesis*) so was probably deemed irrelevant here.

❻ The time ring has a swirling whirlpool emblem attached on the top, which is perhaps intended as a representation of the time vortex.

❼ The camera is on the Doctor as the Time Lord wishes him luck. When the Doctor looks up the Time Lord has gone, we do not see him dematerialize.

❽ They actually appear clambering over rocks.

❾ The 'space-age gun' lying by the soldier was a prop re-used from the 1965 *Doctor Who* story *Galaxy 4*.

❿ The Doctor looks for movement on a ridge above them. As they move away, behind them on the ridge is revealed the figure. It is shrouded and cloaked, one arm outstretched stiffly from its side, probably to make a silhouette roughly approximating a Dalek.

The actor booked to play the Muto – Michael Crane – did not arrive at the location when scheduled. This sequence was filmed when he was later available.

⓫ This was an inserted model shot.

⓬ The exchange between the Doctor and Sarah is spoken over the model shot of the dome. We cut back at Harry's line.

⓭ A dummy was used for one of the dead soldiers in the background (this being cheaper than hiring an extra to play the role). The other two soldiers were played by extras as they needed to be seen standing upright more convincingly.

⓮ There was a recording break here to set up the pyrotechnic effects for the Thal attack. There were several other recording breaks during this complex fight sequence.

⑮　The Kaled troops are young men rather than boys. This may have been partly to hire more experienced actors, and also because there are rules about the hours children are allowed to work in the studio which would have placed restrictions on the scheduling of their scenes.

⑯　The specially made electric train developed by the visual effects team had worked fine at their workshops in Windmill Road, but when Baker and Marter climbed aboard in the studio it collapsed.

⑰　The relief map and symbols were provided by Visual Effects. Depending on required movements of cameras and characters, the table was moved to various predetermined positions referred to by code numbers.

⑱　The Doctor's pockets contain, amongst other things: sonic screwdriver, magnifying glass, yo-yo, biro, eyeglass, catapult, bag of jelly babies, handcuffs, a large yellow crystal and the scientific instruments mentioned in the script.

⑲　The camera directions note at this point that Ravon is left-handed. This is important for the positioning of Ravon and the gun he holds on the Doctor.

⑳　The Doctor uses his sonic screwdriver, not Ravon's gun, to destroy the communications equipment.

㉑　The references to Ravon being a colonel are left over from when the characters of General Greiner and Colonel Ravon were amalgamated.

㉒　This line is unattributed in the script. It seems intended for the Doctor, but is spoken by Harry, who has the gun.

㉓　A note on the camera script suggests that it was at some point intended to insert an effects shot for this, but it was dropped. It is Nyder's escort who fires, not Nyder himself.

㉔　For logistical reasons, this short scene (6A) was recorded *after* the preceding scene (6B).

㉕　Scene 6C was presumably another short insert in the corridor system, and dropped from the script before studio recording.

㉖　The klaxon sound effect actually continues throughout the scene.

㉗　This whole scene was edited out of the final version, presumably for timing reasons.

㉘　We clearly see the Muto shuffling after Sarah.

㉙　The scene opens with a shot of Nyder seen distorted through the Doctor's magnifying glass as he examines the Doctor's belongings.

㉚　Though the script specifies day for this scene, it is shot to appear to be dusk. This ties in better with the scene immediately following, when it is night.

㉛　The wall was erected in the studio, so the end of this scene, while specified for location filming, was actually recorded on video in the studio as part of the subsequent scene.

㉜　While the script refers to this Dalek as a 'primitive' model (as does the Doctor in Part Two), standard Dalek-machine props from previous stories were re-used. A 'Primitive Dalek' was also listed on the original visual effects requirements sheet.

　　The Dalek lacks its sucker arm in this scene, but is otherwise exactly as we know it from preceding stories, with the same gunmetal colour scheme seen before in *Day of the Daleks* and *Planet of the Daleks*.

㉝　CSO was used to inlay blue ray beams when the Daleks fired their weapons.

㉞　The camera direction for the end of the episode is 'Close Shot SARAH reaction'. But the final shot of the episode is actually a crash zoom on to the Dalek.

GENESIS OF THE DALEKS

by Terry Nation

Part Two

OPENING TITLES
Sarah has witnessed the Dalek weaponry test and now crouches into hiding as Davros, in his special chair, accompanied by Gharman and the Dalek ① (under its own uncertain power) exit from the ruined building. ②

DAVROS *(To Dalek)* **Follow.**

They pass quite close to the point where she is hiding. In an effort to crouch still deeper into her cover, Sarah dislodges a piece of stone.

The rattle of the stone makes Gharman glance in her direction. He pauses and takes a step towards her, peering through the fog to find the cause of the sound. He moves uncertainly closer.

DAVROS ~~Come along,~~ Gharman… There is much to be done…

Gharman moves back to join Davros and the Dalek. The trio move off into the darkness.

Sarah allows herself a sigh of relief, and still using caution starts to move out of her cover.

Now it is her turn to be startled by a sound. A slight crunching of a footstep somewhere in the darkness behind her. She spins to face the sound then stays frozen in position. The sinister and ominous dragging footsteps come a little closer. She presses back against the wall.

Sarah is totally unaware that behind her, inching along the wall towards her head is a misshapen and very frightening 'hand'. Spider-

like it edges toward her. The arm is swathed in rags… the body of the creature is not seen.

The hand lightly lands on Sarah's shoulder. She spins around giving a gasp of horror. What she sees (and we don't) terrifies her still more.

The shock is too great and she slumps to the ground in a faint. We widen to show the owner of the hand move in to stand over her body. The creature is a Muto and its actual shape is hidden by a draping of filthy torn rags. A second Muto moves in from the direction in which Sarah was staring. They seem to tower above her unconscious body.

At all times, Mutos try to conceal their awful deformities with wrappings of any kind. We must never know what they look like.

The first Muto stretches a hand down towards Sarah.

2. INT. BUNKER CHECKPOINT. NIGHT.

A small ante-room. A heavy iron door on one side and in it a viewing panel. There is another and less formidable door at the other side of the room. Between the two doors is a console of complex-looking scientific equipment. This equipment is controlled from a desk behind which sits a young officer of the Elite.

On the checkpoint desk are TV monitors, in background two Elite guards stand stiffly at attention.

Behind the desk is a small window and through it we can see a distant view of the Kaled dome. Glowing with light. ❸

The Elite officer at the desk is Tane, an aide stands behind him. Tane is staring at his TV monitor. We do not see the screen. He calls across to the two guards near the heavy door:

TANE Party approaching. Check one.

The guards move to the door. Tane speaks into a microphone on his desk, pressing the switch. We hear his amplified voice booming beyond the closed door.

TANE You will announce your name, rank and serial number. Speak now.

Through a loudspeaker on the desk we hear:

NYDER (VO) Alright, Tane! This is Security Commander Nyder with prisoners and escort.

TANE Yes, sir.

Tane presses a switch on his desk and the heavy door glides open, to reveal Harry and the Doctor escorted by Nyder and a guard. Nyder prods his prisoners forward into the room.

NYDER Tane. I want these two screened and passed to Ronson for full interrogation.

TANE Yes, sir.

Nyder hands over a small but bulky package. ❹

NYDER The prisoners' belongings.

Tane gives the special salute. Nyder formally acknowledges the salute and exits with his armed guard. Tane presses the control on his desk and the large door closes again. The Doctor seems relieved to see the back of Nyder.

DOCTOR WHO Good… Well, now that he's gone perhaps you'll offer us any chance of a cup of tea?

TANE What?

DOCTOR WHO Or any light refreshment coffee. My friend and I have been through the most had a very trying experience, haven't we had a trying experience, Harry?

HARRY Very trying, Doctor.

Tane points to Harry.

TANE Step into the security scan.

Harry makes to take a step forward but the Doctor restrains him.

DOCTOR WHO What, no tea?

TANE Let me point out to you that you have no rights whatsoever. I have full authority to torture and kill any prisoner who does not comply absolutely with my orders. Consider that your first and last warning.

DOCTOR WHO No tea, Harry.

Tane clicks his fingers. The guard standing behind the two prisoners knocks the Doctor aside and pushes Harry forward.

TANE Move into the security scan.

Harry steps between two man-sized cabinets of instruments. The moment he is between them he is engulfed in a coloured light from above. His whole body goes rigid as though he were suffering some electric shock.

There is a whirring sound and clicking noises. After a few seconds the lights go out and the sounds end.

TANE You're cleared. Move forward. (To Doctor) You next.

The Doctor shrugs and steps forward. The same sequence of events, but this time the machine gives out a high-pitched warning shriek.

Tane quickly glances at his instruments.

TANE Scan detects power source. Located below **prisoner's** left elbow.

He presses another switch and the scan check ends.

The Doctor lurches out to join Harry.

TANE Remove object on prisoner's left wrist.

The soldier grabs the Doctor's left wrist and starts to pull from it the bracelet given to him by the Time Lord.

DOCTOR WHO You can't have that…

The soldier hits the Doctor savagely and rips the bracelet free. ⑤

Tane drops it into the envelope along with their other belongings.

The Doctor staggers rubbing his kidneys.

DOCTOR ⑥ That bracelet has no possible use as a weapon…

TANE It remains with the other confiscated items.

While Tane gives his attention to muttering something into a 'communicator', Harry tries to comfort the Doctor.

HARRY Don't make a fuss about it. ⑦

DOCTOR WHO That time ~~bracelet~~ **ring** is our only hope of getting back to the TARDIS. *(Urgently and softly)* Harry, recovering that has got to be our ~~top~~ **number one** priority. You understand me… it's vital!

HARRY I know it's ~~important~~ **vital**, but we don't want them to know that.

Harry nods blankly. Tane replaces the 'communicator'.

As he rises:

TANE The prisoners are to be given into the custody of Senior Researcher Ronson … Here take this with you… **Move!**

He hands a guard the package of belongings. The guards then move to flank the Doctor and Harry.

Tane presses a control and the inner door opens.

Harry and the Doctor are marched through it and the door closes behind them.

3. EXT. SHATTERED WALL. NIGHT. ⑧

One of the Mutos, Sevrin, is crouched beside the unconscious body of Sarah. He reaches out his deformed hand ⑨ *and with great gentleness strokes her face. When he speaks his voice is gentle, almost soothing.*

SEVRIN She is beautiful… No deformities… no imperfections.

GERRILL ⑩ She is a norm. All norms are our enemies… Kill her now for what has been done to our kind…

SEVRIN No… no… why must we always destroy beauty? Why kill because another creature is not in our image..?

GERRILL Kill her. It is the law. All norms must die… They are our enemies.

Sevrin makes no move to harm Sarah.

Gerrill pulls a crude and savage knife from amongst his rags. He makes to push Sevrin aside.

GERRILL Then if you won't, I will…

Before Gerrill can move the protective Sevrin aside there comes from quite close at hand an indistinct blur of voices.

SOLDIER *(VO)* **Listen, there's something over there.**

Both the Mutos are immediately alarmed. They stare out into the darkness.

SEVRIN A patrol… very close.

GERRILL Let's get away from here…

SEVRIN No, no… They're too near… If you move they'll see us…

GERRILL They're coming this way… I'm going… come on.

Gerrill starts to scramble away. Sevrin, keeping his head down, tries to restrain him.

SEVRIN No – I tell you they'll see you.

Gerrill pulls free. He stares into the darkness and then starts to skulk along the wall silently. He has not gone more than a yard or so… when a voice calls from the darkness.

SOLDIER'S VOICE Halt… Stay where you are.

Gerrill is engulfed and held in the glare of a powerful spotlight. He shields his face against the glare.

SOLDIER'S VOICE Stand where you are… Don't move…

Footsteps approach through the darkness behind the beam.

Gerrill's nerve cracks and he tries to run for it. He has taken not more than pace or two when there is a single shot. He falls dead.

Show Sevrin crouching over Sarah's body trying to protect himself and her from view.

Two Thal soldiers in their makeshift uniforms move in to examine their kill. One of them carries the lamp, the other has an old muzzle-loading rifle with a trickle of smoke coming from the barrel.

SOLDIER It's only a Muto… waste of good ammunition…

The soldier with the gun starts to reload. The man with the lamp starts flashing it around the area. Show Sevrin pull still closer to the ground as the light flashes just above him. The beam passes on and then swings back to illuminate him fully.

SOLDIER *(VO)* There's a couple more of them.
Angle of the soldiers.
A rifle is raised to fire.

SOLDIER Hold it… If they've not too badly mutated we might be able to use them… They still need expendable labour for the rocket loading…

One of the soldiers pulls Sevrin to his feet. He appears disgusted at having to touch a Muto.

SOLDIER This one~~'s not bad~~ looks all right… It's got all it needs to carry and walk…

He directs the soldier with the lamp to point it toward Sarah.

SOLDIER No reason why this one shouldn't work… Looks almost a norm…

He roughly prods at Sarah with his foot. She begins to stir.

SOLDIER Come on… ~~get on your feet…~~ Get up… ~~come on~~ Up..!

Sarah recovers enough under the prodding to rise to her knees and is aware enough that she is danger to make an effort. But despite her best efforts the strain is too great for her and she can't stand.

SOLDIER It's too slow… all right, kill it off…
The soldier aims his rifle.
Sevrin moves swiftly to shield Sarah and helps her to her feet.

SEVRIN She'll be all right… I'll help her…

SOLDIER Then move… And move quietly. There are Kaled patrols out tonight.

Sevrin supports Sarah and they start forward. The soldiers stay close urging them forward. They move into the darkness.

4. INT. BUNKER LABORATORY. NIGHT.

A large rectangular room. Around its walls are computers and instruments.

A guard in the uniform of the Elite stands at attention in background.

Scientists are at work at some of the instruments. There is an air of quiet and calm efficiency.

Off to one side is a desk. Standing before it are Harry and the Doctor. Seated at the desk is Ronson. A man in his late forties. He is examining the contents of the envelope. ⑪

Ronson glances up and gestures to some chairs.

RONSON Please sit down.

The Doctor and Harry gratefully take chairs.

DOCTOR WHO Thank you. You are not a part of the military, I assume?

RONSON I am with the science division.

DOCTOR WHO ~~Excellent. Then perhaps we might be able to conduct a conversation without punctuation~~ **Oh good, good. Then perhaps we can talk without interruption** from rifle butts.

RONSON That depends. If you don't answer my questions then I'm afraid I must hand you back to the military. They take rather a pride in loosening tongues.

Ronson pokes amongst the items. ⑫

RONSON Where did you get these things?

DOCTOR WHO Here and there…

RONSON If I didn't know better I'd have to conclude these articles had been made by an intelligence on another planet.

DOCTOR WHO If you didn't know better?

RONSON It's an established scientific fact that in the seven ~~known~~ galaxies only Skaro is capable of supporting intelligent life.

DOCTOR WHO ~~The answer to that is~~ **It is also an established scientific fact** that there are many more than seven galaxies…

Ronson picks up two cards.

RONSON Indeed, when you passed through the security scan the instruments also ran a check

on blood and chemical make up…
encephalographic patterns… physiological
composition and so on, so if you are from
another planet…

He stops talking and actually gapes at the
cards. Then looks slowly up at the two men.

DOCTOR WHO You were saying?

Ronson is quite awed.

RONSON Nothing. Nothing conforms to any
known life form on this planet… only the
external appearance…

DOCTOR WHO ~~Never judge by appearance~~ You
can't always judge by external appearances.

RONSON Who are you? Where have you come
from? Tell me.

DOCTOR WHO It's a long story… Do you have
any inkling of the theory of space dimension
co-related by relative time..?

Before the Doctor can launch into his
explanation a gentle gonging sound emerges
from the loudspeakers. It takes the immediate
attention of all the scientists working in the
room. The sound is followed by an
announcement.

LOUDSPEAKER VOICE Davros wishes all members
of the Elite scientific corps to assemble in the
main laboratory immediately.

More white-coated workers start to filter into
the room.

RONSON I'm afraid our session will have to
wait… Davros is coming.

DOCTOR WHO Your chief scientist.

RONSON He is the supreme commander. When
he calls a full meeting **like this** he obviously
has something of the greatest importance to
tell us.

DOCTOR WHO **Well,** I shall be very ~~interested~~
delighted to meet him.

RONSON **Shut up and keep** quiet.

A silence falls over the room, which is sustained
for quite a few seconds. A door glides slowly
open. More seconds pass. Then into the room
comes Davros.

Davros is contained in a specially
constructed self-powered wheelchair. It has
similarities to the base of a Dalek. Davros
himself is a masterpiece of mechanical
engineering. His chair is a complete life-
support system for the ancient creature.

A throat microphone and amplifier create the
voice he no longer has. (Its sound is not unlike
the voice of a Dalek.) A miniature H and L
machine keeps his heart and lungs functioning.
A single lens wired to his forehead replaces his
sightless eyes. Little of his face can be seen.
Tubes and electrodes attached to what does
show. The upper part of his body is contained
in a harness from which great complexes of
wires and tubes emerge.

The only really human feature we ever see of
Davros is an ancient withered hand that plays
across the switch-packed surface of the control
panel that stretches across the front of the chair.

Davros glides to the centre of the room.
Silently he swings his chair in a slow arc to
view the group.

Through the door behind him come Nyder
and Gharman, sparklingly correct in their
gleaming uniforms. They stand slightly behind
and either side of the chair. Respectfully silent.

DAVROS If I may have your attention. For some
time I have been experimenting with the mark
three project. Details of ~~the~~ modifications will
be distributed later. However I am anxious
that you should see **immediately** the
remarkable ~~progress that has been made~~
~~immediately~~ **results that I have achieved.** And
to that end I have arranged this
demonstration.

Davros turns his chair so that he is facing the
door. The withered hand hovers over a switch
on his control board. He presses it. Moments
later, the 'primitive' Dalek glides into the room.
It has no weapon or arm. It appears to be a
'utility' model. However there is no mistaking
it as a Dalek.

DOCTOR WHO *(Whispers)* A Dalek.

HARRY *(Whispers)* What?

DOCTOR WHO *(Whispers)* A Dalek… Very
primitive but undeniably a Dalek… ⑭

Ronson glances at him.

RONSON You're mistaken… it is a mark three
travel machine…

The Doctor shrugs.

DOCTOR WHO If you say so…

The machine glides up to Davros.

DAVROS Halt. **Forward.**

The Dalek stops.

Creating the Creator

Michael Wisher rehearsed for his role as Davros by wearing a paper bag on his head and sitting in a chair the whole time; this allowed him to perfect his vocal rather than physical performance.

While playing Davros in studio, Wisher wore a kilt to avoid wearing out his trousers with rapid leg movements while sitting inside Davros' wheelchair.

The wheelchair was a prop based on the lower part of a Dalek and constructed by visual effects designer Peter Day and his assistants Tony Harding and Steve Drewett.

Davros' mask was constructed by visual effects sculptor John Friedlander, and Hinchcliffe suggested that this should resemble the evil Venusian genius the Mekon, from the *Dan Dare* comic strips from the *Eagle* comic of the 1950s and 1960s. The mask included a blue bulb which illuminated as Davros' third eye, but this stopped working in some of the recording sessions.

In coming up with the voice, Michael Wisher recalled the tones of the philosopher Bertrand Russell. Wisher's voice was fed through a ring modulator to make him sound like a Dalek.

Terry Nation on Davros: 'Davros served two roles. Firstly he was half man, half Dalek, a sort of mutated missing link between the two species – the Kaleds as they once were and the Daleks they were to become. Secondly, with the Daleks' slow speech patterns, having a Dalek as a spokesperson for their point of view all through would have been dull, and – worse – would have slowed down the pace of the story. I wanted someone who could think like a Dalek, but talk in a more human fashion. I feel very strongly the Daleks themselves should be left to speak in short, snappy sentences, not long speeches.'

RONSON He's perfected voice control, that's magnificent…

As Davros gives orders the Dalek responds albeit a little falteringly.

DAVROS ~~Move left… Halt. Move forward. Halt. Circle… Halt… Turn toward me…~~ ~~Halt…~~ Turn right… Move forward and circle left.

~~As the Dalek completes its display the scientists in the room burst into spontaneous and enthusiastic applause.~~

DAVROS You will agree I think that voice control represents an enormous step forward… However the best is yet to come… Nyder.

Nyder steps forward. He is holding a version of a Dalek gun and a sucker arm. **15** *He slots both items into the Dalek, then moves back to his position.* **16**

DAVROS ~~Thank you.~~ Our machine is now equipped with a weapon ~~of~~ **for** self-defence. Now I am turning the machine over to total self-control.

A gasp from the audience.

DAVROS It will be **entirely** independent of all outside influences. A living, thinking, self-supporting creature.

Davros turns a switch on his panel. At first the Dalek does nothing. Then slowly its arm and gun move. The 'head' moves. Then very slowly, uncertainly, the Dalek begins to move. Uncertain of direction it wanders a bit, then gaining confidence moves a little more certainly. It moves past the scientists and then seems to 'see' Doctor Who and Harry. It makes slowly towards them.

Davros moves his chair to follow the Dalek. The Dalek halts in front of the Doctor. He holds his ground and stares back at it.

DAVROS Brilliant… brilliant…It has detected non-conformity.

The Dalek very slowly begins to raise its gun. Its unsure voice croaks out:

DALEK Aliens. I must exterminate. Exterminate. Exterminate. ⑰

The gun is almost levelled at the Doctor. Ronson shows sudden alarm as he realizes the creature intends to kill.

RONSON No!

He darts forward to Davros and before anyone can stop him throws the switch on the board. The Dalek's life subsides. The gun and arm and eye droop. All movement stops. Davros' voice is furious.

DAVROS You dare to interfere! You have the audacity to interrupt **one of** my experiments?!

RONSON **But** it would have destroyed ~~him~~ **them.**

DAVROS You consider the saving of a worthless life more important than the progress we have made!..? My creature shows a natural desire… an instinct to destroy and you interceded! You will be punished for this… ⑱

RONSON Davros… I'm sorry… but **I believe that** these prisoners… ~~I believe~~ they could be extremely valuable… By all means… when I have finished **my** questioning ~~them your creature can~~ **let the machine** do what it likes to them… But I do need to interrogate them further…

There is a brief pause whilst Davros considers.

DAVROS You will be punished for insubordination… In the mean time you may question ~~your~~ **the** prisoners until first light… After that they will be used to resume the experiment. This meeting is ended.

Davros wheels his chair around and exits swiftly, followed by Gharman and Nyder. The deactivated Dalek remains.

Ronson breathes a sigh of relief.

DOCTOR WHO Thank you. **I'm obliged to you.**

RONSON I was simply doing my duty. I… I believe you might have knowledge that ~~can help us~~ **could be of the greatest assistance to us…** **But,** if you do not co-operate then it is certain that Davros will use you ~~to test~~ **as an experiment with** his machine in a few hours time.

Nyder re-enters and crosses to the group.

NYDER The prisoners are to be taken to the cells… You can continue questioning them there… Davros orders it.

Ronson nods. Nyder motions them all to follow him. The Doctor, Harry and Ronson move away.

We angle on to Ronson's desk to show the Doctor's belongings spread out. Amongst them, and evident is the bracelet from the Time Lord.

Angle to the Dalek where all the other scientists are now grouping to examine it in admiration.

TELECINE 1
EXT. LANDSCAPE AND DOME. NIGHT. (MODEL SHOT)

A distant shot of the Thal domed city. ⑲ Establish and close on it, then:

5. INT. THAL CELL. NIGHT.

At the door a Thal guard dressed from head to toe in radiation-protective clothing. A menacing figure in the silver suiting ⑳ with only his eyes visible through the narrow slit in the helmet. He is armed with a machine gun. ㉑

The exhausted prisoners in the cell are made up of Mutos in their all-concealing rags, and some Kaled soldiers in their makeshift uniforms.

Sevrin is seated beside Sarah who has her back against the wall. Still groggy from her earlier experience and only now becoming totally aware of her surroundings. She is fighting to stop herself slipping into hysteria as she stares around.

The young Kaled leader from Part One sits near Sevrin and Sarah. He shows every sign of total exhaustion.

SARAH Where are we?

SEVRIN Inside the Thal dome. We should think ourselves lucky… Normally the Thals kill on sight…

SARAH Then why the change? Why bring us here?

SEVRIN *(Shrugging)* Perhaps they need slave workers for some project…

LEADER The Muto is right. The work they're making us do kills with the same certainty as a bullet between the eyes…

SARAH What work?

LEADER The Thals have built a rocket. It's used up all their manpower and resources. They're gambling that it will bring them victory in one blow. And if they can make the launch successfully, I don't see how they will fail… My race… the whole of the Kaled people will be wiped out in seconds…

SEVRIN Perhaps we should be happy to work on such a weapon if it ends a thousand years of war.

LEADER You won't be when you find out what it is…

SARAH What is it?

LEADER The nose cone of the rocket is being packed with distronic explosive. We have to put it into position.

SARAH So?

LEADER To reduce weight they are using no protective shielding. Every load we carry exposes us to distronic toxaemia. After a few hours' exposure we'll all be dead.

SARAH We'd better think of something hadn't we?

Sarah stares at him in horror.

Before she can make any comment there is a whirring sound from the door and it slides open. The Thal guard in protective clothing motions to the inmates of the cell and they wearily begin to get to their feet like automatons.

SARAH Now what's happening?

LEADER The rest period is over. We start loading again… I've already done one ~~stint~~ **load** since I was captured.

The prisoners begin to file out of the door. None of them show any hint of resistance.

The Thal guard sees that Sarah and Sevrin are not moving quickly enough with the group and he moves across and prods them to their feet with his gun, directing them to follow the others.

SARAH All right, don't push.

6. INT. ROCKET SILO. NIGHT. 22

The concrete walls of a rocket silo. At its centre we see a section of the bottom of the great rocket. At floor level there is a small open hatchway through which the workers carry the fissionable material.

The area is dimly lit, the furthermost reaches of the silo being lost in shadow. There is a skeleton of scaffolding around the rocket.

We see Sarah and Sevrin emerge from the cell door, followed by the guard.

Sarah stares around, then slowly tilts her head back to look up at the rocket, her face reflecting her awe as she stares.

7. INT. ROCKET SILO. NIGHT. 23

As though seen from ground level and Sarah's VP the towering rocket and around it the framework of scaffold.

Model shot of rocket.

8. INT. ROCKET SILO. NIGHT. 24

Sarah stands staring upward for a moment or two longer. The other workers have formed rough lines and stand waiting with their heads bowed.

Sarah and Sevrin are shoved into the end of the line. Sarah is still staring around the silo area and notices a very large dial on the wall.

It is a clearly marked 'Toxic Level'. The final third of its calibration is marked in red. At the moment the indicator reading is resting safely in the white 'Safe' zone.

There is the clank and chug of a motor and a fork-lift truck *appears from around the rocket base. Its driver wears the same protective clothing as the guard. As the fork-lift moves closer we see it is carrying a load of large 'ingots'. Sarah watches as it drives closer and then looks at the radiation dial. The pointer swings violently across far into the red zone.*

The fork-lift halts and the prisoners file past and each picks up one of the heavy ingots and enters the hatch of the rocket. We watch the line move forward until finally it is Sarah's turn to pick up one of the ingots. **26** *She hesitates for a moment and is prodded by the guard. Very frightened, she picks up the ingot and moves into the rocket.*

Angle again on the radiation register. The needle twitching slightly but not moving out of the red zone.

9. INT. DETENTION ROOM. NIGHT.

Situated somewhere deep in the Elite bunker. Windowless and with only one door. There is a bench along one wall and on it sits Harry, head in hands and worried. He glances up at sounds of approaching footsteps.

A moment later the door is opened and the Doctor is virtually thrown inside by two Elite guards.

The door is closed and locked again. Harry helps the Doctor to his feet.

HARRY Are you all right?

The Doctor is stiff and his movements reflect his aches and pains. He rubs his ribs and winces.

DOCTOR WHO I might be.

HARRY ~~Did you tell them anything?~~ What happened?

DOCTOR WHO ~~Oh yes...~~ They took down reams of notes... Every bit of scientific gobbledegook I could think of... Technical jargon that even I didn't understand...

HARRY That should keep their experts confused for weeks.

DOCTOR WHO I learned a good deal more from them than they did from me...

HARRY About this Bunker?

DOCTOR WHO Yes.

HARRY It is underground, isn't it?

DOCTOR WHO Yes... ~~as we suspected it's mostly underground...~~ And bomb proof... impregnable from attack **from the outside** and about three or four miles outside the Kaled dome.

HARRY What are they doing **down** here?

DOCTOR WHO Years ago the Kaled government decided to form an Elite group... all the best brains in every scientific field...

HARRY A sort of think tank. **27**

DOCTOR WHO ~~Right~~. **Yes.** But over the years the Elite has become more and more powerful and now they can demand ~~anything they want~~ **whatever they like**.

There is the sound of footsteps in the hallway.

RONSON *(OOV)* Open up.

HARRY Perhaps this is the tea.

The door opens and Ronson steps inside. He glances at a uniformed Elite guard behind him.

RONSON You needn't wait... I am armed.

The guard nods and closes the door. We hear his footsteps move away. Ronson only speaks when he is sure the guard has moved out of earshot.

RONSON I'm sorry that they hurt you. I... I lacked the courage to interfere.

DOCTOR WHO But you did save me from becoming the very first victim of a Dalek, **thank you.**

RONSON You used that word earlier... It had never been heard before. Yet... only an hour ago... Davros announced that ~~the~~ **henceforth his** mark three travel machine would ~~henceforth~~ be referred to as... a Dalek... How could you have known that..?

DOCTOR WHO I have an advantage in terms of time. ~~In fact~~ **You see**, we have come here at this time because of... future concern... about the development of the Daleks... I think you're concerned, too, aren't you?

RONSON *(Nods)* Yes, I am concerned and there are **a few** others who think **the same** as I ~~do~~ but we are powerless.

DOCTOR WHO Then let us ~~try to~~ help.

RONSON **You see,** we believe Davros has changed the direction of our research into something that is immoral. **Evil.** You see the ~~Elitist movement was started~~ **Elite was formed** to produce weapons that would end the war. ~~But~~ We soon saw that this was futile and ~~turned our attention to~~ **changed the direction of our research into** the survival of our race. ~~so~~ **But** our chemical weapons had already started genetic mutations.

HARRY And ~~you're the~~ mutations ~~have been~~ **were** banished **out in**to the wastelands.

RONSON Yes.

DOCTOR WHO The Mutos.

RONSON Yes. Davros believed there was no way to reverse this trend ~~so began~~ **and so he started** experiments to ~~find~~ **establish** our final mutational form. He took living cells, **treated them** with chemicals and ~~created~~ **produced** the ultimate creature. Come with me.

10. INT. CORRIDOR. NIGHT.

Ronson leads Harry and Doctor Who down a short section of corridor to a heavy door in which there is a viewing panel.

The shutter is closed over the panel for the moment.

Ronson pulls aside the shutter on the viewing panel.

Beyond it is a dull green glow.

Ronson indicates Doctor Who and Harry should look in.

RONSON ~~That~~ **Now this** is what the Kaleds will become… 28

Harry and Doctor Who move up to the viewing panel. 29

Ronson turns his head away swiftly, sickened by the sight.

Doctor Who stares for a moment longer then gently closes the panel.

This is our future…

DOCTOR WHO ~~Then~~ You've got troubles.

11. INT. THAL CELL. NIGHT. 30

The prisoners are filing back into the cell. They find their piece of floor space and collapse, exhausted.

We favour Sarah, the Kaled leader and Sevrin as they slump to the floor in a group.

Sarah watches as the cell door closes and the armed guard in his protective clothing takes up his position.

SARAH *(Listening)* We have to do something now. If we work another shift we won't have the strength to take any kind of action.

LEADER Action? What do you mean?

SARAH I mean we have to get out of here…

SEVRIN ~~That is impossible~~ **It's not possible**…

SARAH Why? The guard's not expecting trouble from a group of exhausted slave workers.

LEADER So we get out into the rocket silo… But where then..? The only other exit goes out through a command point. ~~It will~~ **And that's going to** be crawling with Thal troops…

SARAH There is another way.

SEVRIN Where?

SARAH Straight up… The scaffolding goes right up to the nose cone of the rocket… If we could get up there then there is a chance we could get out on to the surface of the dome…

LEADER Yes getting down there wouldn't be too difficult… The angle of the dome is quite gentle…

SEVRIN ~~But climbing~~ **I mean** – that scaffolding! It's so high.

SARAH It's the only way ~~out~~… ~~the~~ **It's our** only chance…

LEADER I'd rather ~~fail~~ **die** taking a chance like that than rot away **in here** with distronic toxaemia…

Sarah turns to look at Sevrin, he nods slowly.

SARAH All right… now pass the word to the others…

Each of them cautiously moves out to settle beside other prisoners and begins to talk in low whispers.

12. INT. DETENTION ROOM. NIGHT.

DOCTOR WHO Go on, **Ronson.**

RONSON Knowing our ultimate form Davros began to devise a travel machine… the Dalek.

DOCTOR WHO But now he's trying to change that into a weapon…

RONSON And he is succeeding… he's made a monster utterly devoid of conscience.

HARRY You want to stop him?

RONSON I must. There are ~~men~~ **a few** in the Kaled government who still have the strength to act. If they knew the truth they could end Davros' power… Close down the Bunker… ~~and~~ **finish** the Elite…

DOCTOR WHO Then go to them, Ronson, **go to them.**

RONSON I am not allowed to go to the city… security here is absolute.

DOCTOR WHO Then help us to escape… Give us the names of the men who have power…
HARRY Can you get us out **of here**?
RONSON Yes. There is a way… **Through** one of the ~~ventilation system's~~ secondary ducts **in the ventilation system that** leads to a cave on the edge of the wastelands…
HARRY Well?
RONSON The exit is barred.
~~**HARRY** Yes?~~
RONSON There is something else… Davros' early experiments were with animals… Some of the things he created were… horrific. And they're still alive…
DOCTOR WHO And I have an uneasy feeling you're going to ~~say~~ **tell me** they're in that cave.
Ronson nods.

13. INT. THAL CELL. NIGHT. ㉛
Everything set for the escape attempt.
Sarah gives the Kaled leader a nod. She crosses in front of the guard, sways as though dizzy, then falls against him.
Sevrin and the leader move swiftly and grapple with him. The Kaled chops a blow to the neck. The guard falls.
Sarah pulls the door open as the prisoners crowd forward.
SARAH Quickly!

14. INT. CORRIDOR. NIGHT.
Harry is climbing into the ventilation duct.
Ronson hands the Doctor a sheet of paper with names upon it.
RONSON They are the people you should try to contact.
HARRY ~~Ready, Doctor.~~ Right-ho.
RONSON If anything should ~~go wrong~~ **happen** –
DOCTOR WHO ~~Destroy the list?~~ Don't worry. ~~I~~ **We** won't let it fall into the wrong hands.
RONSON Quick!
He helps the Doctor climb into the duct, replaces the cover and turns away as a guard rounds the corner.
Ronson walks past him.

TELECINE 1A
INT. ROCKET SILO. NIGHT. ㉜
Sarah leads the way to the scaffolding. She and Sevrin start to climb, the other prisoners waiting their turn behind.

16. INT. THAL CELL. NIGHT.
The unconscious guard in the empty cell. He starts to stir.

17. INT. SECTION DUCT. NIGHT. ㉝
The ducting ends at this point. Its opening is covered by a wide mesh grille. The Doctor and Harry crawl up to the grille.
DOCTOR WHO There is where it comes out into the cave. ~~I'll try and get the cover free…~~
They start to hammer and shake the mesh.
Suddenly there is a sinister scuffling sound followed by an animal-like grunting.
DOCTOR WHO Ssh! What was that?
The noise comes nearer.
HARRY *(Whispers)* ~~Must be one of those animal things.~~ **Probably one of Davros's pets.**
A shapeless hunk crashes right past the grille. ㉞
The Doctor and Harry pin themselves back against the wall of the duct. The creature shambles off.
~~**DOCTOR WHO** It's gone. Come on.~~
They raise the grille cover and scurry through.

18. INT. THAL CELL. NIGHT. ㉟
The guard regains his senses. He pulls himself shakily to his feet and reaches out to a warning device on the wall.

TELECINE 2
INT. SCAFFOLD SECTION. NIGHT.
Black backing.
Sarah hauls herself up to the next bars.
Sevrin and the leader are not far behind her.
Sarah pauses to get her breath. She glances down.

20. INT. ROCKET. NIGHT. ㊱
As though from Sarah's VP looking down towards the base of the silo and rocket. A dizzying view.

TELECINE 3 (TK2 cont.)
INT. SCAFFOLD SECTION. NIGHT.

Sarah suffers an attack of vertigo. She sways on the scaffolding.

   Sound effect: Alarm bells.

   The Kaled stares downward and calls urgently.

LEADER That's the alarm… They'll be after us in a moment… come on…

Sarah starts to climb again.

INT. ROCKET SILO. NIGHT. ③⑦

Thal soldiers in their regular uniforms rush into the area.

   They point their firearms upwards and start shooting.

INT. SCAFFOLD SECTION. NIGHT.

Sarah and her group trying to clamber upwards, bullets start to whine around them hitting the metal scaffolding and walls.

INT. ROCKET SILO. NIGHT.

Prisoners hit by the gunfire fall down into shot. One man's body drapes on the scaffolding.

INT. SCAFFOLD SECTION. NIGHT.

In panic now, Sarah is reaching for a horizontal scaffold bar just above and beyond her reach. The Kaled ③⑧ helps lift her slightly

and she gets a grip and begins to pull herself up.

   Just as it appears Sarah is safe, the Kaled is hit by a shot. He releases his hold. Teeters for a moment then begins to topple.

   Sarah and Sevrin can do nothing to help him. Sarah turns her head away in horror as, screaming, he begins to fall.

INT. ROCKET SILO. NIGHT.

The Kaled falls into shot at the feet of the firing soldiers. He is quite dead. Now the Thal soldiers start towards the scaffolding and begin to climb after the runaways.

INT. SCAFFOLD SECTION. NIGHT.

Sarah is frozen into immobility. Unable to move, her eyes tightly closed. Sevrin moves to her side.

SEVRIN They're coming up after us… ~~We~~ **You** must keep ~~going~~ **moving**… ~~we~~ **you** must.

SARAH I can't… I can't move.

SEVRIN Come on… you must!

Sarah nerves herself and makes a desperate clutch for the next rung in the scaffolding. Her hand slips away and, with a scream, she falls from the scaffolding. ③⑨

END TELECINE 3

   CLOSING TITLES ④⓪

---

❶   The single Dalek seen in Parts One and Two was operated by John Scott Martin.

❷   There was no reprise from the previous episode at the start of this one.

❸   The night shot of the Kaled dome was a model. This was added into the letterbox-shaped window in the set using CSO. The camera then panned down from the window (the CSO camera matching its movements) to Tane at the controls.

❹   Nyder hands Tane a transparent plastic tray with the things from the Doctor's pockets on it.

❺   As the guard removes the time ring, the TARDIS key is clearly visible on a chain round the Doctor's neck. Presumably it is not detected by the scan.

❻   Several lines of the Doctor's speech were deleted from here.

❼   Harry's actual line ('Better not make a fuss, Doctor') was followed by more speech deleted before the studio session.

❽   This scene was recorded immediately after Scene 1 (i.e. before the previous scene) as it takes place in the same set.

❾   Philip Hinchcliffe had originally intended that the Muto actors should wear masks made by John Friedlander.

❿   Gerrill is never named within the story, though his name is given in the closing credits.

(11) The scene opens with a close shot of Ronson holding the Doctor's sonic screwdriver.

(12) He takes the time ring.

(14) The main three Daleks seen in the serial were constructed in the 1960s. All the Daleks used in this story were standard 'refurbished' casings, painted in gunmetal grey with black balls (a colour scheme which helped conceal how worn some of the props were getting).

The assistant floor manager sent a memo to Clifford Culley (c/o Visual Effects) on 3 January 1975 (following a letter from George Gallaccio):

'Could we please have all the Daleks painted a dark grey. That is, 3 fully practical Daleks which will be required for rehearsal from 16 January, and 5 non-practical Daleks required for the studio recording from 10 February on.'

Cliff Culley's company, Westbury Design and Optical Ltd, was storing the Dalek props for the BBC – after *Planet of the Daleks* he stored them and repainted them silver for *Death to the Daleks*. They were then returned to him for storage.

The five 'non-practical' Daleks were referred to by the production team and camera scripts as 'goons'.

(15) Nyder takes the Dalek gun from a suitcase with a padded interior (provided by Visual Effects), and hands it to Gharman, who fits it into the Dalek. A cable is inserted and plugged into the socket first, then the gun snapped into the ball-and-socket fitting. (The Dalek was already fitted with a sucker arm.)

(16) Peter Miles (Nyder) and Dennis Chinnery (Gharman) had a fit of giggles when Chinnery could not get the Dalek weapon arm to fit. There is a cut-away reaction shot to the Doctor which masks the recording break when the Dalek prop has the gun inserted.

(17) The single line of Dalek dialogue was pre-recorded by Michael Wisher (Davros) and played back into the studio.

The Dalek voices were created by treating the actor's voice with a 'ring modulator', the same as for every other Dalek story. A ring modulator works by adding and subtracting an input signal's frequency, (in this case the actor doing the Dalek voice) from an internal oscillator's frequency. Unfortunately, the frequency used was never noted, and so Dalek voices tended to alter between stories. (The optimum setting for a Dalek voice seems to be 63hz, while Davros' voice is around 80hz.)

The name of the ring modulator comes from the arrangement of diodes in the analogue circuit (although it is sometimes assumed that the name comes from the fact that setting the modulator at higher frequencies – 1300 hz and above – produces a ringing tone on whatever signal is being passed through it).

(18) Davros' voice becomes more and more like that of a Dalek as he becomes louder and angrier. This was achieved by feeding Wisher's voice through a ring modulator (see above).

(19) In fact just one model was used for both of the domes – Thal and Kaled.

(20) The guards wear dark grey radiation suits.

(21) The guard has a Drahvin gun.

(22) This scene was recorded with Part Three to save re-erecting the set.

(23) As stated in the directions below, this was a model. The model of the Thal rocket seen here and in some other insert shots had been reworked by effects assistants Tony Harding and Andy Lazell, from Peter Day's recovery rocket in *The Ambassadors of Death* (1970).

(24) This scene was recorded with Part Three to save re-erecting the set.

(25) The explosives are driven up to the rocket in a small motorized buggy (called a 'Teddy' in the production notes).

(26) The 'ingots' were cylinders with a stubby handle on the top of each.

(27) The Thinktank comparison was added to refer back to *Robot*.

(28) Ronson says his line before pressing the button that opens the shutter.

(29) The Doctor and Harry are seen from inside the incubator room, looking through the window. The room is lit by a green glow interrupted by the thrashings of the unseen creatures. Sound effects make the effect even more unpleasant.

(30) Since it is in the same set, this scene was recorded immediately after Scene 5.

(31) Since it is in the same set, this scene was recorded immediately after Scene 11.

㉜   All the Thal rocket silo scenes were scripted by Nation for the TV studio but those involving the escape attempt were actually done at Ealing film studios, to facilitate staging and editing the stunt work. Filming of the action scenes in the Thal rocket silo took placed at the BBC Television film studios in Ealing on Monday 13 and Tuesday 14 January 1975. Other scenes have not been renumbered in the camera script to take account of this, so there is no Scene 15, for example.

㉝   This scene was recorded with Part Three to save re-erecting the set.

㉞   The mutated creature encountered by the Doctor and Harry (referred to in the camera directions as 'Muto') was in fact the back of an ice warrior body-shell with some slight modifications. The same sound effect was used as for the Dalek embryo creatures. In the camera script, cast list and other paperwork the creature appears simply as 'Thing!'.

㉟   This scene was moved so that it comes after Scene 20 in the final programme.

㊱   This was a model shot.

㊲   These scenes are not numbered as they are the same telecine film run continuously.

㊳   The Kaled leader (previously called 'Leader') is now referred to simply as 'Kaled'.

㊴   Director David Maloney was reportedly disappointed with the realization of Sarah's fall from the scaffolding. It was performed by stunt woman Tracey Eddon who fell about eight feet on to boxes and a mattress. Elisabeth Sladen herself had already fallen ten feet in rehearsals.

㊵   The episode ends on a freeze-frame of Sarah falling from the scaffolding, the first time an episode had ended with a freeze-frame.

GENESIS OF THE DALEKS

by Terry Nation

Part Three

OPENING TITLES

1. INT. SCAFFOLD SECTION. NIGHT.

Recap. ❶ *Sarah gives a cry of fear and falls. But by a desperate contortion she manages to catch the next rung of scaffolding. She hangs there, struggling to pull herself to safety.*
Sevrin scrambles down to her aid.

~~2. INT. ROCKET. NIGHT.~~

~~*As though from Sarah's viewpoint, we see the dizzying drop to the base of the silo. CSO model shot.*~~

3. INT. SCAFFOLD SECTION. NIGHT.

SEVRIN Are you all right?
SARAH I think so…

4. INT. ROCKET SILO. NIGHT.

Thal soldiers are kneeling and aiming their guns upwards. ❷

5. INT. SCAFFOLD SECTION. NIGHT.

Bullets whine through the scaffolding past Sarah and Sevrin. Another Kaled escaper starts along the scaffold towards the couple. He has almost reached them when he is hit. He teeters for a moment and then plunges down. Sarah and Sevrin stare in horror.

SEVRIN We must go on, Sarah… it's our only chance…

Sarah nodes bravely and readies herself to follow Sevrin.

6. INT. ROCKET SILO. NIGHT.

The bodies of the Kaled leader and the second Kaled lie crumpled on the concrete.

The Thal soldiers are starting to climb after the escapers.

7. INT. SCAFFOLD SECTION. NIGHT.

Sarah and Sevrin climbing upward.

Another angle: pursuing Thal pauses in his climb to aim and fire.

Resume on Sarah and Sevrin. The shot whines close to their heads.

8. INT. SCAFFOLD AND NOSE CONE. NIGHT.

The tip of the cone is only a foot or so away from the fabric of the dome. The scaffolding, at its nearest point, stands several feet away from the sloping cone. To get on to the cone and then to the dome itself is a hazardous leap.

On the nose cone are some metal grips and rungs. Sarah and Sevrin climb into view and stand on the scaffold at the point nearest to the nose cone.

SEVRIN ~~There's~~ A section of the roof ~~that~~ slides open… We ~~could reach~~ **can get to** it from the top of the rocket.

SARAH ~~How… how do we get across?~~ **We've got to get across first.**

SEVRIN We'll have to jump ~~for it~~… I'll go first… *(He tenses for the jump)* You follow ~~as soon as I have a footing. I'll be able to~~ **and I'll** catch you.

Sarah nods without hesitation and looks down at the drop below them.

9. INT. ROCKET SILO. NIGHT.

Again showing the awful drop.

10. INT. SCAFFOLD AND NOSE CONE. NIGHT.

Sevrin jumps. He spread-eagles himself on the nosecone and his hands slither and scrabble around for a grip.

His fingers lock around one of the handholds and he pulls himself into a position of safety.

SEVRIN ~~All right,~~ Come on **Sarah**… come on ~~Sarah~~…

Sarah sways dangerously, filled with terror at the prospect. She stares down.

11. INT. ROCKET SILO. NIGHT.

The vertiginous viewpoint to the base, far, far below.

12. INT. SCAFFOLD AND NOSE CONE. NIGHT.

Still Sarah sways dangerously.

Sevrin urges her on.

SEVRIN You've got to do it… You hear me… Jump!

Sarah glances down.

13. INT. SCAFFOLD SECTION. NIGHT.

Three or four Thal soldiers now climbing swiftly in pursuit of the escapees.

14. INT. SCAFFOLD AND NOSE CONE. NIGHT. ❸

Sarah reacts and braces herself for the jump, screws up her face and launches herself forward. [Her hands slip] and she starts to slither down the nose cone.

Sevrin snatches at her wrist and grabs her. Sarah [manages to get] hold, and finally is safe.

Sevrin begins to climb up to the tip of the nose cone.

Sarah follows cautiously. Almost triumphantly, Sevrin calls back down to her.

SEVRIN We're nearly there… just a bit more and we'll be out on the surface of the dome and safe.

Sevrin continues to climb slowly.

On the scaffolding behind her the first of the Thal soldiers climbs into sight. The second and third follow quickly.

At the tip of the nose cone, Sevrin reaches up to open the section of dome.

[Sevrin sees the closest soldier]. He freezes.

The Thal soldiers are finally positioned on the scaffold alongside the nose cone. Their guns are levelled and they could pick off their targets with ease.

THAL SOLDIER That's far enough…

Sevrin [gazes at the safety outside, then pulls his hands back in]. With no other choice [he sighs and] submits to the orders of the Thals.

THAL SOLDIER Right… come on back down here…

Sevrin moves back down the nose cone. Sarah stays in position.

Sevrin makes the jump – rocket cone back to the scaffold

THAL SOLDIER Now you… come on…move!

Sarah's fear of heights outweighs everything the Thal can threaten. The remaining two soldiers see her fear and start to enjoy it.

The non-speaking soldier has a coil of rope around his shoulders. ❹

The soldier grins.

THAL SOLDIER I'll get her…

With great confidence, he jumps across the gap. He moves up to Sarah. He signals to his companion to toss over one end of the rope. He catches it and reaches his hand out to Sarah.

THAL SOLDIER Give me your hand… **Come on!**

Almost cautiously, Sarah removes her hand and stretches it out to the soldier. He grabs her wrist and grins as he sees her hesitate, unable to move. He prods his feet forward and kicks Sarah's feet off the rim.

She gives a gasp of terror as she starts to slither down.

The Thal soldier, enjoying this torture, holds on to her wrist as she virtually dangles in space.

THAL SOLDIER If I should just slacken my grip… They say people who fall from great heights are dead before they hit the ground… I don't believe that… do you?

He makes a sudden movement to let Sarah jerk downward another few inches, smiling at her terror. Then tiring of his game, he hauls Sarah back up beside him and fastens the rope end around her waist.

THAL SOLDIER You're going back to work… And in a day or so you'll wish I had let you drop…

He calls across to his companion.

THAL SOLDIER ~~Right… Lower her down…~~ *(To Sarah)* Right, get over.

We go close on Sarah's face as she feels the rope tighten around her. For the moment at least her particular terror is over. ❺

15. INT. CAVE. NIGHT.

In the darkness we are only able to discern a section of dank dripping wall. All around are the spluttering gasping sounds that we heard earlier. The Doctor appears after a moment, groping his way forward along the wall. Harry is close behind him.

DOCTOR WHO It's lighter this way.

HARRY Looks as though we've made it.

DOCTOR WHO Look!

From their VP we see a small barred hole ~~through which dim daylight enters the cave~~.

HARRY That's the way out to the wastelands. *(Moving forward)*

He advances, his attention on the exit hole. Something large stirs slightly on the ground ahead of him. Harry steps into it.

There is an unearthly hiss and the top shell of a giant clam closes like a mantrap.

The serrated edges of its shell crunch round Harry's leg and he screams in agony and falls to the ground.

HARRY Doctor, quick!

The creature starts to withdraw back into the gloom of the cave, dragging Harry with it. He is in intense pain. The Doctor fights desperately to lever the clam's jaws apart but it holds remorselessly to its prey, hissing and moaning to itself. Harry is almost unconscious.

The Doctor grabs up a rock and tries to smash the clam's shell. It is iron hard. Finally the Doctor sees a long, spear-like stalactite and uses his rock to smash it loose. He takes this stone spear and frantically thrusts it inside the clam's jaws, alongside Harry's calf. The Doctor lunges and lunges again. The clam screams in agony as the stone twists into its vitals. Its jaws open and it scuttles back into the darkness.

The Doctor drops to his knees to examine Harry's injuries.

DOCTOR One of Davros' ~~early~~ experiments.

HARRY Magnae conchylum.

DOCTOR WHO What?

HARRY Latin.

DOCTOR WHO Never mind the Latin, let's have a look at your foot. It's incredible, nothing seems to be ~~I don't think anything's~~ broken… but you're going to have some ~~bad~~ bruises though, **Harry**.

He starts tearing strips from his shirt. Harry *sits up wearily.*

HARRY ~~Somehow it's~~ **Why is it** always me who puts a foot in it…

He tries a feeble grin. ~~The Doctor is bandaging his wound.~~

DOCTOR WHO You'll be all right~~, Harry~~. Can you stand **up**?

HARRY I think so…

The Doctor helps him to his feet. ⑥

DOCTOR WHO ~~Now we'd better~~ **Let's** get out of here.

HARRY ~~We ought to~~ **Let's** look for Sarah. She's out there somewhere…

The Doctor tests the bars over the exit hole.

DOCTOR WHO We'll find her but we've got to contact the Kaled leaders first.

With great effort he starts to bend the iron bars, widening the gap.

HARRY Try again – they're pretty corroded.

16. INT. MAIN LABORATORY. DAY.

Two Daleks glide along the length of the laboratory. Group of Elite scientists watches with fascination. Davros is in his wheelchair with Nyder, as always, in attendance. The Daleks glide to halt in front of Davros. ⑦

DALEK We await your commands.

Davros approaches. His mechanical voice croaks.

DAVROS Excellent. Excellent.

KAVELL ~~They are~~ Perfect, Davros… Perfect… a brilliant creation.

DAVROS A brilliant creation yes… But perfect no… not yet… I want improvements made in the optical systems. And the sensory circuits… Their instincts must be as accurate as a scientific instrument… You will begin at once… dismantle the viewer circuit.

The scientists swarm around the two Daleks. We angle on Ronson looking worried. Kavell edges up beside Ronson. He speaks in a conspiratorial voice, not looking at Ronson.

KAVELL Does Davros know that the prisoners have escaped?

Ronson looks alarmed. He blusters slightly.

RONSON I don't know what you mean… The prisoners are in the cell…

KAVELL Don't worry… I won't betray you… You're not the only one who is concerned about the morality of the work we are doing here… Now answer me. Does Davros know they have gone?

RONSON The prisoners are in the detention room for further interrogation.

KAVELL Well. I have some news for you. They've reached the city and made contact with leaders whose names you gave them.

RONSON How do you know?

KAVELL There are some advantages to being in command of the communications system…

⑧ ~~Just that…~~ All we can do now is hope they convince the leaders that Davros' work must be ended.

RONSON They must… they must. ⑨

17. ⑩ INT. COMMAND HEADQUARTERS. DAY. ⑪

Statesman-like Kaleds in civilian clothes. Also General Ravon, the Doctor and Harry.
The leader of the civilians is Councillor Mogran.

MOGRAN Fellow Councillors, I asked you to assemble here and not in our House of Congress because our meeting is of a most secret nature. And there are no listening devices here, are there Ravon?

RAVON None that I know of, Mogran.

Mogran turns to the Doctor.

MOGRAN Doctor… Will you please tell the Councillors what you have told me?

DOCTOR WHO Of course. And some of what I will tell you ~~concerns~~ **relates to** events in the future. Events not only on this planet but on others whose existence ~~is not even known to you~~ **you don't even know of**…

A murmur of surprise.

DOCTOR WHO ~~that may be hard to accept~~ But my knowledge scientific fact… Davros ~~is creating~~ **has created** a machine creature… a monster… which will terrorize and destroy **millions and** millions of lives and lands through all eternity. He has given this ~~vile~~ machine a name… A Dalek… it is a word new to you… but for a thousand generations ~~of people it will be~~ **it is a** name that will bring fear and terror…

We angle towards the Thal dome that stands on the relief map on the central table. The Doctor's voice begins to fade.

DOCTOR WHO Davros has one of the finest scientific minds ~~that ever existed~~ **in existence.** But he has a fanatical desire to perpetuate himself, in his creation. He works without conscience, without soul, without pity and his machines are equally devoid of these qualities.

The Doctor's voice fades away and we are firmly on the model of the Thal dome.

18. INT. ROCKET SILO. DAY.

The soldiers in protective clothing supervise chain of prisoners who wait to carry the material into the rocket. We see Sarah and Sevrin amongst them. Sarah puts her hand on her forehead and sways slightly. Sevrin supports her.

THAL SOLDIER What's the matter with her?

SEVRIN She's tired… she needs rest…

THAL SOLDIER This is the last consignment. When this is packed aboard she'll get all the rest she wants… Now… pick up your loads.

Sarah with Sevrin's help manages to stay on her feet and move with the line to pick up one of the ingots and stagger with it towards the rocket.

19. INT. MAIN LABORATORY. DAY.

Like mechanics, a group of scientists are gathered around the Daleks, tinkering and adjusting.

Davros is watching.

Nyder enters from a side doorway to cross urgently to Davros, his mission very evidently important.

From another point in the room where he is working alone, Ronson observes Nyder's arrival and reacts nervously.

Close on Nyder and Davros. Nyder keeps his voice low.

NYDER I've just had word from one of our supporters in the dome. Councillor Mogran has called a secret meeting. The only councillors ~~who have been~~ invited are known opponents of the work we are doing here in the Bunker.

The claw-like withered hand of Davros drums across the control panel of the wheelchair.

DAVROS I want a full report of everything that was discussed. I don't care how you get the information… get it. However, I think we need not be too concerned… Many times in the last 50 years ⑫ factions of ~~our~~ **the** government have tried to interfere with my research **here**… they have failed… they will fail again.

NYDER There's something else. The two prisoners in Ronson's charge. They have been seen in the dome… they are at the meeting.

DAVROS Impossible. There is no escape from here.

NYDER I've checked their cell… They are missing.

Very slowly Davros turns his chair so that he can look directly across the room at Ronson.

Nyder follows his look. Ronson shifts uneasily under their gaze and nervously pretends to be busy at something.

DAVROS Find out how they escaped and report to me immediately.

NYDER What action shall I take concerning Ronson?

DAVROS For the moment none. I will deal with him in my own way.

20. INT. COMMAND HEADQUARTERS. DAY.

The Kaled statesmen are talking quietly amongst themselves.

Doctor Who and Harry are watching the deliberations.

RAVON That was a very impressive speech Doctor.

DOCTOR WHO It was meant to be.

HARRY Let's hope you've convinced them.

DOCTOR WHO I hope so, but sometimes words are not enough, Harry.

HARRY ~~It looks as though they've~~ **Well, they seem to have** reached a decision!

The conversation amongst the councillors is at an end, all but Mogran – exit.

He crosses to Doctor Who.

MOGRAN I am afraid, **Doctor,** the councillors could not agree to halt all experimentation at the Bunker.

HARRY Then the councillors are fools –

MOGRAN Let me finish please… It has been agreed that an independent tribunal will investigate all work that is being done at the Bunker.

DOCTOR WHO But that could take months! ~~Right now~~ Davros already has **several** prototype Daleks ready for action.

MOGRAN It has also been agreed that, pending the result of the investigation, Davros's experiments will be suspended.

DOCTOR WHO It's less than I had hoped **for**… ~~but…~~

MOGRAN I promise you, **Doctor,** that if your allegations are borne out **all work at** the Bunker will be closed down ~~completely~~ – now, I must go with my committee to inform Davros of our decision.

Mogran turns and exits.

HARRY I think it's high time we ~~tried to find~~ **looked for** Sarah, **don't you?**

RAVON The one you left **behind** in the wastelands.

HARRY Yes do you ~~know something~~ **have news of her**?

RAVON I can't be certain, you understand. But our agents inside the Thal dome report a newly arrived girl prisoner who led an attempted break-out. Gave the Thals quite a bit of trouble.

HARRY That's her…

DOCTOR WHO Inside the Thal dome you say?

RAVON The Thals are using prisoners to load their last great rocket.

HARRY Rocket?

RAVON They think they'll win the war with it… What they don't know is that no matter how powerful the rocket, it cannot penetrate our protective dome… Only **a matter of** months ago Davros perfected a new substance which has the strength of 30-foot-thick reinforced concrete. ⑬

DOCTOR WHO ~~It's time we found Sarah. Can you help us?~~ Yes, yes, well never mind about that. **Could** you help us to find Sarah?

RAVON One of my agents could lead you into the service shafts under the Thal city…

DOCTOR WHO Oh good, good.

RAVON But after that you're strictly on your own.

HARRY ~~Understood~~ **Fair enough.**

RAVON Right. I'll give you a map showing how to reach the rocket-silo area.

He exits quickly. Harry and Doctor Who turn their attention to the relief map on the large table. Harry moves his finger from the Kaled dome to the Thal dome.

HARRY Well, Doctor, it look as though we'll have to cross the wastelands again.

DOCTOR WHO Yes! And then our troubles really begin.

He smiles cheerfully at the prospect.

20A INT. MAIN LABORATORY. DAY.

Mogran and two councillors stand confronting Davros.

Nyder is standing behind him.

DAVROS An investigation? But of course Mogran. I welcome any inquiry into our work here. I think the idea is an excellent one.

The councillors look a little taken aback.

DAVROS The Kaled people sacrifice much so that we should have the materials we need. They have the right to know how our work is progressing… and when they learn of our achievements their patriotism will be refired… It is vital that our soldiers know that they and we of the Elite are as one… working together to bring the final victory.

MOGRAN I am grateful that you have accepted this decision so… so patriotically. There is one thing more… until the inquiry all work is to be suspended.

DAVROS If that is your wish… then naturally, I will obey. It will take some time to close down certain pieces of equipment. Shall we say twenty-four hours?

MOGRAN Twelve.

DAVROS It will be difficult… but it will be done.

MOGRAN The members of the tribunal will arrive in that time. ~~I want to~~ Thank you, Davros, for your co-operation. ~~I appreciate it.~~

DAVROS It is simply my duty. The investigation will reveal nothing but our loyalty, and total dedication to the cause of the Kaled people.

Mogran nods politely, then with his companions turns on his heels and exits. As the door closes behind them:

NYDER We cannot allow this investigation! They cannot fail to see the dangers to themselves in the Dalek project.

DAVROS Calm yourself, Nyder. There will be no investigation.

NYDER But you can't stop it now.

DAVROS I can and will. The councill~~ors have~~ **has** signed the death warrant for the whole of the Kaled people... Only we... the Elite... We and the Daleks will go on.

Even Nyder seems shocked the calmness of Davros.

NYDER The whole of the Kaled people? You... you would go that far?

DAVROS Did you ever doubt it?

NYDER No.

DAVROS There is much to do. I want ~~twenty of~~ the genetically conditioned creatures installed in the machines immediately. **Twenty of them.**

NYDER Twenty!

DAVROS They are our troops in this battle for survival~~, Nyder.~~

NYDER But they're still very erratic. Unstable...

DAVROS They will not be allowed self-control... I will prepare a computer program that will limit their actions... After that... we are going on a journey.

Nyder looks at him, puzzled. Davros operates the control on his chair and wheels away towards the end of the room.

21. INT. CORRIDOR AND MANHOLE COVER. DAY.

A small section of corridor. In the floor a metal trap. We see the trap start to inch upward. Then swiftly slip back. ⓮

Two Thal soldiers walk past, their heels echoing on the metal trap. As the sound of their footsteps fades the trap inches open again and we see Doctor Who peer out.

Reassured that he is in the clear, he pushes the trap out of the way and hoists himself out of the manhole. He leans down and assists Harry to climb out. Both of them, looking around warily, replace the trap. Doctor Who refers to a map. He beckons to Harry and they move silently out of shot.

22. INT. CORRIDOR AND DOORWAY. DAY.

There are a few points that will provide hiding places. The principal feature is a door with a top-half glass panel ⓯ *that leads into the 'Rocket launch room'.*

We see Doctor Who and Harry skulk into sight. As they near the doorway they hear approaching footsteps and dive into cover. A senior Thal officer appears and enters the rocket launch room. ⓰ *After a pause Doctor Who carefully looks through the glass. Close on the Doctor's face as he registers astonishment at what he sees. He beckons Harry to join him. Harry reacts in the same way.*

23. INT. LAUNCH ROOM. DAY.

One wall is covered with technical equipment to launch and guide the missile.

There are three senior Thal officers in uniform and two Thal civilians. But the figures who have caused the astonishment are Davros and Nyder. ⓱

24. INT. CORRIDOR AND DOORWAY. DAY.

HARRY What's Davros doing... here in the Thal city!

The Doctor motions him to silence and with great caution opens the door a fraction. ⓲

25. INT. LAUNCH ROOM. DAY.

DAVROS ... and I am no longer influenced by words like nationalism or patriotism. My concern is only for peace. An end to the carnage that has virtually destroyed both our races.

COUNCILLOR Why aren't you telling this to your own government and people?

DAVROS I have tried. Time and again I have tried, but now they will ~~settle for nothing less~~ **be satisfied with nothing other** than ~~the~~ total annihilation of the Thal people.

COUNCILLOR Then they deserve to perish. Or perish they will when we launch our rocket... It is primed and ready. The countdown for firing can begin immediately.

DAVROS And it will fail.

COUNCILLOR It can't fail.

DAVROS The Kaled ~~city~~ dome cannot be penetrated. Your great rocket will hardly scratch it…

26. INT. CORRIDOR AND DOORWAY. DAY.

The Doctor and Harry exchange a puzzled look. Then they both hustle into cover and stay hidden while some Thal soldiers march past. As soon as they have gone, the couple turn silently back to the door.

27. INT. LAUNCH ROOM. DAY.

DAVROS This is a measure of my faith… Nyder.
Nyder produces a folded piece of paper from his pocket. And he offers it to the leading Thal.
NYDER It is a simple chemical formula… If the substance is loaded into ~~normal~~ artillery shells and fired onto the surface of our… the Kaled dome… it will weaken the molecular structure and make it brittle… Your rocket will then be able to penetrate without resistance.
POLITICIAN Why are you giving us this information..? You know that your **own** people… the Kaleds will be utterly exterminated…
DAVROS ~~There can be~~ No price **is** too great to pay for peace… I ask only that when the war is over I be allowed to help in the reconstruction of our ~~world~~ **planet**…
NYDER We want only to see the conflict brought to an end. This formula gives you the power to bring that about.
DAVROS At dawn tomorrow our ~~planet~~ **world** could be at peace.

28. INT. CORRIDOR AND DOORWAY. DAY.

The Doctor and Harry dash back into hiding. Davros and Nyder swing out of the door. It shuts behind them.
NYDER You think they believed you?
DAVROS It is ~~not~~ **un**important. They are hungry for victory… They will use the formula and fire their rocket no matter what they believe ~~to be~~ my motives **to be**… and when they do, Nyder… when they do…
Davros cuts off as the politicians emerge from the rocket launch room.
POLITICIAN I have given orders that a barrage of shells containing the formula should begin as

soon as possible. The rocket launch ~~will follow~~ **can begin** immediately afterwards… and now I'll ~~see that you are given~~ **arrange your** safe escort out of the city…
Davros, Nyder and the politician move away.
HARRY ~~We have to warn the Kaleds.~~ **Doctor, somehow we've got to warn Mogran and the other Kaled leaders.**
DOCTOR WHO **Yes,** and we ~~still~~ haven't found Sarah **yet**… Come on…
The Doctor leads the way, swinging along the corridor.

29. INT. CORRIDOR. DAY.

Two Thal soldiers completely swathed in anti-radiation-protective clothing stand outside the doorway that leads into the rocket silo.
The Doctor peers around a corner, braces himself and then with a very casual air moves forward. He moves past the soldiers, and then turns back to face them. He adopts the slightly blank look of one who is lost. The attention of the soldiers is on him so that their backs are towards the direction from which the Doctor came.
DOCTOR WHO Excuse me… **Can you help me –** I am a spy… ⑲ ~~I wonder if you could help me. I'm looking for the rocket silo.~~
The two guards stare at him in blank amazement. Then as they are jolted into reality they reach out to grab him. Unsuspected by the guards Harry glides up behind them.
He crashes his clenched fists down on to the back of one's neck. The Doctor delivers a blow to the stomach of the other guard. As he doubles up Harry gives him a crack on the back of the neck too.
DOCTOR WHO ~~Well done, Harry. Now…~~ **Their suits, Harry!**
Harry and the Doctor start to pull the protective clothing off the guards.

30. INT. ROCKET SILO. DAY.

A single Thal in protective clothing keeps a casual guard on the prisoners that remain. Amongst them are Sevrin and Sarah.
SARAH The rocket is loaded… why are they **still** keeping us here?

SEVRIN Why ~~should they~~ take the trouble to move us..? It's easier to leave us here…

SARAH But when ~~the rocket is~~ it's fired the exhaust blast will burn us up.

> She realizes what Sevrin means. That they will be incinerated.
>> Two figures in protective clothing shuffle into sight.
>> And cross to the guard.
>> One delivers a smashing punch that floors him.
>> Harry and the Doctor quickly whip off their hoods and free themselves of their protective clothing.
>> The Doctor crosses to Sarah.

SARAH Harry, Doctor!

DOCTOR WHO Are you all right, Sarah?

SARAH I am now. But we've got to get out of here. The Thals are going to launch this rocket.

DOCTOR WHO ~~I know Sarah, go with Harry. He knows the way out. Get to the Kaled dome… tell General Ravon what we have learned.~~ Yes, yes, I know. Listen, I want you and Harry to go back to the Kaled dome. Harry knows the way. **Tell them all we know.** There's a chance that if they launch an all out offensive ~~they~~ I might be able to stop the rocket launch.

SARAH And what are you going to do?

DOCTOR WHO Try to sabotage it or at least delay ~~the launch~~ it… Good luck to you.

SARAH Sevrin, you come with us.

> The Doctor turns to the other prisoners.

DOCTOR WHO Well, don't just stand there – come on, you're free. Go now while you've got the chance, come on! ~~Go on… all of you… you're free… take the chance while you can… go on…~~

> After a brief moment of doubt the prisoners start to run for the door.
> Sarah calls to Sevrin.

SARAH ~~Sevrin… you stay with us…~~

> ~~Sevrin moves up to join the group. The Doctor waves them away.~~

DOCTOR WHO ~~Good luck to you…~~

> ~~There is a brief moment when it seems that they won't go, then Harry nods firmly, turns and heads Sarah and Sevrin from the room.~~

> Alone now in the rocket silo the Doctor walks across to the hatch of the rocket. It is firmly locked against him. He tilts back his head and stares up.

31. INT. ROCKET. DAY.

> As though from the Doctor's VP the rocket towering away, and seemingly gigantic.
> CSO model shot. **20**

32. INT. CORRIDOR AND MANHOLE COVER. DAY.

> Harry and Sarah and Sevrin race into sight. Harry hauls up the manhole cover and Sarah drops swiftly through. As Harry starts to lower himself in, two armed Thal soldiers appear at the corner. They instantly fire. Their bullets whine off the metal cover. Harry drops out of sight, the manhole cover not fully back in position. The Thal soldiers race up and push the cover aside and then start to pour automatic fire down into the cavity below.

33. INT. ROCKET SILO. DAY.

> Tight on the Doctor as he examines a thin metal pipe that runs down the tail fin of the rocket. He is evidently intent on sabotage of some kind. **21**

34. **22** INT. LAUNCH ROOM. DAY.

> As though from the Doctor's VP: as the mists of unconsciousness clear and his vision sharpens he sees the group of generals and politicians standing around a TV scanner.
> The Doctor is in a chair guarded by a Thal soldier.
> Insert: the scene on the scanner is a model shot of the Thal dome. **23**
> The surface of the dome is smoking.
> Occasional explosions of shell fire send up spouts of flame and smoke.

POLITICIAN It's working… the Kaled dome is breaking up… Start the countdown for ~~an immediate~~ the rocket launch.

> The Doctor tries the lurch forward out of his chair.

DOCTOR WHO No, ~~no,~~ you mustn't…

> The guard pulls him back into his seat.

A Thal officer presses a control and we see digital counter, set at 50, begin to tick off the numbers. 24

Helplessly pinned in his chair the Doctor stares in horror at the scanner screen.

We favour the screen.

35. INT. MAIN LABORATORY. DAY.

Opening 25 *on a scanner screen showing the same sequence,* 26 *then widening to show the screen being observed by Davros, Nyder and a grim-faced group of scientists.*

We see Ronson standing a little away from the group.

Kavell stands near Davros.

KAVELL How could the Thals have found the formula to destroy our dome?

NYDER Someone has betrayed us…

KAVELL That's impossible. Only a handful of us knew the formula… No member of the Elite would have given the secret to the Thals…

DAVROS ~~The fact remains that~~ Nevertheless, someone has. And ~~their~~ his treachery has resulted in the total extermination of our people.

We favour the scanner screen again. 27

36. INT. LAUNCH ROOM. DAY.

Linking the scene with a shot of the scanner screen which now cuts to a shot of the rocket on its firing pad.

The digital counter is down to 10 and reducing. 28

A Thal general has his finger poised down over a clearly marked 'fire' button.

The Doctor watches in despair. As the digital counter reaches five he launches himself forward to try to reach a button marked 'destruct'.

His finger hovers over it for an instant and for a moment it seems he might succeed.

Then he is overwhelmed by the others and held firm.

He watches the Thal general push the fire button on scanner.

We see the rocket start its journey. 29

The Doctor stares at the screen in anguish. He murmurs to himself:

DOCTOR WHO I sent Harry and Sarah ~~back~~ in there.

He closes his eyes. 30

37. INT. MAIN LABORATORY. DAY.

The group stares at the screen which shows the Kaled dome still smoking. Then there is the most enormous explosion that totally fills the screen. The utter destruction of the Kaled dome. 31 *We hear the distant rumble of this explosion.*

They all watch for a moment more, then Davros orders:

DAVROS Switch it off.

He turns his chair slightly.

DAVROS We will avenge the annihilation of our people with a retaliation so massive, so merciless, that it will live in history.

Davros' clawed hand reaches across the control panel of his chair and presses a switch.

Immediately a door opens and a group of Daleks 32 *glide swiftly into the room and line up for Davros' commands.*

DAVROS Let the vengeance begin with the death of the traitor, the Thal spy Ronson.

The clawed hand points a finger accusingly at Ronson.

Ronson backs away in terror.

RONSON No… ~~no… no…~~ Davros!

DAVROS Exterminate. Exterminate. Exterminate.

As one the Daleks turn and advance on the cringing Ronson. They fire as one. Go to negative as we hear the crackle of the Dalek weapons. 33

Ronson falls dead.

Davros turns to face the grim group of scientists.

DAVROS Today the Kaled race is ended, consumed in a fire of war… but from its ashes will rise a new race… The supreme creature… the ultimate conqueror of the Universe… The Dalek.* 34

CLOSING TITLES

1 There is no freeze-frame in the reprise, though the film of Sarah's fall is slowed. She lands on a ledge, not far down. Scenes 1, 2 and 14 were actually shot on film at the BBC's Ealing film studios.

2 The Thals are actually on the scaffolding tower.

3 Some of the text in this scene is illegible on the surviving copies of the scripts. Where text is in doubt, it is enclosed in square brackets [like this].

4 While one of the Thals does have a rope, it was not used in the following sequence.

5 The scene ends with Sarah jumping back to the scaffolding.

6 We hear the 'clam' screeching again in the background.

7 A third Dalek, presumably the 'original', is visible in the background as the two new Daleks approach Davros.

8 An interjected line of Ronson's (which motivated Kavell's 'Just that') was cut from here.

9 The scene ends with the camera pulling back past the two test Daleks to show Nyder watching Ronson and Kavell as they talk.

10 An establishing shot of the Kaled dome was inserted ahead of this scene.

11 To save erecting some sets or hiring cast twice, the Kaled command headquarters scenes for Part Three were taped with Part One, reusing the Kaled headquarters set.

12 Davros' reference to 'the last 50 years' suggests that his condition is at least in part due to his great age.

13 The Doctor interrupts Ravon's enthusiastic speech.

14 A Thal soldier is standing with his back to the trap door. The Doctor opens the opposite side of the trap, and doesn't see him until he is midway out, then pushes Harry back down and closes the trap door. The soldier is then joined by another Thal soldier, and they leave.

15 The glass panel is an eye-level round window, like a porthole.

16 The door is opened by touching a circular panel in the left frame.

17 We see Davros and Nyder through the porthole, from the Doctor and Harry's point of view.

18 We hear the first sentence of the next scene as if through the door, before the scene changes.

19 As he finishes speaking, the Doctor bangs the guards' heads together, and they fall unconscious to the floor.

20 The scene cuts back to the Doctor approaching the rocket's hatch.

21 The directions that follow have been erased from the final camera script, possibly when the end of Part Three was reworked and moved.

The camera directions detail what happens as the guard recovers and manages to press a button. The Doctor is slammed to the now electrified scaffolding.

The camera directions read:

FOLLOW DOCTOR in low shot as he moves up steps to door
BCS [big close shot] *GUARD – PAN ALONG his hands as he reaches for control*
DOCTOR moving round rocket
CS [close shot] *DOCTOR reacting – + touching – see him spin*
LOW MS [mid shot] *DOCTOR with electric flames*

A spark generator was used to create the lightning flashes superimposed over close-ups of the Doctor's hands gripping the scaffolding rails.

This was then edited to become the end of Part Three.

22 Scenes 34 to 37 were moved to the start of Part Four during editing, presumably to balance the timings of Parts Three and Four.

23 The scanner picture was inlaid using CSO.

24 The countdown was displayed on a flip-over digital counter, as used for digital clocks at the time.

25 We actually open with a close shot of Davros.

26 Again, CSO was used for the scanner.

27 There was a recording break immediately after this scene was recorded, in order to set up the model film of the rocket launch to be played back on the CSO scanner.

28 The counter and the 'Fire/Destruct' button assembly were both added as insert shots.

29   The rocket lift-off was achieved by the camera tracking down the model rocket as smoke billows up, and the picture is tinged red. The shots of the rocket in flight were achieved by using four feet of silent 16mm stock footage of a rocket provided by NHK Japan.

30   There was a recording break after this scene to set up the effects shot and CSO scanner for the next one.

31   The destruction of the Kaled dome was achieved by blowing up the model.

32   There are three Daleks.

33   The extermination of Ronson was achieved by electronically adding a blue beam of energy from the close-up of a Dalek gun. The picture of Ronson dying was then over-exposed and reversed positive/negative.

34   The end of the episode was moved during editing so that it occurs in Scene 33.

This Week Page 6 In the same week that his latest *Dr Who* story ends (Saturday BBC1), writer **Terry Nation** (*below*, with Daleks) has a new series, *Survivors* (Wednesday BBC1), beginning. 'But they're two very different series,' insists Nation, who talks to Chris Dunkley in our feature. '*Survivors* has its roots in the future, as it were, but it's not science-fiction. It's not going into the realms of the impossible; it's skating very close to the possible.'

Menace . . . ? Terry Nation with his friends the Daleks – the terrors of a million Saturday tea-times. He's the Welsh Guest in Woman's Hour from Cardiff: 1.45 (MW)

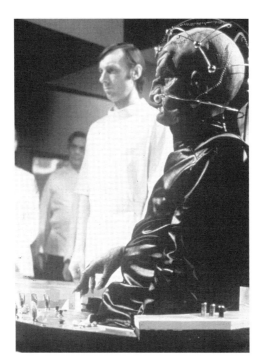

GENESIS OF THE DALEKS

by Terry Nation

Part Four

OPENING TITLES

1. INT. MAIN LABORATORY. DAY.

Reprise:

Davros turns to face the grim group of scientists.

DAVROS Today the Kaled race is ended, consumed in a fire of war… but from its ashes will rise a new race… The supreme creature… the ultimate conqueror of the Universe… The Dalek.

Favour the Daleks.

DAVROS The action you take today is the beginning of a journey that will take the Daleks to their destiny of universal and absolute supremacy. You have been conditioned and programmed to complete a task. You will now carry out that program.

DALEK LEADER We obey.

The Daleks turn and start to file out. They pass a low-angled camera, looming and menacing as they move. They dominate the screen.

2. INT. ROCKET LAUNCH ROOM. DAY.

The uniformed Thal officers and the Thal politicians stand staring at the scanner screen that shows nothing but billowing smoke and flame. The Doctor stands behind the group, his face grim.

THAL POLITICIAN A thousand years of war… and now it's ended… Listen…

We hear distant cheering and excitement.

THAL POLITICIAN The people… they know already.

They listen for a moment with great satisfaction and then the Thal politician becomes more business-like.

THAL POLITICIAN Gentlemen… there is a great deal to be done… I will speak to the people… there must be a victory parade…

He starts to lead the way out of the room. He halts at seeing the Doctor.

THAL POLITICIAN As for him, he must be punished for his attempt to… *(Sudden Inspiration)* No… No, let us now show that whilst we were ruthless in war we are generous in victory… **Let** all prisoners shall be freed. Charges against them dropped. *(To Bettan, female aide)* Issue that statement immediately **at once**…

The politician and the others sweep out. The Doctor is staring again at the scanner screen that shows the billowing smoke and flame.

BETTAN **Did** you had **have** friends in the Kaled city?

DOCTOR WHO **Yes.** Two people very dear to me… and I sent them into that holocaust.

BETTAN What will you do now?

DOCTOR WHO Start again. **Try and** find a way to complete what I came here **set out** to do… Stop the development of the Daleks…

BETTAN Daleks?

DOCTOR WHO Machine creatures that Davros is developing… Monsters…

BETTAN Davros… no, you're wrong. It was he who told us how to destroy the Kaled dome… His only interest is in achieving peace…

DOCTOR WHO Let me tell you something. The Kaled government was about to stop **on the point of stopping** Davros' experiments… Rather than let that happen he helped you to destroy his own race.

BETTAN You'll never convince my people of that… Davros is a hero…

DOCTOR WHO Yes. But for how long, I wonder?

BETTAN I must go. Under the general amnesty you're free to leave whenever you want.

DOCTOR WHO Thank you…

Bettan exits. The Doctor takes one more look at the smoke and fire on the scanner screen and turns to leave.

3. INT. MAIN LABORATORY. DAY.

Scientists at work around the area. Davros hands a slip of paper to Gharman.

DAVROS That outlines the chromosomal variations that are to be introduced into the genetic structuring of the embryo Daleks… It is to be implemented at once, Gharman.

Gharman glances at the paper and begins to react.

GHARMAN But Davros… This will create enormous mental defects…

DAVROS Not defects… improvements.

GHARMAN It will mean creatures without conscience. No sense of right or wrong. No pity… They'll be without feeling or emotion…

DAVROS Correct. Now see that my orders are carried out…

GHARMAN But…

DAVROS *(Angrily)* Without question, Gharman.

Gharman reluctantly moves away. Nyder comes to join Davros.

DAVROS Well?

NYDER The Daleks are in position. They will act on your command.

DAVROS I see no reason to delay any longer…

We see Davros' withered hand hover over the control panel on his chair. Then with great deliberation he presses a switch.

4. INT. SECTION OF CORRIDOR. DAY.

A section of plain walled corridor with a 'T' junction.

The Doctor runs into a group of Thal revellers. ② *They are happy and laughing. He pushes past them and turns the corner into the vertical of the 'T'.*

We can still hear the cheering of distant crowds.

A Dalek appears at the end of the corridor in which the group are moving. For a moment they stare at it in bewilderment. Then the Dalek raises its gun and starts to fire. There are screams and cries as they begin to fall.

DALEK Exterminate. Exterminate.

We hear the crackling of the blast.

The Doctor dashes back to the junction and stares cautiously round the corner.

As he does so, Bettan staggers up to him. She is terrified.

From the Doctor's viewpoint we see the group of Thals lying dead on the ground.

The Dalek advances down the corridor. More follow it. At the far end of the corridor other frightened and confused Thals appear. Instantly the Daleks begin to fire.

DALEKS Exterminate… Exterminate.

Resume on the Doctor. He grabs Bettan's arm and drags her into cover.

BETTAN What are they..?

DOCTOR WHO Keep back. **Get** out of sight…

He pushes Bettan into the cover of a buttress.

We see the Daleks file past the junction. One of them advances down the Doctor's section of corridor for a short distance.

The Dalek seems satisfied that the corridor is empty, turns and makes its way back to join the others.

Bettan is rigid with terror.

DOCTOR WHO We've got to get out of the **Thal** dome…

BETTAN Are those the Daleks?

DOCTOR WHO Out into the wastelands… ~~It's our only chance…~~ Do you know a way?

Bettan nods dumbly.

DOCTOR WHO Yes those are Daleks – ~~then lead us out of here.~~ **Come on, lead the way.**

The Doctor has to shove Bettan into action, but the two begin along the corridor. The moment they are out of sight some Daleks appear at the junction and follow the same route.

5. EXT. MAIN LABORATORY. DAY. ③

Opening close on Davros.

DAVROS The beginning. Only the beginning… From this moment all other research will cease… absolute priority is to be given to building of our Dalek force… Nothing ~~I repeat~~ **absolutely** nothing must delay this **glorious** project!!

6. INT. THAL DOME. NIGHT. (MODEL SHOT)

The interior of the dome glows with the flicker of the flames that consume the City. We see smoke and explosions. ④

The dome begins to melt. We hear the distant sound of the explosions and crackle of flame. ⑤

7. EXT. TRENCH. NIGHT.

The Doctor and Bettan staring in awe. Their faces are lit by the distant flicker of the flames. ⑥

BETTAN ~~It didn't~~ **There was no** need to go that far… When our leaders saw they were beaten they should have surrendered…

DOCTOR WHO Perhaps they did… But the Daleks accept no terms. They're ~~conditioned~~ **programmed** to wipe the Thals from the face of this planet…

BETTAN There must be some who'll escape… Some survivors…

DOCTOR WHO A few perhaps… but they'~~ll have~~ **need** to be grouped together into some ~~sort~~ **kind** of fighting ~~unit~~ **force**…

BETTAN What?

DOCTOR WHO **Well,** destroy Davros and you'll destroy the Daleks.

BETTAN What chance ~~would~~ **do** we have against them…

DOCTOR WHO It's the only chance… Will you do it?

BETTAN Yes

DOCTOR WHO **Good girl!** I'm going to try to get **back** into the Bunker now.

BETTAN Alone?

Doctor Who nods, then as he slides over the edge of the trench he glances back and calls:

DOCTOR WHO Good luck.

We stay on Bettan. She stays in position for a moment and then rouses herself and starts up to the rim. She peers over warily and then instantly ducks down again.

A Dalek glides into sight almost at the rim of the trench.

Bettan presses into the ground as the Dalek scans the area.

It looks huge and menacing, lit as it is from the back by the flicker of flame.

It does not see Bettan and then turns to move away.

7A. EXT. SECTION OF ROCKS. NIGHT.

Doctor Who moves cautiously into sight.

He glances behind him, as if he has heard an unexplained sound. With alarming suddenness a Muto appears behind him and grabs at Doctor Who.

Instantly two other Mutos appear and despite Doctor Who's considerable struggles he is overcome quickly and thrown to the ground.

With two of the Mutos pinning Doctor Who flat on his back, the third finds a large rock and holding it in both hands raises it above his head ready to smash it down on to Doctor Who.

Before the blow can be struck a figure from out of frame dives on to the rock-wielding Muto.

It is Harry Sullivan.

An instant later, Sevrin joins the battle.

The Mutos put up very little resistance.

Sevrin and Harry drive them off into the night.

Sarah slips from the shadows and helps Doctor Who to his feet.

SARAH Doctor!

DOCTOR WHO Sarah..! Harry – I can hardly believe it.

SARAH What's the matter with you?

DOCTOR WHO I thought you were in the Kaled dome when it was hit.

SARAH We didn't get there…

HARRY No, you see halfway across the wastelands we were attacked by a band of Mutos…

SARAH And that's when the rocket was launched.

HARRY And then when the Kaled dome exploded…

SARAH And The Mutos just ran for their lives.

HARRY We came here because Well, of course I knew you'd try to get back into the Bunker… through the cave.

DOCTOR WHO You're were absolutely right, Harry. It's absolutely vital to get we go back into the Bunker.

SARAH Why?

HARRY Because they took the time ring.

DOCTOR WHO That bracelet the Time Lord gave me is our lifeline. Without it there's no way we'll ever we can never escape from this planet.

8. INT. MAIN LABORATORY. NIGHT.

A close shot of Ronson's work desk.

Amongst the items on the desk is the bracelet.

Angle to where Kavell is working at another point. Gharman is at work.

He looks around shiftily.

There are uniformed Elite guards at the doors.

Kavell picks up a piece of equipment from his bench and walks across to Gharman.

GHARMAN I wonder if you'd have a look at this… I'm having a problem with the dimensional thought circuit…

Kavell takes the piece of equipment. Gharman lowers his voice.

GHARMAN We must stop the Daleks, Kavell.

KAVELL I don't want to get involved. You saw what happened to Ronson… Davros wouldn't hesitate to have us killed if he suspected we were plotting against him.

GHARMAN Then we must make our plans so he won't suspect anything.

KAVELL The Elite troops will stay loyal to him.

GHARMAN That's not important… If the whole of the scientific corps act against Davros he can't proceed. We can then demand that the Dalek project be halted. His whole concept is monstrous… It's evil and immoral.

Kavell nods slowly.

KAVELL What do you want me to do?

We angle away from the two men towards a buttress. Behind this, out of their sight stands Nyder, clearly hearing their entire conversation. As we favour Nyder we still hear the voices of the two men.

GHARMAN *(VO)* Spread the word… Convince those who waver how vital it is that the whole Dalek project be ended…

Resume on Gharman and Kavell.

KAVELL I'll do what I can.

Gharman takes the piece of equipment back from Kavell and moves back to his own bench.

After a few seconds, Nyder casually emerges and walks towards the exit showing no sign that he has heard anything.

9. INT. SECTION OF ROCKS. NIGHT.

Doctor Who, Harry, Sarah scramble through the broken-barred aperture. Sevrin is about to follow. Doctor Who stops him.

DOCTOR WHO ~~No~~, Sevrin – will you do something for us – something important?
SEVRIN Yes.
DOCTOR WHO Over in the Kaled trenches there's a Thal, **a** girl – **named** Bettan – trying to ~~organize~~ **form** a resistance group. Join her with as many of your own people as you can get. The idea is to ~~attack the main entrance of~~ **knock out** the Bunker.
SEVRIN ~~We won't get away with that.~~ **Do you think you'll get away with it?**
DOCTOR WHO ~~I know – but~~ It will keep the Elite troops occupied, Sevrin, while I try to ~~complete my mission –~~ find the weakness of the Daleks.
SEVRIN ~~Right Doctor.~~ Good luck, **Doctor.**
SARAH ~~Goodbye,~~ Sevrin… ~~And thanks…~~ **Thank you.**

Sevrin limps away into the darkness of the wastelands. The trio turn to face the cave. We begin to hear echoing and sinister moans from the darkness.

SARAH ~~Doctor – what –~~ What's that?
DOCTOR WHO ~~This cave is full~~ **Just one** of Davros' ~~rejected~~ experiments. I think we'd better stay close together.
HARRY You're not scared are you?
SARAH Of course not.
HARRY **Well,** I am!

10. INT. MAIN LABORATORY. NIGHT.

Gharman is at his bench. Nyder enters and edges up to him. He seems nervous. His mood confidential.

NYDER Gharman – I must talk to you… it's ~~important.~~ **of vital importance.**
GHARMAN Not now, I'm busy.
NYDER Then soon and… Somewhere we can talk in private.
GHARMAN What's this about, Nyder?
NYDER You know… I've served Davros faithfully for many years. I've never questioned anything he has done… but now… He's become a megalomaniac… He's ready to sacrifice everything and everyone including us… just so that the Dalek project can be completed.

Gharman shows great relief.

GHARMAN You're not alone in your fears… Where can we meet in safety?
NYDER The only place Davros never goes is the lower level…
GHARMAN There's the detention room down there.

Nyder nods.

GHARMAN Good. I'll meet you there as soon as I can.

Nyder turns and moves away. Gharman allows himself a grin of pleasure and relief. He turns back to his work.

11. INT. CAVE. NIGHT.

Something moves behind the rocks. We angle close to distinguish two giant clams lurking in the darkness.

The Doctor and his party are approaching. All around we can still hear the eerie moans and slithery noises of unseen creatures.

DOCTOR WHO *(VO)* Not much further now. The entrance to the ventilation duct ~~is~~ **must be** just along here.

They move into front.
Harry stares around.

HARRY Are you sure ~~of that~~, Doctor? It doesn't look familiar.

He prods one of the clams with his foot.
It swings instantly, jaw opening.
Sarah gives a cry of terror.

DOCTOR WHO Look out, Harry!

Harry dodges back.
Sarah, running the other way, almost steps into the second clam.
The Doctor sweeps her aside as its mantrap shell clangs shut. The clams advance surprisingly quickly.

DOCTOR WHO Jump!

They run off into the darkness, the clams pursue them for a few yards and then settle into stillness again. **⑨**
Another angle: the trio staring back.

SARAH I'll never eat oysters again…
DOCTOR WHO Luckily for us ~~their speed is limited.~~ **they're not very fast.**
HARRY **That's obviously why Davros abandoned them.**
DOCTOR WHO ~~So that's why Davros discarded them.~~ Come on – we're there… **⑩**

He points to the open shaft in the cave wall.

DOCTOR WHO Harry.

HARRY Right.

He scrambles up into the shaft.

SARAH Listen, I've been down tunnels before. I've just had a rather nasty thought, Doctor.

DOCTOR WHO Really?

SARAH Yes. Suppose something's in there waiting for us?

DOCTOR WHO ~~Yes,~~ That is nasty. Better not tell Harry. He's going first.

Harry reaches down a hand.

He pulls her up into the vent.

The Doctor takes a last look around the cave, listening to its sounds. Then he turns to clamber up into the vent.

12. INT. SECTION OF CORRIDOR. NIGHT. ⓫

The corridor is dimly lit.

Gharman advances cautiously to the half-open door of the detention room. He peers inside.

GHARMAN Nyder.

There is no reply. He starts to enter.

13. INT. DETENTION ROOM. NIGHT.

There is one pool of light in the room. Its limits are lost in darkness.

Gharman enters the lighted area. He is startled by a sudden sound and spins to see Nyder move from the shadows into the light to join him.

NYDER I had to be sure it was you…

GHARMAN We'll make this as quick as we can… I don't want to be missed…

NYDER What are we going to do?

GHARMAN Look… a number of the scientists ~~feel~~ believe as we do. When we have enough strength on our side we'll give Davros an ultimatum.

NYDER What ultimatum do you suggest?

GHARMAN That we will only continue to work on the Daleks if he restores the conscience to the brain cells. The creature must have a moral sense… a judgment of right and wrong… in fact all the qualities that we believe are essential in ourselves…

NYDER And if he doesn't accept that ultimatum?

GHARMAN Then we will destroy all the work that has been done… everything. It will be as though the Daleks were never created.

NYDER Right. I will try to get some of the Military Elite on our side… Who can you count on?

GHARMAN Kavell… Frenton… Parran… but there'll be more soon. I'm sure of it…

NYDER *(Grins)* Thank you. That's what I wanted to know.

There is an uneasy silence for a moment. Then Gharman is alarmed by a whirring electrical sound ⓬ from the deep shadows and out of the darkness into the pool of light comes Davros.

Gharman realizes he has betrayed not only himself but his friends.

DAVROS That information will prove most helpful.

Gharman looks around desperately and then launches for the door.

Nyder intercepts him and with two fast easy blows drops him unconscious to the ground.

DAVROS A pity. He has a good scientific mind.

NYDER *(Mildly)* Shall I kill him?

DAVROS No. A little surgery on his brain will remove these stupid emotions and still allow us to ~~take advantage~~ make use of his inventive skills…

NYDER And the other plotters?

DAVROS The same for them. But we must move carefully… not force their hands… let us learn who are our allies and who are our enemies… ~~come.~~ Leave Gharman here, safely locked away…

Davros starts for the door when he is halted by a sound. An echoing scuffle and an indistinct murmur of voices, magnified by the place it comes from, the ventilator shaft.

DAVROS What was that?

Both men listen hard. The sound is repeated. Nyder looks up towards the tiny opening of the air conditioner. ⓭ He whispers:

NYDER It's coming from there…

He swiftly climbs up onto a bench and puts his ear near the grating. Then moving back to Davros:

NYDER There is somebody in the ventilator shaft…

14. INT. CORRIDOR. NIGHT.

The Doctor is lowering himself to the ground from a larger air-conditioning grille halfway up the wall. He stares cautiously along the darkened corridor.

Harry and Sarah emerge in turn and quickly drop down beside the Doctor. Between them, Harry and the Doctor swiftly put the grille back in position.

As the Doctor turns to lead the way along the corridor the full lighting is suddenly switched on. In the blazing glare we see Davros with Nyder beside him blocking the way. Nyder keeps a gun on them.

DAVROS Welcome back…

The Doctor sighs.

DOCTOR WHO You were right, Sarah. ~~There was~~ **About there being** something nasty waiting for us.

15. INT. MAIN LABORATORY. NIGHT.

The room is empty of scientists. At one point a special chair has been installed. It is fitted with various pieces of electronic equipment. Cables and wires lead from it to a complex-looking cabinet.

Strapped into the chair is the Doctor. Various cords taped to his body. His arms fastened to the arms of the chair. His ankles securely fixed.

Davros is seated before him with Nyder in attendance.

DAVROS I have read the initial reports of your interrogation. The suggestion that you had travelled through space and time was utterly dismissed by the computer analysis.

DOCTOR WHO I imagine that it had never been programmed ~~to accept~~ **for** such a concept.

DAVROS Precisely. I however… I am perhaps more flexible. Though the power of such travel is beyond my scientific comprehension it is not beyond my imagination. Why did you come here?

DOCTOR WHO To stop the development of the Daleks.

DAVROS Why?

DOCTOR WHO Because, having lived in what you would call the future I have seen the carnage and destruction ~~that they will create~~ **they have caused**.

DAVROS Then my Daleks <u>do</u> go on… They <u>do</u> survive.

DOCTOR WHO **Yes.** As weapons of hate. Machines of war.

DAVROS Fascinating.

DOCTOR WHO **But** there is still time to change **all** that… Why not ~~allow them to become~~ **make them** a force for good throughout the Universe…

DAVROS I could do it.

DOCTOR WHO Then do it… be remembered for that.

DAVROS You have seen ~~the~~ **my** Daleks in battle?

DOCTOR WHO Many times. I have fought against them.

DAVROS And do they win? Do they always win?

DOCTOR WHO **Not always.** They have been defeated, but never utterly defeated… the Dalek menace always remains…

DAVROS If as you say, they become the supreme ~~war machine~~ **creatures of war**, how can they lose… how can they fail?

DOCTOR WHO Misfortune. Lack of information… sometimes overwhelming opposition.

DAVROS ~~Then~~ **Yes, but** tell me – ~~where~~ **how** do the Daleks fail?

DOCTOR WHO No Davros… That is ~~something~~ **a question** that the future must keep secret.

DAVROS What mistakes ~~did~~ **do** they make? You will tell me!

DOCTOR WHO No.

DAVROS You will tell me!

DOCTOR WHO No I will not.

Angry, Davros swings his chair away.

DAVROS Nyder?

Nyder nods.

Davros turns and glides back to the Doctor.

DAVROS You will tell me because you have a weakness. ~~A weakness~~ that I have totally eliminated from the mind of the Dalek… so they will always be superior… ~~and that is why you will~~ **a weakness that will make you** give me the knowledge to change the future. You are afflicted with a conscience.

The Doctor looks very alarmed and strains against his bonds.

16. EXT. TRENCH. NIGHT.

In the crater are about six Thal soldiers. All are tattered and injured and weary. Also Bettan and Sevrin.

BETTAN We don't look much of a fighting force.

SEVRIN I am ~~sorry~~ **afraid** my people won't **be much** help. They don't like fighting.

BETTAN Well, at least we have weapons. And a fair amount of explosive, too.

She indicates some metal canisters.

SEVRIN ~~Will you~~ **Are you going to** attack the main entrance to the Bunker?

BETTAN ~~If~~ **As long as** there are people inside risking their lives to destroy the Daleks that's the least we can do…

SEVRIN When will you attack?

BETTAN As soon as we've rested and picked up any stragglers…

SEVRIN But they need help now!

BETTAN We must wait until we have the strongest possible force… then… we'll attack…

Sevrin shows his worry.

17. INT. MAIN LABORATORY. NIGHT.

Close on the Doctor. Angle away to show his VP.

Harry and Sarah are strapped on to inclined boards.

They are wired up with electrical terminals to various points on their bodies.

The cords from these lead to Davros' chair.

Nyder makes the last fixing and stands back.

DAVROS Nyder?

Davros turns to the Doctor.

DAVROS Let me ~~now~~ tell you what is going to happen… You will answer my questions. **You will** answer them carefully and precisely. The instruments to which you are wired are particularly sensitive… they will detect instantly any attempt to lie.

DOCTOR WHO And if I do lie?

DAVROS If you lie… your friends will ~~be made to~~ suffer ~~the agony. At the touch of a switch~~ I can create in their bodies all the torments and agonies ever known.

SARAH Don't tell him, Doctor!

DAVROS Now, you will tell me the reason for every Dalek defeat. With that knowledge I can program them so they will know their errors and how to avoid them… With that knowledge there will be no defeats. We will begin…

DOCTOR WHO Davros – If I tell you what you want to know then I betray millions of people in the future… I can't do that…

DAVROS But you can. You will tell me. You will tell me! **You will tell me!**

CLOSING TITLES

Alternative Ending

The camera script also includes an alternative ending to the one eventually used:

DOCTOR WHO If I tell you what you want to know then I betray millions of people in the future… I can't do that…

DAVROS But you can. You will tell me the reason for every Dalek defeat. With that knowledge I can program them so they will know their errors and how to avoid them… With that knowledge there will be no defeats. We will begin…

DOCTOR WHO No, Davros. Wait!

DAVROS Either tell me about the Dalek future or watch your friends suffer.

His withered hand moves towards control switch on his chair.

DOCTOR WHO All right… all right… just leave them alone…

DAVROS Begin.

DOCTOR WHO The Dalek invasion of the planet Earth in its year 2000 was foiled because of the attempt by the Daleks to mine the core of the planet…

His eyes tightly shut to drown out the sounds, the Doctor continues and we angle away to the tape on the computer recording his every word.

DOCTOR WHO The magnetic properties of the Earth were too powerful. On Mars the Daleks were destroyed by a virus that attacked the insulation on cables in its electrical circuits…

Bring the music up to drown out the Doctor's halting voice.

CLOSING TITLES

1 The ending of Part Three was moved back to Scene 33. As a result, a reprise of Part Three, Scene 33, and Part Three, Scenes 34 to 37 were moved into Part Four.

2 The Doctor has returned to his usual clothing, and is carrying the radiation suit he was wearing previously. One of the revellers he passes takes it from him and throws it away.

3 This short insert scene was recorded immediately after Scene 3.

4 The destruction of the Thal dome was achieved using a wire frame supported through the bottom of the miniature landscape with rods. When small explosive charges were detonated, the rods were pulled down to make the dome collapse.

5 It was intended to include a further sequence of Thal revellers being exterminated. This was to be recorded after Scene 4, lit with red floodlights, then CSO'd over this sequence of the burning dome, but was dropped due to time constraints.

6 Throughout this scene we can hear the sound of the battle in the background, punctuated by Dalek cries of 'Exterminate!'.

7 As he rises, the Doctor shakes Harry vigorously by the hand, then hugs Sarah tightly.

8 Originally Gharman was to go over to Kavell, but this was changed. In fact, Kavell takes a clipboard over to Gharman, who then shows him a piece of equipment.

9 A planned cut-away shot of a clam following them was omitted – probably as the clams were not as impressive as had been hoped.

10 There was a recording break at this point (as the Doctor, Sarah and Harry move past the camera and out of sight). This was to remove the clams and set in the end of the ventilation shaft. This meant that the same part of the set could be re-used, making the caves seem more extensive than they actually were.

11 These scenes set in the detention room and its adjoining corridor (up to the end of Scene 14) were recorded after Part Two in order to save re-erecting the sets. That also meant that Nyder's iron cross reappeared for these scenes (see production notes, page 205).

12 The technical notes on the camera script also include:
SOUND: DAVROS' CHAIR

But in the event no sound effect was added, as Davros' chair makes no noise. But this does suggest that a sound effect of some sort had been initially planned, though Part Five, Scene 14 describes Davros' chair as moving 'silently'.

13 Nyder simply listens. There was no ventilator grille as scripted.

GENESIS OF THE DALEKS

by Terry Nation

Part Five

1. INT. MAIN LABORATORY. NIGHT. ❶

DAVROS You will tell me. You will tell me. **You will tell me!**

HARRY Doctor – please – don't tell, Doctor!

DOCTOR WHO All right, all right, just leave them alone.

The Dalek invasion of the planet Earth in its year 2000 was foiled because of the attempt by the Daleks to mine the core of the planet... ❷

DOCTOR WHO The magnetic properties of the Earth were too powerful. On Mars the Daleks were ~~destroyed~~ **defeated** by a virus that

attacked the insulation on cables in ~~its~~ **their** electrical ~~circuits~~ **systems...**

Harry and Sarah listen helplessly as the Doctor relates his knowledge of future Dalek history. ❸

We stay on the Doctor for the first few lines of his speech and then angle away to the tape winding on to an almost empty spool.

DOCTOR WHO ❹ ~~The Dalek wars against~~ The Venusians in the space year 17000 was ended by the intervention of a fleet of war rockets ~~sent~~ from the planet Hyperon. The rockets were ~~built~~ **made** from a metal that was ~~totally~~ **completely** resistant to Dalek fire power and the Dalek task force was completely destroyed.

The Doctor's voice fades.

2. INT. MAIN LABORATORY. NIGHT. ❺

Close on the tape spool, now almost filled with tape. The machine clicks to a halt. Davros glances at the machine, and then at the Doctor who appears almost utterly exhausted.

DAVROS This seems an opportune moment to end this session… *(He calls)* Nyder. Release the prisoners and take them to the detention area.

The two guards quickly unstrap Harry and Sarah.

Nyder does the same for the Doctor.

DAVROS ~~We will continue with~~ The interrogation **will continue** later. And I must thank you Doctor… what you have told me will be invaluable. All this information… this foreknowledge will be programmed into the Dalek memory banks…

DAVROS Take them away…

The Elite guards lead Harry and Sarah out.
The Doctor makes to follow, but Davros halts him.

DAVROS Oh Doctor ~~whoever you are~~ stay a moment, sit down… Let us talk together now not as prisoner and captor but as men of science… There is so much I wish to know… Nyder, take ~~that tape to my office~~ charge of the tape.

Doctor shrugs and sits back in his chair.

NYDER Immediately Davros.

DAVROS ~~Its security is~~ It will be your responsibility… And remember it is priceless… its value beyond computation…

The Doctor watches as the tape is lifted from the machine. His eyes follow it as Nyder heads towards the exit.

3. INT. CORRIDOR. NIGHT.

Outside the door of the detention room stands a guard of the military Elite.
Harry and Sarah are shoved along the corridor by their escorts.
The guard produces keys, unlocks and opens the door of the detention room and the couple are pushed inside.

4. INT. DETENTION ROOM. NIGHT.

Gharman rises as the two are thrust into the room and the door slams behind them. ❻

GHARMAN ~~Are you all right?~~

SARAH ~~Yes…~~ Thank you…

HARRY Who are you?

GHARMAN My name's Gharman. Until a few hours ago I was head of the military Elite's scientific corps.

SARAH And now you're a prisoner like us? What happened?

GHARMAN Wait ❼ – I was trying to organize a movement against Davros. He found out… What's happening up there? Has there been any attempt to take control away from Davros..?

SARAH Not that we know of.

GHARMAN Nothing?

HARRY He's still very much in charge.

GHARMAN I don't understand. **You see,** Davros tricked me into giving **him** the names of the group who were plotting against him. ~~I would have thought that there would have~~ **Have there not** been mass arrests by now… ~~even~~ executions?

SARAH It all seems quiet up there.

GHARMAN **But** Davros knows that we're planning action against him. Why hasn't he moved to stop it? Why?

HARRY Perhaps that would be too obvious for Davros.

GHARMAN **Well,** if that's true he's being too clever for his own good. Every moment he delays our movement grows in strength.

SARAH I hope you're right.

GHARMAN I know I am. Many of us feel that production of the Daleks must end… I believe now, we are in the majority… If we act soon we can break his power.

HARRY We're not in much of a position to act **at the moment**, are we?

GHARMAN If only I could get word to them… now!!!

In a fury of frustration he pounds his fist against the wall.

5. INT. CORRIDOR. NIGHT.

Establish the guard at the door.
We take an angle on the corridor behind him.
We see Kavell slide cautiously into view. Silently he moves towards the detention room and pauses in the cover of a buttress. He takes a short truncheon from his pocket. Holding it so that it cannot be seen.
He advances towards the guard.
The guard spins and levels his gun.

GUARD Halt!

Kavell stops instantly.

GUARD State your business.

KAVELL I wish to question the prisoners…

GUARD Nobody is allowed to communicate with the prisoners unless they have a pass signed by Davros.

Kavell makes the pretence of reaching for his pockets and moves forward, hoping to get in range of the guard.

GUARD Stay where you are…

Kavell halts. He rather lamely taps his pockets

KAVELL I… I seem to have mislaid it… I'll come back later…

He starts back the way he has come. The guard lowers his gun and turns away.
Kavell pauses and glances back, his face takes on a new determination. **8**

6. INT. MAIN LABORATORY. NIGHT.

DAVROS Now future errors will be eradicated. Defeats will become victories. You have changed the future of the Universe.

DOCTOR WHO ~~I have committed the greatest act of treachery ever perpetrated. I have betrayed millions.~~ **I have betrayed the future.** Davros… For the last time… Consider what you are doing… **Stop the development of the Daleks.**

DAVROS ~~Stop the development of the Daleks?~~ Impossible. It ~~that~~ is beyond my control… The workshops are **already** automated to produce Dalek machines.

DOCTOR WHO It isn't the machines, it's the minds of the creatures inside them… Minds that you created… They are totally evil…

DAVROS Evil? No… no I will not accept that. They are conditioned simply to survive. They can survive only by becoming the dominant species… When all other life forms are suppressed… when the Daleks are the supreme ~~power~~ **rulers** of the Universe… ~~Unchallenged.~~ Then you will have peace… wars will end… They are the power not of evil… but of good!

DOCTOR WHO ~~Let us do evil that good may come.~~ Davros… if you had created a virus in your laboratory, something contagious and infectious that killed on contact… a virus that would destroy all **other forms of** life ~~forms~~, would you allow its use?

DAVROS It is an interesting conjecture.

DOCTOR WHO Would you do it?

DAVROS The only living thing… a microscopic organism ruling supreme… a fascinating idea…

DOCTOR WHO Would you do it?

DAVROS Yes, ~~yes,~~ yes! To hold in my hand a capsule containing such power… To know that life and death on such a scale was my choice… To know that the tiny pressure of my thumb… enough to break the glass… would end everything… Yes I would do it! That power would set me amongst the gods… And through the Daleks I shall have that power! **9**

The Doctor knows finally that he is looking into the face of madness. He launches himself at Davros. He grasps the single arm and holds it firmly.

DAVROS Release me… ~~release me.~~

DOCTOR WHO No, Davros…

With his free hand the Doctor reaches for the bank of switches on the wheelchair panel.

DAVROS Don't touch that **switch!** **10**

DOCTOR WHO Why not?

DAVROS It controls my life-support systems… I could not survive 30 seconds without them.

DOCTOR WHO Order the destruction of the incubator section. ~~Give the order.~~

DAVROS Destroy the Daleks? Never!

The Doctor presses a row of switches into the off position. **11** *Davros goes totally limp. The Doctor waits a few seconds and then moves the switches into the on position. Davros again becomes animated.*

DOCTOR WHO I mean it, Davros… Next time I press that switch it stays pressed. Now give the order…

DAVROS Even if I do this, there will be no escape for you…

DOCTOR WHO I'll take that chance… **Now, give the order.**

He touches the switches. Davros is convinced.

DAVROS Press the communicator switch.

He indicates a switch on a microphone. The Doctor puts it on.

DAVROS This is Davros. Elite unit seven will go to the incubator room… All survival maintenance systems are to be closed down. The Dalek creatures are to be destroyed…

DOCTOR WHO Tell them the order cannot be countermanded…

DAVROS This order cannot…

A hand swings in from the side of frame on the back of the Doctor's neck. **⑫** *He slumps unconscious. We see Nyder standing behind him.*

Davros quickly speaks into the microphone.

DAVROS **This is Davros, this is Davros.** My last order is cancelled. Repeat **cancelled**… No actions is to be taken.

Nyder indicates the Doctor.

NYDER What do you want done with this..?

DAVROS For the moment he must be kept alive… He has knowledge that is vital to our future… I will drain every last detail of it from his mind… and then… **he** will learn the true meaning of pain…

NYDER I'll take him to the detention room.

DAVROS The dissidents? What progress are they making?

NYDER Feeling against you is rising. Many of the scientific corps are openly speaking against you. Even some of the military are joining them.

DAVROS As I expected. They will take action soon? **⑬**

NYDER Almost certainly. They ~~probably already~~ outnumber those of us who are loyal ~~to you~~ … Davros, why don't you let me take a squad of ~~the~~ Elite~~…~~ men I can trust. In an hour I could wipe out their leaders…

DAVROS You think like a soldier, Nyder. Rebellion is an idea in the mind. Suppress it and it hides away and festers. No. My way is best.

NYDER As you wish.

The Doctor stirs. Nyder prods him with his foot.

NYDER On your feet.

He pulls the Doctor to his feet and drags him towards the exit. The moment the two men are out of the room, Davros operates a switch and begins to speak.

DAVROS All Dalek units… all Dalek units…

7. INT. THAL CORRIDOR. NIGHT. ⑭

Inside the Thal dome. Smoke billows around the area. We can hear the distant sound of Dalek weapons, explosions and cries of panic.

A Thal soldier runs in terror and crouches in the cover of some fallen masonry. A Dalek glides into sight and unhesitatingly fires at the man.

The Dalek turns to seek out new victims. It looks enormously powerful and all-conquering as it stands against the glow of the burning city.

A second Dalek glides into sight.

DALEK Davros has commanded all Dalek units to disengage and return to the Bunker immediately.

DALEK I obey.

The two Daleks turn and move off and are lost in a swirl of smoke.

8. EXT. TRENCH. NIGHT. ⑮

A small group of exhausted Thals lie in the trench hole. Bettan is keeping guard. The skyline glows with flame.

Bettan becomes suddenly alert and crouches lower.

BETTAN ~~Quiet~~ **Shh!** There's something moving out there.

She watches tensely for a moment, then relaxes as Sevrin glides out of the darkness, into the trench.

BETTAN ~~Well?~~

SEVRIN The whole of the Thal city is burning… The Daleks are moving through it section by section, hunting down the survivors.

BETTAN ~~Then we're the only survivors?~~ **Then there's no one left?**

SEVRIN I covered a fairly large area… I found no one. ~~None~~ **No one** living that is.

BETTAN ~~Then we're the only ones left.~~ **So we're on our own.**

SEVRIN You ~~will~~ **are** still **going to** attack the **main** entrance ~~to the Bunker~~ **though, aren't you?**

BETTAN No point in delaying any longer. We'll move more safely under cover of darkness… *(to the men)* Come on, **get ready**… we're moving out…

She gets the soldiers on their feet.

9. INT. CORRIDOR. NIGHT.

Nyder moves down towards the door of the detention room. He half-supports the Doctor who is still very groggy. As Nyder approaches he calls:

NYDER Open up.

The guard turns to the door and begins to unlock it. It is only when Nyder is actually standing next to him that the guard turns and reveals himself to be Harry Sullivan.

Harry makes a grab at Nyder who pulls the Doctor around, between himself and Harry.

Nyder thrusts the Doctor forward, cannoning him into Harry, and races off down the corridor. The Doctor is hardly conscious. The door of the cell opens and Sarah peeks out.

HARRY Not exactly as planned, ~~eh~~ Sarah~~?~~

10. INT. DETENTION ROOM. NIGHT.

The guard, stripped of his uniform, lies on the ground bound and gagged. Kavell, Gharman, Sarah and Harry group round the Doctor.

HARRY He's **a bit** groggy ~~still~~ but he'll be all right…

GHARMAN Come on Kavell, we've a lot to do…

KAVELL What about the ~~soldiers~~ **guards**? Suppose they won't come over to ~~your~~ **our** side?

GHARMAN They'll be disarmed and held in custody until we've presented our ultimatum to Davros…

Gharman and Kavell start for the door. The Doctor rouses himself to call after them.

DOCTOR WHO No – wait…

They hesitate.

DOCTOR WHO Davros knows what you are planning. I heard him talking to Nyder…

GHARMAN But if he knows, why hasn't he taken action against us?

KAVELL *(Confidently)* Perhaps because he knows it is futile… there are too many of us…

DOCTOR WHO No – it's not that… **I don't know what he's got prepared for you,** but believe me ~~he has something ready for you~~ **he's ready.**

GHARMAN Even so… we'll still be too many for him…

DOCTOR WHO Just be careful… **Be careful.**

KAVELL I think we can take care of things. But thanks for the warning.

Kavell and Gharman exit. **16**

SARAH There's no use telling you to rest ~~for a while~~, I suppose.

DOCTOR WHO No there isn't ~~time~~. We have got to recover that time ring.

SARAH Because without it we'll not get off this planet. But where is it?

DOCTOR WHO On ~~Ronson's~~ **the** desk in the laboratory. Then there's the tape recording which Nyder took. ~~charge of. That must be destroyed~~ **We've got to get it back** at all costs. It would make the Daleks ~~totally~~ invincible. Come on.

He leads the way to the door and they all exit.

11. INT. CORRIDOR. NIGHT.

Built into one wall is a section of steel-doored cupboards.

Pacing back and forth in front of these cupboards are two Elite guards. Their uniforms and manner very correct and precise. We establish them, then angle away to the end of the corridor to show Gharman peering cautiously around the corner. He withdraws and we angle on him.

Gharman has three Elite scientists with him.

GHARMAN Ready?

He receives nods in answer.

GHARMAN And remember… we resort to violence only if there is no other way…

Gharman steps around the corner, the others follow. The scientists move very casually giving no hint of what action they are about to take.

As they draw level Gharman swiftly draws a pistol. **17**

GHARMAN Stay perfectly still… Take their weapons.

A scientist moves forward and takes the first guard's gun. As he reaches to take the second gun, the guard explodes into action. He knocks the scientist back against Gharman who is thrown to the floor. (18) *The guard shoots one of the scientists. As the guard swings his gun to bear on the next target, Gharman, from his position on the floor, fires.* (19) *The guard is hit and crumples.*

Gharman swings his gun to cover the remaining guard who cringes back and raises his hands.

Gharman gets to his feet and looks down at the two dead men. He is obviously very distressed.

GHARMAN That was stupid. A stupid waste of life… Our intention has always been to make a bloodless revolution… There's been enough of killing and violence… Take him away and lock him up with the others.

The guard is led away by a scientist. Gharman moves to the steel doors of the cupboards and starts to pull them open. (20) *Inside we see racks of weapons. Gharman starts to take them out.*

GHARMAN Start passing these out to our people…

Kavell hurries into shot from around a corner.

KAVELL Gharman… I've been looking for you Gharman… They're coming over to our side in droves… We have the backing of a good 80 per cent now…

GHARMAN Good… good… What about the hard core Davros people?

KAVELL Most of them have They've all been rounded up… We're winning Gharman… We're winning.

Gharman gives a smile of satisfaction. Hands some weapons to Kavell.

GHARMAN Then let's finish it off.

12. INT. MAIN LABORATORY. NIGHT.

Davros sits alone in the huge empty laboratory. So silent and unmoving he might be dead.

We hear a brief distant burst of gunfire. (21) *Davros shows no reaction. As the camera tracks towards him we see that his single claw-*

like hand is drumming the fingers in slow rhythm.

A door bursts open and Nyder enters at a run. He has a gun in his hand, and we see him for the first time showing panic and fear.

NYDER Davros… They're taking over… We must act quickly. In one another hour they'll they could be totally in control.

Davros remains silent. Only his drumming fingers move.

NYDER Do you hear me Davros..? I've a dozen crack men hiding in section nine… Let me order them into action… Davros?

DAVROS *(Gently)* I hear you.

NYDER Then what are we going to do?

DAVROS I want you to find their leaders. Hand over your weapons to them.

Nyder looks amazed.

NYDER Surrender?

DAVROS Order all members of the **Elite** guard still at liberty to do the same.

NYDER You know what you're saying?

DAVROS *(Hard)* I know precisely what I am saying. Now… I will command and you will obey… You will do as I order.

Nyder is brought to heel. He nods.

DAVROS You will inform the rebel leaders that I have given these orders to avoid bloodshed. Tell them I submit and will listen to their demands… That is all.

NYDER Then we're admitting that we are beaten.

DAVROS That is what they will believe.

Nyder perks up at this evasive answer.

NYDER You mean that…

DAVROS Exactly. You… and they will find out exactly what I mean all in good time… Now carry out my orders.

13. INT. CORRIDOR. NIGHT.

The section with the arms lockers.

Some guns and equipment still remain. Doctor Who, Harry and Sarah appear.

Harry moves quickly to one of the lockers and takes down a gun. (22)

He tosses it to Sarah and then gets a second weapon which he offers to Doctor Who.

Doctor Who starts to search around in the cupboard.

Among the things he collects are some small waxed cartons, some spools of wire and a few other odd items.

DOCTOR WHO Useful… ㉓ Ah, here's ~~There's~~ something ~~here that will prove~~ **rather more** useful…

Sarah glances at the cartons.

SARAH That's explosive, isn't it?

DOCTOR WHO Yes… explosive and detonators seems almost providential.

SARAH Why? What are you going to use it for?

DOCTOR WHO The Time Lords gave me three options… There is only one still open – genocide.

HARRY Genocide?

DOCTOR WHO **Yes.** I'm going to kill everything in that ~~incubator~~ **incubation** room, I'm going to destroy the Daleks for ever.

Harry and Sarah stare at Doctor Who.

14. INT. MAIN LABORATORY. NIGHT.

The laboratory is empty. Through one of the side doors come Gharman, Kavell and two more scientists. With them is Nyder, cool and impassive again.

GHARMAN Where is Davros?

KAVELL You said that Davros had agreed to meet us **here**… ~~Where is he?~~

NYDER He'll be here.

Davros enters. His self-propelled wheelchair moves silently and slowly down the centre of the laboratory.

Nyder detaches himself from the group and moves to cross and stand behind Davros' chair.

DAVROS You have something to say to me..?

Gharman takes a pace forward.

GHARMAN Davros… We wish to make our views plain to you concerning our work here.

DAVROS With what authority do you speak? With whose backing?

GHARMAN We speak for virtually all of the Elite scientific corps and many of the military… We represent the majority.

DAVROS Very well… continue.

GHARMAN Nobody disputes that in the past, under your guidance, we have made incredible progress in many fields of science.

DAVROS You did not come here to flatter me… You came to offer ~~me~~ an ultimatum. Confine yourself to the terms of that ultimatum.

GHARMAN Very well… The initial concept of the Dalek was to build a life-support system and a travel machine for the creature that we know our race will ultimately evolve into.

DAVROS You disapprove of that?

GHARMAN No. But we believe that concept has been perverted. You have tampered with the genetic structuring of the creatures to create a ruthless power for evil. We cannot permit this to continue.

DAVROS *(OOV)* ㉔ Then what do you suggest?

GHARMAN All work on Dalek projects is to cease immediately. The creatures that have been conditioned and programmed are to be destroyed. If these terms are met, we will **then** be proud to work under your guidance on the rebuilding of our society.

DAVROS And if I refuse?

GHARMAN If you refuse you will be placed under arrest. The Daleks will be destroyed and our work here will **then** continue under a new democratically elected leader.

DAVROS Have you finished?

Gharman nods.

Davros remains silent and unmoving. After some seconds Davros has still made no reply.

GHARMAN Well?

DAVROS **You might** at least do me the courtesy of giving me time to consider.

He spins his chair around and wheels swiftly to the other end of the laboratory.

The deputation stand watching him uneasily. We move to a close shot on Davros and see his fingers begin to drum. Very big close-up on the drumming hand.

15. INT. CORRIDOR. NIGHT.

Harry, Sarah and the Doctor move along the corridor towards the heavy door with the glass viewing panel. They halt outside.

Sarah stares at the door uneasily. The Doctor busies himself with the small explosive packets and a coil of wire.

SARAH The Daleks are in there?

DOCTOR WHO The flesh and blood part of them… if indeed ~~it is~~ **they are** flesh and blood…

HARRY ~~They're various stages of development… some in jars and test tubes… Others seem to have freedom of movement… perhaps they're the fully grown ones.~~ **Some of them can move about…**

SARAH How do I see?

~~**HARRY** Press the button.~~

DOCTOR WHO Press the button.

Sarah very determinedly ignores him ㉕ *and moves to look in through the viewing panel. She stares for a moment and slowly at first, registers her horror and loathing.* ㉖ *Then unable to look any longer turns swiftly away in disgust.*

The Doctor hands Harry the spool of wire.

~~**DOCTOR WHO** Pay this out slowly, will you?~~

Harry takes the spool and nods.

Sarah looks at the Doctor in amazement.

SARAH You… You're not going in there Doctor?

DOCTOR WHO *(Nodding)* They're harmless enough, I think. Just unpleasant.

HARRY You don't want me to come ~~with you~~ **in, do you Doctor**?

DOCTOR WHO No need, Harry. ~~It's simply a matter of setting~~ **It just remains to** put the charges where they will do the most damage… ~~A couple of minutes is all I'll need~~ **It shouldn't take me more than a couple of minutes**…

The Doctor braces himself and then pulls the door open. He steps inside.

We go close on Harry's hands, holding the spool as it begins to turn, paying out cable, measuring the Doctor's progress into the room.

16. INT. MAIN LABORATORY. NIGHT.

Close on the members of the deputation. They are whispering amongst themselves. They are suddenly alarmed by the sound of Davros' voice.

DAVROS *(VO)* I have made my decision.

In a wider angle we see Davros move his wheelchair towards the group.

DAVROS I accept your ultimatum on one condition…

GHARMAN Go on…

DAVROS That ~~before any action is taken I shall be allowed~~ **you allow me** to speak to a full meeting of the Elite… both scientific and military. Anyone you elect may speak against me. When that is done a vote will be taken. I will abide by the decision of the majority.

GHARMAN ~~We~~ **You** already know the opinion of the majority. You will lose, Davros.

DAVROS With such confidence you can hardly deny my request… It was you who introduced the word democracy…

The members of the deputation exchange looks.

GHARMAN Very well… it's agreed.

DAVROS The meeting will take place one hour from now. Arrange it. You may go ~~now~~.

The deputation hurries out.

As the door closes Davros swings his chair to face Nyder.

DAVROS Ours is the victory Nyder. We have won… They talk of democracy… freedom… fairness. ~~The creed of the weak~~ **Those are the creeds of cowards**, the ones who will listen to a thousand viewpoints and try to satisfy them all… Achievement comes through absolute power… And power through strength. They have lost!!!

17. EXT. TRENCH. NIGHT. ㉗

On the rim of the trench as Daleks move past swiftly. ㉘

Their progress marked by loud martial music.

As the last moves out of sight we angle down to show Bettan and Sevrin pressed flat on to the soil.

The other troops behind them.

Cautiously they raise their heads.

SEVRIN The entrance to the Bunker is just beyond the next rise. That's where they must be heading.

Bettan glances off in another direction and swiftly presses Sevrin back close to the ground.

~~**BETTAN** More of them coming.~~

We angle up to show more Daleks sweeping past.

18. INT. CORRIDOR. NIGHT.

Close on a very tense Harry and Sarah. We angle to the coil of wire in Harry's hands. Then the camera trails along it to the door of the incubator room.

19. INT. INCUBATOR ROOM. NIGHT.

The lighting gives an overall cast of green. Only certain features of the room are seen with any clear definition. Some laboratory jars and tanks glow with light. Blobs float and swirl in them.

There is a constant liquid squelching sound.

The Doctor stares around with disgust. He kneels beside the leg of a bench and begins to wind the wire around his packets of explosive. He makes a quick startled movement to brush something off his shoulder. Something we never see, but that causes him to give a look of revulsion. He returns nervously to his work, glancing around warily all the time.

An angle very close on the Doctor's feet. From the edge of frame we see a shapeless viscous liquid ooze toward him. **29** *Like a very thick paint being spilt from a can it advances slowly, its dimensions changing constantly.*

20. INT. CORRIDOR. NIGHT.

SARAH What's taking him so long?

HARRY It's a **very** delicate ~~job planting explosives~~ operation, **Sarah.** **Still,** he should have ~~done it~~ **finished** by now.

SARAH Doctor… Doctor! Are you all right ~~Doctor?~~ ~~I'm going to have a look~~

She advances to the door.

Sarah steps into the doorway.

We reverse on to her face to show a reaction of total horror.

Then, showing Sarah's VP the Doctor standing, his back towards the camera. His body from head to toe covered in the viscous fluid, its texture flowing like liquid rubber. **30** *Only his widespread arms are visible.*

DOCTOR WHO Sarah! **31**

Angle on Sarah as she dashes forward.

Harry drops the wire coil and rushes forward to help Sarah get the Doctor out of the room and pulls the door firmly shut after him.

SARAH Harry help me! **32** ~~What is this stuff?~~

~~**DOCTOR WHO** I think it's what they feed on. Got those wires ready Harry?~~

~~**HARRY** Nearly.~~

Harry goes to work on the wire. The Doctor stares back at the door. He stares at it, his face reflecting his doubts. Sarah moves up beside him.

SARAH **Well,** what are you waiting for ~~Doctor~~?

DOCTOR WHO **Just** touch these **two** strands together and the Daleks are finished. ~~Do I have the right~~ **Have I that right**?

SARAH To destroy the Daleks? You can't doubt it. ~~But you know what they'll become.~~

DOCTOR WHO ~~I do but what is most important is that with the Daleks many things could be better~~. **But I do. You see, some things could be better with the Daleks.** Many future worlds will ~~stop warring amongst themselves and~~ become allies ~~only~~ **just** because of ~~the threat~~ **their fear** of the Daleks.

Harry holds the two bared wires in his hand. They are well splayed apart.

SARAH But it isn't like that.

DOCTOR WHO But the final responsibility is mine and mine alone. **Listen,** if somebody who knew the future pointed out a child to you… ~~If they~~ **and** told you that the child would grow up totally evil… **To be** a ruthless dictator who would destroy millions of lives. Could you then kill that child?

SARAH ~~Look~~ We're talking about the Daleks – the most evil creatures ever invented. You must destroy them ~~completely~~. You must complete your mission for the Time Lords.

DOCTOR WHO ~~But~~ Do I have the right? **33**

CLOSING TITLES

1   The episode reprise actually starts earlier with Sarah's inserted line: 'Don't tell him, Doctor'.

2   The Doctor's voice fades out, then back in, the picture fading from one shot of the turning tape reels to another of the Doctor as he speaks, to signify the passage of time.

The production directions indicate:

SOUND OVERLAY VOICES FADING + BEGINNING

3   The descriptions of future Dalek history that the Doctor gives are actually at odds with 'established' Dalek history as seen in *Doctor Who*. For example, he gives the date for events in the 1964 serial *The Dalek Invasion of Earth*, in which the Daleks attempted to mine the Earth's magnetic core, as 2000 although 2167 is suggested in both *The Dalek Invasion of Earth* and *The Daleks' Master Plan* (1965/6) as the date of the story, the actual invasion having occurred ten years previously. The mention of the Earth's magnetic properties is more relevant to the feature film version of the same story (starring Peter Cushing as Doctor Who): *Daleks – Invasion Earth, 2150 AD*.

4   Another audio fade-out/in. The Doctor's voice becomes audible again at '…the Venusians…'.

5   The fact that this is scripted as a separate scene suggests that another scene may have been removed, perhaps in the reworking of the end of Part Four/start of Part Five.

6   Gharman catches Sarah as she is pushed inside.

7   Gharman goes to check at the door. He lowers his voice in case anyone is listening.

8   The scene ends with Kavell raising the truncheon and running back towards the guard.

9   Terry Nation was very pleased with the way Wisher played this key speech: 'Wasn't his delivery on that wonderful? Very Hitlerian… That still scares me, it's a terrific theatrical speech'.

10   The switch for Davros' life-support system is a single black pressure switch.

11   The sound effect for the accompanying alarm is the same as used for the incoming radio message in *The Ark in Space*, Part Four, Scene 57.

12   Nyder coshes the Doctor with a short truncheon.

13   The Doctor actually stirs and wakes at this point.

14   This scene was recorded with Part Four to save re-erecting the Kaled dome corridor set.

15   This scene (together with Scene 17) was recorded with Part Four to save re-erecting the Trench set.

16   In the background, Harry is changing back into his own clothes.

17   He actually has a machine gun.

18   There is a fight in the foreground between a scientist (played by stunt man Terry Walsh) and one of the guards (stunt man Alan Chuntz) while another scientist and guard fight in the background.

19   As recorded, Gharman is knocked groggy at the start of the fight, and it is one of the other scientists (Terry Walsh) who shoots the guard.

20   The doors are unlocked using a remote-control device kept at the side of the cupboard.

21   There is the constant sound of distant gunfire throughout this scene.

22   The Doctor is unable to open a locker, until Harry hands him the remote-control device left in another, now empty, locker. None of them actually take guns.

23   The Doctor hands Sarah a pair of combat trousers and a shirt and jacket from the locker. This sequence was added so that Elisabeth Sladen could change clothes to match what she wore for the (previous) recording of *Revenge of the Cybermen*.

24   Davros' line is over a close shot first of Gharman, then Kavell.

25   This suggests that some dialogue was cut, presumably to the effect that Sarah does not want to see what's inside.

26   Inserted is a shot of the Doctor and Sarah looking through the window as seen from inside the incubator room.

27   This scene (together with Scene 8) was recorded with Part Four to save re-erecting the trench set.

28   Recalling the difficulties of using the Daleks on location during *Planet of the Daleks*, Maloney did not schedule any location work involving them.

29   The liquid was not used or seen. The Doctor is attacked by one of the Dalek embryos, though we do not see this happen.

30 A Dalek mutant embryo wrapped about the Doctor's neck was substituted for the 'fluid'. The fluid is still referred to in the camera directions, and there was a recording break before this scene 'For Doctor's FX'. This suggests that it may have been a late change, perhaps because the effect was not working as well as hoped.

31 The end of Part Five was moved up to this point – so as to end on the Doctor in danger rather than his philosophical doubts about destroying the Dalek creatures. The following sequence formed the opening of Part Six.

32 The Doctor, Harry and Sarah manage to pull the creature off the Doctor and throw it back into the incubator room before closing the door.

33 This continues straight on into the start of the Part Six camera script.

GENESIS OF THE DALEKS

by Terry Nation

Part Six

1. INT. CORRIDOR. NIGHT.

Opening ❶ on a close-up of two bared wires as their tips, held in the Doctor's hands, gradually move together. Harry, Sarah and the Doctor stare at the wires as though mesmerized. All highly tensed.

DOCTOR WHO Simply touch one wire against the other... ~~that's all~~ and that's it... ~~then~~ the Daleks ~~will~~ cease to exist. Hundreds of millions of people thousands of generations ~~might~~ can live without fear... in peace... and never even know the word Dalek.

SARAH They why ~~not~~ wait? If it were a disease ~~Doctor~~ or some sort of bacteria you were destroying, you wouldn't hesitate.

DOCTOR WHO But if I kill... wipe out a whole intelligent life form... Then ~~that makes me~~ I become like them. I would be no better than the Daleks!

SARAH Think of all the suffering there will be if you don't ~~act~~ do it.

The Doctor gives the matter a moment more of tortured reflection then moves the wires nearer.

GHARMAN *(VO)* Doctor!

At the surprised shout from behind them the Doctor turns to see Gharman at the end of the corridor. He hurries towards them.

270

GHARMAN Doctor... I've been looking **everywhere** for you... Davros has agreed to our terms!

HARRY He submitted?

GHARMAN He did. ~~Except for~~ **But he asked only** one thing: ~~he asked~~ that he be allowed to address a meeting of all the Elite... Scientific and military.

DOCTOR WHO He's going to put ~~his~~ **a** case?

GHARMAN Yes... ~~then~~ **but** a vote will be taken. ~~But it's already a foregone conclusion~~. It will be a **complete** landslide against any further development of the Daleks... We've won.

DOCTOR WHO **I'm grateful to you,** Gharman, ~~I'm~~ more grateful than ~~you can ever know~~ **I can tell you...**

GHARMAN The meeting is about to begin. Will you come?

DOCTOR WHO Yes.

He picks up the wire at the point where it begins to slide under the door. He gives it a sharp tug. Then he reels in until we see the other end of the wire appear beneath the door.

He turns and hurries after the others.

2. INT. MAIN LABORATORY. NIGHT.

A fairly large crowd has assembled. ② *They talk quietly among themselves. Separated from them and at one end of the room sits Davros. Behind him, impassive as ever, is Nyder.*

Harry, Sarah and Gharman stand near a doorway. Gharman excuses himself and makes his way down to the front of the crowd. While he is doing this the Doctor enters and joins his friends.

GHARMAN Everybody is here, Davros.

The crowd falls silent. Davros shifts his chair slightly.

DAVROS The issues are simple and clear cut. I have given my life's work to the survival of our race. The travel machine I ~~have~~ designed... the Dalek... will give **the creature into which we will mutate its** ~~us the~~ only possibility of continued existence.

GHARMAN But you have deviated from that intention. You have introduced genetic changes which will alter the mutation into a creature without morals, without ethics...

DAVROS I introduced aggression without which no race can survive!

GHARMAN But aggression without a conscience.

DAVROS History will show that ~~co-existence~~ **co-operation** between different species is impossible. One race must survive all others. To do this it must dominate ruthlessly. I intend that when all the bickering and battling has ended... The supreme victors will be our race... the Daleks.

During this exchange the Doctor whispers to his friends.

We see the group edging across toward Ronson's work area. ③

DAVROS At this very moment the production lines stand ready... Totally automated, fully programmed. The Daleks are no longer dependent on us. The machinery is ready... they are a power in their own right. ~~Would you end all that has been achieved?~~ **If any one of you would destroy everything that we have ever achieved, then...**

Davros suddenly swings his chair and moves it across to a large wall-mounted instrument. In the centre of the instrument is a large red button, shielded by a pane of glass. ④

Whilst he is making this move we angle on to the Doctor and his friends as they start to rifle amongst the equipment on Ronson's work bench. They locate some of their belongings but they cannot find the travel bracelet.

Davros points his withered hand at the red button.

DAVROS This is a destruct button... Press it and ~~we~~ **you** will destroy ~~the~~ **this** Bunker and everything in it... Only this room will remain. Press it and **you will** wipe out our entire race. Destroy the Daleks forever. Which of you will do it? ~~Which of you?~~

There is a shuffling among the crowd but no one moves forward.

DAVROS You are men without courage. You have lost your ~~own~~ right to survive.

A sudden burst of low whispering as the crowd discuss the situation. We favour the Doctor again. With great concern he looks at the others.

HARRY The time ring's not here

DOCTOR WHO What?

HARRY The time ring – it's not here.

Resume on the front of the crowd. Gharman is in consultation with his immediate neighbours.

Davros beckons to Nyder. Nyder bends to listen as Davros says something we do not hear. Nyder glances at his watch and reports the time.

DAVROS Good. Then we have achieved the delay we needed… ~~Give it~~ **Wait** a few minutes and then check that everything is ready.

Gharman moves forward and stands beside Davros to address the crowd.

GHARMAN You have heard Davros' case. What he has not made clear is that there is another way.

DAVROS There is no other way.

GHARMAN Production of the Daleks can continue… We can destroy the genetically conditioned creatures and allow the mutation to follow its ~~natural~~ **own** course… Our race will survive… if it deserves to survive… but… ~~Let it~~ **they're to** have all the strengths and weaknesses that we have… ~~both~~ compassion and hate… **They're to do good** ~~Let it do great~~ things and evil… But we cannot let it become an unfeeling heartless machine! That is our choice… Now we must decide.

Again a burst of discussion from the group.

The Doctor and Harry start to move away from the work bench. Sarah trailing slightly.

DOCTOR WHO We've got to find that time ring!

Sarah glances back.

SARAH Doctor!

She points to a spot beneath the work bench. The travel bracelet has fallen and been kicked almost out of sight. She stoops and recovers it and triumphantly hands it to the Doctor.

DOCTOR WHO ~~Thank you~~ **Good girl**, Sarah. Now ~~if we can only destroy~~ **all we need is** that tape recording, ~~and~~ **so** keep an eye on Nyder.

DAVROS You have heard our cases. I will give you two minutes to decide… then you must answer not only to me… but to the future…

3. INT. BUNKER CHECKPOINT. NIGHT.

A broad section of tunnel leads to some heavy iron doors that stand open. Beyond them is a checkpoint. Little more than a space-age

guardroom. It contains TV scanner screens and other security devices.

Beyond the checkpoint area are more heavy doors that lead to another section of corridor. These doors are closed.

For a moment the tunnel is empty, then the patrol of Daleks swings into sight. They move determinedly and with an obvious sense of mission. They sweep into the checkpoint area and halt at the closed doors on its far side.

We angle back to the tunnel down which the Daleks have come. At the bend we see Sevrin and Bettan peer around cautiously. They spot the Daleks and pull back out of sight swiftly.

Angle favouring Sevrin and Bettan, behind them the tiny, ragged group of Thal soldiers who make up the attack force. From their viewpoint we see the Daleks waiting at the closed iron doors.

4. INT. MAIN LABORATORY. NIGHT.

The debate still continues. The Doctor and company are among the main group, then favour Davros and Nyder, still set aside from the mass.

Nyder glances at his watch, bends and mutters something unheard to Davros. Davros reaches his hand to the control panel of his chair and presses one of the switches. We see this in big close-up.

5. INT. BUNKER CHECKPOINT. NIGHT.

DALEK 1 Advance!

On the doors and the Daleks. The doors hiss open and the Daleks sweep through into the tunnel beyond.

The moment they have all moved through and out of sight, we pan back to the Thal patrol. Bettan and Sevrin lead the group down to the checkpoint.

Bettan quickly examines the area of tunnel just beyond the recently opened doors. She calls an order:

BETTAN Right… bring up the explosives.

The Thal soldiers carrying the explosive canisters and detonating equipment hurry forward. Bettan indicates various supporting roof beams.

BETTAN Now… Lay the charges along all those main carriers… One charge to each beam should be enough…

She turns to Sevrin.

BETTAN You are quite sure this is the only way into the Bunker?

SEVRIN The only other way was from the Kaled dome. Your war rocket caved that in… It can never be cleared.

BETTAN Then if we can do the same here we'll entomb the Daleks and those who created them.

SEVRIN But Sarah and the Doctor are inside ~~too~~… You'll give them a chance to get clear **won't you..?**

BETTAN I must blow the roof as soon as the charges are laid… I can't delay… If the Daleks find out what we're doing and attack I ~~just~~ don't have enough men or arms to stand them off…

SEVRIN How long?

BETTAN Thirty minutes… perhaps less.

SEVRIN Then I must get inside and try to warn them…

BETTAN That's up to you… but you must understand… If you're not back I must go on… You'll die in there with them…

SEVRIN I understand.

Sevrin turns and starts along the route taken by the Daleks.

BETTAN I'll give you what time I can…

6. INT. MAIN LABORATORY. NIGHT.

On Davros as he calls for the attention of the assembled group.

All become silent and turn towards Davros. We see the Doctor and Sarah and Harry off to one side of the room giving their attention.

The physical distance between Davros and the meeting seems greater now. An open area across which Davros' supporters must move.

DAVROS You have had ample time to decide. Those who will remain loyal to me and **to** the future of our race… Move forward to stand at my side…

There is a pause, then two scientists cross the space to stand beside Davros.

They all stare defiantly at the much larger group.

DAVROS No more..?

Favour one man in the group. ❺

DAVROS Kravos… will you betray me?

Kravos looks very shifty but stays in position.

Nyder starts to edge away from Davros.

He moves very casually, slipping towards a door.

DOCTOR WHO Now I wonder where Nyder's going at such a crucial moment…

HARRY ~~It might be a good idea~~ I think we ought to find out~~, Doctor~~.

DOCTOR WHO ~~I think so, too. Come on.~~ So do I. Let's go.

Doctor Who and his group move cautiously to another door off the laboratory.

They go quite unnoticed in the tense atmosphere.

Covering this action Davros singles out another man. ❻

DAVROS ~~Fenatin~~… **Kravos,** I saved your life **once.** In your chest is a tiny instrument that I designed… It keeps your heart beating… ~~Do~~ **Will** you ~~too~~ turn **that heart** against me?

We favour another man who has not the courage to answer Davros, but instead shifts uncomfortably but holds his ground.

7. INT. CORRIDOR. NIGHT.

Nyder has just drawn level with one of the doors when the Doctor and his group step out. On seeing them, Nyder reacts in a panic and starts to run.

Harry takes after him instantly and brings Nyder crashing down.

Nyder struggles to draw a gun, but before he can the Doctor and Sarah join in.

Nyder is dragged to his feet and the Doctor takes his gun. ❼ *Unnoticed, during the struggle, the bracelet is dropped and rolls away.* ❽

DOCTOR WHO *(To Nyder)* Now… where were you going in such a hurry?

NYDER **Davros has lost.** I'm getting out while I can.

DOCTOR WHO That somehow just doesn't ring true…

SARAH Why didn't you just ~~move over and~~ join the other side..?

DOCTOR WHO **Now that's** a good question… Do you have a good answer?

Nyder stays silent.

The Doctor shrugs.

DOCTOR WHO **Evidently not. Well,** then let's try something else… The tape recording you took ~~away~~… Where is it?

NYDER It's put away in a safe in Davros' office.

DOCTOR WHO ~~Let's go and look at it.~~ **Shall we go and see?**

Nyder judges the odds against him.

The Doctor looks very serious and vaguely menaces with the gun.

NYDER Down here…

Nyder still in Harry's grip, they move along the corridor and reach a door. Sarah opens it and they all move inside.

8. INT. SECTION OF CORRIDOR. NIGHT.

The corridor is empty.

Sevrin appears and moves along it quickly. He pauses at the door of the detention room and looks inside. Finding it empty he is about to move on when he is alerted by a sound. He steps behind the door and all but closes it, peering out only a fraction.

Several Daleks move down the corridor and pass. They go out of sight and Sevrin steps out to move on in his search.

9. INT. DAVROS' OFFICE. NIGHT.

Very much a working office. Blueprints and drawings of Daleks. Biological drawings, etc. cover the walls.

There is one heavy door through which our principals entered, and in another wall is a large viewing panel that looks down into the main laboratory. For the moment, however, this is hidden by sliding shutters.

Nyder is standing beside a safe. **⑨** *It is set in the wall quite high up. Nyder stands beside it surrounded by the Doctor, Harry and Sarah.*

DOCTOR WHO Now be ~~a good chap~~ **reasonable** and open it for us.

NYDER ~~I have already told you.~~ Only Davros knows the combination.

HARRY **Come on, Nyder.** You can do better than that…

He releases him reluctantly.

SARAH Perhaps he's telling the truth?

DOCTOR WHO **Oh no, no.** On the contrary…

He moves a chair to the wall below the safe.

DOCTOR WHO **Now,** Davros cannot rise from his chair. Correct?

NYDER Well?

The Doctor sits in the chair.

DOCTOR WHO He has the use of only one ~~arm~~ **hand**… This ~~one~~ **hand**…

The Doctor reaches up his arm at full stretch and demonstrates that the tips of his fingers are some inches away from the dial.

DOCTOR WHO **And** Davros never goes anywhere without you, Nyder, so you must open the safe for him. ~~Now you'll~~ open it for us –

Faced by this threat, Nyder moves to the safe and starts to twist the dial. The safe door opens and he lifts out the spool of tape which he hands to the Doctor.

DOCTOR WHO **Thank you.** Now let's destroy it.

They all start to search around. Harry **⑩** *finds a Dalek gun on the desk. An experimental model, it has cables that lead away to a small power pack.*

~~**HARRY** How would this do?~~

SARAH **How about this?**

DOCTOR WHO A Dalek gun, very apt.

With some sense of ceremony the Doctor drops the tape into a waste bin. He points the gun into it. The action has the attention of all of them.

The Doctor fires the gun. Nyder eases away.

<u>*Insert:*</u> *Showing the tape and its spool virtually melt.* **⑪**

They all stare down into the smoking waste bin, and are alarmed by a sudden noise.

Nyder has taken his chance and has bolted out of the door.

Harry rushes at it but Nyder is through and slamming it before he can reach it.

DOCTOR WHO **It's not** important. **We've got the** time ring, we've destroyed the tape… ~~Now I think our mission is over…~~ Davros' power has been broken… ~~If the Daleks do survive, then Gharman and his people will at least ensure that they are… well… humanized.~~

SARAH What about the Daleks that ~~were~~ **are** already operational~~, Doctor~~?

DOCTOR WHO … I think we can leave Gharman ~~will~~ to destroy them.
HARRY ~~We can leave here…?~~ That means we can leave then.
DOCTOR WHO Yes. ~~Right away if we want. We all~~ All we've got to do is touch the time ring.

He reaches for his wrist, and then with sudden alarm; he realizes the bracelet has gone. His wrist is empty.

DOCTOR WHO ~~It's gone. It must have fallen off during the struggle.~~ I must have dropped it in the struggle in the corridor.
SARAH … Well, now we must get out… Come on.

The Doctor and Harry move to the door to see if their combined strengths can shift it.

10. INT. BUNKER CHECKPOINT. NIGHT.

Thal soldiers are running cables from the charges that are already in position, back through the checkpoint.

Bettan nervously oversees the operation.

BETTAN How many more charges to go on?
SOLDIER Only ~~another~~ four **more**.
BETTAN That won't take long… It doesn't give them much time… All right… carry on…

She advances down the tunnel a little way, desperately hoping to see the group. The tunnel ahead of her remains empty.

11. INT. DAVROS' OFFICE. NIGHT.

Harry and the Doctor are making futile attempts to force the door. 12

DOCTOR WHO Even the sonic screwdriver won't open this door.

At the desk, Sarah knocks against a control. Panels slide back to reveal the viewing window that looks out into the main laboratory. 13

SARAH Doctor… ~~look…~~

They stare through the glass to see:

12. INT. MAIN LABORATORY. NIGHT. 14

The very small group of people who have sided with Davros stand clustered around his chair. The mass of the meeting remain united some distance away.

13. INT. DAVROS' OFFICE. NIGHT.

SARAH ~~Once they get this business over with there'll be somebody to let us out.~~ Why's it going on so long?
DOCTOR WHO ~~And yet…~~ Who knows… It's out of character for Davros to submit **quite** so easily…

14. INT. MAIN LABORATORY. NIGHT.

Davros addresses the group.

DAVROS This is your last chance. Move to join me now or suffer the consequences…
GHARMAN Why don't you just accept the fact you have lost..? It's over for you Davros…
DAVROS Do you believe I would let a lifetime's work be ended by the will of spineless fools like you..? You have won nothing. I allowed this charade to be played out for only one reason. To find those men who… were truly loyal to me… and to discover those who would betray me…

He indicates the group around him.

DAVROS We… I… will go… on!

Gharman speaks very quietly, believing he is listening to the ravings of a madman.

GHARMAN You are insane, Davros… ~~you are totally outnumbered…~~

Davros makes a large gesture of pressing a control of his panel.

All the doors that open onto the main laboratory slide open as one. Framed in each doorway is a Dalek. 15

They all advance a little and we see that there are more Daleks ready to follow at every door.

The crowd falls silent, cringing away from the Daleks.

~~15. INT. DAVROS' OFFICE. NIGHT.~~

~~The Doctor's group watch in horrified silence.~~

16. INT. MAIN LABORATORY. NIGHT.

For a moment the whole scene seems frozen. The Daleks holding their positions, the crowd immobilized by terror.

DAVROS Exterminate! Exterminate! Exterminate!

We go to a series of close-ups of the muzzles of Daleks' guns as they open fire.

We hear the tremendous searing roar of the assault. We briefly show the crowd reeling under the massive fire. The picture is negative.

17. INT. DAVROS' OFFICE. NIGHT.

The trio stare in shocked horror, the flaring light of the Dalek fire playing on their faces.

18. INT. MAIN LABORATORY. NIGHT.

Close on the muzzle of a flaring Dalek weapon. Then briefly isolating Gharman as he writhes and falls under the attack.

Favouring Davros and his group. His supporters showing the same sort of horror at the massacre as the Doctor.

Nyder is now back at Davros' side and he stares at the carnage without emotion.

One of the Elite officers in a panic of hysteria screams at Davros:

ELITE OFFICER 🄯 Stop them, Davros..! You must stop them..!

He hurls himself at Davros and is pulled off by Nyder who powerfully shoves him away and into the crowd. We see the man hit by the blast of Dalek fire.

19. INT. DAVROS' OFFICE. NIGHT.

Harry and the Doctor stand transfixed. Sarah turns her face away.

We angle behind them to favour the door. We see the handle move slowly as someone tries it from the outside. 🄯 *The door begins to inch open. The Doctor and his group totally unaware of it.*

The Doctor, alerted by some sixth sense spins around to face the door. He levels the gun. The door opens slowly and menacingly, then finally reveals Sevrin.

SARAH Sevrin!

After their relief they exchange brief greetings which are cut short by Sevrin.

SEVRIN ~~Come… we have very little time.~~ **We haven't got much time.** The Thals have set explosives at the entrance… they'll detonate as soon as they're ready…

SARAH What?

DOCTOR WHO Give me a moment to find the time ring.

They all move swiftly to exit.

20. INT. CORRIDOR. NIGHT.

The quartet step out into the corridor and the Doctor runs along it to the point where they intercepted Nyder. The others follow.

The travel bracelet is quickly found. Before they can even register relief at finding it a Dalek appears at the end of the corridor.

The group turn and flee, turning a corner in the same instant as the Dalek fires. 🄯

Another angle of the same corridor showing our group in flight. Another Dalek appears in front of them and they have to dive into a side corridor. 🄯

The group finally come to a panting halt in the temporary shelter of buttressed section of the corridor.

SEVRIN We are not far from the entrance now… if we can get through the next section we will be safe…

The Doctor nods, then takes the travel bracelet from his pocket. He presses it into Sarah's hand.

DOCTOR WHO Take this, Sarah… Sevrin, lead them to the main entrance. Get them out of here…

SARAH What are you going to do?

DOCTOR WHO ~~I must get~~ **I'm going** back to the incubator room… this time ~~I will destroy it~~ **I'm going to blow it up.**

SARAH Let us come with you.

DOCTOR WHO No. ~~Now~~ get out of here~~, the three of you~~. Hurry!

Harry looks as though he is about to argue and then realizes it would be futile. He turns to Sevrin.

Sevrin turns and moves off. Sarah hesitates and Harry grabs her arm and pulls her along with them.

The Doctor watches them move away and then turns and starts off in the opposite direction.

21. INT. MAIN LABORATORY. NIGHT.

The Daleks are ranked before Davros. His supporters grouped around him.

DAVROS Dispose of the traitors' bodies… the Daleks will assume all military duties necessary for the security of the Bunker… **as** for ~~the rest of~~ us, work will commence as soon as possible on ~~research and experimentation to improve~~

the improvement of every aspect of Dalek design.

NYDER *(Entering)* Davros, the prisoners I locked **away** in your office have escaped!

DAVROS Then they must be found. Seek ~~them~~ out **the prisoners** and exterminate ~~them~~.

DALEK We obey.

The Daleks start to move off.

22. INT. BUNKER CHECKPOINT. NIGHT.

Most of the Thal soldiers have now finished their work and are grouped in the checkpoint area.

Two more are fixing the final charges in the tunnel. Bettan is staring down the tunnel.

The last explosive charge is fixed and the two soldiers trail a cable from it back towards the checkpoint.

THAL SOLDIER That's the last one in position.

BETTAN ~~Very well.~~ **Right…**

The soldiers move on. She stares hopelessly down the empty tunnel. Then turns and moves to join her men, calling:

BETTAN Prepare to detonate… 20

She is alerted by the sound of running footsteps and spins to see: Harry, Sarah and Sevrin running towards the entrance.

BETTAN I'd given up hope… now quickly move **away,** we're about to detonate…

SARAH You can't! Not yet… the Doctor is still inside…

HARRY Please… you must wait… 21

SEVRIN ~~Give him~~ A few minutes ~~at least~~ please…

Bettan is very unsure. It is only Sarah's desperate plea that moves her.

SARAH Please… ~~please…~~

BETTAN All right… a few minutes… but if there's the least indication of the Daleks ~~coming~~ **moving** up that ~~tunnel~~ **corridor** ~~first~~… then I detonate…

They all turn to stare down the tunnel. Silent and nervous. We see it from their viewpoint, empty and echoing.

23. INT. CORRIDOR. NIGHT. 22

The door of the incubator room is open slightly. The wire stretches across the floor of the corridor and into the room. We see the wire

move. *The Doctor backs out of the room trailing the wire in his hand.* 23 *He closes the door and backs up the corridor. His hand trails along the wire until he has almost got the two bared ends of the wire in his fingers.*

In the same instant a Dalek appears at one end of the corridor. It fires instantly. The wall beside the Doctor blisters with the heat of the blast.

The Doctor dives for the cover of a buttress and presses himself back into it.

24 *The two bared ends of the wire lie on the ground just a little distance from him. Keeping well in cover he stretches his arm along the ground towards it. His fingers almost reach it.*

The Dalek fires a blast and the Doctor withdraws his hand swiftly and clutches it in pain. Knowing he cannot now succeed he gets to his feet and makes a swift dash to new cover, taking him still further from the wire.

The Dalek advances a little, and the Doctor makes his final swift dash around a corner, evading the next blast from the Dalek.

Now the Dalek moves down the corridor at some speed. 25 *Feature the twin tips of bared wire lying on the floor. The Dalek passes right over them, completing the circuit. There is a huge blast from inside the incubator room and the door is blown off in a flurry of smoke and dust. The Dalek is hurtled against the wall. Then the scene is lost in a cloud of dust.* 26

24. INT. BUNKER CHECKPOINT. NIGHT.

The anxious group still staring down the empty tunnel. From the checkpoint area one of the Thal soldiers calls.

THAL SOLDIER We're getting a picture on one of these scanners…

The group move back into the checkpoint. On one of screens is a picture of the main laboratory. 27

We see Davros and Nyder and some Daleks. ~~We can hear the murmur of voices, but no clear dialogue.~~

BETTAN ~~Get some more volume.~~

~~A soldier operates a knob and we hear Davros'~~ ~~voice.~~

DAVROS ~~Move~~ **Send** a patrol of Daleks to the main entrance… This will remain an area of maximum security…

DALEK I obey.

The Dalek wheels around and moves off.

BETTAN ~~That does~~ **That's** it… I can't wait any longer… Some of you get those doors closed… The rest of you move ~~back~~ **away**…

A couple of men move to close the huge iron doors.

This they have to do manually.

HARRY ~~Give it just~~ one minute more. Please.

BETTAN I'm sorry…

~~25. INT. CORRIDOR. NIGHT.~~ ㉓

~~*The Doctor appears at the distant end of the corridor running for his life.*~~

~~*As he passes camera number of Daleks appear in pursuit.*~~

~~**DALEK** Exterminate… Exterminate.~~

26. INT. MAIN LABORATORY. NIGHT.

Davros and Nyder are moving slowly around the laboratory.

Davros' attention is taken by an indicator panel that is flashing a series of lights.

He halts and looks at it.

DAVROS The automated Dalek production line has been started… I gave no such order. Who did?

DALEK I gave the command.

DAVROS You will perform no function unless ~~it is directly~~ ordered by me. You will obey only my commands… The production line is to be halted immediately.

The Dalek makes no move.

DAVROS You heard my order. Obey… Obey!

The Daleks hold their position.

Nyder steps forward towards the panel.

~~NYDER~~ ~~I'll do it…~~

DAVROS Nyder!

NYDER Yes, Davros.

As he moves across to the panel a Dalek swings towards him and fires.

Nyder crumples to the ground.

DALEK Production will continue.

Davros slowly begins to move back from the ranks of Daleks.

27. INT. BUNKER CHECKPOINT. NIGHT.

The iron doors are almost closed.

Harry and Sarah stare through the ever-narrowing gap.

Bettan kneels beside the soldier who controls the plunger detonator.

BETTAN Fire.

The soldier pulls the plunger up.

There is a scream from Sarah.

SARAH No! Wait… he's coming… He's coming.

Sarah and Harry force the almost closed doors apart enough to allow the Doctor to get through.

We see him belting along the corridor toward the doors.

As he reaches the doors and begins to squeeze through, a group of Daleks appear behind him.

The Doctor squeezes into the checkpoint, pulled through by Harry and Sarah.

The doors close.

The Daleks move up toward the closed doors, firing as they come.

BETTAN Now!

The soldier presses the plunger.

We hear the thunder of the explosion on the other side of the doors.

The doors themselves quake with its violence. ㉙

The Doctor's group turn to look at the scanner screen.

We see the Daleks moving around.

Davros has backed away against a wall near the 'total destruct' switch we featured earlier.

The other scientists are edging away in terror towards the doors.

28. INT. MAIN LABORATORY. NIGHT.

DAVROS You must obey me! I created you! I am the master… Not you… I… I… I!

DALEK Our programming does not permit us to acknowledge that any creature is superior to the Daleks.

DAVROS You cannot exist without me! You cannot progress!

DALEK We are programmed to survive. We have the ability to develop in any way necessary to ensure that survival.

A Dalek moves in from one of the doorways and reports to what is now evidently the leading Dalek.

DALEK 2 Main exit blocked by explosion for a length of at least one thousand yards.

29. INT. BUNKER CHECKPOINT. NIGHT.

The Doctor and his group along with the Thals stare at the scanner screen.

Sarah nudges the Doctor.

SARAH The incubator room… were you able to do anything?

DOCTOR WHO Yes. With a little help from a Dalek… **But I'm afraid** I've **only** delayed them for **a short time…** perhaps… A thousand years. In the total time scale it is no more than…

Clicks his thumb and finger.

Harry draws their attention back to the screen.

HARRY Look…

On the screen we see the few of Davros' supporters being forced back into a corner.

30. INT. MAIN LABORATORY. NIGHT.

DALEK All inferior creatures are to be considered the enemy of the Daleks and destroyed.

DAVROS No, wait! Those men are scientists. They can help you… let them live… Have ~~some~~ pity

DALEK Pity? I have no understanding of the word. It is not registered in my vocabulary bank… Exterminate.

The Daleks fire on the group of men.

The leading Dalek moves across to Davros again. **30**

DAVROS For the last time… I am your creator… You must… you will obey me!

DALEK We obey no one. We are the superior beings.

Davros finally realizes the monster he has created.

He spins his chair and moves swiftly to the destruct button.

His one claw-like hand stretches up and smashes the glass on the button.

As his fingers reach to touch it, we are in huge close-up of the hand and the button.

DALEK Exterminate!

We hear a Dalek command 'exterminate'. The hand is lit by the glare of the blast.

It seems to vanish in the blaze, the button untouched. **31**

A Dalek seems to move directly to camera as it addresses the other Daleks.

DALEK We are entombed but we live on. This is only the beginning. We will prepare. We will grow stronger. When the time is right we will emerge and take our rightful place as the supreme power of the Universe.

The screen goes blank. **32**

32. INT. BUNKER CHECKPOINT. NIGHT.

DOCTOR WHO Goodbye, Bettan… Goodbye, thank you…

BETTAN Goodbye, Harry.

SEVRIN Goodbye, Harry.

SARAH Thank you, Sevrin…

The Doctor, Sarah and Harry stand in a small group staring after the Thals who are moving away up the corridor.

Bettan and Sevrin turn and give a final wave.

SARAH ~~We've failed, haven't we?~~

She hands the time ring to him

DOCTOR WHO Hands on the time ring

SARAH You don't seem too disappointed. **We've failed… haven't we?**

DOCTOR WHO ~~Hands on the ring.~~

They all do this. Special effect begins as they seem to start to lose substance. As the Doctor speaks his voice becomes more echoing.

DOCTOR WHO **33** ~~Disappointed~~ **Failed?** No – not really. You see, I know that although the Daleks will create havoc and destruction for millions of years, I know also that out of their evil must come something good. **34**

CLOSING TITLES **35**

Rewriting History

Although Terry Nation attempted not to contradict his original 1963 Dalek serial, in that story the Daleks' forefathers before the neutronic war had been teachers and philosophers called Dals.

In associated merchandise, an origin story for the Daleks had been published in January 1965 in the comic *TV Century 21* where former script editor David Whitaker had written a comic strip for the monsters entitled 'The Daleks'. In this, the Daleks were originally war machines developed by Yarvelling of the short, warlike, blue-skinned Dalek race. The Daleks are planning to destroy the Thals with a neutron bomb which is prematurely detonated by a meteorite storm. Two years later, Yarvelling's dying action is to adapt his war machine to carry the mutated remains of his people. These events were dated as taking place in 2003 by Nation in his Souvenir Press book *The Dalek Pocketbook and Space Travellers Guide* in October 1965.

In 1973, Nation had contradicted these earlier origins for the first time, when writing a short story – 'We Are the Daleks!' – for a lavish *Radio Times* souvenir magazine to celebrate 10 years of *Doctor Who*. In this, it was postulated that the Daleks were in fact the result of an accelerated development of mankind, with specimens of humanity's primate ancestors captured by a scientific expedition from Halldon and taken to the planet Ameron, where their evolution was speeded up.

---

1 The episode opens with a brief shot of the Doctor in the incubator room, followed by Sarah's line: 'What's taking him so long?' before the Doctor emerges from the incubator room being strangled by a Dalek creature.

2 There are six scientists and two guards, as well as the 'named' characters.

3 Sarah hands the Doctor's possessions on Ronson's desk to Harry, who passes them to the Doctor – a yo-yo, the sonic screwdriver…

4 The button is set into the surface of Davros' desk. It is labelled 'TOTAL DESTRUCT'.

5 Kravos is an Elite guard.

6 The character of Fenatin was removed so Davros addresses this whole accusation at Kravos.

7 Actually a short truncheon.

8 This was recorded as a separate shot and edited back into the main scene.

9 The safe was circular, forming the centre of the eye in an embossed Elite symbol – a stylized eye with a lightning bolt through it. It was used on the notepaper and appears on the lapels of the Elite guards.

10 Sarah actually finds the Dalek gun.

11 An effects shot of the tape exploding, with the blue ray of the Dalek gun inlaid. The picture was also flashed to negative to show the effects of the blast.

12 The Doctor is using the sonic screwdriver.

13 It is actually a screen relaying an image from the laboratory (provided using CSO).

14 This scene was recorded to be inlaid into the viewing panel in Scenes 11 and 13, which ran continuously.

15 For the first time the static prop Daleks (referred to as 'goon' Daleks) were used to give the impression of many Daleks arriving. Two were positioned in a doorway revealed as the door opened, another was pushed into view together with a 'real' Dalek.

16 Kravos speaks this line, adding poignancy as we know that Davros previously saved his life.

17 There is no handle on the door. The Doctor hears someone outside and goes to listen.

18 The Dalek gun firing was planned as a brief cut-away shot, but not actually used.

19 There was a short recording break here to allow the actors to reposition themselves as if in a new section of corridor.

20 The first part of Scene 23 was inserted here – as far as the Dalek first firing at the Doctor.

21 Most of Harry's line is lost under the others.

22 The first part of this scene was cut into the previous scene.

23 The Doctor has managed to regain his coat from Part One, and is again wearing it.

24 The scene resumes at this point.

25 There was a brief recording break here to allow Visual Effects to rig the explosion.

26 The screen is whited out by the blast.

27 The screen is a black-and-white TV monitor.

28 This scene was recorded immediately after Scene 20 and featured three Daleks pursuing the Doctor. It was cut for timing reasons.

29 A puff of smoke escapes through the crack between the doors.

30 There was a short recording pause before this, to line up the camera shot on Davros and the chief Dalek.

31 Terry Nation later commented, 'It was absolutely my intention that when Davros was buried in the rubble of the explosion we should see either a glowing light, or his hand move in some way and press a button. Just enough to explain it away when – many years later – we might want to resurrect him. It grieves me that the shot was lost.'

32 The screen is blanked out completely for almost a second.

33 The Doctor's line was dubbed in, with an echo effect added. The travellers spin slowly round before the image fades to the closing shot of them whirling in space.

34 The CSO shot of the travellers with the time ring was edited in at the end, having been recorded with Part Three. While the Doctor has his overcoat when he 'leaves' Skaro, he is not wearing it in this sequence, or in the next story (already recorded) *Revenge of the Cybermen*.

35 At the end of the script, it says:

END OF EPISODE SIX: OVER TO YOU DOUGLAS!

Terror of the Zygons was recorded almost immediately after this story, though held back to open the following season of *Doctor Who*. It was directed by Douglas Camfield.

REVENGE OF THE CYBERMEN

BY GERRY DAVIS

PART ONE first transmitted 19 April 1975 at 17.35
PART TWO 26 April 1975 at 17.30
PART THREE 3 May 1975 at 17.50
PART FOUR 10 May 1975 at 17.35

Overview

Received wisdom has it that *Revenge of the Cybermen* is the least successful story of the 12th season of *Doctor Who*. While it really is a more coherent, exciting and entertaining story than this suggests, the received wisdom is nonetheless correct.

There is actually much to recommend the story. The Cybermen are physically as impressive as ever, although there are only four of them. The sets that are inherited from *The Ark in Space* are excellent. The location film work is exemplary.

But sadly, the story is thin; the Vogans are not convincing aliens; the studio caves don't even come close to matching the extent and splendour of the location; the Cybermen do not come out of the narrative as impressively as they usually do.

There is nothing that bad about *Revenge of the Cybermen.* But it fails to live up to the expectations built up by the rest of this season. It is above-average comic-book entertainment. It is great fun to watch. But for a story that promises the long-awaited return of the Cybermen, and which directly follows the hard-edged, superbly realized *Genesis of the Daleks,* that just isn't enough.

Origin

The idea of bringing the Cybermen back to *Doctor Who* after an absence of some years came from producer Barry Letts, who had previously performed the same exercise in 1971 when he decided to resurrect the Daleks for *Day of the Daleks.* The resulting press and public interest seemed to have paid dividends, so the notion was worth reusing. In this case, the Cybermen – created in 1966 by scientist Kit Pedler for *The Tenth Planet* – had not been the main villains since *The Invasion* in 1968.

The plan to bring the Cybermen back arose during spring 1974, with Letts and script editor Robert Holmes aiming to have them appear in a very cost-conscious four-part serial. The writer whom Letts contacted to provide the script was Gerry Davis, the script editor on *Doctor Who* from 1966 to 1967 who had helped Pedler to develop the Cybermen and who co-wrote several of their serials.

Davis had left *Doctor Who* in spring 1967 to become script editor on *The First Lady* – a prestigious BBC drama series. In 1968 Davis worked with Pedler to develop *Doomwatch,* a BBC drama series about threats to humanity caused by mankind's own use of technology and science. *Doomwatch* entered production in autumn 1969 with Davis as script editor, although he left during its second season in 1970 after differences with the producer, Terence Dudley (later a writer/director on *Doctor Who*). In 1972, Davis became script editor on the BBC police drama *Softly, Softly: Task Force* and then returned to freelance writing, with one of his assignments in early 1974 being an adaptation of the 1967 *Doctor Who* Cyberman story *The Moonbase* for the new range of Target paperbacks. Visiting Holmes and Letts at the *Doctor Who* production office, Davis was delighted to find that the team still carried on a tradition which he had begun in 1966: each serial was represented on the office wall by a photograph and synopsis, allowing easy reference to see if a proposed story idea had been done before.

Storyline

Because Letts and Holmes were keen to develop a linked set of storylines for the new season – allowing the Doctor again to become more of a wanderer in space and time as opposed to the Earth-bound adviser to UNIT – it was decided to link Davis' Cybermen serial into the already delivered but problematic scripts for *Space Station* by Christopher Langley. Davis was asked to set his serial in the same space station as Langley's serial, but at a different point in time. This would allow savings for the production team as only one group of sets needed to be made for both serials and could be re-used with minimal re-dressing.

Davis was commissioned on Thursday 9 May for a four-part storyline to be delivered by Friday 31 May under the title *Revenge of the Cybermen*; at this stage it was suggested that the serial could be made third and it was allocated the production code 4C (thus following on from *Space Station* after the summer break). A cost-conscious writer himself from his script editor days, Davis developed an outline which would be a cheap, studio-bound production that could re-use the *Space Station* sets; at this point in time the satellite would be a space-bound casino with all the Las Vegas trappings, but the Doctor's party would arrive there to find all the gambling tables deserted and strange sets of footprints all over the station. Drawing on elements from previous Cybermen stories, Davis indicated that the gamblers would have succumbed to a plague being spread by Cybermats – small, rodent-like cybernetic creatures which Davis and Pedler had developed for *The Tomb of the Cybermen* with potential merchandising spin-offs in mind. Davis also developed the notion that gold would be deadly to Cybermen, and hence the casino's gold reserves could be used to defeat them at the end of the serial. Davis' storyline was delivered ahead of deadline on Wednesday 29 May.

With gambling felt not to be a suitable subject for the family audience of *Doctor Who*, the casino element of Davis' proposed serial was dropped at a very early stage, although the notion of gold as the major weapon against the Cybermen was retained. By the end of May, *Space Station* had been dropped, and Holmes was in discussions with John Lucarotti to develop *The Ark in Space*, which would again use the same setting. Meanwhile, Holmes commissioned Davis for four scripts entitled *The Revenge of the Cybermen* on Thursday 6 June; the target date for delivery was Wednesday 31 July. The right to use the Cybermen had to be negotiated with Pedler – who had left the field of television drama after his initial *Doomwatch* scripts in 1969/70 – and correspondence regarding this began on Monday 17 June; by Monday 8 July, a payment to Pedler of £120 for use of the Cybermen was agreed.

Scripts

Davis' scripts drew heavily upon *The Moonbase* (1967) for a number of their elements: the Cybermen infiltrate a confined outpost of humanity in space, hiding in the medical unit, and attacking humans with what appears to be a disease and which causes black veins on the victim's skin. Having no point of reference for the new incarnation of the Doctor as played by Tom Baker, Davis wrote the lead character very much in the manner of how the role was portrayed by Patrick Troughton (the new Doctor even retained the earlier Doctor's diary). Davis titled his scripts *Doctor Who and the Return of the Cybermen* (a working title previously used on both *The Moonbase* and *The Invasion*). He was in discussion with incoming producer Philip Hinchcliffe in mid-July about his new story.

The first finished script was sent to Holmes on Saturday 20 July, with Davis observing in a covering letter that he had seen the regeneration of Jon Pertwee into Tom Baker (*Planet of the Spiders* Part Six having aired on Saturday 8 June), and declared Baker to be the 'Best thing that happened to *Doctor Who* in quite a while'. As with Lucarotti's version of *The Ark in Space*, Davis also retained individual episode titles on his scripts (it was during Davis' tenure as story editor that these had been phased out in early 1966). The first instalment was 'The Beacon in Space' in which the Doctor, Harry and Sarah arrive on the Nerva, a former mineral-processing station where all bar four survivors – Commander Stevenson, Dr Anitra Berglund, Bill Lester and Professor Richard Kellman – have been killed by a 'disease' spread by Cybermats. The Doctor soon realizes that the crew are under attack from the apparently extinct Cybermen, and Anitra finds that Cybermats can be neutralized by gold dust. A full synopsis of *Return of the Cybermen* can be found in Appendix B.

The script for Part One was received on Tuesday 23 July. Concerned about the style of narrative, Robert Holmes wrote to Davis the same day with guidelines for the three remaining instalments:

I've gone through this script and discussed it with Barry [Letts] and Philip [Hinchcliffe]. We all feel much the same way – that you have written it only for children. It's too straightforward (particularly in characterization) and therefore rather dull.

Our audience these days is 60 per cent adult and so we need a level of interest behind the 'front' action. I think if you bear this in mind when working on the remaining episodes we shall all be saved a lot of trouble.

'Doctor Who' has probably changed considerably since your connection with it and, these days, we find our audience is ready to accept quite sophisticated concepts.

I am accepting Episode 1 – despite all these wounding strictures! – because I feel the flaws in the script stem more from your mental approach than anything inherently wrong in the story or its structure.

However, in case any heavy rewriting does eventually become necessary, I am sending a copy of this letter to Harvey [Davis' agent: Harvey Unna] so that he is fully in the picture.

With this new guidance, Davis delivered his remaining three instalments of *Return of the Cybermen* on Tuesday 27 August: 'The Plague Carriers', 'The Gold Miners' and 'The Battle for the Nerva' (see Appendix B) which introduced a sub-plot in which a group of miners on a worked-out asteroid of gold were now instrumental in being used by Kellman in his plan as a double agent for the Cybermen. Because Holmes was tied up with work on both *The Destructors* and *The Ark in Space*, it was Philip Hinchcliffe who initially read Davis' scripts. He outlined his thoughts to his script editor in a memo on Wednesday 4 September:

Basically, I think this story will work although I am unhappy about Gerry Davis' 'elementary' style of writing, which never rises above telling the basic plot. We need to improve the dialogue wherever possible therefore, and flesh out the characterization, particularly of Commander Stevenson and in places the Doctor himself. As a general point about the season I am a bit worried that Sarah's role is being reduced too much and she should be given more to do in this story if possible.

Episode 1 is probably quite a large rewrite and I have told Gerry that we will be doing it. In the opening scene there must clearly be references to the Doctor's previous visit to the Ark and the audience must be in no doubt as to the exact time and stage of development on the Ark. Losing the teaser, Captain Warner should be discovered isolated and abandoned, and throughout the episode there should be no direct contact with him (ie: no one in the same room) as this would destroy the motivation of the other crew members in this episode. I think we need to invent something less ridiculous than the Doctor leafing through his diary to solve the mystery of the scratch marks. As written he simply has a mental block for a few hours and then remembers.

As I said, Commander Stevenson's character should be built up – his is a genuine concern to stop the plague spreading throughout the Nerva and the arrival of the Doctor & Co faces him with a difficult moral decision.

I think we need more background (perhaps from the Doctor) about the Cybermen and their attributes and I am a bit unhappy about the references to Kellman as the only surviving scientist aboard and what this is meant to indicate. Gerry Davis says that Kellman conducts experiments which is why there is a room for crushing mineral ore and is his explanation for the rather fortuitous bottle of gold dust which Anitra finds to throw at the Cybermats in Scene 20. I suppose this is just about acceptable but we need to look hard at Kellman's motivation throughout this story and probably build up his greed for gold.

In Episode 2 I think again the Doctor consulting his diary is a clumsy device and it would be better to have more dialogue in this scene between the Doctor and Commander Stevenson building up the background and threat of the Cybermen.

The X-ray 'gun' is nonsense scientifically speaking so we must find a proper explanation because it wouldn't bang and flash.

Evans, the murdered miner, needs to be planted more strongly – perhaps the rest of the crew talking about his disappearance *before* the plague.

Also, I think the climax of this episode is handled badly. The Commander & Co. discover the Doctor and Harry too quickly. There is no tension if we know they are about to be saved. Likewise the revelation of Kellman's evil role is too simple and poorly stage-managed.

I won't go into Episode 3 much except to say that Gerry Davis is rewriting the whole of the 'miners' scenes more closely along the lines we originally envisaged. In this lost colony of humans the gold has acquired a totemistic value and the Doctor has to save them in spite of themselves. On a scientific point we should check whether human life is feasible on an asteroid.

Episode 4 works reasonably well I think, although Harry has more action than the Doctor. Perhaps we could reverse their roles in this episode. I wonder also if it is a bit short. The ending, of course, will have to be rewritten to link up with the next story.

Despite his reservations, Hinchcliffe formally accepted the scripts on Monday 9 September; the next day, the producer wrote to Davis:

First of all let me say thank you very much. I am sure this will turn out to be a
vintage Cybermen story.

As I mentioned on the phone the other day there will be a few changes. In
Episode 1 the opening few scenes and possibly some of the Doctor's lines to
bring his characterization more into line with the rest of the scripts, and in
Episode 3 the mine scenes which I still think can be improved. Episodes 2 and
4 work very well by and large although we may need to make the Doctor more
obviously active at the climax of the story – perhaps giving him some of
Harry's action. Finally, of course, we shall have to rejig the final scene to tie it
in with the next story.

Bob feels he can cope with this all right but I thought I would just keep you
in the picture.

In mid-September, the story's title reverted to its original *The Revenge
of the Cybermen*. However, at the end of September as pre-production got
underway, the production team realized that the revised scripts were not
entirely suitable. The director, Michael E. Briant, was dismayed by the
reworked versions of Davis' scripts, and felt the story existed for no other
reason than the 'resurrection of a boring monster'. It was evident that Robert
Holmes would need to rework the scripts extensively now that he was getting
clear of the rewrites on *The Ark in Space*. Because of these more drastic
changes, Hinchcliffe wrote to Davis on Thursday 10 October to 'keep him
in the picture' about *Revenge of the Cybermen*:

Bob and myself have reviewed the scripts and still feel some changes are required.

As it stands at the moment the serial is almost entirely confined to the space
station and the battle with the Cybermen. From episode two onwards there is
plenty of incident but very little real development and the story runs a very
grave risk of becoming boring. I think Bob and I half sensed this danger when
your episode one came in but it has now become much more apparent in our
discussions with the director.

Basically what is needed is (1) a proper sub-plot featuring the 'miners'
(whom we want to make more alien still) – which will enable us to shift more
of the action on to the 'asteroid' and thus open up the story considerably; and
(2) make more involvement for Harry and Sarah. At the moment Sarah does
very little until episode four and Harry's role overlaps with the Doctor's.

The rest remains the same with Kellman's treachery, the cyberplague and the
Cyberplan to destroy the 'planet of gold'.

I realize in some respects these go beyond our original storyline but I hope
you will view them as additions to your original script rather than rewrites.

At this late stage, of course, it would be unfair and impractical to ask you to do this work and the best thing is probably for us to send you copies of the rewritten scripts as they become ready.

Since there was now more money available than expected, which would allow an extensive location shoot, Davis' studio-bound script could be opened out. For this expansion, Holmes selected the material concerning the miners – which the team had never been happy about – and turned the miners into a new alien race, intending that the material set inside the asteroid could now be pre-filmed in an impressive location. During early October, the asteroid was christened first Alanthea, then Vegan and finally Voga – this final name stemmed from the island of gold which Christopher Columbus, the fifteenth-century explorer, had searched for.

Holmes' rewrites were concurrent with pre-production and occupied most of October. As the scripts took shape, Holmes drafted a set of background notes on *The Revenge of the Cybermen* along with a scene breakdown for the final three episodes. In the new back story, Holmes referred to Voga – 'the fabled Moon of Gold' – being supposedly destroyed 'in the Cyberwar thousands of years before'. Vorus was 'guardian of the gold mines' who 'seeks personal wealth and power' and has hatched a plan to destroy the Cybermen with his missile and 'cover himself in glory and in the process bring inter-galactic attention to the Cybermen's aggression. Other nations will be forced to re-arm using Vogan gold and thus bring vast profits to Vorus'.

In the breakdown for Part Two, an early extra scene appears as the Doctor attempts to mend the transmat:

3. CABIN. Kellman on his private radio (which we will have established in Ep.1) to Vorus, warning him to expect visitors.

4. VOGAN CHAMBER. Vorus sending guards to matterbeam receptors. Important at this vital stage not to let outsiders fall into Tyrum's hands and perhaps give game away.

And just after Harry and Sarah are successfully transmatted to Voga:

6A. CYBERSHIP. Cybermen detect use of matter beam and jam it.

Holmes clarified the roles and differences of his two main Vogans, Tyrum and Vorus:

Tyrum is Prime Minister/City Boss. The ancient guilds – trade unions – give Vorus his power base. He controls the gold galleries and thus the route to the surface.

In Part Three, Holmes' humour showed through in the explanation:

> 4. VOGAN CHAMBER. Vorus insisting that Tyrum's city scum must never enter this holy of holies, the inner sanctum of the goldworkers. (The reason is that he has a CSO rocket the other side of a grille.)

Meanwhile, on the beacon which was now under control of the Cybermen, the Cyberleader wonders what problems Harry and Sarah could have encountered on Voga, which it believes is uninhabited:

> Not uninhabited says the Doctor and refers to cryptic radio call in Ep.1. So?, hisses the Cyberleader. And being a sophisticated Cyberchap he begins to toy with the idea that Kellman might be double-crossing him.

Kellman transmats to Voga and is soon picked up by Tyrum's 'police' and meets Harry and Sarah at Tyrum's HQ.

> 13. TYRUM HQ. Kellman's nerve is failing fast. He knows the Cybermen will be going ahead with the bomb plan and he has no wish to be blown up. Tyrum decides to let Kellman go and have him tailed.

> 14. CAVES. Harry and Sarah have been allowed to escape along with Kellman. The three are temporary allies. Kellman tells them about Vorus' rocket and how it represents the only way of stopping the Cybermen.

> 15. TYRUM HQ. Above conversation picked up on Tyrum's parabolic mike. It decides him to move his musclemen in on Vorus.

> 16. CAVES. Sarah says they must warn Doctor if they're going to start firing rockets. Kellman doesn't want this, naturally, because Cybermen will be alerted. He tries to stop her – Harry intervenes and is stunned. Then Tyrum's men arrive and a melee starts outside the Vogan chambers. During this Sarah slips away to matterbeam.

> 17. CONTROL ROOM. Sarah arrives on space beacon and just has time to hide before Cyberleader enters with bomb-laden captives and sends them down to Voga with two Cybercompanions.

In Part Four's breakdown, Kellman survives the rockfall and is killed when Lester unfastens his explosive belt-buckle to destroy the two Cybermen. The rest of the synopsis was very close to the broadcast episode, with the Doctor unlocking the 'gyro-tillers' on the beacon in the nick of time to save Voga.

It was not until a fortnight before location filming was due to begin that, on Wednesday 6 November, Holmes was able to provide a full set of scripts for *Revenge of the Cybermen*, structured to use the sets built for the recording of *The Ark in Space* and locations which had been selected by Briant for the new film sequences. The start of the serial also now linked back to *Genesis of the Daleks*, which would precede *Revenge of the Cybermen* in transmission but would enter production after it in January 1975. Even at this stage, though, there were great differences between Harry's scripted dialogue and what would end up on the finished programme; the character was still written as a rather extreme *Boys Own* hero, spouting expressions like 'good-oh' and being used far more for comic effect (see Part Two, TK 9).

As it turned out, the person who was probably least happy with the finished serial was Gerry Davis, who disliked Tom Baker's realization of the lead and was unhappy with some of Holmes' changes. The serial was to be Davis' final broadcast work on *Doctor Who*; in the 1970s he moved first to Toronto and then Los Angeles where he worked on series such as *Sidestreet*, *The Great Detective*, *Vega$*, *Quincy* and *Jessie*. Although he submitted a storyline about the origins of the Cybermen to the BBC in the early 1980s, it was never accepted for development. In 1990 Davis formed a consortium with Terry Nation to bid for the licence to make *Doctor Who* for the BBC; the attempt proved unsuccessful. Davis died in August 1991, aged 64.

Production Team

Formally joining production of Serial 4D (as *Revenge of the Cybermen* had now been rescheduled since the late addition of *The Sontaran Experiment*) on Monday 30 September was director Michael E. Briant. Briant had been an assistant floor manager on *The Crusade* and *The Daleks' Master Plan* in 1965, and worked as production assistant on *The Power of the Daleks* and *Fury from the Deep* before his first directorial assignment on the series with *Colony in Space* in 1971. Since then he had directed *The Sea Devils* (1972), *The Green Death* (1973) and *Death to the Daleks* (1974), and had recently been working on the BBC police drama *Dixon of Dock Green*.

Because of his work on *The Ark in Space* and the re-use of his sets, Roger Murray-Leach was again retained as the set designer. On costumes, L. Rowland Warne was requested by Briant after their work together on *Death to the Daleks*, but he was not available and Christine Rawlins was offered instead. Eventually, costume design was undertaken by Prue Handley who, like make-up designer Cecile Hay-Arthur, was a newcomer to *Doctor Who*. Visual effects were to be handled by James Ward whose first major *Doctor Who* assignment had been *Doctor Who and the Silurians* in 1969 (although he had been an effects assistant on the first serial in 1963); he had also worked with Briant on *Death to the Daleks*.

Rather than use Dudley Simpson to provide an incidental music score as on the other stories of the season, Briant opted to hire composer Carey Blyton. Blyton had first scored a *Doctor Who* serial in 1969/70 with *Doctor Who and the Silurians* and had returned to provide a saxophone score for Briant on *Death to the Daleks*. Hinchcliffe attempted to contact Blyton throughout September 1974; on Saturday 21 the composer indicated that he was indeed available to take on the assignment, and was formally contracted on Tuesday 22 October.

When conceiving the Vogans (then called Alantheans or Vegans), it was hoped that visual effects designer John Friedlander would sculpt half-masks for the actors playing these aliens, and a make-up document dated Tuesday 8 October noted that these would be, 'Albino people with 1/3 masks – blind/short-sighted – long white hair – beautiful coloured costumes.'

Unfortunately the masks – as made by Friedlander using a face cast from his assistant Rhys Jones – ended up looking rather comical and were a disappointment to Briant and Hinchcliffe.

In comparison, the 'spacemen' of Nerva would wear 'Royal Space Corps' uniforms. The original intention for the Cyberleader was to reveal the decaying, once-human head inside the metal helmet. An early visual effects list describes the requirement for, 'Big head with gauze front that reveals face (nasty) – Interior lights?'

Hinchcliffe and Briant checked on what Cybermen costumes and Cybermats still existed from the 1960s. No Cybermats from either *The Tomb of the Cybermen* or *The Wheel in Space* (1968) had been retained and Briant found the original designs very dated. There were two very battered and old-fashioned wet-suit-based Cyberman costumes left from *The Invasion*. So it was decided that the freelancer Alistair Bowtell – who had worked on *Robot* – should construct four new Cyberman outfits.

Again based on a wet suit, these used large ribbed rubber tubes with additional piping at the knees and elbows. Pieces of broken television set were used inside the chest units. Not seeing the logic of having the Cybermen carry guns as in previous stories (and in Davis' script), Briant suggested that their weaponry should be part of them. A four-chamber set of flash charges was therefore mounted in the new, larger fibreglass helmets and could be triggered to explode on cue, like the guns used in *The Sea Devils*. Silver-sprayed gloves and wellingtons finished off the costume, and the Cyberleader was given black trimmings on its helmet to indicate its rank. Of the new Cybermats, one effects list indicated that the Cybermats should be 'with fangs (to spread plague)'.

Cast

One of the main guest stars for the serial was Ronald Leigh-Hunt who was cast as Commander Stevenson. Leigh-Hunt had previously guested in *Doctor Who* as Commander Radnor in *The Seeds of Death* (1969) and had played Colonel Buchan in Southern Television's adventure series *Freewheelers*.

Playing Kellman was Jeremy Wilkin, who had starred in *Undermind*, a science fiction thriller series from ABC in 1965, and had worked on several of the Gerry and Sylvia Anderson series since the second season of *Thunderbirds* in 1966 (providing the voice characterization for Thunderbird 2's pilot, Virgil Tracy). Lester was portrayed by William Marlowe, who had appeared as Harry Mailer in *The Mind of Evil* (1971); he later married Kismet Delgado, the widow of Roger Delgado, who played the Master in the Jon Pertwee era of *Doctor Who*.

The other Nerva survivor, Warner, was to have been played by Malcolm Thompson, but the actor dropped out during pre-production, on Tuesday 5 November. In his place, Briant cast Alec Wallis, whom he had previously used as Leading-Telegraphist Bowman in *The Sea Devils*.

For the role of Vorus, leader of the Guardians, Briant's first choice was Dudley Sutton, an actor who had gained a reputation as a 'heavy' in various 1960s television series and was then in the ATV sitcom *Up the Workers*. When Sutton rejected the part on Tuesday 29 October, Briant cast David Collings who had been in the film *Scrooge* and whose extensive television work included *Elizabeth R*. The other prominent Vogan, Tyrum, was played by Kevin Stoney. Stoney had two previous guest roles in *Doctor Who* as villains – Mavic Chen in *The Daleks' Master Plan* and Tobias Vaughn in *The Invasion*. The part of Vorus' engineer, Magrik, went to Michael Wisher, who went on to play Davros – see *Genesis of the Daleks* – and who had provided the Dalek voices for Briant's *Death to the Daleks* the previous year. An accomplished voice artist, Wisher also provided the voices of the doomed Vogan radio operator and the radio operator of Pluto-Earth flight one five.

Inside the costume of the Cyberleader was Christopher Robbie, a tall actor with imposing stature who had appeared in the 1968 *Doctor Who* adventure *The Mind Robber* as a superhero called the Karkus. The other speaking Cyberman was Melville Jones who had previously been a guard in *The Time Monster* (1972); Jones found his Cyberman costume extremely claustrophobic. One of the other Cybermen was regular monster actor Pat Gorman (see *Robot*). Also on hand for the location filming as Vogans and stunt doubles were both Terry Walsh (see *Robot*) and Alan Chuntz (see *Genesis of the Daleks*).

Filming

Model filming took place for the serial at the Puppet Theatre of Television Centre on Tuesday 12 November, the same day that *The Ark in Space* completed studio recording; Tom Baker took time off from camera rehearsals to visit James Ward's visual effects team as they filmed sequences of the Cybership, the Nerva and Vorus' sky-striker rocket (some of which were ultimately abandoned). The Cybership was made from odds and ends by visual effects assistant Tony Harding. Briant had wanted elaborate effects for the serial on the scale of Stanley Kubrick's movie *2001: A Space Odyssey* despite the BBC's limited budget. Two days later, the Society for Film and Television Awards (SFTA) announced that the scripts for *Doctor Who*'s previous season had won an award.

Because of the budget increase and the addition of location filming, Briant had made early recces to find suitable venues for the Voga scenes with his wife Monique (who had appeared as an extra in *Doctor Who* serials since *The Ice Warriors* in 1967, including her husband's *Colony in Space*). Early on in production, Briant settled on using the Wookey Hole caves, an Iron Age cave network which was excavated around 1912 by Herbert Balch. These caverns were created by the River Axe cutting through the Mendip Hills near Wells in Somerset. In the early 1970s, several new caves had been blasted open and the chambers had been opened to the public. The first cave the visitors entered was the Witch's Kitchen, so named because of legends of an old woman accused of practising witchcraft and banished from the caves. One of the rock formations in the cavern looked very much like the outline of a witch. Beyond the Witch's Kitchen were tunnels leading to the Witch's Parlour and the Cathedral caves.

Briant and his team were to find the location a distinctly unnerving one at times, although Monique was intrigued by some Stone Age arrow-heads which she found in one cavern. After discussions with the cave-owners during his visit on Monday 11 November, Briant was allowed to stay at Wookey Hole late at night to make notes on possible camera positions. Around midnight, Briant encountered a man dressed in potholing gear who greeted him briefly before going on his way. The director continued his work and emerged an hour or so later, commenting that he had seen the man – whom he assumed to be one of the cave staff – down in the caverns. However, the owners explained that Briant had been totally alone in the caves… adding that a potholing diver had died in the caves just a few years earlier.

Having sacrificed two days' film rehearsal for extra days on location, Briant's cast and crew travelled down to Wells to start shooting the serial at Wookey Hole on Monday 18 November. Designer Roger Murray-Leach's team had arrived the previous day to dress some of the caves with gold paint and also set up the electric Isocar used by the Vogans. There were strict orders placed on the team that there was to be no smoking inside the caves, which the film schedule described as 'The Oldest Stately Home in England'. Furthermore, many of the rock formations in the cave were unique and one warning in particular was given:

> DO NOT TOUCH the 'Witch' and the 'Witch's Dog' because they are considered to be the prime features of the Caves, and are irreplaceable.

Work on the first day began in the Cathedral cavern with shots of the Doctor's party in Part Three and Harry and Sarah's flight from the Vogans in Part Two. Briant found that Baker was still trying to find the best manner in which to play the Doctor, and could still be nervous over some aspects of his performance. The nerves of the team were not helped by the claustrophobic nature of the caves. The walkie-talkies, which normally gave good communication between team members, did not function in them, and the lack of oxygen caused errors of judgment that resulted in mistakes and minor accidents. Rosemary Hester, the assistant floor manager, was very badly affected by the claustrophobic caves and collapsed. She was driven back to London overnight by production unit manager George Gallaccio, who then collected Russ Karel as her replacement. The caves also had an adverse effect on Jack Wells, the unit armourer, who was ill when he ventured underground.

An element added to Holmes' scripts by Briant was that the Vogan skimmers – referred to in the dialogue for Part Two – should be shown on screen. Given the underwater lakes in Wookey Hole, Briant arranged for his production assistant John Bradburn to have three small motorboats called Sizzlas hired from Mr TS Boorer of Dorhill Ltd., a company based in Henley-in-Arden in Warwickshire. Although Boorer was sure that his vessels would be suitable for the show from the description given of the caves, the boats failed to function properly when tested on the first day. A change to some special spark plugs was suggested and agreed by Briant the following day.

On Tuesday 19, the passage leading into the Witch's Parlour was used for the rockfall sequences, with the matterbeam area set up inside the parlour, reusing the props from *The Sontaran Experiment*. Further scenes were filmed up the steps into Hell's Larder – referred to in the film schedule as the 'battle arch'; this was used for the scenes of the Vogan 'doves' (as Tyrum's followers were referred to on production paperwork) in battle with the Cybermen.

Unfortunately there were still problems with the Sizzlas; even with the modifications made by Boorer one of the three boats refused to operate, and the other two still had engine trouble which meant delays in shooting until the propellers could be altered; the cast and crew had to wear life jackets when on board the Sizzlas, removing them only for the actual take.

Wednesday 20 began with material in the Witch's Kitchen for various scenes of the serial, and a photocall was held for the Cybermen and the series' new aliens, the Vogans, during rehearsals. Also in attendance was a reporter from a local newspaper, the *Evening News*, to cover this regional work by the series. However, it was a day fraught with problems. Ignoring the instructions in the film schedule, some of the electricians could not resist dressing up the supposedly cursed witch rock formation with a cloak and broomstick. At 3.20 p.m. that afternoon, Elisabeth Sladen was shooting a scene using one of the Sizzla boats on the Witch's Parlour lake for Part Three. The Sizzla went out of control, and it seemed to Sladen that the vehicle was going to smash into the cave wall with her on board. To avoid the impact, Sladen dived off the rogue craft into the cold water of the caves, and found herself in more difficulties as she was not wearing a life jacket because it was an actual take. Terry Walsh, who had been uneasy during the shoot, had decided to be on hand for this sequence and dived into the water to save Sladen from drowning. Walsh himself was then very ill after the rescue, and had to return to the surface. A quarter of an hour later, a ladder gave way beneath an electrician who was fixing some lights and he broke his leg in the fall.

The crew completed their work at Wookey Hole on Thursday 21 November with various shots including the battle between the Vogan 'doves' and 'hawks' (the followers of Vorus). There were more production problems when some relatively simple pyrotechnic effects arranged by Tony Harding failed to work. A film crew from *Points West*, a local news programme broadcast on BBC1 from the Wenvoe transmitter for the West Country, arrived to cover the filming of various sequences, and Baker gave an interview about his approach to the role, the horror in the series and how he was attempting to make his Doctor different from Jon Pertwee's incarnation. The report concluded with Baker entering a local pub with the two Cybermen for lunch. The story was broadcast the following day, allowing local viewers a sneak preview of the new Doctor over a month before his debut episode.

Briant believed that the shoot – with its accidents and delays – was jinxed in some way. Disputes over the failure of the Sizzlas to perform as requested dragged on into January 1975, with Boorer claiming that he had not been fully briefed regarding the manner in which his vessels were to be used. Bradburn commented on the situation, recalling that Boorer had not made any comment about adverse humidity when the problems arose at Wookey Hole; he observed that the boats were clearly unsuitable for use. However, it was also suggested that Dorhill had not exercised proper business precautions in preparing for the shoot, and the BBC suggested to Boorer that the experience must have been useful in testing their experimental models. With the filming completed, Briant blamed the bad luck and mishaps on the arrow-heads found by Monique and threw them away.

Recording

By the time rehearsals began at Acton Room 602 on Saturday 23 November, Briant had struck up quite a rapport with Baker, and the two men were seeing each other socially. Following a schedule which he had implemented successfully with *Death to the Daleks*, Briant decided to spend the first day of each of his two-day studio sessions purely on camera rehearsals. He would then record on both the afternoon and evening of his second day. Furthermore, he would divide most of the material in his studios by location. So recording on Tuesday 3 December would cover most of the scenes set on Nerva, leaving the studio scenes from Voga and the Cybership for later on. As such, the first afternoon saw the recording of most of Part One in sequence, with some groupings for scenes on the transom and the crew deck (for Sarah viewing the video loop). It was soon clear that there were costume continuity problems with *The Sontaran Experiment*; the heavy coat worn by Baker at the end of the serial was not used, and Sladen was now sporting a different outfit from that seen in earlier sequences. The latter of these would later be covered by writing a change of costume for Sarah into *Genesis of the Daleks*.

The Nerva scenes for Parts Two and Three were recorded in the evening, with – for the first time – the actors inside the Cybermen costumes also providing the voices; Robbie developed a rather staccato delivery which was then electronically modulated to make it sound more mechanical. When Briant ran late, the last couple of scheduled scenes (Part Three, Scenes 14 and 16) in which Sarah returned to Nerva, if recorded that night, would have run over the 10 p.m. deadline, and so were left for remounting in the second studio session.

After a day off, rehearsals began again on Thursday 5 December, with one double-entendre line of dialogue in Part Four – 'We're heading for the biggest bang in history' (Scene 23) – causing particular hilarity amongst the cast. With some of the other Vogan cast members now joining the team, both Michael Wisher and Brian Grellis decided to play their subterranean characters as asthmatics. Studio recording on Tuesday 17 (with camera rehearsals the previous day) saw Baker pose with one of the Cybermen on the Vogan cave sets for BBC publicity and other press photographers. This was Baker's last work on the show prior to his debut on BBC1 in *Robot* a fortnight later (see the photograph on page 275).

The afternoon was spent on scenes at Tyrum's HQ, in the Cybership and then in the seven interlocking sets which comprised the cave areas and rock tunnel areas of Voga (with the Isocar being re-used from the location shoot). In the meantime, Tyrum's HQ set was re-dressed and most of the scenes set in Vorus' guildroom were recorded back on this set. The more complex scenes were left for the evening, when the bulk of Part Four (and the two scenes from Part Three left over from the previous shoot) were taped using the guildroom and Nerva control room sets. Two inserts were also recorded: the floor of Kellman's room smoking in Part One and CSO shots of a leaping Cybermat. Following this, the cast could take a break until work began in the New Year on *Genesis of the Daleks*.

The editing of *Revenge of the Cybermen* took longer than expected because of Briant's commitment to episodes of the BBC Scotland drama *Sutherland's Law*, so Hinchcliffe took over on some sessions. Part Three notably overran while Parts Two and Four were under time. Cuts and resequences were undertaken as appropriate; first edits of all the instalments apart from Part Two were broadcast (Part Two came from a second edit).

Carey Blyton had been considering his incidental music even before filming. The militaristic Vogan hawks would have music from trumpet, percussion and trombone while the Vogan doves had a softer version of the same melody. The Cybermen had a metallic arrangement of tubular bells, cornet and piccolo trumpet. There were delays in recording some of the music when the edited episodes were not ready, and some episodes were dubbed only days before transmission. Feeling some of Blyton's score had unsuitable comic overtones, Hinchcliffe arranged for Peter Howell, one of the composers at the BBC Radiophonic Workshop, to score extra sections of electronic music for Part Two, Scene 14 and Part Three, Scene 5.

Promotion and Reaction

On its original transmission, *Revenge of the Cybermen* was still against the talent show *New Faces* in most ITV regions, with *Sale of the Century* on ATV in the Midlands and repeats of ITC's *The Champions* on Southern. Part Three of the serial went out in a later slot than usually scheduled because of coverage of the FA Cup Final. Although the audience size was down on *Genesis of the Daleks* (a seasonal change that was usual as the summer months approached), the serial kept *Doctor Who* in the Top 30 shows of the week and gained the highest recorded audience appreciation figures for Season Twelve.

Selected Merchandise

○ NOVELIZATION: *Doctor Who and the Revenge of the Cybermen*: novelization by Terrance Dicks. Published May 1976 by Target Books/Tandem Publishing (paperback) and Allan Wingate (hardback). Included in *The Doctor Who Omnibus* from Book Club Associates in 1977. American edition: June 1979 by Pinnacle Books (paperback) and included in *The Adventures of Doctor Who* from Nelson Doubleday Inc in 1979. Revised Target edition as *Doctor Who – Revenge of the Cybermen* published May 1991.

○ INCIDENTAL MUSIC: *Sherlock Holmes meets Dr Who* (Upbeat Classics URCD 148) issued July 1999; includes incidental music comprising *Vogan Suite, Op 101 for Horn in F & Piano* (new recordings made July/August 1998).

○ VIDEOTAPES (ETC.): *Doctor Who – Revenge of the Cybermen* (BBC Video BBCV 2003/BBCB 2003 [Betamax]/BBCL 2003 [Laserdisc, V2000]) issued in edited version October 1983. Japanese version – subtitled, with brochure (Pony Video V128F1331), 1983. Unedited reissue (BBC Video BBCV 6773) issued April 1999. American edition: (Playhouse #3714) in 1987.

○ CYBERMAN TOY (Denys Fisher Toys UK, © 1976, released 1977).

Production Details

4D: Revenge of the Cybermen

Projects: 2344/7052-7055

Cast

Doctor Who	Tom Baker
Sarah Jane Smith	Elisabeth Sladen
Harry Sullivan	Ian Marter
Kellman	Jeremy Wilkin [1-3]
Commander Stevenson	Ronald Leigh-Hunt
Lester	William Marlowe
Warner	Alec Wallis [1]
Tyrum	Kevin Stoney [2-4]
Vorus	David Collings
Sheprah	Brian Grellis [2-3]
Magrik	Michael Wisher
Cyberleader	Christopher Robbie
First Cyberman	Melville Jones [2-4]

Uncredited:

Bodies [1]: Tony Lord, Pat Gorman
Colville (Voice) [1]: Michael Wisher
Vogan Radio Operator (Voice) [1]: Michael Wisher
Vogan Hawks: Cy Town [1-3], Leslie Weekes [1-3], David Billa [1-3], David Sulkin [2-3]
Vogan Dove Radio Operator [1]: Terry Walsh or Alan Chuntz
Cybermen [1-4]: Tony Lord, Pat Gorman
Monitor Voice [1-2]: Michael E Briant
Vogan Doves and Hawks: Harry Fielder [2-4], Barry Summerford [2-4], Roy Caeser [2-4]
Stunt men/Vogan Doves and Hawks [2-3]: Terry Walsh, Alan Chuntz

Vogan Doves [2-3]: Cy Town, Leslie Weekes, David Billa, David Sulkin
Stunt Double for Doctor Who [3-4]: Terry Walsh
Stunt Double for Commander Stevenson [3]: Alan Chuntz
Stunt Double for Harry Sullivan [4]: Alan Chuntz

Crew

Written by	Gerry Davis
Production Unit Manager	George Gallaccio
Production Assistant	John Bradburn
Title Music by	Ron Grainer & BBC Radiophonic Workshop
Title Sequence	Bernard Lodge
Incidental Music by	Carey Blyton*
Special Sound	Dick Mills
Visual Effects Designer	James Ward
Costume Designer	Prue Handley
Make-up	Cecile Hay-Arthur
Studio Lighting	Derek Slee
Studio Sound	Norman Bennett
Film Cameraman	Elmer Cossey
Film Sound	John Gatland
Film Editor	Sheila S Tomlinson
Script Editor	Robert Holmes
Designer	Roger Murray-Leach
Producer	Philip Hinchcliffe
Directed by	Michael E Briant

* Additional Music by Peter Howell, BBC Radiophonic Workshop [2-3]

Production History

Filming - Television Centre, Puppet Theatre
Tuesday 12 November 1974: 10.00am onwards
- Filmed model shots

Filming - Wookey Hole Caves, nr Wells, Somerset
Monday 18 November 1974: 11.00am onwards
- Cave A - Part Three TK 20 and Part Two TK 14,
- Cave B - Part Two TK 10 and Part Three TK 22

Tuesday 19 November 1974: 9.00am onwards
- Cave C - Part Three TK 23, 24 and Part Four TK 27
- Cave D - Part Three TK 21, 18, Part Two TK 9 and Part Four TK 30
- Cave E - Part Three TK 18 and Part Four TK 30

Wednesday 20 November 1974: 9.00am onwards
- Cave F - Part Two TK 9, Part Four TK 30, 1 and Part Three TK 21, 17, 9, 22, 19

Thursday 21 November 1974: 9.00am onwards

◦ Cave F – Part Four TK 28, 29 and Part Three TK 17

Studio Recording – Television Centre Studio 1
Tuesday 3 December 1974: 2.30pm–5.30pm & 7.30pm–10.00pm

◦ Part One: except scenes 12, 21A
◦ Part Two: except scenes 8, 12, 13, 15-17, 19, 20
◦ Part Three: scenes 1, 6 [transom], 2 [crew deck], 5, 7, 9, 10 [control room 1+2]
◦ Part Four: scenes 9 [transom], 11, 13 [crew deck]

Studio Recording – Television Centre Studio 3
Tuesday 17 December 1974: 2.30pm–5.30pm & 7.30pm–10.00pm

◦ Part Three: except scenes 1, 2, 5-7, 9, 10, 14, 16
◦ Part Four: except scenes 9, 11, 13
◦ Part One: scene 12 [guildroom], 21A [Cybership]
◦ Part Two: scene 16 [Tyrum HQ], 12 [Cyber control deck], 15, 17, 20, 19 [cave areas A-D], 8, 13 [guildroom]

Music

◦ Specially recorded incidental music by Carey Blyton. Recording Dates: Wednesday 19 March (Parts One and Two), Thursday 20 March (Parts Two and Three: cancelled), Wednesday 16 April (Parts Two and Three), Saturday 19 April (Part Four: cancelled), Friday 2 May (Part Four) at Lime Grove. Total: 30'54"
◦ Synthesizer music by Peter Howell, BBC Radiophonic Workshop. Recorded mid-April 1975 at Maida Vale. Total: 5'33"

Original Transmission – BBC1

Part One	Saturday 19 April 1975	5.35pm 5.36pm 24'19"	9.5M 24th 57
Part Two	Saturday 26 April 1975	5.30pm 5.30pm 24'24"	8.3M 28th –
Part Three	Saturday 3 May 1975	5.50pm 5.30pm 24'32"	8.9M 25th –
Part Four	Saturday 10 May 1975	5.35pm 5.30pm 23'21"	9.4M 22nd 58

REVENGE OF THE CYBERMEN

by Gerry Davis

Part One

OPENING TITLES

TELECINE 2 ❶

Sarah, Harry and the Doctor, hands clasped to the time bracelet, whirling in space. ❷

TELECINE 3
MODEL SHOT.

Establishing shot of Space Beacon Nerva
A repeat of Telecine 1, Story 4C. ❸

1. INT. CONTROL ROOM 1.

The Doctor, Sarah and Harry materialize in the clover-leaf kiosk. ❹

SARAH Thank heaven for that. We've made it haven't we?

DOCTOR WHO Of course we've made it, Sarah. Did you think we wouldn't?

SARAH In these past few weeks, yes. Quite frequently.

The Doctor holds up the copper bracelet.

DOCTOR WHO There's really nothing that can go wrong with a time ring. ~~Apart from~~ Except a molecular short circuit.

SARAH Doctor, the TARDIS isn't here.

DOCTOR WHO ~~Perhaps it hasn't got here. We've probably arrived a little early.~~ Well, it probably hasn't arrived yet – we're a little early.

HARRY Hasn't ~~got here~~ arrived yet?

DOCTOR WHO No, you see the TARDIS ~~will be~~ is drifting back through time, **Harry**. We'll have to wait for it to turn up.

HARRY I say, Doctor, do you – er do you want ~~that, Doctor~~ this ring thing?

DOCTOR WHO ~~This?~~ What, that?

HARRY Yes.

DOCTOR WHO No.

HARRY ~~Goodo… I mean, that is,~~ **Well**, I'd rather like **to have** it…

DOCTOR WHO ~~You'd better look after it carefully, Harry.~~ Well, you take good care of it, Harry.

He puts bracelet on table.

HARRY Oh, of course I will! ~~Thanks awfully.~~ Thank you.

The time bracelet has vanished. **5**

The Doctor laughs.

HARRY You knew that was going to happen, **didn't you?**

The Doctor snaps the transom-door release irritably. The door sighs open. A body rolls into the room.

A man in military-type uniform. They stare. Harry bends over him.

HARRY He's dead… been dead some time.

DOCTOR WHO How long?

HARRY A week or two, I'd say, though there's very little putrefaction…

DOCTOR WHO Sterile ~~environment~~ atmosphere, Harry.

HARRY Yes, exactly. No sign of injury. Nothing to indicate cause of death.

SARAH He was just sitting against the door as though he'd collapsed.

DOCTOR WHO But he wouldn't have been left for two weeks unless…

SARAH Unless what?

DOCTOR WHO ~~There must be~~ Unless there **was** something seriously wrong here. Come on.

2. INT. TRANSOM.

The Doctor, Sarah and Harry step out into the transom. They look along it and stand transfixed with shock and horror.

We pull back from them along the transom. Every few feet a man's body lies in the stiff-limbed posture of death. **6** *We keep tracking back until the group, still unmoving, is in*

distant long shot and the corpses might be a strafed infantry column on a French road. **7**

3. INT. CONTROL ROOM 2.

Warner is at the control console **8** *drooping with fatigue. He is in uniform and wears headphones of a futuristic pattern. A sharp asdic-type pinging jerks him awake.*

He goes into action on the controls and picks up a blip on the radar scope. **9**

WARNER This is Nerva Beacon calling Pluto-Earth flight one five. This is Nerva Beacon calling Pluto-Earth flight one five… Pluto-Earth flight one five. Are you reading me?

VOICE **10** *(Filter)* ~~Yes~~ Hello, Nerva Beacon, we read you clear. Our dropover ~~T.O.A.~~ **Tango Oscar Alpha** estimated at thirteen twenty.

WARNER ~~Hullo,~~ Pluto-Earth flight one five. Next notice, **urgent:** This beacon is a quarantined zone. We have a plague infection. I repeat, we have a plague infection.

VOICE *(Filter)* ~~Say again. You have what?~~

WARNER ~~Plague.~~ Your dropover is transferred to Ganymede Beacon, one nine ~~six~~ zero **six** seven **and** zero two. Do you ~~want~~ **require** a repeat on those vectors?

VOICE *(Filter)* **No** thanks, Nerva ~~Beacon~~. We got them. How bad are things there?

WARNER They're… they're pretty bad.

VOICE ~~*(Filter)* Hold contact, Nerva Beacon.~~

~~A few moments of static and then:~~

VOICE *(Filter)* Hullo, Nerva ~~Beacon. One of our crew has a brother doing a tour with you. Crewmaster Colville. Crewmaster Colville – is he all right?~~ Crewmaster Colville, I say again Crewmaster Colville is doing a tour with you. He's my brother – is he all right?

WARNER Hold contact. I'll check.

He works his switchboard.

4. INT. CREW DECK.

Stevenson, an older astronaut, is busy with paperwork at the mess table.

Lester, Warner's opposite number, turns from the intercom. **11**

Kellman, a civilian, is asleep on a makeshift bed.

WARNER *(Distort)* Commander Stevenson.

LESTER Warner wants **to speak to** you, sir.

Stevenson gets up wearily and crosses to the set. Kellman isn't asleep. We see him watching through half-shut eyes.

COMMANDER *(OOV)* Yes, Warner?

5. INT. CONTROL ROOM 2.

WARNER Sir, I'm in contact with the Pluto-Earth flight~~, sir~~. One of the crew wants news of his brother. Crewmaster Colville. What shall I tell him?

6. INT. CREW DECK.

COMMANDER Tell him ~~tell him~~ Colville's fine and say that… our medical staff have got the epidemic under control… ⑫ ~~Yes,~~ just that and nothing else. Thank you, Warner.

He turns away from the set.

KELLMAN Why don't you tell them the truth, Commander?

Stevenson eyes him with dislike.

COMMANDER I'm following the orders I was given by Earth Centre.

KELLMAN Operating the beacon to the last man?

COMMANDER If necessary, yes. You're just a civilian Kellman. You wouldn't understand.

KELLMAN How much longer can you go on – three of you trying to do the work of 50 men?

LESTER We've managed for ~~a~~ one week. We can manage for another ~~week~~.

KELLMAN And another after that..? No, Lester, this beacon's job is finished…

COMMANDER Nerva Beacon has a 30-year assignment. It will be that long before the last inward-bound ship has this new asteroid on its star chart.

LESTER ~~And~~ Until then there'll be a constant danger of space collision.

KELLMAN You deserve a medal for self-sacrifice beyond the bounds of stupidity.

He exits.

COMMANDER I've lost most of my crew in these last months… good friends among them. Yet a thing like that is still alive.

LESTER Probably because he ~~shut~~ locked himself ~~away~~ in that ~~office~~ cabin of his at the first sign of the plague. It's only in these last few days, ~~now we seem to have beaten it~~, that he's **dared** ~~poked~~ his nose outside.

The commander shrugs and turns heavily to his papers.

7. INT. TRANSOM.

The Doctor and his companions find their way barred by a cross shutter. Two bodies lie in the transom just behind them.

The Doctor finds that the shutter doesn't respond to the cell-control set in the wall. ⑬

SARAH Is it jammed~~, Doctor~~?

DOCTOR WHO The control's locked.

HARRY You mean we can't get any further?

DOCTOR WHO These poor chaps couldn't.

The Doctor turns thoughtfully and leans against the shutter.

DOCTOR WHO They were trapped in the ~~aft-section~~ after end, and left ~~here~~ to die. So whatever did it ~~must~~ might be on the other side of this door.

The Doctor takes out his sonic screwdriver and turns to the shutter.

DOCTOR WHO ~~Servicing panel for the magnetic coils.~~ Might be a way of opening ~~this~~ it.

SARAH Look – are you sure we're in the right place, Doctor? **I mean,** this doesn't ~~really~~ look like our Ark.

DOCTOR WHO Of course it doesn't – this is a ~~much earlier~~ different point in time. *(Looking round)*

SARAH How can you tell?

DOCTOR WHO Some of the equipment. ~~Yes, it's a beacon placed~~ This is probably a beacon, put in orbit to service and guide space freighters.

HARRY Then this is before the time of the solar flares when Earth was evacuated?

DOCTOR WHO Thousands of years ~~earlier~~ before, Harry.

SARAH I'm not even going to think about it. I shall only get a headache.

DOCTOR WHO All you have to remember is that this is where we parted company with the TARDIS. ~~Unless…~~

~~HARRY Unless what?~~

SARAH What is it?

DOCTOR WHO If they've changed things around the TARDIS might ~~turn up~~ materialize in the forward control ~~centre~~ rooms!

Down the transom behind them a Cybermat scurries out of a grille. It is triangular in shape

with large red electronic 'eyes' set on top of its
head and a scaled body like a silverfish. **14**

On this appearance, however, we get only a
quick glimpse of the thing.

8. INT. CONTROL ROOM 2.

Warner is nodding at the console. He shakes his
head, fighting off fatigue, and notices a faint
flicker of activity on his spectrum monitor. **15**
It is an unexpected waveband. Puzzled, he
tunes across to it. A thin voice comes faintly
over the ether:

VOICE **16** (Heavy distort)… anyone hear me, I
am calling… Anyone… Can anyone hear me?
I am calling Nerva Beacon…

The voice fades out in a crackle of static.

WARNER This is Nerva Beacon. I repeat, this is
Nerva Beacon. **Hullo, are you reading me?**
~~Hullo, do you read me? This is Nerva Beacon.~~
~~I repeat this is Nerva Beacon.~~

~~**VOICE** (Distort) I read you. I read you is that~~
~~Nerva Beacon?~~

~~**WARNER** Yes, receiving you on 398 kilohertz.~~
~~Strength 2. Please return to 127 decimal 35~~
~~and repeat message.~~

TELECINE 4
INT. CAVE. DAY.

VOICE **17** Can anyone hear me? Can anyone
hear me? Can anyone – **18**

Close on an X transmitter, a limp hand is
dragging down its front.

WARNER (VO filter) ~~Hullo, Voga, do you read~~
~~me? This is Nerva Beacon~~

Pull back to show the radio operator,
a young Vogan, slumping to the ground.
He is dead.

Behind him stand two burly members of the
Vorus SS. One of them replaces a weapon in
his belt. The other reaches forward to pull the
plug on Warner.

WARNER (VO filter) ~~Come in, Voga, This is~~
~~Nerva Beacon, I repeat –~~ This is Nerva
Beacon calling on 398…

The jack plug is wrenched from its socket.

8B. INT. CONTROL ROOM 2.

WARNER ~~This is Nerva Beacon calling on 397.~~
Do you read me?

He looks round and sees Kellman. **19** He
shrugs and stops his work on the transmitter.

WARNER Professor, this new asteroid – this rock
or whatever it is, are you sure there's no life on
it?

KELLMAN On Voga? Of course not! How can
there be?

WARNER I don't know, Professor.

Warner punches up a scanner picture of
Voga. **20**

WARNER But I just picked up a call and that's
the only place it could have come from. It's the
only place near enough.

KELLMAN Hallucinations, Warner. You've been
sitting here too long.

WARNER Where did that rock come from,
anyway? What system?

KELLMAN Nobody knows. It was first detected
in our system 50 years ago when it was
captured by Jupiter.

WARNER So there could be life on it?

KELLMAN Impossible! An asteroid that size
drifting in the vacuum between star systems?
Nothing could have lived under those
conditions.

WARNER All the same, I'd swear that's where the
transmission was from.

KELLMAN Warner, I'm an exographer. I've been
down there. I set up a transmat station there.
I've spent the last six months studying rock
samples from Voga – what are you doing?

WARNER Logging it… **21** Unidentified call
apparently from direction of Voga.

KELLMAN You're mad. I've said all along it was a
mistake to keep this control room operating.

WARNER Commander Stevenson's decision.
Nothing to do with you, is it?

KELLMAN Every time anyone ~~moves~~ **goes** down
that transom there's a risk of spreading the
plague.

WARNER If the commander says this beacon is
staying operational, it stays operational.

Kellman exits.

9. INT. THE TRANSOM.

The Doctor has removed a panel in the
shutter. **22** He knocks out the disc of metal
and reaches through to work the cell control on
the other side.

SARAH Can you reach, ~~Doctor~~?
DOCTOR WHO Yes, I think so… If you two would put your weight against the door and stop it ~~moving~~ opening too suddenly –
~~HARRY Like this?~~
DOCTOR WHO ~~Splendid. (Stretching) I'm greatly attached to my humerus and I'd hate to lose it.~~ I don't want to lose my arm, I'm rather attached to it.
HARRY Like so?
DOCTOR WHO It's so handy. Yes.
The shutter opens. The Doctor pulls his arm back hastily. Beyond the shutter 23 *the transom is empty. They step through and the Doctor operates the control to close the shutter.* 24
~~DOCTOR WHO Right.~~
SARAH *(As Doctor's hand is caught)* Doctor! Get this through… quick.
DOCTOR WHO *(To Sarah)* Thank you.
He glares at Harry.
HARRY Well, what have I done now?

10. INT. CONTROL ROOM 2.

Warner is struggling to keep awake. He gazes fuzzily at the console dials. Something registers. 25 *He takes a closer look, then moves to the intercom.*
WARNER Hullo, Lester? Is the commander there?
COMMANDER *(Distort)* I'm here, Warner, go ahead.
WARNER Listen, somebody has just operated the aft-transom shutter. I know it's impossible but it's happened.* 26

11. INT. CREW DECK.

Lester is staring at the commander.
WARNER The information's right here on the electronic register.
LESTER Everybody in that after-section had the plague, ~~sir~~. Nobody can be left alive.
COMMANDER Exactly… And the shutters were sealed ~~Exactly~~. They couldn't **possibly** be operated from the after-section. **Come on.** We'll have to check the transom.
He hands gun to Lester and leads the way out. Lester follows.

12. INT. GUILD ROOM. DAY. 27

On the body of the radio operator. 28 *The two burly SS members* 29 *stand on either side of the body.*
Ornate golden doors open and Vorus strides in with his chief scientist Magrik. He stares down at the body, prods it disdainfully with his curly-toed golden boot. Magrik is in BG.
VORUS Take it out and bury it. Bury it deep.
The two guards drag the body out. Vorus paces.
VORUS Why?
MAGRIK Your plan frightened him, Vorus. Sometimes it frightens me.
VORUS But would you warn the humans? Do you feel kinship?
MAGRIK No, **no**. It is simply that there are so many things that might go wrong.
VORUS Of course. It is a big plan. But it will work, ~~Magrik~~. You and I together, **Magrik**, will make it work.
MAGRIK Yes, but can we trust our agent?
VORUS We can trust in his greed. Gold buys humans and we have more gold here in Voga than in the rest of the known galaxy.
MAGRIK But he has not communicated.
VORUS Better that he should not at this time. ~~By now,~~ The Cybermen will be monitoring our radio link.
MAGRIK The mention of Cybermen fills me with dread.
VORUS Magrik, you feel fear because we have lived too long in **this underground** darkness. When I lead our people into the light, all those ancient fears will fall away.
MAGRIK **The light…** Yes. I believe you, Vorus.

13. INT. CONTROL ROOM 2.

Warner nodding over controls. A Cybermat creeps out of cover behind him. 30 *It rears up almost on end* 31 *and leaps at Warner's neck.* 32 *Warner stiffens, cries out and knocks Cybermat away as he staggers to his feet. Cybermat scurries away. Warner falls. He struggles to reach alarm and then slumps.*

INT. TRANSOM.

The commander and Lester with guns.
The commander and Lester staring at the shutter. The commander touches the panel the

Doctor operated on. It moves under his hand. He inspects it.

COMMANDER The rivets have been taken out.

LESTER From the other side, **sir**? **That's impossible**, they're blind-headed, ~~sir~~.

COMMANDER They could have been loosened with a sonic vibrator.

LESTER ~~Then~~ Well in that case, Warner was right. Somebody has come through.

COMMANDER ~~Come on~~ Right. We'll **have to** check every section.

15. INT. CONTROL ROOM 2.

Warner is dying. There is a black 'tree trunk' of nerves spreading up from the base of his neck. ㉝ *He is gasping for air.*

Kellman is looking down at him.

Kellman crosses and sits at desk. He takes out tape cassette and pulls out tape. ㉞

16. INT. CONTROL ROOM 1 CORRIDOR.

The Doctor, Sarah and Harry are looking round.

16A. INT. CONTROL ROOM.

SARAH We've just left here.

DOCTOR WHO No, no ~~Sarah~~, this is the forward control ~~centre~~ room.

HARRY ~~And the TARDIS isn't here, either.~~ Well, the TARDIS doesn't seem to be here either, does it?

DOCTOR WHO No. ~~Presumably~~ but the time ring was designed with a slight safety margin. We can expect the TARDIS to arrive soon.

HARRY ㉟ ~~You mean it will just materialize?~~ Doctor, do you expect me to believe that that old police box is going to materialize out of nothing...

DOCTOR WHO ~~(Nods) And it won't wait for us, either, we'll have to catch it while it's in our co-ordinate.~~

SARAH ~~Sounds like a London bus.~~

The Commander and Lester enter.

COMMANDER All right. Get your hands up.

DOCTOR WHO ~~So when it does arrive, Harry.~~

COMMANDER I said get your hands up.

DOCTOR WHO ~~Certainly.~~

Sign Language – Front Axial Projection

The tree-branch lines of plague make-up applied to Warner and Sarah in *Revenge of the Cybermen* were made to 'pulse' by means of a technique called Front Axial Projection (FAP).

Director Michael E. Briant had used the technique before, with limited effect, to make the Exxilon rebels appear phosphorescent in *Death to the Daleks* (1974) and, more effectively, to provide *The Green Death* (1973).

The basic principle of the technique was that particular materials – such as 'scotchlite' – would brilliantly reflect light shone from directly in front back along the same axis. From directly in front, anything coated with such material then appears to shine or glow while everything else is less well lit – the same way that a road sign appears clearly lit to the driver of the car whose headlights are shining directly towards it.

In the studio, a particular camera was fitted with a set of lights around its lens that shone directly at the 'target'. The FAP material then reflected the light straight back along its axis to the camera. If the lights were flashed, then the reflective glow of the material also strobed – so that, in this case, the veins of poison seemed to pulse.

LESTER Who are you and how did you get here?

DOCTOR WHO I'm the Doctor, this is Sarah Jane Smith, Harry Sullivan… We're ~~just~~ travellers.

Kellman enters from control room 2.

KELLMAN You'd better ~~take a look~~ step in here, Commander.

COMMANDER What is it?

KELLMAN See for yourself.

He stands aside. The commander moves the Doctor and company ahead of him.

COMMANDER ~~Move~~. *(To Lester)* Watch them.

17. INT. CONTROL ROOM 2.

Warner is collapsed over the console. The commander follows his line of prisoners. He gives a shocked exclamation and strides over to Warner.

~~**COMMANDER** Warner.~~

He puts out a hand. Warner flops sideways. The tree of nerves is a black tracery almost to his temple.

The commander pulls back, unconsciously trying to wipe the contamination from his hand. He levels his gun and slides the bolt.

The Doctor steps forward.

DOCTOR WHO What are you ~~doing~~ going to do?

COMMANDER Get back. He's ~~caught~~ got the plague – ~~it's~~ this is the only way to deal with it.

DOCTOR WHO The man is sick. He needs treatment.

LESTER There's no treatment. All we can do is try to stop ~~it~~ the infection spreading ~~further~~!

DOCTOR WHO *(Shielding Warner)* I'm sorry, gentlemen. I can't allow ~~that~~ it.

COMMANDER You can't allow it?

DOCTOR WHO My colleague is a doctor of medicine, and I am a Doctor of many things. If we can examine him –

KELLMAN Commander, I'm afraid you'll have to kill these people too. They've brought the plague in here.

DOCTOR WHO Who's the homicidal maniac?

COMMANDER You say you're doctors? Did Earth Centre send you?

DOCTOR WHO Yes. We're from Earth, ~~yes, and~~ we want to help you.

LESTER Help us? **Don't you realize** you've ~~carried~~ brought the infection through from the after-section!

SARAH ~~Oh, use a little commonsense! If you think we carried it, how come~~ Oh don't be ridiculous! How could we have brought it through when he's infected and we aren't?

HARRY ~~Perhaps the virus hopped off us and ran on ahead, eh?~~ It's quite impossible – we've had no contact with him.

DOCTOR WHO ~~You haven't~~ I don't think you've got plague here, Commander.

COMMANDER According to our own medical team, we have.

DOCTOR WHO ~~But~~ Did they identify – it?

LESTER They didn't have ~~much~~ time. They were among the first victims.

DOCTOR WHO Well, now you've got a new medical team… Well, Commander.

COMMANDER ~~I'll allow you to~~ All right, you can examine him.

DOCTOR WHO Thank you.

COMMANDER ~~If you're going to try to treat him,~~ But not here, it'll have to be done in the crew quarters. This control room ~~has to~~ must be kept operational.

KELLMAN *(Ironical)* Oh yes – at all costs!

He exits.

COMMANDER You help the doctors with him Lester. I'll take over the console.

~~**DOCTOR WHO** You two can manage, can't you? I've a few little things to attend to here.~~

~~**HARRY** Sure. Come on, Lester.~~

LESTER Once the infection develops they've got a few minutes to live.

SARAH I'll help **you**.

They carry Warner out.

The Doctor is examining the console. With a finger he traces the outline of a serrated scratch mark left by a Cybermat.

18. INT. KELLMAN'S OFFICE (& CONTROL ROOM 2).

Kellman wearing earphones. He turns up the volume on his bug-control. **36**

DOCTOR WHO Have you noticed these rather strange scratches, Commander? **37**

COMMANDER Can't say that I **have** –

DOCTOR WHO All over your ship. ~~What bothers me is that~~ I've ~~come across~~ seen them before somewhere… If only I could remember **where**.
COMMANDER Is it important?
DOCTOR WHO Everything's important.
He is prowling the deck, studying everything. He stops, staring down at Warner's tape log.
DOCTOR WHO Well, well, well!
COMMANDER **What is it?**
DOCTOR WHO I've just made a third interesting discovery about your plague virus, Commander.
COMMANDER A third?
DOCTOR WHO ~~Oh,~~ Yes – one, it scratches metal. Two, it attacks **its victims** so suddenly ~~its victims are~~ **they become** unconscious before they can even ~~reach an alarm bell~~ **raise the alarm – and three…**
COMMANDER Go on.
DOCTOR WHO ~~Three~~. *(He hands Stevenson the logbook* ㊳ *)* ~~It tears tape out of logbooks~~ **It removes tape from radio-logs**. It must be ~~an inquisitive and literate~~ **a very literate and inquisitive** virus.
The Commander stares at the book.
COMMANDER What **exactly** are you trying to tell me, Doctor?
DOCTOR WHO Whatever it is that's ~~been~~ attacking your crew, **Commander,** it's certainly not ~~any kind of~~ a plague.
Kellman shows fear and hatred of this too-knowing interloper.

19. INT. CREW DECK.

Harry is doing his medical best for Warner. Lester and Sarah are helping.
HARRY Never seen anything like ~~it~~ **this before**. His temperature's just shooting up.
SARAH **Harry,** I make his pulse a hundred and twenty.
LESTER It's always the same. They just seem to burn up. Warner's lasted longer than most.
HARRY ~~He has~~ A very strong constitution.
LESTER ~~Yeah.~~ He's **as** tough as an old boot.
SARAH How long is it since all this started?
LESTER This… **This** is the 79th day.
SARAH And you've had no outside help ~~at all~~?
LESTER Earth Centre decided to isolate us.
HARRY A bit ruthless, isn't it?

LESTER They reckon its better to lose one space crew than chance carrying ~~some~~ **an** extra-terrestrial disease back to Earth. ㊴
Warner chokes, Harry bends over him.

20. INT. CONTROL ROOM 2 (& KELLMAN'S OFFICE).

Doctor Who still weighing things up, pacing and probing.
DOCTOR WHO Who's your civilian?
COMMANDER Professor Kellman? He's an exographer.
DOCTOR How interesting. Planetary survey. Of what?
COMMANDER Jupiter.
DOCTOR WHO I thought Jupiter~~'s~~ **had already** been thoroughly studied?
COMMANDER ~~Kellman's~~ **Yes, he's** interested in its new satellite.
Doctor Who turns from the matterbeam controls.
DOCTOR WHO ~~Fascinating!~~ **What?** You mean there are now 13?
The commander punches up a scanner picture of Voga.
COMMANDER Turned up ~~about~~ 50 years ago – that's why this beacon's out here. A lot of the great circle freighters haven't got it on their charts yet.
DOCTOR WHO What's it called?
COMMANDER Neo-Phobos originally. But Kellman's renamed it Voga.
Doctor Who stares.
DOCTOR WHO Voga..? Of course!
~~COMMANDER What?~~
DOCTOR WHO ~~He's~~ **Has he** been down there?
COMMANDER Kellman? He set up ~~the~~ **a** transmat – why?
DOCTOR WHO Voga – Voga – the planet of gold! Yes, it's all coming back to me
COMMANDER What's coming back to you?
DOCTOR WHO Cybermen!
He looks appalled.
DOCTOR WHO ~~Why have I been so slow? Cybermen, Commander,~~ That's what we're up against, **Commander – Cybermen!**
COMMANDER But surely, **Doctor,** Cybermen died out centuries ago?

DOCTOR WHO They disappeared after their attack on Voga at the end of the Cyberwar. Not the same thing as dying out, Commander. They're ~~totally~~ utterly ruthless. **Total machine creatures.**

21. INT. KELLMAN'S OFFICE.

Kellman still listening.

He removes his headphones. He takes a drawer from his desk and, from behind the drawer, produces a hidden transmitter. ④⓪

It is a compact, futuristic device.

He sets up the telescopic aerial, opens a panel in the wall, plugs the set into the ship's main power line.

He starts tapping out an urgent signal.

TELECINE 5
MODEL SHOT.

The Cyberman spaceship hanging motionless in the blackness of space. It is a long, sinister, rakish-looking vessel.

We hear the rapid staccato whistle of the Morse message.

We track in towards the ship's prow. In close-up the two ducts in the nose look like eyes. The effect is not unlike the headmast of a Cyberman.

21A. INT. CYBERSHIP. ④①

Close shot of the Cyberleader ④② *flanked by two Cybermen. The Morse message is loud and clear. Suddenly the Cyberleader makes a decisive gesture.*

One of his Cybermen immediately reaches out with his huge silver hand for the firing lever.

TELECINE 6
MODEL SHOT.

Flame blasts from the spacecraft's rockets. It moves slowly forward, turning through 90 degrees and then accelerates away at an ever-increasing speed.

22. INT. CREW DECK.

Warner moans softly.
Sarah bends over him.

SARAH ~~Are you sure there's nothing you can do, Harry?~~

The Doctor comes hurrying in, followed by the commander.

DOCTOR WHO How is he?

HARRY ~~Beyond help,~~ I'm afraid **he's had it,** Doctor.

COMMANDER **You'd better** take over the control room, Lester.

The Doctor bends over Warner, takes out a magnifying glass for a closer inspection.

Lester exits and the Doctor studies the base of Warner's neck.

DOCTOR WHO **Yes, just** as I thought.

Hands his glass to Harry.

DOCTOR WHO ~~Take a look.~~

HARRY *(A beat)* ~~There seem to be two punctures~~ You mean the two puncture marks.

DOCTOR WHO Like ~~the bite of a serpent.~~ a snake bite.

SARAH You ~~don't~~ mean venom~~, Doctor~~?

DOCTOR WHO ~~Yes,~~ He's been injected with poison.

Warner convulses, then sighs and is silent.
Harry bends over him.
Harry pulls a sheet up over Warner.

SARAH Poor man.

DOCTOR WHO If only I'd been quicker, I might have saved him.

COMMANDER How? Is there an antidote?

DOCTOR WHO ~~There's the~~ A matterbeam. ~~It~~ disperses human molecules. ~~But this~~ **That** type of alien poison ~~would~~ **might** be separated and rejected.

SARAH Alien?

COMMANDER **Now** where are you going?

DOCTOR WHO I smell a rat.

He exits. The commander looks perplexed.

COMMANDER **You know,** I sometimes ~~I~~ wonder if your friend is quite right in the head. ~~We don't carry rats aboard the beacon.~~

SARAH If the Doctor's scented a rat, Commander, he'll find one.

23. INT. TRANSOM.

The Doctor is stooped, examining another scratch mark he has found on the floor. Ahead of him, down the transom, Kellman emerges from a door. He looks carefully around but the Doctor is below his sight line.

Kellman locks the door and goes off. The Doctor rises and moves to the door.

23A. CORRIDOR.

The Doctor tries the door. Then takes out his sonic screwdriver.

25. INT. KELLMAN'S OFFICE.

The Doctor enters the room. He is searching carefully.

It is simply furnished: a day bed, a locker, a desk/table, filing cabinets and a single chair.

The Doctor leafs through files and papers, finds and inspects the hidden radio, **43** *then turns his attention to Kellman's locker.*

He pulls aside a pair of shoes – checks – balances them. **44**

He tips one shoe over and a string-necked bag drops out. He opens the bag and tips a little of its contents on to his hand.

We see the rich, dull gleam of gold dust.

DOCTOR WHO Gold…

He runs it between his fingers in deep thought. There is a rattle at the door. The Doctor jumps.

26. INT. TRANSOM.

Kellman at the door to his cabin. He puts his key in the lock, turns it, enters.

27. INT. KELLMAN'S OFFICE.

Kellman's POV of the empty cabin. No sign of the Doctor.

Kellman crosses to the desk. He takes out a metal box and puts it down on the desk top… feels a grating under the box. He rubs his fingers on the desk – a smear of gold dust. **45**

Kellman stands quietly. From his face we know he knows. He looks round the cabin. The Doctor has to be under the bed.

Whistling softly, he moves with studied nonchalance to the farther wall.

On the Doctor: face flat to the floor, watching Kellman's boots.

Kellman has opened a panel in the wall. He takes out three fuses, closes the panel, then pulls down the master switch. **46** *Smiling to himself, he leaves the room.*

28. INT. TRANSOM.

Kellman comes out into the transom and locks the door.

29. INT. KELLMAN'S OFFICE.

The Doctor is waiting to be sure Kellman really has gone.

He starts to wriggle from under the bed. A thin wisp of smoke rises from the floor. **47**

The Doctor gazes at it. The smoke thickens. The composition floor starts to bubble. **48** *The Doctor scrambles from under the bed and goes to the door. Again he gets out his sonic screwdriver. The floor is rumbling under his feet. Fumes are filling the room.*

The Doctor coughs. He pulls his scarf over his mouth and nose and bends frantically to work on the lock.

30. INT. CREW DECK.

Harry is holding the door.

HARRY Where are we going to ~~take~~ put him, Commander?

COMMANDER When this trouble first started we turned part of the infrastructure into a mortuary.

LESTER ~~But then it got so that nobody would touch the bodies. They were left where they fell.~~ Yes, we used to leave them where they dropped.

SARAH We saw.

COMMANDER ~~All right?~~

LESTER ~~Yes.~~

They carry Warner out. Harry leaves. Closing door. Sarah sighs. She picks up the old book. **49**

VOICE … constellation of Zeros X Twenty, the intensity of radiation caused severe distortion. When the computer dealt with all original errors, it was found that the intensity was minus –

31. INT. KELLMAN'S OFFICE. **50**

Doctor in Kellman's office.

He swings across cupboard to door. Takes out sonic screwdriver and leans out but can't reach door.

32. INT. CREW DECK.

VOICE Star charts for outer space section four carry a two per cent error factor. Solar readings should be independently taken when patrolling this area…

Sarah is reading. 🔢

Suddenly, from a duct behind her, a Cybermat appears. Its red eye-lights flash and it creeps towards her back. It leaves the now familiar serrated scratch on the wall.

33. INT. KELLMAN'S OFFICE.

Doctor choking. Smoke billowing from the floor.

34. INT. CREW DECK. 🔢

VOICE … magazines which departed from the ship's cell. In the constellation of Zeros X Twenty, the intensity of radiation caused severe distortion. When the computer dealt with all original errors –

Sarah switches off monitor.

The Cybermat appears. 🔢

The Cybermat launches itself at Sarah's throat. She screams. 🔢 *It clings to her neck.*

She screams and beats at it with her hands. 🔢 🔢

35. INT. THE TRANSOM. 🔢

Distant screams from Sarah.

The Doctor hears Sarah's screams. He struggles up.

DOCTOR WHO Sarah!

36. INT. CREW DECK.

The Cybermat drops to the floor. Sarah reels back, clutching her neck.

The Doctor rushes in. The Cybermat whirls towards him.

DOCTOR WHO Don't let it touch you!

He pulls the bag of gold dust from his pocket and flings it at the Cybermat. The Cybermat spins round and round in a spray of gold dust. It comes to a stop. The red eye-lights fade out.

SARAH Ugh. Ugh.

Gasping for breath, she starts to move towards him. Then she collapses. He catches her. He looks at her neck. Already the black tree of nerve lines is spreading upwards. 🔢

CLOSING TITLES

---

① Telecine 1 was the film of the opening titles. This insert sequence lasted a total of 2'30", and was filmed without sound.

② At the start of the episode, the regulars lay on a yellow CSO floor, moving so that it would appear that they were spinning through time and space and were shot from above to be superimposed on a starscape. This was shot through a rotating lens and merged with film of the Nerva model from *The Ark in Space* (Telecine 3) to simulate the journey back to the beacon from Skaro, by time ring. The sequence was recorded with *Genesis of the Daleks* Part Three.

③ The opening model shot of *The Ark in Space*, though this was originally recorded as video footage. Telecine 2 was superimposed over the shot of Nerva.

④ The technique of rolling back the tape and mixing in a new image (roll-back-and-mix) was used for the arrival.

⑤ Roll-back-and-mix was used for the disappearing time ring, with additional blue flashes added in from a spark generator.

⑥ Most of the bodies were mannequins, though Pat Gorman and Tony Lord played two of them. (Gorman and Lord later played the non-speaking Cybermen.)

⑦ The early transom scenes (2, 7, 9, 14) were recorded together, with breaks in between to reposition the dead bodies so as to make it look as though the Doctor, Sarah and Harry were passing through different sections.

⑧ The control desk featured five monochrome monitors showing schematics of Nerva as well as images from the crew-deck set, and also the output of a tiny lynx camera mounted on the control desk itself. Text and main graphics (like the image of Voga in Scene 8B) were shown on a larger CSO screen above the console.

9 For the control room 2 set, the main yellow CSO screen displayed a mixture of a red radar trace from an oscilloscope and also 'Anchor' captioning to give information on Pluto-Earth flight one-five (described in the technical notes as 'mumbo jumbo'):

> PLUTO-EARTH ONE-FIVE
>
> Incoming
>
> Vectors   13.73.74 (para)
>
> 18.00.36 .....
>
> 15.55.31 (para)
>
> Control 00703009 Positive
>
> Last input update at 22.14.5

10 The voice was provided by Michael Wisher.

11 Warner appears on a black-and-white monitor on Lester's console.

12 Stevenson's first words (to this point) are played into the previous scene.

13 There was a recording break at this point to remove all but four of the bodies.

14 The Cybermat prop was pulled along the floor of the transom using a string.

15 The 'Anchor' text on the monitor reads:

> K H 397
>
> Bearing
>
> 172N
>
> 43E

16 The voice was provided by Michael Wisher.

17 Michael Wisher's voice was dubbed over the scene. An extra played the Vogan trying to contact Nerva.

18 The Vogan turns to find two Vogan militia aiming guns. They shoot him.

19 Kellman enters through a door marked 'CREW AREA 3'.

20 A caption slide CSO'd on to the main screen. It was intended to include a caption 'VOGA' but this was not done.

21 The main screen displays:

> 18.57 Hrs.
>
> DAY 3
>
> WEEK 47
>
> LOG unidentified
>
> Call apparent
>
> Direction VOGA.

Though, due a slight mispositioning of the CSO, the first character of each line is off the left of the screen.

22 The scene opens with a view from the other side of the door showing the Doctor's hand wriggling through the hole he has made.

23 The other side of the shutter is labelled 'FORWARD AREA P SECTION'.

24 This sequence was slightly expanded with ad-libs from the regulars, worked out during rehearsals, so that the Doctor's arm was caught in the door.

25 A light flashes on a schematic map of Nerva, accompanied by a warning bleep.

26 Warner's second sentence was included in Scene 11, with Warner reporting on the monitor.

27 The guildroom set featured the circular motif that was later associated with the Time Lords from *The Deadly Assassin* (1976).

28 A trickle of blood was added to the Vogan's forehead.

29 Referred to in the camera directions as 'hawks'.

30 Briant opted to have the movement of the Cybermats achieved by numerous different techniques. The first one seen in the transom was pulled along on a string. CSO was generally used to show a rod puppet being manipulated into a leaping position for the attack shots, and a flexible prop was then held by the actor playing the victim for close-ups. Briant later felt he should have opted for remote-control props only.

㉛ A CSO'd rod-puppet Cybermat was used to show it rearing up. This same shot was used in Part Two, Scene 14 (as was the CSO shot of the Cybermat emerging from behind a pedestal) and Part Four, Scene 13.

㉜ A 'static' prop Cybermat was thrown at Warner. He caught it and 'wrestled' with it.

㉝ After Warner was attacked, Wallis was made up with veins of reflective Front Axial Projection (FAP) material (see panel below); this meant that one camera fitted with an FAP light could make the veins appear to pulse red. More make-up was added as his condition worsened.

㉞ In the original treatment Kellman tore pages from Warner's logbook.

㉟ Harry's line is heard, faintly, over an inserted scene of Kellman in control room 2 as he hears them. This is followed by the commander and Lester arriving in the control room 1 corridor section.

㊱ Kellman enters his cabin and assembles a small viewing screen from some equipment. A small speaker is hidden inside the back of his hairbrush.

㊲ The Doctor and Stevenson are heard through the hairbrush-speaker. Kellman watches them on a small screen, achieved by using yellow CSO and inlaying the picture from a camera with a wide-angled lens positioned above the control room 2 set.

㊳ There is confusion here about whether the log is a book (the original intention) or a tape (which was the case).

㊴ The Cybermen use infected sugar to create a plague in *The Moonbase* (1967). That plague is referred to by the Cybermen as Neurotrope X, and its victims become covered in a tree-like tracery of black lines following the nerves under the skin.

㊵ The communications device is actually in the drawer.

㊶ An 'Anchor' device was used to relay 'Numbers + mumbo jumbo' to the main screen of the Cybership.

㊷ The Cyberleader is distinguished from the other Cybermen by his partially black helmet (see the picture from this scene on page 316).

㊸ The Doctor also finds the hairbrush and reveals its mechanism.

㊹ The bag of gold is in the drawer with the radio.

㊺ Kellman finds the hairbrush with its back left half-open.

㊻ He also attaches crocodile clips and leads to a heating vent close to the floor.

㊼ A small section of floor was built as a model by Visual Effects and smoke was pumped through a crack in it.

㊽ A spark generator was used to add blue flashes between the Doctor's feet as he stands on the floor.

㊾ Sarah actually knocks against a control and switches on a monitor. The film displayed was 13 feet of silent 16mm material called *Rocket Man*; this had been provided by Nassau for the BBC documentary *Thanks For The Frying Pan* broadcast Saturday 11 May 1974, and Michael Briant provided the voice-over.

㊿ This scene was shifted to Part Two.

(51) Sarah is also reading a contemporary issue of New English Library's *Science Fiction Monthly* magazine.

(52) The CSO shots of the Cybermat attacking Sarah and other visual effects shots for this and Scene 36 were all shot at the end of this scene. The visual effects instructions for the sequences were:

> Stick 'Mat':
> 1. In top L rear up. 2. Jump out top R. 3. Fall in from top R. 4. Rear up look R. 5. Throw 'gold dust' on it. 6. Mat. Go potty. 7. Light out. 8. Lie still.

(53) Blue CSO was used to show the Cybermat appearing over a pipe.

(54) Elisabeth Sladen was struck by a fit of giggles during this sequence.

(55) The episode ends here. The subsequent scenes were moved to Part Two.

(56) There was a recording break after this scene to apply make-up to Sarah's neck to show the puncture marks and the plague infection.

(57) Ahead of this is a short sequence of the Doctor finally managing to open the door with his sonic screwdriver.

(58) The episode actually ends as the Cybermat attacks Sarah and she tries to fight it off, in Scene 34.

REVENGE OF THE CYBERMEN

by Gerry Davis

Part Two

OPENING TITLES

1. INT. CREW DECK.

Replay the closing moments of Part One. ❶
Sarah collapses.
Harry, the commander and Lester arrive back.

HARRY ~~Was that Sarah?~~ **That sounded like Sarah.**

He sees the Doctor supporting her.

HARRY What's happened?

DOCTOR WHO That Cybermat**'s happened**, Harry… **Quick, into** the transmat beam. **Quickly as you can.** It's the only way of getting the poison out of her system.

LESTER She's got the plague.

DOCTOR WHO No, **sir** – that's your so-called plague, **Commander.**

COMMANDER Is ~~that~~ **this** thing still dangerous, Doctor?

DOCTOR WHO Not any more. But there are bound to be others around.

The Doctor and Harry exit with Sarah.
Lester lends a hand.
The commander kicks the Cybermat gently. ❷

2. INT. CONTROL ROOMS 1 & 2.

In the matterbeam.

DOCTOR WHO Hang on to her, Harry. You'd better travel with her.

HARRY ~~Right~~. Where are we going?

The Doctor leaps out and goes to the controls.
Lester is watching.
The commander enters.

DOCTOR WHO ~~The beam's set~~ I'll set the beam for Voga. You know how to work the reciprocator~~, don't you~~?

HARRY ~~Oh the switch thing!~~ Yes, I've seen you do it.

DOCTOR WHO ~~Right, then –~~ off you go. ~~Every second counts now.~~ No time to lose.

He works the control.
Harry stands stiffly.
The transmat hums.
Harry stands rigid, holding Sarah, staring at the Doctor. The Doctor stares back.
A beat.
The Doctor yanks the back off the control box.

LESTER Has it ~~broken down~~ gone wrong, Doctor?

The Doctor stares grimly into the intricacies of the box.

DOCTOR WHO Sabotage.

COMMANDER Sabotage?

DOCTOR WHO Somebody has taken the pentalion drive!

COMMANDER But who – ?

DOCTOR WHO Who ~~tore~~ removed the tape from your radio log? Who used Cybermats to murder your crew? **And** who is desperate to cut all connection between this beacon and Voga?

3. INT. KELLMAN'S OFFICE.

Kellman with headset on.

COMMANDER You mean Kellman? ❸

DOCTOR WHO *(VO filter)* Exactly! Kellman. Your friendly exographer must be working ~~with~~ for the Cybermen, **Commander**.

LESTER *(VO filter)* Then what are we waiting for? Let's get him!

Kellman evacuating. He opens the metal box, pockets the pentalion drive. ❹
Opens a desk drawer, takes out a gun, sticks it in his belt.
He hides his radio and bugging gear in the secret compartment at the back of the desk. ❺

6. INT. CORRIDOR TO KELLMAN'S OFFICE.

The Commander and Lester arrive at the other end. ❻
They halt by the door and the commander hammers on it.

COMMANDER Kellman! Kellman..?

No answer. ❼
The commander nods.
Lester evaporates the door lock with a burst from his laser pistol. ❽
They enter.

6A. INT. KELLMAN'S OFFICE.

The commander and Lester burst in.

LESTER He's skipped.

COMMANDER In **quite** a hurry, by the look of it. Come on.

They exit.

6B. INT. THE CORRIDOR.

COMMANDER You take that section, Lester. I'll look ~~in~~ round the transom…

They separate. ❾

6D. INT. CONTROL ROOM 1. ❿

The Doctor has taken a small cylinder, with wires attached, out of the console.

DOCTOR WHO ~~This might work at a pinch~~ Right, this might just work… if I can adapt the monosode to a three-phase output. ~~How is she now?~~

HARRY ~~She's dying Doctor, She's dying, Doctor.~~ Doctor – she's not going to last much longer.

DOCTOR WHO I know, Harry, I know!

HARRY She's **reacting just** like Warner. It's ~~just~~ happening all over again…

The Doctor has inserted his jeweller's glass and is working on the cylinder with some delicate instrument.

⓫ ## 8. INT. GUILDROOM. ⓬

Vorus is staring out of a window at the great Vogan city of CSO. ⓭
Magrik enters.

MAGRIK You sent for me?

VORUS The Cybermen are moving.

MAGRIK What? ~~But~~ it is too soon –

VORUS Our **human** agent reports that they ~~have started~~ **will soon have taken over the beacon.** We have, perhaps, four hours to complete the sky-striker.

MAGRIK That's impossible~~, Vorus~~!

VORUS Four hours ~~to finish it~~, Magrik, or all our dreams are ended.

MAGRIK The **sky**-striker is ~~complete~~ **ready** but the bombhead has not been tested. **And then** it will take four hours to fit.

VORUS Then **we must gamble, Magrik** – the bombhead will be tested when it strikes the beacon. ~~You understand?~~

Magrik swallows.

MAGRIK ~~I'll call every engineer available to the bunker and put them to work at once, Vorus.~~ Very well, I'll send for every available engineer, Vorus – at once. ⑭

9. INT. CONTROL ROOM.

Harry holding Sarah in the matterbeam.

DOCTOR WHO There isn't time to wire this in. I'll have to hold it in position. **Ready?**

He switches on the control. The transmat hums.

CU Sarah.

The 'plague' lines almost to her temple. Harry gazing at her anxiously.

The Doctor takes his little cylinder ⑮ and pushes it into the control-box circuit.

Harry and Sarah dematerialize. ⑯

There is a flash and a bang.

TELECINE 9
INT. CAVE. DAY.

Matterbeam area. ⑰ *Harry holding Sarah. Their position identical to that in Scene 9.* ⑱ *He stares at the side of her neck and face. The vicious black lines have gone. Sarah stirs.*

HARRY ~~I say~~... Sarah?

Sarah's eyes flicker.

SARAH ~~Harry?~~ Mmmm?

HARRY (Shouts) It worked, Doctor! It worked!

SARAH (Wincing) Stop bawling in my ear! ~~I know you're a sailor but you don't have to prove~~ You've got a voice like a foghorn – hey!

HARRY What's the matter?

She straightens up and eyes him suspiciously.

SARAH ~~Get your great maulers off my waist~~. What's going on here~~, anyway~~?

HARRY ~~Isn't it marvellous?~~ Well, **that's marvellous, isn't it?** Here am I, trying to save your life and –

SARAH ~~Oh,~~ **Trying to save my** – I remember ~~now~~! That thing jumped on my neck…

She rubs it tenderly.

SARAH ~~Then the Doctor came in and –~~ Where are we?

HARRY **A place called** Voga, **I think**. The Doctor transmatted us to get rid of the poison. I might tell you, my girl, you were ~~just~~ on the point of popping off.

SARAH ~~Well, now we're here I think we should pop off back, don't you?~~

HARRY ~~Eh?~~

SARAH ~~Up to the beacon. I don't like Voga very much – the bit that I can see of it, anyway.~~

HARRY ~~All right, old thing. Just leave it to me. Simply a matter of turning the old reciprieator whatsit…~~

He has crossed to one of the stainless steel globes. He bends towards it and then stares slightly outwards beyond the circle.

HARRY Oh, I say, **look at that!**

SARAH What is it?

HARRY ~~Looks remarkably~~ Well, **it looks very much** like gold~~, but of course it can't possibly~~… It can't be… I don't believe it…

He reaches out and picks up a golden nugget.

HARRY ~~Oh, my word… Oh, dear…~~

SARAH ~~What have you got there?~~

HARRY ~~Oh, gosh… Oh, look!~~ There's some more of it **over here!** ~~I'm going to faint!~~

SARAH Oh, Harry – ?

But Harry is now consumed with gold fever. He scurries about the cave like a demented squirrel, picking up nuggets, stuffing them into his pockets, inside his shirt, everywhere…

HARRY **Look** gold, ~~Sarah! Gold! Gold! Gold! Lots of lovely – oh, come and get it – come and help me –~~

SARAH Don't be ~~a fool~~ **so silly!** It can't be gold.

HARRY ~~It is, it is! Look at it. Lovely beautiful gold. Tons and tons of glorious gorgeous gold~~ – Sarah – solid gold!

SARAH Harry, stop it! ~~This isn't right.~~ Anyway, **it isn't ours.**

HARRY Well, it isn't anybody's is it, just lying scattered around here. ⓳

HARRY ~~We're going to be rich, Sarah, don't you see?~~ Rich! I'll buy myself out of the navy. I'll buy a **quiet** little practice in ~~Drayton Parslow~~ **the country,** ~~A mink-lined consulting room. A diamond-studded~~ **solid gold** stethoscope – **Uh oh…** ⓴

~~Sarah grabs him and shakes him.~~

~~**SARAH** You're getting hysterical, Harry! Stop it!~~

~~**HARRY** (A beat) Ah… sorry. It's just that there's so much of it. Everywhere you look.~~

~~**SARAH** But it isn't ours, Harry.~~

~~**HARRY** It isn't anybody's. It's just lying about.~~

Suddenly a great beam of light hits them. They turn, blinded, transfixed against the cave wall.

An open truck with a front spotlight blazing whines towards them from the end of the cave. The truck carries a crew of stiff figures. Travelling like firemen ready to jump into action the second the vehicle stops. Each figure holds a carbine.

Harry lets the gold slip from his arms. He shields his eyes, trying to see.

HARRY ~~Oh, dear.~~ That's torn it.

SARAH (*As she is grabbed*) Oh!

HARRY Steady on, old chap.

㉑ 10. INT. TRANSOM.

Kellman and the commander facing each other, guns in hand. Kellman sneers.

COMMANDER Put that gun down, Kellman. *Kellman backs slowly up the transom. The commander edges after him.*

KELLMAN All right, Commander. Go ahead and ~~fire~~ **shoot**. Neither of us can miss at this range… ~~Oh, no.~~

COMMANDER I said, put that gun down.

KELLMAN Oh no.

COMMANDER You can't get away. *Kellman reaches behind him, finding the door he is seeking.*

KELLMAN That's right, Commander… I'm going into ~~this~~ **my** cabin. **You can** lock me in if you like… just don't try to follow. *Lester grabs Kellman's gun hand.*

COMMANDER Well done, **Lester** –

LESTER He walked right into it.

Fighting talk for the struggle scene. Kellman is subdued and dragged off.

TELECINE 10
INT. CAVE. DAY.
Harry and Sarah being roughly loaded on to the truck by guards.

SARAH Let go! Where are you taking us?

HARRY This isn't necessary, you know.

SARAH This is all a mistake.

HARRY A lot of fuss about nothing at all.

SARAH Harry, tell them.

HARRY I'm trying to tell them, but they don't seem to –

SARAH Look – please, where are you taking us?… We weren't stealing your gold **if that's what you're thinking – well,** not really.

HARRY No, **of course we weren't**. We were just – just feeling it. That's all. *A firm hand sends him sprawling to the floor of the truck.*

~~**HARRY** No speaka da English, I guess.~~

The truck whines away into the darkness. Camera pans. A spy straightens up from behind a boulder. ㉒ He stares after the truck and then moves off himself.

11. CONTROL ROOM 2.

~~**DOCTOR WHO** There's Voga, Commander, – what remains of it and somewhere not far away, I fancy, are the remnants of the Cybermen.~~

~~**LESTER** You mean the Cybermen have followed that rock into our system – why?~~

DOCTOR WHO Voga, otherwise known as the planet of gold, is hated **and feared** by ~~the~~ Cybermen because gold is lethal to them.

COMMANDER How?

DOCTOR WHO It's the perfect non-corrodable metal. It plates their breathing apparatus and in effect suffocates them. Doesn't it Professor? *No reply.*

DOCTOR WHO **Now,** Harry and Sarah are down ~~on Voga~~ **there, and** I can't bring them back without that pentalion drive.

LESTER We found these in his cabin. ㉓

DOCTOR WHO ~~To keep in contact~~ Yes… Keeps **in touch** with his masters. What have you

done with the pentalion drive, ~~Kellman~~
Professor?
KELLMAN I don't know what you're talking
about.
DOCTOR WHO ~~I see.~~
LESTER *(OOV)* He's lying.
DOCTOR WHO I think he's lying but why?
KELLMAN What are you doing with that?
DOCTOR WHO ~~Mm~~This? Oh, nothing. Why – is
it ~~something~~ important?
KELLMAN No.
The Doctor shrugs and puts the box down.
DOCTOR WHO Yes... I think our ~~mercenary~~
friend is lying ~~in order~~ to gain time. ~~Am I~~
~~right?~~
KELLMAN I don't know what you mean.
The Doctor who stares at him.
DOCTOR WHO ~~Time, yes.~~ But time for what, I
wonder?

TELECINE 11
MODEL SHOT.
*The Cyberman spaceship speeding through
space.*

12. INT. CYBER CONTROL DECK.
*First Cyberman takes a reading from the
computer.* 24
FIRST CYBERMAN Computer reports heavy
phobic energy discharge between the beacon
and Voga.
CYBERLEADER ~~Then~~ That means the humans
have recently used their transmat beam.
FIRST CYBERMAN Yes, leader.
CYBERLEADER Time to docking?
FIRST CYBERMAN 16 minutes.
CYBERLEADER Good. Order the boarding party
to the forward hatch.

13. INT. GUILDROOM. 25
*Harry and Sarah are captive between the silent
SS guards.*
SARAH The Doctor will be worrying about us.
HARRY I'm worrying about us. What is this
place anyway?
SARAH I can tell you what it isn't. It isn't
uninhabited.
The golden doors open to admit Vorus.

VORUS So – you are from the beacon? Why
have you come to Voga? Was it to escape the
plague?
SARAH Yes. Yes, that's right. The plague.
VORUS ~~That is a lie.~~ You're lying. Now tell me
the truth.
SARAH I'm not lying! I had the plague and –
VORUS When the plague had done its work
there were to be only four humans ~~were to~~
~~have been~~ left alive. That was the plan.
HARRY Plan? You planned the death –
VORUS You were not among the four.
SARAH We arrived after the plague. ~~Then~~ But I
was bitten and the Doctor put me in the
matterbeam to cure me – didn't he, Harry?
HARRY ~~Absolutely right,~~ Yes, that's right. It's
the truth. And I came with her because she
was ~~unconscious, d'you see?~~ dying. And ~~I~~ we
really ~~wasn't~~ weren't trying to steal your gold.
VORUS So, how many humans are on the
beacon now? If you refuse to answer ~~my~~
~~questions~~ you will suffer. Then I shall ask them
again and then you will answer. Do you
understand?
HARRY Yes...
VORUS Humans are ~~reputed~~ reported to have
some intelligence. When Vorus, leader of the
Guardians, asks you a question it is not
~~intelligent~~ wise to refuse to answer.
*Sound effect: melodious chime. Vorus looks
round, then to the guards.*
VORUS ~~Remove them. Place~~ Take them out
and put them in confinement. I will question
them again later.
*The guards lead Sarah and Harry out. Vorus
goes to his panel and touches the button. The
wall disappears and we see Tyrum at his desk.
The room Tyrum is in is more functional,
less ornate than the guildroom. Tyrum is
working.*
VORUS Greetings, Councillor Tyrum.
Tyrum looks up.
TYRUM Ah, Vorus! There are matters of
importance I must discuss with you.
VORUS Yes..?
TYRUM Not over the vision-projector. Here in
the city.
VORUS I am not aware of anything of such
importance, Councillor.

TYRUM I am. And as always, Vorus, I look forward to our meeting with the keenest pleasure. So I have sent our fastest skimmer to collect you.

He touches a button on his desk. The golden wall is as solid as before. Vorus stares at it unseeingly. His mind probing the nuances of their conversation.

14. INT. CONTROL ROOMS 2 & 1. ㉖

Kellman is slumped.
  Doctor Who is fiddling with the small cylinder, now rather badly charred.
  He throws it down.
  The commander walks into FG.

COMMANDER As a space service commander there are certain crimes where I can order immediate execution. **And** you have murdered 47 members of my crew and jeopardized our mission.

KELLMAN You're talking rubbish, **Commander**.

LESTER Shooting's too good for him.

COMMANDER So what's it going to be, Kellman?

KELLMAN Be?

COMMANDER Are you going to die now or are you going to tell us where that pentalion drive is?

KELLMAN You're not frightening me, Commander. You won't shoot.

COMMANDER **But** I have every right –

KELLMAN You can't prove a thing!

The commander indicates the Cybermat control.

COMMANDER ~~There's this.~~ No? Well what about that box you had? The Doctor says it controls the Cybermats.

KELLMAN And I say it's an instrument for analysing mineral elements. Every exographer carries one.

LESTER ~~Hey!~~ Look!

DOCTOR WHO ~~Shhs~~

A Cybermat has appeared from a duct. ㉗ Its eye-lights flash. It heads across the floor. The commander levels his gun. The Doctor holds him by the forearm and gives a nod of complicity.

DOCTOR WHO Leave it, don't shoot.

The Cybermat is heading directly for Kellman. ㉘ He sits up stiffly, staring at it.

He has no chance of getting out of its way. His voice cracks.

KELLMAN Stop it! For heaven's sake… Do something!

The Cybermat is closing on him. Sweat beads Kellman's face. He looks from the Cybermat to the control box. The Cybermat is only a yard from him. It tips back, preparing to launch itself. ㉙

DOCTOR WHO After you've been bitten, Kellman, ~~if you want to live~~ you'll have **just** ten seconds ~~of consciousness~~ to remember where that pentalion drive is. **If you want to live.**

KELLMAN ~~I'll tell you. I'll tell you.~~ All right – all right! It's round my neck.

Kellman's nerve breaks. With a sob of fear, he grabs the Cybermat control box and operates its buttons.
  The Cybermat whirls, its eye-lights fade and it settles into dormancy.
  The Commander strides forward and puts his gun against the broken man's head.

KELLMAN ~~It's here.~~ Take it…

He pulls a chain from his shirt. The pentalion drive is hanging from it. The commander looks at Lester who gives a shrug of disgust.

DOCTOR WHO Splendid. Now we can get Harry and Sarah back.

He takes the crystal and moves to the transmat. Lester follows.

LESTER ~~You whistled that thing in, didn't you? How did you know it would attack Kellman?~~
DOCTOR WHO ~~Very simple. I set the controls to his brainwaves. Now this is much more difficult… (peering) If I put it back the wrong way round the entire beacon could disintegrate.~~
LESTER ~~Ah… right. Well, I – I won't bother you then.~~
~~He backs away.~~

15. INT. CAVE AREA C ㉚. DAY.

Harry and Sarah are sitting chained to the wall.

HARRY **Sarah**, these chains are solid gold~~, you know~~.

SARAH Harry, will you just shut up about your rotten gold?

HARRY 24 carat ~~I think~~ by the looks of it.

SARAH It's all because of the gold that we're in this mess!

HARRY I was thinking…

SARAH **Well,** don't.

HARRY ~~No, what I mean is,~~ Gold's a ~~pretty~~ **very** soft metal, isn't it, **Sarah**? **So,** if we can find a decent bit of rock we might be able to file through ~~it~~.

SARAH Well~~, it's worth a try~~. We can't just sit around glittering, **can we**?

They begin searching within their limited reach.

16. INT. TYRUM HQ. DAY. ㉛

Tyrum facing Vorus.

VORUS You said a matter of importance, Chief Councillor?

TYRUM Yes. I have a report that two aliens – two humans – have been seen in the upper ~~galleries.~~ **gold mines.**

VORUS What?

TYRUM By ancient tradition, your guards control the ~~galleries~~ **gold mines** and the routes to the surface. If humans have set foot on Voga it can only have been with your connivance, Vorus.

VORUS You've no proof of this absurd allegation!

TYRUM Nonetheless, I believe it.

He flings back drapery to reveal the body of the unfortunate radio operator killed in Part One.

TYRUM Whatever is happening in the ~~galleries~~ **gold mines**, Vorus – and strange stories have reached my ears – your guards have never before resorted to murder!

VORUS **It was** a matter of internal discipline.

TYRUM I know your ambitions, Vorus. I know you see Voga as a great power again, trading its gold with other planets in the galaxy –

VORUS And why not? Why should we ~~live~~ **remain** for ever underground, cowering from the memory of something that happened centuries ago?

TYRUM Because this way we survive. While no one suspects that Voga is inhabited – that this is the famous planet of gold – we remain safe.

VORUS Safe! You have the philosophy of a cringing mouse, Tyrum!

TYRUM And you are a gambler with a mad thirst for power. That is why I no longer trust you and the Guardians. My city militia are taking over control of the ~~galleries~~ **gold mines**.

VORUS ~~What!~~ You dare not challenge the traditional authority of the Guardians!

TYRUM To maintain security, Vorus. The militia are moving into the ~~galleries~~ **gold mines** at this moment.

Vorus stares at him bitterly, then spins to leave.

VORUS We shall see.

TYRUM Your men are outnumbered, Vorus, and the troops have orders to crush any resistance. If there is any bloodshed, remember it will be on your hands.

VORUS I'll have you removed from office for this ~~outrage~~!

17. INT. CAVE AREA C. DAY.

Harry has a chunk of jabolite rock ㉜ and is hammering at Sarah's leg-gold. He misses.

SARAH Ow! ~~Watch it!~~ **Careful!**

HARRY Sorry, ~~old girl~~. It's flattening, though.

SARAH So's my ankle~~, you clumsy oaf~~.

HARRY I think you might almost get your foot through ~~that~~ now.

SARAH Let's have a go, **then**.

Harry pulls of her shoe and holds the chain. Sarah tugs.

HARRY ~~And again! Go on – it's moving.~~ **Come on. One more pull** – it's coming.

SARAH It hurts!

HARRY Tibias, or rather fetlocks, like a carthorse. ~~Go on – pull…~~

SARAH My ankles are not thick!

HARRY **Come on, pull!**

With a final effort Sarah manages to withdraw her foot from the flattened hoop.

HARRY Oh, well done! ~~Here,~~ **Now** you **can** have a go at mine ~~now~~.

He offers her the rock.
Sarah is rubbing her ankle. She pulls on her shoe.

SARAH Wait a minute. ~~I've a better idea –~~ if I can break off one of those stalagmites we ~~can~~ **might be able to** use it as a lever, eh?

HARRY ~~Those are stalactites, actually Stalagmites point upwards.~~

~~**SARAH** Thank you!~~

~~She heads towards the stalactite deposits.~~

18. INT. CONTROL ROOMS 2 & 1.

The Doctor completes his work on the control box. He closes the panel.

DOCTOR WHO ~~There!~~ **Right!** Now to see if it works.

He moves the control switch down. The transmat hums but nothing else happens. **34**
The Doctor switches off.

DOCTOR WHO That's strange.

COMMANDER Isn't it working?

DOCTOR WHO ~~Mm?~~ Yes, full power… They must have left the receptor circle.

LESTER Commander!

The commander crosses.

LESTER ~~We're~~ **I'm** getting a signal on the radar screen. **35**

He indicates the control. A blip of light on the screen. **36**
The commander and the Doctor cross to look. Kellman perks up.

COMMANDER It could be an incoming ship.

LESTER Nothing due for another twelve days.

COMMANDER Try to get a contact.

Lester tunes the transmitter.

LESTER ~~This is Nerva Beacon.~~ This is Nerva Beacon to approaching craft. ~~Are you reading me?~~ How do you read me? Over.

After a moment he shrugs and holds the headset for the commander to listen.

LESTER Nothing.

COMMANDER It must be a spaceship. **Look,** it's ~~heading~~ **coming** directly towards us… Keep trying them, Lester.

LESTER ~~Hullo,~~ This is Nerva Beacon to approaching craft. Do you read me? This is Nerva Beacon. ~~Will you please~~ **Would you kindly** give your identity signal?… ~~Hullo, do you read me?~~

On the Doctor staring thoughtfully at the radar.

19. INT. CAVE AREAS A, B, C, D. DAY. **37**

Sheprah and his men advancing. **38**
Vorus and his guards holding the far end of the cave.

VORUS Fire one shot over their heads!

1st guard fires. Sheprah and his men dive for cover.

VORUS (Calls) Stay back! No one enters the Guildroom of the Guardians!

2nd guard fires. Sheprah shifts his position.

SHEPRAH Hold your positions while I take **fresh** orders from Tyrum. **39**

Vorus moves back as far as the golden doors of the Guildroom. Magrik is there.

VORUS They must be kept from this section at all costs. If Tyrum finds our sky-striker, all our years of work will have been for nothing.

MAGRIK I agree.

VORUS As for the two humans from the beacon – have them killed immediately.

MAGRIK Without further questioning?

VORUS If they fall into Tyrum's hands he might learn too much of our plans. They have to be silenced.

MAGRIK Very well. I'll send a detachment to deal with them.

Vorus goes through the golden doors.

20. INT. CAVE AREAS B & C. DAY.

Harry is hobbling round in small circles. Sarah is holding a stalactite. **40**

HARRY ~~Oh, my goodness! I think I'm~~ Maimed for life.

SARAH Honestly, I don't know why you're complaining. I got **you free –** ~~listen!~~ What's that?

Sound effect: distant whine, coming nearer.

HARRY What? ~~That~~ Sounds like ~~one~~ **another** of their Dodgem cars.

SARAH It's coming this way!

HARRY Quick…

They run. The electric car whines to a stop. **41** *Four guards enter carrying their carbines. They stop on seeing the broken chains. Then, at a gesture from the leader, they spread out and start a search.* **42**

21. INT. CONTROL ROOMS 2 & 1.

As before. The commander looks at the radar.

COMMANDER It must be within visual range now~~, Lester~~. Try to get a scanner contact.

Lester works the console controls. The scanner picture sweeps the heavens, then settles on a distant moving dot.

LESTER There she is.

He zooms the scanner in. We see the Cyberman spaceship in head-on shot. *They stare at the scanner.*

COMMANDER I don't recognize that type.

LESTER Never seen ~~one~~ **anything** like it before. ~~Have you, Doctor?~~

DOCTOR WHO ~~Yes, but I never expected to see one again.~~

COMMANDER ~~Those~~ **There** are missile tubes in the nose cone.

LESTER It must be an alien.

He leans to the transmitter.

COMMANDER This is Nerva Beacon. You are approaching Nerva Beacon. We are **in quarantine by orders from Earth Centre** ~~quarantined with space plague~~. I repeat we ~~have plague aboard this beacon~~ **are in quarantine**. Stand away.

The Cyberman ship looms nearer on the scanner.

LESTER They're deliberately ignoring our ~~calls~~ **signals**, Commander. ~~Look,~~ They're moving into a docking orbit!

COMMANDER The fools!...

TELECINE 13
MODEL SHOT.

The spaceship slowly edging its docking link into contact with Nerva Beacon.

21A. INT. CONTROL ROOM 2.

LESTER They're docking.

DOCTOR WHO We've got to stop them getting in –

COMMANDER ~~Stop~~ **But** who –

The Doctor is leaving.

DOCTOR WHO Cybermen!

21B. INT. THE TRANSOM.

The Doctor comes into the transom and runs.

TELECINE 14
INT. CAVES. DAY.

Harry and Sarah on the run. The guards are hunting them. They haven't been seen yet, but discovery is only a matter of time.

HARRY ~~This way – whoops, no!~~ Sorry, old girl. Dead end. Back we go.

SARAH **No** we can't, Harry – look. We're trapped.

They cower behind rocks. Their POV of the guards advancing.

~~**HARRY** The blighters seem to be able to see in the dark, don't they?~~

SARAH Harry – **they're coming**!

She points. A possible escape route over the rocks to another small cave. They start to climb towards it.

On the guards. Suddenly one of them raises his head. He emits an eerie low whistle, unlike any human sound.

All the guards stop and stare in the same direction. They raise their blaster carbines.

On Harry and Sarah climbing, panting. He is pushing her ahead of him.

A sudden whine and bang. A lump of rock explodes behind them. Then another.

~~**HARRY** They've seen us!~~

They scramble desperately towards the cave.

On the guards firing. The cavern echoes with gunfire. The small explosions pepper the rocks behind Harry and Sarah as they dash into the temporary safety of the little cave. Sarah collapses, exhausted. Harry drags her up.

~~**HARRY** Come on, old girl... Can't stop... Got to keep... going...~~

They hurry off into the depths of the cave.

On the guards behind them. They are now running in pursuit of their quarry.

22. INT. AIRLOCK.

The Doctor has a panel open.

He is working on heavy hydraulic piping with a monkey wrench.

Sweat streams from him.

The glands are locked firmly on.

He hears something and looks around apprehensively.

There is a hiss of air from the further side of the lock.

Something clonks against the door.

23. INT. TRANSOM.

The commander and Lester are staring in at the Doctor who is inside the airlock.

~~**COMMANDER** He's trying to shut off the vacuum control!~~

~~**LESTER** He's too late – look!~~

24. INT. AIRLOCK.

The door behind Doctor starts to sigh open.
  He drops the wrench and makes a dive for the transom exit.

25. INT. TRANSOM.

The Doctor bursts out into the transom.
DOCTOR WHO No good.
The commander stares beyond him.
  He makes a dive for his gun.
COMMANDER Good grief!

26. INT. AIRLOCK.

Cyberleader and Cybermen in airlock.

27. INT. TRANSOM.

The Cybermen advance into the transom.
The commander and Lester open fire.

Their laser blasts have no effect on the huge Cybermen, who raise their Cyberweapons. **51**
  One shot cuts down the commander.
  A second shot flings Lester against the wall.
  He collapses in a crumpled heap, apparently dead.
  Doctor Who starts running.
~~**CYBERLEADER** Stop!~~
  Doctor Who looks over his shoulder.
  A single shot hits him.
  He gives a cry, has a fit of the Cagney staggers, then slumps to the ground.
FIRST CYBERMAN All resistance overcome.
CYBERLEADER The beacon is ours.
  And we close on his unpleasant steel mask… **52**

CLOSING TITLES

---

1 The reprise starts with the Doctor in Kellman's office as the floor starts to smoke (Part One, Scene 29). The action then jumps ahead to Part One, Scene 34 as the Cybermat approaches Sarah.

2 There was a recording break here because it was the end of the afternoon recording session, and also to add more plague make-up to Elisabeth Sladen.

3 Although this sequence follows straight on from the previous scene, there was a brief pause to set up the high camera. The actors then played the scene going from the Doctor's closing speech of Scene 2 so it seemed continuous.

4 Kellman puts the pentalion drive on a string round his neck.

5 Two short scenes of a page each were dropped before recording, and so Scene 6D was moved here to cover the time it would take Lester and the commander to get to Kellman's office.

6 The commander and Lester in the transom was recorded with Scene 10 and edited back into the start of this scene.

7 Scene 8 was inserted here.

8 The guns are machine pistols. Visual Effects rigged Kellman's lock so that it is destroyed by bullet fire.

9 With Scenes 6D and 8 inserted earlier, the next scene was Scene 9.

10 This scene was moved so that it followed Scene 3.

11 Either there was no Scene 7, or it was renamed 6D for some reason during rewrites.

12 This scene was moved to the middle of Scene 6.

13 Vorus is looking at his (model) sky-striker rocket on a circular screen, provided using blue CSO.

14 After this scene we cut back to the second part of Scene 6.

15 The camera and visual effects instructions refer to the Doctor's lash-up as 'drive thing'.

16 We do not see Harry and Sarah disappear (though the camera directions suggest that either roll-back-and-mix could be used, or an edit – as was the case). The flash dazzles the Doctor and the camera stays on him as he recovers. He looks towards the transmat and smiles.

17 The matterbeam-globe props created for *The Sontaran Experiment* were re-used here, one of them raised on a low plinth.

18 The materialization of Harry and Sarah was achieved using the roll-back-and-mix technique (see *Robot* Part One, Scene 1 for an explanation). The effect was enhanced by shining a spotlight (concealed behind the globe/plinth) upwards at Harry and Sarah and the cave ceiling.

19   At this point, the Vogans arrive in small powerboats and run along a gallery towards Harry and Sarah.

20   Harry catches sight of the approaching Vogans.

21   A brief insert of the commander and Lester in the transom was recorded ahead of this scene to be inserted into the start of Scene 6.

22   The subplot with the spy was omitted, though Tyrum knows of Vorus' activities from finding the body of the dead Vogan from Part One, Scene 12 and does say that he has heard rumours about outsiders.

23   Lester hands the Doctor a remote-control box.

24   The screen on which the data is displayed was a small 'vignette' set, separate from the main set. Editing made it appear to be in front of the Cybermen at the controls of the ship. Referred to in the technical directions as 'Anchor Mumbo-Jumbo', the screen reads:

> RAD INPUT
> Log.31..08
> Axis. 13..13..051
> Range. 11---42-9
> Analysis.
> Type R"L" Anti-sine
> Energy (Phobic)
> Mag.
> 27 n 09 R'''

25   As well as being on Vorus' tunic front, the device that later becomes the Prydonian Seal in *The Deadly Assassin* (1977) is imprinted on each end of the long table in the room, and embossed on the walls.

26   This was one of the scenes for which Peter Howell scored additional incidental music to augment Carey Blyton's score.

27   The same CSO shot as that used in Part One, Scene 13 showed the Cybermat emerging from behind a pedestal.

28   As it heads towards Kellman the Cybermat was a prop pulled along on a wire.

29   The CSO shots of the Cybermat rearing up were recorded with Part One, Scene 13 and edited in.

30   The cave area and rock tunnel area of Voga, which comprised seven interlocking sets; one of these had a blue CSO area with a colour photo caption of Wookey Hole added behind the actors. The different areas of the set were referred to by letter: A, B, C, D...

31   Tyrum's followers are referred to in the camera directions as 'doves' (to distinguish them from Vorus' 'hawks', or SS).

32   For 'jabolite', read polystyrene.

33   Scene 19 was inserted ahead of this scene.

34   A lighting effect was added so that the transmat cubicles light up.

35   Lester is in the other control room, out of view.

36   The main CSO screen shows a radar 'sweep' with a blip flashing at the 3 o'clock position.

37   This scene was moved ahead of Scene 18.

38   They arrive in one of the small trucks.

39   There was a brief recording pause here to allow two of the 'hawks' to move to another position on the set so it appears there are more of them than there really are.

40   The scene opens with Sarah prising the manacle from Harry's ankle.

41   The car arriving is seen through a 'clump' of stalagmites. These were a model, CSO'd over the main picture of the Vogans' arrival. The car, which moved slowly, was slightly speeded up using a videodisc.

42   Telecine 14, scripted to follow Scene 21B, was inserted here.

43   Telecine 12A – a model shot of the Cybership in space – was CSO'd on to the main screen.

44   As the commander speaks, the Cybership turns and heads straight for the camera.

45   The latter part of Telecine 17, scripted for Part Three, was inserted here.

46   A model of a small section of Nerva's hull was constructed for the Cybership to dock with.

47   This scene was moved forward so that it follows Scene 20.

48   The Vogans fire at Harry and Sarah. Their guns fire bullets, and Visual Effects provided ricochets and bullet hits in the cave walls.

49   The Doctor is trying to hold the locking wheel closed.

50   Warning lights flash above the airlock door.

51   The Cybermen fire from their head units. Visual Effects rigged firing mechanisms linked to the four gun chambers in the head masks. The charges were set off by the actors, and had to be reloaded between takes.

52   We actually close with a zoom in on the Doctor's unconscious face.

REVENGE OF THE CYBERMEN

by Gerry Davis

Part Three

OPENING TITLES

1. INT. TRANSOM.
Reprise. **1**
Kellman runs down transom.
He looks at the bodies.
KELLMAN You haven't killed them?
CYBERLEADER Of course not. **We have neutralized them.** They are necessary to our plan.
Kellman grunts. He bends and begins to search the Doctor's pockets.
CYBERLEADER What are you doing, Kellman?
KELLMAN This is the stranger I reported. Calls himself the Doctor.

CYBERLEADER And because of him our plan was advanced?
KELLMAN Had to be. He was interfering. I'd just like to know who and what he is…
A bag of jelly babies, a half-eaten apple, a string of conkers, a yo-yo. **2**

TELECINE 17 **3**
INT. CAVES. DAY.
Harry and Sarah still being pursued by the guards through a small cave. They are using the rocks and bends to stay out of the sight line of their hunters. But they are very tired, constantly stumbling and tripping over unseen obstacles in

the darkness of the tunnels. The guards on the other hand move with uncanny ease.

SARAH Harry – over there…

The cave is widening. They change direction and run out across a more open, less rubble-strewn cave floor.

Behind them again a guard issues the strange low whistle. The guards fan out in a line as they follow their fugitives.

Suddenly Harry and Sarah stop. A few yards ahead of them the cave floor descends into a lake. There is no way across or round. Or back now.

HARRY Oh, Lord…

SARAH Oh – Harry!

The guards, now certain of success, have slowed to a walk. They are advancing in a tightening circle, carbines pointing. Harry and Sarah look at each other.

HARRY This looks like it, old girl. the end, Sarah.

SARAH One thing about you, Harry – you never miss the obvious.

HARRY Why don't they get it over with just finish us off?

SARAH They're waiting till they can see the whites of our goose pimples.

Suddenly a cross-pattern of beams illuminates both hunters and hunted. The guards start to turn.

SHEPRAH Vogans of Vorus – lay down your weapons. You are surrounded. Throw down your weapons!

The guards hesitate. Then obey the stentorian command from the darkness. Sheprah, captain of the city militia, and two of his men move into the light and advance across the cave floor.

SARAH Now what?

2. INT. CREW DECK. ④

The Doctor, the commander and Lester are sitting up, still groggy but taking notice. ⑤

Kellman and the Cyberleader are studying a map of the Vogan cave system. A Cyberman stands guard at the door.

CYBERLEADER Once our landing is detected the Vogans will attack in force.

KELLMAN They have only light armaments. Nothing that can affect your Cybermen.

CYBERLEADER This is the heart main shaft?

KELLMAN Yes, that's the shaft I explored for you. It runs to the very core of Voga.

CYBERLEADER And how far is the shaft entrance from the transmat receptor area?

KELLMAN Just a matter of yards. I set the receptors as close as possible.

CYBERLEADER Excellent. You have done well, Kellman… The humans will carry the bombs explosives into the shaft.

DOCTOR WHO What's your cut, Kellman – Voga's gold?

CYBERLEADER There will be no gold. Voga is to be utterly destroyed. This time we shall not fail.

DOCTOR WHO Oh really?

CYBERLEADER You three And you, Doctor, and your two friends will help in this task – that is why your lives have been spared.

COMMANDER I was wondering why you hadn't killed us.

LESTER We still don't have to help them. They can't force us.

CYBERLEADER You are mistaken.

LESTER You'll find out discover who's made the mistake mistaken, chum.

CYBERLEADER The heart of Voga is almost pure gold, but gold is hostile to our functioning. Therefore, we asked Kellman was asked to preserve three animal organisms for this purpose.

DOCTOR WHO Isn't it wonderful to feel wanted needed, Commander.

CYBERLEADER Kellman, on our approach run we detected an operational discharge of from the transmat beam area. Explain that.

KELLMAN That was his doing – he beamed his two friends down to Voga. I tried to put the transmat out of action but he managed to fix it somehow.

CYBERLEADER And how much did those humans know?

3. INT. TYRUM HQ. DAY. ⑥

TYRUM A plague?

SHEPRAH They seemed confused. At first they spoke of this scourge as a plague. But then one of them said that the humans were killed by poison.

TYRUM I will see them myself, Sheprah. Are the Guardians resisting our militia?

SHEPRAH Not in the galleries. They are holding a defensive position outside the guild chambers.

TYRUM I expected Vorus would make the guild chambers his strong point. Let him hold that for the present.

SHEPRAH One determined assault is all that is needed to occupy them.

TYRUM Let me see the two human captives. If Vorus has committed treason I might give him the chance to die in battle!

Sheprah goes to the door and signals to a militia guard.

SHEPRAH You think he is a traitor, Councillor?

TYRUM ~~I think he has been holding secret negotiations with these aliens – no doubt promising them gold in return for weapons.~~

SHEPRAH ~~So that he can take over, I understand.~~

TYRUM ~~Vorus has never concealed his ambitions. But I never thought that even he would be reckless enough to reveal Voga to its enemies.~~

SHEPRAH ~~You think the humans are enemies?~~

TYRUM After the cataclysm of our ancient past, Sheprah, we have survived down here only by regarding all outsiders as hostile. ❼ ~~Now I will find out how far this involvement has gone.~~

The guard brings in Harry and Sarah. Tyrum turns to them. ❽

TYRUM I am Tyrum, Chief Councillor of Voga.

HARRY How d'you do? ~~My name's Sullivan –~~ I'm Harry Sullivan – and **this is –**

SARAH Sarah Jane Smith.

TYRUM What is your mission here?

SARAH Mission? We don't have any mission. We just… well, we **just** sort of ~~got~~ **came** here by accident, didn't we, Harry?

HARRY **Yes,** that's right. Nothing to do with us really.

TYRUM Explain.

SARAH We'd better start at the beginning. **Well, our plan was to find the TARDIS…**

4. INT. ROCK TUNNELS AREAS A, B, C. DAY.

A narrow shaft. Sheprah advances cautiously. Two of his men are in position to give covering fire.

SHEPRAH Vorus, **Leader of the Guardians…** I have a message.

VORUS *(VO)* Stay where you are!

Sheprah halts. After a moment Vorus emerges cautiously from the rocks. ❾

VORUS Well, Sheprah?

SHEPRAH Tyrum has given fresh orders. My ~~soldiers~~ **troops** will hold their present positions and we will not attack your guild chambers.

VORUS He has shown sense. Your city scum would be badly beaten.

SHEPRAH Unless we are provoked, Vorus. Then we shall sweep you aside.

Sheprah turns and moves away. Vorus glowers then returns to his own position. ~~He notices Magrik, cradling a gun in the shelter of a rock.~~

MAGRIK ~~Another hour.~~

VORUS ~~We may not have an hour, Magrik. The Cybermen are already on the beacon.~~

MAGRIK ~~I thought the plan was to wait until Kellman was safely off the beacon?~~

VORUS ~~The Cybermen may suspect his story… in which case he will die with them.~~

MAGRIK ~~Very well. I will notify you immediately we are ready to start the countdown.~~

~~He leaves.~~

4A. INT. TYRUM H.Q. DAY. ❿

As before. Tyrum rises.

TYRUM ~~I believe your story.~~

SARAH ~~Well, it's the truth.~~

TYRUM ~~But if you are simply innocent travellers why did Vorus send his guards to kill you?~~

SARAH ~~That's what we'd like to know.~~

TYRUM ~~Clearly~~ You know something, or he thinks you do, that would incriminate him.

HARRY Incriminate him in what?

TYRUM Some plot against the state – against me.

SARAH But we only met Vorus for ten minutes.

TYRUM It is something to do with the beacon. My suspicions about Vorus are hardening into certainty. He has always had great ambitions… This city you are in was once the survival chamber for our people. We have lived here ever since, unseen, safe from further attack **from the Cybermen**. You know of the Cybermen?

SARAH **Well, yes, I've heard of them.** But they're ~~supposed~~ **meant** to have been wiped out ages ago.

HARRY **I remember** the Doctor ~~said~~ **saying that** the thing that attacked Sarah was a Cybermat.

TYRUM I wonder..? Has Vorus, in the madness of his vanity, brought **down** the vengeance of the Cybermen upon us again? *(Decisive)* You will come with me!

HARRY Where to?

SARAH Where are we going?

TYRUM To the gold mines. It is time that Vorus accounted for himself. ⓫

⓬ **5. INT. CONTROL ROOMS 1 & 2.** ⓭

~~The Cyberleader is testing the transmat.~~

CYBERLEADER ~~There is no malfunction at this end.~~

KELLMAN ~~Then it must lie at the Vogan end. A faulty reciprocator diode. … the two Cybermen you are sending to Voga might be unable to return.~~

~~He shifts uneasily under the Cyberleader's probing metallic stare.~~

CYBERLEADER ~~Your concern for Cybermen is interesting, Kellman. Explain.~~

KELLMAN **Look** – I… I've done everything I can to help. I set up the transmat, I directed the Cybermats. You might never have found Voga ~~without~~ **if it hadn't been for** me.

The Doctor and company are brought in by their Cyberguard no. 1.

CYBERLEADER That is true. ~~But~~ **And** you have been promised great rewards for your assistance.

KELLMAN That's why I must go **down** to Voga – to ~~see~~ **make sure** that nothing goes wrong with the transmat.

CYBERLEADER Very well. But return as soon as possible.

He waves Kellman into the matterbeam.

CYBERLEADER Once the detonation cycle commences it cannot be stopped.

He moves the transmat control. Kellman dematerializes. ⓮

⓯ **DOCTOR WHO** What great rewards have you promised Kellman?

CYBERLEADER The matter is of no interest to you.

DOCTOR WHO Everything is of interest to me. And Cybermen possess nothing that a human might want.

CYBERLEADER You are incorrect.

DOCTOR WHO Then what is it? You have no home planet, no influence, nothing. You're just a pathetic ~~collection~~ **bunch** of tin soldiers skulking about the galaxy in an ancient spaceship.

CYBERLEADER You speak unwisely. We are destined to be rulers of all the cosmos.

DOCTOR WHO **No,** I don't think so somehow. You tried that once and **you** were very nearly wiped out.

CYBERLEADER Because of Voga and its gold. If ~~the~~ humans had not had the resources of Voga the Cyberwar would have ended in glorious triumph.

DOCTOR WHO It <u>was</u> a glorious triumph – for human ingenuity. They ~~found~~ **discovered** your weakness, **and** they invented the glitter ~~cannon~~ **gun** and that was the end of the Cybermen – except as gold-plated souvenirs that people used for hatstands.

The Cyberleader moves threateningly forward as though to strike.

LESTER Watch it Doctor! **I think** you've riled him…

CYBERLEADER That is why Voga must be destroyed before we begin our second campaign.

DOCTOR WHO Oh, there's to be a second campaign, is there?

CYBERLEADER We have ~~the~~ **enough** parts in our ship to build **an entirely** new Cyberarmy – and this time, **Doctor,** it will be invincible. ⓰ Cybermen ~~function~~ **can survive** more efficiently than animal organisms. ~~Therefore we must~~ **That is why we will** rule the galaxy.

DOCTOR WHO Loose thinking. The ~~great~~ trouble with Cybermen is that they have hydraulic muscles – and **of course** hydraulic brains to go with them.

This time the Cyberleader does strike. The Doctor is sent rolling across the room. He rolls to the rucksacks ⑰ *and then bounds to his feet, holding one of them threateningly.*

~~DOCTOR WHO~~ ~~Thank you.~~

CYBERLEADER Put that down.

DOCTOR WHO Now if I'm ~~right~~ correct about ~~what's in here~~ what this contains and ~~I~~ should accidentally drop it –

He lets the rucksack drop by the length of its straps. Instinctively, the Cyberleader takes a step back and puts hand on chest.

DOCTOR WHO Now, Cyberleader, I want some information out of you.

6. INT. TRANSOM.

The Cyberman no. 1 is standing on guard. Suddenly a light in its chestpack or head starts to flicker. ⑱ *The Cyberman answers the call. It turns and strides away.*

7. INT. CONTROL ROOMS 1 & 2.

The Doctor still holds the rucksack.

DOCTOR WHO What is Kellman expecting to get out of **all** this?

CYBERLEADER Kellman wants power. He will be ~~the~~ ruler of this solar system when we have conquered it.

DOCTOR WHO Your puppet dictator in other words? Strange. I wouldn't have said his ambitions la~~y~~ in that direction –

COMMANDER Look out, Doctor!

But the warning is too late.

A Cyberman has stepped through from control room 2 and taken the Doctor from behind in its huge steel Cyberhug.

One metal paw holds the straps of the rucksack.

The Doctor struggles but is remorselessly crushed around his chest.

The other Cybermen move in.

The Commander is sent spinning.

Lester, too, is overpowered.

CYBERLEADER Do not kill them.

The Cybermen holding the Doctor takes note and releases him.

He slumps to the floor unconscious.

7A. INT. ROCK TUNNELS AREAS C, D.

Kellman hurrying along. Suddenly lights pin him down. Sheprah and soldiers surround him. ⑲ *Kellman offers no resistance.*

SHEPRAH Another human.

KELLMAN Take me to Vorus.

SHEPRAH Vorus?

KELLMAN Quickly, man. It is vital that I see Vorus immediately!

SHEPRAH Vorus is no longer in charge here.

KELLMAN What?

SHEPRAH Take him away.

The soldiers hustle Kellman off. But now he does start struggling.

KELLMAN No! No, you don't understand! I must see Vorus… ~~I've got something to tell him…~~ You're in danger, all of you…

His voice fades as he is dragged away.

⑳ 9. INT. CONTROL ROOM 2.

The Doctor, the Commander and Lester are being fitted into their rucksacks.

The buckles are snapped into position over their chests.

CYBERLEADER ~~Cobalt~~ Cyberbombs. The most compact and powerful explosive devices ever invented.

DOCTOR WHO Yes. And their use was banned ~~at~~ by the Armageddon Convention.

CYBERLEADER Cybermen do not subscribe to any theory of morality in war, **Doctor**. Our calculations indicate that two ~~of these~~ bombs, placed in the ~~centre~~ central fissure of Voga, will fragmentize the planet.

DOCTOR WHO Fragmentize? Oh well, I suppose we can't expect decent English from a machine.

CYBERLEADER Prime the buckles. Two **bombs** should be sufficient ~~to complete the task we began 427 years ago~~. Three will make certain.

He gestures. His Cybermen move forward and twist the buckles.

COMMANDER Now what ~~are you doing~~ have they done?

CYBERLEADER The buckles are now primed. Any attempt to remove the harness before the countdown ~~enters~~ reaches the red zone –

*He indicates the master clock on the relay
equipment carried by a Cyberman –*

CYBERLEADER will cause a secondary explosion.
Do you understand?

LESTER You mean if we ~~take~~ **attempt to release**
the harness ~~off~~ before then we'll ~~be~~ **get** blown
up.

CYBERLEADER Correct. It is as well to keep that
thought in your minds.

DOCTOR WHO And when we ~~get down to~~ **reach**
the centre Voga we will be fragmentized – as
you put it.

CYBERLEADER Incorrect. You will have 14
minutes – the time period of the red zone – to
~~return to~~ **reach** the surface and save yourselves
by the transmat beam.

COMMANDER That isn't long enough.

CYBERLEADER 14 minutes is considered
adequate.

DOCTOR WHO Anything else before we ~~leave~~ **go**?

CYBERLEADER Yes, Doctor. ~~Remember that we
shall be following~~ Your progress **will be**
followed by radar. ~~Any deviation from the
route indicated~~ **Any attempt to deviate from
the planned course** will be **immediately**
detected – and the bombs ~~will be immediately~~
exploded by means of this manual control.

The Doctor glances at the commander.

DOCTOR WHO Thank you.

*The Cyberleader presses button on the master
clock.*

CYBERLEADER Countdown has commenced.

To Doctor:

CYBERLEADER You, Doctor, will leave first~~, with
one guard~~.

*The Doctor shrugs.
A Cyberman pulls him towards the
transmat.*

DOCTOR WHO Ah-ah! Careful, **careful**, I might,
~~go off~~ **explode**…

The Cyberleader operates the transmat control.

TELECINE 18
INT. CAVES. DAY.

*The Doctor and the Cyberman materialize in
the receptor area.* ㉑ *The Cyberman pushes
the Doctor ahead of him. They move towards
the shaft entrance.*

~~**DOCTOR WHO** All right, my iron friend, I can see
it.~~

*Suddenly they are picked up by a searchlight.
The electric truck* ㉒ *whines out of the
darkness. The Cyberman turns. Armed
militiamen jump from the truck and open fire.*

DOCTOR WHO ~~I think~~ Someone's trying to
attract your attention.

*The Cyberman is struck by concentrated laser
rays* ㉓ *and is unharmed. He fights back,
picking off the Vogans with cool single shots.*

~~**DOCTOR WHO** This is getting dangerous. Must
rush.~~

*The Doctor scrambles into the shaft, trying
desperately not to be hit by a stray shot.
Lester, the commander and a second
Cyberman arrive in the receptor area.* ㉔
*The second Cyberman sets down the relay
equipment and joins the battle. The handful of
Vogans are no match for their invulnerable
enemies. They are quickly destroyed and forced
to flee.
While the battle is in full swing the
commander and Lester duck through the
crossfire and join the Doctor in the tunnel.*

9A. INT. ROCK TUNNELS AREA E.

DOCTOR WHO If only they knew about the use of
gold.

COMMANDER You mean as a weapon.

DOCTOR Yes. It's the only thing that's effective
against Cybermen.

LESTER Did you believe all that guff about
giving us time to escape?

DOCTOR WHO Not a word of it. Once we've
reached the ~~explosure~~ **explosive** zone we'll have
outlived our usefulness.

LESTER So what do we do **now**?

DOCTOR WHO Keep moving. **Give their
radarscope something to follow.** ㉕

LESTER Doctor – why don't we just ~~stay~~ **wait**
here?

DOCTOR WHO I think my idea's better –
They start off down the shaft.

LESTER What **is your** idea?

DOCTOR WHO Mm? ~~Not sure yet –~~ I don't know
yet. That's the trouble with ideas – they only
come a bit at a time.

He strides on. The commander and Lester exchange a glance.

10. INT. CONTROL ROOM 2.

1st Cyberman strides across to his leader

FIRST CYBERMAN Our warriors report that all initial opposition has been crushed.

CYBERLEADER ~~That is good.~~ Excellent.

He looks at the radarscope. Its moving dot represent the Doctor and his friends. ㉖

CYBERLEADER They are now 100 metres below the surface.

FIRST CYBERMAN Kellman has not returned.

CYBERLEADER He is of no importance now. His part in the operation is at an end.

10A. INT. ROCK TUNNELS AREA B.

A couple of the city militia flank Kellman. He is being questioned by Tyrum. Harry and Sarah stand by.

TYRUM What is your connection with Vorus?

KELLMAN We were working together. We wanted to lure the Cybermen into a trap.

TYRUM What trap?

KELLMAN Look, we're wasting time! The Cybermen are planning to blow Voga apart and –

TYRUM What trap?

KELLMAN The beacon, of course! Vorus has a rocket aimed at the beacon –

SARAH What? Harry – ~~We must~~ we've got to warn the Doctor.

The electric truck whines out of the darkness. Sheprah leaps from it before it stops.

SHEPRAH Councillor! The Cybermen are here!

TYRUM What?

SHEPRAH They've landed on the first level. We've suffered heavy casualties and need reinforcements ~~immediately~~.

TYRUM How many Cybermen are there?

SHEPRAH Two, at least. Our weapons have no effect on them.

KELLMAN You'll never stop them ~~now~~ that way! Vorus' rocket is your only chance – that beacon ~~must~~ has to be blasted out of the sky!

Sarah looks at Harry.

TYRUM Sheprah, ~~you~~ we must attack the Cybermen with every weapon we have.

Sheprah swings back on to the truck.

TYRUM The rest of you come with me. We must speak to Vorus.

TELECINE 19
INT. CAVES. DAY.

Matterbeam area. The two Cybermen patrol watchfully. ㉗ *Close on the relay equipment. The countdown clock is ticking steadily round.* ㉘

㉙ TELECINE 20
INT. SHAFT. DAY.

The Doctor, Lester and the commander slipping and staggering down the sloping shaft. They are beginning to feel the weight of their packs. The commander almost falls. The Doctor holds him.

DOCTOR WHO Steady.

COMMANDER I'm getting ~~too~~ a bit old for this sort of thing.

DOCTOR WHO We'll rest **for** a moment…

Lester looks at the duplicate clock above the Commander's pack.

LESTER ~~Have you~~ Had any more bits of that idea, Doctor?

The Doctor prods at a gold-veined wall.

DOCTOR WHO ~~As I expected –~~ The deeper we go the heavier the concentration of gold. Before long it must start affecting their radar picture.

LESTER Then what?

DOCTOR WHO ~~Cybermen are totally logical creatures. So their behaviour is always predictable.~~ Well, it's an outside chance, but if we can get back without being detected we can take the Cybermen from behind. All right now, Commander?

COMMANDER Yes, I think so.

DOCTOR WHO ~~Then let's push on.~~ Let's go. ~~Logical progression, that's the answer, eh?~~

Lester gives a look of total bafflement as he follows the Doctor.

㉚ 11. INT. CAVE AREAS A, B, C. DAY.

Tyrum's party is progressing when, suddenly, guards block their way. ㉛

TYRUM Do you not recognize Tyrum, Chief Councillor of Voga? Stand aside!

KELLMAN We've got to see Vorus.

They move forward. The guards raise their weapons.

TYRUM Stand aside, I say!

His militia rush the guards. The melee develops.

SARAH Harry, I'm going to try to reach that transmat...

HARRY Sarah, you try and reach the transmat.

SARAH And warn the Doctor.

HARRY I'll see if I can do something about this rocket.

SARAH Take care.

HARRY OK. Good luck, old thing... And you.

Sarah slips away. 32

12. INT. GUILDROOM. DAY.

Vorus hears the sound of the fight outside. 33
He goes to the door.

13. INT. CAVE AREAS A, B, C. DAY.

Vorus appears at the end of the cave.
Tyrum's party, outnumbered, is being driven back.
Tyrum sees Vorus.

TYRUM Vorus, call off your guards!

VORUS Enough!

The fighting stops. He moves forward.

VORUS You should know better, Tyrum, than to **try to** use force.

TYRUM Our planet is being attacked, Vorus. At this hour Vogans should fight together, not against each other.

Kellman, bleeding from a head wound, staggers to his feet. 34

KELLMAN The rocket, Vorus – is it ready to fire? Vorus – is the rocket ready to fire?

VORUS The bombhead is being fitted **now**.

KELLMAN Too late! The Cybermen have already landed.

VORUS What? Have you betrayed us?

KELLMAN I tried to warn you to hurry! Once they were on the beacon I couldn't delay them any further.

TYRUM What is this rocket that you speak of, Vorus?

VORUS Come. **Very well**, I will show you.

KELLMAN Where's the girl?

They look at Harry. He shrugs.

HARRY She's gone to warn the Doctor, **of course.**

VORUS Doctor?

HARRY Well, if you're going aim rocket missiles at the beacon, If people are going to start firing missiles at him, what do you expect?

KELLMAN If the that girl reaches the beacon and starts blabbing about the rocket, the Cybermen will explode their bombs.

TELECINE 21
INT. CAVE. DAY.

Matterbeam area. Vogan soldiers firing from cover. The Cybermen are standing their ground and returning the fire.

Sheprah is shouting exhortations to his men who seem daunted by the invulnerability of their massive enemies.

We pick up Sarah on the edge of the battle. She runs, dodging from rock to rock, heading for the matterbeam.

As she lies panting, gathering herself for another run, a hurled grenade falls short of the Cybermen. It bounces off the cave wall and trickles towards her. 35

SARAH Oh, golly!

She scoops the grenade up and flings it away. It explodes further down the cave, showering her in chips of rock and dirt.

Sarah makes a final dash into the matterbeam. She reaches for the control switch.

One of the Cybermen sees her and takes careful aim. 36 *We see Sarah through his gunsight POV. She dematerializes* 37 *a split second before he fires. The Cyberbolt explodes against the wall beyond the matterbeam.*

14. INT. CONTROL ROOMS 1 & 2.

FIRST CYBERMAN Average progression rate is 50 metres per minute.

CYBERLEADER Excellent.

Sarah materializes in the matterbeam behind them. 38

CYBERLEADER Excellent. They will be in the central chamber of Voga in 17 minutes.

Sarah conceals herself.

FIRST CYBERMAN The Distortion on our radarscope is increasing. The three humans carrying our bombs can no longer be identified by separate signals.

CYBERLEADER ~~It is not important~~ That is of no importance now. Even the Doctor believes they will be given time to ~~save them~~ escape – before our bombs explode.

He indicates the master clock.

CYBERLEADER They do not know the detonators will fire when the countdown reaches the red ~~sector~~ zone.

15. INT. GUILDROOM. DAY.

CSO shot of the rocket complex through the 'window'. Vorus, Tyrum, Harry, Kellman gazing at it.

VORUS Magrik and his team have been working on it for two years. And now we have lost the race by minutes!

KELLMAN There might still be a chance. If the rocket can be fired before the Cyberbombs are in position –

Vorus shakes his head and switches off screen.

VORUS Magrik reports a delay in fitting the bombhead. ~~It will be another 20 minutes~~. No. We have lost our gamble, Kellman.

TYRUM You're insane, Vorus. You have brought about the destruction of our race.

VORUS I ~~was going~~ wanted to bring them freedom, Tyrum. Freedom from fear. Freedom to live as Vogans should – on the surface, not cowering like worms in the earth.

TYRUM And this great plan was conceived in the company of such as he… *(Indicating Kellman)* A double agent, a despicable traitor, a murderer of his own kind – a man whose only loyalty is to himself and the gold he hoped to win!

VORUS The plan would have worked – ~~just a little~~ I just needed more time~~, that's all we needed~~.

HARRY Look, all this recrimination is pretty pointless, isn't it. What we've got to do is get into that central shaft and stop these bombs being planted.

KELLMAN The Cybermen ~~are holding~~ hold the entrance. There's no way past them.

HARRY ~~Well, isn't there some other way down? There jolly well should be in a labyrinth like~~ ~~this…~~ I should think there's another way down, wouldn't you, Kellman?

KELLMAN Only that central shaft ~~penetrates so~~ runs that deep. And the galleries do not connect with it.

TYRUM Wait! When it was widened a cross-shaft was bored to provide ventilation. I have seen it in our records.

HARRY Well, ~~for Pete's sake,~~ let's go and ~~see~~ take a look!

TELECINE 22
INT. CAVES. DAY.

Matterbeam area. The battle has died away. The Vogans are licking their wounds. Sheprah straightens from tending a dying soldier.

On the relay equipment. The countdown clock still ticking round towards the red sector.

16. INT. CONTROL ROOM 2. 40

FIRST CYBERMAN Progression rate has slowed to 30 metres a minute.

CYBERLEADER Good. The bombs will ~~be detonated~~ explode in 11 minutes from now.

16A. INT. NARROW ROCK TUNNELS AREA E. 41

~~The narrowest possible. Kellman and Harry struggling along with great exertion.~~

~~**HARRY** Hurry man!~~

~~A crunch of rock behind them. Kellman turns in fear.~~

~~**KELLMAN** These rocks are dangerous.~~

~~**HARRY** One way or another, Kellman, we're going to cash our chips shortly. So it doesn't matter, does it? Keep moving!~~

TYRUM It runs for about 50 metres and the rock's friable. It'll be very dangerous after all these years.

HARRY Well, in that case we'll send our expert on ahead. In you go, Kellman.

TELECINE 23
INT. CAVES. DAY.

The commander staggers to a halt.

COMMANDER Sorry, Doctor… I'm a bit whacked…

DOCTOR WHO Sit down ~~for a minute~~ a moment…

While the others rest he walks over to the wall and prods at it with his pocket knife.

DOCTOR WHO Actually, I think we're very near the centre now. This is pretty well solid gold.

He wanders round a corner.

Lester slumps beside the commander.

LESTER I wonder if these buckles really would explode?

COMMANDER I shouldn't put it to the test. They'll explode all right.

17. INT. ROCK TUNNEL BLOCKED AREAS E, F.

KELLMAN It's blocked…

HARRY Let's see.

He wriggles past Kellman and prises at the rocks.

KELLMAN It's no use. We'll have to turn back.

~~HARRY They're moving… Come on, man, give me a hand! Pull… They're giving a bit…~~

~~KELLMAN You'll have the whole lot down on us!~~

~~Suddenly with a roar the rocks give way.~~

TELECINE 24
INT. CAVES. DAY.
A. ROCKFALL

The Doctor is still inspecting the wall.
He hears the noise of falling rock. He looks up. Half the cave wall is falling. **42**

DOCTOR WHO Look out!

Harry looks through from top of the shaft.

~~HARRY We're there! We've made it, Kellman!~~

He looks round and goes back. **43**

B. AFTER ROCKFALL

Harry reappears at top of shaft and comes down to see Doctor.

HARRY Doctor!

Doctor is unconscious.

HARRY Just a bump on the napper, **Doctor**… nothing ~~serious~~ **to worry about**. ~~Come on, Doctor,~~ let's get you out of this ~~first~~ **thing**!

He reaches for the buckle on the rucksack and fumbles to open it.

CLOSING TITLES

---

1 Part Three starts with the Cyberleader shooting the commander. An extra music cue was added over the Cyberman and Cyberleader's closing words of the previous episode.

2 The scene cuts after Kellman finds the jelly babies and apple core.

3 This scene was moved forward to Part Two, following Scene 21.

4 The latter part of Scene 3 (not used in Part Two) was inserted before this scene, replacing Telecine 17.

5 They are sitting like the three wise monkeys – Lester has his hands over his ears, the Doctor his hands over his eyes and the commander his hands in front of his mouth.

6 The first part of this scene was moved forward to Part Two, following the latter part of Telecine 17, before Telecine 13.

7 At this point the scene cuts back to Telecine 13 in Part Two. The rest of the scene remains in Part Three as scripted.

8 The rest of this scene, from this point on, was moved to follow Scene 1.

9 A photograph of Wookey Hole caves was CSO'd into the background of the sequence of Vorus and Sheprah meeting.

10 This scene was moved back slightly, so that the first part of Scene 5 precedes it.

11 Following this scene we cut to the latter part of Scene 5, starting with the Doctor's line: 'What great rewards have you promised Kellman?'.

12 This was one of the scenes for which Peter Howell scored additional incidental music to augment Carey Blyton's score.

13 The first part of this scene, up until Kellman transmats down to Voga, was moved ahead of Scene 4.

14 Achieved with a lighting effect and roll-back-and-mix.

15 The latter part of this scene – from here on – followed Scene 4, as scripted.

16 This is the point where the Cyberleader grabs the Doctor.

⑰   The Cyberbombs are large, black spherical devices attached to a harness that goes over the carrier's shoulders like a rucksack.

⑱   A pinging sound effect was used for the signal. This scene opens with a close shot of the Cyberman's chest unit, suggesting this is where it receives the signal.

⑲   They fire a warning shot.

⑳   There is no scene 8. It was removed before the studio session.

㉑   Roll-back-and-mix and the lighting effect were used for the materializations. The Doctor leaves the previous scene and arrives in this one playing with his yo-yo.

㉒   The Vogans actually arrive on foot.

㉓   The Vogans have bullet-firing weapons.

㉔   They arrive before the Vogans attack.

㉕   The scene was cut at this point, the rest being inserted after Telecine 19.

㉖   Shown on the main (CSO) screen, the radarscope shows a line sweeping from each side to the next across a diamond-shaped space.

㉗   This is another battle sequence between Cybermen and Vogans.

㉘   The latter part of Scene 9A was inserted here (starting with Lester's line: 'Doctor – why don't we just wait here?'), followed by Scene 11.

㉙   This scene was moved after Scene 15.

㉚   This scene was moved forward to follow the latter part of Scene 9A, which comes after Telecine 19.

㉛   Warning shots send Tyrum and the others into cover.

㉜   There was a recording pause at the end of this scene to reload the 'hawks'' guns ready for the opening of Scene 13.

㉝   He is looking at the sky-striker on his (CSO) screen.

㉞   Kellman is not injured.

㉟   The business with the grenade was dropped. Instead Sarah creeps round behind the Cybermen and uses one of the Vogan speedboats to cross the lake to get round to the matterbeam. This was when she had her accident and had to be saved from the water by stunt man Terry Walsh.

㊱   The Cybermen have moved away from the matterbeam, pursuing the Vogans through the cave system, so this sequence was dropped.

㊲   The usual lighting effect and roll-back-and-mix were used.

㊳   The usual lighting effect and roll-back-and-mix were used.

㊴   This scene was moved to follow Scene 16A.

㊵   This scene was moved into Part Four, following Telecine 27.

㊶   The scripted scene of Kellman and Harry already in the cross-shaft was altered for clarity – in this revised version, Tyrum shows them the shaft.

㊷   Polystyrene rocks were used for the rockfall.

㊸   The instruction of the script at this point is:
        Telecine blanking – cut to studio
    In fact there are three cuts back from the telecine sequence to studio action. As the rocks start to fall and the Doctor shouts 'Look out!', there is a brief insert of Kellman pushing Harry away from the falling rock face. Then, after seeing the commander and Lester diving for cover, we see Kellman (in the studio set) as (polystyrene) rocks fall over him too. Finally, after the rockfall, we see Harry inspecting Kellman's body, and closing the dead man's eyes.

REVENGE OF THE CYBERMEN

by Gerry Davis

Part Four

OPENING TITLES

TELECINE 27
INT. CAVES. DAY. ❶

Harry fumbling to unfasten the explosive buckle round the Doctor.

Lester appears round the rocks.

LESTER No, ~~Sullivan~~ Harry! Don't **touch it!**

HARRY Eh?

He continues trying to tug the buckle apart.

Lester dives forward.

LESTER Open that buckle and you'll be blown to kingdom come!

HARRY ~~Oh, Lord!~~ You mean ~~they're~~ it's booby-trapped?

LESTER These buckles can't be opened till the Cybermen beam the release signal.

The Doctor opens his eyes.

DOCTOR WHO Harry – Were you trying to ~~open~~ undo this ~~Harry~~?

Additional dialogue. ❷

HARRY Well, naturally.

DOCTOR WHO Did you makes the rocks fall, Harry?

HARRY Er, well, I suppose I must have done, yes.

DOCTOR WHO Harry Sullivan is an imbecile! ❸

1. INT. CONTROL ROOM 2. ④

The Cyberleader is watching the radarscope.
He cranes forward to stare more intently.

FIRST CYBERMAN Our surface party report the
Vogan attackers have been driven off with
heavy casualties.

CYBERLEADER Order them to intensify the radar
signal.

FIRST CYBERMAN It is already at maximum,
leader.

CYBERLEADER The signal is difficult to
interpret. ⑤ What depth have the bomb-
carriers reached?

FIRST CYBERMAN 1600 metres. They are eight
minutes from the detonation zone.

On Sarah listening.

CYBERLEADER Eight minutes! In eight minutes
the accursed planet of gold will be ~~totally~~
utterly destroyed. Annihilated. Vapourized! It
is good…

2. INT. ROCK TUNNELS. AREA G. ⑥

DOCTOR WHO So where's Sarah?

HARRY Well, I'm not sure **Doctor. I mean,**
when I last saw her she was trying to get back
to the beacon –

The Commander joins them.

DOCTOR WHO What?

HARRY ~~Well, she~~ Yes, you see, we thought you
were still up there~~.~~ **and** she **naturally** wanted
to warn you about this rocket – sorry. I can see
you're not with me.

DOCTOR WHO ~~No.~~ Harry, I'm not with you.

HARRY No, you see, it seems that Kellman –
he's dead, by the way – **Kellman** was really
working for ~~these~~ **the** Vogan people. And he
got the other lot, **the, er** – whatd'yacallems –

COMMANDER ~~The~~ Cybermen.

HARRY Cybermen, that's right ~~Yes, I'm~~
~~awfully~~ – **terribly** bad on names. He got ~~them~~
the Cybermen up on the beacon so they'd be
sitting ducks for ~~this whacking great~~ **the**
Vogans' rocket. Only the Vogans haven't
finished ~~it~~ **the rocket** yet so things have gone a
bit wrong.

DOCTOR WHO Yes.

Lester looks at the slave clock atop the
commander's pack.

LESTER Doctor – we have about nine minutes
left~~, Doctor. What are we going to do?~~

HARRY And if she starts –

DOCTOR WHO Listen, **listen**. Commander, ~~I~~
~~want you~~ **if you were** to keep **on** ~~moving down~~
going towards the centre. **You could** draw
their radar track away from the rest of us.

COMMANDER ~~Right~~ Yes.

He moves off.

DOCTOR WHO ~~We'll cut through~~ **Meantime,**
Lester and I could take the cross-shaft and
attack the Cybermen from the rear.

LESTER What with?

DOCTOR WHO Gold. **Plain** old-fashioned gold.
~~Come on…~~

COMMANDER Well, Lester? Agreed, right.

DOCTOR WHO Good luck, Commander.

COMMANDER And to you.

DOCTOR WHO Come on…

TELECINE 28
INT. CAVES. DAY.

Matterbeam area. The Cybermen still on
guard. Pan down to the relay apparatus. The
countdown clock is now very close to the red
sector. ⑦

3. INT. CAVE AREA F.

The Doctor, Harry and Lester are sifting specks
and granules of gold from the cave floor,
accumulating them in their hands

DOCTOR WHO How much have we got?

LESTER ~~Only another~~ We've got about five
minutes~~, Doctor.~~

DOCTOR WHO I know we've got five minutes.
~~Oh, dear –~~ I mean how much **gold dust** have
we got? Mm, that might be enough. You know
what to do?

HARRY Yes. Creep as close as we can, then
chuck this ~~gold dust~~ **stuff** into their chest
units.

DOCTOR WHO ~~Right.~~ You've got it, Harry. Come
on…

4. INT. GUILDROOM. DAY.

Tyrum is confronting Vorus.

TYRUM As the human said, recrimination is
pointless now. But I promise you, Vorus, if by

some miracle our planet should survive – you will face trial for treason!

VORUS It is you who should be tried, Tyrum – you and your creeping sycophants in the city.

TYRUM As leader of the Guardians you abused your trust. You opened the route to the surface. You made clandestine contact with aliens. And you beamed radio transmissions out into space. There are no greater crimes in our calendar.

VORUS In your calendar, Tyrum – in your cowering, furtive, underworld life! If we survive I ~~shall~~ will face trial gladly… ~~and let the people hear~~ I will give the people my reasons. I wanted to free them from this tyranny of… dark, dripping rock.

TYRUM Living the way we had for generations, at least we were safe, Vorus. Safe from the genocidal threat of the Cybermen!

VORUS I had a dream…

TYRUM A folly! Conceived out of arrogance through overweening ambition!

VORUS We could have traded with the other worlds. Exchanged **our** gold for armaments. We could have been strong enough to defend ourselves against ~~the~~ Cybermen or any other attacker.

Sheprah enters.

SHEPRAH Councillor, we are beaten! Our people have withdrawn – refusing to attack the Cybermen again –

VORUS Order them back! Command them!

SHEPRAH I'm sorry, Councillor. We need time to regroup.

VORUS There is no time.

TYRUM Come, I will speak to them. ~~If I were younger I'd lead them myself.~~ **8**

TELECINE 29
INT. CAVES. DAY.

On the clock ticking steadily. A minute to the red zone. On the Cybermen pacing steadily. And beyond them a glimpse – the Doctor dropping behind a rock as a Cyberman turns in his direction.

The three attackers are spread out, sneaking forward a yard at a time as in a children's game.

DOCTOR WHO There they are… Wait till I give the signal… Ready?

On the clock. 30 seconds left. Sweat beading on Harry's face. A glint in the Doctor's eye. In his strange way he is enjoying their final gamble.

A Cyberman turns again, moves towards Harry. Discovery is certain. The Doctor tosses a lump of rock. It falls behind the Cyberman and he swings quickly.

DOCTOR WHO ~~Get him, Harry.~~ **Now!**

Harry leaps at the Cyberman's back. He clings on, rubbing gold dust into the Cyberman's chest unit.

The Cyberman swings round, trying to dislodge Harry. The second Cyberman has drawn a bead on Harry. He fires just as the Cyberman turns and hits his compatriot on the head. **9**

The Doctor and Lester are rushing the second Cyberman who is momentarily unsure which way to turn. A double volley of gold catches him in the chest and he staggers back, collapsing beside the relay apparatus. He swings his gun towards the Doctor.

Harry's Cyberman pitches forwards on his face with Harry still clinging leech-like to his back.

DOCTOR WHO Come on, Harry – run for it.

Lester flings himself at the second Cyberman. His hands reach for the buckle of his rucksack. There is an explosion. A lot of smoke. **10**

A Cyberhead comes spinning across the ground out of the smoke. The Doctor traps it with his foot.

Harry gets dazedly to his feet.

HARRY Lester…

He goes forward with the Doctor and bends over Lester's crumpled body. One glance is enough. The rucksack is still intact.

The Doctor picks the broken countdown clock out of the wreckage of the relay apparatus. It shows two seconds to go.

The Doctor bends and puts his ear to the wreckage.

DOCTOR WHO It's still humming!

The faint power hum he hears galvanizes him into action. He rips off a buckled cover plate. **11**

5. INT. CONTROL ROOM 2. ⑫

The Cyberleader stares at the blank radar screen. ⑬

CYBERLEADER We have lost radar contact.

FIRST CYBERMAN ~~My~~ **Our** information flow from the surface has ceased. The countdown has stopped.

The Cyberleader studies his apparatus.

CYBERLEADER Select Video Picture of Voga. Detonation by manual control.

SARAH No! **Don't!**

The Cyberleader is reaching for the plunger as she springs forward. He turns in surprise. Sarah grapples with him. The first Cyberman goes to his leader's assistance. He pulls Sarah off and flings her across the room. She lies senseless.

FIRST CYBERMAN Shall I destroy the human female?

But the Cyberleader has turned back to his bomb controls. Once more he reaches for the plunger.

CYBERLEADER Detonation – now!

He pushes the plunger home and turns expectantly to the scanner, waiting to see Voga disintegrate. The seconds tick past and nothing happens. The Cyberleader hammers his mailed fist on the console. ⑭

CYBERLEADER ~~We have~~ **It has** failed! Why?

TELECINE 30
INT. CAVES. DAY.

On their way to the Matterbeam area the Doctor puts his hands on the rucksack buckle. Thinks about it for a moment. Then flips open the clip. Harry winces. The Doctor smiles and eases the rucksack from his shoulders. ⑮

DOCTOR WHO ~~Well, that's a weight off my mind.~~ Well, I'm impressed. ~~Now, Harry, what about this rocket?~~

HARRY ~~Oh, my gosh, yes! Sarah!~~

DOCTOR WHO ~~We have to stop them firing it. Come on.~~

~~He hurries off. Harry follows.~~

HARRY ~~It's all go, isn't it?~~

6. INT. CONTROL ROOM 2.

Sarah bound, propped against a wall. She recovers consciousness. Sees the Cyberleader staring down at her. She cranes round to look at the scanner and sees Voga is still on the screen. ⑯

SARAH Voga! It's still there…

CYBERLEADER Yes. For the moment.

SARAH Then your plan failed! The Doctor's beaten you! ~~I knew he would –~~

CYBERLEADER Silence! ~~I am not beaten.~~ **We have not failed.** Our computers are assessing an alternative plan.

SARAH Your best plan is to get off this beacon before the Vogans…

CYBERLEADER Continue. The Vogans?

SARAH *(Shrugs)* Kellman led you into a trap. They have a rocket aimed at this beacon.

CYBERLEADER You lie.

SARAH **Well,** stick around and ~~see.~~ –

The Cyberleader takes a worried pace or two.

CYBERLEADER You lie because if ~~Vogans~~ **they** had such a rocket they would have used it ~~before~~ **by** now.

SARAH All I know is when I left Kellman said the rocket was – ~~the only hope of saving the planet.~~

CYBERLEADER Kellman… So they have a rocket. But they have not ~~fired~~ **used** it. Logical conclusion – the rocket has a malfunction. Therefore this information does not affect our ~~alternative~~ plan. We shall proceed. Voga will be destroyed.

7. INT. GUILDROOM. DAY.

Tyrum, Vorus, Harry, the Doctor.

TYRUM We are grateful to you, human, for saving Voga –

DOCTOR WHO Oh, **please,** don't call me human, ~~please –~~ just Doctor will do nicely, **thank you.** ~~So~~ **Is** that ~~is~~ your rocket~~, eh~~? ⑰ ⑱

VORUS The sky-striker. **Yes.** You have delivered our enemies into my hands, Doctor.

He turns eagerly as Magrik enters.

VORUS Magrik, you have news?

MAGRIK Everything is now ready, Vorus. We can start the countdown.

VORUS Excellent!

He presses a switch on his desk and a section of the desk reverses to reveal a simple control fascia.

DOCTOR WHO ~~Now just~~ Before you do anything rash – like pressing another button – ~~can I~~

~~suggest~~ may I make an alternative ~~solution~~ **suggestion**?

VORUS An alternative?

DOCTOR WHO Let me take the transmat back to the beacon and deal with the Cybermen myself.

TYRUM Yourself… You mean alone?

DOCTOR WHO Give me **just** 15 minutes. If at the end of that time, ~~I've not~~ **I haven't** come through on the radio – well, then you can ~~let that~~ **fire off** your rocket ~~off~~.

TYRUM You have already done so much – why should you risk your life again in this way?

DOCTOR WHO I have a young friend on the beacon – Sarah Jane, the girl who was here. She's risked her life trying to save mine. The least I can do is to accept the same risk for her. Just fifteen minutes. Is that so intolerable?

TYRUM Fifteen minutes then, Doctor – but no longer.

DOCTOR WHO Thank you, Tyrum. ~~Then~~ There's ~~only~~ **just** one other thing I need.

TYRUM What is that?

DOCTOR WHO A bag of gold dust.

TYRUM Oh yes.

DOCTOR WHO **Thank you. And Harry?**

HARRY Doctor?

DOCTOR WHO While I'm gone, Harry, you'd better find the commander.

HARRY I'll try.

VORUS I have ~~worked and~~ planned **for this moment** for years ~~for this moment~~ and now **as I close the trap** you ~~ask us~~ **expect me** to wait.

TELECINE 'Z'
INT. CAVES. DAY.

The Doctor running through caves to matterbeam area.

8. INT. CONTROL ROOMS 2 & 1.

Sarah still tied. ⑲ *1st Cyberman and the Cyberleader are going over the computer's figures.* ⑳

CYBERLEADER Point of impact?

FIRST CYBERMAN ~~23~~ 27 Degrees 7 minutes north, 160 degrees 20 minutes east. The crust is weakest at this point.

CYBERLEADER Velocity at impact, 10,000 light units.

FIRST CYBERMAN Calculations indicate at maximum thrust the beacon will attain that velocity seven minutes before impact.

CYBERLEADER What explosive force ~~will be~~ **is** required to sunder the planet at that depth?

FIRST CYBERMAN 1000 kilos per unit.

CYBERLEADER Excellent! Then the plan will be executed.

FIRST CYBERMAN Yes, leader.

CYBERLEADER Order the ~~bomb-load~~ **bombs** to be transferred to the beacon.

The Cyberman exits. The Cyberleader turns to Sarah.

CYBERLEADER ~~Our~~ **The** alternative plan will work. When ~~this~~ **the** beacon crashes into Voga we shall be watching from a safe distance. But you will have a much closer view.

He exits.
Sarah struggles against her bonds.
Suddenly the transmat hums.
She looks round.
The Doctor materializes. ㉑

SARAH Doctor?

DOCTOR WHO Sssh!

SARAH Sorry.

He hurries to her and cuts the flex binding her wrists and feet.

DOCTOR WHO You haven't seen **anything of** the TARDIS, ~~I suppose~~ **have you**?

SARAH The TARDIS? Listen, Doctor, ~~they're going to load~~ **the** Cybermen **are loading** this beacon with bombs and **they're going to** smash it into Voga!

DOCTOR WHO ~~Oh, dear!~~ And we've got ~~exactly~~ **about**… nine minutes before the Vogans ~~fire~~ **aim** their rocket at us.

The Doctor frowns and picks up the dormant Cybermat. He turns it over thoughtfully.

DOCTOR WHO ~~Here,~~ Bring that control box and we'll see what we can do. ~~Quickly now.~~

SARAH Doctor…

DOCTOR WHO Yes?

SARAH ~~Doctor. I am glad~~ **It's good** to see you.

DOCTOR WHO Is it?

SARAH Yes.

DOCTOR WHO Oh, well… Come on – quickly now.

He strides out. Sarah grabs the control box and runs after him.

9. INT. TRANSOM.

Cybermen are carrying cobalt bombs – black, dome-headed metal cylinders, like containers for camping gas – into the transom from their spaceship. The Cyberleader is watching.

CYBERLEADER ~~Take the bombs into~~ **Carry the bombs to** the nose cone. Maximum urgency imperative.

10. INT. GUILDROOM. DAY.

Vorus and Magrik hover over the control fascia. Tyrum stands watching.

MAGRIK Seven minutes, **Vorus**.

VORUS What can the Doctor do in the time? We should never have agreed **to wait**!

TYRUM Stand back from the firing button, Vorus. There is, as Magrik says, another seven minutes.

VORUS Don't worry, Tyrum – I can wait. But when I press ~~this~~ **that** button it will ~~signal~~ **mean** more than the ~~destruction~~ **end** of the Cybermen. It will ~~be~~ **mean** the start of a new life on Voga. A new regime.

TYRUM That will be for the people to decide.

VORUS This was my idea. ~~I created it all.~~ I planned **it all** ~~the details~~… I shall be the people's liberator.

TYRUM You came very close to being their destroyer.

VORUS That will be forgotten in ~~our~~ **my** triumph. The people will turn to me… they will beg me to lead them.

Harry and the Commander enter.

HARRY ~~Have you heard~~ **Any news** from the Doctor ~~yet~~?

VORUS No, and I don't expect ~~we shall~~ **there will be**. ㉒

MAGRIK Five minutes.

11. INT. CREW DECK.

The Doctor is replacing the base plate on the Cybermat. ㉓ *He turns his attention to the control box.*

SARAH ~~What's the point of~~ **There's no point** filling it with gold dust.~~?~~ It won't attack the Cybermen.

DOCTOR WHO Wait and see.

Sound effect: a whining vibration building in volume. ㉔

SARAH What's that?

DOCTOR WHO They've started the engines.

12. INT. CONTROL ROOMS 1 & 2.

The Cyberleader is looking at the spot where Sarah was. The severed flex lies on the floor.

CYBERLEADER She has been freed. One of her friends from Voga… perhaps the Doctor.

FIRST CYBERMAN All engines normal. Thrust zero.

CYBERLEADER Increase ton levels.

He turns and looks at the transmat.

CYBERLEADER If it was the Doctor, he will make ~~some final~~ **a further** attempt to thwart my plan… ~~so~~ **therefore** he will **still** be concealed aboard. Search the forward compartments. Locate and destroy all animal organisms…

The Cyberman moves out.

FIRST CYBERMAN Control response normal. Engine response effective. Thrust 5000.

CYBERLEADER Engage hyperdrive.

The Cyberman selects the hyperdrive controls.

13. INT. CREW DECK.

The Doctor is slotting the control box together. Heavy footsteps along the transom.

SARAH Listen!

DOCTOR WHO ~~Quick – down there!~~ **Come on, let's** hide!

He puts the Cybermat on the floor and joins Sarah in the corner.

The footsteps halt outside the door.

A moment of menacing silence.

Then the door crashes open and the Cyberman stomps in, gun in hand.

His eye-slots search the room.

The Doctor presses switches on his control box.

The Cybermat's eyes light up and it moves towards the Cyberman's back.

The Cyberman turns towards the corner where the Doctor and Sarah are hiding.

He advances a pace or two.

Suddenly the Cybermat launches itself towards the Cyberman's throat. ㉕ *It drives its hypodermic plungers into his neck.*

The Cyberman emits a strange noise. He knocks the Cybermat to the floor and lurches backwards. His knees buckle. He does a little

Cyberjig and collapses, green fluid issuing from his joints.

The Doctor and Sarah emerge and look down at him.

SARAH You did it.

DOCTOR WHO It was nothing…

SARAH Hurry!

DOCTOR WHO ~~The way to~~ Dusty death. Out, out ~~brief candle~~!

We might fear he is going through the whole speech. But there is a sudden change in the engine note and they clutch at the table for balance.

DOCTOR WHO ~~Come on!~~

SARAH Doctor, come on!

He grabs his Cybermat and hurries out.

14. INT. GUILDROOM. DAY.

Vorus leans forward to a speaker.

VORUS Control to firing bunker. Stand by for the countdown.

TYRUM We have another two minutes.

Vorus eyes him balefully.

VORUS The countdown ~~will take~~ –

MAGRIK Vorus, look! The target sensor – it's moving!

VORUS ~~What…?~~ The beacon is in motion!

MAGRIK It's coming towards us. ~~It has been~~ It's set on a collision course.

VORUS Activate firing controls.

He reaches towards the fascia.

Harry jumps forward.

HARRY ~~Now hold on!~~ Vorus – You promised the Doctor 15 minutes –

VORUS ~~Fools!~~

COMMANDER Vorus!

He starts again for the firing button.

Vorus is clearly not going to listen. Tyrum points a gun.

TYRUM No, Vorus~~, stand back~~. No!

VORUS My sky-striker… my… glory.

TELECINE 32

Rocket blasts off.

15. INT. CONTROL ROOM 1.

Voga looming closer on the main screen.

The Cyberleader and First Cyberman at the controls.

CYBERLEADER We must evacuate the beacon in three minutes.

FIRST CYBERMAN Our calculations indicate the fireball will extend 1.5 million miles.

The Doctor and Sarah sneak in with their Cybermat.

A 3rd Cyberman sees them, and the Cybermat leaps at it, latching on the Cyberman's throat. The 3rd Cyberman staggers away in its death throes.

The Doctor throws a handful of gold dust towards the 1st Cyberman.]

3rd Cyberman blundering around in his death throes bobs into its path. The gold dust sprays down its front and it collapses.

DOCTOR WHO All right. **All right – you've made your point.** We surrender.

CYBERLEADER What?

DOCTOR WHO ~~Raynights.~~ **We surrender.**

CYBERLEADER You have interfered once too often, Doctor. **Now, tie her up…** Tie her up.

The Cyberleader and the 1st Cyberman drag Sarah and the Doctor to the console. The Cyberleader hands the Doctor a length of flex.

The Cyberleader looks at the scanner.

Voga is filling the screen now.

~~CYBERLEADER Hurry!~~

16. INT. GUILDROOM. DAY.

Tyrum and the commander are looking at the fascia.

Harry is rubbing his head.

TYRUM The Doctor's time is up. He has failed.

COMMANDER I'm afraid so.

HARRY I wouldn't be too sure. ~~He was pretty confident.~~

COMMANDER Well, his only chance now is to get off that beacon by the transmat. The rocket is due to impact in six minutes.

~~HARRY You understand that set-up eh?~~

~~The commander shakes his head.~~

~~COMMANDER It's not like anything I've seen before.~~

~~TYRUM Look! There is the rocket!~~

~~On the window picture we see the rocket soaring steadily upwards towards the beacon.~~

17. INT. CONTROL ROOM 1.

The Cyberleader tests Sarah's bonds.

CYBERLEADER The beacon is approaching Voga at 10,000 light units. It is time for us to leave.

The Doctor is staring at the scanner in awe.

DOCTOR WHO ~~Ta ta.~~ **Bye bye.**

CYBERLEADER You two are especially privileged.

~~**SARAH** Bye, Bye.~~

CYBERLEADER You are about to die in the biggest explosion ever witnessed in this solar system. It will be a magnificent spectacle. Unfortunately you ~~won't be able~~ **will be unable** to appreciate it.

He exits with 1st Cyberman.

DOCTOR WHO Nice sense of irony. I thought for a moment he was going to smile… ~~The Great tinned ham…~~

SARAH How long have we got, Doctor?

DOCTOR WHO Judging ~~from~~ **at** the speed at which that rocket is ~~closing~~ **approaching**, two or three minutes.

SARAH The Vogan rocket?

DOCTOR WHO Yes, that's right.

TELECINE 35

Cybership undocks from beacon. 🄳🄵

18. INT. GUILDROOM. DAY.

~~**TYRUM** The Cybership is leaving the beacon.~~

COMMANDER They're getting away.

TYRUM **Then t**he sky-striker will simply destroy the empty beacon!

HARRY If it is empty…

19. INT. CONTROL ROOM 1.

The Doctor and Sarah are struggling frenziedly to free themselves.

SARAH **It's no good, Doctor.** They won't budge.

DOCTOR WHO ~~I tied your wrists in a special sheepshank~~ **I used a tangle Turk's head eye-splice with a gromit** I picked up from Houdini – it should ~~give~~ **work**.

SARAH Well, you must have tied it wrong – no, wait a minute! **You're right.** They're loosening! ~~I can feel …~~

She pulls a hand free.

DOCTOR WHO Good girl! ~~Now, Harry.~~ That rocket's getting too close for comfort…

Sarah frees herself swiftly, then helps the Doctor untie himself. He goes straight to the radio.

DOCTOR WHO *(Switching on)* Hullo, Voga! Hullo, Voga! This is Nerva Beacon.

Crackle, crackle.

COMMANDER *(VO)* Doctor! Is that you?

DOCTOR WHO Commander? Listen, tell Vorus the Cybermen have abandoned the Beacon. He's to aim the rocket at the cybership.

20. INT. GUILDROOM. DAY.

COMMANDER But, **Doctor,** Vorus is dead, ~~Doctor.~~ And none of us knows how to operate ~~the control~~ **these controls.**

DOCTOR WHO *(VO)* ~~Just a second…~~ **What?** Let me think…

COMMANDER Let you what?

HARRY **Just** let him think.

21. INT. CONTROL ROOM 1.

The Doctor is concentrating fiercely.
Sarah is staring at the scanner with sick fascination. 🄳🄶

SARAH Doctor, it's going to hit ~~us~~ any second ~~now~~!

DOCTOR WHO ~~Yes, Yes, yes, … I saw that control panel …~~ *(into radio)* Commander!

COMMANDER *(VO)* Yes, Doctor?

DOCTOR WHO There are two ~~quadrant~~ levers on the left of the panel. Got them?

22. INT. GUILDROOM. DAY.

COMMANDER Yes, I've got them.

DOCTOR WHO *(VO)* The top ~~one~~ **lever** controls the angle of flight and the lower one must be the direction and stabilizer control. ~~See if they're working.~~

~~**COMMANDER** Right.~~

He pulls the top lever across its quadrant and then moves the other.

TELECINE 38A

Rocket heads towards us with beacon foreground. 🄳🄷

23. INT. CONTROL ROOM 1. 🄳🄸

DOCTOR WHO Cogito, ergo sum.

SARAH Eh? **What?**

DOCTOR WHO I think, therefore it missed.

Sarah indicates the scanner. The scabs and craters of Voga are now visible.

SARAH Yes, but we're still heading for the biggest bang in history.

DOCTOR WHO ~~Ah~~, **Oh** yes…

He goes to the controls and pulls back the flight trimmers. They move less than an inch. He exerts all his strength. No joy.

DOCTOR WHO Oh, no… They've locked the gyro controls. The flight trimmers are jammed!

SARAH What does that mean?

DOCTOR WHO It means we're heading for the biggest bang in history.

24. INT. GUILDROOM. DAY.

TYRUM The rocket is closing on the Cybermen's ship!

HARRY A touch more starboard rudder, Commander.

On the screen they are watching the rocket arrowing down towards the Cybership. 39

COMMANDER Come on… Come on! Just a few more seconds!

25. INT. CYBERSHIP. DAY.

The Cyberleader and his two Cyberflankers.

~~CYBERLEADER The beacon will impact on Voga in three and a half minutes!~~

A sudden alarm klaxon. 40

FIRST CYBERMAN There is a missile on our port bow!

CYBERLEADER ~~A missile?~~ Engage full thrust! Deploy energy shield!

~~FIRST CYBERMAN It is too late. The missile is about to —~~

Flash white.

TELECINE 41

Explosion in space. 41

26. INT. GUILDROOM. DAY.

Tyrum, the commander and Harry are watching the screen.

HARRY Well, that's ~~your Cybermen finished.~~ the end of your Cybermen.

TYRUM Never again will they be a threat to Voga. At last we can live without fear.

COMMANDER Why doesn't the Doctor put the beacon back on course?

~~HARRY What?~~

COMMANDER I thought he was taking evasive action but **look** – ~~it's still heading~~ He's coming straight ~~for~~ **towards** us.

HARRY Better give him a whistle, **Commander**. He ~~has~~ **does have** these absent-minded moments… 42

He goes to the speaker.

27. INT. CONTROL ROOM 1.

The Doctor has a panel open in the wall. He is using a two-man Stillson wrench on the heavy plumbing inside. 43 *He is gasping with effort and deploying every ounce of strength. So far the nuts have not moved.*

~~SARAH Perhaps you're trying to turn it the wrong way?~~

The Doctor scowls and shoots an anxious glance at the scanner. Voga is rushing upwards now at an appalling speed.

The Doctor shifts his grip and tries again.

HARRY *(VO filter)* Hullo, Doctor? Can you hear me?

Sarah goes to the radio intercom. 44

SARAH Yes, Harry – What is it~~, Harry~~?

HARRY *(VO)* Hullo, Sarah. **Look, old girl, I don't know if you're aware of it, but** you appear to be heading straight for us.

SARAH Yes, we are aware of it, Harry. Very much so. And we're loaded with Cyberbombs.

28. INT. GUILDROOM. DAY.

HARRY What! ~~Cyberbombs. Can't you do something?~~ Well, you'd better do something, old girl, and quickly.

SARAH *(VO filter)* The Doctor's doing his best~~, Harry~~. **But** – 45

29. INT. CONTROL ROOM 1.

SARAH – the Cybermen locked the gyro-controls.

The Stillson moves. The Doctor gives a gasp of relief. 46

29A. INT. CONTROL ROOM 1. 47

DOCTOR WHO That should do it! ~~If she'll answer to the controls…~~

The Doctor springs across to flight trimmers. This time they move. The scanner picture of

Voga's surface tilts. (48) *Sarah clutches at the console for support.* (49)

30. INT. GUILDROOM. DAY. (50)

On the screen. The beacon swinging towards the screen. (51)

COMMANDER ~~She's~~ **It's still** coming straight towards us.

TYRUM ~~She's~~ **It's** going to hit! ~~She's~~ **It's** going to hit!

31. INT. CONTROL ROOM 1.

The crackling roar of the engines bouncing back now from Vogan surface. On the scanner the features of the planet are a crazy blur. (52)

SARAH We're going to crash~~, Doctor~~!

DOCTOR WHO Hang on! If I pull her back ~~too hard~~ at this speed she'll break in half…

Now, on the scanner, peaks and crags are flashing towards the screen at incredible speed.

Sarah shrieks and ducks as collision with a particularly large mountain seems inevitable. (53) *The Doctor is crouched at the controls. He is fighting desperately to beat the odds.*

Suddenly the screen is clear of all but sky. The engine roar recedes. (54)

The Doctor straightens and gives a half-unbelieving shake of his head. He looks at Sarah.

DOCTOR WHO Yes, I think she'll settle ~~back into her~~ **down nicely into** orbit now.

SARAH Oh, good! (55)

Tardis materializes.

DOCTOR WHO **I think** I'll just set the drift compensators. We don't want it slipping through our fingers. (56)

Harry materializes (57)

~~**DOCTOR WHO** Ah, Harry. Don't just stand there. Come along!~~

HARRY I see old faithful's turned up after all.

DOCTOR WHO **Don't just stand there, come on.** (58)

SARAH It's all go, isn't it?

DOCTOR WHO ~~No idea. But~~ I'm needed back on Earth.

SARAH How d'you know?

DOCTOR WHO ~~Because~~ I left the Brigadier a space-time telegraph system and told him not to use it unless he had a real emergency **on his hands**.

SARAH And he's used it?

DOCTOR WHO He has. **Come on, you two.**

HARRY I say, but what about the commander – **aren't we going to stop and say cheerio?** ~~But aren't we going to wait and say cheerio to the Commander?~~

DOCTOR WHO *(VO very loud)* Come along ~~you two~~!

SARAH Don't argue – come on!

Harry and Sarah enter the TARDIS. (59) *The door shuts. TARDIS noise and it disappears.* (60)

CLOSING TITLES

---

(1) The reprise starts with the Doctor approaching the rock face. The rocks then fall, and the film sequence is shown without the studio inserts added to the end of Part Three.

(2) The note 'Additional Dialogue' does appear in the camera script. It may be that this is a direction for the actors to ad-lib dialogue at this point, but it is more likely that there is additional dialogue inserted here that was not scripted. This would reduce the potential for confusion when the film sequence was transferred to videotape and edited into the episode.

(3) Scene 16 from Part Three was inserted here, followed by Part Four, Scene 2.

(4) This scene was moved to after Telecine 28.

(5) The radar sweep has become fuzzy and unclear on the main screen. A different effect – zooming in and out on the radar screen that was inlaid into the CSO area – was also considered, either to enhance this effect or replace it.

(6) This scene was moved ahead of Scene 1.

(7) Scene 1 was inserted here, ahead of Scene 3.

(8) This was the last scene of the afternoon recording. In the break before the evening session, the small stage area where the shots of Tyrum in his office were recorded for CSOing on to Vorus' monitor was

removed. The revolving drum used for the sequence of Nerva plummeting towards Voga (Scenes 29A and 31) was set up there instead.

9 This sequence of the second Cyberman firing was dropped. What happens is that Harry and the Doctor jump on the Cybermen, but are overpowered. Lester hangs back and watches as the Cybermen manage to spill the gold dust. Harry and the Doctor are forced to flee, and then Lester jumps down at the feet of both Cybermen and sets off his buckle-bomb, killing the Cybermen.

10 The explosion was achieved with smoke, and by overlaying a picture of a large flame over the film of the Cybermen.

11 Telecine 30 immediately followed this film sequence.

12 This scene was moved to after Telecine 30.

13 We see the radarscope image shrink and fade to nothing – achieved by the camera feeding the main CSO screen zooming out from the image of the radar trace.

14 A picture of Voga on the main screen shows that nothing has happened.

15 The scene starts with Harry and the Doctor still examining the relay apparatus beside the dead Cyberman.

16 A caption slide CSO'd on to the main screen.

17 Vorus is looking at the circular screen which shows (using CSO) the model sky-striker in its silo.

18 The control panel in front of the screen rolls over to reveal another, similar, panel beneath.

19 A close-up of Voga is on the main (CSO) screen.

20 The text fed to a monitor by 'Anchor' reads:

> 27 Degrees 07 Minutes NORTH
>
> 160 Degrees 20 Minutes EAST
>
> Co-ordinates verified
>
> 003-02-36
>
> Geo-stress minima established

21 The usual lighting effect and roll-back-and-mix for the Doctor's materialization. He cannot see Sarah from the transmat area, so whistles to attract her attention. She whistles back the first half of a wolf whistle, which he completes. (Elisabeth Sladen cannot whistle – her final scene as a regular on *Doctor Who* was miming while someone else whistled 'Daddy Wouldn't Buy Me a Bow-Wow' in *The Hand of Fear*: 1976.)

22 Vorus turns on his (CSO) screen and looks at his (model) sky-striker.

23 The Doctor tips gold dust into the 'tail' of the Cybermat and pushes it down with a spatula.

24 Nerva seems to tip – achieved by tilting the camera to the right as Elisabeth Sladen and Tom Baker lurched to the left. The camera (and actors) then righted themselves.

25 The CSO shot of the Cybermat rearing up used in Part One, Scene 13 was again edited in here. As in that scene, a visual effects assistant threw the Cybermat at its victim from off camera.

26 Nerva lurches the other way at this point – camera tilting left and actors 'falling' to the right.

27 The Doctor delivers this quote from *Macbeth* to the dead Cyberman.

28 Filmed model footage of Nerva (Telecine 31) was CSO'd on to Vorus' screen. As the camera zoomed in on the model beacon, so it seemed to approach.

29 First Harry, then the commander, try to pull Vorus away from the controls.

30 Tyrum takes a gun from one of the guards and shoots Magrik when he tries to fire the rocket, then Vorus. There was a brief recording pause in the struggle to allow Tyrum to be given a new – loaded – gun for the second shot.

31 Filmed inserts, including 13 feet of stock 16mm showing a NASA Saturn V rocket launching, were used to replace some of the sky-striker model shoot (see also the end of Scene 16).

32 One page of the script for this episode is missing from the BBC Archives. To replace it, the small amount of material in square brackets [like this] is transcribed from the completed programme, not reproduced from the camera script.

33 CSO was used to show Voga looming closer outside the main window.

34 A CSO shot was planned, showing a filmed model insert of the rocket approaching Nerva – Telecine 33. It may be that the model sky-striker footage was not considered good enough to use, hence the substitution of stock NASA footage for its lift-off (replacing Telecine 32).

35 This model shot was preceded by a brief model shot of the sky-striker travelling outwards from Voga (Telecine 'D').

36 CSO'd on to the scanner were a picture of Voga against a starscape and the model sky-striker. The camera aimed at the model zoomed in to create the effect of the rocket approaching on the scanner.

37 This model shot was a view, 'through' the ring of Nerva beacon, of the sky-striker approaching.

38 The scene opens with the Doctor and Sarah ducking as the (CSO'd) rocket swoops close on the scanner. Then there was a brief filmed insert of the sky-striker heading away into space.

39 Telecine 40, CSO'd on to the screen, was model footage of the sky-striker approaching the Cybership.

40 Telecine 'A' was CSO'd on to the vignette set of the ship's screen – this showed the (model) rocket approaching.

41 This model sequence showed the sky-striker impacting the after-section of the Cybership and the resulting explosion. There was a brief cut to the stricken Cybermen within the ship (run on from Scene 25), before cutting back to the end of the explosion – the debris falling downwards.

42 CSO'd on to the scanner, Telecine 42 shows the beacon heading towards us.

43 The Doctor turns a crank handle which he inserts into a socket behind a hatch labelled 'SECONDARY SYSTEM'.

44 Sarah speaks into a microphone projecting from the control console.

45 Sarah's dialogue continues straight into Scene 29.

46 There was a recording break after this scene. This scene was followed by Scene 30, before which there was a short model shot of Voga approaching the camera.

47 This scene was moved to after Scene 30.

48 As Nerva crashed towards Voga, the CSO screen showed a revolving drum that simulated the asteroid's surface; Briant was not impressed with this effect.

49 The camera showing Sarah and the Doctor in profile was tilted left so that Nerva appeared to be tilting 'forwards' as the Doctor tries to steer it clear. The camera showing Sarah and the Doctor from behind, together with the main screen, was tilted right so that Nerva seemed to be leaning to the left as it skimmed the surface of Voga.

50 This scene was moved ahead of Scene 29A.

51 Telecine 45, a model shot of the beacon coming straight at the camera, was inserted using CSO on to the circular screen.

52 The revolving drum was used, as in Scene 29A.

53 The camera behind Sarah and the Doctor was tilted the other way (to the left), then back to level as the drum surface of Voga disappeared off the bottom of the screen to show Nerva moving up and away.

54 A brief model shot (Telecine 46) of the Beacon heading off into space was inserted here.

55 The TARDIS materializes at this point, achieved by roll-back-and-mix.

56 As the Doctor enters the TARDIS prop, the mass of ticker tape he will bring out with him is visible behind the left door.

57 As usual, the transmat effect was achieved using a lighting effect and roll-back-and-mix.

58 The Doctor emerges from the TARDIS with a mass of ticker tape wrapped round his shoulders.

59 The dematerialization sound has already started and Sarah drags Harry into the TARDIS.

60 The TARDIS was dematerialized using roll-back-and-mix. Unusually, it leaves without its light flashing.

Other Adventures

A sixth serial (apart from *Space Station*) was commissioned for Season Twelve but not used. This was originally intended to follow *Revenge of the Cybermen* in transmission order, but was actually held over to begin Season Thirteen as *Terror of the Zygons*. This serial was written by Robert Banks Stewart, an old colleague of Robert Holmes from their work together at ATV in the 1960s. The story, which concerned an explanation for the legend of the Loch Ness monster, was commissioned as a six-part storyline under the title *Loch Ness* on Tuesday 12 March 1974 for delivery by Tuesday 26 March (so it was in development prior to all the broadcast Season Twelve stories except *Robot* and *Genesis of the Daleks*). However, the day after this initial deadline, the target was revised to Monday 6 May, allowing Stewart more time to complete his submission. The six scripts, however, were commissioned on Wednesday 3 April.

Loch Ness Part One was delivered on Wednesday 18 September and accepted six days later; Parts Two and Three arrived at the BBC on Monday 2 December, to be accepted on Thursday 5. The fourth and final episode (which counted as the originally commissioned Parts Four to Six since the story had now been shortened) was submitted on Monday 30 December – the weekend after Tom Baker's debut as the Doctor on BBC1. Director Douglas Camfield then called a production meeting on *The Secret of Loch Ness* on Thursday 30 January 1975, since it was intended that the serial should follow *Genesis of the Daleks* into production for broadcast after *Revenge of the Cybermen*. Filming began on Monday 17 March and studio recording was completed on Wednesday 23 April, but by this time it had been decided to drop the serial – now entitled *Terror of the Zygons* – back to start Season Thirteen (although the BBC programme synopses issued in advance by the Royal National Institute for the Deaf in April 1975 still had *The Secret of Loch Ness* due to start transmission on Saturday 17 May – following on directly from *Revenge of the Cybermen*). The reason behind this decision was that the BBC schedulers wanted to move *Doctor Who* forward from the New Year start it had enjoyed since 1970 and shift the six-month run from January to June back to September to March. This was a calculated move in opposition to a new science fiction adventure film series, *Space: 1999*. This had been shot at Pinewood Studios since November 1973, and several ITV regions hinted they would be screening it as part of the autumn 1975 season on Saturday evenings. It therefore made sense to have *Doctor Who* established at the outset of the new BBC season, rather than have it swamped with a New Year debut, should *Space: 1999* have become popular in the ITV schedules.

As a result, *Terror of the Zygons* belongs with the scripts for Season Thirteen, although it was intended, and made, for Season Twelve. The other serials that were under development during the production of Season Twelve were:

- *Pyramids of Mars* by Lewis Greifer; commissioned in July 1974 and produced for Season Thirteen.

- [Title not known] by Robert Sloman; never formally commissioned but under consideration in November 1974.
- *The Enemy Within* (a.k.a. *Return to Sukannan, The Kraals*) by Terry Nation; commissioned in November 1974 and produced for Season Thirteen as *The Android Invasion.*
- *The Haunting* by Terrance Dicks; commissioned in December 1974 and storylined in January 1975.
- *The Beasts of Manzic* by Robin Smyth; commissioned c. December 1974.
- *Nightmare Planet* by Dennis Spooner; commissioned in January 1975.

Also during the production of Season Twelve, on Monday 6 May 1974, the production office was approached regarding a *Doctor Who* stage play by Anthony Pye-Jeary of Robert de Wynter and Anthony Pye-Jeary Ltd, a production company and agency based in Piccadilly. Pye-Jeary indicated that he was interested in staging such a project, and had already spoken to Terrance Dicks about writing a script and Terry Nation about the use of the Daleks; both had agreed in principle. The proposal was that the play would open in early December 1974 for an eight to ten week run and then go on tour around the UK. As Roy Williams, a BBC exploitations manager, commented to Letts:

> As these plans will probably conflict with your own commitments for Tom Baker, Mr Pye-Jeary wondered whether, if Dr Who was seen in outline on a dark stage entering a time machine for 'rejuvenation', the difference in appearance of the character could be explained this way?

By Friday 5 June, Letts had attended a meeting about the play; between August 1971 and October 1973 there had been prolonged discussions with both the Century Theatre Ltd in Lancaster and Dimension Productions about a stage version of *Doctor Who,* which had finally been abandoned because it was too expensive. With *Robot* completed, Dicks worked on the script of the new stage play – *Doctor Who and the Daleks in Seven Keys to Doomsday*; numerous elements from this would later be re-used in his 1975 television script *The Brain of Morbius* and indeed in the 1989 stage play *Doctor Who – The Ultimate Adventure.* Trevor Martin (who had played a Time Lord in *The War Games*) was cast as the Doctor. Martin had trained at the Guildhall School of Music and Drama and been one of the original members of the National Theatre as well as having experience with the Royal Shakespeare Company. One of the Doctor's assistants, Jenny, was played by Wendy Padbury who had co-starred in the television series as Zoe in 1968/9; the other, Jimmy (originally called Dave), was the first West End role for James Matthews. The show's publicity day was Thursday 7 November, with Martin appearing in costume outside the Adelphi Theatre alongside the Dalek Supreme prop which had been borrowed from Terry Nation. Also working on the show was costume designer James Acheson who designed monstrous creatures such as the Daleks' servants the Clawrantulars (named Crocs in Dicks' scripts) and the Grand Master of Karn; Barry Letts oversaw production on behalf of the BBC and the director was Mick Hughes.

Dicks – who had attempted to get a stage musical version of the show, with Jon Pertwee and the Daleks, off the ground some years earlier – found himself developing yet another new version of the Doctor, who was seen to regenerate (on a screen) from the Pertwee incarnation of the Doctor at the start of the play. The newly regenerated Doctor – who exhibited elements of the personae of his three predecessors – was helped into the TARDIS by two 'children' from the audience – Jimmy and Jenny – who then join him in his ongoing quest on the planet Karn to prevent the Daleks from locating seven crystal keys that would allow them to develop an ultimate weapon and dominate the Universe. After mind-battles with the Grand Master of Karn and disabling a Dalek in which Jenny could hide, the Doctor managed to alter the structure of one of the crystals, causing the ultimate weapon to explode, defeating the Daleks.

The show opened on Monday 16 December and was a complex spectacle, involving pre-recorded voices, synchronized slide shows and pre-filmed sequences shown on massive projector screens. The show was well received by theatre critic Irving Wardle in *The Times* on Tuesday 17 December, although he chastised Dicks for implying that the Daleks were not robotic in his script; one scene had Jenny getting into a disabled Dalek after the creature inside had been removed. Dicks responded with a letter in the edition of Friday 20 in which he stated:

> The Daleks are not, and never have been, any kind of robot – a fact cleverly established on television many times, since the Daleks were created by Terry Nation well over ten years ago… In the hope that you will permit me to exterminate this minor inaccuracy, I am,
>
> Yours faithfully
> Terrance Dicks

However, the IRA launched a bombing campaign in mainland Britain over the Christmas period, and bookings for West End shows dwindled. Sustaining serious losses on the complex and expensive production, de Wynter and Pye-Jeary took the decision to close the show after four weeks. The final performance was on Saturday 11 January 1975 (the same day as *Robot* Part Three was broadcast). The play was later revived in December 1981 at the Buxton Opera House in Derbyshire and in New Zealand at Porirua Little Theatre in

Titahi Bay, New Zealand, in November/December 1984.

Christmas 1974 also saw the Doctor appearing elsewhere on BBC1 in his third incarnation – but not played by Jon Pertwee. After years of doubling Pertwee, stunt man Terry Walsh finally got to play the Doctor in *Aladdin*, a pantomime production made by the crew of the long-running children's entertainment show *Crackerjack*. This 60-minute special was written by Bob Headley, Tony Hare and Mort Kingsley, and included a galaxy of stars familiar to young audiences; joining the *Crackerjack* team of comics Peter Glaze (who had appeared in the 1964 *Doctor Who* story *The Sensorites*), Don Maclean and Jan Hunt were guests such as Dana, Deryck Guyler, Derek Griffiths and the Goodies. When Aladdin (Hunt) became trapped in a cave by his evil uncle Abanazar (Griffiths), he was rescued by none other than the Doctor in the TARDIS – with Walsh as the Doctor and the dance group Pan's People as his assistants! Barrie Gosney also appeared as a Dalek in the programme, which was recorded on Tuesday 3 December at Television Theatre and broadcast three weeks later at 4.15 p.m. on Christmas Eve, a few days before the repeat of *Planet of the Spiders*. The producer was Robin Nash.

Crackerjack was not slow to spot the popularity of *Doctor Who*, and when the new series began in spring 1975 and ran concurrently with *Doctor Who* Season Twelve, Headley and Hare wrote a new *Doctor Who* skit entitled 'Hallo My Dalek' for Glaze, Maclean and Hunt to perform in the twelfth show of the run which was taped at Television Theatre on Tuesday 18 March. Running to about eleven minutes, the routine was acted out on an ersatz TARDIS-control-room set with Maclean as the new Tom Baker-style 'Doctor Why', Hunt giving a very credible pastiche of Sarah at her most badly written and Glaze as a suitably pompous Brigadier; evidence of the show being written during Season Twelve comes from a comment about Harry being in hospital because he 'had to have his duffel coat removed' – a reference to the outfit worn by Ian Marter in *The Sontaran Experiment,* which aired in late February/early March. The sketch also featured one of the BBC Daleks in its *Genesis of the Daleks* livery, which was apparently operated by Suzanne Moore. The show was broadcast on BBC1 at 4.55 p.m. on Friday 21 March, the day before *Genesis of the Daleks* Part Three was broadcast.

In addition to the new Doctor's adventures on television, readers of Polystyle Publications' *TV Comic* followed his escapades on two monochrome pages every Monday. Drawn by Gerry Haylock, Tom Baker's Doctor made his debut in a new serial *Death Flower!* in issue 1204 (dated 11 January 1975), and the serial was preceded by a block of text entitled 'The Changing Face of Doctor Who' which covered the events at the end of *Planet of the Spiders,* and hence explained why the Doctor's face had changed since the previous week. The Doctor was now accompanied by Sarah Jane Smith in his comic-strip adventures, and together their first adventure was an Earth-bound affair about a form of alien plant breeding at the Wiltshire factory of the Vegpro Corporation. Martin Asbury took over the art for the next two stories, and started by taking the Doctor and Sarah back out into space for *Return of the Daleks!* (issues 1215–22) which ran in tandem with *Genesis of the Daleks* on BBC1. Drawing upon references regarding the Time Lords as seen in *The Three Doctors,* the tale had the Doctor and Sarah coming up against Shazar, a renegade Time Lord, who aims to steal the Doctor's TARDIS as the first step

in creating a fleet of Time Ships for his allies from Skaro. *The Wreckers!* (issues 1223–31) had the TARDIS materializing on the eighth moon of Gorgas where the Doctor discovered spaceships being dragged to their doom. Behind this scheme were the Vogans, a race of small creatures on hoverchairs who bore no resemblance to the Vogans currently appearing on television in *Revenge of the Cybermen,* but who had previously appeared in a *Doctor Who* strip in *Countdown* during 1971 entitled *The Vogan Slaves.* With the next strip, *The Emperor's Spy!* (issues 1232–38), John Canning (who had drawn the strip between 1966 and 1971) returned to take control of the visuals with a nineteenth-century serial in which the Doctor helps out with an experimental submarine to be used against the French during the Napoleonic Wars.

During the run of Season Twelve, *Doctor Who* also featured on BBC television on several other shows. A clip from *Death to the Daleks* appeared on the children's TV quiz show *Play It Again* on Saturday 22 February; Elisabeth Sladen – then on her break before starting work on *The Secret of Loch Ness* – was interviewed on *Wogan's World* on Sunday 9 March to tie in with the broadcast of *Genesis of the Daleks*; a series of *Doctor Who* monsters made by a keen model-maker, and another clip from *Death to the Daleks* appeared on *Blue Peter* on Thursday 20 March; and Terry Nation was interviewed about the Daleks and his new BBC telefantasy series *Survivors* on Radio 4's *Woman's Hour* on Friday 16 May. Tom Baker did a plethora of interviews and appearances as he worked on the following season: he was heard on BBC Radio Newcastle on Saturday 29 March and Radio 4's *4th Dimension* on Saturday 24 May, a fortnight after the run had ended.

APPENDIX B

Return Of The Cybermen

While the script for *Revenge of the Cybermen* remains credited to Gerry Davis, it was extensively rewritten by Robert Holmes (see the production notes for *Revenge of the Cybermen*). However, the basic story of both scripts is fundamentally the same – which is why it was deemed an 'editing' change rather than a complete rewrite.

The synopsis below is written from Gerry Davis' submitted scripts for *Return of the Cybermen*. Note that, like John Lucarotti with his original *Ark in Space* scripts, Gerry Davis provided titles for each individual episode.

1: The Beacon in Space

The story takes place on the Nerva, a space beacon originally built as a mineral processing station in a group of constantly moving asteroids; however, the Cyberwars have decimated the resources used in the processing, and in any event the asteroids are held to be worked out of their mineral deposits. The beacon now monitors and reports on the asteroids as a navigational hazard.

The story begins during a plague emergency. Captain Warner (a female character) is attacked by a Cybermat during her watch, and she collapses with black veins spreading up her neck. Meanwhile, the Doctor, Sarah and Harry appear in the station's mess room. They recognize it as the Nerva, but it is deserted. The Doctor proposes bringing out the crew by eating all their food. In fact, they are under camera surveillance by the crew: Commander Stevenson, the chemist Richard Kellman, Anitra Berglund and 24-year-old Bill Lester.

The travellers appear to have ignored the quarantine signals, so they must not be allowed to leave the Nerva alive.

In the mess room Sarah catches a fleeting glimpse of a Cybermat, but when the others investigate all they can see is a scratch on the floor. Looking around the corridors, they see Kellman watching them but he runs away when they approach him. They enter the crusher room, which is covered in gold dust, and also has more of the scratches they observed in the mess room. Kellman locks them in and begins to move the ceiling down to crush them, but leaves Anitra in charge; she reverses the process after hearing the Doctor state his identity.

The Doctor introduces himself to Stevenson as a doctor, and he is shown Warner; he recognizes the symptoms, but can't quite place them. Anitra explains that the plague began about a year ago, and (after several unsuccessful attempts to treat it) Nerva has been confined in quarantine until the disease burns itself out, or everyone on board is dead. Sarah is left to help Anitra in the sickbay while the Doctor and Harry are taken to the control room and questioned. Consulting his diary, the Doctor finds a drawing of a scratch mark similar to the ones around the Nerva, labelled 'C on T' and dated 24 October 2248; but his inability to remember what the initials stand for, or find the information in his diary, does not win him the commander's confidence.

In the sickbay, Anitra falls asleep, and Sarah is attacked by a Cybermat which leaves a trail of familiar scratches. Anitra raises the alarm, but by the time Lester, the

Doctor, and Harry arrive the Cybermats are dead, killed by a desperately thrown jar of gold dust – two bottles of acid having proved ineffective. The Doctor identifies the Cybermats as the cause of the plague, and demonstrates that the gold dust killed them by plating their gills so that they were unable to react to the atmosphere. Kellman accuses the Doctor of having brought the Cybermats on board. Meanwhile, Warner dies; and Sarah, too, has been infected. The Doctor reasons that there must be an antidote, since the Cybermen are too logical to create a plague virus without one; his mention of the Cybermen alarms the commander, since they were thought to have died out fifty years before.

Using an electronic detector, the Doctor establishes that there is a Cyberman hidden in the sick bay – in the radiation-suit lockers. Kellman is reluctant to give them the keys and makes a break for the door, but is rugby-tackled by Harry. Inside locker no. 5 they find an array of radiation suits hanging up – and underneath them, the silver boots of a Cyberman, which emerges menacingly from the locker.

2: The Plague Carriers

Harry tries to shoot the Cyberman, but his ray gun has no effect. The Cyberman stuns him while a second Cyberman cuts off the commander's escape. The Cybermen were not ready to meet them, but now they will have to await the Cyberleader. The Doctor asks for the plague antidote, but is told that they 'cannot make requests'. He checks his diary for a list of the Cybermen's weaknesses. This has all the items crossed out except radiation.

The Doctor and Harry set up a ruse involving treating the injured Harry (who plays dead, though recovered), for which they have to alter the sickbay lighting – actually a signal to Lester, who is watching on the monitor screen and who dims the lights on command. The Doctor and Harry

then drive away the Cybermen using radiation from the X-ray machines; the Doctor manages to snatch the Cybermat control box from them. Kellman protests that this will make the Cybermen their enemies without hearing what they have to say; the Doctor counters that it has established the humans in a position of strength from which to negotiate. He also notes that the Cybermen evidently need the remaining Nerva crew members alive, especially the commander; to discover why this is, they will have to find the Cyberleader, who must be hidden on the beacon. They go to look for him while the other Cybermen are recuperating from their dose of radiation.

While they are planning the search of the beacon, the commander comments that the two crew members accompanying Kellman were taken ill after the last search six weeks before; the Doctor and Harry go to search the area they covered. In the storage area, they realize that the liquid oxygen tanks have not been searched, presumably because they are 88 per cent full; but the Doctor points out that a Cyberman could survive inside them, and quotes a colleague of his about eliminating the impossible to leave behind the improbable truth (Doyle, not Holmes, he explains). He demonstrates that the pressure gauge on the tanks has been falsified, and tells the Commander over the radio. Inside the tank they find some caskets, one of which contains a skeleton, apparently of a miner, covered in gold dust, with an initialled locket (JHE); it has been there for about a year, since before the plague began, and the man appears to have been murdered for his gold. Other caskets contain Cybermen, including the two irradiated ones. Using his naval training, Harry lashes the caskets shut; then they find that they are themselves locked into the oxygen tank – and the strong nylon ropes are snapping as the Cybermen inside wake up and struggle to free themselves. Fortunately the others are outside and able to open the external doors of the tank. It emerges that Kellman has a radio-control device with which he revived the dormant Cybermen, and with which he now summons the dome-headed Cyberleader, which is dormant behind one of the gyro-room walls.

The Cyberleader bursts out and releases the Cybermen from inside the oxygen tank. He remarks that the humans forced him and his followers to act before they were ready and will now have to help them in their plan to destroy the asteroid lying beyond the Nerva, using the beacon itself to strike it out of orbit so that it burns up in the nearest star.

3: The Gold Miners

The Cyberleader explains that the target asteroid is a major producer of gold, which can be used to destroy his race. The Cybermen on the Nerva will be destroyed when the beacon impacts, but the Cyber-race will survive, which is what matters; the humans will be allowed to leave on a shuttle if they co-operate. Kellman is to leave for the asteroid to check the point of impact, and must return within four hours, the time it will take to bring the Nerva's reactors to full capacity. The Doctor agrees to help in return for the plague antidote for Sarah, and on condition that no further humans will be killed. Two Cybermen escort him and Harry to the sickbay, while the commander and Lester are taken to operate the reactor – the Cybermen cannot do this themselves because of their sensitivity to radiation.

In the sickbay, the antidote has been administered to Sarah, but it is touch and go whether she will recover. The Cybermen, meanwhile, are wrecking the x-ray machines. Finding the skeleton in the oxygen tank has convinced the Doctor that there is life on the asteroid, and that Kellman is playing a double game. He plans to follow Kellman down to the asteroid, both to investigate and to obtain gold dust

as a weapon against the Cybermen; so Harry and Anitra create a diversion that allows him to escape from the Cybermen. Sarah begins to recover.

The Doctor beams down after Kellman and follows him through the tunnels. The asteroid proves to be inhabited by a group of starving miners, who have been there for 25 years. They were attacked by the Cybermen, who destroyed their surface installations and drove off their relief ships so that the universe forgot them. Then they discovered a giant golden idol to which all their gold is now dedicated, and whom they believe will protect them. Kellman took the son of their leader, Evans, up to the Nerva in order (so he says) to negotiate with the commander for the other miners' rescue; but he demands gold as a guarantee of their good behaviour. The Doctor is caught trying to take some of their gold dust. Kellman attempts to discredit him as a dangerous man responsible for the deaths of several Nerva crew members; and the Doctor in turn tells the miners about the involvement of the Cybermen. Evans is convinced of his veracity when the Doctor produces the skeleton's J.H.E. locket and when the food brought by Kellman, supposedly sent by John Evans, turns out to be fish, to which Evans is allergic. Kellman escapes, but is killed when Evans dynamites the tunnel; the Doctor promises the dying Evans he will make sure the other miners are taken aboard the Nerva. The Doctor takes a sack of gold for use against the Cybermen – he is sure the idol will understand, he says.

On Nerva, Sarah has defied doctor's orders (from both Harry and the Doctor) and got out of bed. The engines have not been powered up for three years, and nobody knows if they can take full power now. The Cyberleader prepares to launch the beacon on its collision course, whether Kellman returns or not. On the asteroid the Doctor is unable to find the exact point from which to beam up.

4: The Battle for the Nerva

The Doctor finds the beam just in time. The Cybermen, concerned that the Doctor has not returned and cannot be found on the ship, take Anitra hostage. The Doctor rejoins Sarah and Harry in time to find them surrounded by Cybermats after Sarah has experimented with the control box; fortunately, when throwing it to Harry, she misses and it hits the wall, which seems to disorientate the Cybermats.

The Doctor arrives at the control room in time to save Anitra; he also tells them of Kellman's treachery, and they appoint him their new scientific adviser. The Cyberleader intends to set the Nerva on course for the asteroid before releasing the humans, as they will be needed to check the course.

The Doctor has reprogrammed the Cybermats to home in on 'Cyberman brain static' rather than human brain waves, and Sarah replaces the plague virus inside their containers with gold dust. Harry goes through the air duct to the gyro room, where he adjusts the controls. Sarah sends the Cybermats after him. Harry's manipulations change the Nerva's course. The Cyberleader stuns the commander when he attempts to conceal this, then sends a Cyberman to deal with Harry. It is killed by Lester, using a captured Cybergun, and the humans plan to capture the control room. Meanwhile the Cybermats are attacking the Cybermen. Lester is knocked unconscious in an exchange of fire with the Cyberleader, who moves to kill him; but the Doctor intervenes, spraying gold dust from a Cybermat over the Cyberleader, who is then killed by gunfire from Harry. The Nerva's course is changed at the last moment.

The time travellers leave, after alerting the Nerva crew to the presence of the forgotten miners. The TARDIS turns out to have been stashed away in the commander's cabin – mistaken for some kind of toilet!

An unscripted TARDIS scene follows…

APPENDIX C

Time-Life Syndication Prints

The versions of *Doctor Who* stories broadcast in the United Kingdom from Season Twelve to Season Fifteen differed from those syndicated in the United States from 1978. In a second attempt to crack the difficult North American market (after a lukewarm response to the Jon Pertwee serials from *Doctor Who and the Silurians* to *The Time Monster* in 1972), a batch of 98 episodes spearheaded by *Robot* were all re-edited by the distributor, Time-Life, to make them more palatable for American commercial stations such as WOR in New York and KDTU in Tucson. To help sell the export and introduce *Doctor Who* for American audiences, a special publicity session was set up at the United States Embassy in London's Grosvenor Square on Tuesday 14 February 1978. With characteristic floppy hat, dangling scarf and voluminous coat pulled on over his civvies of checked shirt and casual trousers, Tom Baker lined up at the front of an array of the strange characters he had encountered in his first four years of adventures in time and space: his trusted robotic dog companion K9 (introduced in

1977's *The Invisible Enemy*), a Dalek, a Zygon (from 1975's *Terror of the Zygons*), Voc Robot V8 (from 1977's *The Robots of Death*), a Sontaran trooper (from 1978's *The Invasion of Time*) and a rather cumbersome Wirrn (from *The Ark in Space…* complete with operator's feet emerging from the abdomen, which had been so cleverly hidden on screen). The notion – as reported by newspapers such as the *Daily Express* the following day – was that 'Dr Who' and his 'crowd of all-star horrors' were queuing for visas which would allow them entry into the US, capitalizing on the massive interest in all things sci-fi generated by the blockbuster movie *Star Wars* the previous summer.

Repackaging shows for the US was routine. *The Benny Hill Show* made by Thames Television was re-edited into new editions and gained massive popularity. Sometimes a title change was necessary; the BBC's self-sufficiency sitcom *The Good Life* became *The Good Neighbors* to differentiate it from Larry Hagman's short-lived 1971 comedy *The Good Life*, which had aired on NBC. And Yorkshire Television's *Flambards* acquired a new opening narration, supposedly from one of the lead characters, to clarify the plot. It was the voice-over aspect that would primarily affect *Doctor Who*.

The voice-over of a narrator was a staple ingredient of many well-remembered American series. Rod Serling's thoughtful and poetic musings were a key element for each visit into the fantasy anthology of *The Twilight Zone,* while the sombre Control Voice had performed a similar role in the more SF orientated *The Outer Limits*. Other potent examples were William Conrad's chronicling of Dr Richard Kimble's adventures to top and tail *The Fugitive* and William Dozier's surpressed terror and excitement which helped to make the comic-strip *Batman* such a camp classic. In the case of *Doctor Who*, veteran actor Howard da Silva was employed to

record all the tops and tails for the 98 syndicated episodes in the space of two days – and without ever having seen an episode (da Silva did not see the show until some years later).

Born Howard Silverblatt in Cleveland, Ohio in May 1909, Howard da Silva began acting in the 1930s. He broke into films in 1935 with various minor roles and by the 1940s was starring in films such as *The Lost Weekend* and *The Blue Daliah*. He had been in the original stage presentation of *Oklahoma!* in 1943 and worked with Unit 891 in major theatrical works such as *The Cradle Will Rock*. Unfortunately, during the early 1950s he was accused of Un-American behaviour, fell foul of the McCarthy investigations and was blacklisted until the mid-1960s. He then started to work on television again, both as a guest star on shows such as *The Outer Limits*, and *The Man from UNCLE* and as lead actor in the short-lived CBS police drama *For the People*. He continued to rebuild his movie career in the early 1970s with films like *1776* (recreating a role he had originated on Broadway). In September 1978, da Silva won an Emmy for his appearance on the PBS series *Great Performances*, and was perceived as a hallmark of quality. Da Silva died in New York of lymphoma in February 1986.

Not only were these narrative additions by Time-Life superfluous (as proved by the original UK transmissions where the audience had no difficulties following the stories), but the copy provided for da Silva to read was poorly written and ill-researched. The result was melodramatic in the extreme and more akin to 1930s cinema serial hokum, which nobody was expected to take seriously. Da Silva's delivery was smug and self-knowing in the same manner as the narratives later applied to old Mack Sennett films – the action on screen was self-evident to the viewer without having plot elements spelt out to them or explained further. For purist fans, da Silva's continual references to the Doctor as 'Doctor Who' or 'our Time Lord friend' were the nadir of these presentations delivered in his rumbling, plummy tones. Another problem was that, because da Silva had no opportunity to view the programmes, his pronunciation of many of the exotic alien names was simply his own phonetic interpretation of the scripts with which he was presented (e.g. 'Darvrose' for 'Davros').

Also, because of the need to sell the series initially to commercial stations such as WOR, the average 25-minute episodes made by the BBC were too long for the slot and a minute to two minutes had to be deleted from each show. Furthermore, there was a need to introduce each new serial with a 'teaser' of dramatic moments from the forthcoming escapade (shows such as *The Fugitive* would use a scene from the middle of the narrative shown out of context to hook the viewer in before the opening titles, while shows such as *I Spy* and *Mission: Impossible* used clips from the show the viewer was about to see in the titles themselves). After each cliffhanger, the American viewer would be treated with a glimpse of what was to come next time (an insertion which frequently destroyed the carefully constructed tension surrounding the predicament which the instalment was building up to). Three commercial breaks also had to be inserted.

A sample first episode for Season Twelve, *Revenge of the Cybermen* Part One, was re-edited along these lines. After the opening credits a one-minute montage sequence appears to sell the product to the viewer, opening with dialogue between the Doctor and Commander Stevenson from Part One, Scene 20:

STEVENSON But surely, Doctor, Cybermen died out centuries ago?
DOCTOR They disappeared after their attack on Voga at the end of the Cyberwar. Not the

same thing as dying out. They are utterly ruthless. Total machine creatures.

The narration from da Silva then cuts in:

Inside a lighthouse in space, a mysterious plague is killing off the crew members one by one, but the Doctor diagnoses it as a case of poisoning instead, and there appears to be no antidote. Is this the work of the Cybermen?

The action then cuts to Voga from Part One, Scene 12:

VORUS Gold buys humans and we have more gold here on Voga than in the rest of the known galaxy.
MAGRIK But he has not communicated.
VORUS Better that he should not at this time. The Cybermen will be monitoring our radio link.
MAGRIK The mention of Cybermen fills me with dread.

Then, over film of the Vogan battle in the caves from Part Three, da Silva gave his second narration – rich in accuracies:

The Cyberscheme unfolds as a plot to take over the galaxy. But the metal men can succeed only if they regain control of their home planet in order to blow it up. Its core is of pure gold – alluring to humankind but fatal to Cybermen.

The montage then cuts to the Doctor and Sarah on Nerva in Part Four, Scene 23:

SARAH Yes, but we're still heading for the biggest bang in history!
DOCTOR Oh, yes… Oh, no! They've locked the gyro controls – the flight trimmers are jammed!
SARAH What does that mean?
DOCTOR It means we're heading for the biggest bang in history.

There is then a commercial break and station-ident option, after which the episode proper begins, but the opening shot of the Doctor, Sarah and Harry whirling through space and time with the time ring is again supplemented by an explanation from da Silva:

Our space-travelling trio take an unusual means of transport back to Space Beacon Nerva. Though the trip is slightly disconcerting, the Time Lord's ring does the trick, spinning them to their destination.

The first 'act' then runs for seven minutes, through to the appearance of the Cybermat in the transom corridor. However, along the way four cuts are made totalling about 30 seconds: deleted are Warner waking up at his post and part of the first message from Pluto-Earth flight one five (Scene 3), the end of the scene with Lester and Stevenson discussing the situation (Scene 6), the start of the next scene with the Doctor's party in the transom and the end of the same scene in which the Doctor ponders where the TARDIS may materialize (Scene 7). The second 'act' runs to six minutes with cuts comprising some material after the Doctor opens the bulkhead door (Scene 9), Warner calling for Stevenson on the intercom (Scenes 10/11), the whole of the scene where Stevenson and Lester find the damaged bulkhead (Scene 14) and loss of the dialogue between Sarah, Harry and Lester as they move Warner (Scene 17). The last 'act' then runs to eight minutes: deletions include the end of the scene with Lester explaining about Nerva's quarantine situation to Sarah and Harry (Scene 19) and the start of the scene where Warner's body is removed from the crew deck and Sarah is left on her own (Scene 30).

Following the cliffhanger of Sarah being attacked by the Cybermat and the sting of the closing theme, there is then a final commercial break and the 30-second trailer for the next episode. A completely recovered Sarah and Harry run around in the caves of Voga, while da Silva informs us:

Next time: Harry and Sarah try to evade their Vogan captors in the subterranean chambers of

the planet of gold. Unfortunately, the resourceful Doctor Who is still on Nerva, just when they could use his assistance!

The cuts made to each episode vary in subtlety and number. *Robot* Part One lost the comedy scene of the Doctor choosing his new outfit, and began da Silva explaining over the regeneration that,

Doctor Who's face is transformed as his friends watch – instant plastic surgery. But the change goes more than skin-deep. The Time Lord, on the brink of death, is inducing a complete physical metamorphosis… Recently returned from a distant planet, where he was exposed to deadly radioactivity, Doctor Who enters into his fourth incarnation – thus saving his own life. But his new personality is erratic and still in transition, so the Brigadier has no alternative but to place him in the care of a mere Earth doctor.

To introduce the serial, the narration explains that,

Doctor Who loses his sense of humour, when a berserk robot goes on a killing spree in the name of humanity… Originally designed to serve mankind, the robot has been reprogrammed by an elite scientific society to act as its henchman… Programmed with a human brain, and perhaps a human heart, the remorseful robot pays a visit to Professor Kettlewell, its creator, to talk out a personal problem!

The Ark in Space began with the voice-over setting the scene as,

Doctor Who is attacked by the wasp-like Wirrn on Space Station Nerva, where the only survivors of Earth sleep in a deep-frozen state. The giant insect-human face gives the Doctor cause for alarm… When Harry and the revived crew find the Wirrn larvae, the Doctor's fears are confirmed. They are seeking human hosts in which to grow to adulthood… The humans still suspended in the deep-freeze chamber are easy prey for the insect army, and a new addition to their group is very dear to Harry and Doctor Who.

The teaser for *The Sontaran Experiment* began with a shot of Sarah during the torture sequence as da Silva set the scene:

Ten thousand years from now, Doctor Who, Harry and Sarah have returned to Earth expecting to find it uninhabited. Actually, they've been lured there by a Sontaran Field Major whose slave robot is instructed to capture humans for torture and experimentations… Doctor Who confronts a Sontaran experiment to take over the human race.

The opening sequence of Part One then had da Silva's narration interacting with the Doctor's party appearing and vanishing at the transmat terminal:

After a solar burst ten thousand years ago, Earth was deserted by human life. Doctor Who, Harry and Sarah are on their way to the uninhabited planet to repair a malfunction in a transmat. Their success will enable the survivors on Space Station Nerva to return. The Doctor is beamed in. [Doctor appears] Then Harry. [Harry appears – then disappears] But there are still kinks in the system. [Harry appears briefly] Sometimes it takes more than a single try.

Genesis of the Daleks began with the narration:

Mutant life forms are only one result of the chemical warfare waged on the planet Skaro. For centuries, the slaughter of the two opposing races has continued, turning the verdant

landscape into a wasteland. The aged scientist Davros is still determined that his side will win. He has developed a new species – the Daleks – whose primary capability is survival at any cost… But Davros' ruthless beings, created without a conscience, predictably turn on all other life forms. The survivors of both races unite for the first time in generations and plot the overthrow of the Daleks.

The opening sequence from Part One then carries the observation:

Two embittered races fight for control of a planet long since destroyed. The inhabitants of Thal city, and their opponents – the Kaleds – have devoted one thousand precious years of life to promoting death.

And for *Revenge of the Cybermen* the opening of Part Three has da Silva explaining:

Caught in a very unpleasant situation, our Time Lord wishes he'd been down to Voga with the others. But he'll be there soon enough as an unwilling agent of the Cybermen.

Fortunately, from the early 1980s when Lionheart took over syndication of *Doctor Who* in North America, revised complete prints of these 98 episodes without narration were issued to stations instead. However, for many devotees of the series who first encountered 'our Time Lord friend' on PBS stations around 1979, the rumbling tones of Howard da Silva and his ill-written narration were an integral and unwelcome part of their early adventures with Tom Baker's Doctor.

APPENDIX D
Television Drama

On Monday 1 April 1974, producer Barry Letts was approached by director Barbara Derkow regarding a proposed BBC Further Education series which would look at the production of *Doctor Who*. She sent a draft outline of the project which was planned for broadcast from Monday 13 January to Monday 10 February 1975 – concurrent with the intended transmission dates for *Robot*. Derkow proposed covering the production of *Robot* in some depth with a film crew, to study its development – notably at the first read-through on Friday 10 May. There would then be some later recording sessions interviewing crew members about production, which would be recorded in Television Centre Studio 5 on Tuesdays from 12 to 26 November. Derkow arranged a meeting with Letts on Thursday 4, and from this initial discussion it was decided that coverage of Tom Baker's first serial should go ahead.

The following day, producer David Hargreaves of the BBC's Further Education Television department outlined his series – which had a working title of *Television Drama* – to the BBC's Copyright Department to assess potential costs and practicality of covering the production of *Robot*.

> I am preparing a series of 5 x 25' programmes (working title 'Television Drama') which will be transmitted on BBC1 at 11.00 p.m., starting Monday 13 January 1975 (Week 3) and repeated on BBC2 at 15.30 on Tuesday 18 February 1975 (Week 8).
>
> The series is about how TV drama is made and it is based around a 4 part 'Dr Who' story, due for transmission in weeks 1–4, 1975. This story has the working title 'Robot' and is being written by Terrance Dicks... The producer of Dr Who is Barry Letts, Television Centre.
>
> I attach a first outline draft of the Further Education series – you will see that in programmes 1 to 4 we will need (a) to show extracts from 'Robot' in its finished form and (b) to show work in progress on scenes within 'Robot'.

The attached document read:

TELEVISION DRAMA
- a series of 5 x 25' programmes closely linked to 'Dr Who'.
   The aim of the series is to increase viewers' enjoyment of TV drama: by giving them some insight into what is special about TV drama and how it gets on to the screen we hope to add a new dimension to their viewing and encourage thought.
   At the centre of the series we envisage an expanded in-depth interview with Barry Letts which, covering all aspects of a TV drama producer's role in general, and 'Dr Who's' in particular, would provide a thread through the first four programmes. In addition to this each programme, closely linked to an episode of Dr Who, would concentrate on a particular aspect of drama production. The visual interest will come from studio demonstrations and illustrative extracts from Dr Who and other TV dramas.

Here is a first draft.

PROGRAMME 1
Tom Baker introduces himself and leads into the hospital sequence from episode 1 of 'Dr Who'. Intercut with Barry (and Terrance?) Tom discusses what problems re-creating the Doctor for the fourth time poses to an actor. There are statements from two of the old Doctors and the topic is broadened out to a more general discussion of what is special about acting in TV drama, using as illustrative material extracts from other plays these actors have been in. The programme would contain a sequence showing a recording in action, an exposition of how a TV studio works by inference rather than explanation.

PROGRAMME 2
The special effects man introduces himself and leads into a scene with the robot from episode 2 of 'Dr Who'. We deal with audience curiosity about the mechanics of monsters by showing an actor being shown how to work a past monster and this exposition is intercut with Barry on the use of monsters within the stories – how much fear they should be allowed to induce, what 'message' can they carry etc. The designer then introduces himself and drawing on extracts from Dr Who (episode 5, depending on transmission dates) illustrates the practical problems of set design and at the same time the influence of a set on the whole attitude of a viewer to a drama – realism v. fantasy: Unit HQ v. the station, Z Cars.

PROGRAMME 3
Christopher Barry introduces himself and leads into an extract from Dr Who (e.g. the robot attacking in episode 3). Chris discusses the practical and ethical aspects of a TV director's job and indicates how the two are inseparable: angles, lighting etc. affect the impact of violence, tension and romance. (An illustrative extract from something else of Chris's – 'Carnforth Practice'?) Intercut with Barry, this programme ends with Chris taking a Dr Who scene from a read-through to three different ways of recording it, closing with the scene the way it was transmitted.

PROGRAMME 4
Terrance Dicks introduces himself and leads into a scene from Dr Who (if episode 4 e.g. scene 10). Terrance and Barry discuss specifically the long-term aims and development of Dr Who and the issues touched on in this series (women's lib, the purity league, computerization, political assassination, etc.) The discussion then broadens out to include other TV dramas within the experience of those taking part. Some general questions are raised.

PROGRAMME 5
The final programme is about the audience. It might include film of a couple of families watching a Dr Who go out, and interviews with, for example, people from a research project into the effects of TV on children. Drawing on extracts, first from Dr Who, and then from other popular TV dramas, there would follow a studio discussion, guided by a 'name' TV chairman: viewers and professionals from the previous 4 programmes discuss TV drama, hopefully illustrating how the contents of the first four programmes may be drawn on to fulfil the aims of the series.

By Friday 5 April, the transmission slots for the series were outlined by Hargreaves; *Television Drama*'s first broadcasts would be on BBC1 at 11 p.m. on Mondays as originally projected; there would then be a run of repeats at 3.30 p.m. on BBC2 starting Tuesday 18 February.

It seems that three days of coverage on *Robot* were planned, and indeed the read-through for the serial on Friday 10 May seemed to have been filmed to illustrate Programmes 1 and 3. Material for Programmes 2 and 3 was also to be gained by having a camera crew covering the recording of Parts Three and Four in Studio 3 over Thursday 6 and Friday 7 June; this complex session would include a lot of CSO effects work which would be worthy of discussion.

It seems that the industrial unrest of the scenery shifter's strike may have helped to put paid to the plans for *Television Drama*; certainly the lack of studio time brought the drama series *The Double Dealers* to an abrupt end, while series such as *Dial M for Murder* struggled to meet their transmission dates. Whatever the reason, the paperwork in the BBC files relating to *Television Drama* concludes with a scribbled note reading 'D.H. This is cancelled 7/6/74'. However, it seems that this notion – linked with an aborted documentary consisting of two 50 minute programmes for Christmas 1976 – started to fuel the project which culminated in the April 1977 edition of *The Lively Arts: Whose Doctor Who*.

APPENDIX E

BBC Audience Research

In addition to the BBC's sampling of both audience size and reaction to programmes (done by noting the viewing habits and comments of a representative sample of the UK viewing audience), key episodes of *Doctor Who* were occasionally subjected to more detailed examination in the form of an audience research report. This document was prepared by the Audience Research Department, and its contents helped producers to tailor their shows in different directions, learning the strengths and weaknesses of a particular series. During the original run of Season Twelve, two such reports were compiled – for Tom Baker's debut in *Robot* Part One and the climax of *Genesis of the Daleks* – and are here reproduced in full:

DR. WHO

Director: Christopher Barry

Robot Part 1

Saturday, 28th December 1974. 5.35-6.00 pm, BBC1

1. <u>Size of audience</u> (based on results of the Survey of Listening and Viewing). It is estimated that the audience for this broadcast was

21.4% of the United Kingdom population. Programmes on ITV at the time were seen by 10.4% (average).

2. <u>Reaction of audience</u> (based on 180 questionnaires completed by 14% of the Viewing Panel)

   The reactions of this sample of the audience were distributed as follows:-

A+	A	B	C	C-
%	%	%	%	%
4	26	51	17	2

giving a REACTION INDEX of 53. Fourteen reported episodes in the previous series averaged 60, ranging from 52 (Week 36, 1973) to 64 (Week 15, 1974).

3. The sample audience did not, on the whole, appear to have strong views about this programme; after all, it was often the children's choice, not theirs. However, a minority of about three in ten felt it was definitely enjoyable (some were long-term followers of the series) while a small group were distinctly unimpressed. It was suggested, here and there, that this episode had been slow – the story had not got very far by the end.

4. Naturally, the main talking point was the new Doctor (Tom Baker). At this early stage, many did not know whether they were going to like him or not; viewers often said he would 'take some getting used to'. First impressions among those who volunteered an opinion were seldom entirely favourable. Some considered the new personality too clownish and eccentric (occasionally, 'too stupid for words') or too unlike the previous Doctor. Also, Jon Pertwee had been a favourite with some viewers and they missed him. On the other hand, a small group seems to have been instantly attracted, and won over by the end of the episode. The new Doctor had 'more life and humour', it was said, and seemed likely to 'buck the series up'.

5. The acting and production in general were mostly considered competent.

6. 86% of the sample saw the whole episode; 6% came in the middle, 3% switched off before the end and 5% tried a bit.

7. Viewers were asked to pass on the opinions of any children under 15 watching with them. More than half the sample did so, often referring to two or more children.

8. Although a few of these children seemed to enjoy Dr. Who less than before, most were judged to be happily entertained. Some of the smaller ones were apparently a little scared, but determined to stick it out.

9. Comments would suggest that some children are mainly interested in the 'monsters and creepy-crawlies' (in this episode a robot) and are not too concerned about the representation of the Doctor and his friends. However, some children obviously thought the new Doctor 'silly', or missed the familiar Jon Pertwee (which did not necessarily mean the episode as a whole failed to entertain them). In several families, adults or older children had a difficult time trying to explain this 'change' to viewers not quite old enough to 'swallow' the idea. Others were as yet unsure or, less often, positively attracted to this 'crazy but comical' figure.

10. Here are a few examples of children's comments and adult's description of their reactions:

    'The new Doctor is not quite as good as Jon Pertwee, but the programme is still just as exciting' (Boy aged 11);

'Above all else, my two boys aged 4 and 6 were distressed about the change of Dr. Who. They were very excited by the episode, but hope the Doctor will change back again next week!';

'I have four children under 15. They thoroughly enjoyed the programme. Admittedly they all in one voice missed Jon Pertwee, but were quite prepared to let the new man have a good chance in the part before saying whether they will like him or not';

'It was nice and creepy but I like the other Dr. Who best' (Boy – 12);

'My 14-year old son thought the Doctor played the part too much for laughs. My 3 1/2-year-old son was very frightened by the robots, but insisted on watching it sitting on my lap. My ten-year-old daughter thought it very good and liked the way the Doctor changed';

'General opinion was that the new Dr. Who is a looney – he is an eccentric always, but the way it was presented made him stupid';

'My little boy didn't like the new Doctor, he thought he was too silly. Loved the Robot';

'I would like him calmed down a bit, because he's crazy' (Boy – 8);

'It was ever so good. I liked that tin thing with the clippy hands' (Girl – 8);

'My two boys (8 and 11) thought the new Dr. Who "dead funny" and liked him very much';

'General reaction: "What a short episode". I think that indicated their immediate involvement';

'My three-year-old took some convincing about the changed face of Dr. Who. The five-year-old accepted this. Both "like" the Daleks and prehistoric monsters'.

Audience Research Department
16th January 1975

DR. WHO
Genesis of the Daleks
by Terry Nation
Producer: Philip Hinchcliffe
Part 6

Saturday, 12th April 1975, 5.30-5.55 pm, BBC1
1. <u>Size of audience</u> (based on results of the Survey of Listening and Viewing).
   It is estimated that the audience for this broadcast was 18.1% of the United Kingdom population. Programmes on BBC-2 and ITV at the time were seen by 0.3% and 18.3% (average).
2. <u>Reaction of audience</u> (based on 228 questionnaires completed by 15% of the Viewing Panel)
   The reactions of this sample of the audience were distributed as follows:-

A+	A	B	C	C-
%	%	%	%	%
11	30	35	21	3

giving a REACTION INDEX of 56. The second, fourth and fifth episodes of this particular story gained figures of 57 or 58, while the average for Dr. Who in general stands at 58.

3. One group thought the episode slow and the conclusion tame and unimaginative. However, although it had, of course, been obvious from the outset that Doctor Who could not permit the Daleks to perish (for one thing, he could not change what had already happened and, for another, as one somewhat cynically put it, 'you would lose your best money-spinner') this was generally regarded as a satisfactory ending to a story that might be dismissed by some as 'absolute rubbish' and 'just for kids', but which had clearly been followed fairly consistently by most reporting viewers, whether or not they had children watching with them.

4. Comment on the acting again centred around Tom Baker, the still comparatively new Dr. Who and, from what was said, viewers appeared to be fairly evenly divided between those who considered him stupid rather than eccentric (his 'sloppy scarf' was a particular irritant, it seemed) and those who liked his 'slightly dotty' interpretation of the part. The other roles were competently taken, viewers felt, and costumes, setting and make-up (particularly that of Davros) were commended, as were the 'special effects'.

5. 85% of the sample watched the whole programme, 8% came in in the middle, 4% tried a bit and 3% switched off before the end.

6. Asked how many of the six episodes in this particular story they had seen, 17% said <u>one or two</u>, 18% <u>three or four</u> and 65% <u>five or six</u>. Despite some who confessed to being 'fed up with them' – 'how many ways are there of skinning a rabbit?' – and would welcome the introduction of new, preferably non-mechanical monsters, the Daleks were clearly among the Doctor's most popular adversaries and viewers quite liked the idea of seeing how they came into being. A little more complex than some Dr. Who adventures, perhaps, and with underlying questions of conscience, the serial had been 'different' it was occasionally felt, and although dismissed in some quarters as far-fetched, long-drawn-out, confused and/or predictable, had provided acceptable escapist entertainment for the majority.

7. About half the sample had children watching with them and here there would appear to be no two ways about it – with few exceptions, the youngsters were enthralled. As was said 'the world stops for Doctor Who' and although being scared at times – some would not watch without an adult near at hand – they enjoyed every minute of it, evidently ('eyes like organ stops'; 'they find it compelling. The minor frights only add to the enjoyment'; 'they hate the monsters but still wouldn't miss it. Typical children!') and were sorry only that the particular story had come to an end. A handful, though, found it too frightening, would have liked more action or did not care much for the new Doctor.

Audience Research Department
5th May 1975